Testing to the Limits

Dedicated to all pilots who have flown for Britain's aircraft manufacturers,
especially those who have ventured into the unknown in a prototype for the first time

For Pam

Testing to the Limits

British Test Pilots Since 1910

2: James to Zurakowski

Ken Ellis

www.crecy.co.uk

Crécy Publishing Ltd

Published by Crécy Publishing Ltd 2016

A CIP record for this book is available from the British Library

ISBN 9780859791854

Printed In Malta by Melita Press

Crécy Publishing Limited

1a Ringway Trading Estate, Shadowmoss Road, Manchester M22 5LH

www.crecy.co.uk

Front cover: Front cover: Instantly recognisable from any angle, Concorde ushered in European co-operation in airliners that crystallised as today's global giant, Airbus. Brian Trubshaw captained the British prototype for its maiden flight on 9th April 1969. *www.airteamimages.com*

Rear cover main image: Typhoon DA.4 ZH590, the first British Eurofighter with EJ200s, was first flown by Derek Reeh.
Copyright Eurofighter – BAE Systems

Small images clockwise from top:

Alex Henshaw in the cockpit of Mew Gull G-AEXF. *KEC*

The Sopwith Schneider under tow at Monaco, April 1914. *KE*

The caption on this public information photo, dated 6th September 1943, declares that this gathering was taken at: "a factory in the North West where [Lancasters] are produced in surprising numbers for the Ministry of Aircraft Production". *via Dean Wright*

The Cierva W.9 was an advanced, but unsung, helicopter prototype. *Weir Group*

The first pre-production Swift, WJ960, saved by David Morgan in a skilful forced landing in September 1951. *Vickers-Armstrongs*

The Hunting 126 being prepared for the static at the Battle of Britain display at Gaydon, September 1966. *Roy Bonser*

The second prototype Optica, G-BLFC, over the Needles, Isle of Wight. *Edgley Aircraft*

Front flap top: A probe-equipped Meteor F.8 having engaged with an early 'solid' basket at low level. *Flight Refuelling*

Front flap bottom: Victor K.2 XL512 of 55 Squadron, ready to refuel Tornado GR.1A of 13 Squadron, circa 1986. *Sgt Rick Brewell – RAF DPR*

Table of Contents

Foreword

When Ken asked me to write the foreword to his second volume on test pilots I was honoured and delighted. He also sent me a copy of Volume One where the foreword was written by Chris Yeo. I read Chris's words three times and decided that not only was it beautifully written but said everything about the essence of test flying and Ken's amazing achievement in putting these books together. Every word Chris wrote also applies to this volume. So take my tip and buy Volume One as well. I say that because whatever made you buy this book (probably a particular pilot's name you knew) then they would certainly want you to get the whole picture of the past and an insight into the trade of test pilot so well described by Chris.

For my part I would now like to give you my thoughts about the future of even more automation in manned aircraft that Chris touched on in his last paragraph.

Airline pilots are just human beings so from time to time make mistakes just like all of us. Very occasionally an airline pilot's mistake can cause an accident – 'pilot error' as it was called. When I was a young test pilot working at the Royal Aircraft Establishment Bedford in the mid 1960s, the 'boffins' there were trying to come up with a system that could automatically land an airliner in bad weather and so remove the possibility of pilot error causing a landing accident.

I can well remember the day back in 1965 when I was acting as safety pilot for an autoland Comet trials aircraft. The safety pilot was there to land the aircraft normally should the experimental automatics fail to do their thing and the tests that day were to see how much cross wind they could deal with. Sitting there and watching the automatics smoothly remove a huge drift angle and sit the aeroplane neatly on the runway numbers over and over again was very impressive and convinced me that automatics could fly an aircraft better than I could. Indeed at one point I said to the crew: "If the autos quit I am not landing here because I can't do that. I am going to a runway with less cross wind."

From that day the issue for me has not been whether computers can fly an aeroplane better than humans but whether they can be made reliable enough. Reliability was of course at the heart of the issue when the boffins wanted to get autoland cleared for use in airliners and they were told by the certificating authority of the day (the Air Registration Board, now called the Civil Aviation Authority) that, because one in every million airliner manual landings resulted in an accident, any automatic system needed to be ten times safer. In other words, it must not fail more than once in ten million landings. Accordingly this sort of amazing reliability was designed in to the production systems. To cut a long story short, autoland has been used in airliners since the early 1970s and today is available as standard in most airliners.

Despite worldwide use for many decades, no autoland system has ever caused a landing accident. Not surprisingly during the same period there have been many pilot error landing accidents.

Moving on with the automation story, in 1988 the Airbus A320 entered service. This was the world's first 'fly-by-wire' (FBW) airliner. With a FBW aircraft the pilot's hands and feet are no longer connected mechanically to the aircraft's control surfaces on the wings and tail but to a computer system. Thus the FBW pilots use their hands and feet as usual but only to tell the computer what manoeuvre they want and the computer adjusts the control surfaces as appropriate. Since the computers also know the limits of what the aeroplane is designed to do, they will not follow any incorrect pilot demands. Thus the FBW system has built in protections against pilot error. Additionally, if the FBW system is also told navigational information about the route required, it will fly the aircraft perfectly to its destination.

The principles that make FBW computer systems safe are quite simple – multiple computers linked together so that if one disagrees with the others it is automatically disconnected by the majority. Additionally, the computers and their software come from different manufacturers to rule out a common fault affecting them all.

Given we have reached this stage of automation, we face three big issues in the future: the accountants would like to save the pilots' salaries, the pilots don't want to lose their jobs and would passengers be prepared to fly without a man or woman sitting in the cockpit?

So much for where we are today. My view of the future is that talk of 'pilotless aircraft' is quite wrong. I want two people up front to manage each flight but I don't want them to steer the aeroplane because computers are better at that. By 'manage' I mean make all the dozens of decisions that are needed during any flight, which is what humans are so good at compared to computers. As to the reliability of the systems that will steer the aircraft then the principles already in use to ensure FBW safety will be used for the 'steering' systems. A principal known in the profession as fail-safe.

Anyhow time will tell and in the meantime enjoy this book!

John Farley

John Farley after a sortie in a US Marine Corps AV-8A Harrier at Whiteman Air Force Base, Missouri, 1980. John first flew the Sea Harrier FRS.1 prototype on 20th August 1978. *via John Farley*

Introduction

My fascination for test pilots and the British aircraft industry was outlined in Volume One and it need not be repeated here. What you have before you is the culmination of many years of assembling references, quizzing sources and crunching keyboards. As the project got increasingly focussed it was pleasing to see just how many people shared interest in the subject and wanted to know more. Everybody seems to have a favourite test pilot, invariably one of the 'household names' from the 1940s and 1950s, probably stemming from reading an autobiography or biography or watching spellbound at an airshow. But there are so many other individuals to discover and that is the rationale driving these two volumes.

During the production of *Testing to the Limit*s various people who got sight of the manuscript remarked on how dangerous the test flying profession seemed to be. I decided that some 'stats' were called for, but it is very important that the reader appreciates that the author is somebody who can't even get his head around percentages and that 'times' and 'gozinters' are very challenging numeric manoeuvres!

In Volume One Chapter Seven there are 164 'biographies' and 213 in Chapter Six in this volume – that's 377 test pilots. Of these, 101 died while going about what could reasonably be called their job definition. Another 12 perished in non-test aviation activities, for example an airline accident, or non-company supported air racing. Research has failed to provide fates for 45 of the pilots studied in the two volumes, but it is *fairly* reasonable to assume that they did *not* die in a test piloting regime in Britain. Of the others – 118 of them – fall into two groups: they either died from other causes, ranging from influenza, motoring accidents, one known suicide through to old-age – the 'top scorer' reaching 103; or they are still with us!

These are very bald statistics: there are flight test observers and engineers (FTOs and FTEs) and other specialist aircrew that can be added to the death toll. If service test personnel – eg from the Aeroplane & Armament Experimental Establishment, the Royal Aircraft Establishment etc who are not part of the remit of this book – are added in, the figures greatly increase. There have been innumerable injuries, ranging from what these days are called 'life-altering' to broken noses. An assessment of flight test hours per accident would be enlightening, but what data exists would be impossible to 'smooth out' and the vast majority of such gen was either *never* collected in the first place, or was assigned to rubbish skips with the latest corporate change around.

The table showing fatalities by decade may or may not be useful. The 'spikes' for World War Two and the 'envelope-pushing' era of the 'Cold War' should hold no surprises. The plummeting figures beyond the 1970s are indicative of the increasing sophistication of simulators, advances in safety and escape systems, and of how little 'first flighting' has been carried out in that time.

BAE Systems Pete 'Wizzer' Wilson – featured in Chapter Seven – has been British Joint Strike Fighter Project Pilot since 2006 and in October 2011, along with three US Marine Corps pilots, carried out the first vertical landings at sea by the F-35B STOVL variant on the USS *Wasp* (illustrated). On 19th June 2015, Pete flew 'ski-jump' take-offs from Naval Air Station Patuxent River, Maryland, for the first time. *Courtesy and © Lockheed Martin*

British Test Pilot Fatalities	
1910 – 1920	18
1921 – 1930	2
1931 – 1940	11
1941 – 1950	39
1951 – 1960	17
1961 – 1970	9
1971 – 1980	2
1981 – 1990	2
1991 – 2000	1
2000 to date	0
Total	**101**

Some readers will be horrified at this level of sacrifice. Most, I suspect, will view it as relatively modest given the nature of the work, especially when in the throes of two world wars. However you view the statistics – such as they are – it serves to remind us all that test pilots will always be needed to put themselves in harm's way in order to expand our knowledge of aeronautics, improve military capability or enhance flight safety.

End of an Era?

When I approached Chris Yeo about writing the foreword to Volume One he was typically self-effacing and wanted to know why I'd chosen him. Born and bred in Lancashire, I have absorbed everything there is about English Electric and the world-beating military aircraft dynasty that it spawned; so a Warton flier was firmly on the list. Eurofighter Typhoon is the latest Warton product and the flagship of BAE Systems and 'UK plc'.

My second reason took Chris aback a little, but he soon got the significance. Checks complete at the end of Warton's Runway 26, Chris eased the throttles forward on Eurofighter 2000 DA.2 ZH588 on 6th April 1994 and entered the history books. When he returned to the ramp, the celebrations began: he had completed the debut of the first British-assembled prototype of what became the Typhoon.

At midnight on 31st December 1999 the world entered a new millennium. As the clocks chimed, that maiden flight that Chris commanded six years previously again became epoch-making. It had turned out to be the last of a huge number of such prototype ventures made by a British-employed test pilot, flying a British-produced *major* aircraft programme from British soil of the 20th century. There have been variants of the Typhoon, BAe 146 airliner, Hawk trainer, Nimrod maritime patroller, Merlin and Lynx helicopters since but it could be argued that nobody has done what Chris did on 6th April 1994 *since then*.

AgustaWestland is potentially the one organisation to change this, but any new design is just as likely to spiral upwards from Vergiate in Italy while boasting a good proportion of Yeovil-built elements. This was underlined on 1st January 2016 when it was announced that the company was taking the name Finmeccanica-Helicopters, after the Italian holding group. As

shown in Chapter Six of Volume One, BAE Systems is a centre of excellence for *unmanned* aircraft: Taranis is pioneering the way for future strike fighters. While such aircraft may not have cockpits, skilled test pilots will *still* be needed to 'first flight' these innovative machines.

Airbus, directly and indirectly, is a massive employer in the UK and the amount of revenue generated by Britain's participation in this world-beating multi-national eclipses all the go-it-alone programmes since 1945. Hence the reader will find Ed Strongman, captain of the prototype A400M on 11th December 2009, and Peter Chandler who was at the helm (if a side-stick can be called a helm!) of the first A350 on 14th June 2013 within the pages of *Tested to the Limits*. Both of these include a significant proportion of British input, design, technology, airframe, propulsion and systems. The venue for the maiden flight may be Madrid and Toulouse respectively, but a 'Brit' test pilot was flying a major British programme.

This brings me to my other choice of foreword-writer: John Farley may not have known it, but I have been 'stalking' him for decades. I cannot remember where I first saw Harrier Mk.52 G-VTOL climb away in that signature extreme angle vertical take-off, but John's polished, perfectly-executed displays never failed to keep me transfixed with excitement and a sense of pride. When I moved from Merseyside to the People's Republic of Rutland in 1984, I was delighted to be under the Wittering approach and couldn't believe my luck when Harriers also populated Cottesmore in 1999. (Don't get me started on why the founder nation of this sensational achievement no longer flies Harriers while India, Italy, Spain and the USA continue to bask in the type's unique capabilities!) So, my only disloyalty to Warton has always come from the direction of Dunsfold!

From the private-venture days of the P.1127 to the pairing of British Aerospace and McDonnell Douglas to create the incredibly potent 'second generation' Harrier GR.5/AV-8B Harrier II this machine has been a head-turner in many ways. As with Airbus, the British element of the Lockheed Martin F-35 Joint Strike Fighter (JSF) is very significant with BAE Systems, Rolls-Royce and others heavily involved from conception to construction and support. (Like many others, I steadfastly *refuse* to call the RAF/Royal Navy F-35Bs Lightning IIs – there has only been *one* Lightning, unless you are referring to the P-38, which the RAF rejected!)

JSF's STOVL F-35B variant has hugely benefitted from British pioneering expertise. This can be traced all the way back to Hucknall's 'Flying Bedstead' of 1953, Short's control system-proving SC.1 of 1957, Bristol Siddeley's development of the first practical VTOL jet engine – the Pegasus – and to everything achieved by the designers and flight test team at Dunsfold. All of these people have helped to make possible the F-35B that, touch wood, will one day fly from the aircraft carrier HMS *Queen Elizabeth*.

This book is dedicated to all of the pilots that have flown for Britain's aircraft manufacturers, especially those who have ventured into the unknown in a prototype. In particular, I hope it highlights the unsung personalities and reminds us that their contribution was just as vital as that of those who became 'household names'. Each and every one has helped to spearhead a world renowned industry.

Acknowledgements

Over the time that this book has been a-brewing many people have helped in one way or another. Test pilots and members of the UK's aviation industry, past and present, will recognise their input within these pages and my thanks go out to them all. Sources referred to are acknowledged in the Bibliography and within the text.

Every effort has been made to secure permissions for quotes from books that appear in the text, but in the over-riding majority of cases there has been a 'nil' return. My thanks go to: Tony Buttler author of *British Experimental Combat Aircraft of World War Two*, John Davis of Grub Street, John Farley for his *A View from the Hover*, James Hamilton-Paterson author of *Empire of the Clouds*, Nigel Walpole author of *Swift Justice* and, of course Crécy Publishing. Likewise, attributions to the origin of illustrations have been made where-ever possible.

The following all threw themselves into helping answer specific questions, or other needs, and I thank them all: Roy Bonser for his exceptional archive; Tony Buttler who helped source images and pin down elusive stats; Brian Cocks purveyor of 'extinct' books; Mary Chapin Carpenter and the Mumfords for varied, but perfect background; Mike Ingham for encouragement and ideas-to-be-pursued; Steve Jones, ace computer 'whisperer'; Rebecca and Jerry Lockspeiser for images of David; Graham Pitchfork for backgrounds on biographies and a source of images; Nigel Price of Key Publishing's flagship magazine *FlyPast* for his patience and understanding; Graham Skillen, Short problem-solver; Julian Temple of the Brooklands Museum; Andy Thomas for images and sleuthings; Guy Warner for imagery and permissions; Les Whitehouse of the Boulton Paul Association. And there will be others...

Alan Curry, Andrew McClymont and Dean Wright checked, revised, added to and above all enriched the manuscript. That said all errors and omissions are to be laid firmly at my door. Alan also supplied material and much of the research on Spitfire test pilot Clive Anderton – see Chapter Two. Former Scottish Aviation and Avro/Hawker Siddeley FTE Andrew provided background material on the **Flight Department of the** Air Registration Board and its successor, the Civil Aviation Authority. Andrew **was involved** in the pioneering joint certification of Concorde and with Airbus beyond that- see Chapter Four.

John Farley and Chris Yeo not only patiently answered my questions, but both honoured me by agreeing to write the forewords – Chris in Volume One, John herewith. Not content with that, they also commented on the manuscript with John especially providing a font of knowledge and guidance. I am indebted to them both.

The incredible staff at Crécy Publishing didn't flinch when this hare-brained scheme was floated in their general direction! Jeremy Pratt whole-heartedly made suggestions, all of which enhanced the book. Gill Richardson guided, cajoled and managed this mostly errant author with great patience. Rob Taylor took pixels and turned them into the finished, polished, product. Finally, and especially, to Pam and feline Rex for their unique brands of support and encouragement during the creation of this mammoth task.

This whole project is a two-pronged assault – if you've not got the first volume, turn to the rear pages and discover how to make amends!

Ken Ellis
People's Republic of Rutland, February 2016

Myddle Cottage, 13 Mill Lane, Barrowden, Oakham, LE15 8EH
sillenek@gmail.com

The last major manned British programme to take place from a UK runway, certainly in the 20th century, is now a museum piece. Eurofighter 2000 DA.2 ZH588 inside the 'Milestones of Flight' gallery at the RAF Museum, Hendon. *Ken Ellis*

CHAPTER ONE

Same Task, Different 'Trades'

This being a two-volume work, some repetition is necessary to set the scene regarding what *Testing to the Limits* intends to do, and perhaps more importantly what it *doesn't* do.

So, what *is* a test pilot? At its widest, it is anyone who takes (or attempts to take) an aircraft into the sky with the aim of seeing if it will fly, or how a new engine makes it perform, or if the new leading edge slots improve the slow speed envelope, or check it out for renewal of its certificate of airworthiness, or how it reacts when a missile is fired from it, or if the veterans who flew it in 1944 were correct about a newly-rebuilt warbird's characteristics on landing. In the most extreme of cases, to discover why a previous example ended in a steaming crater following a deep stall. You get the picture. *Anyone* trying something new with an aeroplane can be considered a test pilot.

Special mission variants can mean putting a well-established type through an entirely new test schedule. In 1973 Shorts was commissioned to adapt Skyvan 3 C-FQSL for base metal survey work by Questor International Surveys of Toronto, Canada. A nose and two rear-mounted probes and attachment points on each wingtip allowed the suspension of an electric current-carrying cable, acting as a giant magnetometer. *Shorts*

For *Testing to the Limits* the defining word is: manufacturer. A pilot who tests the products of a British aircraft company, be that a small workshop or a multi-national giant. At first, it was decided to feature only pilots who carried out the maiden flight on a brand new design, or of a significantly different new variant. This brings to mind all the famous names that put the throttle forward – or twisted the collective in helicopters – to take a prototype into the air while the designer paced up and down, wondering if he had a winner, or a turkey, on his hands.

But the more the author read and enquired, it was clear that there were plenty of wonderful stories about deputy chief test pilots, or more humble aviators in the flight office, and that they also deserved a mention, in one form or another. After all, if the Chief had been unavailable, then the next in line might well have been the one in the limelight. They also took risks and sometimes paid the ultimate price. That last sentence lingered. *Testing to the Limits* also pays tribute to those who lost their lives while putting a new type through its paces. Thus the entry criteria are:

Pilots that have carried out the maiden flight of a new type or *significant* variant.

The prototype CF-105 Arrow, 25201, during its first flight from Malton, Canada, on 25th March 1958 at the hands of former Gloster test pilot 'Jan' Zurakowski. *Avro Canada*

All known chief test pilots and selected others of the flight test office.

Pilots who lost their life while flight testing.

Further notes on inclusion can be found in the opening paragraphs of Chapter Six. *They Also Serve*, Chapter Seven, gives very brief details of other pilots who fall outside of the above parameters.

Pilots born overseas who have tested UK-built types are included. Occasionally a pilot undertaking a first flight of an overseas type as part of his UK-based employment is covered – for example 'Bill' Waterton and the Avro Canada CF-100. This logic is extended to the British pilots who have taken Airbus designs for their debuts – see Peter Chandler for the A350 and Ed Strongman for the A400M. British-born aviators working full-time for overseas manufacturers, other than Airbus are not included. There have been quite a number of these, pioneering for other aircraft industries. For example, 'Jan' Zurakowski took the Avro Canada CF-105 Arrow for its maiden flight, but as he did so as a full-time employee at Malton: that achievement is presented as an aside in his entry in Chapter Six which concentrates on his time with Gloster.

It is vitally important to remind readers that many an inaugural flight, and even more developmental sorties, did not just involve a pilot or two. Always to be borne in mind are what became known as Flight Test Observers (FTOs – later called Flight Test Engineers – FTEs), navigators and others. Depending on the complexity, and/or size of the aircraft, FTOs etc served to reduce pilot workload and bring their own specialist skills and disciplines to analysing a prototype. For major transport programmes a veritable army of FTOs/FTEs could be found amid specially-instrumented consoles and work stations.

Planes and People

That's pretty much defined the personalities dealt with in *Testing to the Limits*, now we should spend some time examining what *sorts* of aircraft are included. The best way to do that is to explain what is *excluded*. Home-designed and built one-offs, plans-built, kit-based, partial-build and all other combinations of light and sport aviation – while frequently pushing the boundaries of format, construction and performance – are beyond the realms of this book. Staying with light and sport aviation, in general microlights, gyrocopters and all lighter-than-air types are not covered. Sailplanes and gliders equally are not included except for assault gliders and those that formed part of an experimental programme, supporting powered projects.

This is not to belittle all those that take such creations into the skies for the first time, because they are, in every sense, test pilots. Several 'names' have carried out such work; for example, take a look at the later exploits of Roland Beamont in Volume One.

Increasingly, aircraft programmes are evolving *without* a human on board. Sometimes the pilot, sitting at a console, can be in a different continent from the runway or the launch pad. These machines come under an ever-widening series of acronyms – UCAS for unmanned combat air system and UAV for unmanned aerial vehicle being the most prevalent as these words are typed. The word 'drone' is frowned upon, but universally used by the 'media'. As might be guessed, the likes of UCASs, UAVs and all other forms of that lexicon are not part of the remit of this book although Chapter Six in Volume One provides a brief resume of the unmanned programmes of BAE Systems.

Testing to the Limits is about *people* and their *endeavours* and far less about the nitty-gritty of aviation nomenclature.

Designer-pilot-entrepreneur Claude Grahame-White seated in a 'Boxkite' at Hendon, 1912. It is difficult to establish just *which* of his pilots tested – rather than displayed, raced and instructed – for him. *Peter Green Collection*

Well-known types are given scant background on the basis that the reader will be familiar with them while more obscure ones are explained, but briefly. No attempt has been made to supply blow-by-blow development histories, or production totals. Registrations, serials numbers and other means of identity are presented to allow those who know these things far better than the writer to get a 'handle' on what is being discussed; they may or may not have been painted on the aircraft during the time mentioned.

Flight Test 'Community'

For completeness, Volume One described other sorts of test pilot and it will be of help to briefly survey these other 'trades'. Within the 'community' there has always been a degree of cross-over, the most established path being for service test pilots to go on to work for a manufacturer.

The initial form of test pilot was the designer-pilot and Volume One profiled the 'prototype': Samuel Franklin Cody the first man to achieve sustained powered flight in Britain, on 16th October 1908. Most pioneers, like Cody, never got beyond the level of a 'cottage industry'; typically using parts and particularly the engine, in the creation of the next design and seldom employing other people. This elite band had no need for a test pilot as they were learning hop-by-hop about the nascent science of aerodynamics in a 'hands-on' manner. Besides, where would they find someone with more experience than themselves? So most of the early 'names' are not included in the main listings as they worked in a solitary manner as designer-pilots. Several are profiled, but only *after* they have founded a company and test flying became part of their employ. For example, Geoffrey de Havilland only

'appears' once he has been appointed as chief designer *and* pilot at the Royal Aircraft Factory.

The Royal Aircraft Factory was the launchpad for the Royal Aircraft Establishment and after that a veritable 'alphabet soup' of other military organisations to test, evaluate or research wide aspects of aviation emerged – these were outlined in Volume One Chapter Five. Of these bodies, the most central to this book is the Empire Test Pilots' School (ETPS), the first course commencing in April 1943. ETPS rapidly increased professionalisation and again it is important to remember that FTOs also go through its comprehensive and demanding courses. Service test is by far and away the largest 'family' of test pilots and the best reference covering the Martlesham Heath, Felixstowe and Boscombe Down days is Tim Mason's superb series of books – see the Bibliography.

Working in a similar manner as the service test organisations in the commercial aviation sector was the Air Registration Board, the forerunner of the present-day Civil Aviation Authority – this aspect is examined in *Airbuses to 'Puddle-jumpers'*, Chapter Four.

Once the test piloting team has ironed out all of the 'bugs' in a new design and it has been accepted by the military, or been granted certification by the civil authorities, the production line kicks in. If demand is small, the resident test pilots, will 'shake down' and 'sign off' aircraft prior to hand over to the customers, and they may carry out the delivery. With major programmes another 'breed' of test pilot takes over, the production test pilot (PTP), handling the output from the factory while the Chief Test Pilot (CTP) gets on with the next new project. Many a PTP has gone on to become an experimental (or developmental) test pilot and ended up as

Service test pilots predominated at Boscombe Down and Farnborough. Illustrated is night vision goggles trials pioneer Hunter T.7 WV383 of the Royal Aircraft Establishment's Flight Systems Department, May 1980. *Ken Ellis*

CTP. As there has been a large number of PTPs, *Testing to the Limits* devotes a chapter to this vital band in each volume. Herewith, Chapter Two, *Mass Production*, examines the work of Alex Henshaw, Geoffrey Alington and Clive Anderton.

Test pilots have also found work in specialist areas, the most well-known being engine development. Volume One examined such aircrew and turned Martin-Baker experimental fitter Bernard Lynch into an 'honorary' test pilot – he was the first 'Brit' to test an ejection seat, thereby putting Martin-Baker on course to – so far – save the lives of around 7,500 aircrew. Chapter Three, *Global Reach*, in this volume looks at the evolution of in-flight refuelling. Other specialist areas for test pilots have included propeller, armament and missiles and systems (eg autoland). Chapter Five takes a look at another major aspect of the test piloting task, the demonstration of a new type's capabilities to customers, and to the general public.

Aero-engine test pilots have to come to grips with the behaviour of new powerplants and how they change the flying characteristics of the chosen test-bed. Armstrong Whitworth-built Avro Lincoln B.2 SX972 was fitted with Bristol Proteus turboprops in the outer positions in readiness for the Britannia. Below it in this 1951 image is the Brabazon, G-AGPW. *Bristol Aeroplane Company*

CHAPTER TWO

Mass Production

While flying inverted, the 23-year-old pilot noticed that the aircraft had burst into flames. He coolly took to his parachute and landed safely; later joining a policeman to inspect the remains of the sporting biplane he had bought just eight months previously. The parachute had been a birthday present, given to him just 54 days before. This was 30th December 1935 and the pilot was Alex Henshaw – the aircraft was Arrow Active I G-ABIX. The parachute was probably given as a gift because on 6th September that year, Alex had ditched Miles Hawk Major G-ADNJ in the Irish Sea during the King's Cup Air Race and a means of escape may have given him other options!

As CTP for the enormous Castle Bromwich Aircraft Factory in the Midlands, Alex also had to 'take to the silk' while testing Spitfire IX MJ190 on 13th October 1943 when the engine broke up while flying at 470mph. The entry in his fifth logbook makes a terrifying experience seem almost run-of-the-mill: "Flung out of machine with badly torn parachute. Three complete panels missing and canopy held together by slender pieces of thread for 15,000ft."

Castle Bromwich test pilots in front of a Lancaster and a pair of Spitfires. Left to right: Flt Lt J Rosser AFC; Alex Henshaw; Captain Olav Ullstad DSO DFC; Flt Lt Venda Jicha DSO CDG DFC AFC.

Alex Henshaw was an exceptional sporting and long-distance aviator who ended up as a gifted and well-respected test pilot on both Spitfires and Lancasters. Always modest about his achievements, Alex managed the almost impossible – to excel in both civil and military aviation.

For the purposes of *Testing to the Limits*, his earlier flying achievements can only be briefly touched upon. Born in Peterborough in 1912, motorcycles and then aircraft dominated his interests. When Alex gained his private pilot's licence, his father – also Alex – presented him with de Havilland Gipsy Moth G-AALN. Alex had a gift for air racing, his first major event being the 1933 King's Cup. Up to 1936 he flew a variety of types, Comper Swifts G-ACGL and G-ABWW; DH Leopard Moth G-ACLO; DH Hornet Moth G-ADMJ; Miles Hawk Major G-ADAW, the unfortunate G-ADNJ and the ill-fated Arrow Active G-ABIX. After all of these he felt he needed an aircraft with more 'poke' and in late 1937 Alex turned to Jack Cross of the Gravesend-based Essex Aero to radically modify Percival Mew Gull G-AEXF. Piloting this machine Alex won the 1938 King's Cup, held at Hatfield over a 1,066-mile course at 236mph.

Alex turned his mind to long distance record-breaking, again in the Mew Gull. He set his sights on an out-and-back flight to the Cape of Good Hope, South Africa. Taking off from Gravesend on 5th February 1939, Alex reached the Cape, some 6,000 miles distant, in 40 hours. He stayed in Cape Town a mere 27 hours before coming back – he was 11 minutes *slower* on the return leg! He broke a string of point-to-point records in many classes along the way as well as the Britain to South Africa out-and-back.

Midland Spitfires

With the advent of World War Two, Alex – then 27 – volunteered for the RAF. While he was waiting for a reply, Vickers approached him to become a test pilot at Brooklands. Alex wrote about the 'culture shock' of testing, he loved every moment of flying Wellingtons but could not believe the paperwork that came with the job. This depressed him to the extent that he was getting ready to talk to the RAF about enlisting again. Then he met Supermarine CTP Jeffrey Quill who saw in Alex the perfect personality for the Spitfire. Jeffrey had him moved to Eastleigh and there Alex sampled the first of 2,300-plus Spitfires that he was to fly. In his book *Sigh for a Merlin* the love that Alex developed for the fighter comes out of every page, for him "it was a sheer dream".

The factories in Southampton and the flight test airfield at Eastleigh were all-too vulnerable to Luftwaffe raids and construction of the giant Castle Bromwich Aircraft Factory was initiated. On 1st June 1940 Alex was appointed as CTP at 'Castle Brom' and this is where he made his *second* reputation in aviation. Alex established a gifted team around him, including several people to look after the admin! At times Alex was signing off 20 Spitfires a day. As well as Spitfires, Castle Brom also produced Avro Lancasters and Alex flew around 300 of these. At least once, Alex barrel-rolled a 'Lanc' and he described the bomber as finely-tuned and exceptionally reliable.

Castle Bromwich was not the limit of Alex's responsibility; he had the output of Cosford, Desford, Cowley and Sywell to oversee. A 'taxi' was essential for Alex and in February 1941 he acquired a 'job lot' from the Leicestershire Aero Club a Braunstone, Hawker Tomtits G-AFIB, G-AFTA and G-AFVV, for use by his team. His personal mount was G-AFTA, which was also used to 'commute' to his home at Henley-in-Arden. The Tomtit was fitted with a windscreen from a Spitfire and a streamlined fairing behind the pilot's head. Tomtit *Tango-Alpha* was sold to Supermarine pilot 'Pat' Shea-Simmonds – see Chapter Six – for a short period in 1946. To celebrate his new job at a test pilot for Hawker in April 1949, Neville Duke – see Volume One – bought G-AFTA and to clinch the deal he had to sell his beloved MG sports car. In July 1950 Neville transferred the Tomtit to Hawker and continued to fly it at many air events. Since 1960, *Tango-Alpha* has been a part of the Shuttleworth Collection.

To launch Birmingham's Spitfire Fund, the Lord Mayor invited Alex to carry out a flypast outside the town hall in front of gathered honoured guests and the public. It was 18th September 1940 and Alex made an unforgettable 'entrance' in Spitfire II P7426. Flying inverted at high speed, the fighter was below roof height! The dignitaries and especially the mayor were not best pleased. To quote Alex's logbook: "Instructed to demonstrate over Birmingham. Chaos ensued!"

After the war Alex took up a post ferrying Miles aircraft to South Africa and helping to market them but he disliked being a salesman. In 1947 Miles foundered and Alex returned to Britain the following year. He threw himself into the family farming and holiday home business and wrote three timeless books that were classics from the moment they went to press: *Flight of the Mew Gull*, *Sigh for a Merlin* and *Wings over the Great Divide*. Alex Adolphus Dumfries Henshaw MBE died, aged 94, on 24th February 2007.

Alex Henshaw – Test Flying Scrapes and Escapes		
1 Jan 1940	Spitfire I N3294	During test dive a seagull penetrated 12in into wing leading edge.
16 Nov 1940	Spitfire II P7673	Engine failure on take-off. Machine forced on to ground prematurely to avoid house ahead. Badly damaged.
23 Apr 1942	Tomtit G-AFVV	Collided on take-off with Spitfire parked on the airfield. Hawker Tomtit – used as a 'taxi' – was written off.
1 Jun 1942	Spitfire V EP499	Engine failure in flight on a test from Cosford; force landing near Wolverhampton.
18 July 1942	Spitfire V EP615	Engine failure over 'The Black Country' at 800ft. During the force landing the starboard wing was torn off by a tree. The engine ended up in the kitchen of a nearby house.
27 Jul 1942	Spitfire V EP616	Engine failure on take off. Force landed near Willenhall.
20 Sep 1942	Spitfire V AD272	Supercharger exploded at 24,000ft over Warwick; dead-stick landing back at Castle Bromwich with no other damage.
1 Jan 1943	Spitfire IX MA233	Engine failure on take-off, force landed on airfield with undercarriage partially retracted.
6 Sep 1943	Wellington III BK272	Port engine failed on test flight out of Sywell – landed with no damage.
13 Oct 1943	Spitfire IX MJ190	Engine broke up in dive test; Alex flung out with badly damaged parachute – landed safely.
3 Mar 1944	Lancaster I HK541	Dinghy tore adrift from its housing in the upper surface of the starboard wing root in a dive at 360mph; the drag forced the dive to steepen and the dinghy fouled the tailplane. Aircraft brought under control when the dinghy broke away but with damage to tail surfaces.
12 Jun 1945	Spitfire II P8196	Tailwheel trials with weighted tail to simulate take-off and landing loadings. Aircraft pitched up on take-off, tail struck ground and aircraft broke up.

Above: The wreckage of Spitfire V EP615, 18th July 1942. On the rear of the print Alex had written: "Spitfire crash in the 'Black Country'. One of the many. Harness saved me from fatal injury." *Peter Green Collection*

Left: Alex Henshaw in the cockpit of Mew Gull G-AEXF. *KEC*

Below: The Lancaster final assembly hall at Castle Bromwich. *KEC*

The flight line at 'Castle Brom', awaiting Alex Henshaw and his team. *KEC*

Maternal Quality Control

With roots in the East Midlands and similar tastes in sporting aviation, it is not surprising that Alex Henshaw and Geoffrey Alington were friends. This extended to their wartime service; both became production test pilots to Ministry of Aircraft Production (MAP) 'shadow' factories in the Midlands. For a while, their activities shared the same airfield. Both Alex and Geoffrey were given parachutes 'just in case'; only Alex used the gift in anger, while Geoffrey had his tested prior to presentation.

Geoffrey's aeronautical background prior to his taking up the post of PTP with Austin Motors at Longbridge can only be briefly dealt with here. In 1994 *A Sound in the Sky – The Reminiscences of Geoffrey Alington* was published, it records his life up to 1943 and is well worth seeking out. Geoffrey was born in 1914 at Swinhope, near Grimsby. He learned to fly at 17 and began studying at the de Havilland Technical School at Stag Lane, Edgware: the school moved to Hatfield the following year. Geoffrey was one of five brothers and in 1934 along with his eldest sibling, William – later Wg Cdr W J Alington DFC* AFC – and with help from his mother, Gladys, bought the first of many aircraft that Geoffrey was to own outright, part-own, rent or borrow. This was DH Moth G-EBWA which cost £175: that's £9,625 in present-day values but if that sounds a bargain, the average annual salary in 1933 was £200. Possession of this Moth was fleeting, it was written off in a forced landing near Buxton on 11th October 1934 – William and his passenger were injured.

With the purchase of the Moth, Gladys travelled to Brooklands to visit the Gregory-Quilter Parachute Company, later known as GQ Parachutes. *A Sound in the Sky* takes up the story, Gladys asked the salesman: "to fit her up and arrange for an aeroplane so that she could try out two parachutes. She received very little instruction and was equipped with no emergency second parachute. Her instructions to jump were: 'when the pilot of the open cockpit Avro 504K gives the signal, hold on to the rip cord handle, climb out, and dive over the side: count ten, and then pull the cord'... She floated gracefully down from 1,500ft. She then put on the second parachute and did *another* jump. Then to the amazement of the Gregory-Quilter's man she said: 'Thankyou. I will have these two. They are for my sons who have purchased an aeroplane.'" Gladys later learned to fly.

Geoffrey entered the Schlesinger Race from Portsmouth to Johannesburg, hiring BA Eagle G-ADID. With Fleet Air Arm Lt P A Booth as second pilot, they set off on 29th September 1936, but the aircraft was damaged during a take-off accident – with Booth at the helm – in Bavaria. In January 1937 Geoffrey completed his time at the DH Technical School and took up a post with Dunstable-based Dart Aircraft – see Alfred Weyl in Chapter Six – demonstrating the company's Kitten single-seater. The following year Geoffrey and friends established Air Touring, a charter operation at Croydon with a small fleet of light aircraft and two Short Scion twins. In July 1938 Geoffrey became the proud owner of DH Puss Moth G-AAZV *Angela*, graduating to Miles Falcon G-AFAY *Angela II* just four months later. *Angela III*, Miles Sparrowhawk G-ADNL, was acquired in April 1939 and there will be more of this anon. (Take a look at the entries for F G Miles and George Miles for further insights into this versatile and enduring airframe.)

Austin at Longbridge

With the outbreak of war Geoffrey joined the Air Transport Auxiliary (ATA), initially working with 2 Ferry Pilot Pool (FPP) at Filton under the Commanding Officer H A 'Tony' Taylor – see Volume One Chapter Five. In the early weeks of 1940 Geoffrey was seconded to the Austin Motors 'shadow' factory at Longbridge which was busy building Fairey Battles. Chief PTP was Neville 'Stacko' Stack but he was enduring an administration role with his deputy, Maxwell Williams, leading the flying team. As related in Chapter Six, Neville had been badly injured in a landing accident in July 1939 and was still walking around on sticks – he did return to flying, ending the war ferrying for the Fleet Air Arm. The massive Austin factory – which built vehicles as well as aircraft – was situated 40ft below the airfield and an incredible lift had been built to bring aircraft up for test. The airfield was not large and frequently a first flight would end at Castle Bromwich – 12 miles to the north east, across Birmingham – or Perdiswell, near Worcester. Both of these offered greater runway and dispersal space.

A Sound in the Sky has a lovely description of a close shave that Geoffrey and the head of the flight shed, Bert Maynard, had in a Battle. "I was doing a dive to maximum speed which was, if I remember correctly, 350mph, and I had started just below the cloud base which was 5,000ft. With my eyes inside the cockpit watching the instrument I waited for the maximum speed to come up. When it did I started winding back on the elevator trimmer to bring the nose up out of the steep dive and, glancing up, was amazed to find the ground much closer than I had expected. It is strange how, after seeing this, my mind took everything in slow motion. I realised that I must pull out very hard from the dive, or I would hit the ground, but not too hard as the aeroplane would 'mush' into it and I would hit the ground anyway.

"Both of us had plenty of time to notice a man pedalling along a lane on his bicycle straight ahead of the aircraft. I saw him look up, and then he slowly appeared to push down on the handlebars and fly gracefully off the bicycle into the ditch – and then we were climbing again. I supposed we must have cleared him by 20ft. On landing we could not help laughing about the incident, but at the same time felt extremely sorry for the bicyclist. If I could have located him, I would have apologised and explained that I was not deliberately 'shooting him up'!"

His secondment over, on 9th April 1940 Geoffrey left Longbridge, having signed off 60 Battles and carried out 90 other flight tests. Returning to 2 FPP at Filton, Geoffrey also spent time at 9 (Service) FPP at Hawarden and he renewed his acquaintance with Tony Taylor who had taken charge of the test flying at the resident 48 Maintenance Unit. 'Stacko' Stack had been impressed with Geoffrey and he campaigned to have him returned to Longbridge on a permanent basis. This he achieved on 12th August 1940 by which time life at Austin was changing dramatically. A new assembly hall was being completed at Elmdon – now Birmingham Airport – there Short Stirlings and Hawker Hurricanes built at Longbridge would be put together and rolled on to the airfield for flight test. At

Longbridge, production of Battles was on the wane, but on 8th October 1940 Geoffrey flew the first of hundreds of repaired and refurbished Hurricanes, Mk.I L1973. Shorts test pilot Geoffrey Tyson (see Chapter Six) captained the first flight of the initial Austin-built Stirling I, W7426, on 22nd April 1941 with Geoffrey Alington as co-pilot.

Lt P A Booth (left) with Geoffrey Alington in front of BA Eagle G-ADID at Portsmouth, September 1936. *Peter Green Collection*

Prime Ministerial visit to Castle Bromwich, 26th September 1941. Left to right: Mrs Clementine Churchill, Geoffrey Alington, Winston Churchill, Alex Henshaw. *Peter Green Collection*

Below: Geoffrey Alington (left) with an unidentified colleague at Ringway in the late 1940s. *Peter Green Collection*

In late 1941 'Stacko' stood down as Chief PTP and Geoffrey took up the post. Flexing his new-found authority, Geoffrey requested former ATA pilot Douglas Cotton join the team and that he be re-united with *Angela III*, his Sparrowhawk. The latter was for use as a 'taxi' to take him to Castle Bromwich, the Short Brothers Repair Organisation (Sebro) facility at Bourn and other flight test and delivery venues. This was granted and, with a coat of camouflage and roundels, G-ADNL became a familiar site at 'Castle Brom', Elmdon and Longbridge. After Stirlings, Longbridge switched to Avro Lancaster Is and VIIs and Geoffrey carried out the final Lancaster test on 27th July 1946.

In 1948 Geoffrey accepted the post of chief pilot for Air Transport SA, a Belgian-based operator flying converted Short Stirling transports. The bulk of the work was on contract to the Vatican, flying missionaries to and from China. He returned to Britain and to test flying, becoming Chief PTP for Fairey mostly flying at Ringway but also from Hamble and White Waltham. Geoffrey also carried out some test flying for Desmond Norman and John Britten on the one-off BN-1 G-ALZE in May 1951 – see Desmond's section in Chapter Six. In 1956 he and his family moved to Sydney, where he was CTP for Fairey Australia. In 1960 Westland acquired the Fairey rotorcraft assets and Geoffrey was out of a job, returning to Britain the following year. From 1973 to 1977 he flew the last of his long line of light aircraft, French-built Cessna 172 G-ASUH, from Binbrook. By the late 1970s Geoffrey had a total 5,910 hours in 176 types. Cyril Geoffrey Marmaduke Alington died on 6th August 1987, aged, 73. As mentioned earlier, *A Sound in the Sky – The Reminiscences of Geoffrey Alington* records his life up to 1943 and is well worth seeking out. It is written in a pleasant 'conversational' style and is a glorious tribute to a man who loved every moment of his time in the air.

'Ramrods' and 'Rhubarbs'

Alex Henshaw is a 'household' name and many readers will have heard of Geoffrey Alington, but it is unlikely that most will know of Clive Anderton. In Volume One Chapter Five Flt Lt Robert W 'Twinkle' Pearson, a test pilot for 5 Maintenance Unit (MU), Kemble, was profiled to highlight the vital role of airmen testing ready for service aircraft fresh from the factories that had been fitted out with operational equipment; or had spent a period of time in store; or had been repaired and/or modified ready to re-enter service. Clive flew for 33 MU at Lyneham almost exclusively on Supermarine Spitfires from various Supermarine production lines. Additionally, he had a two month spell working for Supermarine CTP Jeffrey Quill from High Post. This provides a fascinating insight into the life of a 'jobbing' test pilot, a member of Quill's extensive 'squadron'.

Clive's background prior to joining 33 MU and Vickers-Armstrongs must be necessarily brief: this is a pity because his operational time with 118 Squadron is a story all of its own. Born and bred in Hull, by 1938 Clive was an engineering draughtsman for Blackburn at Brough. With the outbreak of war in September 1939 Clive's job was termed a 'reserved occupation', meaning that he was already undertaking vital war work and he was exempt from call up. In early 1941 he voluntarily enlisted, but used this to influence his RAF service: he insisted that if he was not selected for flying training, he would stay where he was! This

The very first Austin-built Battle, L4935, going up the specially-created lift from the factory to the adjoining airfield at Longbridge, October 1938. *Peter Green Collection*

Geoffrey's 'taxi', Miles Sparrowhawk G-ADNL, at Elmdon in mid-1944. *Peter Green Collection*

Clive Anderton: Spitfire Testing from High Post
July 1944

	Mk	Serial	Hours.Minutes
4 Jul	XII	-	0.15
5 Jul	VIII	MT564	0.20 and 0.10
	VIII	MT949	0.20
6 Jul	XIV	MB691	0.10
	XIV	MB643	0.10
	VIII	MT986	0.30
7 Jul	XI	PL881	1.10
	XI	PL890	0.50
8 Jul	XI	PL889	1.10
	XI	PL887	0.55
	XI	PL891	0.40
11 Jul	VIII	MT989	0.10
	XIV	RM748	0.10 and 0.20
12 Jul	XI	PL892	0.40
	XI	PL893	0.15
13 Jul	XI	PL892	0.40
	XI	PL865	1.30
14 Jul	XI	PL897	1.10
15 Jul	XI	PL894	0.50
	XI	PL895	0.40
	XI	PL896	0.20
16 Jul	XI	PL896	0.20
	XI	PL894	1.00
18 Jul	XI	PL893	1.00
	VIII	MT961	0.50
	VIII	MT575	1.00
	XI	PL899	0.20
19 Jul	XI	PL899	0.30
	VIII	MT577	0.40
20 Jul	XI	PL902	0.20
21 Jul	VIII	MT576	0.50
	VIII	'996'	0.50
22 Jul	XI	PL898	1.00
23 Jul	XI	PL900	1.00
24 Jul	XI	PL901	1.00
25 Jul	VIII	MT579	1.00
	VIII	MT580	0.50
26 Jul	VIII	MV400	0.50
	VIII	MV408	1.10
	XIV	RM761	0.30
	XI	PL901	0.20
28 Jul	XI	PL903	1.00
	XI	PL904	1.20
29 Jul	XI	PL905	0.40
	XI	PL908	0.50

Clive Anderton: Spitfire Testing from High Post
August 1944

	Mk	Serial	Hours.Minutes
10 Aug	VIII	MV410	1.10
11 Aug	VIII	MT581	1.00
	XI	PL909	0.20
12 Aug	XI	PL909	0.20
14 Aug	VIII	MT872	1.00
15 Aug	VIII	MV412	2.00
16 Aug	XI	PL911	1.10
	XI	PL912	0.20
	XI	PL910	1.00
17 Aug	XI	PL912	1.20
	XI	PL910	0.20
18 Aug	XI	PL913	0.40
	XI	PL914	1.00
20 Aug	XI	PL907	1.00
21 Aug	VIII	MV420	0.30
22 Aug	XI	PL915	0.20
	XI	PL907	0.20
23 Aug	XI	PL915	0.20
	XI	PL916	0.20
24 Aug	XI	PL916	0.30
	XI	PL915	0.20
	XI	PL920	1.10
25 Aug	VIII	JF299	1.15
	XI	PL920	0.20
26 Aug	XI	PL923	1.00
	XI	PL917	0.50
27 Aug	XI	PL921	1.10
28 Aug	XI	JF299	1.20
29 Aug	VIII	MV421	1.00
	XI	PL923	1.00
30 Aug	XI	PL949	1.40
	XI	PL919	1.00
31 Aug	XI	PL957	1.40
	XI	PL953	0.40

Notes: All are marked in the logbook as 'Test' or 'Production Test', other than three in late August: 25th and 28th both in JF299 were 'Petrol Gauge Check'; and 29th PL923 'Retest for oil and coolant leaks'. During this time Clive flew three 'comms' aircraft, Percival Vega Gull which Clive recorded as 'X5319', an anonymous Miles Monarch, and an Auster I on five occasions, only once was it recorded as the Vickers-Armstrongs 'taxi' HH987 and it was with these types that Clive visited other airfields; the Spitfires being restricted to High Post. Of these, the Vega Gull was flown the most, but the venues visited on all of the 'comms' flights were: Aldermaston, Castle Bromwich; Chattis Hill, Eastleigh, Farnborough*, Keevil, Northolt*, South Marston – those marked * not being Supermarine or Vickers-Armstrongs sites.

'blackmail' paid off because on 14th July 1941 he was in the cockpit of a de Havilland Tiger Moth at Guinea Fowl airfield, near Gwelo, Southern Rhodesia, ready to commence flying training at 26 Elementary Flying Training School. On 6th August 1941 he went solo in T5489. Clive had moved to Thornhill, also in Southern Rhodesia, in mid-September, this time tackling the enhanced performance of the North American Harvard at 22 Service Flying Training School.

Back in Britain in early June 1942 Fg Off Anderton was posted to 5 (Pilot) Advanced Flying Unit at Ternhill to quickly get him used to the crowded skies and he flew an anonymous Hawker Hurricane on 15th June. By late June Clive's destiny

as a fighter pilot was sealed with his arrival at 61 Operational Training Unit (OTU) at Rednal and Montford Bridge and on 29th June he flew a Spitfire for the first time – Mk.II P7695.

Clive pushed the throttle forward at Zeals in Somerset on 17th September 1942, he was strapped firmly into the cockpit of Spitfire V EP124 'NK-N' *N-for-Nuts* of 118 Squadron for a sector reconnaissance – his first operational sortie. In his time with the unit, Coltishall was to be the longest tenure (January to August 1943) and when Clive left in April 1944 it was at Skeabrae in the Orkneys. Operations were varied but concentrated on 'Ramrods' – escort of tactical bombers – and 'Rhubarbs' – attacks against tactical targets – both of which mostly ranged over northern France and the Netherlands. While flying Mk.V BM514 on 18th July Clive's 'B' Flight engaged a pair of Messerschmitt Bf 109Gs near Den Helder; one was shot down by Flt Lt John Shepherd, in EP549, and Clive, in BM514, shared in the destruction of the second machine with Shepherd. In November 1943 Clive was awarded the Distinguished Flying Medal and on the 21st, at Peterhead in Scotland, he had his first flight in a Spitfire IX, MH737. At Skaebrae in the Orkneys on 24th March 1944 Clive was scrambled in Mk.V BM538 to intercept and identify what turned out to be a Consolidated Catalina. With this 35-minute sortie his operational flying came to an end. Clive was briefly posted to 57 OTU at Eshott but his 'Above the Average' assessment determined he travel south to Wiltshire.

800-plus Spitfire hours

Clive was posted to 33 MU at Lyneham which almost exclusively dealt with Spitfires, his first test being Mk.IX MK570 on 3rd May 1944 for 20 minutes – the classic amount of time for a basic 'shake down'. The Officer Commanding 33 MU Flight Test was Sqn Ldr H A 'Tony' Taylor – Geoffrey Alington's former ATA 'boss' and featured in Volume One Chapter Five. With 748 hours of flying time to his credit, Clive was seconded to Supermarine at High Post for July and August and the table shows the testing carried out in that time and for comparison September 1944 back at 33 MU is also given. The pace at Supermarine was demanding when contrasted with 33 MU. From High Post in July Clive flew 32 hours, 35 minutes on Spitfires, and 16 hours, 40 minutes in the Vega Gull and the figures for August were respectively 29 hours, 35 minutes and 8 hours. September 1944 at Lyneham saw Clive flying 19 hours, 50 minutes on Spitfires, 40 minutes on Seafires and an hour in the Auster 'taxi'. Part of this testing was to determine if the Spitfire would fly straight and level with hands and feet off. If it didn't, the ailerons were appropriately distorted to correct the fault using a mahogany block and a rubber-headed hammer!

Clive served with 33 MU up to September 1945 by which time he had flown Spitfires from Mk.II to F.22 and Seafire IIIs and XVs. With VE and then VJ Days, the nature of Clive's work changed dramatically and in September 1945 he left 33 MU and joined 2 Ferry Pool at Aston Down. He was mostly engaged in ferrying a variety of types to sub-contractors and storage sites – the bulk bound for spares reclaim and scrapping. At Aston Down, in addition to Spitfires and Seafires, Clive flew a Fairchild Argus 'taxi' and sampled a Blackburn type – Firebrand IV EK637 – and Boulton Paul Defiant TT.I target-tug DR945. In late January 1945 Clive had moved to 3 Ferry Pool at Lichfield, which in April the following year moved to Polebrook. On 9th April 1946 Clive ferried English Electric-built DH Vampire I TG345 from its birthplace at Samlesbury to Cranfield – this was his only time in command of a jet. His final sortie was to take Hawker Tempest VI NX173 from Langley to Aston Down, a half-hour flight on 15th April 1946. With that Clive completed 1,180 flying hours, 889 of which were on Spitfires.

Clive Anderton: Spitfire Testing from 33 MU Lyneham September 1944

	Mk	Serial	Hours.Minutes
1	XI	PL955	1.30
2	XI	PL955	0.20
	XI	PL925	0.40
3	XI	PL925	0.40
5	IX	ML400	0.20
	IX	PT967	0.20
	XIV	RM794	0.20
6	XIV	RM794	0.20
	XIV	RM797	0.20
	IX	PT995	0.20
	IX	MH363	0.20
	IX	PT990	0.20
	IX	BS183	0.20
	IX	ML400	0.20
7	IX	PV186	0.20
	IX	MA222	0.20
	VII	MD141	0.20
	XIV	RM759	0.20
8	XIV	RM692	0.20 and 0.20
	IX	PT969	0.20
	IX	PV181	0.20
	VII	MB823	0.20
	VII	MD141	0.20
	IX	ML400	0.20
	IX	PV189	0.20
9	XIV	RM796	0.20
	II	P8257	0.20
10	IX	PV189	0.20
	IX	MA815	0.20
	XII	MB848	0.20
11	XIV	RM799	0.20
	III*	NN308	0.20
	IX	BS463	0.20
	IX	MH323	0.20
12	IX	PT880	0.20
13	XII	MB848	0.20
	IX	PT954	0.20
14	IX	PT954	0.40
	XIV	RM800	0.20
15	XIV	RM650	0.20
	XIV	RM798	0.20
	IX	LZ839	0.20
16	IX	BS183	0.20
	XIV	RM798	0.20
	III*	NN296	0.20
18	IX	RK808	0.20
	IX	PV188	0.20
29	IX	PV249	0.20
	IX	PV234	0.20
	V	BM211	0.20
30	V	AR511	0.20
	IX	PV245	0.20
	IX	PV231	0.20

Notes: * Seafire III. During the month, Clive flew only one 'comms' sortie, on the 3rd in Auster I HH987, used by Vickers-Armstrongs as a 'taxi', from High Post to Aldermaston, returning to High Post, 'clocking' one hour in the air.

Above: Clive Anderton testing Spitfire XIV RM785 on a sortie out of Lyneham on 25th November 1944. *via Alan Curry*

Left: 'My Grandad Flew Spitfires' – the T-shirt proudly worn by grandson Ben in 1989 says it all about Clive Anderton. *Alan Curry*

CHAPTER THREE

Global Reach

Both volumes of *Testing to the Limits* have shown that the definition of a test pilot is very wide. Chapter Four of Volume One highlighted the life-saving work of Martin-Baker and declared 'Benny' Lynch – the first man to try the company's ejection seat in 'anger' – an 'honorary' test pilot. Another pioneering British company that has become a global 'brand' also deserves study: Flight Refuelling Ltd, the present-day Cobham plc. As with Martin-Baker, the technologies needed to develop in-flight refuelling required considerable testing and development, all of which involved the skills of several 'names' mentioned in both volumes: not least the founder, Sir Alan Cobham.

From the early weeks of 1938 the eyes of the press were drawn to the Short-Mayo Composite. The combination of a specially-modified Short 'Empire' flying-boat carrying in 'piggy-back' fashion *Mercury,* a sleek-looking four-engined floatplane, which separated and then headed off across the Atlantic was a great photo-opportunity. In this volume the sections on John Lankester Parker, Harold Piper and Arthur Wilcockson provide more details. The Composite may have been dramatic but in May 1939 it was eclipsed when an aerial

Close up of the Cobham high-speed variable drag drogue and Mk.905E 'fifth generation' refuelling pod under the port wing of a Royal Australian Air Force Airbus Defence A330 MRTT. *Courtesy and © 2015 – Airbus Defence and Space*

tanker topped up a Short 'C-Class' flying-boat over Southampton Water to presage *practical* transatlantic services.

But the story is getting ahead of itself. Alan Cobham was knighted in 1927 for his exceptional long-range 'expeditions': his background and brief test flying career can be found in Volume One. He began in-flight refuelling (IFR) experiments in 1930 using Handley Page W.10 transports from his National Aviation Day (NAD) 'flying circus' fleet and a pair of modified Airco DH.9As. The W.10s had their limitations but had great internal capacity and were easy to modify: the DH.9As turned out not to be suitable as 'receivers' – the top wing blanking the pilot's vision and hampering the 'catcher' in his work.

Alan was not alone in pioneering IFR in Britain; the Royal Aircraft Establishment at Farnborough was also involved in trials, led by Sqn Ldr David Atcherley. Vickers Virginias acted as tankers with Westland Wapitis as receivers. The RAE system proved to be increasingly impractical and was essentially conceptual, not commercial. The Air Ministry eventually backed Alan's trials, providing aircraft and facilities. In the same manner as his African and Australian 'route-proving' flights, Alan decided that the best way to highlight IFR was to stage a 'show-stopper' and eventually he settled on the idea of a non-stop, topped-up flight to Karachi, India (present-day Pakistan). First it was vital to select a suitable receiver aircraft.

Walking stick and balloons

Alan Cobham was one of the founding directors of Airspeed Ltd in 1931 and he commissioned a pair of Ferry tri-motor biplanes for use by NAD. The company also developed the advanced Courier, a four-seater monoplane with retractable undercarriage. The Courier was the answer to Alan's needs; it was the perfect receiver with a spacious cockpit, allowing an operator to stand in a roof hatch behind the pilot to catch the line from the tanker, pull it in and connect it to the fuel system. With a maximum speed of around 150mph and an unrefuelled range of 600 miles it was ideal and the first prototype Courier took to the air in April 1933. (See under George Stainforth in Chapter Six for more on the Courier.)

With Sqn Ldr 'Bill' Helmore braving the slipstream and brandishing a walking stick to hook the line as it dangled from the tanker W.10, the trials began. The line was weighted by a small football, filled with lead shot. It took a long time to perfect the Courier flying underneath the W.10, all the while Bill trying to grasp the line, haul it in, connect it up and stay coupled long enough to take on fuel. In *Airspeed – The Company and its Aeroplanes*, Don Middleton describes a dicey early moment: "The four-pound weight on the trail rope was near to the Courier with Helmore ready to catch it. Cobham banked slightly to bring it within reach, when suddenly the machine was in a violent slide slip with a jammed aileron control. The weight had entered the aileron gap and wedged itself solidly on the port side. Attempts to centralise the stick and stabilise the Courier only jammed the controls more tightly, height was being lost at an alarming rate and six turns of a spiral dive had been completed before it was realised what had happened. Cobham threw the stick violently to starboard and the weight dropped out, but by that time the aircraft was perilously close to the ground."

The football stuffed with lead shot was potentially lethal and it was replaced by a rubber balloon filled with water attached to a thinner rope. If it impacted with anything, damage would be minimal and it was unlikely to cause a control lock. Use of the walking stick to catch the rope continued! A flow of about 18 Imperial gallons per minute was achieved – the present-day Mk.905E pod can transfer at the rate of 350 Imperial gallons per minute.

Cobham and Helmore took off from Portsmouth on 22nd September 1934 in Courier G-ABXN bound for Karachi. Two hook ups were achieved but beyond Malta the Armstrong Siddeley Lynx radial would not respond and Alan set up a glide to Malta, landing with the wheels up at Hal Far – a brilliant bit of flying. For the want of a cotter pin to secure a joint on the throttle linkage, the attempt was over. This blow was as nothing to the content of a telegram received from Britain. After topping up the Courier for the first time, W.10 G-EBMM had been flown to Ford to have the IFR gear removed and seats for 16 'punters' installed so it could resume joy-riding duties for NAD at Coventry. En route, near Aylesbury, the W.10 reared upwards, reeled over on its back and crashed in flames. Pilot C H Bremridge, engineer J Donovan, rigger A Littlejohn and apprentice D A Harington were killed instantly. The mishap that befell the Courier and the W.10 tragedy were not directly related to the IFR process, but it was a severe blow to the project.

Looped hose across the Atlantic

Undaunted, Alan formed Flight Refuelling Ltd (FRL) on 29th October 1934 and took up the lease on Ford airfield on New Year's Day 1936. Air Ministry co-operation increased with the 'loan' of a pair of Virginias (J7711 and K2668) in 1936 and the following year Armstrong Whitworth AW.23 K3585, Boulton Paul Overstrand J9770, Handley Page HP.51 J9833 and Vickers 19/27 J9131 joined the expanding fleet. By this time FRL was assessing the 'Wing Tip' method whereby the tanker line touched the leading edge of the receiver and was then 'encouraged' to move to a latched hook at the wing tip whereby a connection was achieved via special 'plumbing'. Intensive experimentation proved the process was too complex and it gave way in turn to the 'Nose Contact' and then the far more promising 'Looped Hose' system.

Nose Contact turned the tables and made the tanker the one doing the picking up of the rope. A Handley Page Harrow with a hose reel mounted in the lower forward fuselage and a tubular V-shaped rig on the nose would 'catch' a weighted line from the receiver, which was flying ahead and above. The line would then be pulled into the tanker, hooked up to the reel which was then dragged up to the recipient and fuel was pumped upwards.

Looped Hose became the favoured method, up to and beyond World War Two. The receiver would trail a line behind with a grapnel and a bayonet coupler at the end. The tanker flew astern, lower and to one side of the receiver. The tanker fired a light line out sideways, which connected with the one trailing from the receiver, the grapnel and the bayonet would then ensure link up. The tanker would then climb into a position above the receiver while the line would allow the fuel pipe to unreel and be coupled up to the receiver's fuel system. Topped up, the two aircraft would break away in opposite directions.

This system appealed to Imperial Airways and initial trials with Short 'C-Class' flying-boat G-ADUV *Cambria*, flown by Captain Arthur Wilcockson, having hooked up with AW.23

Handley Page W.10 G-EBMR after successfully linking up with the prototype Airspeed Courier G-ABXN, 1933. *Flight Refuelling*

K3585 piloted by Geoffrey Tyson (see Chapter Six) in April 1938 were very promising. The decision was taken carry out transatlantic trials and three Harrows were readied: G-AFRG and G-AFRH were shipped to Newfoundland. Operating out of Shannon airport in Ireland was the very appropriately registered G-AFRL. Over Southampton Water on 24th May 1939 Geoffrey flew G-AFRL and successfully hooked-up with John Lankester Parker piloting *Cabot* G-AFCU. The first transatlantic run was made on 5th August 1939 with *Caribou* G-AFCV being flown by Captain J C Kelly Rogers, topping up off the Shannon estuary from a Harrow flown by Geoffrey Tyson. This was the first of 17 crossings before the war brought the experiment to a close.

Wartime neglect

To Sir Alan Cobham's consternation, the IFR concept was not embraced by the RAF for much of the war. This was all the more remarkable as Coastal Command struggled to provide coverage to convoys as the Battle of the Atlantic developed. In his engaging autobiography, *A Time to Fly*, Sir Alan Cobham expressed his frustration after again attending the Air Ministry to implore the powers-that-be to let him implement an IFR programme: "The Battle of the Atlantic was so crucial that this plan deserved attention at least, but I couldn't get it taken seriously. Perhaps I oversold it: perhaps I put people off by making myself a bore and nuisance. I remember waiting to see two Air Marshals at the Ministry, and chancing to overhear one of them saying: 'Oh God, here comes Cobham and his bloody refuelling again!' 'I'll leave it to you to tell him that there's nothing doing', said the other." From Ford and Staverton FRL carried out varied and vital war work, becoming one of the 'go to' companies that could tackle complex requirements speedily and efficiently.

After Pearl Harbor, the USA found itself with two enemies, each an ocean away. From April 1943 the USAAF undertook trials of the FRL Looped Hose system, with a Consolidated B-24 Liberator as tanker and a Boeing B-17 Flying Fortress as receiver. Staged from Eglin in Florida,

Short 'C-Class' flying-boat G-ADUV *Cambria*, flown by Captain Arthur Wilcockson, having hooked up with the Flight Refuelling Armstrong Whitworth AW.23 K3585, piloted by Geoffrey Tyson, April 1938. *Flight Refuelling*

Handley Page Harrow tanker G-AFRH at Gander, Newfoundland, as part of the western end of the transatlantic experiments of 1939. Note the early hose unit under the forward fuselage. *Peter Green Collection*

these tentative steps were to have a massive effect on both the USAAF and FRL. The RAF finally turned its attention to IFR as it contemplated its part in the bomber war that would bring Japan to surrender. 'Tiger Force' was to be composed of Avro Lincolns and Lancasters, supported by tanker-configured Lancasters. Hundreds of conversion kits were ordered from FRL and plans were made for a speedy conversion programme. As US forces made better than expected headway in the 'island hopping' campaign, the fleets of Boeing B-29 Superfortresses came within reach of the Japan and the atomic hammer-blows of early August 1945 rendered Tiger Force unnecessary.

Airline IFR finale

With World War Two over, FRL turned its attentions again to airliner IFR techniques, but commercial aviation had dramatically evolved. Long runways had been established across the Pacific, through Africa, the Middle East, Asia and into South America – unrefuelled range was less critical than it had been. Britain had largely abandoned the construction of transports during the war and the US had ploughed ahead to dominate the late 1940s and the 1950s with Boeing Stratocruisers, the exceptional Douglas four-engined family – DC-4, -6 and -7 – and Lockheed Constellations and Starliners. All of these had transatlantic reach. Commercial flying-boats rapidly became a niche market.

Attempts to persuade British airlines that IFR had a place in their operations resulted in a series of trials using Lancaster tankers and receivers based in the Azores and Bermuda during 1946-1947. This was followed by crossings of the North Atlantic with BOAC Liberator IIs in the spring of 1948 –

Lancaster IIIs G-AHJW (tanker) and G-AHJU (receiver) hooked up using the 'Looped Hose' technique during the South Atlantic trials of 1946-1947. *Flight Refuelling*

including some night-time top-ups. These were the last gasps of civilian IFR. The 'Cold War' gave FRL an immediate re-direction and then a long-term one. The Berlin Airlift (1948-1949) provided a use for its Lancaster fleet and with the jet age IFR became a wholly military marketplace, one that FRL has dominated ever since.

Birth of the 'Hoodoo'

USAF planners remembered the success of the B-24/B-17 trials of 1943 as they contemplated what would be needed to allow the bombers of the newly-established Strategic Air Command to strike at the Soviet Union. FRL received a lucrative licence agreement in April 1948 with B-29s adopting the Looped Hose system hardware that had been intended for Tiger Force. As this was happening FRL was moving in to Tarrant Rushton airfield, which offered much more room than Ford.

The jet age raised average speeds but also rid the recipients – initially fighters and later bombers – of propellers. The IFR system could be radically rethought and simplified. Gloster Meteor F.3 EE397 was fitted with a fixed probe on the nose in 1949 and trials began with a Lancaster B.3 with a hose reel mounted in the bomb bay. Quickly a funnel-shaped drogue was put on the end of the hose, providing a larger 'target' for the recipient to aim at. Once the probe was within the 'funnel' it could be guided towards a coupling, uniting the hose with the Meteor's fuel system. Among the many engineering challenges this presented, the greatest was that as the probe entered the drogue there was no resistance and the probe merely pushed the

A probe-equipped Meteor F.8 having engaged with an early 'solid' basket at low level. *Flight Refuelling*

Below: A pair of Meteor F.8s from 245 Squadron (WA829 off the starboard wing, WA826 off the port wing) and Flight Refuelling's own F.4 VZ389 hooked up to the USAF Boeing YKB-29T, 1951. *Flight Refuelling*

drogue away. The solution was to put a motor on the hose reel to provide resistance to the probe enabling a smooth coupling. This IFR system became known as a hose-drogue unit – HDU, inevitably Americanised into 'Hoodoo'. The funnel-like drogue became more and more 'open' and is frequently called a 'basket'.

To prove that FRL had a fully working system that could transform military aviation, FRL test pilot Pat Hornidge took EE397 into the history books on 7th August 1949 establishing a jet endurance record of 12 hours 3 minutes. Tom Marks piloted Lancaster tanker G-33-2 around and around the Isle of Wight, with the Meteor taking a 'drink' whenever required with ease.

The existing HDU could fit into a wide range of bomber and transport types to provide a single-point tanker, but the challenge facing FRL's engineers was to make the HDU small enough to be mounted under a wing or at a wing tip to increase the efficiency of individual tankers. The result was the Mk.20 pod and in 1951 conversion of KB-29M 45-21734 was completed at Tarrant Rushton in 1951 to produce the world's first three-point tanker. From 1953 FRL set to work on English Electric Canberra B.2 WH734 to install a Mk.20 into its bomb bay to create Britain's first jet tanker. Podded HDU's gave rise to many more IFR combinations, including 'buddy-buddy' refuelling from fighters to fighters and for the first time shipborne assets were capable of IFR.

Left: No.214 Squadron combined the nightjar from its badge with the Flight Refuelling logo on its Victor BK.1s – XA937 illustrated in 1968. *Roy Bonser*

Below: Victor K.2 XL512 of 55 Squadron, ready to refuel Tornado GR.1A of 13 Squadron, circa 1986. *Sgt Rick Brewell – RAF DPR*

Latest application for Cobham air refuelling pods is the Airbus A330 MRTT programme. Illustrated is the first flight in RAF service of Voyager KC.2 ZZ330, on 12th April 2012. *Courtesy and © 2015 – Airbus Defence and Space*

The USAF went on to adopt the Boeing-developed 'flying boom' technique: a complex process requiring an operator to 'fly' the rigid boom down to the receiver which required a receptacle that was built in to the airframe whereas the FRL system could use 'bolt on' probes. The US Navy stayed loyal to the HDU system, providing its aircraft with far more potential 'filling stations'. Since then the USAF has hedged its bets with the ability to fit a drogue unit on the end of the flying boom – the so-called 'limp dick' option. The Airbus Multi-Role Tanker Transport (MRTT) programme, based on the Airbus A330 widebody, also offers its own version of the flying boom and HDUs underwing.

As well as the home market, FRL established a vibrant export trade for its IFR and other fuel system-related products. The company was renamed Cobham plc to honour its founder in 1994 and to emphasize that it has a vast portfolio that goes well beyond what would be understood via the name 'Flight Refuelling'. Cobham is a major partner in the present-day Airbus MRTT and the Boeing KC-46 Pegasus programmes. Ever since the early trials with Canberra WH734 FRL has provided the RAF with its IFR equipment for the tanker fleet ever since: Vickers Valiant, Handley Page Victor, the interim Avro Vulcans and Lockheed Hercules, Vickers VC-10, Lockheed Tristar, all the way through to today's Airbus A330-based Voyager.

CHAPTER FOUR

Airbuses to 'Puddle-jumpers'

When Specification 1/20 was issued by the Air Ministry to the Bristol Aeroplane Company in 1920, test piloting took a major leap forward both in capability and the way civil and military aircraft could be judged. The document outlined a need for a 'Spares Carrier', a euphemistic way of generating interest in a civil version of the Braemar triplane long-range bomber – see under 'Freddie' Raynham and Cyril Uwins in Chapter Six for more on this huge machine. As the system extended, Air Ministry specifications provided a set of parameters – performance, weight, load-carrying, range etc – against which test pilots could carry out evaluations of how good, or bad, was the aircraft they were testing.

Prior to this a manufacturer test pilot was essentially using his gut feelings about how an aircraft might meet what the customer was looking for. Before the outbreak of the Great War in 1914 private buyers adopted a 'suck it and see' method of discovering if a type was acceptable – or not – and the War Office was not much more sophisticated in its procurements. With the war, the Royal Aircraft Factory became the arbiter of

the success or otherwise of military aircraft and, more often than not, the final 'shake down' occurred at airfields on the Western Front. With the Armistice of November 1918 and the Versailles Treaty of June 1919 Britain established peacetime aviation on a firm and more regimented footing, and the specification system was a part of this process. With this a manufacturer test pilot could devise flight profiles that proved the machine in question could reach such-and-such an altitude, carry a certain bomb load, take-off and clear an obstacle so high and many more targets, all with safety. This process would probably involve a lot of to-ing and fro-ing to the design office, but it helped to consign gut feelings to the history books.

Martlesham Heath and Felixstowe, respectively home of what became the Aeroplane & Armament Experimental Establishment (A&AEE) and the Marine Aircraft Experimental Establishment (MAEE) in 1924 acted as the 'receipt' end of the test pilot process. Aircraft were delivered from manufacturers and Air Ministry test pilots would then take a prototype and see if it met the increasingly complex requirements of the specifications. Rejection may come with recommendations and an invite to bring it back again, or it may be the end of a type's chances.

The first two Hawker Siddeley 748s in the air together during late 1961: G-APZV (background) and G-ARAY. *British Aerospace*

Civil independence

'Proper' civil aviation was only months old when the ink on Specification 1/20 was drying. On 1st May 1919 the Certificate of Airworthiness (CoA) was introduced for civilian aeroplanes and the first permanent registration sequence was begun with G-EAAA for an Airco DH.9 of Aircraft Transport and Travel. The Air Council looked after the development of civil aviation in Britain while the Air Ministry oversaw the issuing of CoAs and was the body that gave approval to new types. In 1926 the Air Ministry produced a two-part handbook for civil aircraft in an attempt to standardise on the minimum requirements. As civil aviation expanded and matured, demand arose for a wholly independent body to administer what became a major source of commerce. The Gorrell Commission published its findings in the summer of 1934 and it recommended a new organisation be created. In 1936 the government created the Air Registration Board (ARB) to certificate and monitor civil aircraft, large and small, private and commercial.

ARB had a brief existence before the outbreak of World War Two and what civil flying there was beyond late 1939 once again became the remit of A&AEE and MAEE. By 1945 the Civil Aircraft Test Squadron was set up within A&AEE to prepare the way for a return to full-blown civil aviation. It was led by Sqn Ldr Hedley Hazelden, later CTP for Handley Page, and among its early 'clients' were the DH Dove and Vickers

Viking. The Civil Aircraft Test Squadron existed through to 1949. ARB continued to oversee certification renewals for the small fleet of civil aircraft that operated during the war, returning to its full remit in 1946. In exactly the same manner as A&AEE, it established its own test aircrew to monitor the airworthiness certification of new types.

Along with service test pilots and other specialist evaluators, ARB test pilots are beyond the remit of *Testing to the Limits*, but the role is a vitally important one and deserves outlining. Initially the workload was small and pilots were called in as needed, Sqn Ldr Douglas Weightman was the first CTP to be appointed in 1947. Tragically he was killed while testing a Brigand B.1 for Bristol on 14th October 1948 – see Chapter Six. Former Fleet Air Arm pilot David P Davies joined ARB in 1949, taking up the role of CTP.

In 1972 the Civil Aviation Authority (CAA) Safety Regulation Group took over the role of the ARB. Between them, since the late 1940s the ARB/CAA Flight Department has been involved in the certification of many civil types, an ever diminishing number of which are wholly UK-built, the majority later coming from overseas.

Several ARB/CAA test pilots are profiled within Chapter Seven of Volume One and Chapter Six herewith. In common with all aspects of test piloting, the work of the ARB and CAA is not without sacrifice; for example CAA test pilot Al Greer and FTE David Morgan were killed, along with a Dornier test pilot on board Dornier Do 228 D-IFNS which crashed in West Germany on 26th March 1982 during UK certification trials.

Former Botswanan Air Force Scottish Aviation Bulldog 120 G-BHXA getting airborne from a Northamptonshire airstrip in April 2014. It is operated by Airplan Flight Equipment, a sister company to *Testing to the Limits* publisher Crécy Publishing. *Ken Ellis*

Cosmopolitan flight test

The title of this chapter really does take in the remit of the civil aviation authorities: airliners of all sizes, from BN Islanders to Airbus A380s, corporate jets large and small, flying school Beagle Pups to a huge variety of sport aviation types; helicopters ranging from North Sea oil rig 'shuttles' and air ambulances to personal 'taxis'. Some areas of civil aviation have been vested with specialist approved organisations; eg the Light Aviation Association (previously the Popular Flying Association) and the British Microlight Aircraft Association.

The certification process concludes with the award of a Type Certificate after a long and rigorous testing and evaluation regime. Each individual aircraft is then granted a Certificate of Airworthiness, or Permit to Fly for certain lighter types, which shows that it conforms to the build standard as prescribed in the Type Certificate.

The ARB/CAA was involved from the very start in the joint Concorde certification programme. The Anglo-French supersonic transport pioneered cross-nation processes and the Concorde certification book was known as the 'Grand Livre'. The achievement of the joint Type Certificate involved a huge team, at Filton and Toulouse, and with the ARB/CAA and the French equivalent, the Direction Générale de l'Aviation Civile and the Centre d'Essais en Vol. It is often forgotten that Federal Aviation Administration certification was also achieved for Concorde's operation by US airline Braniff International.

There were many new aspects covered during the flight testing and assessment of Concorde, as distinct from the contemporary swept-wing jet transport aircraft. A selection of these challenges provides an illustration of enormity of the task facing the manufacturers and the certification bodies.

■ Defining equivalent climb performance limiting gradients for a slender delta wing layout to establish take-off, climb, approach and landing weight/altitude/temperature limits for the Flight Manual.

■ The use of a single point centre of gravity (cg) near the aft limit for take-off was found to be acceptable because of the very accurate cg control system using the equally precise fuel quantity measuring system needed for the supersonic speed operations.

■ Assessing handling characteristics and control systems for transonic acceleration, including necessary cg movement and appropriate ranges of speed, altitude and cg to operate safely and efficiently up to and beyond Mach 2 for significant time periods. Also deceleration back to subsonic speed and lower altitudes, again with cg movement.

■ Establishing acceptable handling of system failures, including engines and intakes, in the normal and abnormal supersonic and subsonic flight envelope; to ensure safe return.

■ Defining landing speeds and procedures to enable the scheduled landing distance required performance to fit the preferred landing runway, such as the 8,400ft Runway 22L at New York's John F Kennedy (JFK), normally used in low visibility weather. The landing distance required would usually be well within the take-off distance required on a defined runway. At JFK, and some other airports, the preferred landing runway was not necessarily the same as the take-off runway.

These tests and procedures required many sorties and close co-operation between the manufacturer test pilot teams and the certification body flight test teams. All involved in Concorde were aware that the programme was forging new European links; few could have foreseen what it would lead to. The overall certification process paved the way for Joint Airworthiness Requirements and the present-day European Aviation Safety Agency. Perhaps Concorde's greatest unforeseen legacy was to provide the launch pad for the creation of the multi-national, world-beating, giant, Airbus.

Certification runs through to such things as evacuation times, seat anchoring and many more items: the interior of a corporate-configured BAe 146. *British Aerospace*

CHAPTER FIVE

Pilot, Salesman, Diplomat

Without sales there is no production line and nothing to test. Part and parcel of the job of a test pilot is to help the marketing team sell aircraft. This is not restricted to devising a flying routine that is impressive yet honest, it will almost certainly involve flying customer pilots, 'top brass' or managing directors and the occasional celebrity – providing there's room of course! The flying could develop into much more than an 'introduction'; military airmen may want a fulsome briefing on capabilities and to fly a series of operational profiles – this could take a 'detachment' of days or even weeks in-country. Airlines would want route-proving flights, possibly with cabin crew and even 'passengers', to examine how quick turnarounds can be and if the fuel burn is really what is claimed – or perhaps just a 'jolly' for the shareholders.

Flying displays also have to be staged at 'trade shows', where the industry gathers with guests and the press to entertain, cut deals and get the 'word' across. The home-spun 'showcase' is the biennial Farnborough, once an all-British affair but these days wholly cosmopolitan, and there are similar events often with specialist themes dotting the calendar and the planet. There is a broader interpretation of marketing that is frequently labelled 'awareness' – flying for the public at airshows. Apart from the 'public relations' angle, you never know who may be in the audience ready to influence decision makers or even to pounce with an enormous chequebook!

At all of these occasions, the test pilot is never off duty. Once the flying is done there are press conferences, endless questions from customers, support crews to be briefed, hands to be shaken, documentation to be checked, names to be remembered, flight lines to be 'walked', air traffic procedures to be adhered to, dinner jackets to be squeezed into, speeches to deliver and a good night's 'kip' to be achieved! Throughout it all, the test pilot is probably the most demanded of his company's team – sometimes the *only* representative – and constantly an ambassador for his employer and country.

John Farley flying Harrier Mk.52 demonstrator G-VTOL from the helicopter deck of the marine assault support vessel HMS *Fearless* moored on the Thames alongside the Royal Naval College, Greenwich, 24th June 1975. *via John Farley*

From 1932 to 1937 Hendon was the shop window for Britain's aircraft industry, as the SBAC staged an event following on from the RAF Pageant. 'Wing walkers' guiding the Bristol 120 ready for is display slot, June 1933. *KEC*

Curtain up – Display flying

During the research for this book, the author enjoyed interviewing Harrier test pilot John Farley and, as his airshow flying had never ceased to impress, much of the conversation centred on display and demonstration. Accordingly, this chapter is based upon John's patient answering of questions and from plundering his incredible autobiography *A View from the Hover*, which should be on everyone's 'must read' list. While this section is gloriously Harrier-centric, the procedures and disciplines relate to any type, or circumstances.

For the purposes of this chapter a 'display' is a flying presentation of the aircraft and there is little difference in the routine presented to the 'top brass' or to the public. A 'demonstration' is a far more role-specific sequence designed to show the aircraft in a very particular manner, perhaps staged as part of major presentation at Dunsfold, or in the customer's own country, or with the Harrier's shipborne ability, on a vessel. Such a demonstration may also involve 'kit' or weaponry requested by the nation involved and unique to that requirement.

With any new type, a display routine is built up, using a series of manoeuvres designed to highlight the particular attributes of the aircraft. With something as revolutionary as the Harrier there was considerably more scope as to what could be done, but at the same time it was important to show what was *routinely* achievable, not a one-off airshow 'trick'. John Farley: "Above all, the display pilot should understand the limits of his aeroplane." For example, John's 'signature' nose-up rotation immediately after a vertical take-off into a steep climb at the beginning of his routine was completed with a gentle adoption of level flight. While this looked spectacular and always transfixed the audience, showing off the top side silhouette, it was a safer manoeuvre for the crowd as it was staged on the 'B' axis – at right angles to the audience and

going *away* from them. (A normal flat take-off and horizontal transition parallel to the crowd was clearly less impressive.)

Having worked up a display and talked it through with other members of the flight test team, for many shows, be they 'trade' or 'public' there is a Flying Control Committee (FCC) to satisfy. Rehearsals at Dunsfold would be followed by an 'audition' at the show airfield, for example Farnborough or Le Bourget, in front of the host's FCC which will have well-established safety parameters that must be adhered to. This is not always the case, standards can vary. In *A View from the Hover* John outlined how a colonel addressed the pilots before 'curtain up' in Latin America in 1973: "...one of us asked what the minimum display height was and he replied: 'Above ground level'. When questioned as to exactly what he meant by this he looked somewhat pained and said: 'Don't hit the ground'. After the brief, a few of us Europeans decided we would use 50ft and so what if the locals flew lower than us."

Because the Harrier was such a radically new concept, much thought was given as to how to highlight the rotating nozzles of the Pegasus engine to the audience. In *A View from the Hover* John explained a scheme for the 1976 SBAC airshow at Farnborough: "John Fozard, our chief designer, decided that G-VTOL should have a smoke system fitted to show the crowd the nozzle angle in use at any point of the show. Sadly it did not quite work like that. If the aircraft had any forward speed when the nozzles were fully down the smoke immediately turned the corner and streamed behind the aircraft. During my first rehearsal in front of the Flying Control Committee, I had the smoke on and was doing about 200 knots when I lowered the nozzles to the vertical to decelerate to the landing pad. At this 'Bea' Beamont remarked to the committee: 'What is John doing now? It looks like an inverted run by the *Flying Scotsman*!'"

Held at Radlett in 1946 and 1947, the SBAC settled on Farnborough in 1948. Pre-production Bristol Belvedere HC.1 XG451 demonstrating its capabilities at the 1960 airshow. The load is a perfect piece of product-placement, a Bristol Bloodhound surface-to-air-missile. *Bristol Siddeley*

G-VTOL mentioned above is the aircraft most associated with John – it can be seen today at the Brooklands Museum. It was part of a long line of company-owned demonstrators, going back to Hawker Hart G-ABMR of 1931 and concluding with Hawk Mk.50 G-HAWK of 1975. John thinks G-VTOL was a very important investment and that it was essential for it to be a two-seater. It allowed operational pilots to safely experience V/STOL flying at first hand and – if it was necessary – non-pilots could be given a ride. G-VTOL was not solely financed by Hawker Siddeley, as John remarked: "the subcontractors threw in their bits for free – it was very cost effective..."

John added another 'routine' to his display flying in 1978, although it involved a vast amount of preparation and was necessarily a one-off. Having carried out the maiden flight of the prototype Sea Harrier FRS.1, XZ450, at Dunsfold on 20th August 1978, John began planning for the following month when he would not only display the fully navalised Harrier at Farnborough but he would also present the first public demonstration of the 'ski-jump' carrier take-off technique. John was well versed in 'ski-jumping', having carried out his first such take-off from the adjustable ramp at the Royal Aircraft Establishment, Thurleigh, during the summer of 1977. Using portable girder bridge units, a ramp had been built at Farnborough and impressively bombed-up Harrier GR.3 XV789 and debutant XZ450 astounded the audience with the simple but effective way of doing away with catapult launches for a 'conventional' take off from the deck of an aircraft carrier. The author is very proud to declare that he was one of the thousands gob-smacked by what he saw!

Leap of faith

Presenting an aircraft to an air arm or a government involves an element of display flying, but this is just one element of the complex presentations and negotiations. Initial approaches can result in something as simple as the hand over of brochures and specifications. It may be years, if at all, before the sales team gets a 'bite' and a demonstration becomes part of the marketing 'pitch'. It's at this point that the CTP and his team start to hone their display and plan for any customer-specific exercises. John explained that in its simplest terms, the flying was dictated by the answer to a straightforward question: "What do these blokes want the aeroplane for?"

A potential customer will have churned through the finances, the performance figures, support requirements and endless other figures and projections. With the Harrier, an important part of the sale 'drive' was the RAF, as the first air force to operate the ground-breaking machine. Talking to air and ground crew helped considerably to get across the 'how to' and this was also where the test piloting team came into their own – in the early years they had more experience of Harriers than anyone else. John: "You are there to encourage and re-assure and one of the best ways to get message across

is to let [the customer] know the limits of the aeroplane, you must tell the truth." He added: "this openness can put you in conflict with the 'party line' – to sell the machine – but honesty is the best sales tool."

Spain is a long-term Harrier operator, initially taking 'first generation' Harriers, which were designated AV-8S Matadors and now flying AV-8B Matador IIs. A Harrier purchase would transform operations by the Spanish Navy, which previously had been an all-helicopter organisation. Selling the Harrier would require planners in Madrid to take a leap of faith and change the scope and structure of the naval air arm. Since the late 1960s the Spanish Navy had been using the carrier *Dédalo* as a base of operation for Sikorsky Sea King anti-submarine helicopters. Early in the negotiations about acquiring Harriers, it was clear that a demonstration of the type flying from the deck of the *Dédalo* was essential.

A *View from the Hover* outlined Spain's introduction to the Harrier at sea: "With the *Dédalo* cruising somewhere off the east coast of Spain, the flight was a fair old jaunt from Dunsfold so I had asked the hangar to fit a couple of 330 gallon ferry tanks [to GR.1A XW770] to give me plenty of reserves should a game of hunt the ship be necessary. ...this had happened to me once before, so I had learned the hard way to include such an eventuality in my fuel sums.

"After a dull high level flog across France, I coasted out again and in due course started my let down. Once I got below cloud, there she was, exactly where she said she would be and pressing on in a calm sea. She even answered my radio call at once on the briefed frequency, completing a truly class act. After burning off some of the remaining fuel with a few passes at a little above normal helicopter speeds I was welcomed aboard following a simple vertical landing on the stern.

"The next day the weather was forecast to close in so we lost no time in flying three sorties, culminating in a gun attack on a splash target. Only one of the 30mm ADEN guns was functioning nevertheless the rounds the other gun sent into the splash seemed to satisfy the onlookers."

On board *Dédalo* John was quizzed by an admiral who had an obvious enquiry: "our pilots are helicopter pilots, how do we convert?" John knew that there was rivalry between the navy and the air force – the latter seeing itself as having the 'exclusive' on fixed wing types. John dispensed with the mystique, explaining that flying helicopters at sea was an excellent background for Harrier operation. Knowing the Spanish navy had training links with the US Navy, he suggested that they be extended to include fast jet conversions, perhaps on Douglas A-4 Skyhawks, to provide the mid-way point in conversion to V/STOL operations.

Left: A thoughtful John Farley preparing himself before displaying a Sea Harrier at the 1981 Paris Salon, at Le Bourget. *via John Farley*

Below: John Farley carried out the first flight of the prototype Sea Harrier FRS.1, XZ450, on 20th August 1978 and the following month was demonstrating ski-jump take-offs at the Farnborough airshow. The 'jump' was adapted from medium girder bridge by Fairey Engineering and erected by 32 Field Squadron Royal Engineers. *British Aerospace*

The third prototype HS.146, G-OPSA, was used in 1984-1995 by Pacific Southwest Airlines for route-proving , often another role for a test pilot team. *British Aerospace*

As well as demonstrations John and his team would be involved in presentations and flying at Dunsfold for delegations as deals got closer to signing. He praised the determination of the sales team, facing a long, painstaking process that most times came to nought but every so often brought about a contract. Typically self-effacing, John explained that there was never any pressure prior to a demonstration sequence: "I was the icing on the cake; I knew the real work had been done in the conference room". Marketeers, government agencies and the flight test team all combine to make a successful export contract – providing yet another aspect of the test pilot's job.

CHAPTER SIX

Throttle Forward – Britain's Test Pilots

Chapter One – *What is a Test Pilot?* – defines what a manufacturer's test pilot is for the purposes of this book. Readers should refer there, but to recap: the main rationale for inclusion is at least *one* maiden flight of a type, or *significant* sub-variant. All known chief test pilots, whether or not they achieved a 'true' first flight, are also detailed. Several other individuals appear by virtue of other exploits or achievements. Sadly, the other criterion for an entry is to have been killed while performing a debut flight. Chapter One also outlines what *sort* of aircraft are dealt with.

Space precludes entries for *all* test pilots and production test pilots, even though their work is very important, not without risk and thoroughly deserving of study: Chapter Seven provides the *briefest* details. Index I gives test pilots by manufacturer and Index II lists not only types, but who 'first

A pair of throttles in this case, controlling two 4,300lbst Garrett TFE731 turbofans on a Hawker Siddeley HS.125-800. The story of the 125 is told via the following test pilots: Chris Capper, Mike Goodfellow, Peter Sedgwick. *Raytheon Corporate Jets*

flighted' what as another means of cross-reference. To help keep track of changing names within the UK aircraft industry, Appendix A is a *brief* 'genealogy' of who-became-who of the main players.

Test pilots are listed alphabetically, by 'basic' name, often by nickname. Ranks, full names, decorations/honours, where applicable, are given within the narrative. (Academic or membership qualifications, eg MA, RAeS, etc are *not* given.)

Where applicable, a 'log' of that pilot's maiden flights with the following information: date, type (with serial/registration if applicable), number of engines, power and engine name/series. (hp – horse power, to denote piston engines, shp – shaft horse power to denote turboprops and turboshafts and lbst – pounds of static thrust to denote turbojets and turbofans, and rated *dry*, ie without reheat/afterburner.) This is presented by way of a quick guide and to prevent repetition of data within the main narrative, particularly when a lot of prototypes listed. While every effort has been made to make this 'log' comprehensive,

TESTING TO THE LIMITS

in many cases it has been impossible to get multi-source confirmation. Where a pilot is known to have been a chief test pilot for a particular period, unlike in some publications, no 'blanket' assumptions have been made that *all* significant maiden flights in that timeframe can be attributed to him.

This is followed by *brief* notes on their background, presented in *italics*; before a detailed examination of their career as a test pilot is examined. Pilots mentioned within the narrative that have their own section within this volume, or in Volume One are denoted with an asterisk (*) upon *first* mention within each biograpahy. Other than in the 'brief background' notes, abbreviations have been kept to a minimum; those frequently used are given in Appendix B.

'Jimmy' James

25 Sep 1913	James-Caudron biplane 1 x 40hp Anzani
late 1917	Siddeley Deasy RT.1 B6625 1 x 200hp Hispano-Suiza
20 Jun 1921	Gloster Mars I G-EAXZ 1 x 450hp Napier Lion
21 Aug 1923	ANEC I G-EBHR 1 x 26hp Blackburne Tomtit
Aug 1924	ANEC II G-EBJO 1 x 35hp Anzani

Notes: Caudron flown from Clynderwen, Wales; the RT.1 from Radford; the Mars I from Hucclecote and the ANECs from Brooklands. Blackburne was a Surrey-based motorcycle engine manufacturer and not to be confused with the Brough-based aircraft and engine manufacturer, Blackburn.

John Herbert James (known to his family as 'Hebbie'), born 1894. He and his elder brother, Henry Howard James (born 1891) built and flew a series of box-kites and in 1912 were among the first to enrol in the International Correspondence School's new course in aeronautics; both graduated. The pair went to Hendon and they were taught to fly on Blériots and Caudrons at the W H Ewen School. Jimmy was awarded Aviators' Certificate No.315 on 15th October 1912 and Howard No.344 on the 22nd. They returned to their father's farm near Clynderwen in Wales and built a modified Caudron biplane with plans supplied by W H Ewen, British agent for the type. The machine was first flown on 25th September 1913, but it crashed on its second flight, with Jimmy piloting. Rebuilt, the Caudron flew in Pembrokeshire skies until the advent of war in August 1914.

During August 1914 the brothers moved to Hendon, becoming instructors at the Felix Ruffy school, taking the Caudron with them. In January 1916 Howard joined the RNAS and is thought to have instructed at Eastbourne. (After a spell at the Royal Aircraft Factory – see below – Howard served with 64 Squadron at Sedgefield with DH.5s. The unit crossed the Channel in October 1917 but in December Howard was either shot down or involved in a traumatic accident. He was invalided out of what was then the RAF in October 1918. Howard died in 1958.)

'JIMMY' JAMES became a test pilot at the Royal Aircraft Factory, Farnborough, and was joined there in July 1916 by his elder brother Howard. In March 1917 the pair became Second Lieutenants in the RFC Special Reserve with Jimmy

'Jimmy' James with the Gloster 'Bamel' during the 1922 Coupe Deutsch de la Meurthe. *Peter Green Collection*

going to 1 Aircraft Acceptance Park at Coventry, testing aircraft from Longbridge, among others. In late 1917 he carried out the first flight of the Siddeley Deasy RT.1, a much revised version of the Royal Aircraft Factory RE.8, at Radford. On that inaugural sortie the designer, John Lloyd, flew as a passenger.

Jimmy settled in Ruislip in May 1919 and started work for Nieuport and General Aircraft Ltd (N&G) at Cricklewood, under CTP Leslie Tait-Cox* and its gifted designer Henry Folland, whom Jimmy would most likely have met at Farnborough. An early assignment was to travel to India and demonstrate Nighthawk G-EAEQ; Jimmy returned in March 1920. That year N&G folded and both Jimmy and Folland moved to Hucclecote, joining the Gloucestershire Aircraft Company (later Gloster).

On 20th June 1921 Jimmy made the first flight of the Mars 1 G-EAXZ, at Hucclecote. A high-performance racer, this machine was designed to put the new company 'on the map'. It went under the curious nickname of 'Bamel', apparently because it exhibited some characteristics of a bear, but others of a camel! Below the cockpit G-EAXZ carried a cartoon of Jimmy, complete with signature silk scarf, riding a half-bear, half-camel. Piloted by Jimmy, the Bamel won the sixth Aerial Derby race around London at an average speed of 163mph. Jimmy picked up a trophy and £600 – £33,000 in present-day values – for his employer. He flew the Bamel to Étampes in France to compete in the Coupe Deutsch de la Meurthe in October 1921, but did not finish. During trials at AEE Martlesham Heath, Jimmy got the Bamel up to an average of 196mph – a British record; one of the four runs made reached 212mph, exceeding the world record. On 7th August 1922 Jimmy won the Aerial Derby, this time at 177mph; but again did not complete that year's Coupe Deutsch de la Meurthe. During this time, Jimmy was involved in production testing Sparrowhawks, Nighthawks (Mars VI) and Nightjars (Mars X), all derived from the original Nieuport. Jimmy parted company with Gloster in 1923 and Larry Carter* took over. (Carter went on to fly the 'Bamel' in much rebuilt state – which see.)

Jimmy became the test pilot of the newly-established Air Navigation and Engineering Company (ANEC) of Addlestone, Surrey. On 21st August 1923 he flew the company's first product, ANEC I G-EBHR, at Brooklands. This tiny machine was one of two built for the Air Ministry's Light Aircraft Trials at Lympne, to be staged the following month. Jimmy coaxed the ANEC I to an incredible 87.5mpg, sharing the Duke of Sutherland's prize of £500 for the most fuel-efficient aircraft with the English Electric Wren, flown by W H Longton. The following year, Jimmy was flying the two-seater ANEC II G-EBJO at the Lympne trials, but it was withdrawn. He *very probably* made the first flight of this aircraft, which today flies as part of the Shuttleworth Collection at Old Warden. Beyond 1924 Jimmy seems to have stopped flying, taking a full-time post with instrument makers S Smith and Sons at Cricklewood. He joined the RAF in a non-flying capacity in 1940 but was taken ill and died in hospital on 4th February 1944.

Colin Jarred

BY AUGUST 1941 Fg Off Colin Robert Jarred was flying Supermarine Spitfire Vs with 41 Squadron from Marston. He *may* have flown with 616 Squadron prior to this. By June 1942 he had been seconded to Supermarine as a PTP. A test flight on 18th June 1942 ended in disaster when the engine of Spitfire IV BR643 failed and Colin attempted a forced lading near Midhurst. The Spitfire hit trees and burst into flames, killing the 27-year-old. The sortie originated at Henley-on-Thames, also known as Crazies Farm, which may not leap to the mind as a Supermarine test flight venue. This was the home of final assembly for the Reading Group of factories, hence Colin's fateful flight test from the airfield.

'Andy' Jones

Andrew Philip Shetler Jones, born in 1939. After graduating from the RAF College Cranwell in 1959 he became an instructor at 4 FTS, Oakington. His next tour was an on EE Lightning F.2s with 92 Squadron, then as a Lightning weapons instructor on 226 OCU at Coltishall. He graduated from No.25 Course ETPS at Farnborough in 1966. A tour on 'A' Squadron A&AEE Boscombe Down was followed by an exchange posting to the USAF at Tyndall, Florida, on Convair F-106 Delta Darts.

'ANDY' JONES recruited to join the Hawker Siddeley Dunsfold test team in 1970, initially working on Harriers under CTP Duncan Simpson*. With the advent of the Hawk he became the type's Project Pilot in 1974 and was responsible for the test and development programme that saw the RAF Hawk T.1 released to service in 1976. On 17th May 1976, company-owned demonstrator Hawk Series 50 G-HAWK had its maiden flight. This hard-working machine was used to help develop the

Andy Jones, with his boss John Farley, and a Hawk in the background.
British Aerospace via Tony Buttler

various export versions of the Hawk and Andy led these efforts as well as flying several overseas sales tours with the aircraft.

John Farley*, Dunsfold CTP from 1978 (with HSA becoming BAe the year before), takes up Andy's story: "With flying in general, as well as test flying, it is so often what you least expect that gets you. On a 'routine' flight in a Hawk T.1 to test nothing more demanding than the range of the radio at high altitude, Andy was in the back with the front seat occupied by an inexperienced Hawk captain getting some time in before carrying out overseas delivery flights. In the way of things and shortly after losing radio contact over the sea beyond the Scillies, the engine made grinding noises and quit. Being the perfect gentleman Andy offered to take over as captain from the front-seater – an offer that was not surprisingly accepted. They set off gliding towards Culdrose only to find that the airfield was closed that day and they would need to go to St Mawgan. A successful forced landing with a seized engine on the main runway was followed by air traffic asking them to taxi clear as they had other aircraft that wished to use the runway!

"A much more potentially serious incident occurred when Andy was doing another 'routine' trip at Dunsfold. This time he was flying an export Hunter on a production 'ceiling climb' to measure climb performance. At high altitude he started to feel unwell and selected 100% oxygen flood flow before starting a quick descent and turning for home. The next thing he knew was regaining consciousness, pointing at the ground, supersonic and not that high. He recovered and later back at base it became clear that his oxygen bottles had been filled with nitrogen. Sometimes the good guys win regardless of what is thrown at them!"

Andy became Deputy CTP in 1978 and succeeded John Farley as CTP at Dunsfold in 1983 before retiring and handing over to Mike Snelling* in 1985.

Fairey Long Range Monoplane J9479 – Sqn Ldr Arthur Jones-Williams was its first and last pilot. *KEC*

Arthur Jones-Williams

14 Nov 1928   Fairey Long Range Mono J9479
                 1 x 570hp Napier Lion XIA

Arthur G Jones-Williams, born 1898 in Canada. After training at Sandhurst, joined the Welsh Regiment, fighting on the Western Front 1916. He was seconded to the RFC in 1917, with 29 Squadron on Nieuport 17s and 23s and, from mid-1918, with 65 Squadron on Sopwith Camels, both units based in France. Between April 1917 and October 1918 Arthur is credited with 11 aerial victories, 2 destroyed and 9 out-of-controls. The latter were 7 Albatros D.IIIs, a single D.V and one Fokker D.VII; the destroyed were a pair of D.VIIs. Arthur took a permanent commission in the RAF and in the mid-1920s was CO of 23 Squadron at Kenley, with Sopwith Snipes and later Gloster Gamecocks.

IN 1928 Sqn Ldr Arthur Jones-Williams was chosen to pilot a new type designed specifically for record-breaking long-range flights. This machine was commissioned from Fairey and under the design leadership of Hollis Williams* an advanced monoplane with a span of 82ft was created. Initially it was referred to as the 'Postal Aeroplane' in an attempt to throw the Treasury off the scent, but eventually the RAF came clean and designated it, prosaically, Long Range Monoplane. J9479 was taken to Northolt and assembled and Arthur took it on its maiden flight in November 1928. Fairey CTP Norman Macmillan* would ordinarily have done the job, but it seems the RAF were keen for Arthur to get familiarised from the earliest opportunity. Norman did carry out some flights before J9479 was ferried to Cranwell, which offered the RAF's longest flying field. Flt Lt N H Jenkins OBE DFC DSM was detailed to act as navigator on the record-breaking sorties.

On 22nd-23rd March 1929 Arthur was at the helm of J9479 for a 24-hour endurance test. Along as an observer was Hollis Williams. The monoplane landed having flown 1,950

miles. Cranwell was again the venue on 24th April 1929 when Arthur and Flt Lt Jenkins took off heading east. They completed the first non-stop flight to India, landing at Karachi after 50 hours, 37 minutes and 4,130 miles. The pair embarked in J9479 again on 16th December 1929, this time bound for South Africa from Cranwell's turf. The large monoplane impacted on high ground to the south of Tunis in North Africa, killing Flt Lt N H Jenkins and the 31-year old Sqn Ldr Arthur G Jones-Williams OBE MC* CDG.

'Pee Wee' Judge

27 Aug 1964	Beagle 242X G-ASTX
	2 x 195hp RR-Continental IO-360-A
27 Apr 1967	Beagle Pup 100 G-AVDF
	1 x 100hp RR-Continental O-200-A
19 May 1969	Beagle Bulldog G-AXEH
	1 x 200hp Lycoming IO-360-A

John W Charles Judge, born 1922. Joining the RAF, by 1943 he was serving with 33 Squadron in the Western Desert, on Hawker Hurricane IIs and Supermarine Spitfire Vs. He was posted to 245 Squadron, flying Hawker Typhoons, from July 1944 stepping through France and the Netherlands into Germany. He stayed on with the RAF initially ferrying within Europe and then as a maintenance unit test pilot in India. Leaving the RAF in 1948, he freelanced as a delivery pilot.

KNOWN universally as 'Pee-Wee', John Judge joined Supermarine as a production test pilot in 1950, working on Seafires, Spitfires, Attackers, Swifts, through to Scimitars. In 1959 he was testing with Rolls-Royce at Hucknall, types flown included the Airspeed Ambassador Tyne test-bed G-AKRD. Along with several others ('Dizzy' Addicott*, Les Colquhoun*, Jasper Jarvis, David Morgan*) Pee-Wee was involved in a series of wet runway braking trials for the Ministry of Supply using Supermarine Swift F.7 XF114, these lasted from 1958 to 1962.

In 1961 Pee-Wee joined the newly-established Beagle Aircraft at Shoreham as CTP. He missed out on 'first flighting' the prototype Beagle 206 twin – see John Nicolson – but was in command of the pre-production example, G-ARXM, on 12th August 1962. Beagle was developing a family of light aircraft and following the cancellation of the composite construction Beagle 218 twin – see George Miles – a conventional all-metal version was built, the four-seat 242 twin. Pee-Wee carried out the maiden flight at Shoreham in August 1964 and demonstrated it at the Farnborough show the following month. The 242 programme was axed in 1967. The two-seat aerobatic Pup 100 appeared in 1967 and Pee-Wee flew the prototype and demonstrated it widely. The three/four seat Pup 150 tourer followed, the first example, G-AVLM, flying on 4th October 1967. In May 1969 the Bulldog military trainer version had its maiden flight with Pee-Wee again at the controls. Beagle ceased trading in December 1969 and the Bulldog became the responsibility of Scottish Aviation – see John Blair. (The Bulldog prototype, G-AXEH, is on show at the National Museum of Flight Scotland, at East Fortune.)

In 1961 Beagle started a collaboration with Ken Wallis*, the light autogyro pioneer, who had developed the WA-116 single-seater. Five of these were built at Shoreham, mostly for evaluation by the Army Air Corps. Ken carried out the bulk of the flying with Pee-Wee clocking up nearly 15 hours over 137 sorties between late 1961 and December 1963. Following the collapse of Beagle, with his experience of Wallis 'gyros Pee-Wee was engaged by Airmark Ltd of Storrington, Sussex, as test pilot. The company intended to revitalise the marketing of Wallis-designed autogyros and in March 1970 took on WA-117 G-AXAR, which had been built by in 1969 by Ken's cousin, Geoffrey.

For the SBAC airshow at Farnborough that year, Pee-Wee displayed *Alpha-Romeo* on 7th, 8th and 9th, with Ken taking over on the 10th. The following day, the last of the 'trade' days, Pee-

The one-off Beagle 242X G-ASTX at Shoreham, 1964. *Beagle*

Here come the Pups!
the most exciting aircraft of all

✳ LUXURIOUS ✳ TOUGH ✳ AEROBATIC ✳ STABLE ✳ EASILY MAINTAINED

Beagle AIRCRAFT LTD
SHOREHAM AIRPORT · SUSSEX · ENGLAND · TELEPHONE: SHOREHAM-BY-SEA 2301
REARSBY AERODROME · LEICESTER · ENGLAND · TELEPHONE: REARSBY 321

Basic monochrome advertising of December 1968, featuring the first four Pups. Top to bottom: No.2 G-AVLM the prototype 150 first flown 4th October 1967; No.3 G-AVLN the second 150, 17th January 1968; No.1 G-AVDF the prototype, 8th April 1967; No.4 G-AVZM the second 100, 23rd February 1968 – all flown by 'Pee Wee'.

The prototype Bulldog, G-AXEH complete with Scottish saltire at East Fortune, 1984. *KEC*

Wee again displayed G-AXAR, but the little rotorcraft crashed, killing its 48-year-old pilot. The Accidents Investigation Branch published Report 7/74 on 21st March 1974, within its 10 pages was the following summary: "After a high speed downwind run parallel to the runway the aircraft first pitched rapidly nose-up, then nose-down, and went out of control, the rotor blades striking the propeller, fin and rudder as it fell to the ground. The pilot was killed instantly." At the time John W Charles Judge had a total of about 9,300 flying hours. The report concluded that the accident: "resulted from a loss of control due to the effect of negative 'g' when the pilot attempted to control a nose-up pitch that occurred during a manoeuvre in which the aircraft's speed exceeded the authorised maximum."

Stuart Keep

Nov 1918	Westland Weasel F2912 1 x 340hp ABC Dragonfly
Jul 1919	Westland Limousine I K-126 1 x 275hp RR Falcon III
Jun 1920	Westland Limousine III G-EARV 1 x 450hp Napier Lion IA
Feb/Mar 1921	Westland Walrus N9500 1 x 450hp Napier Lion II
9 May 1924	Westland Dreadnought J6986 1 x 450hp Napier Lion II

Arthur Stuart Keep, born 1891 to British parents in Australia. A university graduate, he joined the Warwickshire Regiment in September 1914. By late 1915 he was on the Western Front, but was invalided back to Britain in 1916. Stuart transferred to the RFC, gaining his 'wings' in August 1916, going on to serve as a ferry pilot. From January 1917 he worked as a test pilot checking aircraft off maintenance or repair, perhaps in the Middle East. By April 1918 he was flying Airco DH.4s with 55 Squadron at Azelot, France, and was engaged on 'ops' including a raid on Cologne in May 1918. He was wounded and returned to Britain in July 1918.

CAPTAIN ARTHUR STUART KEEP MC was posted to Yeovil by the Air Ministry to act as a test pilot for Westland succeeding F Alexander*. In 1919 Stuart became the company's inaugural full-time CTP. His first prototype was the Weasel two-seat fighter which – like others – suffered from adopting the temperamental ABC Dragonfly engine. During one flight, Stuart had managing director Robert Bruce in the gunner/observer's compartment when the ABC stopped, a long way from the comparative safety of the Yeovil circuit. Stuart managed to bring the Weasel all the way back to the airfield, clipping trees on the approach. With or without the Dragonfly, the Weasel was unlikely to enter production. It was intended to replace the Bristol F.2B Fighter, but the RAF had already realised that the best replacement was more of the same!

The next design recognised the need to enter the civil market: the Limousine accommodated 3 to 5 passengers in sumptuous conditions – a Lear Jet of its day. To meet the demands of the Air Ministry's Commercial Aeroplane Competition to be held in August 1920, the type was so altered that the six-passenger Limousine III showed only a family resemblance to its forebear. This was a three-bay, no longer two-bay, biplane, with a length of 33ft 6in (Limousine I – 27ft 9in), span of 54ft (was 38ft 2in) and another 175hp. At Martlesham Heath, the Mk.III came away with the £7,000 first prize in the 'small' category – that's a hefty £385,000 in present-day values. Demonstrations to customers included Stuart joining them in the aircraft's cabin which may have been a graphic way of showing how stable the Limousine III was without a pilot at the helm, but the message was likely neutered by the initial alarm or panic! Production of all models of the Limousine came to just eight units.

The prototype Westland Walrus, with its flotation bags deployed. *Peter Green Collection*

Stuart's new 'first' was the Walrus, a much re-engineered Airco DH.9A for shipborne fleet reconnaissance duties. The Yeovil factory had great experience building DH.4s, DH.9s and 'Ninacks' as the DH.9A was nicknamed. The resulting Walrus was fitted with an under-fuselage observation/gun gondola, three separate 'cockpits' for the crew, detachable mainplanes and arrester wire 'jaws' for deck landing. The undercarriage included a hydrovane to prevent tip-over and jettisonable wheels for ditching and pneumatic flotation bags along the engine cowling to aid stability in the water. Not surprisingly, Stuart found the first example, N9500, very difficult to control. For the maiden flight the erecting shop foreman, Harry Dalwood, was 'volunteered' to go along with Stuart. On chopping the throttle, N9500 assumed a pronounced nose-down attitude. Harry was persuaded to climb aft, along the top of the fuselage until the centre of gravity was restored allowing for a hasty return to terra firma. With enlarged rudders, 36 Walruses were built at Yeovil.

A 450hp Napier Lion II also powered the next project, but other than that the Walrus and the Dreadnought could not have been more different. Inspired by the thoughts of Russian designer M Voevodskii, the RAE at Farnborough and the Aeronautical Research Committee had tested some models in 1919. The Russian proposed a very deep aerofoil to create an all-metal cantilever monoplane wing that blended into the fuselage. Issuing Specification 6/21 the Air Ministry chose to call the required machine a 'Postal' aeroplane and asked for accommodation for eight passengers. (The 'Postal' ruse was again used with the Fairey Long Range Monoplane -see Arthur Jones-Williams.) In modern day parlance, the Dreadnought would be regarded as a pioneer of the Blended Wing Body (BWB) concept.

On 8th May 1924, with Robert Bruce as a passenger, Stuart carried out initial taxying trials of the Dreadnought. The following day, with most of the factory out on the airfield to watch, Stuart – alone this time – carried out a few 'straights' and then elected to take-off. Very quickly J6986 assumed a steep nose-up attitude, the starboard wing dropped and the Dreadnought crashed; the 960lb Napier Lion crushed the cockpit. There was no such thing as a 'response vehicle' in those days. This was not an example of Westland parsimony; such things were almost universally unheard of. The factory nurse, Sister Thomas, proved to be both quick on her feet and cool-headed. Pinned in the wreckage by his legs, Stuart was given life-saving tourniquets before he was extracted and rushed to hospital. Both of his legs were amputated and his long convalescence included getting used to life on prosthetic limbs. The Dreadnought was quietly forgotten; knowledge of such aerodynamics was many decades away. When fit enough, Stuart returned to work at Yeovil, initially as technical supervisor and, from 1934, as business manager. Laurence Openshaw* took over as CTP. In a shake up at Westland he was 'retired' in 1935. Captain Arthur Stuart Keep MC died on 3rd December 1952, aged 61.

'Ronnie' Kemp

8 Aug 1911	Flanders F.2 Monoplane 1 x 60hp Green
early 1916	Short Bomber 3706 1 x 225hp Sunbeam
Jul 1916	Short 310 floatplane 1 x 310hp Sunbeam
23 Jan 1917	Short N.2A floatplane N36 1 x 200hp Sunbeam

Notes: Flanders tested at Brooklands, the Type 310 and the N.2A from the Medway at Rochester.

Ronald Campbell Kemp, born 1890. Learned to fly with the Avro school at Brooklands, initially on the Type IV triplane and then Type D biplane. He was granted Aviators' Certificate No.80 on 9th May 1911.

'RONNIE' KEMP was retained by Avro and in July 1911 was to pilot the specially-modified Type D in the potentially lucrative *Daily Mail* 'Circuit of Britain' race with a £10,000 prize. The biplane was given extensions to both the upper and lower wings; the former bolstered by additional struts extending diagonally to the shorter lower wings. Ronnie was second away from the start line at Brooklands and reached about 700ft. In a strong wind the aircraft lost height, then at about 100ft the port lower wing extension detached and the biplane spiralled into the ground. Miraculously, Ronnie suffered only scratches and bruises. After this Alliot Verdon Roe decided that no 'mods' would be made by 'eye' and the small company needed to hire a stressman.

This experience did not diminish his enthusiasm; the following month Ronnie tested at Brooklands the second monoplane designed by Howard Flanders – a previous assistant of Roe's. With a second seat and other modifications, this craft was renamed the F.3 and Ronnie entered it into the British Empire Michelin Cup, with awards for closed-circuit and non-stop cross-country flights. He was unsuccessful in both categories. During 1912 and 1913 Ronnie worked for the Lakes Flying Company at Bowness, Windermere; there he met up with John Lankester Parker*.

Towards the end of 1913, Geoffrey de Havilland* gave up his post as chief designer and CTP for the Royal Aircraft Factory and Ronnie was appointed in the latter role. On 23rd February 1914 Ronnie had another close shave. Flying a Royal Aircraft Factory FE.2, with E T Haynes acting as observer, Ronnie was carrying out stalls when the pusher biplane spun in near West Wittering: Haynes was killed and Ronnie suffered a broken leg.

By August 1914 Ronnie had moved on to Shorts at Rochester, taking over as CTP from Gordon Bell*. Much of the work was centred on the very successful Short 184 patrol floatplane. In this capacity, he came under the eye of his elder brother, William Pitcairn Kemp, who worked for the Admiralty checking on the workmanship of suppliers to the RNAS. ('Peter', as William Pitcairn preferred to be known, became works manager at Rochester in 1918.) The Type 184 was produced by several manufacturers and it was Ronnie's responsibility to test the first-of-kind from sub-contractors; for example he was at Great Yarmouth in January 1916 trying out 8368, first 184 built by Phoenix Dynamo. As work expanded at Shorts, so did the need for additional test pilots and John Lankester Parker joined Ronnie in 1916; this was the start of 'Lanky's' incredible career. The Type 184 led to the Short Bomber, an increasingly large landplane used for long range sorties by the RNAS. Ronnie found its lifting capacity disappointing – it was intended to carry a bomb load of close on to 1,000lb care of a 225hp Sunbeam. A partial solution was to extend the 72ft wing span by 6ft, but with a fuselage length of half that – 36ft 6in – it was not surprising that the tail

Proudly declaring it was built by Short Brothers, Aeronautical Engineers of Rochester, England, torpedo-laden Short 320 N1393 also displayed its constructor's number, S.402, under the serial number. The warning under the cockpit appeared on every production example: 'Very Important – The Removable Rear Crossbar Must always be in Position Before the Wings are Folded'. *KEC*

'feathers' had little effect on pitch and yaw. Service acceptance flights by Wg Cdr Arthur Longmore produced exactly the same conclusion as Ronnie had come to – with a longer fuselage the tail surfaces would have a much greater turning moment from which to influence the rest of the airframe!

C H Barnes in *Shorts Aircraft since 1900* takes up the plot: "...Horace Short [chief designer] refused to make the change without re-stressing the whole airframe, and Longmore was anxious to get the German [coastal] batteries silenced as quickly as possible. So he arranged for Horace to receive an invitation from the Admiral commanding naval forces in Belgium to visit the RNAS at Dunkerque." With Horace out of the way Ronnie and Arthur set to with affirmative action at Eastchurch and cut the fuselage of the prototype Bomber, 3706, off just behind the rear cockpit! A new fuselage section was scarfed in, increasing the length by 8ft 6in. Before the pair could test the modified machine Horace's secretary sent her boss a telegram saying that she thought something untoward was going on! The great man returned and refused to talk to Ronnie, who naturally thought his employment was a thing of the past. The following morning Ronnie and Arthur awaited the wrath of Horace. But, as C H Barnes explained: "...Horace had stayed up all night checking the strength of the lengthened fuselage, and they were greeted with one of his broadest smiles and an announcement that the job was already cleared for production..." The Short Bomber was built by four other companies in addition to Shorts and was involved in a number of crucial raids – all down to a bit of 'cut and shut'!

The Type 310 was tested by Ronnie in the summer of 1916 and was another extrapolation of the Type 184 family, for torpedo attack or patrol. The designation was taken from the power rating of its Sunbeam engine; so, when fitted with a 320hp Sunbeam Cossack the type became the 320. A shortened, single-seat version of the family, the N.2A, was intended as a scout floatplane. Try as he might, Ronnie could not get the prototype to leave the water and as the second example showed poor characteristics development was stopped. The redesigned N.2B had slightly better prospects.

Ronnie left Shorts and was succeeded by 'Lanky' Parker in January 1918. By 1920 Ronnie was running his own company, Air Survey Ltd. Initially operating Airco DH.9 floatplanes a contract to chart the Irrawaddy River in Burma was followed by another in Sarawak, Borneo. By 1928 fellow former test pilot 'Freddy' Raynham* had joined Ronnie and a major commission gave rise to a new organisation, the Indian Air Survey and Transport Ltd, headquartered in Calcutta. Ronnie went on to become an aeronautical engineering consultant to the Indian Government. He returned to the UK in 1947 and bought a boat yard on the Hamble. In 1963 former BAC test pilot Peter Hillwood* tracked Ronnie down to seek his opinion on an Avro type to be used in the film *Those Magnificent Men in their Flying Machines*. The intention was to build a replica of the Roe Type III triplane, but Ronnie suggested the Type IV – on which he had started to learn to fly 52 years previously – as he felt it had far better flying characteristics and was more robust. Ronnie was taken at his word and as the surviving replica still delights crowds at Old Warden each season, he was spot on! Ronald Campbell Kemp died in 1978, aged 88.

Hugh Kendall

| 21 Jul 1949 | Miles Marathon II G-AHXU
2 x 1,010shp AS Mamba |
| 8 Oct 1955 | Somers-Kendall SK.1 G-AOBG
1 x 330lbst Turboméca Palas 1 |

Notes: Both flown from Woodley.

Hugh McLennan Kendall, born 1915 in Canada. Active as a sporting and racing pilot in the pre-war years and from 1939 served with the Air Transport Auxiliary, piloting a wide range of types including amphibians.

BY 1946 Hugh Kendall was a test pilot for Miles at Woodley, his work involving Aerovan and Marathon development and production sign-off. While calibrating the accelerate-to-stop distance of Aerovan V G-AISJ at Woodley on 15th July 1947 Hugh reached take-off speed, chopped the throttles and applied the brakes, only for the nosewheel to collapse. The aircraft skidded along on its nose, its cockpit being increasingly demolished. As rescue crews approached the scene they fully expected the worst. Hugh was extracted from *Sierra-Juliet* with just cuts and bruises – the anchor points for his seat had come adrift and he was propelled away from the carnage occurring in front and beneath of him.

The Miles company foundered in late 1947 and in June 1948 Handley Page took over most of the aviation assets at Woodley; Hugh was appointed as CTP to Handley Page (Reading) Ltd. In January 1950 he set off in Marathon G-ALUB on a 40,000-mile demonstration tour of Australia and New Zealand with sales manager Gp Capt 'Bush' Bandidt as co-pilot. Sales prospects for the original four-engined Marathon were not looking good and the decision was taken to re-engineer it as a twin turboprop. Hugh was in command of the prototype Marathon II, G-AHXU, for its maiden flight on 21st July 1949. *Xray-Uniform* became the largest aircraft Hugh had ever raced when it was entered into the *Daily Express* coastal air race of 16th September 1950; he averaged 280mph and came seventh.

Hugh left Handley Page in 1950 and worked as a freelance consultant. In response to a 1947 design competition staged by the British Gliding Association, Hugh entered the K.1 glider – nicknamed 'Crabpot' – and it won. In 1953 he commissioned Elliotts of Newbury to build a redesigned version, with a V-tail. This was first flown at Lasham in March 1954 but it did not enter production. In response to a request from racing pilot 'Nat' Somers in 1951 Hugh designed and supervised the construction of the SK.1 two-seat jet under the aegis of Somers-Kendall Aircraft Ltd. Hugh flew SK.1 G-AOBG for the first time on 8th October 1955. A mid-air turbine failure on 11th July 1957 put paid to the SK.1's prospects and it was donated to the so-called 'Library of Flight' at the College of Aeronautics, Cranfield. The fuselage is believed extant amid hopes that it may one day take to the air again.

By the early 1960s Hugh was living on the Isle of Wight and working for the Air Registration Board. He became involved with Britten-Norman (see Desmond Norman) in the mid-1960s as a consultant and on 1st January 1970 became

Above: The one-off Marathon II wearing Handley Page logo on the nose.
Handley Page (Reading)

Right: The Somers-Kendal SK.1 G-AOBG at the College of Aeronautics,
Cranfield, Beds, May 1963. *Roy Bonser*

the company's experimental test pilot on Islanders and
Trislanders. Work with BN was varied, including tropical
performance trials on the first from-new Trislander, G-AYTU,
at two locations in Eritrea: Asmara (7,500ft above sea level)
and Massawa (at sea level) in September 1971. He was
appointed CTP in 1979, semi-retiring to the role of consultant
test pilot in 1983, finally retiring from the Bembridge-based
enterprise in 1989 at the age of 73. From 1964 to 1992 Hugh
commuted to his work in SAN Jodel D.150 G-ASRT, from a
tiny airstrip close to his home in Yarmouth, this included the
'hop' to Bembridge! Hugh Kendall MBE died in 1999.

Reginald Kenworthy

May 1918	Blackburn Blackburd N113 1 x 350hp RR Eagle VIII
1920	Blackburn Swift N139 1 x 450hp Napier Lion IB
1922	Blackburn Blackburn N150 1 x 450hp Napier Lion IIB
26 Sep 1923	Blackburn Pellet G-EBHF 1 x 450hp Napier Lion

Notes: All but the Pellet flew at Brough, the Pellet made its
first flight from Hamble Water.

REGINALD WATSON KENWORTHY was born in 1891 and by
mid-1912 he was working for Robert Blackburn, being
involved in the abortive two-seat Type E monoplane. He was
flying as a passenger of Sydney Pickles* in the Type I
monoplane in July 1914. Reginald was granted Aviators'
Certificate No.1222 in 1915 and became an instructor, very
probably with Blackburn. By 1916 he was testing for
Blackburn and in May 1917 took over as CTP following the
death of Rowland Ding*. His first work was checking out
Blackburn-built Sopwith Baby floatplanes from the slipway at
Brough into the River Humber.

The Blackburn Blackburd (that's no spelling error!) was a
single-seat torpedo-attack biplane and this was Reginald's first
'first'. Trials included the dropping of dummy torpedos in the
Humber and jettisoning the mainwheels, to allow for a ditching
on the 'hydrovane' that was part of the main undercarriage
struts. Only three Blackburds were built.

In the slump of the immediate post-war years, Blackburn
diversified by establishing the North Sea Aerial and General
Transport Co Ltd from April 1919 and Reginald was the chief

One of three dual-control Dart civilian seaplanes used for training by Blackburn at Brough, 1926. *KEC*

pilot. Initially converted Blackburn Kangaroo bombers were used but a small fleet of Avro 504Ks was added to cater for the 'joy-riding' market. The first recorded charter for the new company was flown by Reginald on 10th May 1919 taking freight from Gosport to Leeds, via Hounslow. While flying two passengers for a 'trip around' the bay at Scarborough on 3rd August 1920 the engine failed in Avro 504K G-EAGV and Reginald had to make a hasty force-landing. He and his passengers escaped unscathed, but the Avro was a write off.

Another attempt was made at creating a torpedo-attack aircraft in the form of the Swift in 1920. On the maiden flight of N139 the centre of gravity was far too far back as Reginald discovered from the steep climb-out and the useless elevator. He was able to throttle back and crab his way around a wide circuit using a dropped wing and rudder. The Swift attracted orders for a pair from the US Navy and five from Japan. As the Dart it entered production for the Fleet Air Arm. After the adoption of the name Blackburd, it was perhaps inevitable that the three-seat shipborne general reconnaissance biplane would be called the Blackburn *Blackburn*. This large 45ft 6in span biplane was built for the Fleet Air Arm from 1922 to 1925.

Robert Blackburn decided that the Schneider Trophy competition, due to be staged at Cowes in September 1923 was a worthwhile venture and the Pellet single-seat biplane flying-boat was created for the purpose. G-EBHF was launched into the Humber in early September but the 'boat was caught by the tide and rolled over, Reginald received a drenching – it was not to be his last. The contest was scheduled for the 28th, with the previous day set aside as the 'last possible' moment for acceptance trials. The Pellet was sent by rail to Southampton and from there on the back of a truck to Hamble. A test flight on the 26th revealed that G-EBHF was *very* nose heavy and then the Lion engine over-heated. Reginald put it down abeam Calshot seaplane station and it was towed to Cowes by a motorboat. The following day, Reginald tried again on the waters of the River Medina but the Pellet started to violently porpoise, then reared into the air and crashed back into the water. Reginald was trapped inside the cockpit but managed to extricate himself and clambered onto the up-turned wreck to await rescue. With this, Reginald's career for Blackburn came to an end. 'George' Bulman* took on the testing of new types, on loan from Hawker, as and when needed.

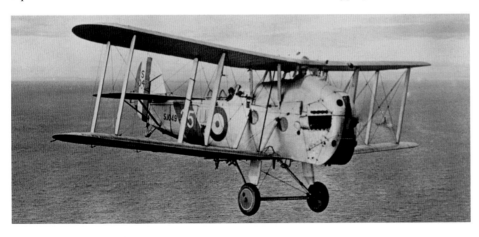

Blackburn Blackburn II S1049 of 420 Flight, as operated from HMS *Furious*, 1926-1927. *KEC*

Pat King

23 Mar 1926	ANEC III
	1 x 350hp RR Eagle VIII

F G OFF PATRICK J R KING tested the first of three ANEC III transport biplanes built for the Australian market at Brooklands on23rd March 1926. The Air Navigation and Engineering Company (ANEC) of Addlestone, Surrey, had picked up the contract after the Handasyde H.2 (see Frank Courtney) had failed to come up to the requirements of the agents, Larkin Aircraft Supply. By 1928 'Pat' King was a flight commander with 22 Squadron, the resident service test unit within A&AEE at Martlesham Heath. By September 1936 Pat was a Squadron Leader, in command of 64 Squadron, equipped with Hawker Demons. He finished his RAF career as an Air Vice-Marshal.

'Archie' Kingwill

Feb 1926	Beardmore WB.XXVI
	1 x 360hp RR Eagle IX
3 Sep 1936	CLW Curlew G-ADYU
	1 x 90hp Pobjoy Niagara III

C APTAIN ARCHIBALD NORMAN KINGWILL was appointed as CTP to the re-established aircraft division of William Beardmore & Co by 1924. The company had secured the services of former ANEC designer William Shackleton and he came up with a radical all-metal two-seat fighter, the WB.XXVI, which had attracted interest from the Latvian government. The biplane had no bracing wires, a hexagonal section fuselage and the company claimed that the WB.XXVI could not be spun. The issue of *Flight* magazine for 25th February 1926 described a demonstration by 'Archie': "The throttle was then closed and the control stick pulled right back. The machine assumed an attitude of approximately 60 degrees to the horizontal and commenced to sink on an even keel. By way of showing that the machine was still under control in this fully stalled condition, Captain Kingwill rocked it laterally and pitched it fore and aft." Today, that would be called a high-alpha manoeuvre, or high angle-of-attack. Despite this promise, it was rejected as lacking in performance by the Latvians: the WB.XXVI remained a one-off.

The one-off CLW Curlew of 1936; an all-metal light aircraft in a world dominated by wood and fabric construction. *Peter Green Collection*

A decade later Archie had been engaged by CLW Aviation, a company set up by Stanton Cole, providing the finance, and designers Arthur Levell and Francis Welman to develop a new lightweight method of all-metal construction. The Curlew two-seater served as a demonstrator of the concept and was aimed at the sporting and primary trainer marketplaces. Archie flew the prototype, G-ADYU, from Gravesend in September 1936 and it was well received, but was considered expensive. The Curlew remained a one-off. In May 1939 Archie was demonstrating another civil prototype, the twin-engined, twin-boom, Willoughby Delta G-AFPX and it is *likely* that he had carried out the first flight from Witney.

Don Knight

Donald M Knight, born 1931. National Service with the RAF 1949-1951, training ending with conversion to Gloster Meteors at Middleton St George and then Stradishall. He was posted to 603 (City of Edinburgh) Squadron RAuxAF first on Supermarine Spitfire F.22s, then DH Vampire FB.5s at Turnhouse and briefly at Leuchars. He stayed on with 603, as a reservist, until 1954.

'D ON' KNIGHT joined English Electric on 1st June 1953, initially as a PTP on Canberras from Samlesbury. With the jet bomber programme in full swing, life was busy: Don carried out six sorties on 7th September 1955. He took a major part in B(I).8 development flying. On 27th July 1958 Peter Hillwood* flew the first 'true' Canberra PR.9, XH129, at Sydenham, Northern Ireland. (See also Mike Randrup for the 'big-wing' prototype, WH793, of 1955.) After shake-down at Sydenham, XH129 was ferried to Warton on 11th September 1958 and there it became Don's domain, as he had been appointed as project pilot for the PR.9 programme. With Don at the controls and P H Durrant as FTO in the nose, XH129 took off on a low-level structural test sortie on 9th October, 1958. Off Blackpool's 'Golden Mile', Don pulled hard for a high-'g' turn and a wing broke off outboard of the engine nacelle. Don had just enough time to eject, his parachute only fully deploying just before he hit the water. The FTO – with no ejection seat – stood no chance: Durrant's body was discovered still strapped in his seat in the wreckage. As explained in Chapter One, Volume One, the PR.9 was strengthened and redesigned, the navigator gaining an ejector seat.

That was not the only time that Don had to thank Martin-Baker. He converted to Lightnings and, by the time of his retirement, had clocked 1,000 hours on type. At the helm of the fifth pre-production P.1B XG311 on 31st July 1963 the starboard undercarriage leg refused to lower. After several attempts, it was clear it was not going to budge and that a landing in such a configuration was far too risky. Don pointed XG311 out into the Irish Sea and 'banged out', to be rescued by Warton's own search and rescue Westland Whirlwind HAS.7 XG597.

Prior to this incident, Don had been in the USA as part of the run-up to the maiden flight of the TSR.2. He flew Lockheed NT-33A 51-4120 which had been converted into a variable stability test-bed by Cornell University and operated initially by the institution's Aero Lab at Buffalo, New York. Later this 'T-Bird' was used by NASA, boasting among its pilots Neil Armstrong. It had an incredibly long flying career, retiring in April 1997 to join what is now the National Museum of the USAF at Dayton, Ohio. Promoted to DCTP under Jimmy Dell* in January 1964, Don flew two sorties in TSR.2 XR219 – both with Peter Moneypenny – on 10th February and 27th March 1965. In January 1968 Don retired for medical reasons and he became a much-travelled member of BAC's sales department and was appointed Executive Director, Marketing in 1980. He retired in 1990.

Frederick Koolhoven

1914	Armstrong Whitworth FK.1
	1 x 50hp Gnome

FREDERICK KOOLHOVEN was born circa 1886 in the Netherlands. He learned to fly in 1910 on Farmans in France and joined Armard Deperdussin's Société Pour les Appareils Deperdussin at Reims as an assistant designer. By 1912 he had moved to the UK to work within the UK off-shoot, The British Deperdussin Aeroplane Syndicate, in London. He joined Armstrong Whitworth's newly-established aircraft manufacturing division at Gosforth, Newcastle upon Tyne, in 1913, initially as assistant works manager. His capabilities in design were soon recognised and his first creation was a private-venture single-seat military biplane, the FK.1. With this machine he became a designer-pilot (see Chapter Two in Volume One) by carrying out the maiden flight. He does not appear to have repeated this function with the series of types he created for Armstrong Whitworth. In 1917 Frederick moved to the British Aerial Transport Company (BAT) as chief designer. Joining him at BAT was Peter Legh*, who had tested Koolhoven's FK.6 in 1916. By late 1919 Frederick had returned to his native Holland, working for the state aircraft industry, Nationale Vlietuigindustrie, before establishing his own company, Koolhoven Vliegtuigen in 1934. He designed a series of military and civil types up to 1940. (See Frank Courtney and Marcel Desoutter, who flight tested for Koolhoven during this era.) Frederick Koolhoven died in the Netherlands in 1946.

Robert Kronfeld

10th Aug 1943	Baynes Carrier Wing RA809 glider
13th Nov 1944	General A/c GAL.56 TS507A glider

Robert Kronfeld, born 1904 in Austria. The first glider competitions were staged at Wasserkuppe, Germany, in 1924 and Robert became fascinated by soaring flight and enrolled in Austria's inaugural gliding club. In 1926 he designed and built a glider, called Wien (Vienna) to attempt the 5,000 Deutsche Mark competition staged by German newspaper Grüne Post for the first glider flight of at least 100km. In a five-hour sortie, Robert managed a distance of 102.5km and won the prize. He used the money to build

another glider of his own design, the 30m span Austria. His exploits, including display flying and distance and altitude records made him a celebrity. He was invited to Britain in 1930 for the Daily Express-supported glider meeting at Itford in Sussex and Robert flew 50 miles, landing near Portsmouth. On 20th June 1931 he became the first person to fly a glider across the English Channel. Hitler became Chancellor of Germany in January 1933 and among many edicts, Jews were banned from flying. Robert re-located briefly to Austria, before settling in Britain. In May 1933 Charles Lowe-Wylde was killed and Robert took over the latter's Feltham-based British Aircraft Company (BAC), manufacturers of gliders and light aircraft. In 1936 BAC was renamed Kronfeld Ltd, but it ceased trading the following year and Robert took up the post of instructor and manager of the Oxford University and City Gliding Club.*

WITH the advent of war in 1939 Robert Kronfeld adopted English citizenship. His extensive gliding experience was not put to waste; he joined the Airborne Forces Experimental Establishment (AFEE) at Sherburn-in-Elmet in 1942, taking the rank of Squadron Leader. An extreme example of AFEE experimentation was the deliberate ditching of General Aircraft Hotspur II BT771 into Tatton Mere, near Knutsford on 20th June 1942; almost certainly on a sortie originating from Ringway. The main undercarriage was jettisoned but on touchdown the front section of the Hotspur fragmented; Robert and an unnamed observer were injured and rescued. The flight was to assess the use of gliders making water landings for commando-type raids; no more similar trials were attempted.

In 1943 a tail-less glider was delivered to Sherburn for tests of a radical scheme to *fly* tanks into battle zones. This strange device may have raised eyebrows at AFEE but was not a surprise to Robert, who had flown several tail-less gliders designed by the German pioneer Alexander Lippisch during the 1920s and early 1930s. Glider and light aircraft designer Leslie Everett Baynes had conceived what he called the Carrier Wing while working for research and development specialist Alan Muntz Ltd at Heston. The Carrier Wing was a 100ft all-wood sweptwing with fins and rudders as 'endplates' on the wingtips. The wing would be attached to a light tank and the combination would be towed to a landing zone by a Handley Page Halifax, or Short Stirling, and released. The pilot-cum-tank-commander would then guide the contraption in to a landing, using the tank's tracks as 'undercarriage'. The wing would be jettisoned during the landing roll and the tank would go off to war. A one-third scale version of the planned wing, with a small cockpit in the centre section was built by Slingsby Sailplanes for aerodynamic trials. Officially designated the Baynes Carrier Wing, its format meant that it was universally referred to as the Bat. Low-level tows behind a Jeep at Sherburn were followed by the first flight on 10th August 1943 with an Avro Tutor as tug. Robert was favourable about its flying characteristics but nothing further came of the Carrier Wing as the much more orthodox General Aircraft Hamilcar assault glider was adopted for carrying tanks and heavy equipment into battle.

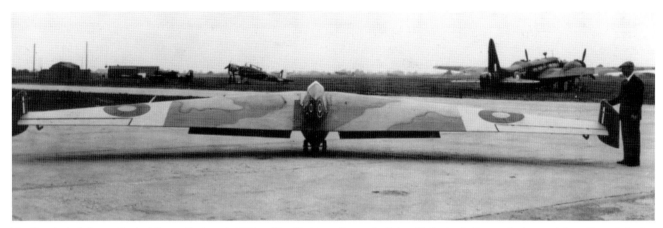

The Slingsby-built Baynes Carrier Wing at Sherburn in 1943 – with a Blackburn Skua and a Vickers Wellington in the near background. *Peter Green Collection*

The first GAL.56 tail-less glider, TS507, with canted-back main undercarriage. The mainwheels came from a Westland Lysander. *Peter Green Collection*

During November 1944 Robert was at Radlett to test the Handley Page Manx tail-less aircraft – see 'Jamie' Talbot for more. Sqn Ldr Kronfeld's second 'first' occurred that month and was also tail-less. Hanworth-based General Aircraft had been contracted to build a series of two-seat gliders with different wing planforms to investigate the slow-speed characteristics of the sweptback, tail-less format. Three GAL.56 versions with a 'conventional' fuselage on top of the wing and the much more advanced GAL.61 with minimal 'fuselage' and the pilot seated within the thick centre section underneath a small canopy were completed.

First was GAL.56 TS507 – the serial appearing as TS507A at the rear of the fuselage – which featured a sweep back of 28.4-degrees and a planform that was termed 'Medium V'. Towed aloft behind an Armstrong Whitworth Whitley from Farnborough on 13th November 1944, TS507A proved to be a nightmare on take-off and Robert demanded that the undercarriage be canted backwards to allow for improved ground handling. Handling trials behind a Halifax were followed by being towed to 20,000ft from Wittering behind a Supermarine Spitfire IX. Captain Eric 'Winkle' Brown (see Chapter Five in Volume One) was scathing of the GAL.56's behaviour, both under tow and particularly in the stall. The second GAL.56, TS510D, featured an unswept centre section and outer wings with a sweep of 28.4-degrees and was known as the 'Medium U' accordingly. Robert took this for its first flight, from Aldermaston, on 27th February 1946.

GAL.56 TS507 was delivered by air to Lasham on 28th August 1947 for another period of flight trials. Towed to 10,000ft by a Halifax on 12th February 1948, Robert was detailed to conduct stall trials with FTO Barry A G McGowan in the rear seat. After release from the tug the glider entered a spin from which Robert recovered, but it quickly went into another spin and inverted. Robert announced it was time to abandon TS507 and Barry managed to extricate himself. Sqn Ldr Robert Kronfeld AFC, aged 43, was not successful and was found in the wreck near Alton.

In 1932, Carl Theodor Haanen and Robert Kronfeld had collaborated on the book *Ein Segelflieger* ('A Glider') and in that same year, J Manchot translated it and it was published as *Kronfeld on Gliding and Soaring: The Story of Motorless Human Flight*.

Carrying the serial 'TS510D' on the rear fuselage, the second GAL.56 tail-less glider, with an unswept centre section and swept outer wings, hence its designation 'Medium U'. *KEC*

Peter 'Sheepy' Lamb

Peter Melville Lamb, born 1923. Joined the Fleet Air Arm in 1941, training at Pensacola, Florida, in 1942. Delivering Supermarine Seafire II MB315 from storage at Donibristle to Christchurch on 25th June 1943, 'Sheepy' overshot and attempted a go-around, only to crash through the perimeter fence and demolish a bungalow: he was badly injured. By September 1943 he was with 808 Squadron, flying Seafire IIs from HMS Battler and covered the amphibious landings at Salerno, Italy. By March 1944 he was with 807 Squadron, with Seafire IIs and later Mk.IIIs operating from HMS Hunter off the French coast and then engaged on strikes in the Aegean. August 1944 was eventful: piloting Seafire III NF645 the fighter nosed up in the barrier and was badly damaged on the 21st. Four days later, while flying Mk.III NM999 he landed heavy and the Seafire bounced over the barrier and collided with the carrier's island; NM999 was written off; Peter was OK. During 1945 Hunter sailed to the Indian Ocean and took part in the re-capture of Rangoon in May.

Post-war, Sheepy 'signed on' and after a stint with 780 Squadron on Fairey Firefly Is in 1946, he was back at sea with 800 Squadron on HMS Triumph by the summer of 1949, flying Seafire F.47s and later FR.47s. Triumph's air group was involved in strikes against communist terrorists in Malaya before moving on to the Sea of Japan for ground attack sorties during the UN-led counter to North Korea's invasion of South Korea. On 4th July 1950 Sheepy was flying FR.47 VP472, post-strike it took a hit and over-heated, he carried out an emergency landing on Triumph, and the Seafire returned to service. No.800 disbanded in November 1950 and the following year Sheepy graduated from No.10 Course ETPS at Farnborough and went on to a 3-year tour with A&AEE, Boscombe Down. In 1954 he found himself back with HMS Triumph, a cadet training ship since 1953, instructing on Boulton Paul Balliol T.21s of the Triumph Ship's Flight, shore-based at Lee-on-Solent. After combat in World War Two, Malaya and Korea, Sheepy had not finished with 'ops'. Converting to Hawker Sea Hawk jets, in July 1955 he took command of 810 Squadron with FGA.4s embarked on HMS Albion, sailing to the Far East. In October 1956 the Sea Hawks of 810 were on HMS Bulwark in the eastern Mediterranean. At dawn on 1st November Sheepy led a flight of 810 in a strike on Cairo West airfield, personally claiming an Ilyushin Il-28 Beagle destroyed – the pre-emptive phase of the Suez conflict had begun. Sheepy and his unit were heavily engaged in strikes against airfields and army installations, his last 'op' was on 5th November when, while flying XE389, he destroyed a motor torpedo boat and damaged another at Port Said. His final posting was as CO of the trials and development unit 700 Squadron, flying Sea Hawks from Ford.

INEVITABLY nicknamed 'Sheepy', combat veteran of four conflicts Lt Cdr Peter Lamb DSC* AFC joined Saunders-Roe (Saro) as what was to turn out to be its last CTP in 1958. His predecessor, John Booth*, had been killed in the second prototype Saro SR.53 mixed-power interceptor, XD151, on

The prototype SR.53, XD145, joined the RAF Museum collection in 1969 and went on display at Cosford in 1982. *KEC*

5th June 1958. It was not until 23rd February 1959 that the project was cleared for flight again and on that day Sheepy took the first SR.53, XD145, up for a familiarisation flight from Boscombe Down. Since late 1957 the SR.53 had been down-graded to a research project only, so Sheepy's remit with the solitary XD145 was exploratory only, with a view to handing the aircraft on to RAE. As such Sheepy expanded the envelope of the rocket-powered interceptor with a turbojet to return the aircraft to base. (Respectively, an 8,000lbst DH Spectre 1A rocket and a 1,640lbst Armstrong Siddeley Viper 8 turbojet.) On 11th May, Sheepy's sixth flight, he took the SR.53 to supersonic speeds for the first time, reaching Mach 1.14 and on 13th September Mach 1.46 in level flight. On the sortie of 20th October 1959 the Spectre blasted XD145 to 56,900ft and, with the rocket expended, it was down to the Viper to bring the delta back to Boscombe. The turbojet flamed out and Sheepy spent the next 46,000ft trying to re-light it. On the third attempt the Viper kicked in and XD145 touched down at Boscombe Down. It was never to fly again: XD145 accumulated just 17 hours, 45 minutes of flying time, split between John Booth, Jack Overbury* and Sheepy. Today, XD145 is preserved at the RAF Museum, Cosford.

Westland acquired Saro in 1959 and the future at Cowes lay with the Black Knight rocket programme and the world-beating hovercraft. Sheepy had converted to rotorcraft while awaiting his moment to fly the SR.53 and also took to the new discipline of flying *extremely* low on a cushion of air with ease. The 'official' first 'flight' of the world's first practical hovercraft, the Saro SR-N1, was on 11th June 1959 when it was shown off to invited guests at Cowes. It wore the Saro B Condition (or 'trade-plate') identity G-12-4 as at the time hovercraft were treated administratively as aircraft, but soon were eventually to become a breed all of their own. Sheepy piloted (perhaps more in the *nautical* than aeronautical sense!) the SR-N1 across the Solent on 22nd June 1959 and on 25th July he was at the helm as it crossed the English Channel. The date for the Channel crossing was deliberate: it was the 50th anniversary of Louis Blériot's aerial 'invasion' of Britain. (The SR-N1 is kept by the Science Museum at its storage site at Wroughton.) Lt Cdr Peter Melville Lamb DSC* AFC died in August 2000, aged 77.

John 'Jo' Lancaster

John Oliver Lancaster, born 1919. Took up an engineering apprenticeship in October 1935 with Armstrong Whitworth at Whitley Abbey. In 1937 he enrolled in the RAFVR and learned to fly at 6 E&RFTS, Sywell. In July 1940 he was streamed for bombers, going to 20 OTU at Lossiemouth on Vickers Wellingtons. Posted to 40 Squadron at Wyton he flew Wellington Is and completed a tour of 30 'ops'. 'Jo' was 'rested', becoming an instructor at 22 OTU, Wellesbourne Mountford, still on Wellingtons – he and the OTU took part in the 'Thousand Bomber' raids to Cologne 30/31st May and Essen on 1/2nd June 1942. A brief posting to 28 OTU at Wymeswold followed before the inevitable happened – Flt Lt Lancaster was sent to an Avro Lancaster unit, 12 Squadron at Wickenby in October 1942. Jo completed his second tour, and had a total of 54 'ops', including his OTU sorties. He was posted to A&AEE, Boscombe Down, from October 1943 for a two-year stint, before graduating from No.3 Course ETPS at Boscombe in 1945.

'Jo' Lancaster in the cockpit of a Meteor. *via J O Lancaster*

LOOKING out of the window while having a shave at his home in Long Itchington, Warwickshire, on 30th May 1949, Joe Dell was horrified to see a man descending by parachute. Still clutching his razor, Joe ran outside to help the pilot. The aviator declared that he was also known as 'Joe' and worked for Armstrong Whitworth (AW) – this was John Lancaster. Neither of them was to know it at the time, but they were respectively witness and participant in the first-ever emergency use of a Martin-Baker ejection seat. The pilot appeared to have suffered only bruises and scratches and enjoyed a cup of tea courtesy of the Dell household, before he was driven back to Bitteswell. The 'bang-seat' – now part of the Science Museum's collection – described by Martin-Baker as a "pre-Mk.1" had landed half a mile away. Four miles to the east, lay the wreckage of AW.52 TS363, the famous 'Flying Wing'. It had narrowly missed the village of Broadwell: a ewe and her lamb were the only casualties of the incident. (The two jet-powered AW.52 'flying wings' had their debuts at the hands of Eric Franklin*: TS363 on 13th November 1947 from Boscombe Down.)

In two conversations with 'Jo' Lancaster, the author inevitably asked about being Martin-Baker's first 'customer'. Jo was very happy to discuss it, but wanted to point out that several published sources had made a "very stupid, invented account" of the reasons why he parted company with the AW.52 that day. The flying wing was claimed to have suffered asymmetric flutter, starting at one tip and spreading across the whole span, only to damp out when Jo ejected allowing TS363

Nene-powered Armstrong Whitworth AW.52 TS363 over a snow-clad Leicestershire in January 1948. *Peter Green Collection*

to glide down and land almost intact. At that time, Jo was particularly scathing of a book on British flight test accidents and later, material arrived to "put the record straight". He also told a heart-warming story about Sir James Martin – of which more anon. Before we go on to his career as a test pilot, we'll stick with Jo's experience as it serves to illustrate the perils of a historian and his 'victim'.

As described in his section in Volume One, Bill Else and FTO Arthur Payne experienced a frightening situation while flying the second AW.52, Rolls-Royce Derwent-powered TS368, at Baginton in the spring of 1949. Bill encountered an oscillation in pitch (up and down) of about 2 cycles per second (2 CPS); this was damped out when he chopped the throttles. During this time, Rolls-Royce Nene-powered TS363 was undergoing modifications to increase structural stiffness. When it was ready to resume tests, in the light of Bill's incident, TS363 was given a limited speed that Jo thinks was around 350mph. At the time TS363 was not fitted with any test instrumentation, or flight recorders, not even of the basic NACA-developed Velocity-Gravity kind. The AW.52 was a two-seater, with an FTO in the back without the luxury of a 'bang-seat', to provide 'organic' records along with the pilot's knee-pad notes.

Back to the sortie of 30th May 1949, Jo's third in TS363. He wrote: "I was detailed for [solo] familiarisation flights and to investigate behaviour up to the revised limiting speed... There were lofty cumulus clouds about, and quite a lot of turbulence. At about 5,000ft and in a shallow dive, I had reached about 320mph when the oscillation in pitch set in. My estimate is that it was again about 2 CPS, but the amplitude built up almost instantaneously to become of such extreme violence as to almost incapacitate me both physically and mentally. It was accompanied by a very loud noise, which at the time seemed to suggest that structural failure was imminent. In my very confused mental state I decided to eject.

"With manually controlled elevons, harmonisation in pitch and roll was always going to be a problem. The wingspan was 90ft while the effective control moment [or arm] in pitch was only about 16ft... As a result, fore-and-aft stick forces were extremely light." Jo also remarked that the recent structural 'beef up' given to TS363 may have altered the machine's resonance characteristics. (Both AW.52s being powered by different engines would also give each airframe individual attributes –

KE.) Jo concluded: "Turbulence in the atmosphere most probably triggered flutter in the elevons, which almost instantaneously excited a pitching oscillation at the airframe's natural resonance frequency, about 2 CPS. This rapidly increased in amplitude to extremely violent proportions. ...had [powered flying controls] been available for the AW.52 I believe that they might have transformed it into a very different aircraft."

In the above description of the crash of TS363 it was noted that Jo *appeared* to have suffered only bruises and scratches. Jo was of course sent to hospital and it was found that he had compression fractures of the first and second lumbar vertebrae; he'd chipped the socket of a shoulder bone and was badly bruised around the shoulders and knees. The doctors also believed that the vertebrae showed signs of having been damaged some time prior to the accident. Jo put the previous compression down to his trying out the Martin Baker test rig at Denham (see Chapter Four in Volume One) in January 1947 when he was getting ready to fly the SR.A/1 jet flying-boat fighter – see below. RAF Form 624 – Medical Inspection Report issued by the Halton-based 1 Central Medical Board dated 8th August 1949 assessed Jo for his continued fitness to test Ministry of Supply aircraft after he had recovered. It declared him fit: "but not to be exposed to hazards of Martin-Baker ejector seat". Jo noted that this endorsement: "caused some amusement at the time but was, of course, completely ignored!"

With the initials 'J' and 'O', John Lancaster could hardly have avoided being nicknamed 'Jo'. After graduating from ETPS, Jo was posted in 1945 to Pendeford as a test pilot for Boulton Paul under Cecil Feather*. In *Men with Wings*, 'Sandy' Powell notes that Cecil was about to retire and: "Jo was offered the job of [CTP], which he accepted, only to find that someone else had received a similar offer before him!" That was Lindsay Neale*. Les Whitehouse of the Boulton Paul Association records that Jo's appointment was approved by the Boulton Paul board on 19th October 1945, but his tenure was short.

Upon leaving the RAF, Flt Lt Lancaster DFC was determined to stay in test piloting and he secured a post with Saunders-Roe (Saro) in early 1946. The renowned flying-boat specialist was based at Cowes on the Isle of Wight, with Geoffrey Tyson* as CTP. Jo needed to convert to seaplanes and the RAF chipped in with a course on Short Sunderlands. Initial work at Cowes included refurbished Supermarine Walrus and Saro-built Supermarine Sea Otter amphibians. An interesting diversion was to test Auster VI VF517 in March 1947. This had been built as a

The first AW.52 outside Hangars 5 and 6 at Bitteswell. *KEC*

landplane by Auster at Rearsby in 1946 and was fitted with Saro-built floats and given a ventral fin to increase directional stability. It was transferred to MAEE at Felixstowe where it was found to be very underpowered and was written off on 7th August 1947 when the float structure deformed during touchdown.

As related above, Jo also converted to the Saro SR.A/1 jet-powered flying-boat fighter and he demonstrated the third prototype, TG271, at the 1948 SBAC airshow at Farnborough. The SR.A/1 had retractable wing floats to balance the 'boat in the water and a sortie in 1948 called for some quick thinking. About to land on the Solent, Jo pulled the control to lower the floats, but nothing happened. A series of dives, where he activated the lowering of the floats as he started to climb, failed to pull the errant items out of their housing under each wing. One last try resulted in the port float coming down and locking. In this state, the SR.A/1 would carry out the equivalent of a ground-loop as soon as it began to slow and settle on the water. Joe worked out a solution. Sliding the canopy back, he removed his harness. He made a perfect landing and as the 'boat slowed down, he cut the two Metropolitan-Vickers Beryl turbojets and bounded out on to the port wing. With this human ballast the SR.A/1 did not drop its starboard wing and Jo stayed where he was until the Saro duty tender came alongside to sort things out.

Work at Saro was diminishing whereas in the East Midlands, the company that had given him an apprenticeship, Armstrong Whitworth, was flourishing. In January 1949 Jo took up the post of test pilot under Eric Franklin and his deputy Bill Else. At Baginton, Avro Lincolns were being manufactured and Avro Lancasters and Yorks were under refurbishment. The company was gearing up to build a series of two-seat night-fighter versions of the Gloster Meteor for the

Rare image of Derwent-powered AW.52 TS368. *Key Publishing collection – www.keypublishing.com*

RAF and export, starting off the NF.11 from late 1950. As part of this programme, Jo carried out the maiden flight of the prototype of the tropicalized NF.13, WM308, on 21st February 1952. As well as the AW.52s, the AW.52G glider that had presaged the jets, were under development and Eric Franklin was to take the AW Apollo four-turboprop airliner for its maiden flight in April 1949. To be able to fly the AW.52G, RG324, Jo turned to Ron Clear* of Airspeed at Christchurch for a conversion course on a Horsa assault glider. He and Ron had met up at ETPS in 1945. Jo handed over the AW.52G to AFEE at Beaulieu in June 1950.

Auster VI VF517 on Saro-built floats, moored on the Medina at Cowes, March 1947. Jo Lancaster tested this conversion. *Saunders-Roe*

Having been involved in many Bitteswell production programmes including Hawker Sea Hawks and Hunters, Gloster Javelins and AW Argosies, Jo retired from what had become Hawker Siddeley in 1965. By then he had amassed over 2,300 hours on 68 types. He became general manager for Meridian Air Maps, operating Avro XIXs and Ansons from Shoreham. He retired from an incredible life in aviation in 1984, remaining in Sussex.

Jo provided a charming endpiece to the AW.52 ejection. Martin-Baker managing director and chief designer, James Martin (Sir James from 1965) wrote to Jo on 22nd July 1949: "I am taking the opportunity of expressing my congratulations to you in some tangible way since you have been the first person in England to use this ejection seat in an emergency, and I would like to commemorate the event by the enclosed little parcel..." Jo explained that the 'little parcel' was a beautifully-made wooden box marked: 'Danger – High Explosive'. Inside was an engraved gold Rolex watch. Sadly, this was stolen in the 1980s, but in 1999 – to mark the 50th anniversary of the event – Martin-Baker presented Jo with another watch, this time a Garrard. Grinning away, Jo said that the box had been sent to the Baginton headquarters of AW without causing a stir. He declared that: "...it was different in 1949, today [2004] the building would have been evacuated and 'Jimmy' Martin would have got five years [imprisonment]!"

Ralph and Allan Lashmar

Aug 1916	Wight Quadruplane
	1 x 110hp Clerget

Ralph Oliver Lashmar, born 1887. Joined J Samuel White and Co at the company's East Cowes, Isle of Wight, shipyard prior to 1913. The firm decided to have him trained as a pilot and he went to the Northern Aircraft Company at Windermere, receiving tuition from Rowland Ding* and gaining his Aviators' Certificate in February 1915.

Allan Frank Lashmar, born 1892. Enlisted with the RNAS as a mechanic in September 1914. He was discharged in July 1915 to join J Samuel White and in November 1915 qualified for his Aviators' Certificate.

The Lashmar brothers were born and bred on the Isle of Wight and it seems that Ralph was determined that his younger brother join him at J Samuel White's works at East Cowes. Trading under the name 'Wight', the company was producing aircraft designed by Howard Wright* and licence-building Short seaplanes. Prior to Ralph's appointment as CTP, Eric Gordon England*, 'Freddy' Raynham* and even Howard Wright had carried out testing. During August 1916 Ralph 'first flighted' a private-venture single-seat quadruplane scout from the aerodrome at Somerton. This machine was wrecked in a forced landing on approach to Somerton in September 1916: Ralph was unhurt. On 7th September 1916, Ralph took Wight Landplane Bomber 9841 up for its second test flight from Somerton with Allan acting as observer. The 76ft span biplane crashed at Gurnard, killing 29-year-old Ralph and his brother Allan, aged 24. Flight testing of the second Wight Quadruplane was passed on to a RNAS pilot called Evans and the role of CTP was fulfilled by Marcus Manton*.

Head on view of the first version of the Wight Quadruplane at Somerton, 1916. *via John May*

Peter 'PG' Lawrence

1 Apr 1947	Blackburn YA.1 RT651
	1 x 2,475hp Bristol Centaurus 59
20 Sep 1949	Blackburn YA.7 WB781
	1 x 2,000hp RR Griffon 56
19 Jul 1950	Blackburn YB.1 WB797
	1 x 2,950shp AS Double Mamba

Notes: B.48 flown from Leconfield, the YA.7 and YB.1 from Brough.

Peter Godfrey Lawrence, born 1920. He was apprenticed to Handley Page in 1937. He joined the Fleet Air Arm in 1939 and by 1940 he was flying Fairey Swordfish with 819 Squadron on operations in the Eastern Mediterranean from HMS Illustrious. Later in 1940, Peter transferred to 824 Squadron, also with Swordfish, on HMS Eagle and in November he took part in an attack on the port of Tripoli, Libya. Eagle later cruised the Indian Ocean and the South Atlantic, returning to the Mediterranean and was sunk off Malta on 11th August 1942. Peter, and others from 824, returned to Britain later in the month. By January 1943 he was with 778 Squadron, a service trials unit, based variously at Arbroath and Crail; types flown included Fairey Barracuda, Firefly, Fulmar and Swordfish, plus Supermarine Spitfire V and Seafire. By late 1944 Peter was at Lee-on-Solent with 708 Squadron which had been set up as the Firebrand Tactical Trials Unit to bring the Blackburn Firebrand torpedo-fighter into service. Peter was involved in intensive deck landing assessments from HMS Pretoria Castle.

LT PETER LAWRENCE – 'PG' to his friends and colleagues – joined Blackburn as a test pilot in July 1945 as deputy to Charles Flood*. Peter's work on the company's major development and production programme, the Firebrand torpedo-fighter, certainly held him in good stead. Blackburn sent him to ETPS at Cranfield and he graduated from No.4 Course in early 1946. On 7th March 1946 Peter was up at 20,00ft in Firebrand TF.IV EK739 investigating aileron oscillation. The problem seemed to kick in as altitude increased yet was restricted to a 30-knot speed range, below and above this band it did not occur. On that sortie, the flutter was getting worse and at 25,000ft it did not stop; Peter noted that the wingtips were flexing through about 3ft up and down! He noticed cracking in the upper wing surface and then the windscreen and a side panel cracked. In *British Test Pilots*, Geoffrey Dorman quotes 'PG': "I prepared to bale out, to do which I reduced speed. When I reduced speed to under 100 knots the flutter suddenly stopped and I was able to bring the machine back to Brough for a thorough investigation. It took a long time to come down from 20,000ft at a speed of 100 knots!"

In September 1946 Peter was piloting a Firebrand in far happier circumstances, demonstrating TF.IV EK742 at the SBAC airshow at Radlett. With an all-up weight of 15,671lb and a wing span of 51ft 3in, the Mk.IV was a big beast and under its centre section it carried a 1,850lb torpedo. Peter effortlessly showed off the 'fighter' part of the aircraft's designation with a low-level aerobatic sequence. Racing was one of Peter's passions and at Elmdon on 30th June 1950 he flew TF.5 EK621 at 304mph to win the Challenge Cup.

In March 1948, Peter became CTP for Blackburn, succeeding Charles Flood. Interestingly, the first maiden flight he carried out was while he was DCTP – such sorties usually being the domain of the 'boss'. Geoffrey Dorman noted that Peter's appointment, at the age of 25, made him the youngest CTP in the country at that time. The Firebrand had suffered

Firebrand TF.IV EK601 carrying a 1,850lb torpedo – in similar configuration to Peter Lawrence's aerobatic routine in EK742 at Radlett in 1946. EK601 was used for deck landing trials on HMS *Pretoria Castle* in 1945 – Lt Peter Lawrence took a major role in these flights and was awarded an MBE for his endeavours. *Peter Green Collection*

from a protracted development and as early as February 1944 a specification was issued for an improved version. The response from Brough was the YA.1 which for a while was known, unofficially, as the Firecrest. The new machine had only its overall format in common with the Firebrand and Peter took the prototype, RT651, into the air from a much longer runway at Leconfield on 1st April 1947. The B.48 was not adopted, only two were completed; the Westland Wyvern took on the Firebrand's role.

Competition for the Navy's first dedicated carrier-borne anti-submarine aircraft was intense, and Blackburn put a lot of effort in to the B.54 programme. Initially intended to be powered by a Napier Double Naiad coupled turboprop, the design needed swift adaptation when that powerplant was axed. Peter flew the first prototype, a two-seater powered by a Rolls-Royce Griffon, from Brough in September 1949. This was WB781 which was mostly referred to by its SBAC designation YA.7; it and the three-seat YA.8 WB788 were intended as stop-gaps while the definitive YB.1 with an Armstrong Siddeley Double Mamba was perfected. This latter machine, WB797, was 'first flighted' by Peter in July 1950. Fairey swept the board with this requirement, with the spectacularly successful Gannet.

On 1st January 1949 Blackburn merged with General Aircraft and Peter found himself working under 'Timber' Wood*, who had been the General CTP. Timber concentrated on the Universal Freighter project (which became the Beverley) and left Peter to his abundant experience of naval aircraft. While the 'work split' seemed amicable, in June 1952 PG headed across the Pennines to join English Electric and work in the comparatively lowly post of PTP on Canberras at Samlesbury.

Samlesbury was only an interlude as the Gloster CTP, Bill Waterton*, had his eyes on Peter, not just as an addition to his flight office at Moreton Valence, but eventually as his successor. PG started work in the autumn of 1952. The Meteor was in full production and the Javelin all-weather fighter was the dominant development task. On its 99th flight, 29th June 1952, Bill had encountered elevator flutter with the prototype Javelin, WD804, and had been awarded the George Medal for bringing it back, in a very risky force-landing, and not abandoning it. The second prototype, WD808, was grounded early in 1953 for modifications to the wings to improve manoeuvrability at height and Bill re-flew it on 28th May 1953. Fourteen days later, on his second flight in WD808 that day Peter called: "I'm in trouble". The wreckage of WD808 came down on a playing field near Flax Bourton in Somerset. PG's body, still strapped in his ejector seat, was found nearby.

Gloster put out a press release, declaring that Peter had died "in heroic circumstances". The document continued: "At this point he was over 20,000ft. If he had baled out then he would have been safe, but he elected to crash-land with minimum damage to the aircraft and homes and people on the ground. He came down in a glide, seeking to avoid built-up areas with houses, and just before landing found himself over playing fields where teams of boys were playing cricket. He stayed with the aircraft all the way down to 250ft, put it into a straight slow run in, and baled out, using his ejector seat. However, he had waited too long, and he was killed on impact with the ground. The aircraft swept over the heads of the boys and landed in a field, flat. The wings and tail were undamaged on landing."

As will be seen in the section on Bill Waterton, his autobiography, *The Quick and the Dead*, is essential reading for all interested in test piloting and the aircraft industry. In the book Bill notes that on 11th June 1953 he: "left instructions that

Peter Lawrence flying the first Blackburn B.48, RT651. *Rolls-Royce Bristol*

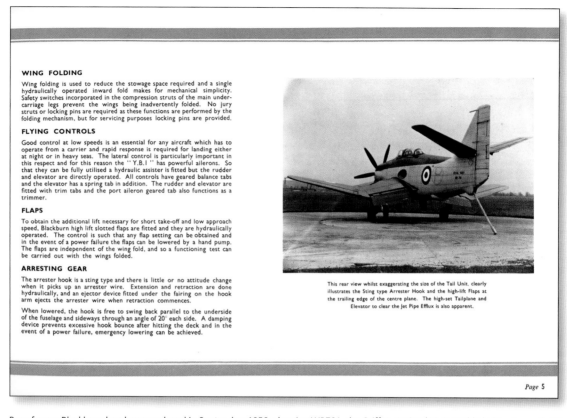

WING FOLDING

Wing folding is used to reduce the stowage space required and a single hydraulically operated inward fold makes for mechanical simplicity. Safety switches incorporated in the compression struts of the main under-carriage legs prevent the wings being inadvertently folded. No jury struts or locking pins are required as these functions are performed by the folding mechanism, but for servicing purposes locking pins are provided.

FLYING CONTROLS

Good control at low speeds is an essential for any aircraft which has to operate from a carrier and rapid response is required for landing either at night or in heavy seas. The lateral control is particularly important in this respect and for this reason the " Y.B.I " has powerful ailerons. So that they can be fully utilised a hydraulic assister is fitted but the rudder and elevator are directly operated. All controls have geared balance tabs and the elevator has a spring tab in addition. The rudder and elevator are fitted with trim tabs and the port aileron geared tab also functions as a trimmer.

FLAPS

To obtain the additional lift necessary for short take-off and low approach speed, Blackburn high lift slotted flaps are fitted and they are hydraulically operated. The control is such that any flap setting can be obtained and in the event of a power failure the flaps can be lowered by a hand pump. The flaps are independent of the wing fold, and so a functioning test can be carried out with the wings folded.

ARRESTING GEAR

The arrester hook is a sting type and there is little or no attitude change when it picks up an arrester wire. Extension and retraction are done hydraulically, and an ejector device fitted under the fairing on the hook arm ejects the arrester wire when retraction commences.

When lowered, the hook is free to swing back parallel to the underside of the fuselage and sideways through an angle of 20° each side. A damping device prevents excessive hook bounce after hitting the deck and in the event of a power failure, emergency lowering can be achieved.

This rear view whilst exaggerating the size of the Tail Unit, clearly illustrates the Sting type Arrester Hook and the high-lift Flaps at the trailing edge of the centre plane. The high-set Tailplane and Elevator to clear the Jet Pipe Efflux is also apparent.

Page 5

Page from a Blackburn brochure produced in September 1950, showing WB781, the Griffon-engined YA.7. Visible below the cockpit is the jet exhaust intended for the original powerplant, a Napier Double Naiad turboprop.

after one trip in the Javelin Peter and I would talk things over. But when I returned to Moreton Valence after lunch I found Peter in the cockpit [of WD808] ready to start up again – on the firm's instructions, not mine. I discussed the morning's flight with Peter, and since it had apparently gone smoothly and he was an experienced experimental pilot who would only be covering old ground, I did not pull him from the cockpit and raise merry hell with all responsible. I wish I had..."

During its reconfiguration in 1953, WD808 had been fitted with a flight resonance monitoring system, reportedly the first of its kind in a British aircraft. Analysis of the accident showed that the Gloster press release had been wildly optimistic about what had transpired. Bill put it graphically in *The Quick and the Dead*: "...it appeared that the Javelin had got into some sort of stabilized stall – had dropped almost vertically like a brick at more than a mile a minute, with very little forward speed. Such records as were salvaged indicated that Peter had come down to a speed where warning of the stall was given, recovered, then approached it for a second time, with flaps down. It then seemed to have rapidly and suddenly got into a condition from which he did not regain control of the 'plane, although he fought it all the way down, only ejecting himself at the last possible moment. He was too low to get clear of his seat and use his parachute."

In later years, Peter's plummet would be known as a 'super-stall'; the delta wing masking the tailplane. Bill concluded: "As a result of the accident the firm altered the flaps. It was little consolation to me that it took the death of my number one to effect modifications that my talking and

reports had been unable to achieve since the aeroplane's earliest flights." Bill Waterton and Gloster were shortly to go their separate ways.

Lt Peter Godfrey Lawrence MBE was 32 when he died on 11th June 1953: he had over 3,000 hours spread across more than 80 types.

'Jerry' Lee

Jeremy John Lee, born 1939. Learned to fly with Liverpool University Air Squadron; joining the RAF in 1960. Operational flying on Hawker Hunter FGA.9s in Aden with 208 and then 43 Squadrons. In 1967 he was posted to the École du Personnel Navigant d'Essais et de Réception (EPNER) at Istres, France prior to joining A&AEE, Boscombe Down in 1968. He became Jaguar Project Pilot at A&AEE in 1970.

SQN LDR JERRY LEE AFC joined BAC at Warton in 1973 becoming the company's Jaguar Project Pilot in 1975. Trials work included soft field and unusual surface take-offs conducted at Farnborough and Boscombe Down. Jerry was appointed as Tornado Project Pilot in 1977 undertaking development flying on terrain following radar and on 'buddy-buddy' refuelling, among other tasks. He was promoted to DCTP BAe Warton in 1979 and in 1983 he became CTP. Jerry Lee retired from test piloting in April 1985, having accrued over 4,300 flying hours, on 40 types. He took up the post of General Manager Oman, and later the same for India. Jerry retired from BAe in 1996.

Peter Legh

1916	AW FK.6 7838 1 x 250hp RR Eagle
19 Jan 1918	BAT Bantam I B9945 1 x 100hp Gnome
10 Jan 1919	BAT Basilisk F2906 1 x 320hp ABC Dragonfly
Apr 1919	BAT FK.26 K-102 1 x 350hp RR Eagle VIII

Notes: FK.6 first flew from Gosforth, Newcastle upon Tyne; all BAT types from Hendon.

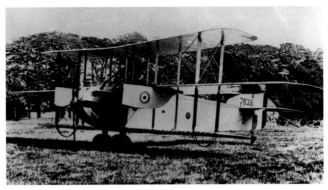

The one-off FK.6 'Zeppelin Destroyer' of 1916. The port nacelle for one of the gunners carries a roundel. *Peter Green Collection*

The BAT Bantam II prototype under evaluation at Upavon in 1918. *Peter Green Collection*

RNAS Lt Cdr Peter Legh was detached to the Armstrong Whitworth (AW) works at Gosforth, Newcastle-upon-Tyne, to test FK.8 general purpose biplanes. AW's designer was the Dutchman Frederick Koolhoven* and he and Legh began a friendship that was to outlast the former's tenure at Gosforth. In late 1916 Peter flew the three-seat FK.6 'Zeppelin Destroyer'. This was a triplane with the pilot in a conventional cockpit behind the wings, and a pair of gunners in small nacelles suspended under the middle wing where the idea was they enjoyed a wide field of fire. Only the prototype FK.6 was built.

Koolhoven left AW in 1917 and began work for the British Aerial Transport Company (BAT) and conceived the FK.22 Bantam biplane fighter. Peter had joined him by this time and he was at the helm of the first example at Hendon in January 1918. Further development of the Bantam produced the FK.23 Bantam II, but ultimately only nine were completed. Another single-seat fighter, the FK.25 Basilisk, was flown by Peter in September 1918. The FK.26 was a large biplane seating four passengers in the cabin and the pilot in an open cockpit well to the rear. It had the distinction of being the first from-scratch post-war civil transport produced in the UK: four were built. On 3rd May 1919, Peter Legh was killed will attempting an altitude record in the Basilisk at Hendon – the aircraft crashed in flames. His friend, Christopher 'Mad Major' Draper* took over as test pilot for BAT.

'Mike' Lithgow

14 Jul 1948	Supermarine Seagull ASR.1 PA143 1 x 1,815hp RR Griffon 29
29 Dec 1948	Supermarine 510 VV106 1 x 5,000lbst RR Nene 2
1 Aug 1951	Supermarine 535 VV119 1 x 5,100lbst RR Nene 3
31 Aug 1951	Supermarine 508 VX133 2 x 6,500lbst RR Avon RA.3
27 Apr 1954	Supermarine 525 VX138 2 x 7,500lbst RR Avon RA.7

Notes: Seagull first flew from the waters of the River Itchen; all of the others from Boscombe Down.

Michael John Lithgow, born 1920. His father, Colonel E G R Lithgow, gained Aviators' Certificate No.414 on 4th February 1912 in a 'Short' under instruction at Salisbury Plain and served with the RFC. 'Mike' joined the Fleet Air Arm in January 1939 and by 1941 was posted to 820 Squadron, equipped with Fairey Albacores. While flying X9170 on night

simulated torpedo attacks from HMS Formidable in the South Atlantic on 7th March 1942 the Albacore was caught in the slipstream of a line of returning Albacores and plummeted into the wake of the carrier. Mike and his two crew members floated courtesy of their Mae Wests and were picked up by Formidable five hours later; all were OK. Formidable later deployed to the Indian Ocean and the Albacores of 820 Squadron were in action during the landings on Madagascar in May 1942. By early 1943 Mike was at A&AEE Boscombe Down. One day short of a year after the ditching in the Albacore, on 6th March 1943 Mike suffered a 'wheels-up' in Fairey Barracuda I P9677. On take-off the Barracuda started to bounce violently (Boscombe was a very 'lumpy' airfield) and as it had achieved unstick speed, Lt Lithgow elected to lift off and tuck the gear up, only to have P9677 sink back to the ground. Mike was unhurt; the Barracuda was repaired. He graduated from Course No.2 ETPS at Boscombe Down 1944-1945.

AFTER ETPS, Lt Cdr 'Mike' Lithgow was seconded to Chattis Hill, working under Jeffrey Quill* as a PTP, mostly working at clearing Supermarine Spitfire VIIIs and

XIVs. This was a brief, but important, interlude. He was appointed to act as a test pilot with the British Air Commission (BAC) at Patuxent River, Maryland, USA, in late 1945. This was his second time at 'Pax', having been posted to the BAC there late in 1943, returning in February 1944. During his second US stint, Mike flew such types as the Ryan Fireball, a piston engined fighter-bomber with a jet engine to augment its performance, and the Bell P-59 Airacomet jet fighter.

On return to the UK, Mike accepted an invitation from Jeffrey Quill to join his staff full-time and he started work for Supermarine on 1st January 1946. Early testing included: Spitfire Mk.22s and Mk.24s, Seafire Mk.45s and Mk.47s and development work on the Spiteful and Seafang prototypes. The major programme was the Attacker naval jet fighter, which Jeffrey had first flown in July 1946. Mike succeeded Jeffrey as CTP in 1947 and on 14th July 1948 he flew the first of two prototype Seagull amphibians. The type was intended to replace the venerable Walrus and Sea Otter in the air-sea rescue role, but the requirement was not taken up and the Seagull turned out to be the last Supermarine marine aircraft. While the Seagull went nowhere, the Attacker was a success: Mike flew the first production example, F.1 WA469, from Chilbolton on 4th April 1950.

The Attacker provided Supermarine chief designer Joe Smith with the ability to move step-by-step to sweptwing fighters. By fitting an Attacker fuselage with a 40-degree sweep, Supermarine created the first British jet with swept main wing and tailplane: Type 510 VV106, which was briefly known as the Swift. Mike 'first flighted' the 'tail-dragger' VV106 at Boscombe Down on 29th December 1948 and was soon taking it to Mach 0.9. Mike suffered his second wheels-up landing, at the scene of his previous such accident Boscombe Down, in VV106 on 16th March 1949. The jet was back in the air 55 days later. The Type 510 was modified for carrier deck landing and on 8th November 1950 Lt 'Jock' Elliot* became the first to land and take-off a sweptwing jet from an aircraft carrier – HMS *Illustrious*. Mike also flew

Supermarine test pilots, left to right: Jeffrey Quill, Les Colquhoun, Mike Lithgow. *via Tony Buttler*

VV106 on and off *Illustrious* that day. VV106 survives, it is held in store by the Fleet Air Museum at Yeovilton.

Next step in the evolution was to take the second Type 510, VV119, which had its maiden flight in Mike's hands on 27th March 1950, and considerably rebuild it. The changes were extensive, but boiled down to a lengthened and re-contoured forward fuselage, larger intakes and a tricycle undercarriage. In this guise VV119 became the Type 535, the *real* prototype of the Swift and it was first flown by Mike on 1st August 1951. Along with the Hawker Hunter, the Swift was one of Britain's 'super-priority' projects – the Korean war having broken out in June 1950 – and the pace of development was, well, swift! Mike flew the first pre-production Swift, WJ960, on 1st August 1951 and production examples were ready in the spring of 1953.

The second prototype Seagull ASR.1, PA147, taking the wire on HMS *Illustrious* during A&AEE deck landing trails, October 1949. *KEC*

Between 1961 and 1964 the Supermarine 517 VV106 was displayed at 2 Recruit Centre at Cardington in a bizarre RAF-like colour scheme. (By 1952 VV106 had been given a variable incidence tail assembly and was redesignated as the Type 517.) *KEC*

The performance of the Swift was such that the world airspeed record was achievable. Mike had already experienced such exacting flying. On 26th February 1948 he had taken the 100km close-circuit record in the prototype Attacker, TS409, to 560.6mph. Not content with this, two days later, he raised it to 564.8mph. In 1953 it was decided to have a crack at the world record, using the prototype Swift F.4, WK198. This represented the main production specification and presented an ideal way of showing what an 'off-the-shelf' Swift could achieve. On 5th July 1953, flying WK198, Mike travelled 212 miles from London to Pairs, raising the 'city pair' record to 669.3mph.

Ten days later Mike and WK198 had another appointment. They had been chosen to close the procession of aircraft at the Royal Coronation Review of the RAF at Odiham. After WK198 had flown past a compressor blade failed in the Rolls-Royce Avon. With a run-through altitude of 700ft, Mike turned his estimated 667mph into more height to carry out a dicey power-off landing at Chilbolton, 21 miles to the south-west. For a Swift that was a long way to glide! Thankfully, Mike had experience of 'dead-sticking' the fighter so the day was not marred by a mishap.

On 22nd September 1953 Mike took WK198 out of Chilbolton, bound for Idris in Libya, the base for the world record attempt. Fifteen days previously, Neville Duke* of arch-rivals Hawker took Hunter Mk.3 WB188 to 727.6mph to secure the world record. No pressure there, then! In his definitive history of the type, rightly titled *Swift Justice*, Nigel Walpole outlines some of the complexities involved in the Libyan record attempt. "The course was surveyed by the Ordnance Survey Office and the runs supervised by the Royal Aero Club (RAeC) according to Fédération Aéronautique Internationale (FAI) rules. However, even with additional coloured smoke markers and flares, Mike found exact positioning difficult at the speeds and heights he flew. Two miles above, Les Colquhoun*, who had accompanied Mike to Libya in an Attacker, orbited at height to provide an airborne relay for any messages to or from

the low-flying Swift while an Anson and a Meteor T.7, carrying RAeC observers, orbited 1km from either end of the 3km course to ensure that Mike did not exceed the 500m ceilings at these points. On the ground, a network of observers manned the electronic timing apparatus and cameras. To ensure accuracy and security the observers packed their 60-valve electronic clock with dry ice and it was guarded day and night by six auxiliary policemen." Mike's run on the afternoon of 25th September produced a speed of 735.7mph and the world record went to Supermarine. Such was the nature of record-breaking in the 1950s that the ink was hardly dry on the FAI's certificate when it was announced that *just two days* later a Douglas F4D-1 Skyray had seized the record again for the USA, this time at 752.9mph. The fuselage of WK198 is displayed at the Brooklands Museum, Weybridge.

Following the success of his autobiography *Mach One* in 1954, Mike presented a follow-up in 1956 with *Vapour Trails* in which he acted as editor and wrote the foreword. Also published by Allan Wingate, this was a compilation of stories from colleagues, carrying the sub-title *Thrilling Exploits of the Men who Fly at Supersonic Speeds*, at least in the Panther paperback edition of 1957. *Vapour Trails* was not all about the jet age and it is still a very engaging read. Mike's role was to select ten pilots and to supply "somewhat unnecessary introductions". For completeness, his 'victims' were, in order with their companies as given in the book: Jimmy Orrell* (Avro), Sandy Powell* (Lockheed), Henri Biard* (Supermarine), Neville Duke* (Hawker), Roland Beamont* (English Electric), Jeffrey Quill* (Supermarine), Dave Morgan* (Vickers Armstrong), Teddy Tennant* (Folland), George Errington* (Airspeed) and Ben Gunn* (Boulton Paul).

In parallel with the Swift programme, Supermarine was developing a twin-engined strike fighter for the Fleet Air Arm; this was to result in the Scimitar – the last aircraft to carry the Supermarine name. An unswept wing prototype, featuring a 'butterfly' tail, started the process: this was Type 508 VX133

Opposite top: The Supermarine 535 VV119 on display at the 1950 SBAC airshow at Farnborough. *Shell Photographic Unit*

Bottom: Mike Lithgow flying world record-breaking Swift F.4 WK198 in 1953. *Vickers-Armstrongs*

Stepping stone to the Scimitar, the butterfly-tailed Supermarine 508 VX133. *Vickers-Armstrongs*

which Mike took into the air for the first time on the last day of August 1951. This was followed by the sweptwing and conventionally-tailed Type 525 VX138 on 27th April 1954 which was effectively the Scimitar prototype. The first pre-series Scimitar, Type 544 WT854, was flown by Mike from Boscombe Down on 19th January 1956 and he also flew the initial production F.1, XD212, from South Marston on 11th January 1957. Prior to that, in 1956 Mike was appointed as

DCTP Vickers-Armstrong (Aircraft) Ltd under 'Jock' Bryce* as Supermarine was subsumed into the company that had owned the 'brand' since 1938.

Scimitar production came to a halt in 1960 and by that time Mike was at Wisley, testing Vickers Vanguards and Viscounts. On 20th August 1963 Jock took the new 'Vickers' airliner into the air from Hurn for its maiden flight – this was the so-called 'Bus Stop Jet', BAC One-Eleven G-ASHG. Mike was the captain of *Hotel-Golf*'s 53rd flight on 22nd October 1963 along with Richard 'Dickie' Rymer* as co-pilot, Dick Wright Senior FTO, Gordon Poulter FTO, D J Clark FTO, B J Prior Assistant Chief Aerodynamicist and C J Webb Assistant Chief Designer. Among the tasks for the sortie was a series of stalls; *Hotel-Golf* crashed near Chicklade, Wiltshire, killing all on board. The accident investigation report, published in late March 1965 concluded: "During the fifth stall, the angle of incidence reached a value at which the elevator effectiveness was insufficient to effect recovery ...the aircraft entered a stable stalled condition. Recovery from which was impossible." The document was critical that no stall-recovery parachute was fitted and that, given the experience of T-tailed aircraft, including the company's VC-10: "stalling tests should have been more cautiously approached, more closely controlled and more carefully correlated with wind tunnel and flight recorder data." Apart from the loss of life, this was a massive blow to the One-Eleven and it was not the last accident the programme suffered – see Peter Baker.

Lt Cdr Michael John Lithgow OBE was 43 when he died. A stained glass window in Cheltenham College, where he was educated 1934 to 1938, serves as a memorial, it concludes with five poignant words: "A famous and gallant pilot".

Mike Lithgow bringing Supermarine 525 VX138 in to land at Boscombe Down at the end of its maiden flight, 27th April 1954. *Vickers-Armstrongs*

Ian Little

2 Feb 1942	AFEE Rotachute I rotor-glider
27 11 1943	AFEE Rotabuggy B-415 rotor-glider

Ian Malcolm David Little, born 1918. He interrupted studies at Oxford and joined the RAF in 1939. After training he flew Avro Rotas (Cierva C.30A) with 1448 Flight at Duxford and, from 1943, with 529 Squadron at Halton and later Henley-on-Thames. As and when needed Ian was seconded to the AFEE to test experimental rotorcraft.

A Rotachute being tested from a fixed rig on the back of a lorry at Ringway, early 1942. *KEC*

During his time at the Airborne Forces Experimental Establishment (AFEE), Ian Little was responsible for the testing of two of the most bizarre rotorcraft. Austrian-born Raoul Hafner designed two helicopters in the early 1930s before relocating to Britain in 1932. His AR.III gyroplane of 1937 was tested by Valentine Baker*. With the onset of war, Hafner worked with the Central Landing Establishment (CLE) at Ringway, tasked with developing airborne forces equipment in readiness for the liberation of Europe. During January 1942 CLE became AFEE and that July moved to Sherburn-in-Elmet.

Hafner devised a one-man fully steerable rotorcraft 'parachute' using bicycle frame construction techniques, a very simple twin-blade rotor and a basic plywood tail section. This was the Rotachute, weighing just 48lb unladen. After early trials, from the back of a speeding truck, Ian Little piloted a Rotachute off tow at Ringway on 2nd February 1942, fluttering back to earth under full control. The Rotachute was progressively developed and the Mk.IV, weighing almost twice as much as the Mk.I, with wheeled landing gear and an instrument panel, had its maiden flight on 29th April 1943. Over 20 Rotachutes were built, but testing was brought to a close on 18th November 1943. A Rotachute III is on show at the Museum of Army Flying, Middle Wallop.

From the Rotachute concept, the Rotabuggy emerged. By installing a rotor pylon attached to a large 46ft 8in 'free-wheeling' two-blade rotor, adding a simple box-like rear fuselage with fins for an element of directional control, a means of towing a Willys Jeep behind an aircraft to a battle zone was created. Once it had landed – on its own wheels – the rotors and fuselage would be discarded and the Jeep and its crew could go to war. Hafner argued that an Airspeed Horsa assault glider cost £2,450 (£134,750 in present-day values) to transport a Jeep on what was more than likely a one-way trip. But with a Rotabuggy, the job could be done for as little as £500.

Engineering specialists R Malcolm Ltd created the Rotabuggy at Slough. (The company became ML Aviation in late 1943.) Officially designated AFEE 10/42, the unique vehicle-rotorcraft crossbreed was also known as the 'Malcolm Blitz Buggy'. The amazing contraption was first flown under tow behind a Bentley, no less, at Sherburn on 27th November 1943 with Ian Little piloting. The contraption made about 60 flights at low level. A sortie on 11th September 1944 resulted in Ian being granted the AFC which a biographer noted was: "awarded almost posthumously". The reported circumstances of this incident vary, from being towed to 1,700ft only to find that the tow line could not be detached and having to make a hazardous landing *behind* the converted bomber. Another version of the story was that at 1,700ft the tow was let go for the first time and the rotorcraft proved very difficult to control. Trials proved that the Rotabuggy needed a very skilled pilot and the plan had been that quickly trained Army drivers would fly them into action. By the time of the final tests, D-Day had been and gone and the Rotabuggy project subsided. Hafner went on to become the founding designer of the helicopter division of Bristol. A replica of the Rotabuggy is on show at the Museum of Army Flying.

Ian Little returned to academia in 1945 and went on to become Professor of Development Economics at Oxford. Sqn Ldr Ian Malcolm David Little CBE AFC died on 13th July 2012, aged 93.

The Rotabuggy at AFEE Sherburn in 1944. Behind is the device that actually flew Jeeps into battle, an Airspeed Horsa assault glider. *ML Aviation*

David Lockspeiser

24 Aug 1971	Lockspeiser LDA-01 G-AVOR
	1 x 85hp Continental C85

David Lockspeiser, born 1927. He volunteered for the RAF in late 1944 but upon being told there was a diminishing need for pilots and he would very likely become "a cook or an orderly attendant" he decided to enter the aircraft industry. He studied design at the Miles Aeronautical Technical School at Woodley from 1945 to 1947 where he met the Miles brothers (Fred* and George*). Miles Aircraft collapsed in 1947 and David moved to Armstrong Whitworth at Coventry to continue his studies and flying training at Air Service Training, Hamble. David joined the RAF in 1949 and flew Gloster Meteor F.8s with 118 Squadron at Fassberg in West Germany and 245 Squadron at Horsham St Faith.

David conducted trials on the EP.9 Prospector during 1959, including flight characteristics with crop spraying booms and a wind-driven pump attached. Illustrated is the third example, G-AOZY. *via David Lockspeiser*

DAVID LOCKSPEISER was featured in Chapter Two, *Giving an Idea Wings*, in Volume One, dealing with designer-pilots: turn to that for a wider look at this charismatic test pilot and the innovative aircraft he created. A chance meeting in 1955 with Hawker CTP Neville Duke*, who was having a meal in a pub near Leconfield with his wife, Gwen, proved pivotal. Praising the Hunter, David told Neville: "you've got the most beautiful aeroplane in the world". Neville told him to pop into Dunsfold to see the operation. Frank Bullen was a PTP at Dunsfold and David had flown with him on Meteors in West Germany and would be pleased to see him. The RAF was a *very* different set up from what it is these days and David borrowed a Meteor and flew from Horsham St Faith down to Dunsfold. He liked what he saw. Neville offered him a post as test pilot and Flt Lt Lockspeiser became a civilian.

What did David think when he got to fly the fighter of his dreams – the Hunter – for the first time? He described it laconically as: "no big deal, a delight". *The* Hunter that David flew during his time at Dunsfold was the company-owned two-seater T.66A G-APUX he was: "very fond of that aeroplane". (See under Bill Bedford for more on 'PUX.) In the mid-1950s about 30 Hunters a month were being built and there was plenty of production and development work for the small Dunsfold team. David was heavily involved in several sub-variants of the Hunter, including the naval T.8C prototype, XL604, in July 1961, which was the first with a TACAN – tactical air navigation – system housed in place of the ADEN cannon. In April 1962 David was at the helm of the prototype Hunter GA.11, XE712, a conversion of a 1955 Blackpool-built F.4 for Fleet Air Arm strike attack training.

David Lockspeiser in his favourite 'office', a Hunter at Dunsfold. *via Rebecca and Jerry Lockspeiser*

There were other types to be flown; during 1959 David was in charge of signing off the target-tug conversion of the Sea Fury T.20 for Deutsche Luftfahrt Beratungsdienst, to be used on contact to the Luftwaffe. As well as sleeve target towing trials, David carried out cable release tests. While working in India, helping the Indian Air Force introduce its large order of Hunter Mk.56s into service, David heard that the Burmese Air Force had grounded its fleet of Sea Furies following a spate of fatal accidents. Burma had a mix of FB.11s and T.20s acquired in 1958. Dunsfold asked him to investigate and it "took some tact" to get to the bottom of it. The Burmese pilots disliked oxygen masks and made few – if any – radio calls, so flew with the mask permanently dangling away from the face. Poor maintenance meant that carbon monoxide seeped into the cockpit and the pilots blacked out. David did his best to instil better procedures but was not sure that much flying was done after his departure. Activity was intense and varied and David praised his CTP: "Neville let us all have a go at everything. He saw us as his chaps; he made us a very real team."

In preparation for the sale of Edgar Percival Aircraft, established by the famed pre-war designer-pilot Edgar Percival*, to what became Lancashire Aircraft in 1959, David was 'loaned out' to fly the general purpose and agricultural EP.9 Prospector for renewed certification. Flying included general handling, maximum weight trials, forward and aft centre of gravity envelope investigation, stick-shaker assessment and flight characteristics with crop spraying booms and a wind-driven pump attached.

David had been seconded to the Buccaneer programme, working on autopilot and the nav-attack systems out of Holme-on-Spalding Moor. He was also engaged in weapons delivery trials, including the Low-Altitude Bombing System. Detached

to Hatfield, he was engaged by de Havilland on Gyron Junior turbojet performance, surge investigation and specific fuel consumption calibration, using the third prototype, XK488. David and FTO R A 'Tony' Buxton were strapped into XK488 on 24th July 1961 at Hatfield, ready to roll. The Buccaneer had a revolutionary boundary layer control (BLC) system that blew air at very high pressure through perforations in the wing skin to dramatically increase lift. For the 24th July sortie, David was to make an 'unblown' take-off; not engaging the BLC. Throttles forward, XK488 blasted off down Hatfield's runway but refused to unstick no matter what David did. He abandoned the take-off, knowing that the safety barrier would come into action. XK488 hit the net and a combination of 115 knots and a loaded weight of around 42,000lb combined to let the Buccaneer shoot straight through. It careered off the end of the runway, impacting in a set of greenhouses. After the sound of breaking glass finally stopped came the realisation that neither of the crew were hurt, nor was anyone on the ground. Buccaneers are made of stern stuff and XK488 was salvaged and repaired and is today held in store at the Fleet Air Arm Museum, Yeovilton. Fourteen months after David's mishap, test pilot George Aird* 'visited' the very same greenhouses!

While with Hawker at Dunsfold, David crystallised long-held thoughts about a utility aeroplane capable of undertaking a wide range of tasks. He came up with a radical single-engined pusher, with a rear-mounted main wing and a canard foreplane. The tandem-wing layout provided for the maximum possible centre of gravity range and placing the engine in the rear allowed the pilot an exceptional view, particularly important when crop dusting or spraying. David called his concept the Land Development Aircraft (LDA), but he liked the name 'Boxer' and mostly referred to it as such. Lockspeiser Aircraft Ltd was founded and David decided to embark upon the construction of a 70% scale version, LDA-01 G-AVOR, to prove the concept.

Blackburn NA.39 XK488 where it finished up after failing to take-off at Hatfield on 24th July 1961. *Hawker Siddeley Dynamics*

The scale proof-of-concept LDA-01 Boxer G-AVOR. *via David Lockspeiser*

David built *Oscar-Romeo* in a Nissen hut at Dunsfold from 1966, under the aegis of the Popular Flying Association and the Permit to Fly scheme. On 24th August 1971, designer-builder David reverted to his full-time occupation as test pilot and took *Oscar-Romeo* for its maiden flight from his then workplace, Wisley. "It was airborne in just 300ft and flew much as I expected." In June 1975 David took G-AVOR to the Paris Salon at Le Bourget and in September 1976 it was at the SBAC display at Farnborough. Despite a lot of interest in the LDA, nothing concrete came about and David was unable to finance further development. In 1986 fortunes seemed to change and there was the possibility of investment from Malaysia and perhaps licence construction of the full-scale version, which David referred to as the "Boxer 1000". *Oscar-Romeo* was re-registered as G-UTIL and moved to Old Sarum. Tragically, there was a hangar fire and among the aircraft consumed on 16th January 1987 was the LDA. David was deeply annoyed at the loss, especially after having his hopes raised that all of his endeavours might well finally be rewarded.

Hawker had morphed into Hawker Siddeley in 1963 and from September 1967 David moved to the civil division of BAC, under CTP Brian Trubshaw. Based at Filton and also at Wisley, he was involved in the BAC One-Eleven programme, including noise abatement procedures, wet runway trials, extreme aft centre of gravity behaviour as well as much time on simulator development. Leaving BAC in 1976, the following year found David flying his favourite type, the Hunter, again. He joined Lockheed Aircraft Services at Tengah, Singapore, to upgrade the capabilities of the Singapore Air Force's fleet of FGA.74s, FR.74s and T.75s. From May 1977 to May 1980 David was in charge of the flight test regime which included undertaking full sign-off, including weapons release, of a new centre-line pylon and two new wing pylons for AIM-9

Sidewinder heat-seeking air-to-air missiles. During his Dunsfold days, David had spent some time studying the famous Sidewinder, putting forward a proposal to arm Hunters with a pair mounted on a modified version of the ADEN gun pack – the missiles being carried in a similar manner to the Lightning's Firestreaks or Red Tops.

With the end of the Singaporean contract, David retired from flying. Flt Lt Lt David Lockspeiser died on 23rd March 2014. He had amassed 7,160 flying hours on 160 types. David had for some time lived in a house alongside Farnborough airfield: he had been born in the town 85 years earlier.

Maurice Longbottom

LEARNING to fly at the Bristol Flying School in 1935, Maurice V Longbottom – 'Shorty' to his colleagues – joined the RAF in 1939 and was a pioneer Supermarine Spitfire photographic reconnaissance pilot. By early 1943 Sqn Ldr Longbottom DFC was posted to Vickers as a PTP. He was involved in development of the Vickers-produced 'Bouncing Bombs' and on 13th May 1943 he flew a fully-modified Avro Lancaster from Manston for the first live drop of an UPKEEP weapon – just three days before the famous 'Dam Buster' raids. On 5th January 1945 'Mutt' Summers* was testing Vickers Warwick III HG364 out of Brooklands when he encountered a chronic directional stability problem. Mutt and his FTO escaped without serious injury. The very next day, Maurice took up Warwick V PN778 solo and, while making his approach to Brooklands, experienced considerable rudder over-balance. PN778 span into the ground, killing its 29-year-old pilot. Twenty-six days later Maurice Summers* (younger brother of Mutt) suffered the same problem in Mk.V PN777; he and his FTO survived.

Arthur Loton

Aug 1924	Blackburn Bluebird I G-EBKD 1 x 35hp Blackburne Thrush
14 Nov 1927	Blackburn Turcock G-EBVP 1 x 450hp AS Jaguar VI

Note: Blackburne was a Surrey-based motorcycle engine manufacturer and not to be confused with the Brough-based aircraft and engine manufacturer, Blackburn.

IN May 1924 Blackburn began operating a reserve school at Brough and 27-year-old Wg Cdr Arthur George Loton was appointed as its first CFI. (In 1935 it was designated 4 Elementary and Reserve Flying Training School.) As with several organisations, occasionally tutors were seconded to carry out test flights. In August 1924 Arthur was tasked with 'first flighting' the Blackburn entry for that year's Lympne Light Aeroplane Trials. The Bluebird was a side-by-side two-seater let down by its extremely underpowered engine and did not travel to Kent for the contest. It did give rise to the successful Bluebird series of biplanes, culminating in the all-metal Mk.IV, first flown by 'Dasher' Blake* in 1929. The Turcock was a single-seat fighter, one example of which was ordered by Turkey and flown by Arthur in November 1927. For his services to reserve flying training, Wg Cdr Arthur George Loton was awarded the AFC in January 1938.

Allan Love

Allan McEwan Love, born 1936. Gained his private pilot's licence via an Air Cadet scholarship and joined the RAF in 1953. Operational flying included 65 Squadron on Hawker Hunter F.6s from 1959, 1 Squadron Hunter FGA.9s from 1961 and 23 Squadron with EE Lightning F.3s from 1964.

ALLAN LOVE joined BAC at Warton in January 1969, becoming Lightning Project Pilot. He was heavily involved in deliveries of Lightnings and Jet Provosts to Saudi Arabia and later instructed on Lightnings for both Kuwait and the Saudis. As part of the Tornado programme Allan flew Blackburn Buccaneer S.2A XT285, which had been specially modified to incorporate the new aircraft's radar and nav-attack systems, mostly on low-level sorties out of West Freugh in western Scotland. On 5th July 1978 Allan and Roy Bigland were killed when XT285 crashed shortly after take-off from West Freugh. Roy was a technician from BAC-owned EASAMS (the former Elliott Automation), he and Allan McEwan Love were both 42.

George Lowdell

1939	R&S Snargasher G-AEOD 2 x 205hp DH Gipsy Six II

George Edward Lowdell, born 1901. He joined the RFC in November 1917 as a mechanic and by 1919 LAC Lowdell was a fitter. He learned to fly in 1923 and became an instructor at 2 FTS, Digby. In 1924 he sent 'Mutt' Summers* solo. Sgt Lowdell was posted to A&AEE Martlesham Heath in September 1927 and during this time he was a part-time instructor at the Suffolk Aero Club, Hadleigh. George also managed the time to demonstrate Blackburn Bluebirds and the Lincock I. In 1930 he was instructing part-time at the Brooklands School of Flying and the following year took up the post of CFI. George returned to testing in 1933 with Wolseley Aero Engines which was developing the AR.9 series of radials. George took up the post of CFI at the Reid & Sigrist-run 7 E&RFTS at Desford in 1935.

ONE of Sqn Ldr George Lowdell's tasks at Desford was to test Reid & Sigrist's (R&S) entry into aircraft manufacturing, the Snargasher twin-engined, three-seat, crew trainer. Flown for the first time from Desford early in 1939, it failed to find a market and was used by the company for communications until it was retired in 1944. In July 1945, R&S had another go at this concept with the Desford – see A G Bullmore and C F French. George was promoted to Wing Commander in 1939, becoming the commanding officer of RAF Desford.

During 1941 he joined Vickers as a PTP, working under his former pupil, 'Mutt' Summers*. He worked where the demand was, be it Brooklands or Squires Gate on Wellingtons or Castle Bromwich and Eastleigh on Supermarine Spitfires. In February 1942 he famously signed off 21 Spitfire Vs in a single day! While test Warwick II HG516 out of Wisley on 11th March 1946 along with FTO W H Langdon George was forced to feather the starboard propeller; while making an asymmetric landing he overshot and he put it down beyond the airfield boundary. The crew were uninjured; HG516 was scrapped. By 1950, George was Chief PTP at Brooklands, having graduated to Vikings, Valettas, Varsities and Viscounts. At that point he had over 8,500 hours on around 150 types. He retired from testing in 1953 liaising with Viscount customers, later taking a role in maintenance training, until leaving Vickers in 1956. Wg Cdr George Edward Lowdell AFM died in 1974, aged 73.

George Lowdell in the cockpit of the one-off Reid & Sigrist Snargasher.
Peter Green Collection

Charles Lowe-Wylde

WHEN Charles Herbert Lowe-Wylde was 14, he designed, built and flew his first glider. (See the section on Hollis Williams for a digression involving him and Lowe-WyIde.) In 1930 Charles founded the Kent Gliding Club and the British Aircraft Company (BAC), the latter at Maidstone. His first product, the BAC.I primary glider, was put into limited production and other sailplanes followed. In 1932 he adapted a two-seat BAC.VII glider by converting it to single-seater status and mounting a pusher 600cc Douglas engine on the wing centre section. This was called the Planette, a self-launching glider, and it is *very likely* that Charles first flew this machine, as he had done with his non-powered creations. (That said, Captain E D Ayre, who by 1939 was assistant works manager for Miles at Woodley, also flew and demonstrated Planettes.) On 13th May 1933 the 32-year-old Charles Herbert Lowe-Wylde was flying a Planette at West Malling when it side-slipped, recovered and then plummeted into the ground, killing its pilot. The inquiry deemed that he had been taken ill in the air. Robert Kronfeld* took over the running of BAC.

D Lowry

21 Nov 1949	Chrislea Skyjeep G-AKVS
	1 x 155hp Blackburn Cirrus Major 3

IN 1948 R F Stedman*, CTP for the Exeter-based Chrislea Aircraft left the company and D Lowry took his place. Chrislea was building the four-seat Super Ace tricycle undercarriage light aircraft, but its purchase price and unconventional control system was inhibiting sales. The Super Ace was re-egineered as a 'tail-dragger' with 'normal' control inputs. As well as four seats the rear decking hinged upwards to allow the carriage of limited amounts of cargo, or a patient on a stretcher in the rear fuselage. Mr Lowry carried out the first flight at Exeter in November 1949. Only four more Skyjeeps were produced; Chrislea had faded away by late 1951.

Philip Lucas

14 Jun 1938	Hawker Hotspur K8309
	1 x 1,025hp RR Merlin II
6 Dec 1939	Hawker Tornado P5219
	1 x 1,760hp RR Vulture II
24 Feb 1940	Hawker Typhoon P5212
	1 x 2,100hp Napier Sabre I
2 Sep 1942	Hawker Tempest V HM595
	1 x 2,180hp Napier Sabre IIA
28 Jun 1943	Hawker Tempest II LA602
	1 x 2,520hp Bristol Centaurus V
1 Sep 1944	Hawker Fury NX798
	1 x 2,300hp Bristol Centaurus XII

Note: Other than the Hotspur, all took place from Langley.

Philip Gadesden Lucas, born 1902. By 1924 he was an engineering apprentice with Vickers, learning to fly at Stag Lane, becoming a founder-member of the London Aeroplane Club. He joined the RAF in 1926 flying Bristol F.2B Fighters and Sopwith Snipes, among others. Fg Off Philip Lucas was posted to A&AEE Martlesham Heath in 1929.

DURING the summer of 1931 Philip Lucas left the RAF to join Hawker at Brooklands as a test pilot under 'George' Bulman* and his deputy 'Gerry' Sayer*. The three became a great team and there was an exceptional amount of work for them; it was the hey-day of the Hawker biplane family and the transition to the incredible Hurricane. In January 1932 Philip was on a Royal Navy vessel heading for Japan, with Hawker Nimrod prototype S1577 and first production example S1578 on board. Philip demonstrated the shipborne fighter and the entire effort was rewarded by an order for a *single* Nimrod in 1934. In June the Bulman-Sayer-Lucas combo delighted the crowds at the SBAC display at Hendon. Philip was flying the company-owned

The Chrislea Skyjeep had a fold-up rear top-decking, allowing the carriage of a stretcher, or bulky items. Chrislea Aircraft

The prototype Hotspur K8309 at Brooklands, 1938. *Peter Green Collection*

Hart G-ABTN, fitted with a Bristol Jupiter radial. Unbeknown to Philip, an appreciable length of balloon cable snagged on the Hart's tail skid and it trailed behind throughout his vigorous aerobatic routine, at times whip-cracking on the ground close to the crowd as he pulled out of dives. There are many other facets from this intensive time but two more will have to suffice: Philip carried out the maiden flights of the first production Demon, K2842, on 10th February 1933 and the first production Hind, K4636, on 4th September 1935.

When George Bulman flew the prototype Hurricane on 6th November 1935 everything changed for Hawker and the RAF. Sydney Camm and his design team had taken all of the experience of the Hart family and the company was set to apply the same logic and create a dynasty of monoplane fighters. In 1937 Philip was promoted to CTP when George Bulman retired ('Gerry' Sayer became Gloster CTP in 1934). Development of the Hurricane became Philip's domain; he took L1547, the first production Hurricane I, on its inaugural flight on 12th October 1937. He was in the 'chair' for the debut of the prototype Hurricane II, P3269, on 11th June 1940 and the Mk.IV, KX405, on 14th March 1943. During 1938 Philip and his expanding team moved out of Brooklands to the new test centre at Langley. Philip's first from-new prototype was the Hotspur turret fighter, K8309, which he flew from Brooklands on 14th June 1938. Like the Henley light bomber before it, the Hotspur employed a lot of Hurricane structure and fittings. The contract went to the Boulton Paul Defiant and the Hotspur remained a one-off.

"Lucas displayed great courage and presence of mind during a test flight and by his skill and coolness saved an aircraft from destruction." So read the citation accompanying the award of the George Medal bestowed upon Philip in late 1940. The medal was instituted by King George VI to recognise acts of bravery carried out by civilians in September 1940; Philip was one of the first recipients of the award. The aircraft Philip brought back was P5219, the prototype Hawker Tornado. From 1937 Sydney Camm embarked upon a new fighter, based on Hurricane philosophy, in two versions both powered by 24-cylinder engines: the Tornado with X-format Rolls-Royce Vulture and the Typhoon with H-format Napier Sabre. Philip 'first flighted' Tornado P5219 on 6th December 1939, with a Hurricane-like radiator under the centre section. Early tests revealed that at high speed the radiator housing caused severe air flow problems. P5219 was re-flown by Philip on 6th December 1939 with a 'chin'-mounted radiator that was to become a hallmark of the Typhoon and Sabre-engined Tempests. While flying P5219 on 9th May 1940 a structural failure of the rear fuselage looked set to make the entire tail section break away. Philip was faced with a classic test pilot dilemma: baling out would save his life but very likely destroy evidence of the cause of the catastrophe; or he could stay with it and nurse it back knowing that as he descended, the parachute he was sitting on would cease to be an option. In a miraculous piece of flying Philip landed P5219 and a structural strengthening programme was carried out.

The Vulture engine was curtailed by Rolls-Royce and on 23rd December 1941 Tornado HG641 fitted with a Bristol Centaurus was first flown by Philip, but the decision was taken to concentrate on the Sabre-powered Typhoon. Philip 'first flighted' the prototype Typhoon, P5212, on 24th February 1940. The Typhoon proved to be a failure as an interceptor but after a demanding development period the type became a first rate ground attack platform. Camm returned to the idea of a high-speed interceptor and took the Typhoon fuselage and tail, married it to a thin-section, elliptical wing and powered it with a Sabre IV cooled by radiators in the leading edge. This was the exceptionally clean-looking Typhoon II, quickly renamed Tempest I as it was a new type and not a variant. As with the

Invasion-striped Typhoon I at an unknown location. *KEC*

Tornado/Typhoon, the plan was to create two versions, with the Sabre and – after the experience gained with Tornado HG641 – the Centaurus radial. The complexities of the Tempest I's cooling system meant that the 'chin' radiator-equipped Tempest V was the first of the new breed to take to the air: Philip took HM595 skyward on 2nd September 1942. It was not until 24th February 1943 that Tempest I HM599 was flown for the first time, again by Philip. The prototype Centaurus-engined Tempest II, LA602, was flown by Philip on 28th June 1943 and, despite its numeric designation, became the last of the Tempest family to enter production. Both the Tempest II and V gave exceptional service with the RAF and the Mk.II enjoyed post-war exports to India and Pakistan. The final extrapolation of the monoplane fighter dynasty was the Fury, which was extensively used by the post-war Fleet Air Arm as the Sea Fury and became a major export success. The Centaurus-powered prototype, NX798, had its debut in Philip's hands on 1st

September 1944. Experimentation with a Rolls-Royce Griffon 85 driving a contra-rotating, six-bladed propeller assembly was first flown by Philip on LA610 on 27th November 1944 and this airframe was later fitted with a Sabre VII with a similar cooling system to the Tempest I. But it was the round-engined Sea Fury that had the honour of being the last of a long line of Hawker piston-engined fighters.

Hawker's jet era was to be the responsibility of Bill Humble*, who succeeded Philip as CTP in 1945. By that time Philip had a total of 3,450 hours on 120 types. In 1946 Philip became a director of Hawker and was appointed as its general manager before he moved in 1947 to take up the post of technical sales manager for de Havilland. Philip G Lucas GM died in 1981, aged 79.

The Centaurus-engined Tornado prototype, HG641 at Langley. *Peter Green Collection*

Above: With its radiators in the inner wing leading edges, the Tempest I prototype HM599 was an exceptionally smooth looking. *Hawker Aircraft*

Right: The second prototype Fury, NX802, late 1945.
 Peter Green Collection

With a six-bladed contra-rotating propeller, the Griffon 85-engined Fury prototype at Langley, January 1945.
Hawker Aircraft

The one-off, high-flying Vickers F7/41 DZ217. *Vickers-Armstrongs*

'Tommy' Lucke

24 Dec 1942	Vickers F7/41 DZ217
	2 x 1,565hp RR Merlin 61

Douglas Webster Lucke, born 1909 in Mexico. He came to Britain in 1929 and joined the RAF. Leaving in 1934, he worked for the Ethyl Export Corporation supplying fuels and lubricants to the worldwide aviation industry. By 1937 he was at Filton, instructing for Bristol.

KNOWN to friends and colleagues as 'Tommy', D W Lucke was working for Vickers at Brooklands by 1939. Most of his time was spent on Wellington and Warwick production testing and he is known to have been involved in testing the Wellington DWI mine-countermeasures variant. On Christmas Eve 1942 Tommy had the honour of 'first flighting' the last Vickers fighter to take to the air, the Type 432 high-altitude interceptor, from Farnborough. Designed to Specification F7/41 the Type 432 was a very advanced, all-metal, design but it failed to rouse any interest; the requirement being met, at least in part, by the Westland Welkin. The prototype, DZ217, remained a one-off and the programme was cancelled in late 1943.

Work on Warwicks included trials with air-droppable lifeboats. While Tommy was testing second production Warwick B.I BV215 at Farnborough on 18th February 1943, a fire broke out in the starboard Pratt & Whitney Double Wasp during a re-start. The blaze engulfed the aircraft and Tommy made a hasty exit. With FTO J M Warner, Tommy took production Warwick GR.V PN780 for its first test flight on

27th March 1945, from Brooklands. This machine had what was hoped would be the definitive 'fix' for a long series of directional instability problems with the type, centred on a dorsal fin fillet. Readying for asymmetric flight at 7,000ft the rudder started to severely oscillate and the decision was taken to bale out. Tommy landed successfully, Warner was slightly injured: PN780 impacted near Cobham. It was discovered that the dinghy had been ejected on its lanyard due to an electrical circuit malfunction; it had fouled the rudder.

Tommy joined BOAC as a test pilot until 1948 when he moved to Egypt to take up an instructor contract with the Royal Egyptian Air Force. He retired from flying in 1950, becoming a sales manager for Export Packing Service Ltd at Slough. Douglas Webster Lucke died in 1972.

Jim Ludford

7 Apr 1994	McDD/BAe Harrier T.10 TX01 ZH653
	1 x 23,800lbst RR Pegasus 105

FLT LT JAMES S LUDFORD graduated from ETPS Course No.44 at Boscombe Down in 1985. By 1994 he was serving a test pilot with British Aerospace at Dunsfold and Warton. On 7th April 1994 Jim piloted the maiden flight of the prototype Harrier T.10, the two-seat equivalent of the GR.5, GR.7 and GR.9 family. This event was also the first time that a Harrier had been first flown from Warton, instead of Dunsfold. By 2002 Jim was flying airliners from East Midlands Airport.

The one-off Avro
Antelope J9183 was first
flown by 'Lux' Luxmoore
at Hamble in 1928.
Peter Green Collection

Francis 'Lux' Luxmoore

Nov 1928	Avro Antelope J9183
	1 x 480hp RR F.XIB
18 Jun 1947	Portsmouth Aerocar Major G-AGTG
	2 x 155hp Blackburn Cirrus Major III

Notes: Antelope flown from Hamble, the Aerocar from
Portsmouth.

*Francis L Luxmoore, born 1898. By 1917 he was with 46
Squadron flying Royal Aircraft Factory BE.2s and later
Sopwith Pups on the Western Front. Early in 1918 he was
shot down and taken prisoner. Repatriated, he signed on
with the RAF; his service including the Versailles Peace
Conference in 1919 and he was part of the escort for the
interment of the Unknown Warrior in Westminster Abbey
on 11th November 1920. By the early 1920s he was with 1
Squadron flying Sopwith Snipes from Hinaidi, Iraq. His Snipe
was modified with an extra cockpit behind the pilot, this
was for Lux's dog, Raggis! Based at Hinaidi, Major
Luxmoore was awarded the DFC in 1925.*

The Portsmouth Aerocar was an advanced design but failed to attract any
buyers. *Portsmouth Aviation*

Francis Luxmoore, known also as 'Frank' and most often
as 'Lux', joined Avro at Hamble in 1927, under CFI 'Sam'
Brown*. One of his first tasks was the test of the Avro Avocet
single-seat shipboard fighter N210, in landplane form, and Lux
may have carried out the first flight. Lux was at the controls
for N210's first ever flight as a floatplane, in April 1928. In
November that year, he 'first flighted' the Antelope two-seat
day bomber prototype, J9183. The Hawker Hart won the
competition and the Antelope remained a one-off.

Lux became a director of Portsmouth, Southsea and Isle of
Wight Aviation in 1931, a regional airline and charter service
based at Portsmouth. He established the company's
engineering subsidiary, Portsmouth Aviation, at Christchurch.
In 1936 Lux acquired Comper Swift G-ACTF from George

Errington*, operating it until the end of the war. (*Tango-Fox*
was acquired by Ron Clear* in 1949; today the Swift is part
of the Shuttleworth Collection.) During the war, Portsmouth
Aviation was part of the Ministry of Aircraft Production's
Civilian Repair Organisation, working on Airspeed Oxfords,
among other types. With the end of the war, Lux was
determined that Portsmouth Aviation turn to aircraft design
and manufacture. The result was the Aerocar Major, a twin-
engined, twin-boom six-seater for small airline, charter and
private owner operation. Lower-powered Junior and Minor
versions were also to be offered. Lux was at the controls for
the first flight of the Aerocar Major, G-AGTG at Portsmouth
on 18th June 1947. Despite much effort at marketing the
project came to nought and G-AGTG was scrapped in 1950.
Major Francis L Luxmoore DFC retired from Portsmouth
Aviation late in 1947 and he bought a farm near East
Grinstead, Sussex.

75

Leslie Macdonald

Leslie F Macdonald was a motor racing enthusiast who competed at Brooklands. He joined British and Colonial (ie Bristol) at Filton as a mechanic in 1910 and in July went with Maurice Edmond* to the Lanark aviation meeting with a Boxkite. He learned to fly at Lanark and then with the Bristol school at Brooklands, gaining Aviators' Certificate No.28 on a 'Bristol' dated 15th November 1910 – the first pupil of the school to achieve this status.

THE ink was hardly dry on Leslie Macdonald's Aviators' Certificate when he was offered a position with British and Colonial as a test and demonstration pilot – good promotion from mechanic. He was then told to pack his bags and was dispatched, along with 'Joe' Hammond* to Australia for a sales tour, using Boxkite No.10, in November 1910. Leslie was back in Britain by May 1912 and was 'poached' by Vickers and appointed as chief pilot. Much of his time was instructing from the flying field at Erith, alongside the Thames, in Kent. He flew the early Vickers Monoplanes, including the two-seater and flew Monoplane No.6 at the Military Aeroplane Trials Competition on Salisbury Plain in June 1912. Early in January 1913 Leslie took off from Erith in Monoplane No.6 with Harold England as a passenger. The engine failed and the aircraft came down in the Thames. Leslie, aged about 20, and his passenger, both drowned. His post at Vickers was taken by Harold Barnwell*.

Donald Maclaine piloting Wildcat ZZ400 on its maiden flight at Yeovil, 12th November 2009. *Courtesy and © 2015 AgustaWestland*

R M Mace

SQN LDR R M MACE RCAF was posted to Armstrong Whitworth at Baginton for PTP duties flying the Avro Lancaster Is being built there. On a routine test flight on 16th December 1944 Mace was flying with an FTO called Morgan in Lancaster I NG435. The bomber was seen in a steepening dive from around 12,000ft. It impacted at Long Marston, Warwickshire, killing both of the crew.

Donald Maclaine

| 12 Nov 2009 | Westland Wildcat ZZ400 |
| | 2 x 1,281shp LHTEC CTS800 |

AGUSTAWESTLAND CTP Donald C Maclaine and senior test pilot Dick Trueman were at the helm of a new variant of the EHI Merlin at Yeovil on 3rd July 2007. Donald succeeded Colin Hague* as CTP for AgustaWestland in 2003 (Westland and Italian rotorcraft manufacturer Agusta merged in 2000). A consortium of AgustaWestland, Bell and Lockheed Martin had won the competition to replace the US Marine Corps-operated Presidential Flight's long-serving Sikorsky VH-3As. Unofficially referred to as the 'US-101', officially designated VH-71 Kestrel, and known at Yeovil as TV-2, the helicopter flew with B Condition (or 'trade-plate') marking G-17-101. Sadly the entire VH-71 programme was terminated in June 2009.

The successful Lynx programme entered the second generation at Yeovil on 12th November 2009 when Donald took the AW159 Lynx Wildcat prototype into the air for the first time. A major evolution of the original Lynx, the British

Army Air Corps and the Fleet Air Arm have started to replace earlier versions of the Lynx with what is now named Wildcat, having dropped the 'Lynx' prefix. Donald Maclaine was replaced as AgustaWestland CTP by Andy Strachan*.

Norman Macmillan

19 Sep 1920	Saunders Kittiwake G-EAUD 2 x 200hp ABC Wasp II	C
19 Nov 1920	Parnall Puffin N136 1 x 450hp Napier Lion II	G
1923	Parnall Plover N160 1 x 436hp Bristol Jupiter IV	Y
Apr 1923	Bristol Bloodhound G-EBGG 1 x 425hp Bristol Jupiter IV	F
19 Jun 1923	Parnall Possum J6862 1 x 450hp Napier Lion II	F
13 Sep 1923	Parnall Pixie I 1 x 3½hp Douglas	F
28 Nov 1924	Fairey Fremantle N173 1 x 650hp RR Condor III	H
3 Jan 1925	Fairey Fox I J9515 1 x 480hp Curtiss D-12	He
5 Jun 1925	Fairey Ferret N190 1 x 400hp AS Jaguar IV	N
9 Nov 1925	Fairey Firefly 1 x 480hp Curtiss D-12	N
19 Mar 1926	Fairey IIIF N198 1 x 500hp Napier Lion VA	N
4 Oct 1926	Fairey Flycatcher II N216 1 x 400hp AS Jaguar IV	N
16 May 1929	Fairey Fleetwing N235 1 x 490hp RR F.XI	N
25 Oct 1929	Fairey Fox II J9834 1 x 480hp RR F.XIB	N
25 Nov 1930	Fairey Night Bomber K1695 2 x 525hp Bristol Jupiter XF	Hw

Notes: Airfields decode: C – Cowes, the River Medina; F – Filton; G – Isle of Grain; H – Hamble Water; He – Hendon; Hw – Harmondsworth, Great West Aerodrome; N – Northolt; Y – Yate. The Night Bomber was named the Hendon in late 1934.

Norman Macmillan, born 1892. Enlisted in the Highland Light Infantry in 1914 and fought on the Western Front. Transferred to the RFC in 1916, joining 45 Squadron flying Sopwith 1½ Strutters, and from mid-1917, Camels. The unit was initially based in France, but moved to Italy in late 1917. He was credited with three aerial victories: a DFW (Aug 1917), an Albatros D.III (Sep 1917) and a D.V (Oct 1917) plus six 'out of control'. 2nd Lt Macmillan was awarded the MC in July 1918.

Norman Macmillan, experienced test pilot and gifted author.
Peter Green Collection

Norman Macmillan set himself up as a freelance test pilot during 1919. At Filton, Roy Fedden's Cosmos Engineering Co was developing radial engines and Norman was engaged as a pilot. Avro 504K G-EADL was converted to act as a test-bed for the three-cylinder 100hp Cosmos Lucifer. In January 1920, with an engineer called Swinchatt as a passenger, Norman was flying G-EADL from Yeovil to Filton in increasingly bad weather. Close to Filton the little Lucifer failed and the Avro was wrecked in a forced landing; Norman and his passenger walked away from the hulk. While at Filton, Norman carried out some flying for the Bristol Aeroplane Co and it was that organisation that recommended him to the US Naval Commission, which was looking for a test pilot to sign off the pair of Parnall Panthers that it had acquired in 1920. This was to lead to commissions from Parnall, of which more anon.

Norman's first maiden flight did not end well. Sam Saunders at Cowes commissioned him to test the two crew, seven passenger, Kittiwake twin-engined biplane amphibian. The Kittiwake had many novel features, including mechanisms that allowed almost all of the leading edge of the upper wing to change camber – this was long before the advent of slots. The trailing edge was a full-span flap; the ailerons being located between the wings, pivoting from the fourth and third struts of the four-bay layout. Norman began sea trials on the waters of the River Medina and then out on to the Solent on 11th September 1920.

Norman Macmillan at the helm of the Saunders Kittiwake on its ill-fated first flight, 19th September 1920. *Peter Green Collection*

Five days later Norman was ready for the 'off' in the Kittiwake. He had with him a Saunders mechanic, an Irishman called Rafferty, who had volunteered on hearing that Norman could not operate the amphibian single-handed. In his book *Freelance Pilot*, Norman described events after take-off: "The altimeter showed 600ft as we climbed towards the shore. I looked out towards the starboard engine. An instant later the upper surface of the leading edge of the wing stripped off and blew away like paper. Kittiwake lurched and heeled to the right. I kicked the rudder, threw the wheel hard across. As we swerved to the left, Rafferty gripped my arm. 'Good God! Look!' he shouted, and pointed toward the left wings. The front covering pulled out of its socket, stood upright for a moment, then tore from the spar and disappeared. Rafferty's face was white."

Norman brought the 68ft 3in-span amphibian down for a reasonably controlled forced landing but was unlucky to hit a rock outcrop in his 'chosen' landing zone. The hull was holed and the aircraft sank up to its lower wing; Norman and Rafferty were rescued from the upper wing. To return to *Freelance Pilot*: "It was Rafferty's first flight. He swore to some of his friends in the works that he would never go into the air again." Late in September 1920 modifications and repairs had been made, but Norman was unable to get the Kittiwake airborne; the notoriously problematically ABC engines contributing to a string of problems. Flight testing began again in March 1921, but Norman was busy on more productive work: the one-off Kittiwake was broken up later in the year.

In July 1921 Spain was plunged into a conflict in Morocco, the so-called Riffian War. Orders were placed hastily for aircraft to bolster the armed forces. In September Norman ferried Bristol F.2B Fighter M-MRAK down to southern Spain, from Filton. On return he picked up an Airco DH.4 that had been acquired from the Aircraft Disposal Company and headed for Spain. Then it was the turn of another F.2B, M-MRAG, and he took with him war correspondent and adventurer Major W T Blake. Having delivered the aircraft, the two of them endeavoured to cross to North Africa to observe the battles. Then some time was spent advising the Spanish Navy on how to ready its neglected Felixstowe flying-boats for return to service.

The prototype Parnall Puffin amphibious fleet reconnaissance biplane. *Peter Green Collection*

Third prototype Parnal Plover, N162, powered by an Armstrong Siddeley Jaguar. *KEC*

Major Blake had devised an elaborate stage-by-stage around-the-world flight and engaged Norman as pilot. The attempt set off from Croydon on 24th May 1922 in three-seat Airco DH.9 G-EBDE. A force-landing near Istres, France, on the 28th necessitated repairs but after a test flight the Siddeley Puma was still defective. The Major had two more DH.9s; G-EBDF which had been positioned in Vancouver for the cross-Canada section, and G-EBDL which was ready to be freighted to where it was needed. This latter machine was flown to France and, with two careful strokes of a paintbrush was transformed from G-EBDL into 'G-EBDE' so as not to compromise the continuity of the documentary film being made! The 'new' G-EBDE reached Calcutta on 12th August where Fairey IIIC floatplane G-EBDI awaited the team for the over-water stages to the west coast of Canada. Blake, cameraman L Broome and Norman departed Calcutta on 19th August but engine failure forced them down at Lukhidia Char in the Bay of Bengal amid a tropical storm. Norman tried again on the 22nd, but the Rolls-Royce Eagle let them down and after 20 minutes they were adrift. Overnight G-EBDI capsized, with the trio clinging to the wreckage. Miraculously they were picked up on the 25th and the entire venture was abandoned.

Prior to his engagement on Major Blake's global venture, Norman had undertaken the first of a series of commissions for George Parnall and Co. The Puffin was a two-seat general duties amphibian intended to be flown from aircraft carriers as well as capable of operating from the sea. The format was such that the observer/gunner had an unobstructed field of fire as the fin and rudder was sited *below* the rear fuselage. Norman made the maiden flight from the airfield at the Isle of Grain, Kent, on 19th November 1920, and the following day

flew N136 from the water. Early trials revealed that the Puffin rode badly and spray thrown back by the central float damaged the propeller, which broke up. Harold Bolas, the designer, flew with Norman to see for himself and largely solved this problem by extending the central float forward, well beyond the propeller. No further orders were placed beyond the three prototypes.

Norman's next job for Parnall was the Plover single-seat shipboard fighter of 1923. The Fairey Flycatcher took the main contract: after three prototypes, ten production Plovers were built. Designer Harold Bolas was on board another of his creations on 19th June 1923 when Norman took the Possum 'Postal' triplane for its maiden flight. The 'Postal' label was a blatant diversion, the machine boasted gun positions fore and aft! The Air Ministry was experimenting with the 'engine room' concept, placing the engine in mid-fuselage driving a pair of contra-rotating propellers via geared shafts. This allowed for a cleaner airframe and for an engineer to tinker with the powerplant in the 'comfort' of the fuselage. Harold Bolas was keen to observe but, as has been mentioned before, if all went wrong the loss of designer and test pilot could have proven catastrophic, not just to the project in hand, but to the company. Norman piloted the Pixie I and II ultralights entered for the October 1923 Light Aeroplane Trials at Lympne; succeeding in gaining the speed award, at 76.1mph for the Pixie I. After the Lympne trials, Norman left Parnall and his place was taken by another prolific freelancer, Frank Courtney*. During 1923 Norman also carried out flight testing of the private-venture Bristol Bloodhound two-seat fighter at Filton. This led to an order for three more for Air Ministry trials, but no production contract.

The King's Cup air race was hosted by A&AEE Martlesham Heath in August 1924 and with the proximity of MAEE Felixstowe, the opportunity was taken to allow seaplanes to compete. A pair of Supermarine Seagull III amphibians were flown by Colonel, the Master of Sempill (see Chapter Seven), and Henri Biard*. The MAEE commissioned Fairey to specially modify Fairey IIID floatplane N9777 ready for the event and Norman was asked to fly it, along with Belgian Ernest Oscar Tips as engineer. Norman piloted N9777 to second place, the race was won by Alan Cobham* in de Havilland DH.50 G-EBFN. The Fairey IIID was the first, and only, floatplane to race in the King's Cup. Norman had been freelancing with Fairey since 1921, but took up the full-time post of CTP January 1924, succeeding Vincent Nicholl*. The Fairey III series of floatplanes and landplanes was the centrepiece of the organisation's success and Norman 'first flighted' the final iteration of the family, the IIIF, in March 1926.

The first Parnall Pixie, No.9, at Lympne during the 1923 trials.
Peter Green Collection

Following Norman's involvement in the abortive Blake around-the-world flight of 1922, Fairey was commissioned to build a large (69ft 2in-span) floatplane to have another crack at the venture. By the time that Norman flew the one-off Fremantle on 28th November 1924, the purpose had vaporised as the USAAS had succeeded with its trio of Douglas World Cruiser floatplanes between April and September 1924. Norman was responsible for the maiden flights of three hopeful Fairey naval biplanes: the Ferret two-seater general purpose type (three built); the Flycatcher II single seat fleet fighter (with only format relating it to the previous Flycatcher, this was a brand new design) and the Fleetwing spotter-reconnaissance floatplane. Both the Flycatcher II and the Fleetwing were one-offs.

Crowds lined the seawall at Stranraer as Fairey IIID N9777 took on fuel during the 950-miles King's Cup on 12th August 1924. *KEC*

Fairey Fox I J7943 was issued to 12 Squadron in June 1926. No.12 was the only Fox unit and to celebrate the type's exceptional performance adopted a Fox's head as a badge and the motto 'Leads the Field'. *KEC*

By far and away the most important aeroplane that Norman 'first flighted' was the private-venture Fox of 1925. The Fox was probably the first time that the 'industry' got to show that it was in a better position to judge what was needed than the ponderous Air Ministry. Having witnessed the success of the American Schneider Trophy team at Cowes in September 1923, the 12-cylinder Curtiss D-12 'Vee' format engine offered the prospect of exceptional streamlining and power output. While Charles Richard Fairey sought to purchase a stock of D-12s and the rights to build them; the Fairey boss told designer Marcel Lobelle to tackle the requirement that gave rise to the Fairey Fawn day bomber, but without the pedantry

written into every paragraph. There was uproar at the need for an American engine, but as Norman showed the prototype had the same armament as the 1923 Fawn but was 50mph *faster* at 10,000ft and the *bomber* Fox was on a par with contemporary RAF *fighters*: it was 5mph faster than the Gloster Gamecock at 10,000ft. A production order for 28 was placed, almost reluctantly but the type's role in invigorating development of V-12s in Britain was its lasting legacy. The Fox spawned a fighter variant, the Firefly, which was not adopted in Britain but became a staple of the Fairey Belgian subsidiary, as did the much refined and developed Fox II, powered initially be a Rolls-Royce Kestrel, which Norman first flew in late 1929.

Norman Macmillan piloting the Firefly II prototype, 1930. *Peter Green Collection*

A production Fairey Hendon with Rolls-Royce Kestrels, 1938. *KEC*

The final prototype that Norman was involved in was only his second twin-engined machine – the first was the problematical Saunders Kittiwake. This was the Night Bomber, which took the name Hendon in late 1934. Powered initially by Bristol Jupiter radials, the prototype was flown by Norman from the newly-acquired Harmondsworth aerodrome on 25th November 1930. On board was Hollis Williams* who had masterminded the creation of the RAF's first all-metal cantilever monoplane. The type entered service in 1936, powered by Rolls-Royce Kestrels but the hoped for large order book, settled on a dismal 14.

All was not well with Norman and his employer. He resigned verbally in October 1930 and put it in writing the following month, but was persuaded to stay on and fly the Night Bomber prototype on 25th November 1930. His last flight for the company was made the following day. Norman explained his reasoning for resigning as Fairey CTP: "I could no longer tolerate [Charles Richard] Fairey's way of dealing with matters that concerned me; he had many good points, but I could not consent that he should have me body and soul – so I slipped my mooring and have never regretted it..." He was succeeded by C R McMullin*.

Norman was snapped up by Armstrong Whitworth, appointing him as foreign sales agent and consultant test pilot. In January 1931, engaged by Avro as a demonstration pilot, Norman was bound for Argentina with Avro 626 G-ABFM. The 626 was a multi-purpose version of the Tutor military trainer, aimed at export markets. Norman displayed G-ABFM both as a landplane and a floatplane. While he was on this tour, Norman and the 626 became the first all-British combination to fly over the Andes, during a trip to Santiago in Chile.

Norman returned to the RAF during World War Two, acting as a historian and war correspondent; he retired from the RAF as a Wing Commander in 1958. He was a prodigious and gifted writer; his works ranging from combat derring-do, piloting textbooks, biography to his four-volume history of the RAF at war. Several of his works included autobiographic material, chiefly his exceptional *Into the Blue* (1929) and

Freelance Pilot (1937). His first title was *The Art of Flying* (1928), others included: The Air Travellers' Guide to Europe (1929), Sir Sefton Brancker (1935), *The Air Cadet's Handbook on How to Pilot an Aeroplane* (1942), *The Royal Air Force at War* (four volumes 1942, 1944, 1949 and 1950), *Wings of Fate* (1967) and *Offensive Patrol: The Story of the RNAS, RFC and RAF in Italy 1917-1918* (1973). Wg Cdr Norman Macmillan OBE MC AFC died on 5th August 1976, aged 84.

Victor Mahl

15 Jul 1914	Sopwith Circuit of Britain
	1 x 100hp Gnome
12 Aug 1914	Pemberton Billing PB.9
	1 x 50hp Gnome

VICTOR MAHL trained as a motor engineer and by 1913 was working for Sopwith, as an engineer. Victor tended to the 100hp Gnome that powered the Tabloid floatplane with which Sopwith test pilot Howard Pixton* took victory in the second Schneider Trophy contest, staged at Monaco on 20th April 1914. The following month Victor gained his 'ticket', Aviators' Certificate No.784, on a Sopwith at Brooklands and he was rewarded by becoming deputy to Harry Hawker. Victor was designated as the pilot for the Sopwith entrant in the 1914 Circuit of Britain contest staged by the *Daily Mail* and offering £5,000 to the winner. He first flew the 'Circuit' biplane in landplane form at Brooklands on 15th July 1914, but with the outbreak of the Great War 13 days later, the contest was cancelled. Harry Hawker 'loaned' Victor to Noel Pemberton Billing's company at Woolston and in August 1914 he flew the PB.9 single-seater scout. The type remained a one-off. By October 1914 Victor was helping to test a batch of ten Sopwith Type 860 floatplanes for the Admiralty on the Solent. On 1st November 1914 disaster befell the first of these, No.851, which dived into the water. Victor was rescued, but R J Alston, of Sopwith's design department, was drowned. Unrelated to the accident, Victor went into hospital for an operation on his appendix: the 25-year-old died of complications of 2nd April 1915.

'Dickie' Mancus

Richard B Mancus, born 1919. He joined the Fleet Air Arm in 1939 and by mid-1942 was flying Sea Hurricane Is with 804 Squadron, initially at Yeovilton. Lt Mancus was injured when he forced landed Z4847 in Cornwall on 30th June 1942. Converting to Seafire Is with 748 Squadron in the summer of 1944, by May 1945 he was flying Grumman Hellcat IIs with 808 Squadron on the aircraft carrier HMS Khedive *involved in operations off Malaya and Sumatra. 'Dickie' graduated from No.6 Course ETPS at Cranfield in 1946 and began three years of trials work, mostly with RAE Farnborough. This included rocket-assisted take-off gear (RATOG) experiments. On 30th July 1948 a RATOG test in Supermarine Spitfire F.17 SX312 went wrong when a rocket pack ignited early and broke loose, hitting the propeller assembly and the Seafire swung violently. SX312 was badly damaged; Dickie was OK. Six months later, also at Farnborough, Dickie was carrying out RATOG trials on the interim Sea Fury FB.11 prototype, VB857, when it was caught by a downdraught, stalled on to the runway and the port undercarriage collapsed. By January 1949 he was conducting rocket projectile launch trials, based at Boscombe Down.*

Lt 'Dickie' Mancus joined Boulton Paul (BP) as a test pilot under 'Ben' Gunn* on 9th May 1949. The main testing work at Pendeford, Wolverhampton, was the Balliol advanced trainer programme and Dickie's naval background was ideal for navalised, deck-landing Sea Balliol T.21 which appeared in late 1952. Final deliveries of the Balliol were made in 1954 to Ceylon and aircraft production by BP came to a halt. The company pioneered electronic powered flying controls – today the computer-controlled equivalent would be called fly-by-wire. From the early 1950s, BP began to convert the Tay-engined Vickers Viscount VX217 at Seighford to act as a test-bed. Once transformed, VX217 was taken on a careful, phase by phase series of tests, initially with the electronic control system deactivated. During the summer of 1957 Dickie was flying using the 'electric' controls while George 'Loopy' Dunworth backed up on the mechanical input. The pair made approaches and landings on a 'virtual' runway at an altitude of 5,000ft. As such Dickie captained the world's first fully FBW controlled flight. It fell to Ben Gunn to make the first official 'hard' landing – at Defford – in VX217 on 2nd January 1958.

By 1966 Dickie was struck with the debilitating disease multiple sclerosis and he became wheelchair-bound but far from despondent. He worked tirelessly at first as the company's Naval Liaison Officer and later as Assistant Liaison Manager with Dowty Boulton Paul at Wolverhampton. Not long after he took retirement, Richard B Mancus MBE died on 1st May 1977, aged 58. Les Whitehouse of the Boulton Paul Association remembered meeting the gifted and inspiring man in his office: "Queried about a part number from months ago Dickie would still remember who called and when and would reel the multi-digit part number off the top of his head. The body might be mangled but the brain was still magnificent – a wonderful chap..."

'Dickie' Mancus (middle) towering over a gathering at Pendeford in front of Sea Balliol T.21 WL721. The gent on the left is unknown, the naval officers unnamed, but on the right is 'Ben' Gunn*. The labelling 'J.O.A.C.' is not a rival airliner, but refers to the Junior Officer's Air Course, operated by 781 Squadron at Lee-on-Solent. *Les Whitehouse-Boulton Paul Association*

Marcus Manton

26 Sep 1917	Wight Type 4 N14
	1 x 130hp Clerget

Marcus Dyce Manton, born 1900. Learned to fly on a Howard-Wright biplane with the Grahame-White school at Hendon, gaining Aviators' Certificate No.231 on 4th June 1912 and he became an instructor at the school. On 27th November 1913 Marcus was the pilot for the first demonstration of a machine-gun fired from an aeroplane in Britain; while flying a Grahame-White Boxkite over the rifle range at Bisley, Lt Stellingwerf of the Belgian Army fired a Lewis gun at a target on the ground. During the early months of 1914, Marcus joined 'Benny' Hucks on his tours of Britain, performing aerobatic routines to large audiences. With the outbreak of the Great War, Marcus volunteered for the RFC but was not accepted; he continued as an instructor for the Grahame-White school.

In early 1917 Marcus Manton took up the post of CTP for J Samuel White at East Cowes, Isle of Wight, following the death of Ralph Lashmar*. Most of this involved signing off 'Converted' Seaplanes for the RNAS; this work was completed in March 1918. By April 1917 Marcus was testing the second Quadruplane single-seat fighter, N546, only to suffer a drenching when he had to put it down in a reservoir near the company aerodrome at Somerton. (A full-scale replica of the Wight Quadruplane is on show at Solent Sky, Southampton.) By June the single-seat triplane flying boat, the Type 4, was ready for its maiden flight. Try as he might, on its first outing on the Medina on the 27th, Marcus could not get the craft to unstick. After modifications to the lower hull, on 26th September Marcus succeeded in getting N14 airborne. On his return he declared it to be dangerous and shortly afterwards it was abandoned.

During 1919 Marcus joined the Aircraft Manufacturing Company's airline subsidiary, Aircraft Transport and Travel Ltd. He flew for a while on the London-Paris route, which was inaugurated from Hounslow Heath in November 1919 using modified DH.4s. By the following year, Marcus was aerodrome manager at Hounslow Heath. The story now skips to 1924 when Marcus was appointed as superintendent of the aircraft department of English Electric (EE). The company had a contract for six Kingston flying-boats and these were assembled at Lytham St Anne's and tested from the Ribble Estuary. As well as the Kingston, EE had come up with the Ayr biplane flying-boat, N148. Powered by a tractor 450hp Napier Lion II, the Ayr's lower wings also functioned as sponsons, so doing away with the need for stabilizing floats. During February 1925 Marcus made attempts to get the Ayr to fly, without success. On 16th March 1926 Marcus was at the helm of Kingston III N9713 and as he ferried it to MAEE at Felixstowe he was doing himself out of a job. With the departure of the last Kingston and nothing to follow up with, English Electric called it a day on aircraft production – but it was to return in 1939.

After EE, Marcus took up a post as an area manager for Shell's aviation fuel and lubricants division. He took to the new sport of gliding and became a founder-member of the British Gliding Association. During World War Two he was Service Liaison Officer for Armstrong Whitworth and in 1945 took an administrative post with the Hawker Siddeley Group, retiring in 1946. Marcus Dyce Manton died in April 1968, aged 68.

Alan Marsh

May 1934	Weir W.2 1 x 50hp Weir Dryad II
9 Jul 1936	Weir W.3 1 x 35hp Weir Pixie
25 Feb 1938	Cierva C.40 G-AFDP 1 x 175hp Salmson 9Ng
Jun 1945	Cierva W.9 PX203 1 x 205hp DH Gipsy Queen 31
27 Jul 1947	Bristol 171 Mk.1 VL958 1 x 450hp P&W Wasp Junior
10 Oct 1948	Cierva Skeeter G-AJCJ 1 x 110hp Jameson FF.1
7 Dec 1948	Cierva Air Horse VZ724 1 x 1,620hp RR Merlin 24

Notes: The Weirs were flown from Abbotsinch; the C.40 from Hanworth; the Bristol 171 from Filton; the W.9, the Skeeter and Air Horse from Eastleigh.

The Weir W.2 on display at the Museum of Flight, East Fortune, 1999: today it is on show at the National Museum of Scotland, Edinburgh. *Ken Ellis*

Henry Alan Marsh, born 1901. Joined the RAF as a mechanic in 1918. He took his 'wings' in 1923, serving in Iraq and then in Britain with fighter units, flying AW Siskins, ending up as Flight Sergeant instructing at CFS. Leaving the RAF in 1930 he became an instructor for Hampshire Aero Club and among its members was Juan de la Cierva*. Early in 1932 Alan was briefly an instructor at the Scarborough Aero Club.

ALAN MARSH, also known as 'Harry', joined the Cierva Autogiro Company (CAC) on 5th April 1932 as a test pilot to assist CTP 'Reggie' Brie* at Hanworth. The following year he was appointed as CFI to the CAC-operated Autogiro Flying School, also at Hanworth, and among his pupils was the 16-year-old 'Jeep' Cable*. As outlined in the section on Juan de la Cierva* the great rotorcraft pioneer was also very much involved in testing the many designs that carried his name. The first Autogiros that Alan tested were not Ciervas, but the product of the associated G & J Weir Ltd – James G Weir was chairman of CAC. The W.2 was first flown by Alan in May 1934 and it helped to pioneer features transferred to the more advanced W.3 of July 1936. The W.3 had the ability to 'jump start'; leaping vertically into the air before translating to forward flight. (The W.2 survives and is on show in the National Museum of Scotland in Edinburgh.)

Alan 'first flighted' the last of the classic Cierva format machines, the C.40. Built by British Aircraft Manufacturing at Hanworth, the C.40 featured the Autodynamic rotor, dual controls and side-by-side seating within a semi-enclosed cockpit. As with most of its forebears, the C.40 required 'mastering'. Ground running commenced on 4th January 1938 and on the 7th Alan went for a conventional 'rolling' take-off, only to encounter considerable resonance and G-AFDP was badly damaged before it got airborne. It was swiftly repaired and Alan got it flying from the roll on 25th February; four days later he achieved a 'jump' take-off and with further attention to the rotor head, the C.40 prototype was regularly leaping vertically into the air by June.

In late 1939 Alan was recalled into the RAF and was posted to RAE Farnborough where he flew a wide variety of types. In 1941 he joined the Avro Rota/Cierva C.30 equipped 1448 Flight on radar calibration duties, under Sqn Ldr Reggie Brie – his colleague from his CAC days. Alan became the unit's commanding officer: 1448 Flight was re-numbered as 529

The prototype Cierva C.40 being demonstrated at Hanworth, very likely by Alan Marsh, 1938. *Peter Green Collection*

Squadron in June 1943. Alan converted to helicopters in 1944, flying Sikorsky Hoverflies, in readiness for his return to 'first flighting'. In 1943 the rotorcraft interests of G & J Weir Ltd and CAC were merged, adopting the iconic Cierva name. A design team was established at Thames Ditton to develop an experimental helicopter, the W.9. To avoid the complication of a tail rotor to counter the torque generated by the main rotor, the team came up with a ducted fan driven off the Gipsy Queen powerplant. The airstream from this vented to port at the extreme tail; the rudder pedals controlled the thrust through this nozzle so that the pilot could control yaw. To achieve this, the W.9's fuselage was effectively a long tube, hence its nicknames, 'Flying Drainpipe' or 'Flying Stovepipe'. Add to this automatic collective control and the W.9 was a challenging project. Alan Marsh was *the* man to debut the W.9 and he was seconded from his duties with 529 Squadron in 1944. Initial trials were unsuccessful and the W.9 was badly damaged; the anti-torque duct was redesigned several times. It was the middle of 1945 before Alan had mastered the helicopter, by which time it had gained a conventional rudder to augment the 'jet' efflux.

Sqn Ldr Alan Marsh left the RAF in 1946 and took up the post of manager and CTP at CAC. The company embarked on a family of helicopters, the W.9, the W.11 Air Horse three-rotor transport and the diminutive W.14 Skeeter aimed at the training and private owner market. As the most experienced rotorcraft pilot in Britain, Bristol turned to Alan to carry out the initial flying of the Type 171 – later to be named Sycamore – and he flew the prototype on 27th July 1947. Following its early sorties in 1945, the W.9 was further refined and fitted with dual controls and it was ready on 20th January 1948. Alan took it aloft but it rolled upside down and crashed. Unscathed, Alan had the strength of character to admit that he was disorientated by being in the 'wrong' seat – dual controls being a novelty to him. The accident was the end of the road for the W.9 – CAC was cash-strapped and the other projects offered more promise. The Skeeter took to the air in October 1948 and, after considerable development, entered production with Saunders-Roe when it acquired the assets of CAC in 1951.

The Cierva Skeeter prototype, G-AJCJ, during early trials, 1949. *KEC*

Air Horse VZ724 performing at the 1949 Farnborough airshow. *KEC*

Below: The Cierva W.9 was an advanced, but unsung, helicopter prototype. *Weir Group*

Front cover of a brochure for the Air Horse, 1949.

When the Air Horse was rolled out at Eastleigh, superlatives were lined up in the press releases and the brochures. It was the largest helicopter, had the greatest payload and was the first with fully-powered flying controls – in the world. A twin-engined version, the WT.11, was already on the drawing boards. Alan took the three-rotor machine for its first flight on 7th December 1948 after a period of extensive ground-running. The Ministry of Supply (MoS) was backing its development and on 13th June 1949 Alan was captaining a flight out of Eastleigh with his former pupil, 'Jeep' Cable in his capacity as MoS rotorcraft CTP, as second pilot and Joseph Unsworth, previously of Cunliffe-Owen, as FTO. At around 500ft the forward rotor hub failed and the Air Horse began to tear itself apart, crashing a couple of miles from Eastleigh; killing Sqn Ldr Henry Alan Marsh AFC (48), Sqn Ldr Frederick John Cable AFC (33) and Joseph Unsworth (41). At the time, Alan Marsh had around 6,400 hours to his credit, over 4,000 of those rotary.

Dickie Martin piloting the Shuttleworth Trust's former Afghan Air Force Hawker Hind at Old Warden, July 1983. *Roy Bonser*

'Dickie' Martin

Richard Frewen Martin, born 1918. After passing out of the RAF College, Cranwell, 'Dickie' Martin was deployed to France with 73 Squadron in September 1939. Oxygen starvation while intercepting a Luftwaffe reconnaissance sortie in Hawker Hurricane I L1959 on 8th November 1939 brought about a forced landing in Luxembourg. Pilot and L1959 were interned, but Dickie managed to escape and caught up with his unit on 26th December. He was involved in the early combats during the Battle of France and shot down two Junkers Ju 87s on 14th May 1940. He returned to Britain to instruct at an OTU in late May 1940 and by April 1941 he re-joined 73 Squadron, in Libya, still equipped with Hurricane Is. This was only very brief as he moved to the Hurricane-equipped 250 Squadron in Egypt, as a flight commander. In actions over Tobruk, Dickie added to his tally of victories with a Messerschmitt Bf 109 on 22nd April 1941 and eight days later an Italian Fiat G.50 and a Macchi MC.200. After a period instructing with a Middle East OTU, he was posted to 107 Maintenance Unit at Kasfereet, Egypt, testing many different repaired, overhauled or modified types. Dickie returned to Britain in 1943 and converted to transports, going to India to fly Douglas Dakotas and Consolidated Liberator VIs with 52 Squadron. Wg Cdr R F Martin graduated from ETPS No.4 Course at Cranfield in 1946 and was posted to RAE Farnborough that year. He was back at ETPS, by then at Farnborough, in 1949 as an instructor, before attending the College of Air Warfare at Manby and then a position with the Air Ministry in 1951.

Wg Cdr 'Dickie' Martin left the RAF in July 1953 and in the following December was taken on by Bill Waterton* to help with the troubled Gloster Javelin all-weather delta-winged fighter. By late March 1954 Bill had resigned from Gloster and Dickie was appointed as the new CTP, with Peter Varley (see Chapter Seven) as his assistant. Dickie flew the fifth Javelin prototype, WT836, on 20th July 1954 from Hucclecote and two days later the first production FAW.1, XA544. The

workload to ready the Javelin for RAF service fell mostly on Dickie and Peter, with Dickie completing nearly 200 spin recoveries as an example of the huge effort needed to clear the delta. During this period, there was a moment when Dickie made headlines, as explained by Don Middleton in *Test Pilots*: "Dickie Martin achieved some notoriety in the press when he was named as the pilot who aimed a sonic boom at London, causing questions to be asked in the House of Commons! Newspaper reports had stated that the new Javelin was unable to fly at supersonic speeds. Gloster naturally, apologized for the unseemly intrusion but the point had been made!"

Development of the Javelin ran from the Mk.1 to the Mk.9 and with the exception of the T.3 dual-control trainer, all featured radar or armament changes, upgraded engines and aerodynamic refinements. Dickie undertook the initial flying of each variant, for example the first FAW.2 XD158 on 31st October 1955, but he left the honours on the Mk.4 to Peter. On 8th April 1960 Dickie was in command of Javelin FAW.8 XJ128, taking off from Hucclecote and finishing at the flight test airfield at Moreton Valence. This was the final maiden flight of the long line of Gloster fighters. Upgrades would occupy Gloster for a while, but there was little to keep Dickie in Gloucestershire: Geoff Worrall* took up the post of CTP.

Dickie moved to Woodford and Avro, working for CTP 'Jimmy' Harrison* from late 1960. He retired from what had become Hawker Siddeley in 1967, starting a career as a commercial pilot with Autair – renamed Court Line Aviation in 1969 – flying BAC One-Elevens. Court Line ceased operations in August 1974 and afterwards Dickie continued piloting One-Elevens, with Air Malawi and then Monarch Airlines – he retired in 1984. From 1948 Dickie was deeply involved with the Shuttleworth Collection at Old Warden, both as a display pilot and as part of the executive committee. Wg Cdr R F Richard Frewen Martin OBE DFC* AFC died on 1st September 2006, aged 88. He had accrued over 19,000 hours on 240 types.

Charles Masefield in front of a Nimrod AEW.3. *British Aerospace*

Charles Masefield

16 Jul 1980	BAe Nimrod AEW.3 XZ286
	4 x 12,140lbst RR Spey Mk.250

CHARLES BEECH GORDON MASEFIELD was born in 1940 and gained his private pilot's licence in 1957. He flew with Cambridge University Air Squadron while studying at Cambridge. In 1964 he started with Beagle Aircraft on production test and delivery work. (Beagle was run by Peter Masefield – Sir Peter from 1972 – Charles's father.) In 1967 at Tollerton he won the King's Cup air race at 277.5mph in North American Mustang N6356T. With the collapse of Beagle in 1970 Charles was appointed as a test pilot with Hawker Siddeley at Woodford, under Tony Blackman*, working on HS.748s, Nimrods, Victors and Vulcans. In 1976 he became DCTP and CTP in 1978. By this time the major project was the airborne early warning version of the Nimrod, the AEW.3. On 16th July 1980 Charles captained the prototype Nimrod AEW.3, XZ286, with John Cruse – AEW Project Pilot – as co-pilot and four other crew for a 3½ hours maiden flight. The Nimrod AEW programme was beset with developmental problems and the entire project was axed in late 1986. Charles was appointed as Production Director at the British Aerospace Chadderton plant in 1980 and followed with a glittering career within the aviation industry, including: President BAe Commercial Aircraft (1990), Senior Vice President (Commercial) Airbus Industrie (1993), Vice Chair GEC (1998) and President BAE Systems (2003). Charles was succeeded as CTP at Woodford by 'Robbie' Robinson*. Charles was knighted in 1997. He left BAE Systems in 2007 and has held a variety of posts in business since.

The prototype Nimrod AEW.3, XZ286. *British Aerospace*

Frank McClean

18 Sep 1911	Short Triple-Twin
	1 x 50hp Gnome
10 Jan 1912	Short S.36 Tractor Biplane
	1 x 70hp Gnome
24 Jul 1912	Short Triple-Tractor
	2 x 50hp Gnome

Francis Kennedy McClean, born 1876. Known as 'Frank', he trained as a civil engineer and worked on major projects in India in the late 19th century, returning to Britain by 1902. He was fascinated by astronomy and travelled widely studying eclipses and visiting observatories. He also embraced ballooning and through this met up with the Short brothers. He visited France in November 1908 and was flown in a Wright Flyer by Wilbur Wright. Inspired, he commissioned a biplane from Shorts and in the following year became a founder member of the Aero Club (the Royal Aero Club – RAeC – from February 1910). In 1909 he decided that land at Leysdown on the Isle of Sheppey was suitable for a flying field and Shorts established its factory to build Short-Wright biplanes there. McClean also acquired nearby Mussel Manor as headquarters for the Aero Club and in early 1910 bought land at Eastchurch, close by, as a flying ground for the RAeC and Shorts also moved to the new site. The biplane he commissioned in late 1908 – the Short No.1 – proved to be unsuccessful in trails at Eastchurch in September 1909. Frank acquired the Short-Wright No.3 and on 20th September 1910 he gained Aviators' Certificate No.21. Frank generously began to lend out his aircraft – initially the S.26 and S.28 Farman-type Short biplanes – so that Royal Navy personnel could be taught to fly, with Cecil Grace* at first carrying out the tuition.

WITH the death of Cecil Grace* in December 1910, 'Frank' McClean took on the unpaid post of test pilot for the nascent Short brothers factory at Eastchurch. On 29th July 1911 Frank flew the first dedicated dual-control two-seater, the Farman-type S.32: two similar machines followed in 1912. A pair of twin tractor versions to the 'Farman' format followed in the autumn of 1911, both of which were tested by Frank: the S.39 Triple-Twin and the more successful Tandem-Twin, based on Frank's own S.27. Both of these had propellers mounted on forward inter-plane struts on the wing, driven from the centrally-located powerplant via chains. On 10th January 1910 Frank piloted the S.36 Tractor Biplane which broke all of the moulds previously adopted by the Shorts. This was a classic biplane which, as it evolved, a partially covered nacelle, with tractor engine in the nose and a pair of cockpits behind the wings. Frank tested another version of this layout on 24th July 1912, the Triple-Tractor which featured a pair of Gnome rotaries mounted in tandem in an extended nose section. One Gnome drove a tractor propeller in the nose, the other drove a pair of tractor propellers mounted between the wings, via chains in a similar manner to the Triple-Twin and Tandem-Twin. By August 1912 Frank was testing the S.33 pusher biplane on floats and on the 10th caused a sensation by flying this machine along the Thames and between the towers of Tower Bridge.

By April 1913 Frank had expressed the desire to cease testing Short-built aircraft: the company was becoming successful and the output was too much for the philanthropic volunteer. Charles Gordon Bell* became the first full-time test pilot for Shorts. By late 1913 Frank was involved in his ambitious seaplane expedition down the River Nile. The specially-commissioned S.80 Nile Seaplane was shipped out to Alexandria and was launched there in January 1914. With Alec Ogilvy backing him up as pilot, Frank had an eventful expedition; returning the Britain in March 1914. Frank owned no less than 17 different aircraft, ranging from the unsuccessful Short No.1 of 1909 to the S.80 of 1914. In August 1919 Frank enlisted in the RNAS, transferring to the RAF in 1918. He left the service in 1918 and was knighted in 1926. Lt Col Sir Francis Kennedy McClean AFC died in 1955, aged 79. *Frank McClean: The Godfather of British Naval Aviation* by Philip Jarrett was published in 2011 by Pen & Sword.

The Short Triple-Twin at Eastchurch in late 1911. *Peter Green Collection*

'Al' McDicken

Alistair McDicken joined the RAF in 1965 and started his operational career with 9 Squadron on Avro Vulcan B.2s at Akrotiri, Cyprus. The following year he joined 50 Squadron at Waddington, also with Vulcans. He graduated from ETPS Course No.33 at Boscombe Down in 1974, joining A&AEE thereafter, eventually becoming Senior Pilot.

"*MARSHALL 15* is ready for departure." Bruntingthorpe, Leicestershire, 12:26 local time on 18th October 2007. In terms of the maiden flights recorded within *Testing to the Limits*, this was not an occasion to normally receive a mention, but the emotions were as high as any first foray by a prototype. Avro Vulcan B.2 XH558 – civil registration G-VLCN – took to the air and completed a wholly successful test flight. With this, the world's most complex return-to-the-sky restoration was achieved. Flight crew were: Sqn Ldr 'Al' McDicken captain; Sqn Ldr David Thomas, Vulcan to the Sky Trust chief pilot; Sqn Ldr Barry Masefield, air electronics officer.

These days Alistair 'Al' McDicken is probably best known for captaining the world's last airworthy Vulcan and this tends to overshadow what is thought to be another unique achievement: Al has been the CTP at Woodford on *two* occasions. Al joined BAe at Woodford in 1983, replacing Peter Henley* as CTP in 1993. Work during this time centred on ATP twin-turboprops and the HS.146 regional jetliner. From 1998 to 2000 Al took on a management role, J E Davies* taking his place in the flight office. Al was re-appointed CTP in 2000, by which time BAE had morphed into BAE Systems and his main role was to ready the Nimrod MRA.4 project for flight. During this time the Nimrod office moved from Woodford to Warton. Al departed in 2003, with John Turner* taking on the role of CTP and captaining the maiden flight of the MRA.4 in August 2004. With over 10,000 flying hours on 90-plus types, Al McDicken today is a freelance pilot and consultant.

Sqn Ldr 'Al' McDicken in celebratory mood following the return to flight of Vulcan XH558, 18th October 2007. *Duncan Cubitt – Key Publishing – www.keypublishing.com*

Charles McMullin

Charles Richard McMullin, born 1894. He volunteered for the Army in 1915, transferring to the RFC in 1917. Charles flew operationally on the Western Front with 22 Squadron, on Royal Aircraft Factory FE.2bs. In 1919 he joined Aircraft Transport and Travel flying DH.4s on the pioneering London to Paris route until it was wound up in 1920. The following year Charles was instructing in China and advising on possible airliner operations on contract from the British Air Ministry. In 1923 he flew for Major Jack Savage's aerial skywriting company, based at Hendon, but travelling widely on the Continent. Charles also carried out a stint with the subsidiary Skywriting Corporation of America: both organisations flew modified versions of the Royal Aircraft Factory SE.5A.

CAPTAIN CHARLES RICHARD McMULLIN was appointed as CTP for Fairey Aviation, succeeding Norman Macmillan*. In September 1931 Charles accompanied Fairey inspector Kenneth Wright (previously with RAE Farnborough and older brother of Maurice Wright*) on a visit to the Fairey associate company at Gosselies, Belgium. They were travelling in Kenneth's own Blackburn Bluebird III G-EBWE. On 9th September 1931 the pair dropped into Nivelles to inspect Fairey-built aircraft recently taken on charge by the Belgian Air Force. On take-off the aircraft suffered a mechanical failure and it crashed, killing outright Kenneth V Wright and Captain Charles Richard McMullin, aged 37. He was succeeded by Chris Staniland*.

Angus McVitie

23 Aug 1976	Cranfield A1 G-BCIT
	1 x 210hp RR-Continental IO-360-D
14 Dec 1979	Edgley Optica G-BGMW
	1 x 160hp Lycoming O-320-B2B
12 Dec 1988	CMC Leopard G-BKRL
	2 x 300lbst Noel Penny NPT301-3A

Notes: The A1 and Optica were first flown from Cranfield; the Leopard had its maiden flight from Thurleigh.

Angus McKinnon McVitie, early life spent in Argentina. Sailed to Britain in 1943 and started an apprenticeship with Bristol at Filton and learned to fly with the Bristol University Air Squadron. Joined the RAF in 1950 and served with Transport Command, including HP Hastings with 511 Squadron and Vickers Valettas with 114 Squadron. Graduated from ETPS Course No.15 at Farnborough, 1956 followed by a posting to RAE Farnborough. This was followed by a stint as test pilot with the National Gas Turbine Establishment, the flying element of which was also resident at Farnborough. By 1960 Angus was the CO of Aero Flight at RAF Thurleigh and he later was seconded to the Royal Malaysian Air Force.

SQN LDR ANGUS MCVITIE left the RAF in 1968 and took up the post of CTP at the College of Aeronautics at Cranfield, which the following year was rebranded as Cranfield Institute of Technology. As well as piloting the organisation's 'flying laboratory' HP Jetstream G-AXUI and other types used for trials and contract work, in August 1976 Angus flew the Cranfield A1 single-seat aerobatic aircraft which had been under development on the campus since the late 1960s. (The A1 has not flown for many years and is stored at Cranfield.) Angus was able to offer his services to other organisations and warbird restorers as a test pilot. He was at the controls of the prototype Edgley Optica three-seat, ducted-fan, observation aircraft at Cranfield for its first flight on 14th December 1979. Despite early promise, only 19 Opticas were completed. On 28th March 1980 Angus was at Prestwick where he was co-pilot to Len Houston* for the first flight of the prototype British Aerospace Jetstream 31 G-JSSD. Angus returned to Thurleigh in December 1988 to use the generous runway for the maiden flight of another radical design, the four-seat, twin-jet Chichester-Miles Consultants Leopard prototype, G-BKRL. A second airframe was built, but did not fly and *Romeo-Lima* remained a one-off. (G-BKRL is today on show at the Bournemouth Aviation Museum, Hurn.) Sqn Ldr Angus McVitie retired as CTP at Cranfield in 1990; he died on 13th January 2004 having flown over 11,000 hours.

Angus McVitie in the cockpit of Supermarine Spitfire XIV NH749 (G-MXIV) in conversation with a past master of the type, Sqn Ldr James Henry 'Ginger' Lacey DFM*, at Bruntingthorpe in June 1984. Angus carried out the post-restoration maiden flight of this Spitfire, at Cranfield on 9th April 1983. *Roy Bonser*

The Cranfield A1 at Farnborough, September 1978. *KEC*

The second prototype Optica, G-BLFC, over the Needles, Isle of Wight. *Edgley Aircraft*

The CMC Leopard prototype G-BKRD at North Weald, June 1991. *KEC*

Hugh Merewether

Hugh Christopher Henry Merewether, born 1924 in South Africa. In 1942 he joined the South African Navy, transferring to the Royal Navy and the Fleet Air Arm. He learned to fly in the USA, trained by the US Navy up to 1945. Demobbed in 1948 he worked with Vickers as a junior technician under Dr Barnes Wallis while studying for a degree in engineering. Hugh left Vickers in 1953, working as a freelance ferry pilot. In 1951 Hugh joined 615 (County of Surrey) Squadron RAuxAF, operating Meteor F.4s – later F.8s – from Biggin Hill. At that point, the unit's CO was Sqn Ldr Neville Duke*.

At the invite of Neville Duke*, Hugh Merewether joined Hawker at Dunsfold as a test pilot in 1954. Bill Bedford* became CTP in October 1956 and Hugh was appointed as his deputy. He contributed considerably to the development of the Hunter, helping to refine its powered flying control units and carrying out much work on inverted spin recovery. As related in Volume One, the latter half of the 1950s at Dunsfold was devoted to creating the latest Hawker project, which became the incredible V/STOL P.1127, the Kestrel 'transition' and the world-beating Harrier. CTP since October 1956, Bill Bedford* along with Hugh prepared for a very demanding, and different, maiden flight. The pair learned how to fly a helicopter on a civilian Hiller 360. NASA's Ames Laboratory in California offered up its Bell X-14 twin-jet to give Bill and Hugh some experience. This open cockpit machine first took to the air in 1957, using deflectors to drive the efflux from a pair of nose-mounted turbojets either backwards for thrust or down for lift. Hugh was first to have a go, succeeding in bending its undercarriage when he could not correct a roll due to its slow control response. Then they visited Shorts at Sydenham to try out the VTOL SC.1 XG900. Great emphasis had been placed on well harmonised, simple, manual controls on the P.1127; so the clumsy X-14 and the auto-stabilized SC.1 were not much help in 'prepping'.

Bill carried out the first tethered hover on the prototype P.1127, XP831, on 21st October 1960. Three days later he let his deputy try out the new machine – still on the tether. Trials continued in this manner, with Bill handing on to Hugh as soon as the CTP was happy with the characteristics of each flight regime. This was a wise procedure, allowing Hugh to 'shadow' his 'boss' and not leave all the experience of the precious prototype on just one set of shoulders. By the end of 1961 the pair had taken XP831 through all of its flight permutations: taking off and landing vertically, conventional take-offs and vertical landings, short take-offs, grass landings etc. Hugh piloted the third P.1127, XP972, on its maiden – conventional – flight at Dunsfold on 5th April 1962 and was the first to perform a vertical ascent in it, on 29th August. On XP972's 49th sortie the aircraft suffered an engine failure at 3,000ft and Hugh managed to put it down in a force-landing at Tangmere. He was safe, but it was declared beyond economical repair.

Hugh Merewether in the cockpit of a Hunter.
Hawker Siddeley via Graham Pitchfork

Hunter T.66A G-APUX escorting the third prototype P.1127, XP972, to the Farnborough airshow in September 1962. *Hawker Siddeley*

This was not to be Hugh's only in-flight engine failure. In XP984, the sixth P.1127 prototype on 19th March 1965, he was diving through 28,000ft when the Pegasus packed up; a helpful gap in the overcast at 4,000ft revealed Thorney Island and Hugh made an emergency landing there. With a new engine, XP984 was back in the air in late October.

In 1967 Hugh took over from Bill Bedford as CTP. In turn, he retired from test flying in 1970, Duncan Simpson* taking on the V/STOL baton. Hugh turned his hand to becoming an art dealer, specialising in maritime subjects. He acquired a boat and sailed around the world, mostly solo, over six years. In 1998 his book *Prelude to the Harrier: P.1127 Prototype Flight Testing and Kestrel Evaluation*, published by HPM Publications was well greeted, providing a detailed insight into the creation of the Harrier. Hugh Christopher Henry Merewether OBE died on 13th September 2006, aged 82.

'Midge' Midgley

Frederick Ronald Midgley, born 1907. He initially worked with Vulcan Motor Engineering and later Lea-Francis Motors, both with facilities in Southport. 'Midge' learned to fly on Avro Avians at Merseyside Aero and Sports at Hooton Park. By 1932 he was working for Brooklands Aviation and its short-lived airline off-shoot Brooklands Airways, later moving to charter operator Maddox Airways. In 1934 he joined Croydon-based Olley Air Services, continuing through to the wartime National Air Communications and the Associated Airways Joint Committee network.

'MIDGE' MIDGLEY switched from DH Dragon Rapides to Hawker Hurricanes in late 1940, joining the team at Brooklands, signing off the constant flow from the production line. In October 1941 Midge moved north to Armstrong Whitworth (AW) at Baginton, working under CTP Charles 'Toch-H' Turner-Hughes*. Most of the work was on Whitley, Lancaster and Lincoln production but Midge also found himself helping out the Armstrong Siddeley engines division on development and experimental flying. Upon the retirement of Turner-Hughes in the spring of 1946 Midge was appointed CTP for AW. With his promotion Midge wisely recognised the role of chronology, he was 39 and he created the post of Senior Test Pilot for Eric Franklin* who, at 27, was to take on the flying of the AW.52 jet-powered 'flying wings' from November 1947. In late 1946 Midge's prospects changed dramatically, he lost control of his car and it cartwheeled and plummeted down a small bank. He had broken his back in two places and he recuperated within a complex plaster cast. By this time Midge had clocked up around 7,500 flying hours on 64 types. Frederick Ronald Midgley retired from AW in 1948 with Eric Franklin taking over: Midge died in 1985, aged 78.

A famous gathering at Woodley, 1947 with Southern Martlet G-AAYX behind. Left to right: Don L Brown, long-term associate of the Miles brothers and author of *Miles Aircraft since 1925*; Harry Hull, master woodworker, the man that built the first Hawk; George Miles, F G Miles; Maxine Mary 'Blossom' Miles, F G's wife who assisted him in design. *Miles Aircraft*

F G Miles

26 Jun 1929	Parnall Elf G-AAFH 1 x 105hp Cirrus Hermes I
10 Jul 1929	Southern Martlet G-AAII 1 x 75hp ABC Hornet
Mar 1931	Miles Metal Martlet G-ABJW 1 x 110hp Cirrus Hermes
31 Jul 1932	Miles Satyr G-ABVG 1 x 75hp Pobjoy R
29 Mar 1933	Miles Hawk G-ACGH 1 x 95hp Cirrus III
23 Jun 1934	Miles Hawk Major G-ACTD 1 x 120hp DH Gipsy III
28 Jun 1934	Miles Hawk Speed Six G-ACTE 1 x 200hp DH Gipsy Six
12 Oct 1934	Miles Falcon Major G-ACTM 1 x 130hp DH Gipsy Major
27 Jul 1935	Miles Falcon Six G-ADLC 1 x 200hp DH Gipsy Six
20 Aug 1935	Miles Sparrowhawk G-ADNL 1 x 140hp DH Gipsy Major
3 Jun 1937	Miles Kestrel U5 1 x 745hp RR Kestrel XVI
14 May 1936	Miles Whitney Straight G-AECT 1 x 130hp DH Gipsy Major
28 Jan 1937	Miles Mohawk G-AEKW 1 x 200hs Menasco Buccaneer B6S
20 Mar 1937	Miles Magister U2 1 x 130hp DH Gipsy Major
4 Sep 1937	Miles Hobby U2 1 x 140hp DH Gipsy Major 2
4 Dec 1938	Miles M.18 U2 1 x 130hp DH Gipsy Major
26 Oct 1945	Miles Gemini G-AGUS 2 x 100hp Blackburn Cirrus Minor II

Notes: The Elf and the Satyr were first flown from Yate, the Martlets from Shoreham and all the others took place at Woodley. The Metal Martlet originally flew with the incorrect identity G-AAJW (which was a DH Moth). As with Sydney Camm's Hart 'family', it is difficult to single-out which airframes constitute a 'full' prototype and not a development of an established variant. Several types first flown by F G Miles, for example the M.2 Hawk, led to several variants and the Kestrel spawned the very successful Master lineage. Although a version of the Hawk Trainer III, the Magister *is* included in the above, because of its enormous importance to the Miles organisation and to flying training.

Frederick George Miles, born 1903: elder brother of George Herbert Miles*. Living in Portslade, by 1916 'FGM' was a projectionist in local cinemas and diversified into motorcycle hire and a delivery service using a converted Ford Model T ambulance. FGM was fascinated by aviation and in 1922 took a 'joyride' in an Avro 504 and with help of friends, *particularly Fred Wallis, embarked upon the construction of a single-seat biplane, the Gnat, in premises at the rear of his father's laundry business in Portslade. FGM heard of aviation pioneer Cecil 'Pash' Pashley who, along with his brother Eric, operated a three-seat pusher biplane of their own design, powered by a 50hp Gnome, at Shoreham from the summer of 1914. Cecil was persuaded to bring his Avro 504K G-EATU from Northolt and to start tuition and 'joyriding'. To formalise this, the Gnat Aero & Motor Company was formed. A barn used by the short-lived Sussex County Aero Club in a small field at Shoreham was leased and Pash began to teach FGM to fly from November 1925 and on 19th May 1926, he went solo. By mid-1926 George Miles also joined in the activities. A small and eclectic fleet was gathered, including: three Avro 504s, a Grahame-White Bantam and Boxkite and a pair of Central Centaur IVs. In mid-June a move was made to a field to the north of the railway line and the present-day Shoreham Airport was born. That year also saw Miles start up the Southern Aero Club and by this point no further reference was made to the Gnat biplane. A large amount of material was acquired when Avro closed down its Hamble plant in 1927 and among this was single-seat Avro Baby G-EAUM: this machine marked the transition to original design. Miles fitted a 60hp ADC Cirrus in place of the 35hp Green and enlarged the cockpit to take two people: the Baby was flown by FGM in this guise on 13th November 1927. In 1929 Southern Aircraft Ltd was established to reflect the intention to design and build aeroplanes.*

As Frederick George Miles was known to everyone as 'Miles', to avoid confusion with the organisation he founded, here he will be referred to as 'FGM'. The bulk of the story of the Miles brothers lies with design, diversification and expansion, and the trials and tribulations of business and industry. For this work, we shall endeavour to stick to the subject in hand, that of flight testing the output of the brothers; much of which they did themselves.

FGM's first maiden flight was not an aircraft of his own design. He was engaged by George Parnall & Co at Yate for test piloting duties and on 26th June 1929 he flew the prototype Elf two-seater biplane. He continued testing at Yate, mostly on Elfs, until 1932. The following month, at Shoreham, he was aloft in one of his own, the prototype Southern Martlet. Having turned Avro Baby G-EAUM into a viable sportsplane (see above), Miles improved on the concept and created the Hornet Baby – a single-seater powered by an ABC Hornet loosely based on the Avro design. Upon seeking permission from Avro, FGM was given the company's blessing, but there could be no connection with what today would be called the design authority. Anyone studying the Martlet and the Baby would realise that proportions and format were essentially all they shared. Out went all reference to 'Baby' and the name Martlet started the Miles 'brand'. Another version, boasting wing-folding and metal tube construction followed in 1929, but remained a one-off. The first from-scratch Miles design was the diminutive M.1 Satyr. Construction was contracted to Parnall and FGM became a true designer-pilot on 31st July 1932 when he took the 21ft span biplane aloft at Yate.

Parnall Elf II G-AAIN is kept in airworthy condition by the Shuttleworth Collection at Old Warden. It was first flown by F G Miles on 2nd June 1932 at Yate. *Roy Bonser*

The Miles Satyr at Martlesham Heath in December 1932 – the measuring pole alongside gives testament to its small size. *KEC*

A meeting with Charles Powis* at Woodley in August 1932 gave FGM the facilities he needed to make the transition from designer to manufacturer. Along with Jack Phillips, Charles Powis had developed a motorcycle and small car building organisation, along with other enterprises. Phillips & Powis Aircraft (Reading) Ltd was established, becoming a large flying school, aircraft dealership and maintenance organisation. FGM teamed up, Miles acting as chief designer and manager with Phillips and Powis providing production facilities. The first Woodley product was the ground-breaking M.2 Hawk, a two-seat, wing folding, monoplane trainer/tourer in a world dominated by the de Havilland Moth and similar biplanes. With the Hawk, a family could be created leading all the way through to the Magister military trainer and the M.18 intended to provide a 'second generation' of the format. 'Thinned down' single-seaters for racing produced such types as the Hawk Speed Six and the Sparrowhawk. Widened fuselages provided enclosed seating for two (Whitney Straight) or four (Falcon Major) people were developed. As mentioned in the notes given with the 'logbook' of FGM's first flights, defining *exactly* what constitutes a brand-new type is open to debate.

Not content to design and test an ever increasing family of light aircraft, FGM was keen to prove his machines whenever the occasion presented itself. He entered the prototype Sparrowhawk, G-ADNL, in the King's Cup air race, staged at Hatfield on 7th September 1935. At 163.6mph FGM came eleventh overall, but won the speed prize. That race produced a 1-2-3 for Miles types – see under 'Tommy' Rose for more details. (G-ADNL was owned and flown extensively by Geoffrey Alington – see Chapter Two. It also morphed into a jet that was 'first flighted' by George Miles – see his own section, below.) The Mohawk was a special commission for American solo transatlantic flyer Charles Lindbergh for his personal use when visiting Europe. (The Mohawk is now part of the RAF Museum collection.)

M.2P Hawk Major de Luxe G-ADLO, July 1935. *Peter Green Collection*

After the M.2 Hawk, the most important FGM design was the private-venture Kestrel, a visionary response to the then unaddressed need for an advance trainer to meet the increased performance and retractable undercarriage of the up-coming new breeds of fighter and bombers. Fully militarised to Specification 16/38 and renamed Master, an order for an astonishing 500 was placed on 11th June 1938. This was claimed to be worth £2.2 million – £121 million in present-day values – and it shot Phillips & Powis from a 'batch' manufacturer into a full-blown industrial complex with a pioneering moving assembly track. All of these pressures were to increasingly put FGM in the board room and not in the flight test shed. Just prior to the huge Master order, FGM carried out what was to be his last maiden flight until World War Two had ended – piloting the M.18 prototype – see Walter Capley in Chapter Seven. 'Bill' Skinner* had been taken on as a test pilot and others followed, including 'Freddie' Stent*, Tommy Rose and FGM's brother, George, took on some very challenging debuts during the war years. In 1943 the share structure of Phillips & Powis was re-allocated and the company became Miles Aircraft.

Publicity shot of a Rolls-Royce, an anonymous Falcon Major and probably 'Blossom' Miles outside the Falcon Hotel at Woodley, 1935. *Miles Aircraft*

The prototype Sparrowhawk G-ADNL, with race number '9', July 1935. *Peter Green Collection*

Above: Charles Lindbergh flying the one-off Mohawk during the spring of 1937. *RAF Museum*

Left: Miles test pilot Bill Skinner in the prototype Kestrel in June 1937. The '2' is its 'new types' number for that year's Hendon display. *Miles Aircraft*

The Hobby, wearing the B Condition marking U2, at Woodley in September 1937. *Miles Aircraft*

FGM returned to flight testing in 1945 when he took the first Gemini twin into the air on 26th October 1945. The wartime boom could not be sustained and Miles Aircraft ceased trading in late 1947. FGM established himself at Redhill in 1949 as a design consultant, trading as F G Miles Ltd. The tables of history were changed in 1952 when the company re-located to Shoreham and in December that year the two Miles brothers were re-united. In February 1961 the aviation interests of the Miles brothers were acquired by Beagle, initially in the name of Beagle-Miles Ltd, and a tempestuous time began that resulted in FGM and George withdrawing from the organisation in 1963. The pair set up shop at Ford engaging in a series of projects. In 1975 the Hunting Group acquired the majority of the varied assets of F G Miles Ltd. Frederick George Miles died on 15th August 1976 having enjoyed 73 eventful, energetic, innovative and extremely full years.

One of a handful of Geminis still airworthy in Britain, Mk.1A G-AKKH, built in 1947. *Roy Bonser*

George Miles

11 Jul 1941	Miles M.28 U-0232 1 x 130hp DH Gipsy Major 1
1 May 1942	Miles M.35 Libellula U-0235 1 x 130hp DH Gipsy Major
12 Sep 1942	Miles Messenger U-0223 1 x 140hp DH Gipsy Major
22 Jul 1943	Miles M.39B Libellula U-0244 2 x 140hp DH Gipsy Major
3 Jun 1945	Miles LR.5 U-0253 1 x 100hp Blackburn Cirrus Minor
22 Aug 1947	Miles Boxcar G-AJJM 4 x 100hp Blackburn Cirrus Minor II
14 Dec 1953	Miles Sparrowjet G-35-2 2 x 330lbst Turboméca Palas
15 May 1957	Miles Student G-35-4 1 x 880lbst Turboméca Marboré
19 Aug 1962	Beagle M.218X G-35-6 2 x 100hp RR-Continental O-200-A

Notes: M.28 to Boxcar all had their maiden flights from Woodley; Sparrowjet, M.28 and Student all from Shoreham.

George Herbert Miles, born 1911, youngest brother of Frederick George Miles (FGM). Much of the background given in the section on FGM is relevant to George. By mid-1926 George joined FGM at Shoreham, initially helping to maintain the Avro 504K that was being used for tuition and 'joyriding'. With instruction from FGM, George went solo in Avro Avian G-EBVA 9th June 1928 at Shoreham. All of this was unpaid: it was 1936 when he took a salary with Phillips & Powis at Woodley.

WHILE George Herbert Miles was positively introverted when compared with his flamboyant older brother, Frederick George Miles (FGM), this was not the case when it came to aircraft design. George was responsible for the most radical of the types produced under the Miles banner and was behind the plethora of projects of the wartime era and the late 1940s. As with the section on FGM, it is important to note that the bulk of the story of the Miles brothers lies with design, diversification and expansion, and the trials and tribulations of business and industry. For this work, we shall *try* to stick to the subject in hand, that of flight testing the output of the brothers; a lot of which they did themselves. Much of the background given in the section on FGM is relevant to George. The first Miles type designed by George was the Monarch of 1938, a three-seater based upon the Whitney Straight cabin monoplane of 1936. By 1940 his official title was Manager, Repair and Service Department, but like his elder sibling, his responsibilities were wide, including design, production test flying, problem-solving and forecasting future requirements and technologies.

George was appointed as Technical Director and Chief Designer in 1941, as FGM took a greater role in management and strategy. That year saw George take the helm of a Miles

prototype and one he had designed, the elegant, two-seat retractable undercarriage M.28. Classic of how the Miles brothers approached projects, the M.28 was not aimed at any current requirement and was completed as a private-venture in an era when resources – including time – where supposed to be carefully shepherded by the Ministry of Aircraft Production (MAP). The M.28 revived plans that George had schemed in 1939 for trainer/tourer. He took the M.28 on its maiden flight on 11th July 1941 at Woodley. The following day FGM flew it, only to disgrace himself – he completely forgot the undercarriage tucked up in the wings and belly-landed the prototype! Six M.28s were built, but they paved the way for the Messenger, which was aimed initially at an airborne observation post requirement but became the backbone of post-war light aircraft production for the company and the basis for the twin-engined Gemini. George flew the LR.5 – so designated because it was conceived at the Liverpool Road design annexe – in June 1945. It had been created 'under the radar' as a project by members of the design team in their spare time. It would not have looked out of place on a 1970s flightline, unfortunately its flying characteristics were poor and it was quietly put aside.

In late 1941 George spent a lot of time in pondering tandem wing layouts, especially for operation from aircraft carriers. Both the fore and aft wings contributed to lift and are not to be confused with types fitted with foreplanes, such as the Eurofighter Typhoon, which is a means of placing control surfaces that contribute little to lift on the forward fuselage. George envisioned a fleet fighter with a pilot in the nose with a commanding view, a pusher powerplant, a centre of gravity much further aft than previously achieved and of much reduced span. Actions speak louder than words and he started to design and then build a prototype at the Liverpool Road facility, away from the gaze of men from the Ministry! Using as many parts raided from the production line as possible, in *six weeks*, he had the M.35 Libellula ready for testing. (The tandem-winged dragonfly insect is generically known as *Libellula*.)

The story goes that the CTP – that would have been 'Tommy' Rose* – expressed incredulity that he might be asked to fly it; *not* the flat refusal quoted in some sources. More likely, George was already determined that as it was his concept, it should be his neck. Attempts to get airborne from Woodley on 1st May 1942 met with repeated failure. Using a field near the final assembly hall for acceleration before *turning* on to the aerodrome it was hoped the necessary distance for flight could be achieved. Don Brown is his engaging *Miles Aircraft since 1925* takes up the plot: "Having covered three-quarters of the length of the main field still with no tendency to lift off, George hurriedly closed the throttle, having left himself only just sufficient length of field in which to pull up. As he closed the throttle, the M.35 literally leapt into the air to a height of about 10ft. George just managed to get it back on the ground in time..." After a few more such attempts, George eventually summoned up the courage to apply the throttle *again* after the initial leap, then the M.35 stayed aloft and he made a cautious circuit, at no greater 'altitude' than 30ft! Eventually, the little Libellula proved to be more controllable. Needless to say, George was hauled over the coals by MAP for his flagrant departure from procedure.

The prototype M.28, U-0232, July 1941. *Miles Aircraft*

George started to churn out tandem wing designs, including six- and eight-engined strategic bombers and the shapely M.39, a rival to the DH Mosquito featuring a swept rear wing, which carried the engines. Once again, George elected to build what today would be called a proof-of-concept aircraft, designated M.39B, it was a five-eighth scale version of the proposed bomber. George flew this much more advanced machine, it had flaps and retractable undercarriage, on 22nd July 1943 and it was found to be far less of a handful than the crude M.35 had been. Assistant test pilot Hugh Kennedy* flew it the same day, allowing the pair to compare notes. The M.39B was evaluated by RAE Farnborough and jet-powered versions were schemed but it remained an aeronautical cul-de-sac.

On 7th August 1947 Ken Waller* took the prototype Merchantman, a four-engined growth version of the Aerovan, on its first flight at Woodley. Fifteen days later George carried out what turned out to be his last maiden flight from Woodley in a radical alternative to the conventional Merchantman. This was the Boxcar which had a detachable centre fuselage that doubled as a trailer, thereby avoiding the need to unload the cargo for road transport. Should the Boxcar not have a return load, the rear fairing was connected to the rear of the cockpit and the tadpole-like aircraft could still fly. When the Boxcar flew, Miles Aircraft was less than four months from collapse. The Boxcar and the Merchantman remained one-offs.

In 1949 George joined Airspeed at Christchurch, replacing Arthur Hagg as chief designer. de Havilland had acquired Airspeed in 1940 and other than the Ambassador airliner the factory was acting as an annexe of Hatfield. Among the projects that George worked on was the DH.115 Vampire trainer: John Wilson* flying the prototype, G-5-7 on 15th November 1950. As the T.11, the side-by-side trainer entered service with the RAF in 1952 and it was ordered in large numbers, including the T.22 for the Fleet Air Arm and T.55 export version. George resigned his post at Christchurch and joined his brother's F G Miles Ltd at Shoreham in December 1951. The previous year racing pilot Fred Dunkerley had contracted FGM to convert the prototype Sparrowhawk into a jet-powered racer and G-ADNL had been delivered to Redhill, where F G Miles Ltd had been established. The company moved back to its roots at Shoreham in 1952 and George lent a hand on

George Miles undertook arrested landing trials using netting to bring the prototype Messenger, U-0223, to a stop, June 1943. *Miles Aircraft*

The incredible M.39B Libellula, the second Miles 'dragonfly' design to fly. *Miles Aircraft*

Frontal aspect of the M.35 Libellula; the perspective doesn't help but, at 20ft 5in, the rear wing was only 5in inches shorter than the forward example. *Peter Green Collection*

The unsuccessful LR.5 prototype languishing at Woodley post-war: note the car-like access door. *KEC*

The Boxcar with the roadable container that acted as the centre section of the fuselage attached to a car. When 'unloaded' the rear fairing was attached to the rear of the cockpit, producing a tadpole-like appearance, *Miles Aircraft*

the extensive transformation. George carried out the maiden flight of the Sparrowjet on 14th December 1953 – his first time piloting a jet. Flown by Fred Dunkerley G-ADNL won the King's Cup at Baginton in 1957 at 228mph. (G-ADNL is extant and may well be used as the basis for a fascinating restoration *back* to Sparrowhawk status at a workshop in Gloucestershire.)

George's experience of the Vampire gave him a good view about the future for jet trainers. Hearing that the RAF was keen to introduce what was called 'all-through' jet training – basic to advanced tuition on jets types – George set about design studies for a simple, economic yet adaptable, solution. This was the M.100 Student which had the ability to be used for communications and forward air controller roles and to 'grow' into a four-seater for military or private-owner use. With limited financial resources, development of the Student was slow and overtaken by events. The prototype Hunting Jet Provost took to the air in June 1954 and began operational evaluation the following year. In 1957 the 'JP' was ordered into volume production in the same year as George 'first flighted' the Student. Despite further development and offers of licence production, the M.100 remained a one-off. (Re-registered as G-MIOO – for M.100 – in 1996 the Student is now on show at the Museum of Berkshire Aviation at Woodley.)

In February 1961 the aviation interests of the Miles brothers were acquired by Beagle, initially in the name of Beagle-Miles Ltd, and a tempestuous time began that resulted in FGM and George withdrawing from the organisation in 1963. George had been appointed as Technical Director of the new organisation. Among the design studies handed over was the M.114 single-seater, which went on to form the basis of the Pup, and the M.115 four-seat twin. George refined the M.115 into the M.218, which had a metal main spar and 'keel' but the bulk of the airframe was composed of reinforced glass-fibre. George flew the prototype on 19th August 1962 and it showed great promise. Certification would have been a major, and costly, hurdle and Beagle had the over-engineered B.206 twin as its priority and permanently lacked cash reserves. The M.218 was shelved and within a year both of the Miles brothers had left Beagle. Establishing a new set-up at Ford, they were contracted in 1964 to build two flying and one 'studio' replica Bristol Boxkites for the film *Those Magnificent Men in their Flying Machines*. Powered initially by

Based upon the original Sparrowhawk, the Sparrowjet was a radical transformation that first appeared in 1953. *Peter Green Collection*

George Miles, designer and test pilot of the Student, G-35-4, outside the airport building at Shoreham, 1957. *Miles Aircraft*

Rolls-Royce-Continental C90 'flat-fours', George carried out the maiden flights of the two 'flyers'. (The first of these is still flown regularly by the Shuttleworth Collection at Old Warden.) As well as F G Miles Ltd, George established Miles Aviation and Transport Ltd by 1966 and the brothers had interests or ownership of a number of specialist companies. George Herbert Miles died on 18th September 1999, aged 88, ending an aviation dynasty like no other. He had over 2,000 hours on 88 types – a goodly number of those that he had either helped to design, or were wholly the product of his drawing board – that's quite a remarkable achievement.

George Miles piloting the M.218 G-ASCK, behind is the second prototype Beagle 206, G-35-5, which had first flown seven days before the M.218. *Beagle Aircraft*

One of the two Miles-built Bristol Boxkite replicas used for the film *Those Magnificent Men* at Filton in 1964 – where the originals were built in 1910. *Rolls-Royce*

Gordon 'Dusty' Miller

| 6th Sep 1946 | Auster J/3 G-AHSY |
| | 1 x 65hp Continental C65-12 |

DESPITE the prodigious output of Auster, the charting of its test pilots has proven to be a difficult task. Geoffrey Edwards* and George Snarey* are prominent in the 1940s, but the name of Gordon 'Dusty' Miller also appears. In September 1946 Dusty took the prototype J/3 – the so-called 'Atom' – on its debut outing from Rearsby. With surplus wartime models becoming available and a Dollar-strapped economy, the J/3 was not the answer and *Sierra-Yankee* was the only example of its type to fly.

Paul Millett

14 Aug 1974	Panavia Tornado P.01 D-9591
	2 x 8,500lbst Turbo-Union RB.199-34R-2
30 Oct 1974	Panavia Tornado P.02 XX946
	2 x 8,500lbst Turbo-Union RB.199-34R-2

Paul Millett, born 1931. Joined the Royal Navy in 1949, transferring to the Fleet Air Arm. He flew 175 operational sorties during the Korean conflict, on Fairey Firefly FR.5s with 821 Squadron from HMS Glory. *Returning to the carrier in WB366 on 9th February 1953, the wing dipped as Paul 'chopped' for touch down, he attempted a go-around, but the aircraft ditched; he and Captain R Bury were picked up by HMS* Comus. *By 1954, Paul was instructing, including time at Lossiemouth with 736 Squadron on DH Sea Vampire T.22s. Paul graduated from ETPS No.17 Course at Farnborough in 1958 and served with RAE Farnborough until 1961 when he transferred to Aero Flight at RAE Thurleigh. Among the types flown was Bristol 188 XF923 Paul becoming one of only three pilots to have flown it – Godfrey Auty* and Ian Williamson* being the other two.*

"The aircraft handled superbly well, there were no problems... It really felt like an aircraft that has been flying for many years and from the time of leaving the ground was one of the nicest I've ever flown." These were some of the comments made by Paul Millett after the maiden flight of the Panavia MRCA – Multi-Role Combat Aircraft – and shortly to be officially named Tornado. As BAC CTP and Tornado Project Pilot, Paul was in the front seat and Nils Meister of Messerschmitt-Bölkow-Blohm in the back of P.01 D-9591, when it flew from Manching, West Germany, on 14th August 1974. (The first two prototypes were not fitted with dual controls.) At the time, the Luftwaffe was the largest

Paul Millett, test pilot of the exceptional Tornado. *BAC*

British Tornado prototype P.02 XX946 was installed in the RAF Museum at Hendon in 1994. It is presently undergoing a restoration programme at Cosford. *RAF Museum*

customer, so it was deemed that the German-assembled prototype should be the first to fly, but with a British test pilot at the controls. Back at Warton, on 30th October, Paul was again at the helm for the maiden flight of the UK example, P.02 XX946, this time with Aeritalia's Pietro Trevisan in the rear seat. Paul had inaugurated what was to become the most successful European collaborative project of its time and a formidable, battle-proven, warplane. (P.01 is kept at Erding, Germany, P.02 is held by the RAF Museum, at Cosford.)

Lt Cdr Paul Millett DSC left the Fleet Air Arm in 1965, taking up a post with Hawker Siddeley testing Buccaneers at Holme-on-Spalding Moor. His introduction to the work was dramatic; on 13th May 1965 he and FTO J R Harris were tasked with a trial of extended chord ailerons on S.1 XK524. In the circuit at Holme, XK524 developed an increasingly nose down attitude which Paul could not correct, then the tailplane stalled and the next few seconds were vital. Paul called for ejection and he and Harris were blasted upwards as XK524 plummeted downwards, crashing in open ground.

Paul crossed the Pennines in 1968, joining BAC at Warton as Senior Experimental Test Pilot. At first he was involved with Lightning and Strikemaster work. He converted to the Jaguar in 1969 and became the type's Project Pilot. On 1st December 1970, Paul took over from 'Jimmy' Dell* as Warton CTP and he was immersed in the lead-up to the first flight of MRCA. BAC became British Aerospace in 1977 and the following year Paul was appointed Executive Director of Flight Operations as 'Bea' Beamont took up a post at Panavia. Paul's last flight was in GR.1 ZA402 – the 100th British Tornado – on 23rd December 1982. He was succeeded by Dave Eagles* and Paul took on the role of Chief Executive BAe Saudi Arabia. Lt Cdr Paul Millett OBE DSC died on 2nd September 2009, aged 78. He had flown 111 types and 'clocked' over 7,000 flying hours.

A 1970 brochure explaining the multi-national management of MRCA – Multi-Role Combat Aircraft – the nascent Tornado.

The prototype Luton Minor, G-AFMU, at Denham, 1939. *Peter Green collection*

Edward Mole

12 Mar 1939	Luton Major G-AFMU
	1 x 62hp Walter Mikron II

Sᴏ̨ɴ Lᴅʀ Eᴅᴡᴀʀᴅ Lᴜᴄᴀs Mᴏʟᴇ (1906-1997) carried out the first flight of the prototype Luton LA.5 Major light aircraft at Denham in March 1939. The company had previously designed and built a series of single-seat ultralights, and the Major was intended to break into the two-seater market. Production of other examples was stopped with the outbreak of war. The type was offered as a homebuilt post-war.

David Morgan

David William Morgan, born 1923. Started flying training with the RAF in 1942 in the UK then South Africa, where he achieved his 'wings'. Returning to the UK in early 1944 he was posted to Woodhall Spa for air traffic duties prior to being given a flying appointment. He persuaded the local unit, no less than the Lancaster-equipped 617 Squadron, to let him fly on at least two operations. The first was as 'second dickie', the second as mid-upper gunner. David penned Chapter VII of Mike Lithgow's Vapour Trails *and he recorded the advice given by the tail gunner: "Don't let it revolve for more than five times to the left, chum, or you'll unscrew the bloody thing!" He was posted to 18 (Pilots) Advanced Flying Unit at Snitterfield, training on Airspeed Oxfords. David transferred to the Fleet Air Arm eventually joining 809 Squadron embarked on HMS* Stalker *shore-based on Ceylon, in November 1944. He flew Supermarine Seafire IIIs with the unit until September 1945. Back in Britain he instructed and in 1948 graduated from No.7 Course ETPS at Farnborough. He then flew DH Sea Vampire F.20s with 703 Squadron at Lee-on-Solent, completing his service with the Handling Squadron at Manby, helping to devise and revise Pilots' Notes.*

Lᴛ Dᴀᴠɪᴅ Mᴏʀɢᴀɴ joined Supermarine in June 1950, initially tasked with delivering Supermarine Spitfires and Vickers Wellingtons. On 4th August 1950 David cleared customs at Blackbushe in Supermarine Attacker prototype TS409 which was to be flown by Air Marshal Richard Atcherley at the head of the Pakistan Independence Day flypast on the 14th. An electrical fault resulted in the starboard undercarriage leg refusing to come down on approach to Nicosia, Cyprus, on the 5th. A repair team was

David Morgan in front of a Scimitar. Please note: The image attributed to Les Colquhoun on page 115 of Volume One is actually of David Morgan. *via Tony Buttler*

flown out and David arrived in Pakistan in time to hand over TS409 for the big event. Along with Les Colquhoun*, David flew Type 535 Swift VV119 for sequences used in the David Lean film *The Sound Barrier*, released in 1952.

On 6th September 1951 David was flying the first pre-production Swift, WJ960, and he was due to demonstrate it at the SBAC airshow at Farnborough in five day's time. In his exceptional book *Swift Justice*, Nigel Walpole quotes David who recalled: "Returning to Chilbolton, I made a fast run down the runway followed by high 'g' turns and fast rolls, ending with a rapid deceleration using the powerful airbrakes, lowering the undercarriage on the downwind leg at 1,000ft. Descending in the final turn on to runway heading, I lowered full flap at 600ft and to compensate for the marked increase in drag I advanced the throttle whereupon there was a loud bang and a cloud of vapour, momentarily, around the intakes. The engine was still running but it did not respond to the throttle and was giving very little thrust, so with an alarming rate of sink I selected undercarriage up and flap [setting] to maximum lift..."

"Confronted with the valley of the River Test, below Chilbolton airfield, I turned toward less threatening countryside but as I descended towards farmland to the right of the ridge I could see that I was going to be squeezed by a line of large power cables crossing diagonally from the right. I was not sure that I could clear these cables so decided to go under them; this appeared quite easy at the time but although the airspeed indicator showed 160 knots they seemed to pass so slowly overhead! ...I found I was heading straight for a house with a barn to one side. I managed to steer between the

The first pre-production Swift, WJ960, saved by David Morgan in a skilful forced landing in September 1951 – with an outside 'loo' as the only real casualty!
Vickers-Armstrongs

two but the gap proved to be too small and my wing tip dismantled a brick-built lavatory – which was fortunately not occupied at the time. I flopped down hard in the stubble field beyond and began a rough, seemingly endless ride, although it was probably no more than about 150 yards... The option of ejecting never entered my mind and in any case I was too low for the seat we had then." WJ960 was flying again within three months; David flew the following day; getting VV119 ready for display at Farnborough.

David flew WJ960 in very different circumstances in July 1952 when he established a record 'city pair', flying London to Brussels at 667mph in a sizzling time of 18 minutes. Along with several other pilots ('Dizzy' Addicott*, Les Colquhoun*, Jasper Jarvis, John Judge*,) David was involved in a series of wet runway braking trials for the Ministry of Supply from 1958 to 1962. Supermarine Swift F.7 XF114 was modified, including the removal of the main undercarriage doors, for the purpose at Wisley. This Swift still survives, held in reserve for Solent Sky at Southampton. David was involved in the Scimitar programme all the way through to the final example coming off the production line at South Marston in 1960. Beyond that he moved to Brooklands to prepare for the advent of the BAC TSR.2. David had been appointed as project pilot for the nav/attack system, but the project was axed before David got to fly in the type. He then turned his hand to marketing the SEPECAT Jaguar project and was Far East sales

manager for the Rapier surface-to-air missile system. He retired in 1988 to a farm in Devon. Lt David William Morgan MBE died on 3rd February 2004, aged 81.

'Johnny' Morton

| 25 May 1972 | Westland Lynx 05-01 XX469 |
| | 2 x 830shp RR BS.360 |

John George Peter Morton, born 1925. Joined the Fleet Air Arm in 1942, training at Pensacola, Florida, USA. By the summer of 1945 'Johnny' was flying Vought Corsair IVs with 1835 Squadron bound for the Far East, but the end of the war intervened. By January 1947 he was at Donibristle, testing modified Supermarine Seafire XVs; on the 28th he suffered a crash landing in SW917, but was not injured. Shortly afterwards, Johnny was posted to 804 Squadron, operating Seafire XVs from HMS Theseus. He was involved in a tragic accident on 20th July 1947 when Seafire XV SW851 drifted into the barrier on Theseus, killing an aircraft handler. The Seafire ended up with this rear fuselage dangling over the side of the carrier, but again Johnny was uninjured. In 1949 he joined 705 Squadron which had become the specialist helicopter training unit and in 1952 was instructing with CFS, before moving to A&AEE Boscombe Down.

The second naval prototype Lynx, XX510, was intensively flown by 'Johnny' Morton, 1973-1976. *Peter Green Collection*

IN 1955 Lt Cdr 'Johnny' Morton was seconded to Fairey as a test pilot and he joined the company on a permanent basis, under CTP Ron Gellatly*. Johnny played an active part in proving and demonstrating the Ultra-Light Helicopter. He was co-pilot on the first flight of the Rotodyne on 6th November 1957 and also heavily involved it is development. With the acquisition of the Fairey aviation assets in 1960 by Westland, Johnny became the project pilot for the Wasp anti-submarine helicopter. Beyond the Wasp programme he was put in charge of the development flying of the naval version of the Lynx and, with David Gibbings as FTE, Johnny was at the helm of the naval prototype, XX469, on 25th May 1972. Johnny and FTE P Wilson-Chalon were injured on 21st November 1972 when tail rotor control was lost on XX469 at Yeovil. The helicopter came down heavily and rolled on to its side: after just six months it was withdrawn from the test programme and used for ground instructional purposes. It was March the following year before the second naval prototype, XX510 came on stream. Johnny retired from test flying in the early 1980s, going on to instruct on helicopters before emigrating to New Zealand. Lt Cdr John George Peter Morton OBE died on 4th May 2014, aged 88.

Llewellyn Moss

Llewellyn Oliver Moss, born 1895. He served with distinction in the Army on the Western Front during World War One, transferring to the RFC by 1917. He served on with the RAF until July 1933. At 44, he was considered too old to re-join the RAF in 1939 and instead he joined the Air Transport Auxiliary, flying with 2 Ferry Pilots Pool at Hucclecote.

FG OFF LLEWELLYN MOSS MM was recruited by Gloster in 1943, to work as a PTP at Hucclecote on Hawker Typhoons. By May 1946 he had been appointed as Chief PTP and based at nearby Moreton Valence, testing Meteors. On 9th

May 1946 he took off in the second production Meteor IV EE518 and headed north. At RAF Defford the Meteor was noted to pull out of a shallow dive over the airfield and carry out a sharp, climbing turn. At around 1,500ft the starboard wing detached and the aircraft broke up, killing outright its 51-year-old pilot. A programme of wing strengthening was instigated on the production line.

'Frank' 'Spud' Murphy

Francis Murphy, born 1917; his family emigrated to New Zealand in the early 1920s. By the time of his second birthday 'Frank' was afflicted with poliomyelitis – polio, or 'infantile paralysis'. This would have meant that the chances of the word 'pilot' appearing as one of his life achievements were remote, but Frank was a man of considerable character. As an adventurous teenager an 'experiment' with chemicals went horribly wrong and one of his fingers was mutilated and he lost the use of a thumb. In March 1941 the 24-year-old persuaded the RNZAF to take him on and he trained as a pilot. Just over a year later Sgt Murphy was flying Hawker Hurricanes from Wittering with 486 Squadron RNZAF. He stayed with the unit until February 1944, piloting Hawker Typhoons from mid-1942 and helping to introduce the Hawker Tempest V before he left, with the rank of Squadron Leader. On 17th December 1942 Frank opened 486's 'account' by shooting down a Messerschmitt Bf 109F. His confirmed victories, all on Typhoons, included two more Bf 109s and a Junkers Ju 88.

AMONG friends, Francis Murphy became 'Frank' but with his air force colleagues he was inevitably nicknamed 'Spud' because of his Irish-sounding surname and folklore about that nation's diet. Indeed, with 486 Squadron, Frank was known as 'The Flying Potato'. As a seasoned Hawker 'client', a

Frank Murphy carried out the maiden flight of the first production Hunter F.1, WT555, at Dunsfold in May 1953 – the first of many. *Peter Green Collection*

secondment to Langley was providential and Frank set to on signing off Hurricane IIs, Typhoons and Tempest Vs, under CTP Philip Lucas*. On 20th March 1945 Frank was flying the Sea Fury interim naval prototype, SR661, a month after Philip had 'first flighted' it. The Centaurus failed and Frank carried out a skilful wheels-up landing at Redhill: he was unharmed and the Sea Fury was back in the air within two months. Frank clearly excelled at the work and an early demobilisation was arranged; in July 1945 he joined Hawker. He made the headlines on 7th May 1947 when the engine of another Sea Fury, F.X TF903, packed up on him. This time the venue for the wheels-up was the famous Long Walk in the grounds of Windsor Castle. Later that year Frank was in India, helping the Indian Air Force with its Tempest IIs.

Promoted to Chief PTP in 1948, Frank was ready for the jet age and the advent of the Sea Hawk. In his book *Test Pilot*, Neville Duke* described how a typical day at the flight office evolved: "The day at Dunsfold begins with the provision of a weather forecast by 'Bertie' Coopman [air traffic], and with this we also receive a list of aircraft available for flying both at Dunsfold and Langley... Fred Sutton [flight test section manager] may report that four Furies will be ready at Langley at 11am and that two production Sea Hawks will be available at Dunsfold. As chief production test pilot Frank Murphy arranges for a [DH Dragon] Rapide to be provided to take him and Frank Bullen [PTP, he succeeded Spud as Chief PTP in 1955] to Langley to clear the Furies; or he may decide to send Bullen to Langley and deal with the Sea Hawks himself at Dunsfold."

On 16th May 1953 Frank took the first production Hunter F.1, WT555, on its maiden flight at Dunsfold, it was to be the first of many. (WT555 survives with a London-based private owner.) It was a Hunter that brought an end to Frank's flying career. Carrying out a high-altitude – above 40,000ft – gravity feed-only fuel flow assessment in Hunter F.4 WT707 on 25th January 1955 the Avon turbojet began to run rough and Frank descended. By 30,000ft Frank initiated the re-light procedure three times, to no avail. He decided that Ford would be his best option – he had successfully force-landed Sea Hawk F.1 WF159 there on 19th December 1952. He broke through the cloud layer at about 6,000ft and prepared for a flapless belly-landing, crossing the threshold at around 230mph. Don Middleton described the final moments in *Test Pilots*: "Eyewitnesses counted 15 bounces and the Hunter then slewed sideways through a caravan park... It hurtled over the Clymping road where it broke into three pieces. The cockpit went rolling for another 100 yards; the weight of the gun pack underneath caused it to be to rest in an upright position... Marks of all the bolt ends in the cockpit canopy were found in the sides and top of Frank Murphy's helmet, which was split from front to back. This was the first occasion on which a new British 'bone dome' had been tested in a crash." Tragically, bone domes could not prevent the deaths of three people who were in the path of the wreckage as it scythed through the caravan site. Frank was seriously injured and rushed to hospital. A severed wire had prevented the re-light button from functioning.

By the end of 1955 Frank took up a new role in technical sales with Hawker and he was appointed foreign sales manager in 1959. The name Hawker was subsumed within Hawker Siddeley in 1963 and Frank became the organisation's international military sales manager. Retiring in 1976, Sqn Ldr Frank 'Spud' Murphy OBE DFC died on 11th May 1997, aged 80.

Phillip 'Spud' Murphy

Phillip Murphy, born 1926. Joined the RAF in 1945 and served with 56 Squadron on Gloster Meteor F.4s at Thorney Island from 1948 and with 66 Squadron at Linton-on-Ouse, also on Meteor F.4s until 1951.

*A*NOTHER 'Spud' was Frank Murphy – see above – and two 'sources' morph the careers of these two pilots into one! Among friends and colleagues Philip was inevitably nicknamed 'Spud' because of his Irish-sounding surname and folklore about that nation's diet. That said, in his superb *Handley Page Aircraft since 1907*, C H Barnes is alone in calling Philip Murphy 'Paddy'! Spud left the RAF in August 1951 and joined the Vickers flight test team at Wisley. An early 'diversion' was to fly a Wisley-based Valetta as the photo-ship capturing images of Supermarine Swift VV119, playing the role of the 'Prometheus' prototype in David Lean's 1952 film *Sound Barrier*.

Spud was also involved in trials with the Red Dean pulse Doppler-guided missile developed by the missile division of Vickers. English Electric Canberra B.2 WD935 was one of three such machines used and it was first flown with the big missiles hung from pylons under the wings in January 1954. Later Gloster Meteors and Boeing Washingtons (B-29 Superfortresses) were also used on the programme and based at Wisley – see Colin Allen and Brian Trubshaw. The Red Dean project was cancelled in 1956. Spud also took part in Valiant V-bomber trials, including rocket-assisted take-off (RATO) using de Havilland (DH) Super Sprite rocket packs fitted under the inner wings. The one-off Valiant B.2 WJ954 initiated such flights in October 1954, followed by the second prototype B.1, WP215, in 1956 and 1957. Other Valiant development work that Spud engaged in was in-flight refuelling (IFR), using WZ376 and WZ390 in late 1955 and early 1956.

Left: Captain Phillip Murphy in the left hand seat of Air Anglia Fokker Friendship Series 200 G-BCDN on the ramp at Norwich Airport in 1974. *via Don Middleton*

Below: English Electric Canberra B.2 WD935 carrying two Red Dean missiles underwing. Phillip Murphy carried out most of the trials with this large weapon. *Peter Green Collection*

Dramatic image of Victor B.1 XA930 taking off with the aid of a pair of jettisonable DH Spectre rocket packs. 'Spud' Murphy was in command of XA930 for much of this work. *de Havilland*

The RATO and IFR experience Spud had built up at Wisley made him very attractive to the Handley Page test team, where the Victor V-bomber was due to go through similar trials and in February 1958 Phillip made to the move to Radlett. His first sampling of the Victor was the second prototype, WB775, which he flew in September 1958. For RATO the Victor employed bulky DH Spectre packs, attached to the inner wings; after use these were jettisoned, using a parachute to bring them back for re-use. Victor B.1 XA930 was allocated for RATO and IFR trials in 1959. Spud was captain for Spectre trials in April 1959 and the following month drops of the packs were carried out. The Spectres were expensive and were easily damaged in drops; the programme was soon terminated.

On 23rd March 1962 Spud was captaining Victor B.2 XL159 for low speed handling with the production standard fixed drooping leading edges. His crew were: Sqn Ldr John W Waterton of A&AEE, John Tank as air electronics officer and FTOs M P Evans and P Elwood. At 16,000ft Spud set the Victor up for a stall in landing configuration – flaps down, gear down. The big jet entered a stable stall, but this developed into a flat spin. Spud and John ejected and John Tank managed to extract himself from the crew access door/escape hatch on the port side of the cockpit. Tragically, the FTOs failed to get out

and died when XL159 impacted on a farm at Stubton, near Newark, where Mrs A Gibson and her daughter, C P Gibson also perished and two others on the farm were badly injured. Appointed a DCTP in 1965, Spud also tested Heralds and Jetstreams up to the collapse of Handley Page in 1970.

Phillip Murphy joined Air Anglia from its inception in 1970, as Chief Pilot. Based at Norwich Airport, the airline flew Douglas Dakotas and Fokker Friendships: in his honour a Friendship 100 was registered as G-SPUD between 1979 and 1982! Later Spud became the Operations Manager and with the restructuring of the business as AirUK in 1980 he was Operations Director. He returned to flight testing in 1981, moving to Prestwick to assist British Aerospace Scottish division CTP Len Houston* working on certification of the Jetstream 31. Spud returned to commercial flying in 1983, finally retiring in 1992; he died in 2011, aged 85.

Lindsay Neale

26 May 1947	Boulton Paul Balliol VL892
	1 x 810hp Bristol Mercury 30
24 Mar 1948	Boulton Paul Balliol VL917
	1 x 1,000shp AS Mamba

Robert Lindsay Neale, born 1912. He was a salesman and inaugurated the aviation department of Selfridges by 1930, moving to Brian Lewis and Co, de Havilland dealers at Heston. Lindsay learned to fly at Croydon in 1931 and in 1935 established Lindsay Neale Aviation Ltd as a consultancy and became a director of Dart Aircraft at Dunstable (see Alfred Weyl) in 1937. He enlisted in the RAF in 1939.

ROBERT LINDSAY NEALE – 'Robin' to family and colleagues – suffered a motorcycle accident that necessitated the insertion of a plate in one of his legs and this, and his age, may have precluded the 27-year-old from taking up flying with the RAF. Instead, he joined Boulton Paul (BP) at Pendeford as an assistant to CTP Cecil Feather* in February 1940. As well as signing off Defiants, Lindsay tested Pendeford-built Blackburn Rocs and Fairey Barracudas. 'Fluffy' Feather retired as CTP in September 1945 and Lindsay replaced him.

In early 1946 Lindsay was given the task of inspecting and selecting an Airspeed Oxford from a batch that was up for disposal at 15 Maintenance Unit at Wroughton. He singled out two de Havilland-built examples, his favourite being V3388 with a bid of £1,250 (£37,500 in present-day values) and the back-up was V3870 at £750. He got his way and V3388 was registered to BP as G-AHTW on 9th May 1946. Lindsay spent a lot of time in this aircraft and he referred to it as 'his'. It was destined to be the last airworthy Oxford being disposed of to the Wolverhampton Aero Club in 1960 and then to the Skyfame Museum at Staverton in 1964. Today, painted in wartime colours, it is displayed at the Imperial War Museum, Duxford.

The next BP project was the Balliol, intended to be turboprop-powered from inception but problems with the powerplants, initially it was to be the Rolls-Royce Dart but the AS Mamba was eventually chosen, led to the prototype being fitted with a Mercury 30 radial piston engine. Lindsay took this for its maiden flight on 26th May 1947.

Boulton Paul test pilots in front of a Defiant. Left to right: Lindsay Neale, Colin Evans, 'Fluffy' Feather. *Les Whitehouse-Boulton Paul Association*

Taking his wife, two children and sister-in-law on holiday in France on 28th June 1947 Lindsay borrowed Miles Messenger 2A G-AJEY. All was well until near Montignac when there was a disturbing noise from up front – the propeller had fractured and the unbalanced remains shook the Cirrus Major, cowlings and engine mounts clean off the airframe. Quick as anything, Lindsay got his passengers to clamber forward bringing the luggage with them, in an attempt correct the massively aft centre of gravity. He performed a miraculous forced landing and his family was shocked but otherwise unharmed. When Miles Aircraft learned of this, Lindsay was presented with a desk-top model of a Messenger – minus its engine of course!

In the spring of 1948 the Mamba-powered Balliol prototype, VL917, was ready to test. The take-off on 24th March put Boulton Paul and Lindsay into the record books: VL917 was the world's first single-engined turboprop aircraft – but not for long. On returning to Pendeford, the propeller went into fine pitch and there was no response from the throttle. Lindsay put the flaps up and retracted the undercarriage, but VL917 was destined to belly-land short, going through a hedge and writing itself off on the airfield. Lindsay had broken a leg and a couple of ribs. Lessons

Superb image of Lindsay Neale flying the prototype Balliol, VL892, powered by a Bristol Mercury. This was taken from Oxford G-AHTW. *Les Whitehouse-Boulton Paul Association*

Lindsay Neale strapping in to the first Mamba-powered Balliol, the short-lived VL917. *Les Whitehouse-Boulton Paul Association*

Below: The former Boulton Paul 'hack', Airspeed Oxford G-AHTW, returned to wartime colours at the Imperial War Museum, Duxford. *Ken Ellis*

learned, while Lindsay recovered, the second Mamba Balliol, VL935, was test flown by the engine manufacturer's CTP Waldo Price-Owen* from the long expanse of Bitteswell's runway.

Peter Tisshaw*, Lindsay's assistant since August 1947 took the first Merlin-powered Balliol, T.2 VW897, on its maiden flight in July 1948. The variant was found to suffer so-called 'reversal' of the elevator at high speed. On 3rd February 1949 Lindsay *and* Peter took VW897 up for stability trials. During a high speed dive the port windscreen collapsed and the entire canopy was wrenched from the airframe. It would seem that both pilots were incapacitated and the Balliol crashed at Coven, near Wolverhampton. Robert Lindsay Neale (37) and Kingsley Peter Henry Tisshaw (25) were killed instantly. 'Ben' Gunn* took over as CTP in the worst possible of circumstances. At Lindsay's funeral a eulogy read as follows: "As a test pilot he was outstanding. Completely fearless and quick at decision in emergency, he brought to his task a cool detachment from the purely mechanical business of flying. Always serious in

discussing official business, Robin was a light-hearted companion in his leisure hours. He retained a boyish sense of fun – almost frivolity – and was a tireless addition to our company."

John Neilan

6 Apr 1977	BN Turbo-Islander G-BDPR
	2 x 600shp Lycoming LTP101

By 1968 veteran test pilot John Neilan had come out of semi-retirement and joined the Britten-Norman (BN) team at Bembridge helping out James 'Jim' Birnie meet the surge of BN-2 Islander production. (For more on the incredible BN-2, see Desmond Norman.) John had worked as a PTP with Blackburn, initially on Bothas from Brough, later moving to the Blackburn-managed factory at Dumbarton building Short Sunderland IIIs and Vs, which were tested off the Clyde. In early 1976 John was back on the water, taking a flying-boat conversion course – with Hugh Kendall* – on a Lake Buccaneer in preparation for testing the proposed floatplane version of the Islander. That version did not materialise but John was at the controls of a much-demanded turboprop version of the Islander at Bembridge in April 1977 with Bob Wilson as FTO. Designated BN-2A-41, G-BDPR featured Lycoming turboprops mounted further out on the wing and a Trislander-like extended nose. *Papa-Romeo* was an interim step, the definitive Allison 250-B17C BN-2T Turbine Islander, G-BPBN, flying from Bembridge on 2nd August 1980. John had retired from flight testing by 1986.

'Jimmy' Nelson

James C Nelson, born 1920 in Colorado, USA. 'Jimmy' joined the American-crewed 133 'Eagle' Squadron at Coltishall in August 1941, flying Hawker Hurricane IIs and chalking up three 'kills' in the process. On 29th September 1942 the unit was disbanded, most of its personnel going on to form the 336th Fighter Squadron, USAAF. 'Jimmy' elected to stay with the RAF and in January 1943 he was appointed CO of 124 Squadron, flying Supermarine Spitfire VIIs from Martlesham Heath initially. He left the unit in June 1943 and graduated from ETPS Course No.1 at Boscombe Down, going on to serve with RAE Farnborough. On 13th May 1944 Jimmy, along with F/Sgt G L Gould and Mr Tovey as FTO, was flying AW Whitley V Z6649 when a propeller over-sped during a dive; fire broke out and the wing began to break up. All three baled out successfully. Worse was to follow: the port engine failed on take-off at Farnborough on 23rd August 1944 in DH Mosquito B.XVI PF390. Jimmy attempted a circuit but PF390 impacted into trees and both Jimmy and FTP Mr Shirley were seriously injured. Jimmy had a leg amputated and was invalided out of the RAF. By 1945 he was working for the sales department of Miles Aircraft, flying light aircraft whenever possible.

'JIMMY' NELSON was determined to return to test and flying and in 1948 Avro CTP 'Jimmy' Orrell took him seriously and appointed him as a PTP at Woodford, initially on Lincolns, but he later flew Athenas, Ashtons and Shackletons. His disability was not allowed to hold him back, he demonstrated Athena T.2 VR569 at the SBAC airshow at Farnborough in September 1950 and on 20th February 1953 he 'first flighted' the second prototype Avro 707A, WZ736, from Waddington. Sqn Ldr James C Nelson AFC returned to the USA in 1953 and he died there in 1989, aged 69.

Vincent Nicholl

14 Sep 1917	Fairey N10 1 x 260hp Sunbeam Maori II
8 Aug 1919	Fairey IIIB 1 x 260hp Sunbeam Maori II
7 Jul 1920	Fairey Pintail N133 1 x 475hp Napier Lion V
Aug 1920	Fairey IIID N9450 1 x 365hp RR Eagle VIII
28 Nov 1922	Fairey Flycatcher N163 1 x 385hp AS Jaguar II
Mar 1923	Fairey Fawn J6907 1 x 470hp Napier Lion II

Notes: N10 flown from the Isle of Grain; all others from Hamble or Hamble Water. N10, IIIB, Pintail and IIID all floatplanes. Flycatcher debut as landplane, later as floatplane. Fawn was a landplane.

SUB LT VINCENT NICHOLL learned to fly with RNAS and took his 'ticket' on 8th October 1914. He became a master of anti-Zeppelin patrols; flying mostly from Yarmouth from late 1914 through to at least April 1918. His first experience of plodding climbs to height and often fruitless searches was in a Farman Pusher from the Isle of Grain, but he later flew Royal Aircraft Factory BE.2c or BE.2e, plus Sopwith Schneiders, Short 184 and Short 827 floatplanes and finally Airco DH.4s. At times he was asked to carry out tests at the Isle of Grain and his first contact with Fairey types was the N10 experimental two-seat biplane floatplane in September 1917. By 1919 Lt Col Vincent Nicholl had been retained by Fairey as a test pilot and he was re-united with the N10, which by that time had become known as the Type III, the sire of a long and successful series of general purpose sea- and landplanes. Civil registered as G-EALQ, it was entered into the third Schneider Trophy contest, at Bournemouth on 10th September 1919. As well as Nicholl in the Fairey III, Harry Hawker* flew the Sopwith Schneider and Basil Hobbs* the Supermarine Sea Lion I. Guido Jannello of Italy was the only overseas competitor, with a Savoia S.13. The race was declared void, a thick sea fog making the event at times farcical or downright dangerous.

Prior to the abortive Schneider event, Vincent had conducted his first flight as a Fairey employee, not as an Admiralty pilot. This was the IIIB prototype and in August 1920 it was the turn of the IIID, the latter effectively becoming the baseline for the series. In between, he flew the Pintail, a two-seat general duties amphibian intended to be flown from aircraft carriers as well as capable of operating from the sea. The format was such that the observer/gunner had an unobstructed field of fire as the fin and rudder was sited *below* the rear fuselage. In 1921 Vincent fell ill, to the extent that Norman Macmillan* was brought in and he completed test flying of the troublesome Pintail. Redesigned as a landplane day bomber, the Pintail became the Fawn and Vincent took it up for its debut in March 1923 – the type entered service with the RAF, with 70 being built. Vincent had returned to work in late 1922 and he 'first flighted' another Fairey success, the Flycatcher single-seat shipborne fighter, capable of flying from carrier decks, or as a seaplane. Vincent flew N163, the landplane version, in November 1922 and the second example, N164, as a floatplane on 5th May 1923. The 'sea-booted' Flycatcher was probably Vincent's last flight debut as he was appointed Deputy Managing Director of Fairey in late 1923 and Norman Macmillan took his place as CTP. Lt Col Vincent Nicholl DSO DSC died in October 1928, he was in his mid to late 30s.

The Fairey III series were not much to look at, but a very successful and long-lived type. Type IIID Mk.II N9571 of the Seaplane Training Flight, Calshot, 1928. *KEC*

Line-up of Flycatchers of 405 Flight in mid-1929. Behind are Fairey IIIF Mk.IVs. *KEC*

John Nicholson

31 Jun 1961	Gloster Javelin FAW.1 XA552
	2 x 10,000lbst DH DGJ.10 Gyron Junior
15 Aug 1961	Beagle B.206X G-ARRM
	2 x 260hp Continental IO-470D

JOHN M NICHOLSON flew Bristol Beaufighters operationally in the Middle East, then instructed in Rhodesia before flying Douglas Dakotas. He left the RAF in 1946, but re-joined in 1949 and was posted to A&AEE in 1951. In 1954 he joined the de Havilland engine division at Hatfield as a test pilot, being appointed as CTP in January 1957. John's main responsibility was development of the Gyron series of turbojets. As a good example of the work of a powerplant test pilot, he flew a Gloster Javelin converted at Hatfield to test the Gyron Junior intended for the Bristol 188 research aircraft. Had this work have been carried out by Gloster at Moreton Valence, XA552 would certainly have been regarded as a prototype. The Javelin paved the way for the Godfrey Auty* to fly the first Type 188, XF926, in April 1962.

On 5th June 1961 John was appointed as Flight Operations Manager for Beagle Aircraft at Shoreham, where 'Pee Wee' Judge* was in place as CTP. John was at the helm of the debut of Beagle's 'flagship' design, the Beagle 206 twin G-ARRM. John demonstrated the prototype at the SBAAC airshow at Farnborough the following month, where his previous mount, Javelin XA552, was also displayed. (*Romeo-Mike* is held in Farnborough Air Sciences Trust collection.) By the summer of 1963 John had retired from test flying and set up a business marketing 'still' and cinema film. He had clocked up more than 4,000 flying hours on around 50 types.

The prototype Beagle 206, G-ARRM, on an early test flight, 1961. *Beagle Aircraft*

A brochure for the seven-seat and much redesigned B.206 Series 1, 1962.

Jack Noakes

5 Mar 1928	Beardmore Inflexible J7557
	3 x 650hp RR Condor II

Jack Noakes, born 1894. Joined the RFC, gaining his pilot's 'ticket' in 1915. By early 1916 Sgt Noakes was flying Royal Aircraft Factory BE.2s with 5 Squadron on the Western Front. He was with 29 Squadron with Airco DH.2s by May 1916 and on the 19th he engaged an enemy aircraft and downed it. By 1919 Fg Off Jack Noakes AFC MM had taken on a permanent commission and was gaining a reputation for skilful 'crazy flying', performing with vigour at the 1920 and 1921 Hendon displays. In July 1927 Sqn Ldr Noakes took command of 22 Squadron, which acted as 'B' Squadron A&AEE at Martlesham Heath.

AMONG the roles carried out by Sqn Ldr Jack Noakes AFC MM during his time leading 'B' Squadron A&AEE at Martlesham Heath was to 'first flight' the huge Beardmore Inflexible, which inevitably earned the nickname 'Impossible'. The tri-motor was not the only one with a nickname, Frank Courtney* in his excellent book *Flight Path* refers to Jack as 'Ouije'. This is a reference to the so-called 'spirit board' used to contact departed souls by those who believe in such things. Perhaps Jack was good at predicting the future, or even used the board? One wonders if Jack realised how eventful 1928 was destined to be.

The Glasgow-based shipbuilding and engineering business of William Beardmore and Company had established an aviation department and acquired the British rights to German designer Adolph Rohrbach's stressed skin construction that allowed for the creation of very large wings. Sqn Ldr Rollo Haig AFC* left the RAF in 1926 and took up the post of general manager for Beardmore's aviation venture. The Inflexible was intended to pave the way for a giant long-range bomber. This incredible machine had a wing span of 157ft 6in – that's 12ft 3in *greater* than that of a Boeing 707! It was decided that Martlesham was the best place for testing and that it should fall to A&AEE to provide the pilot – Jack. After a prolonged period of ground runs and 'straights' Jack took the 'Impossible' up for its maiden flight on 5th March 1928. It caused a sensation when it appeared at the Hendon display in June that year. The monster was woefully underpowered and it was dismantled in 1930 – a main undercarriage wheel continues to make jaws drop in the Science Museum in London!

In July Jack was at Hendon, competing in the King's Cup air race, flying Blackburn Lincock I G-EBVO. Back with the 'day job' Jack was evaluating the prototype Parnall Pipit single-seat shipboard fighter, N232, that had been first flown by Hubert Broad* in July 1928. On 20th September Jack was in N232, at about 2,000ft in a slight dive, when the tailplane collapsed. Jack could keep a semblance of control by pushing the stick all the way forward and he attempted a forced landing; at the last moment the Pipit lurched downwards. Jack was thrown out and broke his neck. He spent several months in the RAF hospital at Halton; giving up command of 22 Squadron in January 1929. During 1939 Wg Cdr Noakes was promoted to Group Captain and eventually he rose to the rank of Air Commodore.

Sqn Ldr Jack Noakes in front of Blackburn Lincock I G-EBVO which he flew in the King's Cup, July 1928. *Peter Green Collection*

A motor car and a biplane provide scale for the awesome Beardmore Inflexible at Martlesham Heath, 1929. *Peter Green Collection*

Louis Noël

1913	G-W Military Biplane
	1 x 120hp Austro-Daimler
Sep 1913	G-W Charabanc
	1 x 120hp Austro-Daimler
Nov 1913	G-W Lizzie
	1 x 50hp Gnome
May 1914	G-W Warplane
	1 x 100hp Gnome

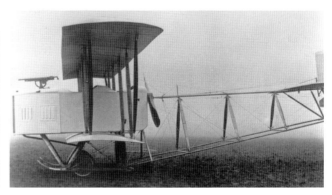

The unsuccessful Grahame-White Military Biplane. *Peter Green Collection*

Frenchman Louis Noël learned to fly in Britain and by September 1912 he was displaying at Hendon, including night demonstrations. By the end of the year he had been appointed as instructor at the Grahame-White school at Hendon, with Marcus Manton* as his assistant. Soon he was testing aircraft built by the Grahame-White (G-W) factory. In his superb autobiography *Flight Path* Frank Courtney* describes the first flight of the Military Biplane at Hendon: "At last it lumbered along under its own power, slowly gathering speed as it approached the hedge at the far end of the field. Somehow Noël hauled it into the air in a soggy stall, barely clearing the hedge. It sat down heavily on the other side – and never flew again." This was almost certainly the Type 6 Military Biplane which boasted a Colt machine-gun in the nose, the engine mounted mid-way in the nacelle driving the pusher propeller via an extension shaft. The complexity peaked with

The hybrid Lizzie sporting biplane. *Peter Green Collection*

the upper part of the triangular structure supporting the tail connecting to the propeller boss. Control wires for the rudder and elevators also ran through the propeller boss. All of this may explain Frank's description of its flight!

The Charabanc (or coach) was designed as a reliable biplane to take larger numbers of the public up on 'joy-rides' at Hendon events. On 22nd September 1913, Louis took seven passengers and kept them aloft for 17 minutes 25 seconds – this broke the previous endurance uplift record by a comfortable 11 minutes 36 seconds. Record-breaking didn't stop there, on 2nd October Louis managed to find room for *nine* passengers and extended the record to 19 minutes 47 seconds. The Lizzie single-seater was specifically developed for aerobatics, the promise of which never ceased to swell the audience at the regular Hendon flying days. Using as many Morane-Saulnier parts as possible (G-W built the French-designed monoplanes under licence) the machine was also known as the 'Teatray' because its sesquiplane format meant that the lower wings were attributed to be merely the size of tea trays. Not long after it had been finished Louis flew the Lizzie in a cross-country handicap race out of Hendon and was the winner. The Warplane of 1914 was another attempt at a gun-carrier, but was of much more conventional 'Gunbus' layout – it did not receive any production orders.

Louis flew a G-W-built Morane-Saulnier monoplane in the London to Paris and return air race of 11th July 1914, routing Hendon-Buc-Hendon, but was unplaced. A month later Britain and France were allies in a war against Germany and Louis returned to his homeland. During the conflict he was awarded the Croix de Guerre, Médaille Militaire and the Légion d'Honneur.

The Warplane of 1914 was a more conventional pusher, but failed to gain a production contract. *Peter Green Collection*

Desmond Norman

4th Aug 1950	Britten-Norman BN-1 G-ALZE	1 x 40hp JAP J-99
13th Jun 1965	BN Islander G-ATCT	2 x 210hp Continental IO-360
14th May 1969	BN Nymph G-AXFB	1 x 115hp Lycoming O-235
11th Sep 1970	BN Trislander G-ATWU	3 x 260hp Lycoming O-540
26th May 1977	NDN Firecracker G-NDNI	1 x 260hp Lycoming AEIO-540
17th Dec 1981	NDN Fieldmaster G-NRDC	1 x 750shp P&W PT6A-34

Note: All from Bembridge, other than the Firecracker which flew from Goodwood and the Fieldmaster at Sandown.

Nigel Desmond Norman, born 1929. After RAF national service he continued in the RAuxAF, flying Gloster Meteor F.8s with 601 (City of London) Squadron from North Weald. Attended the de Havilland Technical School at Hatfield from 1947, meeting up with John Britten and the two formed a business partnership.

"ABSOLUTELY delightful, it flies like a fully developed aircraft that has been in service for a couple of years." This was the comment issued by the directors of Britten-Norman Ltd (BN) – Forrester Robin John Britten and Desmond Norman, after the maiden flight of the BN-2. As the Islander, the type adopted the name in August 1966, this became spectacularly successful – over 1,270 built up to 2014. *Charlie-Tango* was not Desmond Norman's first 'first', he had made tentative flights in the BN-1 (see below) and he was to have another four 'maidens' – making him the most prolific designer-pilot of the second half of the 20th century.

John Britten and Desmond Norman's early ventures included the revolutionary Micronair atomiser for aerial crop-spraying and they also dabbled in hovercraft development. The pair's first design was the BN-1, a single-seat, parasol monoplane. Flown by Desmond, it made its first 'hops' on 4th August 1950 but it was badly damaged following engine failure upon take-off from Bembridge, on a later flight. It was substantially redesigned and rebuilt as the BN-1F, with a Lycoming 'flat-four'. Geoffrey Alington – see Chapter Two –

BN-1 G-ALZE Bembridge 1951. *Peter Green Collection*

BN-2 Islander prototype, G-ATCT, 1965. *Britten-Norman*

tested it on 26th May 1951, also at Bembridge. The BN-1 is displayed today at Solent Sky, Southampton.

With John as second pilot and A J 'Andy' Coombe as FTO, Desmond flew the prototype BN-2, G-ATCT on 13th June 1965 and four days later it was in the static at the Paris Salon. (See under Peter Hillwood for more on *Charlie-Tango*.) While it was obvious that the Islander had considerable development potential, the pair also conceived a four-seat tourer, the BN-3 Nymph and both were at the controls for its maiden flight. The following year, Desmond and John were again side-by-side, this time for the debut of the radical BN-2 Series III. Named Trislander in January 1971 it was an 18-seat, three-engined development with the extra engine mounted on the fin; 72 were built. As a company, BN has had its ups and downs and several owners; both John and Desmond left the concern they had founded in February 1976.

John Britten was awarded the CBE in 1970 and was very proud to become the High Sheriff of the Isle of Wight in 1976. Along with Denis Berryman, John had designed a four seat light twin and, given his appointment, he called it the Sheriff. Forrester Robin John Britten died on 7th July 1977, aged 48. The Sheriff project was continued by Aircraft Designs (Bembridge) Ltd and Sheriff Aerospace. The prototype was registered in John's honour as G-FRJB but was not finished and today is displayed at the East Midlands Airport Aeropark.

Desmond formed NDN Aircraft in 1977 and the Norman Aeroplane Company in 1985. He developed an improved version of the Nymph, the NAC-1 Freelance, in 1984. Two were completed but the type did not enter production. (BN-3 G-AXFB was rebuilt as the prototype NAC-1 G-NACI, it is airworthy with an Isle of Wight-based owner.) Taking off from Goodwood in May 1977, Desmond was at the controls of prototype No.5, the

The one-off BN-3 Nymph G-AXFB. 1969. *Britten-Norman*

A radical solution to 'growing' the Islander, the prototype Trislander G-ATWU, 1970. *Britten-Norman*

piston-engined Firecracker military trainer. It was followed by three turboprop examples, aimed at the RAF's requirement to replace the Jet Provost but was unsuccessful. His final design to take to the air capitalised on Desmond's knowledge of agricultural aviation. This was the large, turboprop-powered Fieldmaster crop-sprayer which was also developed as a fire-fighter, known as the Firemaster. Acting as observer in the rear seat was NDN chief aerodynamicist and author of the seminal *The Story of the British Light Aeroplane*, Terence Boughton. Half-a-dozen NDN-6s were built in the UK. (The prototype Fieldmaster is part of the Aerial Application Collection, based in Lincolnshire.) Awarded a CBE in 1970, Nigel Desmond Norman died on 23rd November 2002, aged 73.

Firecracker prototype G-NDNI in 1977. *NDN Aircraft*

The Fieldmaster turboprop agricultural prototype, G-NRDC in 1981. *NDN Aircraft*

J A C Northway

SPONSORED by his employers, Bristol, J A C Northway graduated from ETPS No.2 Course at Boscombe Down in 1944-1945 and upon return to Filton became the Assistant CTP to Cyril Uwins*. Bristol 170 Freighter Mk.21 prototype G-AIFF (originally completed as a Mk.XI) was converted at Filton in 1948/1949 to Mk.31 status and on 6th May 1949 Northway was captain for a propeller and engine test flight to allow for an increase in all-up weight. During asymmetric (one engine feathered) flying over the English Channel off Portland personnel on a surfaced Royal Navy submarine, HMS *Truculent*, watched the aircraft break up and crash. Northway (41), John M Radcliffe (47) Head of the Flight Research Department and the following FTOs E J N Archbold (27), R H Daniels (40), C W E Flook (36), J L Gundry (37) and R M Pollard (35) all perished. Only the bodies of Archbold and Gundry were ever recovered. Just over a year later, Freighter Mk.21 G-AHJJ was lost during an air test for certification renewal on a sortie out of Llandow, Wales, and was lost in similar circumstances during an engine-out test. Fin fillets and strengthened fins were introduced to subsequent Bristol 170s to prevent failure of the fin/rudder in high-yaw regimes.

'Mike' Oliver

R Michael Oliver, born 1921. Joined the RAF during World War Two and flew fighters, for some of the time based on Malta. Post-war he was a member of 600 (City of London) Squadron. A keen motor racer with a Bugatti, he was co-founder with Rodney Clarke (another former RAF pilot) and Kenneth McAlpine of Connaught Engineering in 1949, building Formula 2 cars for private owners, and sports cars. Connaught closed its doors in 1957, although the name has recently been revived.

WITH the closure of the Connaught 'works' team, 'Mike' Oliver was appointed as test pilot for Folland at Chilbolton in 1957. By 1961 he had become CTP, succeeding 'Teddy' Tennant*. The final single-seat fighter version for India was first flown on 1st April 1960, the last for Finland on 12th October 1960; production of Gnat T.1s for the RAF ran from 1959 to 1965. Folland was taken over by Hawker Siddeley in 1963 and testing moved to Dunsfold, Mike making the transition. The very last Gnat flight out of Chilbolton was pre-production T.1 XM706, following modifications, on 22nd April 1965.

Stanley 'Olly' Oliver

26 Mar 1963	Hunting 126 XN714
	1 x 4,850lbst BSE Orpheus 805

Stanley Blackbourne Oliver joined the RAF in 1942 and transferred to the Fleet Air Arm in 1945, becoming an instructor. He served with 762 Squadron at Ford on DH Mosquito T.IIIs and then North American Harvards with 780 Squadron at Culdrose. By early 1948 he was operational on DH Sea Hornet F.20s with 801 Squadron, shore-based at

The Hunting 126 being prepared for the static at the Battle of Britain display at Gaydon, September 1966. *Roy Bonser*

Lee-on-Solent and mostly deploying on board HMS Implacable. 'Olly' graduated from ETPS No.9 Course at Farnborough in 1950 and then joined naval test at A&AEE, Boscombe Down, 1951-1952.

LT STANLEY OLIVER was bound to get the nickname 'Olly', but doubly so with a first name of Stanley in honour of the legendary cinema comedy duo, Laurel and Hardy. Olly joined Hunting Percival at Luton in January 1954 and succeeded 'Dick' Weldon* as CTP in 1958 – the company having become Hunting Aircraft the previous year. Output of Jet Provosts for the RAF and export was lively and there was plenty of work, including deliveries and demonstrations. Apart from a small batch in 1969, 'JP' production phased out at Luton in 1965. Hunting became part of BAC in 1960 and further developments took place at Warton.

It fell to Olly to pilot the last of the Percival Hunting line, the H.126 jet-flap research aircraft. Envisaged at first as a propulsion system, jet-flaps bled air out of the trailing edge of the wings to either replace a conventional jet exhaust, or complement it. In May 1959 a contract was issued to Hunting to build two H.126s, although the second one was never completed. Powered by a Bristol Siddeley Orpheus turbojet, the H.126 was propelled via two outlets low down on each side of the fuselage, a rear exhaust nozzle and through two ducts under each wing. It first flew on March 26, 1963 and had a relatively short trials life including evaluation in the USA by NASA. Following the 18-minute maiden flight from Luton, Olly described flying XN714 as: "an entirely new sensation, it just floats off the ground and then you go up like a lift." The oddly-shaped one-off is displayed at the RAF Museum, Cosford. Lt Stanley Blackbourne Oliver died in 2003.

Gordon Olley

| Oct 1923 | HP-Sayers Monoplane No.25 |
| | 1 x 8hp ABC |

Gordon Percy Olley, born 1893. With the advent of the Great War he joined the Army in August 1914, but transferred to the RFC as a mechanic, later serving as a despatch rider. He was posted to 1 Squadron, equipped with Morane Parasols, on the Western Front. He was often engaged as an observer and he elected for pilot training. By the summer of 1917 Gordon had re-joined 1 Squadron, by then equipped with Nieuport 17s, and later 27s. Between June and October 1917 he claimed ten victories: three destroyed, one unidentified, one DFW and an Albatros D.V and seven out-of-control, including an LVG on the 23rd. He was awarded the Military Medal in September 1917. By the end of 1917 Gordon was back in Britain, ferrying aircraft. Lt Gordon Olley MM left RAF service in June 1919.

GORDON OLLEY became a test pilot because of his slight build and also is another example of how canny Frederick Handley Page was when it came to 'engaging' men to try out his products! By 1920 Gordon was at Cricklewood working for Handley Page Transport (HPT) initially on 'joy-riding' and then with the airline fleet, O/400s, O/10s and W.8s. He worked briefly with Dutch airline KLM, flying Fokker IIIs. At the Itford glider competition in 1922, he flew a biplane glider designed by Anthony Fokker, before re-joining HPT. For the light aeroplane competition to be staged at Lympne in October 1923, Handley Page decided to enter three powered-gliders designed by W H Sayers, each was to a different format, but only one, No.25, flew successfully. CTP for Handley Page at the time was Arthur Wilcockson* but it was clear from his stature that he would not fit the task in hand: the hunt was on for a smaller, lighter pilot! First port of call was HPT, where Gordon was an ideal candidate. Test pilots were paid a bonus for putting a new type into the air and Frederick was keen to avoid such an outlay. Gordon insisted, but in the end accepted that he could pocket a third of any winnings. With the *Daily Mail* offering up to £1,000 (£55,000 in present-day values) and other concerns throwing in smaller amounts, this seemed like a reasonable prospect. Trials at Cricklewood proved that No.23 and No.26 were impractical: only No.25 made the journey to Kent. The odds on Gordon making any money were shortening and there was no prize money to be had for the Handley Page team. Beyond this Gordon is known to have 'first flighted' a couple of Hendon torpedo-bombers at Cricklewood, but that was the extent of his sojourn into testing.

In March 1924 Imperial Airways came into being, having swallowed HPT, among other airlines. Gordon flew with Imperial until 1934, by which time he had come to fame as the first pilot to have flown a million miles. In 1934 he founded his own airline, Croydon-based Olley Air Services, and his autobiography, *A Million Miles in the Air*, was published. Gordon sold Olley Air Services to Morton Air Services in 1953. When he stopped flying he had amassed over 13,000 hours. Captain Gordon Olley MM died on 18th March 1958, aged 65.

Laurence Openshaw

17 Sep 1924	Westland Woodpigeon I G-EBIY 1 x 32hp Bristol Cherub I
22 Sep 1924	Westland Widgeon I G-EBJT 1 x 35hp Blackburne Thrush
early 1926	Westland Wizard 1 x 275hp RR Falcon III
early 1927	Westland Wapiti I J8495 1 x 420hp Bristol Jupiter VI

Notes: All flown from Yeovil. The Wapiti first flew prior to 12th March 1927. Blackburne was a Surrey-based motorcycle engine manufacturer and not to be confused with the Brough-based aircraft and engine manufacturer, Blackburn.

Laurence Pratt Openshaw, born 1892. Joined the RNAS and tested aircraft at the Isle of Grain and Eastchurch, under Harry Busteed. Post-war he took a degree at Cambridge before managing a marble quarry in Italy. Laurence's pride and joy was a Fiat Grand Prix racing car, his Brough Superior motorcycle running a close second with his affections.*

MAJOR LAURENCE OPENSHAW took over as CTP at Westland following the horrific accident that befell Stuart Keep* while testing the Dreadnought at Yeovil in May 1924. Within the space of six days Laurence 'first flighted' a pair of two-seater prototypes, the Woodpigeon biplane and the Widgeon parasol monoplane. Both designs were entered in the light aeroplane trials at Lympne in September-October 1924: two Woodpigeons and the Widgeon I proved to be underpowered and were all unplaced. With more power, the Widgeon showed promise and the Mk.III – which included design input from Harald Penrose* – entered production with 24 being built.

In June 1925 the Westland Yeovil single-engined day bomber was ready to test, but the Air Ministry decreed that

The second Woodpigeon entered by the Seven Aero Club in the Grosvenor Challenge Race at Lympne in 1926. *Peter Green Collection*

Laurence had insufficient test piloting time to his credit – Grain and Eastchurch being seven years distant. Frank Courtney* was brought in for this task and the freelancer also took the honours in September 1926 with the Westbury twin-engined 'heavy' fighter. Laurence was given his head with the private-venture Wizard single-seat parasol monoplane fighter prototype in early 1926. He was critical of the controls, especially the rudder and a series of 'fixes' were tried out. An air lock in the Rolls-Royce Falcon's fuel system on take off gave Laurence few options and it was wrecked when it went through a hedge and turned over, slightly injuring its pilot. The Wizard needed a complete rebuild and the opportunity was taken to replace its wooden fuselage with a metal one; Louis Paget* took the practically new fighter into the air in November 1927.

Laurence's next maiden flight was crucial to Westland and set the company on a path of mass manufacture, becoming a specialist in general duties aircraft. In his exceptional *Adventure with Fate*, Harald Penrose described the scene at Yeovil on a Sunday morning as Laurence took the prototype Wapiti for its first flight. "We watched enthralled as though he was a gladiator about to meet his fate, for even with so commonplace a machine there could be trouble: and there was. After Openshaw landed we saw him in confidential enclave with Bruce, Davenport and Hill. 'Rudder hardly works at all,' he told them." The trio Laurence was discussing the Wapiti's lack of directional control with were: managing director Robert Bruce, chief designer Arthur Davenport and tail-less aircraft designer Geoffrey Hill*. The rudder was enlarged, but to no avail. Then it was discovered that J8495 was two feet *shorter* than it should have been! There was no time for what would have been a major rebuild, so off went the precious prototype to Martlesham Heath on 12th March 1927 for initial trials. Truncated the prototype may have been, the Wapiti was victorious and it was followed by 500-plus of its elongated siblings produced from 1928 to 1932.

During the summer of 1926 the Westland-Hill Pterodactyl I J8067 had been fitted with smaller 'controllers' at the wingtips – all-moving flying surfaces in modern parlance – capable of acting as ailerons and elevators. Laurence took the machine up for its first excursion in the new guise but it hit a bump on the all-grass aerodrome and bounded into the air only to enter an incipient spin at about 10ft and swing to port, crumpling up as it hit the ground. The slow speed and lack of

The last Widgeon, Mk.III G-AADE with a DH Gipsy I, was completed in 1930. *Westland Aircraft*

height saved Laurence from serious harm. Although the pioneering machine was rebuilt, the accident spurred on the decision to create more advanced versions.

Laurence piloted the much-rebuilt Widgeon II G-EBJT at Lympne in the hotly-contested Grosvenor Challenge Cup race on 18th September 1926. He was unplaced but the 60hp Armstrong Siddeley Genet allowed him to achieve the fastest time over the 75-mile course at 105mph. (The prototype Woodpigeon also with a new powerplant – a 34hp ABC Scorpion – flown by Flt Lt A P Ritchie of 7 Squadron's Seven Aero Club was one of the competitors.) The so-called 'Pub Crawl Races' named because of the support of the Bournemouth and District Hotels and Restaurants Association, staged at Ensbury Park, Bournemouth, over 4th to 6th June 1927 got off to a bad start. On the first day de Havilland DH.37A G-EBDO flown by Major Harold Hemming crashed, killing his passenger, C S J Plevins. Worse was to follow. During the Medium Power Handicap on the 6th the prototype Blackburn Bluebird I G-EBKD, flown by 34-year-old Sqn Ldr Walter Hunt Longton DFC AFC and Laurence in Widgeon III G-EBPW collided; the hulks bursting into flames upon hitting the ground. Longton was killed instantly; Major Laurence Pratt Openshaw, aged 35, took some time to succumb to horrific burns. Louis Paget took his place as CTP at Yeovil.

Wapiti IIA K1142, delivered to the School of Photography at Farnborough in June 1930. *KEC*

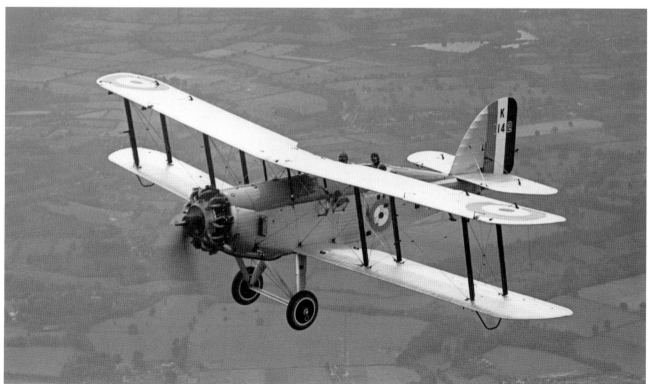

Augustus Orlebar

10 Aug 1929	Supermarine S.6 N247
	1 x 1,900hp RR 'R'

Augustus Henry Orlebar, born 1897. Served with the 1st/5th Bedfordshire Regiment from January 1915 and in September he was at Gallipoli. Wounded by an Ottoman sniper, Augustus was returned to Britain for treatment. Transferred to the RFC, he gained his 'wings' in September 1916. Operational service with the following: 19 Squadron on SPAD VIIs, downing two Albatros D.IIIs on the Western Front; 44 Squadron on Sopwith Camels at Hainault Farm, Essex; back on the Western Front with 73 Squadron on Camels (shooting down a Fokker Dr.I and three Albatros D.Vs); 43 Squadron on Camels and Sopwith Snipes (downing a Fokker D.VII with a Snipe). The Fokker Dr.I was flown by none other than Lt Lothar von Richthofen who was badly wounded in the crash. As Shores, Franks and Guest record in Above the Trenches, *despite seven 'kills', one of which was a Richthofen, Augustus was not decorated for his valour during the Great War: it was 2nd January 1922 before he received an AFC. Posted to AES Martlesham Heath in July 1919, he transferred to 22 Squadron, the resident test unit for AEE, in July 1923 as a Flight Commander. Transferred to MAEE, Felixstowe, in January 1929 and that December Augustus took command of the Flying Boat Development Flight, also at Felixstowe.*

SQN LDR AUGUSTUS HENRY ORLEBAR AFC was posted to the High Speed Flight in readiness for the Schneider Trophy contest, to be staged at Calshot on 12th September 1929. In a similar manner to Wg Cdr Jack Henderson* of the RAE making the first flight of the Handley Page HP.115 slender delta research aircraft (see Volume One, Chapter Five) in 1961, Augustus represented both the client *and* acceptance authority so was ideally placed to carry out the maiden flight of the two Supermarine S.6 seaplanes on which so many hopes rested. Beside that, designer R J Mitchell and engine manufacturer Rolls-Royce were making constant modifications and 'tweaks' and a highly experienced test pilot was vital. Then there was the pressing nature of time: Augustus flew S.6 N247 just 28 days before the competition and sister-ship N248 a mere 13 days before

The machine that won the Schneider Trophy in perpetuity for Great Britain: S.6B S1595 afloat off Calshot, 1931. *Rolls-Royce*

the 'off'. The contest was won by Flt Lt Henry Waghorn piloting S.6 N247 at 328.6mph against a very strong Italian contingent with Macchi M.52 and M.67 seaplanes. On 12th September Augustus, also flying N247, seized the Fédération Aéronautique Internationale-recognised world absolute speed record at 357.7mph. (S.6A N248 is preserved at Solent Sky, Southampton.)

Calshot was the venue for the 1931 contest; the rules were that any country that won three times in a row would keep the Schneider trophy in perpetuity. Augustus took command of the High Speed Flight on 11th May 1931. For this contest two S.6Bs, fitted with 2,300hp Rolls-Royce 'R' engines, had been ordered and the S.6s upgraded to S.6A status. Augustus first flew S.6B S1595 on 29th July 1931. The contest, held on 13th September 1931 was an outright win for Great Britain, as the Italians could not field a team. Flt Lt John Boothman averaged 340.08mph to take the contest and on that same day Flt Lt George Stainforth piloted S1596 to 379.05mph taking the world air speed record, previously held by his 'boss'. (S.6B S1595 and the Schneider Trophy are on show at the Science Museum, London.)

Augustus was appointed Officer Commanding Northolt in December 1937, by which time he was a Group Captain and in July 1941 Air Commodore Orlebar was Air Officer Commanding 10 Group. In March 1943 he became Deputy Chief of Combined Operations but was hospitalised in the summer of that year: AVM Sqn Ldr Augustus Henry Orlebar CBE AFC* died there on 4th August 1943, aged 46.

Supermarine S.6A N248 masquerading as 'S1596' at Horse Guard's Parade, London, September 1968. *Roy Bonser*

'Jimmy' Orrell

12 Jun 1948	Avro Athena VM125
	1 x 1,010shp AS Mamba 1
1 Aug 1948	Avro Athena T.2 VW890
	1 x 1,280hp RR Merlin 35
6 Sep 1948	Avro Tudor 8 VX195
	4 x 5,000lbst RR Nene 5
9 Mar 1949	Avro Shackleton VW126
	4 x 2,450hp RR Griffon 57/57A
10 Aug 1949	Avro Canada Jetliner CF-EJD-X
	4 x 3,600lbst RR Derwent 5/17
1 Sep 1950	Avro Ashton 1 WB490
	4 x 5,000lbst RR Nene 5

Notes: All had their debuts at Woodford other than the C102 Jetliner which first flew at Malton, Canada.

Joseph Harold Orrell, born 1903. Began work with maritime engineers C & H Crichton Ltd in Liverpool. 'Jimmy' joined the RAF in April 1919 as a mechanic/draughtsman, initially training at Halton. Transferred to pilot training and went solo on an Avro 504K at 5 FTS Sealand on 23rd April 1926. (Jimmy used to cycle to Sealand in 1918 to watch the flying and it was where he became determined to be a pilot. He returned to Sealand in 1929-1931 as an instructor.) He was posted to 25 Squadron at Hawkinge on Gloster Grebes in February 1927. Jimmy left the RAF in April 1931 and took up a job with 'joy-riding' company Berkshire Aviation Tours, flying Avro 504Ks. After a brief spell as an instructor at Barton in 1932, Jimmy became senior pilot with Midland and Scottish Air Ferries, based at Renfrew, in April 1933. He flew a wide variety of aircraft, including: Airspeed Ferries, Avro 618 G-ACGF, DH Fox Moths and Dragons.

The caption on this public information photo, dated 6th September 1943, declares that this gathering was taken at: "a factory in the North West where [Lancasters] are produced in surprising numbers for the Ministry of Aircraft Production". Left to right: G Phillip Andrews, publisher of *Air News* and *Air Tech* of New York City; Thomas Martin, manager of a radio station at Waterton, New York; test pilot Jimmy Orrell; H E Hollensbe, editor of *Industry and Power*, St Joseph, Michigan. *via Dean Wright*

JOSEPH HAROLD ORRELL was 'Jimmy' to all who met him. When his previous employers, Midland and Scottish Air Ferries, folded in July 1934, Jimmy was employed briefly by the airline's founder, John Sword, as his private pilot. In December 1934 Jimmy took up a post at Avro's Chadderton factory as a draughtsman, but his experience was too good to miss and he was quickly moved to Woodford as a test pilot, under 'Sam' Brown*.

His spell was short-lived as the airline industry had a strong 'pull' on him; he signed up with Croydon-based Imperial Airways in February 1935; captaining an impressive number of types, including: Armstrong Whitworth Ensign, Avro 652 (Anson predecessor), DH.86, DH Albatross, Handley Page HP.42, Westland Wessex. He brought an Ensign out of France on 17th June 1940, bringing 40 Czech and French airmen with him as France collapsed in the face of the German blitzkrieg. The following month Jimmy joined the Air Transport Auxiliary and was based with 2 Ferry Pilot's Pool at Whitchurch, flying a bewildering variety of aircraft. Jimmy's airline skills were again compelling and he moved to British Overseas Airways Corporation (BOAC) to embark on the perilous 'Ball Bearing Shuttle' from Leuchars to Stockholm

in neutral Sweden from April 1941. With BOAC he mostly flew Lockheed Electras and Hudsons.

In April 1942 Jimmy returned to Woodford and it was to be his 'home' for the next 16 years. Lancasters dominated the work and he achieved a 'double' in January 1944: clocking up his 1,000th 'Lancs' flight and his 700th individual example. Jimmy graduated from ETPS Course No.2 at Boscombe Down in 1944. He was the test pilot for the first flight of the 'airline' version of the Lancaster, Lancastrian G-AGLF, on 17th January 1945 which was destined for BOAC. Jimmy was co-pilot to newly-appointed CTP 'Bill' Thorn* on the maiden flight of the Tudor I airliner G-AGPF, 14th June 1945 at Ringway. The Tudor programme began to take up more and more of Jimmy's time and then on 23rd August 1947 came disaster and much greater responsibility. Piloted by Bill Thorn Tudor II G-AGSU crashed after take-off at Woodford on 23rd August 1947: Thorn, Wilson, radio operator John Webster and Avro's legendary designer, Roy Chadwick, perished. Jimmy became Avro CTP almost overnight.

Jimmy's first maiden flight was the prototype Athena trainer, powered by an Armstrong Siddeley Mamba turboprop, on 12th June 1948. Two months later he was at the helm for

The prototype Dart-powered Athena, VM125, in 1948. Note the fairing behind the tail wheel for the glider-towing hook, a requirement of the original specification. *Rolls-Royce*

the prototype of the 'insurance' version, the T.2 with a Rolls-Royce Merlin. The Athena was up against the Boulton Paul Balliol – the Wolverhampton-based company got the major order, but oddly the Merlin Athena was also ordered, in limited numbers. The Tudor programme had proven to be a major disappointment, but the second prototype was used to good effect and made history. Rebuilt with four Rolls-Royce Nene turbojets in twin nacelles as the Tudor 8, Jimmy 'first flighted' the world's first four-engined jet aircraft on 6th September 1948. Taking off from Woodford, Jimmy flew VX195 to Boscombe Down, completing the 124-mile flight in 20 minutes, averaging 372mph. All the way the airspeed indicator was not working, but it failed to faze Jimmy! The following day Jimmy displayed VX195 daily at the SBAC airshow at Farnborough up to the 12th.

In turn, the Anson, the Lancaster and the Lincoln had helped to turn Avro into a huge concern. On 18th February 1949 Jimmy took the next great hope out for its first trials – the Shackleton prototype VW126. That day he did the first 'angry' engine and taxi runs. Despite the increase in complexity, in 1949 'straights' – full-blown runs or even 'hops' down the runway – were still very much part of the test sequence as they had been four decades earlier. Problems with the rudder needed addressing but on 9th March he carried out the maiden flight, of 40 minutes duration with his deputy, 'Red' Esler*, as co-pilot and A Blake as FTE. The trio taking the prototype up again that afternoon. The Shackleton was to become a mother-lode programme for Avro with the MR.1 and MR.2 'tail-draggers' leading to the

The world's first four-jet aircraft, Avro Tudor 8 VX195 touching down at the Farnborough SBAC display in September 1948 with Jimmy Orrell at the controls. To the left is the prototype Merlin-engined Athena, VW890. *Peter Green Collection*

much-refined MR.3; each requiring major upgrading of systems during their long operational life. Jimmy flew the first production Mk.1, VP254, on 28th March 1950.

Before that event, Jimmy was 'posted' to Canada. At Malton, Ontario, Avro Canada had an ambitious project, the C102 Jetliner designed by James 'Jim' C Floyd and capable of carrying up to 50 passengers. With his experience of flying the 'tail-dragger' Tudor 8 and with Woodford well into creating the Ashton tricycle undercarriage four-jet research test-bed, Jimmy was the ideal candidate to fly the C102. ('Red' Esler 'ran the shop' at Woodford in his absence, making the debut of the Dart-powered Athena and the prototype Avro 707 and perishing in it; all during September 1949.)

In the first chapter of Mike Lithgow's *Vapour Trails*, Jimmy provided a graphic description of his experience of the C102. Typically, Jimmy expressed his dislike of the intrusive behaviour of the press trying to get an exclusive, one paper describing him as a "Shy, tubby Englishman"! After initial taxi runs on 8th August 1949, the first flight took place at Malton two days later with Jimmy in command, Donald H Rogers as co-pilot and A William Baker as FTE. The 30-minute sortie was a great success and it was the first flight by a jet transport in North America. It was only the second inaugural flight by a dedicated jet transport anywhere in the world; 15 days previously John Cunningham* had lifted the prototype de Havilland Comet into the skies at Hatfield.

Jimmy wrote of the debut in the September 1949 issue of the in-house *Avro News*: "...she was the perfect lady and gave us a very fine flight. Smooth – as smooth as a surface plate. Noise – we could talk to each other in ordinary voices, used the [cockpit] loudspeaker with the volume turned down instead of headphones." And concluded: "We were mighty happy with our experience and ready to continue with the schedule of tests that are necessary for a prototype. As a matter of fact 'a piece of cake' and we are ready to take another piece."

This euphoria was not repeated on the second flight on 16th August for which all of Avro Canada's personnel were invited to spectate. During low-speed trials, try as the crew might, the main undercarriage refused to come down. Consultations with air traffic and eventually with Jim Floyd failed to produce anything that would change the situation. Jimmy realised that that a wheels-up was inevitable and invited Don and Bill to bale out. Both declined and the emergency services at Malton got ready. On finals Jimmy still had time for levity, as he wrote in *Vapour Trails*: "Ahead on the road I could see a woman in a white dress running first left then right. 'Don, I'll hit that woman if she doesn't keep still!" A textbook landing was made and the C102 proved to be a robust design; it was back in the air on 20th September. Jimmy flew a total of 16 sorties in the Jetliner, returning to Woodford in November 1949. The C102 project was dropped in December 1951 and the only prototype scrapped. The forward fuselage of CF-EJD-X is displayed in the Canada Aviation Museum at Rockcliffe, Ottawa.

Upon his return from Canada, Jimmy prepared for what would be his final maiden flight. The design office had toyed with an improved Tudor 8 with tricycle undercarriage as an airliner, but the advent of the DH Comet had put paid to that. The Tudor 8 showed great promise as a trials aircraft, offering

The prototype Shackleton, VW126, first flown by 'Jimmy' Orrell on 9th March 1949. *Avro*

jet speeds with a high-capacity fuselage. With this in mind, the Type 706 Ashton was schemed to meet a Ministry of Supply requirement for a specialist test-bed airframe and six were ordered. Jimmy was at the controls of the prototype, WB490, on 1st September 1950, in time to show it off at that month's Farnborough display.

Since January 1950, Jimmy had been working with 'Roly' Falk*, who had been brought in to take over the Avro 707 delta test-bed programme after the death of 'Red' Esler. Effectively, Roly was project pilot for Avro 698 V-bomber that took the name Vulcan in December 1952. Such was Roly's level of experience that his appointment was rationalised as Superintendent of Flying, instead of DCTP, in the spring of 1954. This explains why it was not Jimmy that was in command of the prototype Vulcan, VX770, for its first flight on 30th August 1952. It was the following year, on 23rd July, when Jimmy got a taste of the mighty delta.

Three months before the prototype Vulcan flew, Jimmy was the pilot for another significant Avro milestone. He carried out the first flight of Anson T.21 crew trainer WJ561, on 13th May

The one-off Avro Canada C102 Jetliner at Malton. *Peter Green Collection*

With nose-mounted pitot head, the prototype Ashton research aircraft, WB490, in 1950. *Avro*

125

Anson T.21 crew trainer WJ561, first flown by 'Jimmy' Orrell on 13th May 1952, over Woodford. It was the last of an incredibly long line of 'Annies'.

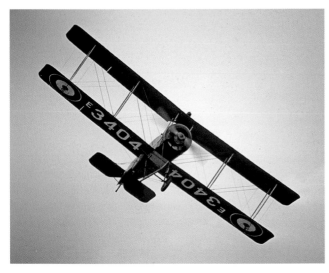

The Shuttleworth Collection's Avro 504K E3404 displaying at Upavon in June 1962. *Roy Bonser*

Jimmy Orrell in front of private-owned Anson T.21 WD413 (G-BFIR) at Woodford on 25th March 1985, during the celebrations of the 50th anniversary of the first flight of the type. *Alan Curry*

1952. It was the last of an incredible 10,996 'Annies', including licence manufacture in Canada. There was still Lancaster work to be had, Jimmy flew French Navy WU48 (previously RAF TW921) for a test after refurbishment on 11th January 1954- this was his 917th and last 'Lanc'. In 1955 Jimmy stood down as CTP, leaving that post to Roly Falk, and he took on the role of Flight Superintendent of the Guided Weapons Division. He signed off in fine style with a very different flight test from Woodford. The apprentices has been restoring Avro 504K E3404 for the Shuttleworth Collection and Jimmy carried out the honours on 19th August 1955 – he'd soloed in the type 29 years previously and had last flown one in 1931. (The venerable Avro is still a 'regular' at Old Warden displays.) The Guided Weapons Division was developing the Blue Steel stand-off bomb – what would be called a nuclear cruise missile by the 1990s – and Jimmy flew a trio of Vickers Valiants used in the early stages of the project, including ferrying one to Woomera in Western Australia in July 1958. On 30th August 1958 Jimmy was flying the Woodford 'hack', Avro Nineteen G-AGPG. It was his last flight: Jimmy's latest medical grounded him the following day. The 'Nineteen' was the name given to the purely civilian version of the Anson C.19 and Jimmy knew G-AGPG very well, he had piloted it on its maiden flight on 28th August 1945. Known to all at Woodford as 'Aggie-Paggie' from its registration, the cockpit of G-AGPG is cherished by a private collector based in the north west of England.

Joseph Harold Orrell OBE died on 3rd August 1988, aged 85. Published in 1989 by the Museum of Science and Industry, Peter V Clegg's *The Quiet Test Pilot -The Story of Jimmy Orrell OBE – One of Britain's Greatest Test Pilots* is well worth seeking out, it includes impressive appendices and is an exceptional biography of a self-effacing but remarkable man. Jimmy had clocked up 8,174 flying hours on *at least* 77 types. Peter Clegg records that Jimmy tested 1,314 separate aircraft in 2,936 flights during his time with Avro. As mentioned earlier, he piloted 917 different Lancasters, which Peter calculates as 22% of all the 'Lancs' built at Woodford!

Jack Overbury

Jack R S Overbury was with 766 Squadron, an FAA operational training unit, at Rattray learning to master Fairey Firefly Is by March 1946. By January 1948 he was on Firefly FR.1s with 816 Squadron off HMS Ocean. A take-off accident from Ocean on 22nd January 1948 ended with PP595 ditching off Malta; Jack and Lt R B Smith were picked up. During 1949 he was serving with 810 Squadron, on Firefly AS.5s, from HMS Theseus. He was with 781 Squadron at Lee-on-Solent in 1951, getting time in on several types, including Supermarine Sea Otters. Jack graduated from ETPS Course No.12 at Farnborough in 1953; going on to serve with 'C' Squadron A&AEE at Boscombe Down. Flying a Hawker Sea Hawk on 29th July 1954 he established a new point-to-point record, London to Amsterdam (Bovingdon to Schiphol) taking 23 minutes, 39 seconds over 224 miles, averaging 571.5mph. Not content with this, while ferrying a DH Sea Venom FAW.21 destined for the Royal Australian Navy to Idris in Libya for trials, he broke the Rome-Malta record. With Lt Cdr Garvin Kable RAN, Jack flew WZ894 from Ciampino to Luqa in 47 minutes, 24 seconds averaging 538mph over the 422 miles on 2nd July 1955.

L T CDR JACK R S OVERBURY joined Saunders-Roe (Saro) as a test pilot in 1956, in readiness to join the SR.53 mixed powerplant interceptor project, under CTP John Booth*. All flights of the SR.53 were staged from Boscombe Down and Jack made his first flight, in XD145, in September 1957. Jack was flying a Druine Turbulent single-seat light aircraft at an airshow at Sandown, Isle of Wight, on 26th May 1958. After a series of tight turns, it dived and crashed on a couple of cars – thankfully with no injuries to any spectators. Jack had a compound fracture of a leg, head and internal injuries. He underwent several operations and spent four months in hospital. Ten days after Jack's crash, John Booth was killed in a take-off crash of the second SR.53, XD151, at Boscombe.

In 1959 Jack left Saro – Peter 'Sheepy' Lamb* taking over the SR.53 programme – and he moved to Luton to become a test pilot with Hunting on Jet Provosts. On 16th November 1960 Jack was flying the private-venture, one-off Jet Provost T.2, G-AOUS and during a maximum design speed dive the nose leg descended, only for it and its doors to be ripped away. The 'JP' began to pitch up and the wings broke off; Jack was killed when G-AOUS crashed near Biggleswade.

Hubert Oxley

| 9 Nov 1911 | Blackburn Mercury |
| | 1 x 60hp Renault |

Hubert Oxley, born 1886. He joined the Roe school at Brooklands and began his tuition on a Roe Type IV triplane. On 17th October 1910 he took off downwind and ended up in the famous sewage farm. Perhaps because of this, he changed his loyalties and completed his flying on a Hanriot, also at Brooklands, gaining Aviators' Certificate No.78 on 9th May 1911. Beyond this he travelled to Filey, Yorkshire, where Robert Blackburn had set up a school, using monoplanes of his own design.

R OBERT BLACKBURN was impressed with Hubert Oxley and offered him the position of chief pilot previously occupied by 'Benny' Hucks. Hubert tried out the Mercury I, which Benny had flown in May 1911, on 3rd September. On 9th November 1911 Hubert first flew the three-seat Mercury, the so-called Type III. This was considerably developed from previous iterations and soon proved to be capable of 70mph. There were high hopes that with this not only could instructional flights be made, but a greater 'uplift' of 'joy-riders' from the beach could be achieved. On 6th December 1911 Hubert took up one of his pupils, Robert J Weiss, and proceeded to climb to 600ft or so and then dive down the face of the cliffs, pulling up over the sea. He had carried this manoeuvre several times before but on this occasion, the machine broke up, killing both occupants. Despite this, Robert Blackburn went on to build five more three-seater Mercuries.

Louis Paget

Nov 1927	Westland Wizard I J9252
	1 x 490hp RR F.XI
30 Jan 1928	Westland Witch J8596
	1 x 420hp Bristol Jupiter VI
Jun 1928	Westland-Hill Pterodactyl IA J9251
	1 x 34hp Bristol Cherub III
Aug 1928	Westland Interceptor J9124
	1 x 440hp Bristol Mercury IIA
22 Feb 1929	Westland IV G-EBKX
	3 x 95hp ADC Cirrus III
Dec 1930	Westland F29/27 J9565
	1 x 485hp Bristol Mercury IIIA
Feb 1931	Westland PV.3 P3
	1 x 575hp Bristol Jupiter XFA
Mar 1931	Westland-Hill Pterodactyl IV K1947
	1 x 120hp DH Gipsy III

Notes: The Witch and the Pterodactyls flew from Andover, all else from Yeovil. J9251 had its maiden flight on either the 13th or the 14th of June 1928.

Louis George Paget, born 1891. Awarded an AFC in 1919. By 1924, as a Flight Lieutenant, he was flying Vickers Vernons with 45 Squadron in Iraq – his CO was Sqn Ldr Roderic Hill – the brother of Geoffrey Hill who designed two of the aircraft Louis 'first flighted'.

W ITH the death of Westland CTP Laurence Openshaw* while racing a Widgeon in June 1927, tail-less aircraft designer Geoffrey Hill* recommended a colleague of his brother, Roderic Hill*, from their mutual days with 45 Squadron in Iraq. This was the tall, monocle-wearing Flt Lt Louis George Paget AFC and in November 1927 he flew the dramatically rethought private-venture Wizard single-seat parasol-winged fighter. A fuel problem during a test flight in 1926 had caused Laurence Openshaw to force land the prototype and it had been extensively damaged. Convinced the

A gathering for the press at Yeovil in 1929 in front of the Westland IV prototype, G-EBXK, which has its Cirrus IIIs running, ready to take Sheikh Hafidh Wahba flying. Left to right: E M Benjamin; Louis Paget; Percival 'Percy' Waddams Petter, managing director of Westland; Sheikh Hafidh Wahba of Hejaz (which became part of Saudi Arabia in 1932); Ali Shukry Bey, T D Cree, R C Petter, Geoffrey Hill, R J Norton. *Westland*

Wizard had great potential, Westland approved its rebuild, with an all-metal fuselage and a Rolls-Royce F.XI – soon to be called the Kestrel – giving the fighter another 215hp. In this guise the Wizard had a top speed of 188mph, at least 30mph faster than the contemporary Gloster Grebe II. Despite the increase in performance, the Wizard remained a one-off, as did the next two fighter prototypes from Yeovil.

The purposely-named Interceptor was aimed at an Air Ministry requirement for a fast-point-defence fighter – which the Wizard would have admirably exceeded – but the Bristol Mercury radial was specified. Louis was not pleased with the Interceptor's flying characteristics, as he was vividly quoted in

British Aviation – The Adventuring Years by Harold Penrose*: "The little beast turns round and looks at you if one attempts a loop – it's a flying corkscrew!" An open cockpit monoplane fighter based on the Interceptor but with a longer fuselage was conceived for an Air Ministry attempt to create a 'bomber destroyer'. The miracle weapon of the day was the 37mm cannon developed by the Coventry Ordnance Works; hence it was referred to as the COW gun. The gun was mounted within the starboard side of the fuselage just in front of the cockpit, angled at 55 degrees upwards, so that it could fire its 1½lb shells into the belly of an enemy bomber. Neither of these types got beyond the prototype stage.

The radically redesigned and re-engined Wizard I fighter at Yeovil, 1928. *Westland*

The one-off Witch, 61ft-span parasol monoplane day bomber. *Peter Green Collection*

With a wingspan of 61ft the single-engined Witch day bomber was the first all-new design that Louis 'first flighted'. Sticking with the parasol layout, the machine also boasted an internal bomb bay. The Witch did not attract orders but it helped prepare the way for the Type IV trimotor, which was later named Wessex. With two crew, the type offered luxury travel for four or, with the baggage area removed, eight passengers as a 'feederliner'. Ten were built at a leisurely pace between 1928 and 1933.

Capitalising on the format of the successful Wapiti, but using all-metal construction, the private-venture PV.3 was intended as a two-seater for torpedo-attack. While it was well greeted at Martlesham Heath, the PV.3 matched no Air Ministry need but it was ideal for the Houston Mount Everest Flying Expedition of 1933 – this story is told in the section dealing with Harald Penrose.

Geoffrey Hill, the man who had helped Louis to take the post of CTP at Yeovil, had designed a new version of his tail-less Pterodactyl and it fell to Louis to take it aloft for the first time. Confusingly designated Mk.IA, while following the format, this was an entirely new design. As with the Witch, the Pterodactyl IA was taken by road to Andover, where the large, unrestricted flying field offered greater safety for the debut of large or radical prototypes than the built-up environs of Yeovil. During a sortie with Harald Penrose on board as observer, the geared control that activated the Pterodactyl IA's flaps slipped and Louis reacted quickly as J9251 plunged downwards, he pulled off a good landing but the monocycle main wheel collapsed. The machine was repaired and eventually given a tandem main undercarriage, among other modifications.

While the initial Hill-built Pterodactyl and the Mk.IA existed to prove the concept, Geoffrey Hill needed to move to practical applications. The first design to this end was the Mk.IV, a cabin three-seater with an aft baggage bay. Geoffrey dispensed with the wing-tip 'controllers', placing rudders at the ends of the wing and elevons acting as both ailerons and elevators, where conventional ailerons would be. Most radically, the Pterodactyl IV had a variable sweep wing, which

Complete with pterodactyl logo on the nose, the side-by-side Pterodactyl IA of 1928. *Peter Green Collection*

Head-on view of a Cirrus Hermes-engined Westland IV with its tail up on a trestle at Yeovil. Among the excrescences are fuel gauges mounted on the leading edge inboard of the wing engines, a large rear view mirror above the captain's position and a large wind-driven generator offset on the cabin roof. *Westland*

The F29/27 fighter at Martlesham, 1931. The barrel of the upward-firing 37mm COW gun can be seen above the cylinders of the Bristol Mercury. *KEC*

could be moved 4¾ degrees aft or forward to alter the centre of gravity depending on the number of occupants in the cabin. While Louis was getting accustomed to this exceptional machine he demonstrated Widgeon III G-EBRL to school children who were visiting the Yeovil factory on 2nd June 1931. While carrying out one of his characteristic low-level spins, Louis failed to pull out and he was seriously injured in the ensuing crash. It looked as though he would make a full recovery, but complications set in and it became clear that he would remain crippled. Harald Penrose took over, at first temporarily and then permanently. Louis George Paget AFC departed for a new life in the USA, but had died by the time that World War Two broke out.

The Pterodactyl IV had an enclosed cabin and wing tip-mounted rudders. *Westland*

Wilfred 'Parky' Parke

14 Mar 1912	Avro 500
	1 x 60hp ENV
1 May 1912	Avro Type F
	1 x 35hp Viale
7 Aug 1912	Avro Type G
	1 x 60hp Green

Notes: Type 500 and the 'F' first flown from Brooklands; the 'G' from Larkhill.

Wilfred Parke, born 1889. Joined the Royal Navy as a midshipman in September 1905 and was a Lieutenant by 1910. Learned to fly at the Avro school, Brooklands, with Howard Pixton as his instructor. He took his first 'hop' on 11th April 1911 and was awarded his Aviators' Certificate, No.73, on the 25th flying a borrowed 'Bristol'.

"To Inventors – Why break your aeroplane yourself, when we can do it for you?" So ran a classified advertisement in *Flight* magazine for 6th May 1911 for an outfit called Bois-Cassé Unlimited. It is unlikely that the man behind the advert, Lt Wilfred Parke – inevitably nicknamed 'Parky', was launching a career as a freelance test pilot. Bois-Cassé translates as 'broken wood' and many 'inventors' were doing just that with their creations. From his very first moment at the controls of an aeroplane, it was obvious that Parky was gifted and passionate – and very likely tongue-in-cheek – about aviation innovations.

At Brooklands, Avro was beginning to move from the creation of one-offs to machines with good prospects for production. By early 1912 the Avro chief pilot, Howard Pixton*, left for pastures new at Bristol and Parky took on the task of instructor and test pilot. In her exceptional *Testing Time*, Constance Babington Smith (CBS) explains his status and why the gifted aviator would especially appeal to Alliot Verdon Roe: "As a serving officer, Parke did not receive any

The Avro Type F at Brooklands, 1912.
Museum of Science and Industry – Manchester

fees for his test flying. He did it for the sheer love of the thing." CBS is strong in her praise of the young naval officer, declaring that Parky should be recognised along with: "Dunne and de Havilland and Busk, as one of the men who, all unawares, brought real test flying into being." In May 1912 Parky joined the Naval Wing at Eastchurch and was flying all week and in his spare time was to be found at Brooklands.

All three of the Avro types that Parky 'first flighted' were of great significance. The Type 500 was also known as the 'Military Biplane' and was aimed at the War Office's first-ever specification, issued in 1911. Nine days after the first flight, 23rd March 1912, Parky was happily taking the biplane to 'height', including an ascent with a passenger to 2,000ft in just 13 minutes – spritely performance for the time. Engine failure on 20th April resulted in substantial damage: Parky was slightly injured and his passenger – W H Sayers – had to be cut out of the wreckage. Rebuilt in double quick time, the Type 500 was ferried to Farnborough by Parky on 9th May for trials; an initial three were ordered and others followed. With the Type 500 Avro had perfected the format that was to lead to the superb Type 504.

On 1st May 1912 Parky made world history when he flew the Type F from Brooklands. This was the first ever aeroplane with a totally enclosed cockpit. On the 25th, a trip to Hendon got as far as Weybridge when the engine failed and the 'F' flipped over in the forced landing. The concept of the cabin stuck and the Type G was an enclosed tandem two-seater and the company's entrant in the Military Aeroplane Competition to be staged at Larkhill in August 1912. Parky flew the machine for the first time at Larkhill; there was not enough time to try it out in the well-known surroundings at Brooklands. Flying the endurance test on 7th August, Parky had to abandon the sortie after 30 minutes or so as the wind increased in severity. Returning to Larkhill he landed downwind and paid the penalty; the 'G' ended up on its back.

The Type G with the competition number '7' at Larkhill, 1912. *Avro*

Parky was flying the repaired 'G' on 25th August with Lt Le Breton as passenger. At about 700ft, Parky put the 'G' into a downward, gliding spiral to lose height. Down went the nose, the machine entered a spin and Parky was in trouble. Power on, he pulled the centred stick hard back and pushed the rudder *into* the direction of the spin – the spiral tightened its grip. The sheds at Larkhill were getting bigger and bigger, his time shorter and shorter and the altitude less and less – perhaps 70ft. He was more aware of the spin than the loss of height and the nose-down attitude so felt that the rotation was the most compelling crisis to be addressed. Rudder in the direction of the spiral had not worked; Parky tried *opposite* rudder at the last possible moment. The 'G' came out of the spin and Parky landed successfully.

This had all been witnessed by those on the ground that early morning. It was the first time that a pilot had succeeded in recovery from a spin *and* had others watch how he did it. By late 1912 Parky had flown in 29 different types and his observational skills were matched by his prose; he wrote up his air tests in *Flight* and a compilation of them was published under the title *Aviaticanda* – were both of these ventures 'firsts in Britain, if not worldwide? The spin of 25th August 1912 became known as 'Parke's Dive' and he wrote about it eloquently and forcibly, but it was a long time before the recovery mantra of rudder-stick-power was drilled into trainee pilots.

Parky had long had his eye on the Handley Page Type F crescent-winged monoplane. Like the Avro 'G' this machine had been damaged during the Larkhill trials when its 70hp Gnome rotary proved troublesome; it was damaged when HP pilot, Peter 'The Painter' Petre* force-landed it. After repairs, Parky air tested it on 9th November 1912 and thereafter frequently. With the HP work's manager, Arkell Hardwick, as passenger, Parky took off from Hendon in the HP 'F' on a trip to Oxford on 15th December 1912. The Gnome was far from on form, blue smoke trailing the monoplane. Over a wooded area near Wembley Parky was down to about 40ft and faced nothing but trees ahead. He turned around and, inevitably, the 'F' stalled and plunged into the wood. Arkell Hardwick was found in the wreck, dying; 23-year-old Lt Wilfred Park had died instantly – he was the first British naval officer to perish while aviating.

'Sailor' Parker

21 Jun 1951	Handley Page HP.88 VX330
	1 x 5,100lbst RR Nene 3

Gartrell Richard Ian Parker, born 1918. He joined the RAF in 1934, becoming a wireless operator/air gunner and his first frontline unit was 59 Squadron in 1937, on Hawker Hectors at Old Sarum. From 1938 he was with 3 Anti-Aircraft Co-operation Unit at Kalafrana, Malta, with detachments to Gibraltar. In 1940 he transferred to the Fleet Air Arm, initially with 830 Squadron at Hal Far, Malta, on Fairey Swordfishes and then with 800 Squadron's 'X' Flight, also at Hal Far, flying Fairey Fulmars. Back in Britain in late 1941, he was Gunnery Leader at 7 Air Gunners School at Stormy Down. Retraining as a pilot, mostly in Canada, Flt Lt Parker joined 219 Squadron RAF flying DH Mosquito XVIIs, initially from Bradwell Bay, before moving on to the Continent in October 1944. The unit started to change to Mosquito 30s from June 1944. During his time with 219 Squadron 'Sailor' – inevitable as former naval officer serving in the RAF – was credited with nine aerial victories: one Focke-Wulf Fw 190, three Junkers Ju 87s, one Ju 88, three Ju 188s and a Messerschmitt Bf 110 plus six V-1 'Doodlebugs'. Sailor left 219 Squadron in September 1945 and was posted to the RAE, becoming Flight Commander of the Radio Flight at Farnborough.

FLT LT GARTRELL 'SAILOR' PARKER DFC* DSM left the RAF in the spring of 1948 and worked for General Aircraft, testing DH Mosquito TT.39 conversions at Hanworth and continuing the work of the late Robert Kronfeld* with GAL.56 tail-less gliders at Lasham. In 1949 Blackburn and General Aircraft merged and Sailor moved to Brough, testing Beverley transports. As part of the Victor V-bomber programme Handley Page devised a test-bed for the crescent wing based on a Supermarine Type 510 fuselage and designated HP.88. The work was sub-contracted to Blackburn, as the YB.2, and the aircraft was roaded from Brough to Carnaby for testing. Sailor flew VX330 for the first time on 21st June 1951. The flight lasted just five minutes, the aircraft being very prone to porpoising. It took 17 flights to iron this out and the HP.88 was handed over to Handley Page. 'Duggie' Broomfield* was killed flying VX330 on 23rd August 1951. The HP.88 did little, if anything, to help the Victor, the prototype of which took to the air on 24th December 1952.

While competing in the National Air Races out of Baginton on 18th June 1954 in the Blackburn 'hack', Percival Proctor 5 G-AHWR ran out of fuel and Sailor had to force land. He was unhurt, but the Proctor was a write off.

Sailor joined the Buccaneer programme, becoming DCTP to CTP Derek Whitehead. The runway at Brough was far too small for the mighty Buccaneer and the big jets were roaded out to nearby Holme-on-Spalding Moor, which became the company test centre. On an autopilot trial sortie on 5th October 1960, Sailor was piloting the prototype Buccaneer, XK486, with D Nightingale as FTO. Near Holme the attitude indicator (or artificial horizon) started to malfunction – rotating violently – and the autopilot seemed to want to 'follow' its gyrations. Disorientated, Sailor decided it was best to abandon XK486 and

Using the fuselage of a Supermarine 510, the HP.88 was intended as a test-bed for the Victor V-bomber's crescent wing.
Blackburn and General Aircraft

the pair ejected safely. Standby artificial horizons became standard fit in Buccaneers after this incident. First flown on 12th February 1963 production S.1 XN952 was up again on the 19th with Sailor and Senior FTO Gordon R Copeman and among the tests being carried out was a LABS – low-altitude bombing system – manoeuvre over Holme. While rolling off the top XN952 went into an upright spin, stalled and impacted close to the control tower. Both Gordon Copeman and 45-year-old night-fighter 'ace' Flt Lt Gartrell Richard Ian Parker DFC* AFC DSM initiated ejection, but perished as the aircraft exploded.

John Lankester Parker

27 May 1918	Short Shirl N11** 1 x 385hp RR Eagle VIII
10 Dec 1919	Short Sporting Seaplane* G-EAPZ 1 x 160hp Beardmore
20 Aug 1920	Short Silver Streak** J6854 1 x 240hp Siddeley Puma
19 Apr 1921	Short Cromarty N120 2 x 600hp RR Condor I
19 Apr 1923	Short Springbok** J6974 1 x 400hp Bristol Jupiter IV
26 May 1923	Gnosspelius Gull** G-EBGN 1 x 16hp Blackburne
19 Sep 1924	Short Satellite** G-EBJU 1 x 32hp Bristol Cherub
7 Nov 1924	Short Cockle G-EBKA 2 x 16hp Blackburne Tomtit
5 Jan 1925	Short S.2 N177 2 x 375hp RR Eagle VIII17
6 Apr 1926	Short Mussel* G-EBMJ 1 x 60hp Cirrus I
17 Aug 1926	Short Singapore I N179 2 x 700hp RR Condor IIIA

14 Mar 1927	Short Chamois** J7295 1 x 400hp Bristol Jupiter IV
22 Jun 1927	Short Sturgeon* N199 1 x 550hp Bristol Jupiter VI
20 Feb 1928	Short Calcutta G-EBVG 3 x 550hp Bristol Jupiter IXF
16 Apr 1929	Short Gurnard II* N229 1 x 525hp RR Kestrel IIS
27 Mar 1930	Short Singapore II N246 2 x 525hp RR Kestrel IIMS tractor 2 x 515hp RR Kestrel IIIMS pusher
21 May 1930	Short Valetta G-AAJY 3 x 550hp Bristol Jupiter IXF
24 Sep 1930	Short Rangoon S1433 3 x 550hp Bristol Jupiter IXF
10 Oct 1930	Short -Kawanishi KF.1 M-2 3 x 825hp RR Buzzard IMS
24 Jan 1931	Short Kent G-ABFA 4 x 580hp Bristol Jupiter XFBM
30 Jun 1932	Short Sarafand S1589 6 x 825hp RR Buzzard IIIMS
18 Aug 1933	Short Scion G-ACJI 2 x 85hp Pobjoy R
30 Nov 1933	Short R24/31 K3574 2 x 660hp RR Goshawk VIII
26 Mar 1934	Short L.17** G-ACJJ 4 x 580hp Bristol Jupiter XFBM
25 Jun 1935	Pobjoy Pirate G-ADEY 1 x 85hp Pobjoy Niagara III
22 Oct 1935	Short Scion Senior* VT-AGU 2 x 85hp Pobjoy Niagara III
3 Jul 1936	Short Empire Boat G-ADHL 4 x 900hp Bristol Pegasus XC
27 Jul 1937	Short-Mayo S.21 G-ADHK 4 x 900hp Bristol Pegasus XC
5 Sep 1937	Short-Mayo S.20* G-ADHJ 4 x 365hp Napier-Halford Rapier VI
16 Oct 1937	Short Sunderland K4774 4 x 950hp Bristol Pegasus X
19 Sep 1938	Short S.31** M-4 4 x 90hp Pobjoy Niagara III
14 May 1939	Short Stirling** L7600 4 x 1,420hp Bristol Hercules X
21 Jul 1939	Short G-Class G-AFCI 4 x 1,380hp Bristol Hercules IV
14 Dec 1944	Short Shetland DX166 4 x 2,400hp Bristol Centaurus VII

Notes: All are flying-boats other than those marked * which were floatplanes at the time of first flight, or ** landplanes at the time of first flight. All had their maiden flights from the River Medway at Rochester, apart from: Shirl – Isle of Grain; Springbok – Martlesham Heath; Gull, Satellite and Chamois – Lympne; Scion – Gravesend; L.17, S.31 and Stirling – Rochester. Blackburne was a Surrey-based motorcycle engine manufacturer and not to be confused with the Brough-based aircraft and engine manufacturer, Blackburn. And through all that, did 'Lanky' miss a first flight? Yes, just one. 'Bert' Hinkler* at the insistence of the Air Ministry flew the Short-Bristow Crusader racing floatplane from Felixstowe on 4th May 1927.

John Lankester Parker, born 1886. He suffered from poliomyelitis – polio virus, or 'infantile paralysis' – as a child and spent a long time in a wheelchair. With funding from an uncle, John joined the Vickers school at Brooklands and was taught by Harold Barnwell on a Vickers Boxkite. He received Aviators' Certificate No.813 on 18th June 1914 just as his money was running out. Because of his medical history, John could not enlist so instead he became an unpaid instructor/mechanic at Hendon. Then came a crucial move, he headed to Windermere to learn to fly floatplanes*

John Lankester Parker, long-term flying-boat specialist. *Shorts*

Below: John Lankester Parker, in the forward hatch/gun position of the prototype Singapore I N179, about to catch the mooring rope. *Shorts*

with the Northern Aircraft Company (NAC), run by Rowland Ding*. John was taken on as an unpaid instructor but soon was on the payroll. In 1916 he began to teach Royal Navy personnel. It was at Windermere that John first met Cmdr Murray Sueter, the man who had set up the RNAS, and Shorts test pilot 'Ronnie' Kemp. Both were impressed by John's capabilities and Murray suggested that he go and see Horace Short to talk about testing at Eastchurch.

AGED 20, John Lankester Parker – known as 'Lanky' but here we'll refer to him as JLP – motorcycled his way to Eastchurch from Windermere. Cmdr Murray Sueter thought he was talented enough to help out Shorts pilot 'Ronnie' Kemp* who was close to being overwhelmed with the output of the factory. Kemp accepted him on a part-time basis on 17th October 1916, but the formidable Horace Short was not taken with the youngster. C H Barnes in *Shorts Aircraft since 1900* takes up the story: "At first Horace Short refused to allow 'that bit of a boy' to fly at all, but when in desperation Parker tendered his resignation, Horace pointed out six [Short] Bombers waiting to be tested and said, 'Go and break your bloody neck on those' then drove quickly away so as not to witness the ensuing disaster." That day JLP flew three of the 84ft span 250hp Rolls-Royce Eagle-powered biplanes and another three on the 18th – he had won over Horace!

By late December 1916 JLP had helped clear the back-log, but this was counter-productive in terms of earning a living. He signed up with the Prodger-Isaac Aviation Company in early 1917. This was a freelance test pilot agency, managed by Bernard Isaacs, founded by Clifford Prodger* principally to handle work for himself and Sydney Pickles*. Prodger-Isaac had a contract with the Phoenix Dynamo Company at Bradford. (Phoenix became part of English Electric in 1918.) JLP helped to test a batch of Phoenix-built Maurice Farman Longhorns from Killingholme: the last of these were signed off in April 1917. Beyond this Clifford Prodger took on Phoenix-built Short 184s. Another parcel of work that JLP picked up – probably via Prodger-Isaac – was testing Norman Thompson flying-boats at Middleton-on-Sea, near Bognor Regis. In January 1918 John was piloting one when the pusher propeller flew off the hub and so damaged the tail that the machine plunged into the Solent. JLP clung to the wreckage for eight hours before he was picked up by a minesweeper. (This *most likely* was the two-seat fighter flying-boat N.1B serial number N37 which had been rejected by the Isle of Grain and had been fitted with a 200hp Hispano-Suiza in an attempt to gain acceptance. It suffered an accident in January 1918 and was written off.)

While JLP was recovering from his ditching, Ronnie Kemp retired from Shorts and "that bit of a boy" took up a post that he would not relinquish until 1945, after an exceptional career. As with other test pilots with a barrage of types 'first flighted' to their credit, a blow-by-blow narrative will be avoided, with only the lesser known types receiving detailed treatment – the reader should not require chapter and verse on Sunderland and Stirling variants and development.

JLP's first maiden flight was the Shirl single-seat torpedo-attack biplane. While ferrying the prototype – complete with an inert Mk.VIII torpedo under the centre section – to AES

The first Sporting Seaplane, G-EAPZ, up on the step on the Medway, 1920. *Peter Green Collection*

The one-off Silver Streak, pioneering all-metal construction. *Short Brothers*

Martlesham Heath JLP proved his determination and skill. The petrol pump sheared en route, JLP carried out a forced landing and fixed the problem. Back in the air, he discovered that he had accidently displaced the throttle adjustment while working on the Rolls-Royce Eagle and he had only one power setting – flat out! JLP was not to be defeated, he realised that the engine would be damaged in level flight, but in a climb it would be fine. By the time he got to Martlesham JLP was at 12,000ft, he chopped the engine and glided down for a perfect power-off touchdown. A Shirl with a bigger wing, the S.538, was built to have a crack at the *Daily Mail* transatlantic challenge with a flight from Ireland to North America by Major J Wood. JLP tested the 'special', named *Shamrock*, on 8th April 1919. Ten days later, en route to Ireland, Wood had to ditch the *Shamrock* and the attempt was abandoned.

Oscar Gnosspelius, head of the Short experimental department, devised the Gull ultra-light in 1923. It was powered by a 697cc converted motorcycle engine mounted behind the pilot and driving a pair of pusher propellers. *Peter Green Collection*

The S.2 was a stepping stone to the all-metal big 'boats from Shorts. It was a hybrid of Felixstowe F.5 wings and tail feathers with a new, duralumin hull. *Peter Green Collection*

The next landplane 'first flighted' by JLP was of vital importance to the future of Shorts, and the British industry in general. Oswald Short was convinced that all-metal aircraft were the future and designed the private-venture Silver Streak to prove the point. The aluminium skin over the duralumin frame proved too flexible and was replaced by duralumin, but other than that the machine was well greeted by sceptical pilots at Martlesham. Air Ministry attitudes were changed by the Silver Streak and knowledge of all-metal construction at Shorts leapt forward. The endeavour of the Silver Streak was rewarded with a contract for an all-metal replacement for the Bristol F.2B

Fighter. This emerged as the Springbok: only five were ordered. One of these, the first Mk.II, J7295 was extensively reconfigured as the Chamois, again chasing the elusive F.2B requirement. This was followed by the shipborne floatplane Sturgeon and the Gurnard fleet fighter. None entered service.

The Sporting Seaplane of 1919 was exactly that, an attempt to break into the civil market for tuition or charter. Only three were built, but the concept lingered and in 1926 the Mussel appeared, a twin-float two-seater that was also tested by JLP as a landplane on 15th September 1926. Mussel G-EBMJ was 'adopted' by Eustace Short, the middle of the three brothers (Horace, Eustace and Oswald – Horace had died in 1917) and JLP taught him to fly, letting Eustace go solo on 19th October 1927. An improved version, the Mussell II, followed, later fitted with a central float for amphibious operation. Completing a solo flight on 8th April 1932, Eustace was observed making a good landing on the Medway, only for G-AAFZ to run on. When the boat crew caught up, Eustace was found dead in the cockpit: a heart attack had taken the 57-year-old.

Three ultralight types were tested by JLP. Shorts had established an experimental department with the 'hydroplane' pioneer Oscar Gnosspelius at its head. Oscar had built two monoplanes to his own design and flown them off Lake Windermere. He also designed a two-seat floatplane for the Lakes Flying Company, which went on to become the Northern Aircraft Company, where JLP had instructed during the Great War. Oscar designed an all-wood glider but he re-thought this as an ultralight, powered by an 18hp Blackburne, for the Light Aeroplane Trials of August 1923 at Lympne. He commissioned Shorts to build two examples for him. The single-seat, twin-engined Cockle originated as an order for a sporting aircraft for an Australian customer. The Satellite was entered by Shorts in the 1924 Light Aeroplane Trials, but like the Gulls of the year before, was unplaced.

The second Mussel of May 1929 had amphibious landing gear. As well as its registration, G-AAFZ, it carried its B Condition – 'trade-plate' – identity M-1 on the fin and rudder. *Short Brothers*

Below: The second Springbok II, J7295, was transformed into the Chamois army co-operation type, first flying in March 1927 in the new guise. *KEC*

It is with big flying-boats that JLP and Shorts were most associated from the 1920s to the late 1940s and his first taste came with the John Porte*-designed Felixstowe F.3 and F.5 that the company built at Rochester from 1918. The Imperial Japanese Navy was a customer and JLP was at Yokosuka in August in the summer of 1921 testing the first example and instructing aircrew. The relationship with Japan extended to the creation of the Short-Kawanishi KF.1 – a three-engined version of the Calcutta – for licence production. A much-improved F.5, the Cromarty, was flown in 1921. As Shorts gained more and more expertise in all-metal construction and the Air Ministry embraced the concept the S.2 acted as a half-way-house, a metal-hulled F.5 – hence its nickname, the 'Tin Five'.

The S.2 led to the successful Singapore family. The prototype Singapore, N179, had a very brief debut on 17th August 1926. JLP was accompanied by Eustace Short, George Cotton and A E Bibby. After two minutes a cowling detached from the port engine and the flight was curtailed. The Mk.II and Mk.III avoided the enormous span that would be required for a conventional four-engined layout by putting the Rolls-Royce Kestrels in a tandem, 'pull-push' arrangement. This format was taken to the extreme with the six-engined Sarafand of 1932. For the first flight of the Sarafand, Oswald Short was in the co-pilot's seat in case the forces on the control column were too much for JLP. It turned out the giant was well harmonised, indeed on only its fifth flight JLP carried out a spirited demonstration to the press of the 120ft span, 70,000lb all-up weight biplane. The Calcutta was a civilian development of the Singapore I and the military Rangoon was an enlarged Singapore. The Kent was adopted by Imperial Airways and it generated the pair of L.17s, *Scylla* and *Syrinx,* landplanes which had the wings and tail of the flying-boat, mated to a capacious fuselage.

With a wing span of 107ft, the Valetta tri-motor monoplane was the largest floatplane of the early 1930s; JLP lifting it off from the Medway on 21st May 1930. He flew in landplane configuration on 13th May 1932 from Croydon. The first large monoplane flying-boat from Shorts was the R24/31, K3574. The cranked wing and large steam condensers mounted above the Rolls-Royce Goshawks gave rise to the nickname 'Knuckleduster'. The debut of the R24/31 was another two-minute affair; with JLP were George Cotton and Howard 'Dinger' Bell. JLP felt that the fins and possibly the rear fuselage were flexing, so pulled the 'boat around for the briefest of circuits. The Knuckleduster needed much redesign before it was acceptable and the Goshawks proved to be very troublesome throughout.

With an all-up weight of about 18,500lb, JLP climbed to 15,000ft on 26th March 1934 and embarked on a dive to maximum design speed – 200mph – in the Knuckleduster. According to Harald Penrose* in *British Aviation – Widening Horizons*, this was the first time that a flying-boat had been put through such a test. Air Publication 970 – *Handbook of Strength Calculations: Design Requirements for Aeroplanes; Separation of Basic Requirements and Acceptable Practice* was first published in 1930. Through this and other 'APs', the Air Ministry was laying down strict parameters to meet, providing test pilots – and manufacturers – with a rigid procedure for testing and calibration. On 7th June 1934 the Knuckleduster underlined the folly of a company putting all its personnel 'eggs' in one 'basket'. With JLP were Oswald Short and the chief designer Arthur Gouge, four minutes in the starboard Goshawk ground to a halt and the sortie ended with a skilful high-speed down-wind touchdown. Had things gone badly, Shorts would have been stripped of its top talent in an instant.

Preparing the first Calcutta flying-boat, G-EBVG, outside the Rochester factory, February 1928. Moored to the left is the second Sturgeon, N200.
Short Brothers and Harland

Singapore III K4577 at MAEE Felixstowe in April 1935 for armament trials. The tandem engine layout is evident. *KEC*

Don Middleton's superb *Test Pilots* relates a story about JLP and the ironies of the job as told to him by Shorts CTP Tom Brooke-Smith* in the 1950s. Bless him, Don, or perhaps Tom, had mashed up two events well separated in time, but the conclusion is unaffected. On 1st August 1928 JLP flew the prototype Calcutta, G-EBVG to Westminster, alighting on the Thames and mooring opposite the Houses of Parliament. For the next four days it was open to inspection by the great and the good. JLP compared that trip with the maiden flight of the Knuckleduster: "It was a frightening experience; the machine would not climb so [I] staggered back to put it down on the Medway. On that trip I nearly killed myself for a paltry fee of £5, for the ...flight to the House of Commons I was given a gold cigarette case with my initials in diamonds!"

With a wing span of 107ft, the Valetta tri-motor was the largest floatplane of the early 1930s. 'Lanky' Parker flew this one-off both as a floatplane and landplane. *Peter Green Collection*

The twin-engined six-seater Scion and the four-engined ten-seat Scion Senior were devised to meet the smaller capacity market. Both used Douglas Pobjoy's lightweight Niagara engines and were available in landplane and floatplane versions. In 1936 Empire flying-boat production looked set to force the Scion line to close and Pobjoy was granted a licence to produce the two types from its own facility at Rochester. In the previous year, Pobjoy had entered the aircraft market with the Pirate three-seater. JLP was 'volunteered' to test it: G-ADEY remained a one-off. On 18th October 1939 JLP flew a test-bed version of the Scion Senior, L9786. This was to investigate the planing bottom for the Sunderland III and had a half-scale lower hull fitted to the lower fuselage, with stabilising floats under the wings.

Canopus, the first of the prestigious Empire flying-boats for Imperial Airways was flown off the Medway by JLP on 3rd July 1936, ushering in a brief glory period for long-range travel and providing the springboard for the Sunderland, a phenomenally successful maritime patroller and submarine killer. *Golden Hind*, the prototype for the G-class, with a deepened hull and other refinements, took to the air for the first time in July 1939, but the type's potential was overtaken by the outbreak of war.

The most spectacular element of the Empire Boats was the Short-Mayo Composite which attracted worldwide interest in 1938. Former Martlesham Heath test pilot Major Robert Mayo was in charge of technical development at Imperial Airways – he had brought about the Empire flying-boat specification. Mayo next turned to how the airline could look westwards: services to Africa, the Middle East, India and Australia were

Above: The prototype Rangoon, S1433, moored on the Medway, 1930. *Short Brothers and Harland*

Right: An airman perched on the bow provides scale to the six-engined Sarafand S1589. *KEC*

The prototype Scion, G-ACJI, a total off 22 of the six-seater type was built. *Shorts*

The cranked wing on the R24/31, K3574, and large steam condensers mounted above the Rolls-Royce Goshawks gave rise to the nickname 'Knuckleduster' for the one-off. *Peter Green Collection*

well established, but North America and the West Indies presented many challenges. Initially it was decided to pioneer transatlantic operations with a mail-only service. Sir Alan Cobham's* proposal for in-flight refuelling was given a lower priority than Mayo's own proposal for a flying-boat to take a smaller machine to height and launch it. This was not new; it was the *scale* of Mayo's proposal that was radical. For example, John Porte flew a Bristol Scout from a Porte Baby in May 1916 and Rollo Haig* did likewise with a DH Humming Bird from the airship R-33 in October 1925. Arthur Gouge and his team had to create an Empire Boat with a much greater wing area, modified rear fuselage and strengthened centre section and an entirely new four-engined floatplane capable of nearly 4,000 miles range and taking at least 1,000lb of mail. When the two aircraft were joined as a composite, the controls of the upper component were locked. As the moment came for release, the pilot of the 'mother' would disengage one of three hooks. Once this was done, he would inform his colleague perched above and a second hook would be released. A third hook was automatic, sensing a pre-set loading as the upper element got ready for independent flight. Separation procedure was for the mail-carrier to rise in level attitude, while the launch-ship dived away. There was an agonising number of seconds when neither pilot could see one another. JLP and his deputy, Harold 'Pip' Piper, had to learn to command the two elements separately, then as a unified entity and to perfect the separation process. The table outlines the step-by-step testing involved. The Short-Mayo Composite turned out to be a 'blip' in history, JLP taking part in *one* of the reasons why the experiment came to nought. Over Southampton Water on 24th May 1939 Geoffrey Tyson* flew Handley Page Harrow tanker G-AFRL and successfully hooked-up with JLP piloting Empire Boat *Cabot* G-AFCU. This proved that Imperial's flying-boats could be topped up en route without the need for mother-ships and the cumbersome infrastructure they required. Chapter Three covers the story of in-flight refuelling in more detail.

The first Empire Boat, G-ADHL *Canopus*, moored on the Medway, as L.17 G-ACJJ *Scylla* flies overhead, in 1936. *Short Brothers and Harland*

One of John Lankester Parker's 'offices', the flight deck of an Empire Boat. *Shorts*

The prototype Sunderland, K4774, at the top of the Rochester slipway, 1937. *Shorts*

Togetherness and Separation – Testing the Short-Mayo Composite

27 Jul 1937	First flight of the S.21 G-ADHK *Maia,* by JLP
10 Aug 1937	First flight of *Maia* with the attachment gantry on the centre section
5 Sep 1937	Fight flight of the S.20 G-ADHJ *Mercury*, by JLP
1 Jan 1938	Both aircraft as composite, first taxi trials. JLP in *Maia*, Harold Piper in *Mercury*; this combination of pilots remained constant until the hand-over to MAEE
20 Jan 1938	First flight as composite – basic weights, no separation
5 Feb 1938	Second flight as composite – basic weights, no separation
6 Feb 1938	First separation
23 Feb 1938	Second separation, with film crews in chase aircraft. Captain Arthur Wilcockson* of Imperial Airways as co-pilot to JLP
4 Mar 1938	Full-load tests as composite
17 Mar 1938	Ferry flights to MAEE Felixstowe – separately
6 May 1938	Full-load tests as composite
9 May 1938	Full-load separation by MAEE Sqn Ldrs L G 'Pincher' Martin and Flt Lt Pickles – first time with no Shorts crew in command
Jun 1938	Handed over to Imperial Airways
21 Jul 1938	First commercial separation and service, operating out of Foynes, Ireland to Boucherville, Montreal, Canada. Don Bennett flew *Mercury* to Montreal, Arthur Wilcockson piloted *Maia*.
12 Jan 1939	Last flight as composite

The complex task of lowering *Mercury* on to *Maia*. This labour-intensive and time-consuming process was one of the many reasons that doomed the Short-Mayo Composite to become a one-off. *via Dean Wright*

A pair of Miles Falcon Sixes, G-AEDL (left) and G-AFAY (right) escorting the Short-Mayo Composite during the first flight in 'piggy-back' guise in 1938. 'Lanky' Parker flying the S.21 G-ADHK, *Maia*, with 'Pip' Piper in the S.20 G-ADHJ *Mercury. via Dean Wright*

From the Empire Boats, the Sunderland was a logical step and JLP took the prototype, K4774, on its maiden voyage on 16th October 1937. Sunderlands were to dominate JLP's time through to the end of World War Two. As well as day-to-day testing from the Medway, JLP needed to liaise with the new factory at Sydenham, Northern Ireland, and the Blackburn-managed Dumbarton, Scotland, production line. There was also a need to return to the place where JLP honed his 'waterplane' techniques – Windermere. Shorts established a small factory and overhaul facility on the lake and in September 1942 JLP tested the first Windermere-built Sunderland, Mk.III DP176. Inaugural flights from Windermere did not end back at the lake, unless there was a problem, to keep disturbance to the area to a minimum. JLP took DP176 down to south-west Wales, landing at Pembroke Dock. JLP's final 'first' was the Shetland, DX166, at the time the largest British flying-boat and intended as a Sunderland replacement, but the programme was shelved with only two built. Along with JLP on the flight deck of DX166 was Geoffrey Tyson, who eight years later capitalised on the experience by captaining the largest-ever British 'boat, the Princess.

Through designer Arthur Gouge, Shorts had become past-masters at taking elements of one aircraft to help create another – the Kent flying-boat morphing into the L.17 airliner being an example. The wing of the Empire Boats was used on what became the Stirling, Britain's first heavy bomber. It was felt that a scale version would help as a pathfinder for the full-size version and JLP flew the S.31 on in September 1938. With JLP for the first flight of the prototype Stirling, L7600, were Sqn Ldr Eric Moreton, on loan from the RAF, as co-pilot and George Cotton acting as FTO and 'wheel-winder' should the electrical system fail and the massive, stalky undercarriage needed to be brought up – or down – manually. The 20-minute debut on 14th May 1939 went well, the Stirling had good characteristics. Harald Penrose in *British Aviation – Ominous Skies* eloquently explained why JLP "found no difficulty, for in effect this bomber was an Empire Boat on wheels". As L7600 touched down at Rochester the big machine spun around, the undercarriage crumpled and collapsed. Nobody was hurt and it was discovered that a brake had seized. It was 21st November 1939 before the second prototype, L7605, was ready and JLP took his time testing the bomber through increasingly faster taxis and 'straights'. It was 3rd December before he ventured skywards in it.

JLP was appointed Director of Flight Operations in 1943 and retired from testing in 1945, handing over to Geoffrey Tyson. John Lankester Parker OBE remained as a much-loved and respected member of the Shorts board into the 1950s, having contributed so much to the history of the oldest aircraft manufacturer in the world. He died on 22nd August 1965, aged 79. In the words of Constance Babington Smith he was: "Britain's greatest tester of flying-boats".

Rare image of the S.31 half-scale Stirling in flight during 1939 with the B Condition marking 'M-4' on the fin and rudder. *Peter Green Collection*

Marked up with black and white 'Invasion Stripes' airborne forces Stirlings on the eve of D-Day ready to tow assault gliders and drop supplies in Normandy. June 1945. *KEC*

Above: Golden Hind, G-AFCI, the first of the G-Class 'boats, at rest on the Medway, 1939. *Shorts*

Left: Under spoken, but striking, Shorts Brothers advert of 1939.

Below: John Parker's last new type, Shetland I DX166 moored on the Medway, spring 1945. *KEC*

H J Payn

Sep 1924	Vickers Vagabond G-EBJF
	1 x 32hp Bristol Cherub

H J Payn was commissioned into the Royal Engineers by 1915, transferring to the RFC in 1916. By February 1917 he was serving on the Western Front with 29 Squadron, flying Airco DH.2s alongside James McCudden. On 23rd February 1916, Major Payn – nicknamed 'Agony' – was involved in a dogfight and was on the receiving end of the guns of an Albatros piloted by Werner Voss: Payn escaped with damage to his DH.2. Sqn Ldr H J Payn AFC left the RAF in 1923 and joined the staff of Vickers at Brooklands.

WITH an excellent background in engineering, H J 'Agony' Payn was appointed as technical assistant to Vickers chief designer Rex Pierson at Brooklands. He was also involved in flight testing, initially alongside 'Tommy' Broome* and, from 1924, with CTP 'Tiny' Scholefield* whenever required. At Brooklands in September 1924 H J Payn is *very likely* to have 'first flighted' the Vickers entry for that year's Light Aeroplane Trials – he certainly flew it at Lympne. The Vagabond, a two-seater biplane, was unplaced.

When Vickers bought Supermarine in 1928, H J Payn was seconded to Woolston and by 1930 was an executive with the company, acting as Reginald Joseph Mitchell's technical assistant. 'Agony' kept his hand in on testing, flying Seagull and Walrus amphibians in 1935, for example. When 'RJ' died in June 1937, Rex Pierson was given overall charge of the design offices at both Brooklands and Woolston and H J Payn was appointed as Manager of the Design Department of Supermarine, the latter perhaps only as an interim position. In the exceptional *Spitfire – A Test Pilot's Story*, Jeffrey Quill describes a disturbing facet of Britain's increasing worry about security, particularly on a vital programme such as the Spitfire. "Payn came under investigation by the security services as a result of a divorce and re-marriage to a lady of foreign origin. The immediate and direct result was that the Air Ministry withdrew their approval for Payn to hold his position of high responsibility in an area where security was obviously of the utmost importance. McLean [Sir Robert McLean chairman of Vickers (Aviation) Ltd] dismissed him..." Jeffrey added that: "Payn became unemployable in the industry and had a very hard time during the ensuing years."

'Bill' Pegg

4 Sep 1949	Bristol Brabazon I G-AGPW
	8 x 2,500hp coupled Bristol Centaurus XX
16 Aug 1952	Bristol Britannia 101 G-ALBO
	4 x 2,800shp Bristol Proteus 625

Arthur John Pegg, born 1906. Joined the RAF as a Boy Apprentice at 15½, becoming a fitter. In 1925 he was accepted for pilot training, going on to fly Sopwith Snipes with 43 Squadron at Henlow, followed by instructing at 5 FTS Sealand and at CFS. By 1933 Bill had been posted to A&AEE

'Bill' Pegg and Brabazon designer 'Archie' Russell in an informal moment during flight testing, October 1949. *Bristol Aeroplane Co*

at Martlesham Heath. On 21st March 1933 he was flying A&AEE Avro Tutor K3191 when its wings broke up during a dive; he baled out successfully.

CAPACITY for 100 passengers in spacious, luxurious surroundings, a dozen crew, range well beyond 5,000 miles, eight coupled engines driving contra-rotating propellers providing a cruise of 250mph, 290,000lb all-up weight, length 177ft and span of 230ft. All this added up to the largest and most complex commercial aircraft ever built – anywhere – at the time. How many more challenges would you expect for a first-ever maiden flight from a test pilot? That was what faced A J Pegg – 'Bill' to his colleagues – on 4th September 1949 as he lined up the prototype Bristol Brabazon at Filton. Then there's economics and politics to stir into the mix. Other than Air Ministry blessing for the prototype and a second, Bristol Proteus turboprop-powered, example sanctioned, not a whiff of an order. The new airliner was not given a powerful, international name, instead it honoured Lord Brabazon of Tara's committee that decreed in February 1943 what civil aircraft would need to be built after the war was won – classic British 'branding'! The preferred construction site, Weston-super-Mare, was ruled out as a heavy load-bearing long runway was impossible given the make up of the sub-soil. So the runway at Filton needed extension,

Unusual aspect of the Brabazon. *Bristol Aeroplane Co*

necessitating the almost total demolition of the village of Charlton and a bypass to cater for existing main roads. A massive new assembly hall, with a 'footprint' of 8 acres, was created. When Bill put the throttles forward that Sunday the whole project was estimated to have cost between £12 and £15 million (£360 to £450 million in present-day values) – an eye-watering financial commitment in a country still suffering food and fuel rationing. Inevitably the axe fell and only the prototype – undeniably an incredible technical achievement – flew, clocking up around 400 hours.

Most remembered for his captaining of the Brabazon, Fg Off A J Pegg joined Bristol at Filton in November 1935, under CTP Cyril Uwins. Duties in those days were not restricted to production and prototype testing; Cyril was also chief instructor with the Bristol Flying School and Bill's background as an instructor *and* A&AEE made him very well suited. There was plenty of work to come: Blenheims, Beauforts, Beaufighters, the Brigand 'family' and the Type 170 Freighters. Very early in the Beaufighter programme, Bill suffered an engine failure on take-off from Filton – *probably* in Mk.I R2064. A circuit would put him over houses and factories, jeopardising more necks than just his. Bill put it down immediately on the adjacent golf course and walked away from it; he had disturbed a game and written off the 'Beau' but the consequences could have been disastrous. Cyril Uwins retired in 1947 and Bill took his place as CTP.

Preparations for the Brabazon were extensive and included trying out a USAF Convair B-36 Peacemaker. Powered by six 3,500hp pusher piston engines, the bomber was more unconventional than the Brabazon, but in terms of size – same wing span, similar cruise, greater all-up weight – it was a good introduction to a very large machine. Rolled out in December 1948, Brabazon I G-AGPW soon started ground running and taxi trials but it was 4th September 1949 before Bill and his flight crew were ready for the maiden voyage. As well as Bill and his deputy, 'Wally' Gibb*, on board were Chief Flight Engineer L D Atkinson; Flight Engineers A Cowan and H J Hayman; Electrical Engineer Ken Fitzgerald; Chief FTO M J Penison; FTOs J M Cochrane, J Sizer and M W West. Flight testing was largely uneventful, the only major incident happening on the 13th sortie – and Wally's first as captain – in January 1950 when a hydraulic failure required a flapless landing, but the reverse pitch propellers easily prevented an over-run. Bill and Wally – the only pilots to fly G-AGPW – demonstrated the Brabazon at Heathrow Airport in June 1950 and at the SBAC Farnborough airshows in 1950 and 1951. The prototype and the unfinished second example were scrapped in 1953.

Prospects for the next Bristol airliner, the Britannia, were far better although engine problems dominated the flight testing. As well as Bill, crew on G-ALBO for the 30-minute

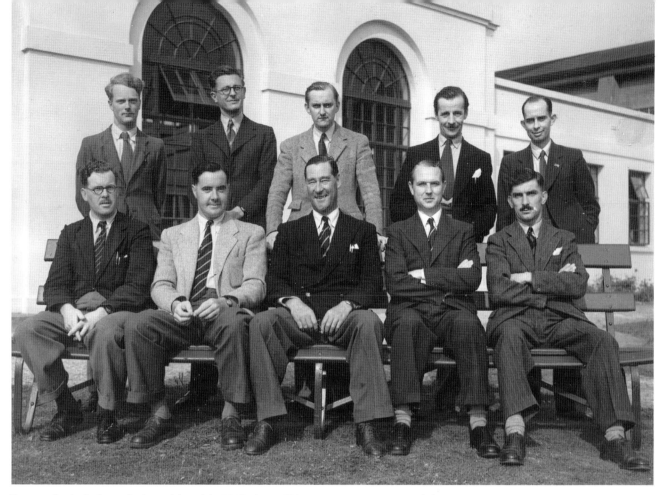

Test crew for the Brabazon. Back row, left to right: J M Cochrane, FTO; M W West, FTO; A Cowan, Flight Engineer; J Sizer, FTO; K A Fitzgerald, Electrical Engineer. Front row, left to right: L D Atkinson, Chief Flight Engineer; 'Wally' Gibb, co-pilot; 'Bill' Pegg, pilot; M J Penison, Chief FTO; H J Hayman, Flight Engineer. *Bristol Aeroplane Co*

debut on 16th August 1952 was: FTEs L D Atkinson and Charles Harding, Electrical Engineer Ken Fitzgerald, Chief FTO M W West; FTO G Taylor. Atkinson, Fitzgerald and West all experiencing déjà vu from three years before; interestingly there was no co-pilot.

Bill's forced landing technique was required one more time. On 4th February 1954 he was piloting the second prototype Britannia G-ALRX – which he had 'first flighted' 53 days and 51 flying hours previously. There were eleven others on board: FTEs Ken Fitzgerald and Gareth Jones and

alongside Bill was Captain D Malouin from Dutch national airline KLM with other worthies from its management in the cabin. Keeping them company was Dr Archibald Russell, chief designer, Dr Stanley Hooker, chief engineer of the Bristol engine division, and Mr Farnes, senior sales manager – no pressure there, then! The reduction gear on the starboard inner Proteus failed and the turboprop disintegrated, starting a severe fire. Sanctuary at Filton was impossible – the rationale that Bill adopted in the Beaufighter in September 1940 still applied. The tide was low in the Severn Estuary and Bill shut

Brabazon G-AGPW inside the hangar that was built for it at Filton, providing scale for both the airliner and the building. *Bristol Aeroplane Co*

Britannia prototype G-ALBO in 1953. *Bristol Aeroplane Co*

down the starboard outer and was committed to a forced landing. James Hamilton-Paterson, in his superb *Empire of the Clouds – When Britain's Aircraft Ruled the World* describes what followed: "Shouting to everyone to brace, Pegg brought the aircraft with flames and thick black smoke trailing from its starboard wing down on its belly in the glistening mud to a flawless crash landing. G-ALRX slid 400 yards with uncanny smoothness until the last moment when it turned abruptly right towards the sea and stopped. With yet another stroke of luck the mud seemed to have put the fire out and the entire party was able to scramble out uninjured before wading through the silt to safety. It was a tribute not only to first-rate piloting but to an immensely strong airframe." So robust was that airframe

that the cockpit still exists, awaiting the opening of the Bristol Aerospace Centre at Filton in 2017, which will celebrate the aeronautical achievements of the region. In all, 85 Britannias were built; oddly KLM never took delivery of one!

At the time of his flying *Bravo-Oscar*, the prototype Britannia, Bill had clocked over 5,000 hours on about 150 types. On 1st January 1957 he handed over to Wally Gibb and took up the post of general service manager of the Weston-super-Mare division. Bill's autobiography, *Sent Flying*, published by Macdonald, is a great read, which probably explains why copies are as rare as hen's teeth! Arthur John Pegg OBE died in 1978, aged 72.

Britannia second prototype G-ALRX down on the mudflats of the Severn Estuary after the forced landing of 4th February 1954, with an Auster making a low run past. *Bristol Aeroplane Co*

'Russ' Pengelly

Russell Pengelly born 1945. Joined the RAF in 1962, going on to fly EE Lightning F.6s with 23 Squadron at Leuchars from 1968. From 1970 he piloted the Lightning F.1As of the Wattisham Target Facilities Flight and became the RAF solo Lightning display pilot – creating some of the most sizzling routines. In 1973 he graduated from ETPS Course No.23 at Boscombe Down and this was followed by a posting 'across the ramp' to A&AEE.

'Russ' Pengelly joined BAC at Warton in June 1977, initially on his beloved Lightning, but by the end of the year he was Tornado Project Pilot and BAC had become BAe. As well as considerable experimental and production flying, Russ went on to perfect stunning display routines in the Tornado. During a weapons release sortie on 12th June 1979 Flt Lt Russell Pengelly AFC and A&AEE navigator Sqn Ldr John Gray were killed when Tornado P.08, XX950, crashed into the North Sea. This was the first loss of a Tornado.

Craig Penrice

Craig Penrice, born 1959. Joined the RAF via the University of Glasgow and Strathclyde Air Squadron, training on SAL Bulldogs from 1977. By July 1983 Flt Lt Penrice was flying EE Lightning F.3s and F.6s with 11 Squadron from Binbrook. On 19th September 1985 in F.6 XS921 Craig encountered severe control restrictions and the Lightning entered a high speed dive. He ejected while XS921 dropped into the North Sea off Flamborough Head. Craig had injured a leg and was suffering hypothermia when he was picked up by a 202 Squadron Sea King HAR.3 from Leconfield and he spent a year recovering. After a posting to the Tactical Weapons Unit at Chivenor on HS Hawks, Craig was sent on an exchange to Tyndall Air Force Base, Florida, flying McDonnel Douglas F-15A Eagles, 1990-1993. He was back in the USA in 1994, attending the US Navy Test Pilots' School at Patuxent River, Maryland, graduating the following year. Upon return to the UK he served from Boscombe Down, becoming RAF Typhoon Project Pilot.

Craig Penrice joined the BAe (BAE Systems from 1999) test team at Warton on 1st May 1998 and took a major role in development of the Typhoon. On 9th April 2002 while piloting Typhoon DA.4, ZH590, with weapons systems operator Stan Ralph, the pair carried out the first fully-guided live firing of a Raytheon AIM-120 AMRAAM missile against a SELIX Galileo Mirach target drone. As well as his 'day job' Craig flew for the Exeter-based Hunter Flying Club and on 1st June 2003 he was flying Peter Hellier's Chivenor Memorial Flight's Hawker Hunter F.6A XF516 (G-BVVC) out of Squires Gate, Blackpool, to perform at an airshow in Northern Ireland before returning to base at Exeter. En route, *Victor-Charlie* suffered a major electrical failure and then its Rolls-Royce Avon 207 flamed out and could not be re-lit. Hoping to make a power-off arrival at Llanbedr on the North Wales coast, it became clear that this was not possible and for the second time he summoned up a 'Martin-Baker moment'. *Victor-Charlie*

impacted into marshland on the Dyfi Estuary, near Borth. Craig came down in shallow water not far away and was again lifted away by a SAR Sea King. He had broken his back and another long period of recuperation followed. Craig's days of fast jet flying were over, his spine could not take another 'bang out'. In 2004 he took up a post with the Joint Strike Fighter project office at Fort Worth, Texas, and then his current role of Aircrew Adviser – Business Development with BAE Systems. For quite some time it looked as though the 4,142 hours he had accrued, including around 500 on Typhoons, was indeed a total, but in 2012 he resumed flying in light aircraft.

Harald Penrose

31 Oct 1932	Westland PV.6 P6 1 x 655hp Bristol Pegasus IV
30 Oct 1933	Westland PV.7 P7 1 x 722hp Bristol Pegasus IIIM3
23 Mar 1934	Westland F7/30 K2891 1 x 600hp RR Goshawk IIS
24 Jul 1934	Westland-Hill Pterodactyl V P8 1 x 600hp RR Goshawk I
15 Jun 1935	Westland Lysander K6127 1 x 890hp Bristol Mercury XII
Aug 1935	Penrose Pegasus glider
11 Oct 1938	Westland Whirlwind L6844 2 x 885hp RR Peregrine I
27 Jul 1941	Westland Lysander P.12 K6127 1 x 890hp Bristol Mercury XII
1 Nov 1942	Westland Welkin DG558 2 x 1,560hp RR Merlin 61
16 Dec 1946	Westland Wyvern TS371 1 x 2,690hp RR Eagle 22
18 Jan 1949	Westland Wyvern VP120 1 x 4,000shp RR Clyde

Harald Penrose in one of his many 'offices' – a Lysander. *Peter Green Collection*

Notes: PV.6, PV.7, Lysander P.12 and Welkin first flew from Yeovil; F7/30 and Pterodactyl from Andover; Pegasus *probably* from Kimmeridge; all others from Boscombe Down.

Harald John Penrose, born 1904. Inspired by the crossing of the Channel by Louis Blériot in 1909 he became an avid modeller and aviation enthusiast. In 1919 he had a 'joy-ride' in an Avro 504J, flown by none other than Alan Cobham*, and determined to have a career as a pilot. At the end of a four-year course in aeronautics at Northampton Engineering College, he had work experience as a wind tunnel assistant at Handley Page, Cricklewood, and then at Westland, Yeovil. By June 1925 Westland CTP Laurence Openshaw* had 'adopted' Harald as an FTO. With another student, Harold began to build a biplane hang-glider at Yeovil, but this does not seem to have flown. Harald took up a full-time post at Westland in September 1926, initially on general workshop duties and, from early 1927, overseeing construction of the prototype Widgeon III, G-EBPW. Openshaw took G-EBPW for its first flight in March and invited Harald on board for the second sortie. In the spring of 1927 Harald became an assistant to Geoffrey Hill*, who was developing tail-less designs for the company and acted as FTO to the new CTP, Louis Paget. Under the Reserve of Air Force Officers scheme he learned to fly at Filton – the school was managed by Cyril Uwins* – from June 1927 and Harald went on to gain a commercial pilot's licence.

AUTHOR, biographer, historian, philosopher, skilled sailor, naval architect (scheming 36 yachts and boats), architect (creating his house at Nether Compton near Sherborne), built and test flew his own sailplane (the Pegasus), RAF reservist, FTO, aircraft engineer and designer, demonstration pilot, sales executive... oh yes, and Westland CTP for 23 years! So, we turn to the doyen of the doyens – the test pilot so often mentioned by others of his profession as *the* character they admire and probably *the* one who has been most read by his colleagues: Harald John Penrose – 'Hal' to colleagues, 'Mr Pen' to the Yeovil workforce.

In March 1928 Harald was appointed as assistant test pilot to Louis Paget*, Westland CTP and by the summer he was promoted, becoming manager of the civil aircraft division. Harald embarked on a demonstration tour to Argentina with Wapiti V G-AAWA being shipped out in January 1931; it was to be shown off in both landplane and floatplane guises. Louis Paget narrowly escaped death in a Widgeon at Yeovil on 2nd June 1931 and as the extent of his injuries became clear, Harald was offered the post of CTP.

Harald's first 'first' was the much modified Argentina demonstrator. It had been rebuilt as a private-venture to replace the Westland cash-cow, the Wapiti, and became the Wallace. This machine, designated PV.6, was given its maiden flight by Harald on the last day of October 1932. During late 1932 the PV.6 and another Westland biplane, PV.3 G-ACAZ, were adapted for extreme high-altitude flying, having been selected for use by the Houston Mount Everest Flying Expedition, which was sponsored by Lady 'Poppy' Houston. With an electrically-heated flying suit, Harald took G-ACAZ up for an acceptance flight. In his book *Adventure with Fate*, Harald explained the nature of the sortie and demonstrated his mastery of prose: "The altimeter paused, moved, hesitated, while height changed from 35,000ft to 36,000ft and then to 37,000ft. The thermometer was showing a stupendous minus 65 degrees. Here at last, where the temperature fell no more, was the edge of the stratosphere and the threshold of the mysteries of space of which astronomer, poet and scientist had so long dreamed." While testing the PV.6, re-registered as G-ACBR, there was drama at 37,500ft when the solitary fuel pump failed (the back-up having been removed, with other items, to save weight): "Within moments the pulse of life that vibrated through the machine became uncertain. ...Ten seconds later the power faded and vanished and the propeller became stationary, a mere carved block of wood." Harald made a silent descent to an uneventful touch down at Hamble, describing the venture as: "the world's longest emergency glide of those days". On 3rd April 1933 Lt David McIntyre and Air Cdr Lord Clydesdale successfully flew the PV.3 and PV.6 over Everest.

The Westland PV.3 caught on camera through the bracing wires of PV.6 Wallace G-ACBR as the two near the summit of Everest, 3rd April 1933. *Westland Group*

The PV.6 at Yeovil in late 1931. *Westland Aircraft Works*

Testing the PV.3 and PV.6 at stratospheric heights gave Westland and Harald unprecedented experience in high-altitude flight. This was put to good use on 11th May 1934 when he took Wapiti I J9102 to 27,453ft to establish a world record for a diesel-powered aircraft. J9102 had been adapted as a test-bed for the 485hp Bristol Phoenix II – an attempt to introduce diesels into British aviation. This achievement appears to be unbeaten by a *manned* aircraft; although several diesel-powered unmanned devices have gone much, much higher.

While the PV.6 was an extrapolation of the well-proven Wapiti format, Harald's second maiden flight was of a wholly-new design. The PV.7 monoplane was aimed at an overly-ambitious Air Ministry requirement for a catch-all capable of light bombing, general reconnaissance, army co-operation and even casualty evacuation. With the leading edge almost in line with Harald's shoulders, he had a commanding view of the wings twisting when the ailerons were employed at speed. Designer Arthur Davenport was doubtful of Harald's claims but agreed to go up and see for himself from the gunner's position. Putting the PV.7 into a slight dive, Harald heard the designer begging him to put the prototype back down on the ground so it could be modified before it fell apart!

Having delivered the PV.7 to A&AEE at Boscombe Down, Harald was asked to carry out a test with the aircraft fully loaded and the centre of gravity well aft on 25th August 1934. With a borrowed parachute Harald got airborne but, as he did so, a telegram was received from Yeovil forbidding the test as it was beyond the airframe's parameters. Radios were a rarity in 1934 and certainly they were not applied to private-venture prototypes, so recalling Harald was not possible. In a dive the port wing broke off, Harald found that the enclosed canopy was jammed but thankfully he forced a side glazing panel and made an exit. This was the first bale out from a British enclosed cockpit military aeroplane. The PV.7 project was not revived.

Earlier in 1934 Harald had flown an advanced biplane interceptor prototype powered by a problematical steam-cooled Rolls-Royce Goshawk mounted within the fuselage, driving the propeller through an extension shaft. The Westland F7/30 was doomed to being a one-off. Harald had another first flight during 1934, the most radical of his career – the tail-less Pterodactyl V. Also Goshawk-powered, it was a fighter, with fixed machine-guns firing through the propeller disc and a turret in the rear of the pod-like fuselage. The machine had been through a long gestation, but by May 1934 it was ready for taxi trials and 'straights'. On the second run the port wing failed and collapsed – worrying enough on the ground, most likely fatal at any stage of flight. Two months of strengthening followed and the maiden flight, on 24th July, was relatively uneventful. Like the F7/30, this was staged from the wider and safer boundaries of Andover. The Mk.V was constantly modified, but was destined to be the last of Geoffrey Hill's* tail-less Pterodactyls to leave the drawing board.

The F7/30 with an enclosed cockpit. The exhaust stubs show the location of the Goshawk engine. *Westland Aircraft Works*

The incredible Pterodactyl V, the last of Geoffrey Hill's tail-less designs to be built. *Peter Green Collection*

During the summer of 1935 Harald was elevated to the status of designer-pilot when he flew the diminutive Pegasus single-seat sailplane. Designed and built by Harald over a three-year period, the all wood Pegasus had a span of 34ft 4in – its dimensions were kept moderate so that sub-assemblies could fit in a workshop at his house. Sadly, the original did not survive beyond the late 1940s but a replica Pegasus is on show at the Norfolk and Suffolk Aviation Museum at Flixton.

The most famous of Westland's wartime products, the Lysander, was 'first flighted' by Harald from Boscombe Down, three years before the airfield became the busy home

of A&AEE. The Lysander was the first design by 27-year-old 'Teddy' Petter, son of Westland co-founder Sir Ernest Petter. While it showed exceptional promise, Harald was unhappy with instability issues, particularly during an overshoot when the aircraft could rear upwards alarmingly with a stall very likely and no 'room' for recovery. With Britain re-arming rapidly and a large production order placed, finessing the design was overlooked. Harald flew the first production Lysander, L4673, on 25th March 1938 and to help with output, George Snarey* was appointed as deputy TP by the end of the year. Harald was engaged on several trial versions, the most extreme being the P.12. This was a tandem-winged reconstruction of the prototype, K6127, with a four-gun turret at the ear of the fuselage. Despite its dramatic change of layout, Harald found that the P.12 flew remarkably well, so much so that he looped it on its maiden flight.

Teddy Petter's second design was the exceptional-looking, but high-risk and complex Whirlwind twin-engined, single-seat fighter. In *Adventure with Fate* Harald highlighted the yawning gap between the practicality of the pilot and the designer's adherence to aerodynamic purity: "...I had emphatically disagreed with Petter's perilous decision to run the exhaust pipes *through* the petrol tanks in the wing to avoid parasitic resistance. ...I stressed that this was a *fighting* machine and one bullet through the tank and exhaust would set the whole thing on fire, for [Petter] coldly told me: 'You

Lysander II R2007 of 225 Squadron with its message hook down ready to engage the 'trap'. *KEC*

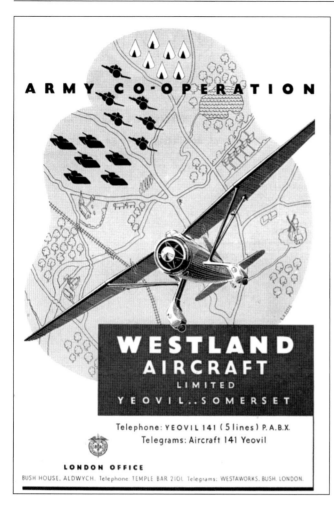

Above: Harald Penrose in the second prototype Whirlwind, L6845. *Rolls-Royce*

Left: Lysander advert from 1936.

pilots have to accept a *few* risks you know.'" (Author's italics.) The 20-minute first flight from Boscombe Down was one of mixed feelings for Harald; there were control issues but the slate-grey L6844 seemed to offer great potential. The Rolls-Royce Peregrines, driving opposite rotating propellers, added to the problems that needed shaking down. It was December 1940 before the Whirlwind entered operational service and by then orders had been slashed to just 112 examples.

The future at Westland, for the time being, lay with building other concern's designs. Yeovil went on to champion production of Supermarine Spitfires and especially Seafires, as well as Fairey Barracudas. The next in-house project was what Harald described as "the world's biggest single-seater", the Welkin high-altitude interceptor. Featuring automated cockpit pressurisation and other sophisticated systems, the Welkin was a challenging project. Harald took the 70ft span prototype for a ten-minute maiden flight on 1st November 1942. Interestingly, this was at Yeovil and not from Andover or Boscombe; perhaps because of problems of transporting the big machine by road.

In the space of just over a year the two prototype Welkins suffered five forced landings. Not all of these had Harald at the helm, but the most spectacular did. Returning from Boscombe Down in DG558 on 23rd September 1943 Harald realised that much of the Yeovil workforce was exiting for lunch and that a 'flat' approach was impossible without putting innocents at risk. He piled on the coals for a go-around only

for the starboard Merlin 61 to pack up; both pilot and prototype survived the inevitable wheels-up in a nearby field. Development of the Welkin was protracted and Harald flew the one-off NF.II, PF370, on 23rd October 1944 in an attempt to offer it as a two-seat, radar-equipped, night-fighter. No Welkins entered operational service, but that did not stop Yeovil churning out 75 examples, most of which were ferried to a maintenance unit to await the scrapman's axe.

The last fixed-wing project for Westland was the Wyvern naval torpedo-attack and strike fighter which overlapped with the company's visionary evolution into Britain's leading helicopter manufacturer. Two contending turboprops, the Armstrong Siddeley Python and the Rolls-Royce Clyde, were beset by developmental delays so the prototypes flew with 2,690hp 24-cylinder H-format RR Eagle 22s. The Wyvern programme faced many problems and more than its share of tragedy. Peter Garner* and Mike Graves*, both appointed by Harald to assist him, were killed in Wyverns. Harald flew the Eagle-powered TS371 on 12th December 1946. Lightning-like reactions were needed early in TS371's testing when the starboard aileron failed on finals, plummeting Harald downwards until he applied power and gained height to assess his predicament. He brought TS371 around for a landing while hoping that local atmospherics would generate no conditions that required ailerons.

First of the Clyde-engined Wyverns, VP120, was ready at Boscombe Down in January 1949. The inaugural excursion was brief and traumatic. Smoke filled the cockpit, taking out all forward visibility and threatening to choke Harald. Out of the side of the cockpit he kept his eye on the runway, completing a four-minute circuit. A fuel leak was the culprit and quickly fixed, so that Harald could make another, more purposeful, sortie that day. (Harald had deputed Python testing to Mike Graves, who had introduced him to the Gloster Meteor jet in early 1945. VP109 first flew on 23rd March 1949.)

The Python won out over the Clyde, but it was May 1953 before the production-standard Wyvern S.4 entered service, with 813 Squadron. During the testing of TF.2 VW867 on 8th January 1952, Harald experienced severe control problems while landing at Merryfield and a belly-landing resulted. It was discovered that only the port flap was operating. Forty-six days later, Harald had to 'park' yet another Wyvern on its belly. The oil pressure decayed away on S.4 VW880 and Harald aimed for Weston-super-Mare, only for the Python to seize giving him no option but to slither into a field prior to the threshold.

Above: Welkin prototype DG558 in mid-1943. *KEC*

Left: The Eagle-powered Wyvern prototype, TS371. *Rolls-Royce*

Below: A production Wyvern S.4 of 813 Squadron believed to be on HMS *Albion*, early 1956. *Armstrong Siddeley*

A loyal friend of 18 years, personal 'taxi' for Harald Penrose, Hermes-powered Widgeon IIIA G-AAGH met its end at Merryfield in July 1948. *Westland*

In late 1945 Harald was given a brief introduction to helicopters at Beaulieu by 'Sox' Hosegood* in a Sikorsky Hoverfly. Harald went on to pilot Dragonflies and Whirlwind helicopters as Westland transformed its business. An accident in 1948 at the flight test airfield, Merryfield, was deeply saddening for Harald. Built in 1930 at Yeovil Widgeon IIIA G-AAGH was retained by the company and Harald used it as a personal 'taxi', particularly to 'commute' from Yeovil to Merryfield and back. With a volunteer to hold the tail, on 27th July 1948, Harald swung the prop and the Cirrus Hermes fired at once and *Golf-Hotel* began to move forwards. Harald tried to throw the cockpit switches, but failed and as his helper let go, Harald fell on to the concrete, breaking his nose. The Widgeon – a loyal friend of 18 years and a type that Harald had helped develop – raised its tail and hurtled into a hangar wall, bursting into flames. In May 1959 Harald invested in a new runabout, purchasing an aircraft that looked as though it belonged in the 1930s but was just a year old: Currie Wot G-APNT. Naming it *Airymouse*, Harald had many memorable adventures in this single-seater biplane, all captured lyrically in his third book. *November-Tango* was sold on in April 1964; it is still airworthy with an appreciative Southampton-based owner.

In 1946 the opportunity of buying into a partnership in a Cornish boatyard was too good to resist and shortly afterwards Aero Marine Ltd was established with Harald as the principal at Emsworth in Hampshire. (The 'Aero' part of the name was in the hope that a tandem-winged light aircraft Harald was scheming might be produced – this did not transpire.) Always a gifted sailor, Harald proved equally good at designing sail- or motor-powered vessels. This business was expanded and renamed the Emsworth Yacht and Motor Company in 1953 and, aged 49, Harald retired from test flying that year. He took up the post of sales manager in 1953, relishing the challenges of convincing operators that helicopters were vital to the modern world – his place as CTP was taken by 'Slim' Sear*. With books and boats increasingly occupying his time, Harald retired from Westland in 1966.

Harald's books are all worth seeking out; his style is engaging and expressive. His autobiographical titles remain as 'classics' and his five-volume history of British aviation is an exceptional and trusted reference. Autobiographical: *I Flew with the Birds,* Country Life, 1949; *No Echo in the Sky,* Cassell, 1958; *Airymouse,* Vernon and Yates, London, 1967; *Cloud Cuckooland,* Airlife, 1981; *Adventure with Fate,* Airlife, 1984. Biographies and histories: *British Aviation – The Pioneer Years 1903-1914,* Putnam, 1967; *British Aviation – The Great War and Armistice 1915-1919,* Putnam, 1969; *British Aviation – The Adventuring Years 1920-1929,* Putnam, 1973; *British Aviation – Widening Horizons 1930-1934,* HMSO, 1979; *British Aviation – Ominous Skies 1935-1939,* HMSO, 1980; *Wings Across the World – An Illustrated History of British Airways,* Cassell, 1980; *Architect of Wings – A Biography of Roy Chadwick,* Airlife, 1985; *An Ancient Air – A Biography of John Stringfellow of Chard, The Victorian Aeronautical Pioneer,* Airlife, 1988.

By 1993 Harald had 5,500-plus hours on 309 types. Harald James Penrose died on 31st August 1996, aged 92. Another quote from *Adventure with Fate* provides an insight into Harald's philosophy and not a bad one to adopt, be you test pilot or not: "We are little more than flotsam on the stream of time so it is the living moment that enthrals and counts". He had lived to the full and his writing legacy continues to enthral.

Currie Wot G-APNT, Harald Penrose's *Airymouse* of 1959 to 1964, in the mid-1980s. *KEC*

Edgar Percival

Oct 1929	Hendy Hobo G-AAIG 1 x 35hp ABC Scorpion II
1930	Hendy 302 G-AAVT 1 x 105hp Cirrus Hermes I
1932	Saro-Percival Mailplane G-ABLI 3 x 120hp DH Gipsy III
Feb 1932	Percival Gull G-ABUR 1 x 130hp Cirrus Hermes IV
22 Mar 1934	Percival Mew Gull G-ACND 1 x 165hp Napier Javelin 1A
Nov 1935	Percival Vega Gull G-AEAB 1 x 200hp DH Gipsy Six
14 Sep 1937	Percival Q.6 G-AEYE 2 x 205hp DH Gipsy Six II
21 Dec 1955	Edgar Percival Prospector G-AOFU 1 x 270hp Lycoming GO-480-B1

Notes: First flight venues: Hobo – Shoreham, Hendy 302 – Yate, Mailplane – Cowes (but see main narrative), Gull and Vega Gull – Gravesend, Q.6 – Luton, Prospector – Stapleford Tawney. Vega Gull initially incorrectly marked 'G-AEAD'. Charles Hughesdon* had his share of adventure in this Vega Gull.

Edgar Wikner Percival, born 1897 in Australia. Cousin of Geoffrey Wikner. From 14 he worked with horses before becoming an engineering apprentice and during this time he designed and built his own gliders. He enlisted in the Australian army in late 1915 and by April 1916 he was in Egypt with a cavalry unit. Edgar transferred to the RFC and by the spring of 1917 was with 60 Squadron on the Western Front, flying Nieuports. He was invalided out of France, perhaps suffering from an ear problem, and was transferred to Palestine, joining 111 Squadron by September 1917, with Bristol M.1s. Edgar was back in Australia by the spring of 1920 and he set up a small business with an Avro 504K and an Airco DH.6, in Richmond, New South Wales. Selling this outfit in 1926, Edgar ran an agency for Avro Avians from 1928. He departed again for the UK in 1928.*

EDGAR WIKNER PERCIVAL set himself up as a freelance test pilot upon arrival in Great Britain in 1928. He first flew the Hendy Hobo single-seater, designed by Basil 'Hendy' Henderson and built by his Hendy Aircraft Company at Shoreham. Hendy's next product was the two-seat cabin tourer Type 302 and Edgar participated in the design of this machine. Construction was subcontracted to Parnall at Yate and it was from there that Edgar carried out the maiden flight in 1930. At that year's King's Club air race, staged from Hanworth, Edgar averaged 121mph. Both the Hobo and the 302 remained as one-offs.

Having trained in engineering, Edgar won a major prize in an aircraft design competition hosted by the Australian government just before he left for the UK – this probably funded his relocation to Britain. He approached Saunders-Roe (Saro) at East Cowes with a proposal for a three-engined mailplane with the potential to become a small airliner. A joint venture was initiated and the resulting Mailplane, G-ABLI, was first flown from Cowes in early 1932. It is *believed* that designer/test pilot Edgar Percival flew this, but two sources also quote the SARO CTP Stuart Scott* as doing this. Striving to set up his own business, Edgar sold his share in the Mailplane. Design rights moved to the Saro associate organisation, Spartan Aircraft, and the much modified Cruiser airliner entered limited production in 1932.

Edgar embarked upon the creation of a family of aircraft, all designed to out-perform existing types. The prototype two/three seat Gull tourer was first flown by its designer – wearing his hallmark trilby hat – from Maidstone in 1932. Meanwhile, discussions were completed for the Percival Aircraft Company to be established at Gravesend and production began in 1933. Meanwhile, Edgar gained 12th place in the 1932 King's Cup at Brooklands. His next design was to become a legend among racing aeroplanes, the Mew Gull, which Edgar first flew at Gravesend in March 1934. At that year's King's Cup, staged at Hatfield, Edgar achieved the fastest speed – 191mph – but the handicapping precluded a 'place'. See Chapter Two for the pilot most linked with the Mew Gull, Alex Henshaw. The Vega Gull of 1935 offered four seats and dual control and provided the basis for the Proctor aircrew trainer that first appeared in late 1939. Percival Aircraft moved to larger facilities at Luton in early 1937 and it was from there that Edgar 'first flighted' the prototype Q.6

The one-off Hendy Hobo, first flown by Edgar Percival in late 1929. *KEC*

Above: Production Spartan Cruiser II G-ACSM, a much developed version of Percival's Mailplane. *KEC*

Right: Wearing his hallmark trilby hat, Edgar Percival at the helm of the prototype Mew Gull, G-ACND. *KEC*

Below: The prototype Vega Gull G-AEAB, temporarily masquerading as 'G-AEAD', at Martlesham Heath in 1932. *KEC*

Edgar Percival flying the first Q.6, G-AEYE, 1937. *Percival Aircraft*

Edgar Percival piloting the prototype Prospector, G-AOFU. *Edgar Percival Aircraft Ltd*

cabin twin. Edgar left the company he founded in March 1940 and Leonard Carruthers* took on the role of CTP.

Involved in the US-UK Lend-Lease programme, Edgar moved to the USA and in 1948 he was granted American citizenship. By the early 1950s he was in New Zealand, perfecting airborne seed and fertilizer dispersal systems and he began to work on the format of a crop-duster which could also be used for other purposes with the minimum of adaptation. Edgar returned to the UK in 1954, setting up Edgar

Percival Aircraft in late 1954 at Stapleford Tawney to produce what had gelled into the EP.9 Prospector. The first example, G-AOFU, was flown on 9th December 1955 with Edgar – complete with trilby – doing the honours. Edgar sold the rights to the EP.9 in 1958 to Samlesbury Engineering/Lancashire Aircraft and up to 1961 a total of 27 EP.9s were completed. After the sale of his company, Edgar worked as a design consultant; he died on 21st January 1984, aged 87.

Edward 'Peter the Painter' Petre

Apr 1912	Handley Page Type E
	1 x 50hp Gnome
Aug 1912	Handley Page Type F
	1 x 80hp Gnome

IT was colleagues at Brooklands that nicknamed the well-regarded Petre brothers after contemporary mobsters from London's East End: the older of the two, Henry A Petre after the Bible-quoting, knife-toting 'Peter the Monk' and Edward after the Latvian-born one-time political agitator 'Peter the Painter'. The relationship that Frederick Handley Page had with his test pilots and airline captains is reflected through the two volumes. Soon after Frederick sacked Robert Fenwick* because he crashed the Type D monoplane in July 1911, he reached an agreement with the brothers; Edward being taken on as chief pilot, with Henry helping out with construction. In true HP style, it is unlikely either received a salary.

The pair first came to prominence when they exhibited their skeletal monoplane at the Olympia Aero Show in 1909; taking it to Brooklands after the event for completion. The Petre Monoplane was powered by a 35hp NEC in the nose, but it drove a pusher propeller in the tail via a long extension shaft. Trials at Brooklands ended in Henry crashing their creation on 23rd July 1910. Prior to the accident the brothers and Howard Flanders had been rebuilding the Neale Monoplane after it had been 'pranged' at Brooklands on 21st May 1910.

The brothers helped Frederick Handley Page to repair the damaged Type D monoplane at Barking. In April 1912 Edward was at the controls for the maiden flight of the improved, two-seat, Type E, at Fairlop. He later damaged it when flying to the HP workshop at Barking, but avoided the wrath of the proprietor and it was rebuilt. It was on this machine that Edward gained Aviators' Certificate No.259 at Fairlop on 24th July 1912. Henry Petre had achieved his Aviators' Certificate, No.128, earlier than his younger sibling, on a Hanriot at Brooklands on 12th September 1911. Henry built the side-by-side seating Type F monoplane for the Military Trials at Salisbury Plain in August 1912 and this was given its maiden flight by Edward. It was damaged while flying and withdrawn from the contest. (Ronald Whitehouse* continued testing the Types E and F for HP.)

Edward 'Peter the Painter' left HP not long after the trials and took up flying for Martin-Handasyde. On Christmas Eve 1912 he embarked on a flight from Brooklands to Edinburgh – a dream he had cherished for some time and he had a self-imposed deadline of the end of 1912 to achieve. Piloting an unspecified Martin-Handasyde he got as far as Marske-by-the-Sea on the North Yorkshire coast, after an epic three-hour, 200-mile flight. In the teeth of a gale, the monoplane was seen to come down to about 500ft, then rise rapidly after which the wings collapsed and 'The Painter' was killed in the crash. In December 1912 Henry 'Peter the Monk' sailed for Australia, having accepted an offer to become a founder instructor for that nation's School of Military Aviation.

George Pickering

| 29 Sep 1938 | Supermarine Sea Otter K8854 |
| | 1 x 745hp Bristol Perseus XI |

SUPERMARINE designer Reginald Joseph Mitchell spotted the talents of MAEE pilot Flt Lt A G Pickering AFC and in 1934 he recommended George join Supermarine to help with the increasing production of flying-boats and amphibians. George entered the RAF in 1924 and by 1929 was at MAEE Felixstowe. He took the prototype Supermarine Scapa, S1648, on a three-month 'cruise' to the Mediterranean in 1933. Mostly based at Kalafrana on Malta, he and his crew carried out performance and armament trials.

George joined Supermarine, under 'Mutt' Summers*, in late 1934. On 25th June 1935 he carried out the maiden flight of Seagull V A2-1, the first for the Royal Australian Air Force. With the RAF and the Fleet Air Arm (FAA) the Seagull V was named Walrus and on 18th March 1936 George took K5772, the first production Walrus down the slipway and on to the Solent for its debut. Jeffrey Quill* had been appointed as deputy to Mutt in November 1935. In his exceptional *Spitfire – A Test Pilot's Story*, Jeffrey describes the test pilot he 'inherited' who had two year's seniority in the company, but held no grudges at the younger man's appointment: "George was a very practical and down-to-earth man, both in his general character and his approach to flying, and he was prone to call a spade a spade with no sort of equivocation. At a time when some test pilots tended to adopt a somewhat *prima donna* attitude if they thought they could get away with it, George's approach – even if sometimes a little over-expressed – was refreshing and healthy."

Originally named Stingray, the Sea Otter was conceived by Mitchell to supersede the Walrus, even though the latter was only two years into its service life. George had problems tempting the prototype, K8854, off the water in September 1938. On the 23rd, a run of just over a mile resulted in the amphibian going up on

George Pickering piloting a flying-boat. *via Don Middleton*

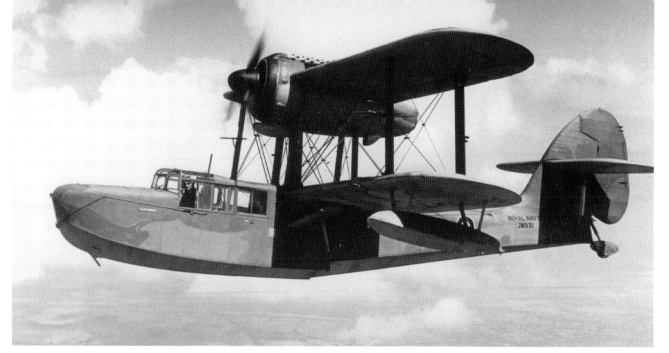

A Saunders-Roe built Sea Otter I in 1944. *KEC*

the step, but it would not wholly unstick. The two-bladed propeller was blamed and a three-blader was fitted. In this guise George got K8854 in the air six days later, but after an unacceptably long run. Experimentation with propellers, including a four-bladed 'scissor' with the blades at 35 degrees to one another instead of 90, continued until 11th January 1939 when George pronounced its performance was satisfactory. Priorities had shifted dramatically to the Spitfire and the Sea Otter took a back seat; it was not until January 1943 that the first production example appeared. The type never supplanted the Walrus in wartime service but did linger with the FAA until the early 1950s.

Although marine aircraft were initially George's priority, Supermarine and Vickers philosophy had always been to share skills and George taught Jeffrey to handle flying-boats and amphibians. After Mutt flew the prototype Spitfire on 6th March 1936, both George and Jeffrey had flown it before the month was out. The agonising hiatus until the first production Spitfire I flew (K9787 on 14th May 1938 by Jeffrey) has been well documented as have the lingering worries that Supermarine was not capable of mass production. Inevitably, George's work became that of signing off Spitfires: the first record of him debuting a Mk.I was K9798 from Eastleigh on 30th July 1938 and it was issued to 19 Squadron at Duxford 18 days later.

George eased the throttle forward at Eastleigh on Mk.V AA876 for its first flight on 25th October 1941. A terminal velocity dive was a routine part of the sign-off but on this occasion it all went horribly wrong: the Spitfire is believed to have reached 520mph and broke up. George was thrown clear and subconsciously deployed his parachute, or the canopy was dragged out of its bag, either way it did not fully open and it took a descent through trees to assist in slowing his fall. George was badly injured and began a long and painful recuperation. The wreckage of AA876 was taken to Farnborough for analysis. By early 1943 George was cleared to return to work. He had befriended an officer in the Irish Guards and took up the offer of a ride in a Bren Gun Carrier – a light tracked vehicle. While attempting to surmount a steep obstacle the tracks slipped, the carrier rolled over, killing Flt Lt A George Pickering AFC.

Sydney Pickles

16 Feb 1917	Fairey Campania N1000
	1 x 250hp RR Mk.IV
17 May 1917	Fairey F.2 3704
	2 x 190hp RR Falcon

Notes: The Campania floatplane most likely flew from Hamble, but *may* have ventured skywards from the Isle of Grain. H A Taylor in *Fairey Aircraft since 1915* notes that the F.2 *may* have flown as earlier from Hartlington, without naming a pilot. The 17th May is declared as the 'official' first flight, taking place at Northolt.

Sydney Pickles, born 1894 in Australia. He settled in Great Britain in 1912 and learned to fly with the Bristol school at Brooklands, going solo on 29th May 1912 and qualifying for Aviators' Certificate No.263 on 30th July and Special Certificate No.8 at Hendon on 1st July 1913 on a Caudron.

ARMED with his Aviators' Certificate, Australian Sydney Pickles began to offer his services as a test pilot. On 1st February 1913 he was at the newly-established Handley Page workshop at Cricklewood trying out the Type E monoplane with a new fin. In typical Handley Page fashion, he was up flying fare-paying joy-riders to keep the coffers healthy the following day! He was flying it again in May, demonstrating its virtues at Winchester on the 10th and he raced it at Hendon seven days later.

In August Sydney responded to a call from Thomas Sopwith to take over from the incapacitated Harry Hawker* in the 'Circuit of Britain' challenge. The weather was against Sydney and Harry recovered in the meanwhile. Eric Gordon Bell* survived an accident at Brooklands in June 1913 although tragically his passenger was killed. Because of this Shorts was left without a test pilot and Sydney stepped in. Among his duties at Eastchurch was taking up the much rebuilt S.39 Triple-Twin on 24th July 1913 in the guise of a much more conventional biplane. Referred to as the S.39 Nacelle Type, it was handed on to the Admiralty.

Sydney was at Hendon on 20th September 1913, *possibly* engaged by Grahame-White, and he took up pioneer British aviatrix Mrs Cheridah de Beauvoir Stocks in a French-built Champel. The rudder bar jammed and the biplane spun in; seriously injuring Mrs Stocks while Sydney broke a leg. Mrs Stocks, the second woman to gain an Aviators' Certificate – No.154 in November 1911 – recovered but did not fly again. Sydney was back helping out at Eastchurch by April 1914 and flying his Blériot XI at events around the country. By the end of 1914 Sydney had joined the RNAS and was reported to be involved in coastal patrols along the East Coast.

Leaving the RNAS by late 1915, Sydney joined the Prodger-Isaac Aviation Company. This was a freelance test pilot agency – perhaps the first of its kind – managed by Bernard Isaacs, founded by American Clifford Prodger*. Early work for Sydney included testing a batch of Fairey-built Short 827 floatplanes from Hamble which continued into early 1916. He then moved to Eastchurch signing off Short 184s along with Clifford and later John Lankester Parker*. In 1917 Sydney flew the first two in-house designs for Fairey, the Campania floatplane – the start of a dynasty of such types for the company – and the three-crew, 77ft span F.2 which was to remain a one-off.

Superb watercolour proclaiming the virtues of the prototype Heron 2, with retractable undercarriage, 1953. At the bottom are the logos of the aircraft, engines and propellers divisions.

After this the story of Sydney Pickles resumes in Australia, perhaps as early as 1918. By 1920 he was instrumental in establishing the Victoria Aero Club and he became its chief instructor. A pupil wrecked its only aircraft and the business is reported to have foundered and Sydney seems to have stopped aviating. In later life he was deeply involved in helping handicapped people; he died on 23rd November 1975, aged 81.

Maurice Piercey

Sep 1924	Beardmore Wee Bee I
	1 x 32hp Bristol Cherub I

MAURICE W PIERCEY piloted the ANEC I No.18 at the 1923 Lympne Light Aeroplane Trials and succeeded in gaining the Wakefield prize of £200 for a climb to 14,400ft. He was engaged by Beardmore to fly the company's entry in the following year's competition – the two-seat Wee Bee, No.4. Averaging around 70mph, this machine carried away the main award, £2,500 from the Air Ministry – that's £137,500 in present-day values. From 1926 to 1927 Maurice was employed by Gloster, testing production Grebes and Gamecocks.

Geoffrey Pike

29 Sep 1945	DH Dove G-AGPJ
	2 x 330hp DH Gipsy Queen 70
28 Aug 1949	DH Vampire NF.10 G-5-2
	1 x 3,350lbst DH Goblin 3
10 May 1950	DH Heron G-ALZL
	4 x 250hp DH Gipsy Queen 30

GEOFFREY HAIG PIKE joined de Havilland as an apprentice at Hatfield in 1934 and learned to fly two years later. He flew for the DH aero engine division from 1940, transferring in 1942 to aircraft production. He worked as an assistant test pilot under Geoffrey de Havilland JR* on Mosquitos – he reportedly flew over 500 of these by 1945 – but also flew Hornets and Vampires. Geoffrey was nicknamed 'Iser' at Hatfield, owing to his habit of starting many of his sentences with "I suggest..." On 23rd April 1945 Geoffrey took off in the prototype Vampire LZ548 only for the fuel pump to fail and he made an immediate forced landing just outside the Hatfield perimeter. Geoffrey was slightly injured, LZ548 was written off.

With the death of Geoffrey de Havilland JR in September 1946, John Cunningham took over as CTP*. Geoffrey continued to fly Hornets and Vampires and assisted with the DH.108 project. Having been returned from A&AEE Boscombe Down, Hornet F.3 PX383 was used to investigate behaviour of the 200-gallon drop tanks. On take-off from Hatfield on 25th March 1949 in PX383 Geoffrey discovered that the starboard Merlin's boost had failed and the underwing tanks could not be jettisoned. Control got increasingly difficult and he took to his parachute and was slightly injured on landing. The Hornet impacted near Royston and several locals were hurt where it came down. On 28th August 1949 Geoffrey carried out the maiden flight of the two-seater night-fighter Vampire, NF.10, G-5-2.

Bristol Siddeley Engine's communications fleet at Filton, circa 1965, Doves G-AJGT and G-AMZY flanking the first HS.125 Series 1 G-ARYC. *Bristol Siddeley*

The second prototype Vampire NF.10, G-5-5. *de Havilland*

By way of marking the 25th anniversary of the founding of de Havilland Aircraft, Geoffrey captained the first flight of the twin-engined Dove, on 25th September 1953. The Dove was very significant, spearheading the transition to peacetime production: the last of 542 examples was delivered in 1967. The Dove was developed into the four-engined, initially more utilitarian, Heron on 10th May 1950 with the retractable undercarriage Series 2 G-AMTS following on 14th December 1952. Ten years later, the HS.125 executive jet was first flown by project pilot Chris Capper* and Geoffrey flew in support of the new programme. The Hatfield operation was taken over by Mike Goodfellow* when Geoffrey Haig Pike retired from test flying in 1969; he died in 1981, aged 65.

Harold Lord 'Pip' Piper

6 Oct 1938	Handley Page Hereford L7271
	2 x 1,000hp Napier Dagger VIII
22 Jan 1948	Short Sealand G-AIVX
	2 x 345hp DH Gipsy Queen 70-2

Harold Lord Piper, born 1899 in New Zealand. He joined the Royal New Zealand Air Force in 1917 and learned to fly before being 'demobbed' in 1920. He became a sheep farmer, while continuing to fly with the Air Force Reserve. Harold sold up his farm in 1927 and came to Great Britain, entering the RAF. After training, he flew AW Atlases with 26 Squadron at Catterick. With Fg Off Cyril 'Cyrus' Kay, Harold asked for permission for a visit to New Zealand and he purchased Desoutter I G-AATI and had it fitted with long range tanks, all for £750 (£41,250 in present-day values) and named it Aorangi. The pair set off on 9th February 1930 and reached Sydney, Australia, on 23rd March. The Desoutter was shipped to New Zealand while the RAF officers visited their families; G-AATI was sold for £250 and

became ZK-ACJ. Upon his return, Harold returned briefly to 26 Squadron before being posted to 503 (City of Lincoln) Squadron, a special reserve unit, with HP Hyderabads at Waddington. Harold left the RAF in 1933 and instructed with the Gravesend Flying Club before taking a post with Shorts as a demonstration pilot on Scion light transports.

Fg Off Harold 'Pip' Piper's job of showing off Scions came under the remit of Short CTP John Lankester Parker* (JLP) who quickly recognised the new man's flying skills and he became JLP's deputy. Initially he was put in charge of the last of the Singapore III flying-boats for the RAF. Pip was alongside JLP on the flight deck of the prototype Sunderland on 16th October 1938 and *above* him in the S.20 element of the Short-Mayo Composite in the spring of 1938 – full details under John Parker's section. During 1938 Shorts was establishing the Northern Ireland business, Short and Harland, and Pip was dispatched to take charge of flight testing at Sydenham, under JLP's guidance.

The first two types built in Northern Ireland were not Short designs: Bristol Bombay bomber-transports and the Napier Dagger-engined version of the Handley Page Hampden, the Hereford. The second prototype Hampden, L7271, was

The second production Hereford, L6003, at Luton for Napier trials, early 1940. *G Napier & Son*

Three Sealands in 1951: YU-CFK and 'J bound for Yugoslavia, and G-AKLV in the background. *Shorts*

delivered to Sydenham on 16th July 1937 for stripping down and converting to Hereford status. Pip was at the controls for its debut on 6th October 1938 and on 19th May 1939 he flew the first from-new example, L6002. The first Short-built Bombay, L5808, had its maiden flight 3rd March 1939 with Pip as pilot. Short and Harland then turned to manufacturing Stirlings and Sunderlands, with Pip and Geoffrey Tyson* testing most of the output – Pip accounted for over 800 examples of the bomber and around 100 of the flying-boat.

Geoffrey Tyson succeeded JLP in 1945 but moved on to Saunders-Roe in 1946 and Pip became Shorts CTP. He presided over the maiden flight of the second Shetland, Mk.II G-AGVD. This civil-configured version was launched at Rochester on 15th September 1947 and with Tom Brooke-Smith* as co-pilot, Pip flew it from the Medway two days later. The first post-war Short design to take to the skies was the Sealand, a twin-engined amphibian capable of a wide variety of tasks. In flying-boat form, Pip took the prototype up from Belfast Lough on 22nd January 1948 before it returned to the works to have its retractable undercarriage fitted. In March 1948 Pip – aged 49 – handed in his resignation and set off for his homeland: Tom Brooke-Smith took over as CTP. At that point Harold Lord Piper had 6,372 hours on 91 types; he died in his native New Zealand in 1965, aged 66.

Howard Pixton

1 Apr 1911	Avro Type D
	1 x 35hp Green
17 Feb 1914	Sopwith Sociable 149
	1 x 80hp Gnome

Cecil Howard Pixton, born 1885. Studied engineering and worked, in turn, as an assistant draughtsman, for a company building dynamos and industrial engines and as a motor mechanic. All the time Howard's passion for aeroplanes was growing and this climaxed when he saw Claude Grahame-White and his Farman in a field near Lichfield in April 1910. After this, Howard applied to as many aviators as he could think of asking if they could teach him to fly while mentioning

his mechanical engineering background. In June 1910, Howard received a reply from Humphrey Verdon Roe, Edwin Alliott Verdon Roe's brother and business partner in A V Roe and Co, proposing that Howard work as a mechanic for Alliott at Brooklands, in return for flying lessons. He learned to fly on an Avro Type IV triplane, initially with 'rolling straights' – fast taxying and then 'hops', building to 'eights' – flying in a figure of eight across the flying ground – to maximise the number of turns and keep them relatively tight. On one of these in November 1910 he side slipped and badly damaged the Type IV and set about its repair. On 24th January 1911 Howard qualified for Aviators' Certificate No.50.

WITH his proven determination and his pilot's 'ticket', Howard Pixton was rewarded by his boss, Edwin Alliott Verdon Roe, by making him the first of a long and distinguished line of company test pilots. In February 1911 Howard tested E V Hammond's large, twin tractor propeller triplane but he could not make it venture skywards. Roe was busy creating a more durable biplane – this became known as the Type D – and on 1st April 1911 Howard took it for its maiden flight at Brooklands and was very pleased with its stability. The new aeroplane inspired so much confidence that Alliott's wife, Mildred, was taken up in it by Howard. He started building hours on the Type D, with his eye firmly on the Manville Prize (see below), competing in the Brooklands to Shoreham air race on 6th May and demonstrating it to the Parliamentary Aerial Defence Committee at Hendon on the 12th. In June the first Type D was sold to the Admiralty to become a floatplane but it was followed by another six examples – Avro was in the 'mass' production business!

On 4th October 1911 a welcome windfall came the way of Howard and his employer. The Manville Aggregate Prize of £500 (a factory worker in that year would typically earn £250 per annum) was for endurance with a passenger on board with a closing date of 4th October 1911. Samuel Franklin Cody was in close contention but Howard had been carefully 'clocking' time on the Type D and a Bristol Boxkite. On the very last day of the contest Howard steamed ahead, beating his rival by nearly two hours and as well as the main prize, clinched an extra £150 for the greatest aggregate achieved throughout the year. Avro and Bristol shared in the prize money and it was

The first Avro Type D, as flown by Howard Pixton, was put on floats in August 1911 tested at a floatplane at Barrow-in-Furness. *A V Roe & Co C201*

from his introduction to Sir George White, founder of British and Colonial Aeroplane ('Bristol') that Howard left Avro. Harry Holmes in *Avro – The History of an Aircraft Company* explains the departure: "[Howard] was happy to work for Avro, but as the firm's finances were always tight he was only receiving £2 per week from [Alliott Roe]. In an amicable agreement he left to join [Bristol] for a salary of £250 per annum plus one-third of any prize money." (Sir George was known to pay well, but without prize money, he was only shelling out about what an industrial worker could expect).

Howard moved to Filton, initially demonstrating Boxkites, but he was not going to spend much time there. He was much in demand during a tour of likely military clients: he flew a Bristol-Prier Monoplane in Madrid, Spain in late 1911; a Bristol-Coanda Monoplane in Bucharest, Romania, also in late 1911 and a Bristol-Prier in Berlin, Germany, in March 1912. Howard was also engaged by Bristol to fly a Bristol-Coanda at the July 1912 Military Aeroplane Competition on Salisbury Plain, netting the company £500 for joint third place.

With Harry Hawker* touring in his native Australia with the prototype Tabloid, Thomas Sopwith* turned to Howard to fill

in as chief pilot. Thomas referred to Howard as 'Picky' and this seems to have stuck, at least in some quarters. His first task was to debut an enlarged, two-bay, version of the Tabloid for a special commission. The machine was destined for the Navy as No.149 at the specific order of the First Lord of the Admiralty, Winston Churchill. Howard tested it at Brooklands on 17th February 1914 and later that day took the man designated as Churchill's pilot, Lt Spenser Grey, up. It was handed over at Hendon two days later and Grey flew Churchill in it on the 20th. Seating was side-by-side, like the Tabloid, within a generous cockpit and No.149 was renamed by Sopwith as the Sociable, but the RNAS referred to it as the 'Tweenie'.

The second Schneider Trophy contest for floatplanes was to be staged at Monaco on 20th April 1914 and Thomas Sopwith had entered a special, single-seat Tabloid, which he claimed had been diverted from an RFC order. Howard was to be both test pilot and competitor. With a central float and balancing floats under each wing Howard tried out the Tabloid at Hamble in March but it promptly cartwheeled and sank. The float was positioned too far aft and it became clear that the layout was cumbersome. Frenetic activity followed, with time

With Howard Pixton, perched on the leading edge of the port lower wing, and a mechanic on the floats to help keep the tail at least partially out of the water, Sopwith Schneider under tow at Monaco, April 1914. *KEC*

ever-pressing. The Tabloid was roaded from Hamble to Kingston-upon-Thames and there Fred Sigrist supervised a piece of adaptive genius: the float was cut down the middle and turned into a pair and a new four-unit mounting was created and attached at the bulkhead and the centre section. There was no time to run the Tabloid back to Hamble; it was launched on to the Thames near Glover's Island with Howard carrying out the last test on 8th April. The Tabloid was packed and shipped to Monaco and flown again on the eve of the competition. In the competition the little Sopwith astonished the remainder of the competitors and Howard was declared the winner at an average of 86mph. Not content with this, Howard flew for another two laps of the course to establish a world air speed record for floatplanes of 92mph. 'Picky' was so modest about what had been achieved that in the grandeur of the Monaco Sporting Club when asked by Jacques Schneider what Howard would like to drink he asked for a small Bass beer!

Howard continued testing for Sopwith until September 1914 when he joined the Farnborough-based Aeronautical Inspection Department (AID) signing off aircraft, taking delivery of them and ferrying them to units including the Western Front. This work was under the aegis of the RFC and he was given the rank of captain. Howard was engaged by Boulton and Paul to fly the first Royal Aircraft Factory FE.2b, 5201, built by the company at Mousehold, near Norwich. A grand occasion had been arranged on 1st October 1915 with a marquee for guests and 'bubbly' on hand to celebrate. Try as he might, Howard could not get the machine to start and the guests left disappointed. The following day, an errant ignition lead was sorted and Howard carried out the maiden flight. In the spring of 1917 the work of the AID was reorganised with inspectors/pilots stationed at a series of Aircraft Acceptance Parks across the country and Howard was sent to 9 AAP at Newcastle. By early 1918 he was in Dublin as Inspector of Aeroplane and Landing Grounds before taking a post at AID's headquarters in London.

Avro set up a joy-riding and tuition business at Lake Windermere with a pair of Avro 504K floatplanes from 4th August 1919. Howard was involved with this from the start and the work also included a short-lived service flying newspapers to the Isle of Man. This was probably Howard's first visit to the island that was later to be his home. By the end of 1919 Howard appears to have given up flying, but not aviation: he worked as an engineer, including a spell as chief engineer for the Lancashire Aero Club. Settling on the Isle of Man in 1932 Howard became a leading light in aviation on the island, helping to establish Ronaldsway as an airport. It is possible that he re-joined AID during World War Two, but not in a flying capacity. Cecil Howard Pixton died on 7th February 1972, aged 87. In 2014 *Howard Pixton – Test Pilot and Pioneer Aviator* was published and the book sticks rigidly to those areas of his life, concluding at the Armistice in November 1918, although there is clearly much more of the man to be explored. Written by his daughter Stella Pixton – although she chose to call it 'ghosted' as it is in the first person – it is a long-overdue tribute to a real pioneer.

John Porte

John Cyril Porte, born 1884 in Ireland. Joined the Royal Navy in 1898 and by 1906 was with the Submarine Service, taking his first command of a sub in 1908. He contracted pulmonary tuberculosis and Lt Porte was discharged from the Navy in 1911. John learned to fly in France and trained on a Deperdussin at Reims, gaining a French licence on 28th July 1911.

JOHN PORTE brought a Deperdussin monoplane to Great Britain in 1911 and took on the roles of joint managing director and test pilot for the Hendon-based British Deperdussin Aeroplane Syndicate Ltd, which was established in April 1912. Porte taught pupils at Hendon and the company built two-seat Deperdussins for private owners. John flew an Anzani-powered British-built Deperdussin in the Military Aeroplane Competition at Larkhill in 1912. The company closed in April 1913 and John joined White and Thompson at Middleton-on-Sea as test pilot.

In October 1913 John and Gordon England* met up with Glenn Curtiss who was handing over a single-engined Curtiss flying-boat to Ernest Bass, the man who had acquired the British production rights for the American's designs. In 1914 John took up a post with Curtiss at Hammondsport, New York, assisting in the design of flying-boats and he was nominated as the pilot for *America*, a twin intended to fly the Atlantic. Testing began in June 1914 but with the outbreak of the Great War in August, John Porte hurried back to Britain.

His medical history was no longer an impediment and John was accepted into the RNAS. The two America-class flying-boats were bought up by the Admiralty, as Curtis H.4s. Based at Felixstowe John began a series of modifications to create a much more seaworthy, robust, patrol aircraft. As well as further imported Curtiss-built 'boats, several concerns built a series of Porte/Felixstowe versions, designated F.1 through to F.5, some of which remained in service into the mid-1920s. As noted in the section on John Lankester Parker, Porte carried out the first British composite aircraft experiment. Bristol Scout C 3028 was mounted on the top wing of a three-engined Porte/Felixstowe Baby flying-boat. On 17th May 1916 with John Porte piloting the Baby and Flt Lt M J Day in the Scout, the combination took off from off Felixstowe and at 1,000ft Flt Lt Day detached the Scout and flew off to Martlesham Heath. No further trials were undertaken. While flying the one-off F.2C N65 out of Felixstowe on 24th July 1917, John attacked and sank the German submarine UC-1.

Allegations of war profiteering during the summer of 1917 did not help John's state of health: in November it was announced he had no case to answer. John was appointed as chief designer for Gosport Aircraft, planning a long-range civil development of the Porte/Felixstowe series. Illness caught up again and John Cyril Porte died on 22nd October 1919, aged 35.

Ranald Porteous

2 Mar 1937	Luton LA.3 Minor G-AEPD 1 x 35hp Anzani
16 Apr 1937	Chilton DW.1 G-AESZ 1 x 32hp Carden-Ford
2 Aug 1938	Taylor-Watkinson Dingbat G-AFJA 1 x 32hp Carden-Ford
8 Dec 1955	Auster Agricola G-25-3 1 x 240hp Continental O-470-B
late 1957	Auster Atlantic G-25-2 1 x 185hp Continental E-185-10
16 Apr 1961	Beagle Airedale G-25-11 1 x 180hp Lycoming O-360-A1A
18 Aug 1961	Beagle E.3 G-25-12 1 x 260hp RR-Continental IO-470-D

Notes: Minor flew at Barton-in-the-Clay; Chilton at Witney; Dingbat at Heston; all others at Rearsby. With a family of aircraft like most of the Auster designs, it is difficult to decide which is radically different enough to truly be called a prototype from the 'baseline' machines of the late 1930s and 1940s.

Ranald Logan Porteous, born in 1916. He went on to study at the de Havilland Technical School, Hatfield, and learned to fly there in 1934. On 16th November 1936 Ranald was flying the one-off Luton Buzzard G-ADYX at Christchurch when its Anzani engine failed and the single-seater came down in trees. Ranald suffered a fractured spine and other injuries.

HAVING recovered from the accident in Luton Buzzard G-ADYX at Christchurch on 16th November 1936, Ranald Porteous piloted Luton Aircraft's next product, the LA.3 Minor single-seat parasol monoplane. The prototype, G-AEPD, was flown from grounds near the company workshop at Barton-in-the-Clay. It *may* have been that Ranald had been engaged by the small company as a test pilot and that was why he was flying the Buzzard the previous year. The LA.3 was refined into the LA.4 Minor and Ranald flew the prototype, G-AFBP, powered by a 40hp ABC Scorpion, at Denham in April 1938.

The prototype Chilton DW.1 G-AESZ at Rendcomb shortly after being test flown by Roger 'Dodge' Bailey on 14th September 2001. It had been painstakingly restored after 48 years on the ground. *Ken Ellis*

While at the de Havilland Technical School, Ranald befriended fellow students 'Reggie' Ward and Andrew Dalrymple who went on to found Chilton Aircraft. The pair created the exceptional DW.1 single-seat sporting aircraft and Ranald carried out the maiden flight of the prototype on 16th April 1937. Ranald went on to extensively demonstrate and race G-AESZ and he returned to the type after World War Two. Eric Watkinson and Cyril Taylor also studied at Hatfield and designed another single-seater, the Taylor-Watkinson Dingbat. Ranald again carried out the honours, piloting G-AFJA on 2nd August 1938. This machine remained a one-off and is believed to be still extant, stored in Hampshire.

At the Lympne race meeting of 31st August 1947 Ranald flew Chilton DW.1 G-AFSV to take the Fédération Aéronautique Internationale Class A 100km closed-circuit speed record at 123mph. When he joined Auster (of which more anon) Ranald briefly owned and flew DW.1 G-AFGH from September 1948 to March 1949. All three of these delightful Chiltons are still extant: prototype G-AESZ flies on loan with the Shuttleworth Collection while G-AFGH and G-AFSV are stored with owners in Sussex and Warwickshire, respectively. Ranald had great affections for the little aircraft, in his 1950 book *British Test Pilot* Geoffrey Dorman quotes him: "I think these Chilton episodes gave me more pleasure than anything aeronautical I have done, before or since."

When he left Hatfield in 1937 Ranald became a freelance charter pilot and signed up with the Reserve of Air Force Officers, flying Hawker Harts and later experienced Handley Page Harrows with 75 Squadron at Driffield. He moved to Woodley in 1938 taking up an instructing post with the Phillips & Powis-operated school and occasionally undertook production testing of Miles types. Called up in late 1939, after initial training in Britain, he was posted to Rhodesia and Ranald spent the rest of the war with the Rhodesian Air Training Group, ending up as a squadron leader. 'Demobbed' in late 1945, Ranald took up charter and ferrying commissions before accepting the post of chief flying instructor at the Derby Aero Club, Burnaston.

From mid-1948 Ranald was back in the test flying business, succeeding George Snarey* as CTP for Auster at Rearsby. Based on the American Taylorcraft, and constantly Anglicized and improved from 1939 under founder 'Lance' Wykes, the family ran in one form or another throughout the history of the company and via the Terrier and Husky into the Beagle era.

The one-off Taylor-Watkinson Dingbat at Sywell in the late 1960s. *Roy Bonser*

The prototype Agricola, G-25-3, later G-ANYG, demonstrating its crop-dusting ability to the press at Rearsby, 1956. *Auster*

From the beginning, Ranald had a marketing remit as well as that of CTP and in 1950 he became director of sales. At the 1948 SBAC airshow at Farnborough Ranald demonstrated J/1 Autocrat G-AJIZ and he quickly developed a reputation for the originality of his displays. For the 1952 event he perfected an aerobatic routine in J/5 Aiglet Trainer G-AMMS in which he flicked from inverted at the top of a loop to inverted again so fast that he could continue the downward arc almost as though nothing had happened. Ranald called this manoeuvre the 'Avalanche' but it was soon named the 'Porteous Loop' in his honour. His signature 'sign off' from a demonstration was a landing on just one of the mainwheels.

Auster's greatest departure from the well-trodden 'formula' was the all-new Agricola agricultural aircraft for which a large amount of market research was carried out, with particular concentration on the potentially large market in New Zealand. Ranald flew the 240hp, 42ft-span, 3,840lb all-up weight prototype on 8th December 1955. (A typical 130hp Aiglet Trainer measured up at 32ft span and a top weight of 1,950lb.) Only eight Agricolas were completed at Rearsby and the cash burden stunted the company through to the acquisition by Beagle in 1960. Despite several sources quoting that the four-seat tricycle undercarriage Atlantic prototype never flew, this was not the case. Ranald and Trevor Howard (see Chapter Seven) took it into the skies in late 1957, but the type ended up on its nose early in testing and remained a one-off.

When Auster melded into Beagle in 1960 Ranald continued his role as CTP but now it was for the Rearsby 'end' of the otherwise Shoreham-based operation. The Atlantic was warmed over and the Airedale was the result, Ranald flying the prototype at Rearsby on in April 1961 and this was followed by the ultimate Air Observation Post Auster, the E.3 or AOP.11, in August. Both

An aircraft with a future in farming' – a brochure for the Agricola, 1956.

Ranald Porteous piloting first Beagle Husky 180, G-ASBV, in 1962. *Beagle*

The prototype Airedale, G-ARKE, peeling away from the photographer's lens, 1961. *Beagle*

Ranald Porteous at the helm of the E.3 in military guise as XP254. The cowling declares it to be a 'Beagle-Auster AOP Mark Eleven'. *Beagle*

were shown off at the Farnborough airshow the following month, with Ranald performing his hallmark Porteous Loop in the E.3. A total of 36 Airedales was built; the E.3 remained a one-off but is still airworthy, as G-ASCC, with a Cambridge-based owner. Days after Ranald had dazzled the 1968 Farnborough audience with an eight-turn spin in a Beagle Pup he was dismissed in a cost-cutting purge of staff.

Beagle collapsed in December 1969 and the following month Ranald took a marketing post with Scottish Aviation in readiness for the Prestwick-based company taking over production of the Bulldog military trainer. Ranald left Scottish in January 1977 to join Britten-Norman, also on the sales side, until he retired in 1981. Sqn Ldr Ranald Logan Porteous died in 1998, aged 82.

G Powell

| 16 Aug 1920 | Beardmore WB.X G-EAQJ |
| | 1 x 160hp Beardmore |

ALL that is known about test pilot G Powell is his once, and once only, maiden flight in the Beardmore entry for the Air Ministry Commercial Aeroplane competition staged at Martlesham Heath in August 1920. Powered by an in-house six-cylinder in-line, derived from an Austro-Daimler design, the two-seat all-metal biplane used airship construction techniques. With no time to test it at Dalmuir, Glasgow, it was trucked to Martlesham and assembled. Powell took it up on 16th August only for the radiator not to work. The WB.X never flew again, the seized engine being impossible to replace before the competition closed.

'Sandy' Powell

| 13 May 1948 | Percival Prince G-ALCM |
| | 2 x 520hp Alvis Leonides 501 |

Harry Proctor Powell, born 1911. After studying mine engineering, he took up a post as a school teacher. 'Sandy' joined the RAF in 1936 and began training at 5 E&RFTS at Hanworth under the instruction of Flt Lt 'Willie' Wilson*. His first unit was 104 Squadron, converting from Hawker Hinds to Bristol Blenheims at Hucknall in the spring of 1938. Via 13 OTU at Bicester, he flew 'ops' within the Advanced Air Striking Force during the Battle of France in early 1940, followed by an instructor's course at Central Flying School, Wittering. After CFS he was posted to A&AEE at Boscombe Down, joining the 'C' Flight of the Performance Testing Squadron under its Flight Commander, Sqn Ldr R G Slade*. While conducting a night test in North American Mitchell II FL191 on 1st October 1942, Fg Off Powell suffered what he described in Mike Lithgow's Vapour Trails *as an engine failure immediately after take-off at around 110mph over Boscombe. The twin-engined bomber cartwheeled and ended up in a pile close to a block of hangars. Miraculously, Sandy and the two crew suffered only bruises. Tim Mason in* The Secret Years – Flight Testing at Boscombe Down 1939-1945 *provides more detail: "FL191 ...was written off in spectacular fashion the night it arrived in October 1942 when it cartwheeled... following premature retraction of the rapid-acting (7 seconds) undercarriage on take-off." By 1943 Sandy was CO of 'C' Flight, A&AEE and in 1944 Wg Cdr Powell was appointed Assistant Commandant of ETPS, under Gp Capt 'Sam' McKenna ready for the intake of No.2 Course. By early 1946 Sandy took up the post of test pilot at Air Service Training, Hamble; types flown including Mosquitos and Spitfires.*

NICKNAMED after a famous 1930s British comedian, Wg Cdr Harry Proctor Powell joined Percival Aircraft at Luton early in 1948, taking over from Leonard Carruthers*. (Sandy's middle name could not be more appropriate, the Luton factory was completing the final Proctor Vs, ending a production run for the type that began in 1939.) Prentice

The second Prince was first flown by 'Sandy' Powell on 7th January 1949 and was delivered to Brazilian operator Aeronorte as PP-XEG in August 1950. It is illustrated on air test out of Luton with the starboard Leonides feathered. *Percival Aircraft*

trainers for the RAF and export were rolling out of the factory and Sandy was set to carry out the maiden flight of the next production success for the company, the twin-engined Prince. A larger and more powerful version of the one-off Merganser, the Prince was designed for a wide range of civilian and military roles and later versions were named Pembroke and President. On board *Charlie-Mike* with Sandy at Luton on 13th May 1948 was its designer, Arthur Bage.

Sandy left Percival in early 1950, briefly taking up the post of test pilot for the aviation division of Dunlop before joining the brake and hydraulics division of Lockheed at Leamington Spa as sales manager. At Luton, Sandy was succeeded by 'Dick' Wheldon*. Sandy contributed a chapter to Mike Lithgow's *Vapour Trails*, published in 1954, and this seems to have inspired him to create what have become two 'standards' in test pilot writing: *Test Flight* and *Men with Wings*, appearing in 1956 and 1957, respectively. Wg Cdr Harry Proctor Powell AFC died in 1986, aged 75.

Charles Powis

| 12 Sep 1936 | Miles Peregrine U9 |
| | 2 x 205hp DH Gipsy Six II |

WITH F G Miles on his way to the USA on business, there were several pilots available at Woodley to carry out the maiden flight of the twin-engined, six-passenger Peregrine prototype. When Charles Owen Powis said that he'd like to do the honours, it was hard to turn him down even though he had never flown a twin before! Charles was Managing Director of Phillips & Powis Aircraft (Reading) Ltd, the company that built the aircraft designed by F G Miles. No corners were cut because of his position in the organisation; Charles was a very competent pilot and he regularly helped out on the flying side of the business. It was agreed that the retractable undercarriage would remain down throughout the first flight. There was also a potential issue with the prototype's centre of gravity (CG); so technician Roy Bournon went along. Roy positioned himself behind Charles and, if needed, could move aft in the cabin until his weight trimmed out any problems with wayward CG! Only two Peregrines were built. Charles resigned his post in 1937 and by 1940 was an RAF squadron leader.

The first of two Miles Peregrines, U9 – later G-AEDE – on an early test flight. *Miles Aircraft*

Waldo Price-Owen

Waldo B Price-Owen, born 1916. Joined the RAF in 1937 and trained in Britain and Egypt. Posted to 8 Squadron at Khormaksar, Aden, in 1938, he flew Vickers Vincents against dissident tribes in the Yemen. In May 1939 he was transferred to Egypt, to 33 Squadron and then 112 Squadron, both with Gloster Gladiators. He was shot down by an Italian Air Force biplane and parachuted to a safe landing in the desert; re-joining his unit some time later. Still flying Gladiators, Waldo moved to Greece, with 80 Squadron until the unit was withdrawn from the theatre in April 1941. Having been shot down in North Africa, Waldo helped to 'balance the books' during the Greek campaign, claiming two Italian Fiat CR.42s as 'probables', one each in November and December 1940. With his knowledge of Egypt, he was next stationed at Takoradi on the Gold Cost of Africa acting as Convoy Leader, escorting aircraft on delivery across Africa to Egypt. After this he was a test pilot with the following Maintenance Units: 117 at Port Sudan, Sudan; 133 Eastleigh, Kenya; 107 Kasfareet, Egypt. Posted to 118 Squadron at Coltishall in February 1943 Waldo flew Supermarine Spitfire Vs for three months. He was OC 9 Group Communications Flight at Samlesbury before graduating from ETPS No.2 Course at Boscombe Down 1944-1945. Waldo spent a month testing Fireflies for Fairey as part of the syllabus.

AFTER completing his ETPS course in January 1945 Sqn Ldr Waldo Price Owen – also known as PO (ie 'Pee-Oh') to his colleagues – was seconded to Westland at Yeovil for three months, under CTP Harald Penrose*. In April 1945 he was posted to A&AEE at Boscombe Down, 'A' Flight. Waldo was appointed as CTP for Armstrong Siddeley (AS) Engines at Bitteswell in August 1947. The bulk of this work is beyond the remit of the book but, unlike many powerplant specialists, he got to handle the first flight of a prototype.

Boulton Paul CTP Lindsay Neale* had flown the first AS Mamba turboprop Balliol, VL917, from the company airfield at Pendeford on 24th March 1948 only to write it off in a forced landing after the prop went into fine pitch and there was no response from the throttle. With Lindsay recovering from a broken leg and other injuries, it was felt that testing the second Mamba-powered Balliol, VL892, would be better placed with the engine's manufacturers and that the long runways at Bitteswell would also be an advantage. The third prototype, VL935, was trucked to Bitteswell and re-assembled. It seemed that the Mamba-powered examples were jinxed. Waldo took VL935 up for its maiden flight on 17th May 1948 for an uneventful first 20 minutes. Again the prop went into fine pitch and the power fell away. Approaching from the west, slipping over the A5 road into Bitteswell, VL935 struck a metal pole on the perimeter hedge, the Balliol undershot and thumped down into the grass before the threshold. Waldo was unhurt; the Mamba-Balliol was repaired and re-joined the test programme.

By 1950 Waldo had amassed 1,800-plus flying hours on 82 types. Sqn Ldr Waldo B Price-Owen left AS in 1951 and died in 1969, aged 53.

Clifford Prodger

Feb 1917	PB Nighthawk 1388 2 x 125hp Anzani
Dec 1917	Blackburn Kangaroo B9970 2 x 250hp RR Falcon II
Apr 1918	AW Armadillo X19 1 x 230hp Bentley BR.2
4 Aug 1918	EE Cork I N86 2 x 350hp RR Eagle VIII

Notes: PB – Pemberton Billing, flown from Eastchurch. The Kangaroo flew from Brough and the Cork used the slipway at Brough, flying from the Humber. The Armadillo flew from Cramlington and as the well-respected Oliver Tapper in *Armstrong Whitworth Aircraft since 1913* notes that it was *probably* flown by Clifford, it deserves a listing.

Clifford B Prodger, born 1889 in Minnesota, USA. He learned to fly at fellow American George W Beatty's school at Hendon in 1915 on Beatty-Wright biplanes. By 1916 he was chief instructor and began to offer his services as a test pilot.

"PRODGER and Parker dashed hither and thither, testing landplanes and seaplanes; monoplanes, biplanes, triplanes – even a quadruplane; everything from single-seaters to some of the Handley Page giants… The average fee for testing production line aircraft was £10 an hour, but special fees were arranged for prototypes." This is how Constance Babington Smith introduced the work of the Prodger-Isaac Aviation Company in her ground-breaking book *Testing Time*. Clifford Prodger set up the company in 1916 as a freelance test pilot agency and it was perhaps the first of its kind. It was run by the energetic Bernard Isaacs, former assistant manager of the Claude Grahame-White Aviation Company and the man behind the barrage of special events at Hendon before the war broke out. As well as Clifford's services, the agency also handled Sydney Pickles* and later John Lankester Parker* – who is mentioned in the quote above.

The incredible Pemberton Billing Nighthawk, designed to destroy Zeppelins. *Supermarine Aviation Works*

An early production Blackburn
Kangaroo, 1918. *KEC*

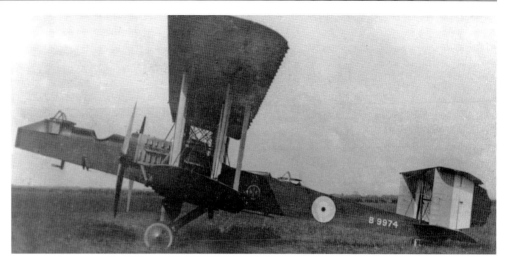

An early commission was with Short, testing Type 184 floatplanes, with Pickles and Parker sharing in the work. Regular work for Clifford was to be found at Handley Page; he was still handling that company's output of large bombers in 1919 – his last recorded flying in Britain. Clifford was at the helm of the second HP O/100 1456 (see John Babington) at Cricklewood in April 1916 following major redesign. Frederick Handley Page was determined to make as much capital out of this as possible and on 23rd April Clifford took ten passengers to 10,000ft in just shy of 40 minutes. A contingency of Admiralty 'brass' arrived on 7th May 1916 to view the acceptance trials of the new O/100. Onlookers were astonished when 16 passengers boarded 1456 – a load of 3,395lb – and Clifford conducted a spritely take-off and climb to 3,000ft. This was a world record uplift and very impressive – Frederick neglected to reveal that only sufficient fuel for the carefully planned sortie had been carried to ease the margins! The following month Clifford took 20 passengers airborne in 1456.

Vernon Busby* had been killed in the prototype HP V/1500 in June 1918. Frederick Handley Page wanted to put the expensive programme back into a good light and turned to Clifford, who had flown the second example, B9464, at Cricklewood on 3rd August 1918. In November Clifford demonstrated the third machine, F7136, by taking up journalists and members of the workforce: 40 people, a world record passenger load. Clifford was at Aldergrove on 20th December 1918 to test the first Harland and Wolff-built V/1500, E4307. He spent the early months of 1919 ferrying other examples from Northern Ireland to England.

Designated PB.31E, the quadruplane mentioned above by Constance Babington Smith was the most bizarre of the prototypes flown by Clifford. The 'PB' relates to Noel Pemberton Billing, the founder of what became the Supermarine Aviation Works in 1916. Named Nighthawk, the PB.31E was envisaged as patrolling waiting for the arrival of a Zeppelin, illuminating the enemy with a searchlight powered by a 5hp ABC auxiliary power unit and then attacking with 1½lb shells from a Davis gun. The Nighthawk did not get beyond the prototype stage. The Blackburn Kangaroo was a landplane development of a large floatplane and entered limited production, going on to become a backbone of pioneer airline operations in 1919. The Armadillo was a private-venture fighter from Armstrong Whitworth which remained a one-off. The Cork was a patrol flying-boat initiated

by the Phoenix Dynamo Company, which became part of English Electric in 1918. Clifford carried out the maiden flight from the Humber on 4th August 1918 with Lt Cdre Hume and Capt Slater as observer and engineer, respectively. Clifford B Prodger died on 22nd August 1920 at Redwood City, California in an unspecified accident – he was 31.

Raymond Pullin

7 Jun 1938	Weir W.5
	1 x 50hp Weir Pixie I
26 Oct 1939	Weir W.6
	1 x 200hp DH Gipsy Six II

THE name Raymond A Pullin hardly trips off the tongue as a test pilot, let alone one who flew a major national breakthrough – he was at the helm of the first British helicopter to achieve controlled flight. Bob Graham* made the first, tentative helicopter 'hops' in the Brennan in 1924. But while the flight time of that venture could be measured in minutes and ended in a crumpled heap; the Weir W.5 and W.6 tandem-rotor designs clocked over 150 flying hours before the pressures of World War Two brought the project to a close in July 1940.

Following on from a series of increasingly advanced autogyros, tested by Alan Marsh*, the Glasgow-based J & G Weir company capitalised on its experience of rotors and rotorheads by developing a practical helicopter. (James G Weir was also chairman of the Cierva Autogiro Company but the two organisations continued to carry out parallel development programmes until full amalgamation in 1943.) Weir designer C G Pullin adopted a single-engine, twin-rotor design with the rotors carried on outriggers on either side of the fuselage. Powered by a Pixie four-cylinder in-line, the W.5 was piloted by Raymond Pullin – the designer's son – on 7th June 1938. Trials were very successful and the larger, two-seat W.6 took over the flying programme on 26th October 1939. The rotors on the W.6 could be declutched, allowing autorotation in the event of an engine failure. The Weir helicopter programme was terminated in July 1940 and C G Pullin worked at the Fighting Vehicle Research Centre and later with Frank Whittle's Power Jets company. And with that the name of Raymond Pullin faded.

Flying helmet in hand, a superb portrait of Jeffrey Quill. *via Tony Buttler*

Jeffery Quill

10 Nov 1938	Supermarine 'High Speed' Spitfire N17 1 x 2,100hp RR Merlin II Special
27 Nov 1941	Supermarine Spitfire IV DP845 1 x 1,445hp RR Griffon IIB
4 Jul 1942	Supermarine Spitfire VI X4942 1 x 1,415hp RR Merlin 47
20 Nov 1942	Supermarine Spitfire VIII JF274 1 x 1,580hp RR Merlin 61
4 Oct 1942	Supermarine Spitfire F.21 DP851 1 x 2,035hp RR Griffon 51
12 Oct 1942	Supermarine Spitfire V Special W3760 1 x 1,440hp RR Merlin 45
20 Jan 1943	Supermarine Spitfire 'XIV' JF316 1 x 2,025hp RR Griffon 65
Nov 1943	Supermarine Seafire XV NS487 1 x 1,750hp RR Griffon VI
30 Jun 1944	Supermarine Spiteful NN660 1 x 2,375hp RR Griffon 61
27 Jul 1946	Supermarine Attacker TS409 1 x 5,000lbst RR Nene 3

Notes: With its many variants and modifications, determining which Spitfire versions represent sufficient differences to call a true prototype has always been a matter of great debate. Several of the examples chosen here represent a modification of a previous variant acting as the interim prototype. For the table, the author has followed Jeffrey Quill's own estimations of the most important 'stepping stones', as outlined in his superb *Spitfire – A Test Pilot's Story*. First flight venues: N17 and X4942 at Eastleigh; DP845 and DP851 at Worthy Down; W3760 from the waters off Hamble – it was converted by Folland to a floatplane; NN660 from High Post; TS409 from Boscombe Down. JF274 was the first production Mk.VIII; 'Special' JF316 was designated Mk.VIIIG as the interim Mk.XIV, Jeffrey carried out the maiden flight of the first production Mk.XIV, RB140, in October 1943.

This is also a good place to remind readers the many variants of the Spitfire encouraged a major change in the designation system in 1944. Roman numerals (eg Mk.XVI) were to continue but once Mk.XX had been reached, the change would be made to Arabic, hence Spitfire Mk.21 etc. In 1948 the decision was taken to adopt Arabic numerals no matter what. For example Spitfire PR.XIXs became PR.19s.

Jeffery Kindersley Quill, born 1913. He joined the RAF in October 1931 and during his training was rated as 'Exceptional'. He joined 17 Squadron, flying Bristol Bulldog IIs, at Upavon on 27th September 1932. He joined the RAF Meteorological Flight at Duxford, with Armstrong Whitworth Atlases and Siskin IIIAs, and in November 1934 he was appointed its CO upon the departure of George Snarey*. On 14th March 1935 Jeffrey crashed an unidentified Siskin when he encountered bad weather and tried to let down through cloud, the biplane made a very hard landing and ended up on its back: Jeffrey injured his nose and was bruised. His last sortie with the 'Met' Flight was in Siskin J8882 on 28th December 1935. Three days later he joined Vickers at Brooklands.

THERE are many names that can be closely linked with the Spitfire and a goodly number of them appear in these two volumes. But if asked to bring that down to the most crucial there are four: two designers and two pilots. Reginald Joseph Mitchell conceived the Supermarine Type 300 Spitfire, but died on 11th June 1937, aged 42, having seen only the prototype, K5054, fly. The man who made that first flight was 'Mutt' Summers* and his association with the type was also brief, in his role of CTP for the entire Vickers organisation – Supermarine having been acquired by Vickers in 1928. By contrast the other two names of the 'essential' quartet were part of the Spitfire story from beginning to end and beyond into the jet age. Joseph 'Joe' Smith took over from Mitchell, overseeing the programme from prototype to mass production, to the laminar flow technology of the Spiteful and on to the Attacker. Paralleling Joe Smith was Jeffrey Quill who took on the bulk of the prototype and development flying, creating and managing the large production test organisation required to meet the output.

On 1st November 1935, Flt Lt Jeffrey Quill flew an Armstrong Whitworth Siskin from Duxford to Brooklands to have a word with Mutt Summers about a job with Vickers. Mutt was impressed and asked him to return for a more formal

A line-up to celebrate the Seafire XVII entering service, September 1945. Fourth from the left is Supermarine chief designer Joseph Smith; sixth from left is Jeffrey Quill, then: Admiral Sir Denys Boyd and Sir James Bird of Supermarine. *Vickers-Armstrongs E2604*

chat with himself and Sir Robert McLean. Jeffrey described in *Spitfire – A Test Pilot's Story* how that meeting went: "I flew to Brooklands again on 18th November and lunched with Mutt Summers and Sir Robert, followed by a short interview with the latter. The result was that I was offered the job of Assistant to the Chief Test Pilot at a salary of £500 a year, conditional on my applying for immediate release from the RAF." Jeffrey was not bowled over by this as he saw himself as a career RAF man; but he could not get a confirmation that a permanent commission was coming his way. This uncertainty and Mutt revealing that the Supermarine division was working on a new monoplane fighter helped Jeffrey commit to leaving the RAF.

At Brooklands there were Vildebeests and Vincents to test and Wellesleys would start to come off the production line in the spring of 1937. On 5th February 1936 Jeffrey was at Woodley where he carried out an acceptance flight on Miles Falcon Six G-ADTD which was the new 'hack', particularly for flying down to Eastleigh where the Spitfire was being readied. Based in Southampton was the Supermarine test pilot, George Pickering* who had begun to teach Jeffrey to fly amphibians and flying-boats. On 5th March 1936 Jeffrey flew Mutt in G-ADTD to Eastleigh where he first took the prototype Spitfire, K5054, into the skies. Twenty-one days later Jeffrey piloted K5054 – the start of an association where he uniquely went on to fly every Spitfire and Seafire variant.

There was an agonising wait for the first production Spitfire – K5054 being the only prototype. In between, Jeffrey started to sign off Wellesleys, a type with what he called "ladylike behaviour". The first flight of K7737 on 5th July 1937 was to be very different from the rest. *Spitfire – A Test Pilot's Story* explains: "...whilst K7737 was wallowing at about 12,000ft and I was scribbling on my knee-pad, waiting for her nose to drop and for us to pick up speed, she suddenly lurched into a right-hand spin. I was taken completely by surprise for the Wellesley had never shown the slightest tendency to do this before. I immediately took recovery action but it was to no avail. ...The Wellesley treated everything I did with scornful disdain and continued solemnly spinning down and down. Somewhere around 3,000ft I decided I would have to go." During Jeffrey's parachute descent he watched the monoplane crash and the emergency services driving full pelt to the scene. He landed in the garden of a Brooklands Flying Club member!

Promoted to CTP for Supermarine in May 1938, on the 14th Jeffery conducted the maiden flight of K9787, the second Spitfire and first production example. "As soon as I climbed into the cockpit I felt entirely at home in this apparent twin sister of K5054. The first flight of only 35 minutes was devoted to checking that everything was working as it should, and produced no surprises or anxieties. Thereafter we got down to a full flight testing programme." Getting production flowing was a traumatic experience and it was the Castle Bromwich Aircraft Factory that was to transform the creation of Spitfires. As related in Chapter Two, in 1939 Jeffrey appointed a sure pair of hands to take on the challenges of Castle Bromwich – Alex Henshaw. The maiden flight table and the notes provide only the slightest insight into Jeffrey's work, which involved vast numbers of flying hours ironing out new variants. Readers will be familiar with the Spitfire and its development, so we will not deal with production sequences, numbers and variants in detail here.

The High Speed Spitfire, N17, in its striking blue and silver colours scheme, running up at Eastleigh 1938. It was developed in response to a series of world air speed records generated by Heinkel and Messerschmitt types, but eventually the attempt was abandoned as the war loomed. *Key Publishing collection – www.keypublishing.com*

In September 1940 the Woolston factory was bombed by the Luftwaffe and a dispersed production system was introduced. At the same time Worthy Down was taken over as the main centre for development and production testing. Jeffrey arranged for 'sample' aircraft from other factories to be brought to Worthy Down to check on quality across the entire production run. Thousands of hours of testing brought about many dramatic moments for Jeffery, but only one sortie ended in a write off. Flying the interim Mk.21 prototype DP851 on 13th May 1943 the starboard undercarriage failed on landing at Boscombe Down; the aircraft whipped around, removing the port leg in the process. Travelling on its belly backwards, DP851 was beyond repair when it came to stop; Jeffrey was unhurt. Built originally as a Mk.IV prototype, DP851 well illustrates the step-by-step evolution of Spitfire variants: the first true F.21, PP139, appeared in November 1943.

Jeffrey put great pressure on the RAF to be allowed to join an operational Spitfire squadron so he could appreciate how a test pilot could help make the fighter exactly what its pilots were looking for. Eventually, the logic of his request was recognised and on 5th August 1940 – in the height of the Battle of Britain – Jeffrey was attached to 65 Squadron at Hornchurch. Jeffrey made it clear he was not just an observer; on 16th August he shot down a Messerschmitt Bf 109E and two days later shared in the downing of a Heinkel He 111. Jeffery returned to Eastleigh on 24th August.

The flight line at Eastleigh during the summer of 1941. A Spitfire I had been painted up as the prototype for a 'starring' role in the Leslie Howard film *The First of the Few*. Behind is a General Aircraft Monospar and a Miles Falcon – the latter very probably the Vickers-Armstrongs 'hack' G-ADTD. *Peter Green Collection*

This 'hands-on' attitude extended to the Fleet Air Arm (FAA) in early 1944. Other than a couple of landings on HMS *Indomitable*, Jeffrey had little experience of aircraft carriers, yet he was testing a fighter designed to do just that. He was appointed as a supernumerary Lieutenant Commander and by the spring of 1944 he was at Easthaven – which the Navy called HMS *Peewit* – to experience the delights of aerodrome dummy deck landings (ADDLs, pronounced 'addles'). While the Scottish airfield could not turn into wind or pitch and roll in rough seas, the instructors did their best to make the exercise as convincing as possible, so much so that there was a mock-up island structure to the side of the runway. As Jeffrey wrote in the chapter he contributed to Mike Lithgow's* *Vapour Trails* this subterfuge gave Easthaven an alternative name to *Peewit* – HMS *Spurious*! Steaming in the Clyde a *real* carrier was on station, this was the veteran HMS *Argus*, used for deck landing training. Jeffrey had an appointment with the commander of the Easthaven training wing who was ensconced on *Argus*. On 9th March 1944 Jeffrey arranged to borrow 731 Squadron Hawker Sea Hurricane Ib Z4921 and was told that – subject to him successfully completing a couple of addles – he could fly over to the ship. The weather was not co-operative on the east coast at Easthaven, but was clear in the Firth of Clyde. Time became pressing and Jeffrey decided that addles could be dispensed with, took off and headed west. 'Batted' down to the deck, he failed to chop the throttle immediately, missed the arrester wires and Z4921 crumpled as it engaged the barrier. The Hurricane was a write off and Jeffrey's embarrassment total – especially as the officer he needed to see had been the one 'batting' him in!

After this inauspicious start, and more than a few addles, Jeffrey spent an intensive time with the FAA, flying Seafire IIs with 879 and 886 Squadrons, from HMS *Attacker* and *Ravager* and the trials carrier *Pretoria Castle*. He also got to sample Grumman Wildcats and Hellcats and Vought Corsairs.

Flt Lt G S White of the RAE was killed on 4th September 1939 when the Spitfire prototype, K5054, stalled on approach to Farnborough. Despite this unfortunate double loss, an all over blue-grey Spitfire marked K5054 again graced the flight line at Eastleigh during the summer of 1941. The airfield was

Spitfire I X4942 was taken off the production line and converted into the prototype high-flyer Mk.VI. *Key Publishing collection – www.keypublishing.com*

one of the locations for *The First of the Few*, a tribute to R J Mitchell and the Spitfire. This was directed by, and starred, Leslie Howard, who played 'RJM'. David Niven had the role of 'Geoffrey Crisp', the test pilot. Jeffrey flew some incredible aerobatic routines in the reincarnated 'K5054', a borrowed Spitfire I with three-bladed propeller.

Joe Smith's ultimate development of the Spitfire was so much of a transformation that it was renamed: Spiteful for the RAF and Seafang for the FAA. The Spiteful provided the means for Supermarine, and Jeffrey, to make the transition to jets. By marrying the Spiteful wing and undercarriage to a new fuselage, the first operational Royal Navy jet fighter, the Attacker, was born. Jeffrey conducted the debut of TS409 from Boscombe Down on 27th July 1946. The following year, Jeffrey handed over to his friend and colleague Mike Lithgow*. Jeffrey went on to an impressive 'desk' career with Vickers and, from 1960, BAC, concluding as Director of Marketing at Panavia: During his working life he had evolved from Bristol Bulldogs to swing-wing Tornados. In 1983 Jeffrey's autobiography *Spitfire – A Test Pilot's Story* was published and remains in print. Along with Alex Henshaw's *Sigh for a Merlin*, these two books combine to provide the most human and engagingly written story of Mitchell's exceptional fighter.

In May 1955 Vickers-Armstrongs (Aircraft) Ltd acquired Spitfire V AB910 (civilian registered G-AISU) and Jeffery was able to keep his hand in on the type. On Battle of Britain day 1965 BAC donated AB910 to the Battle of Britain Flight at Coltishall and the Spitfire still flies with the present-day Battle of Britain Memorial Flight at Coningsby. With the handing over of AB910, Jeffrey assumed that his days of piloting a Spitfire were over, but in 1966 he was invited to Coltishall to fly AB910 one more time, for a documentary being made by a French film company. Jeffery's words in *Spitfire – A Test Pilot's Story* sum up the emotions of that last sortie: "As I taxied in afterwards and shut down the engine, I remained in the cockpit listening to the gentle ticking noises as the engine cooled off and savoured the indefinable yet so familiar smells. It had been 30 years since my first flight in a Spitfire and 18 since I had been an active test pilot, although I had flown AB910 from time to time when I could escape from the not inconsiderable preoccupations of my post-war job. My mind went back to the day in 1936 when I stood with R J Mitchell and Mutt Summers around the unfinished prototype in the old works at Woolston – and to the day, some two months later, when as a very young test pilot [aged 23] I had made my own first flight in it."

Mk.IX MJ892, the last of the Spitfire floatplanes, at Beaumaris, Anglesey, mid-1944. *KEC*

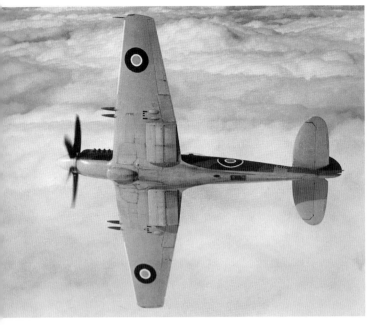

Spiteful XIV RB515 was the initial production example, flying in May 1945. Note the angular lines of the laminar flow wing and large under wing radiator housings. See the section on 'Pat' Shea-Simmonds for more on this aircraft. *Key Publishing collection – www.keypublishing.com*

The prototype Attacker, TS409 – compare the wing with that of the Spiteful. *Key Publishing collection – www.keypublishing.com*

Flt Lt Jeffery Kindersley Quill OBE AFC died on 20th February 1996, aged 83. At one stage in the war, the press called him 'Hell-Diver Quill' which the quiet, modest pilot must have hated. When he died he was universally referred to as 'Mr Spitfire' with deep respect and affection.

Roy Radford

H R Radford joined the RAF in 1946 and instructed on Vickers Valiants and HP Victors in the late 1950s. Roy Graduated from ETPS Course No.18 at Farnborough 1959 going on to fly for A&AEE up to 1964.

ROY RADFORD joined BAC at Hurn and Wisley, under CTP Brian Trubshaw* in 1964. He was heavily involved in the BAC One-Eleven programme, becoming Project Pilot and, by 1967, was Deputy CTP. On 30th June 1967 Roy was co-pilot to Brian for the first flight of the stretched One-Eleven 500, G-ASYD, from Hurn. G-ASYD had originally flown on 13th July 1965 as a standard length 400-series but was given the 8ft 4in increase in fuselage length from early 1967. 'Syd', as this One-Eleven was universally known at BAC, proved to be a very adaptable test and trials airframe. It returned to Hurn in 1969, had the fuselage extension removed and was remodelled as the prototype 475-series, optimised for 'hot-and-high' operation. Roy was at the helm for its maiden flight in this guise on 27th August 1970 and when it was upgraded to 670-series on 13th September 1977, by which time BAC had become BAe. 'Syd' is preserved at the Brooklands Museum, Weybridge.

Roy was also a part of the BAC/Sud Concorde programme, from Filton and Fairford. He was appointed as CTP in 1981, overseeing the final deliveries of One-Elevens, the last example flying from Hurn in 1984. At Filton the VC-10 tanker conversion programme for the RAF got into swing on 22nd June 1982 when Roy captained ZA141, the first K.2. In 1985 Roy became Flight Operations Manager at Filton, retiring in 1989. As a former Concorde and VC-10 pilot, Roy is much in demand; he was a guest at the 50th anniversary of the maiden flight of the VC-10 prototype at Brooklands on 29th June 2012.

Michael Randrup

Michael Randrup was born in Moscow, Imperial Russia, in 1913 to Danish parents: the family settled in Great Britain in 1917. Inspired by a joy-ride in an Avro 504K at Blackpool in 1931, he attended the College of Aeronautical Engineering at Chelsea in 1937, graduating in 1939. During this time, he learned to fly at the Kent Flying Club, Bekesbourne. Joining the RAF in 1940, he became an instructor, in Britain and in Southern Rhodesia. In 1942 he was flying Supermarine Spitfire Vs with 234 Squadron and he succeeded in downing a Focke-Wulf Fw 190. In 1944 he was testing repaired Spitfires at Air Service Training, Hamble, under Eric Greenwood. In 1944 he was posted to RAE Farnborough and he flew a wide variety of aircraft with the Engine Research and Development Flight (ERDF), including a captured Heinkel He 162A jet fighter. With the acting rank of squadron leader, Mike was OC of ERDF by 1945. On 28th July 1945, Mike was flying Spitfire XIV RB176 at Farnborough when the port undercarriage failed and the aircraft broke its back; Mike was not injured.*

Mike Randrup flew the aerodynamic prototype of the Canberra PR.9, converted PR.7 WH793, on 8th July 1955. *BAC*

With his engine test background at Farnborough, Michael Randrup joined D Napier and Son's trials and development flight in March 1946. (He became a naturalised British citizen the following year.) Again, he was involved in flying a wide range of aircraft, of which the bulk lies beyond the remit of this title – by 1950 Mike had over 3,500 hours on 80 different types. As part of the development of the Canberra PR.9 high-altitude photo-reconnaissance aircraft, Napier was sub-contracted by English Electric to create a hybrid aerodynamic prototype. Canberra PR.7 WH793 was converted to near PR.9 status and Mike first flew it from Cranfield on 8th July 1955. Peter Hillwood* piloted the true PR.9 prototype, XH129, on 27th July 1958. On 28th August 1957, Mike and FTO Walter Shirley crewed Canberra B.2 WK163 which had been converted as a test-bed for the Napier Double Scorpion rocket booster, taking it to a world record of 70,310ft. (WK163 is now part of the Classic Air Force collection at Coventry.) Mike was manager for BAC's major contract in Saudi Arabia 1966-1973; he died in 1984, aged 71.

P E Raw

Flt Lt P E Raw was seconded to Hawker at Langley as a production test pilot. On 20th January 1944 he was testing Tempest V JN747. In unknown circumstances, JN747 crashed and burned, killing the pilot instantly.

Arthur 'Dizzy' Rawson

| 18 Feb 1935 | Kay 33/1 Gyroplane G-ACVA |
| | 1 x 75hp Pobjoy R |

Flt Lt Arthur Harold Charles Rawson became CTP for the Cierva Autogiro Company (CAC) in July 1928, succeeding the part-time George Thomson (see Chapter Seven). The story of the Autogiro – the name termed by its inventor Juan de la Cierva* – is outlined in depth in the first volume in the section on the Spanish-born pioneer. Arthur was given the nickname 'Dizzy', very likely because of his extensive experience of whirling rotors – he became the first pilot to achieve 1,000 rotary hours. Demonstrating and publicising the

Cierva C.19 Mk.I G-AAGL at Haldon in Devon on 21st September 1929 after it was blown over and written off during an air rally – 'Dizzy' Rawson was unharmed. It had only received its certificate of airworthiness 30 days before. The twin fin and rudder tail could be canted upwards to deflect airflow into the rotors to get them spinning. *Peter Green Collection*

new form of flight was the highest priority and Dizzy was kept very busy in this manner. James Weir, chairman of CAC, had entered Dizzy and C.8L Mk.II G-EBYY in the July 1928 King's Cup – the first of its breed to do so. Ironically, it had to retire when it force landed near Nuneaton in a field so small that even it could not fly out of.

In January 1929 Dizzy delivered a C.8L Mk.III to the Italian government in Rome and in October he flew two-seat C.19 Mk.II G-AAKZ to Le Bourget, Paris, for extensive demonstrations. At Hounslow Heath on 20th November 1930, Dizzy was displaying C.19 Mk.III G-ABCL but it hit a tree on take-off and was wrecked; Dizzy broke an ankle. He was in Bremen, Germany, in June 1931 to carry out the maiden flight of the first C.19 to be built by Focke-Wulf. Also in 1931 he wrote, with C J Sanders, *The Book of the C.19 Autogiro* – all part of the task of altering minds about rotary-winged flight. Dizzy left CAC in 1932, handing over to 'Reggie' Brie*.

Dizzy was commissioned by David Kay to test fly the single-seat gyroplane, Kay 33/1 G-ACVA, which featured a four-bladed rotor and hub of advanced design. Dizzy flew it for the first time from Eastleigh on 18th February 1935. The Kay survived and is now part of the National Museum of Flight Scotland and is presently on show in Edinburgh.

The Kay Gyroplane survives as part of the National Museum of Flight Scotland. *Ken Ellis*

'Freddy' Raynham

22 Dec 1912	Flanders B.2 1 x 40hp ABC
28 May 1913	Avro 503 floatplane 1 x 100hp Gnome
28 Jul 1913	Avro 504 1 x 80hp Gnome
1914	Avro 511 'Arrowscout' 1 x 80hp Gnome
1916	Avro 521 1 x 110hp Clerget
14 Jul 1916	Bristol M.1A 1 x 110hp Clerget
Jan 1917	Avro Pike N523 2 x 160hp Sunbeam
Mar 1917	Avro 529 3694 2 x 190hp RR Falcon
13 Aug 1918	Bristol Braemar C4296 4 x 230hp Siddeley Puma
1919	Martinsyde Raymor 1 x 285hp RR Falcon
1923	Hawker Woodcock J6987 1 x 385hp AS Jaguar II
9 Sep 1923	Handasyde Monoplane No.13 1 x 15hp Douglas
Sep 1924	Hawker Cygnet G-EBJH 1 x 34hp ABC Scorpion
Sep 1924	Hawker Hedgehog N187 1 x 390hp Bristol Jupiter IV

Notes: First flight venues: Flanders, Avro 504 and 511, Handasyde, Raymor, Woodcock and Hedgehog – Brooklands; Avro 503 – from the River Adur off Shoreham; Avro 521 – Trafford Park; M.1A and Braemar – Filton; Pike and 529-Hamble; Cygnet – Lympne. The Avro 511 was later rebuilt as the Type 51 with unswept wings and first flown by Freddy from Southport Beach in July 1914.

Frederick Phillip Raynham was born in 1893 and had a brief spell as an office junior to an agricultural college in Shropshire 1909. By 1910 – aged 17 – he was at Brooklands, working for the pioneer John V Neale. John created a series of aircraft from 1909 and it is likely to have been the second monoplane (sometimes referred to as the Neale VI or 6) that 'Freddie' was associated with. This machine was wrecked at Brooklands on 21st May 1910 – it is not recorded if Freddie had anything to do with this – and it was rebuilt by the Petre* brothers and Howard Flanders. By 1911 Freddie was learning to fly with the Avro school at Brooklands and on 9th May 1911 he qualified for Aviators' Certificate No.85 on a Type IV triplane. During 1912, Freddy was managing Tom Sopwith's school at Brooklands.

The Avro 503 floatplane beached at Shoreham in June 1913. *Peter Green Collection*

"F P RAYNHAM, who was to become one of the greatest test pilots in the world, took his certificate on the Avro machines, together with Messrs Conway-Jenkins and Ronald Kemp*." The words are those of R Dallas Brett as he introduced 'Freddy' Raynham in the narrative of his *History of British Aviation 1908-1914*. In a sub-chapter entitled 'The First Spin?' Dallas Brett relates an undated incident while flying an Avro Type D biplane at about 1,500ft, Freddy looked down at his compass only to find himself: "standing upright on the rudder pedals and whirling around. After two complete turns, he succeeded by some chance in pulling out and found himself down at 500ft." Dallas Brett asserts that Freddy was the first British pilot, possibly the first in the world, to recover from a spinning nose dive with engine on. On 25th August 1912 Wilfred Parke* recovered from a spin, but in full view of onlookers so that what he did to regain control could be assessed. 'Parke's Dive' technique was still a long time off becoming a routine part of training.

As 'Freddy' Raynham gained experience, both in terms of flying hours and types, he was engaged by Howard Flanders to test his B.2 biplane which had been entered in the August 1912 Military Aircraft Trials at Salisbury Plain. Although the B.2 was taken to the contest, its ABC engine arrived late and Freddy managed only a hop at the event. Back at Brooklands, he flew it on 22nd December 1912 and to show his confidence in it, Freddy took two passengers up that day. Freddy continued to fly the B.2 into 1913 as it was refined, but it remained a one-off.

In 1913 Freddy cemented his relationship with Avro, taking over as resident test pilot from Wilfred Parke and remaining with the expanding company until 1916. Flying from the River Adur near Shoreham on 28th May 1913, Freddy took the Avro 503 floatplane on its maiden flight; with him as a passenger, was Jack Alcock*. On 10th July 1913 Freddy was at Cowes on the Isle of Wight where he was to test another floatplane, built by J Samuel White. The company's designer, Howard Wright*, had embarked on the debut of the Seaplane No.1 on 13th May 1913 but it stalled on take-off from the River Medina and was wrecked; Wright was injured. Rebuilt and refined, the

prototype was ready on 10th July 1913 but as Freddy got it airborne a gust of wind caught it and the machine cartwheeled into the water. Freddy was rescued unscathed and the company went back to the drawing board.

The Type 503 was the stepping stone to the prototype 504, which Freddy had the honour of 'first flighting' from Brooklands on 28th July 1913 and is reported to have declared it: "just perfect". From this machine Avro was transformed from a workshop to an industry by the end of the Great War.

With sponsorship from the *Yorkshire Evening Post*, Robert Blackburn's test pilot (and no relation) 'Harry' Blackburn took part in a race that was dubbed 'The War of the Roses' between the Blackburn Type I and its Lancashire rival, the prototype Avro 504. Staged on 2nd October 1913, the 100-mile course ran from Leeds to York, Doncaster, Sheffield, Barnsley and back to Leeds. Harry flew with the Type I's owner, M G Christie, while for Avro, Freddy had A V Roe's younger brother, Humphrey, as passenger. Avro and Blackburn were neck and neck until poor weather forced Freddy to make a precautionary landing near Barnsley.

To prove the capabilities of the 504, Freddy had a crack at the British solo height record on 4th February 1914. He climbed to 15,000ft, easily eclipsing the record set the previous December by J M Salmond, then switched off and glided towards Hendon, 20 miles distant. Freddy made a perfect, power-off, landing having made the longest glide up to that time. What he hadn't done was achieve a *recognised* British altitude record, and six days later, with Royal Aero Club observers in attendance this time he tried again, taking the record with a passenger at 14,420ft.

The revolutionary Type 511 was a private-venture single-seat scout featuring sweptback wings, ailerons on both upper and lower wings and flaps. It was referred to as the 'Arrowscout' because of its wing shape, but it did not attract orders. The Type 521 was a development of the 504 intended as a fighter-trainer. Flight trials from Trafford Park included assistant designer Harry Broadsmith standing in the rear cockpit/gunner's position so that changes in airflow could be assessed.

Avro 504s were built and rebuilt in many varieties. E9265 was built by Grahame-White at Hendon as a 504K in 1918. It was modified at Hamble (illustrated) in 1922 as one of the 504N prototypes, with an Armstrong Siddeley Lynx engine. *KEC*

The Avro Pike bomber was powered by a pair of Sunbeam pushers and it was Freddy's first twin. In *Architect of Wings*, Harald Penrose's biography of Roy Chadwick, Freddy is quoted as discounting the safety aspects of two powerplants declaring they gave: "twice the chance of engine failure"! While engaged in acceptance testing at the Isle of Grain in May 1916, Freddy was flying the Pike with Roy Dobson acting as observer in the gunner's position behind the wings. The aircraft proved to be exceptionally tail heavy and Freddy realised that throttling back could precipitate a stall. 'Dobbie' – also a pilot – soon grasped the predicament and the nature of Freddy's hand signals. He climbed along the top of the fuselage, over Freddy's open cockpit and deposited himself in the nose gunner's 'office', transforming the centre of gravity! Freddy made a safe landing. Dobbie went on to become the driving force of Avro and later Hawker Siddeley as Sir Roy Dobson. Three Pikes were created, one with tractor propellers. Freddy also flew the much-developed Type 529 in 1917: only two were built. Freddy embarked on a career as a freelancer in 1916: he was succeeded at Avro by Harold Hammersley*.

First commission for Bristol was the private-venture M.1, the so-called 'Bullet', a single-seat monoplane scout designed by Frank Barnwell to break the line of pushers that were becoming increasingly vulnerable. Freddy was clearly delighted with the M.1, first flown in July 1916 it reached 132mph and to celebrate he flew it underneath the Clifton Suspension bridge! Despite its radical boost of performance, only 130 M.1s were built. The other machine from Bristol was another response to German bombing sorties over the UK and

the quest to return the compliment in Berlin. Powered by four Siddeley Pumas mounted in tandem – one pulling one pushing – the Braemar was an 81ft 8in-span triplane. Another Braemar and a civil version, the Pullman, followed in 1919 and 1920.

Freddy also worked for Brooklands-based Martinsyde, testing G.100 and G.102 'Elephants' and, from 1917 F.3 and F.4 Buzzards. While flying an unidentified Martinsyde – Harald Penrose believed it was a "'revised' G" – the machine went into wild gyrations and crashed near Weybridge: Freddy was lucky to come away with bad cuts to his face. Along with several other manufacturers, Martinsyde entered the *Daily Mail's* transatlantic flight challenge of 1919 in the hope that it could change the company's fortunes in the post-war downturn. A special two-bay version of the F.4 was created and named in honour of its crew as the Raymor – for Freddy Ray̲nham and navigator Charles Fairfax 'Fax' Mor̲gan. Freighted to Newfoundland, the Raymor was assembled at Qidi Vidi airstrip, where 'Jack' Alcock* and Harry Hawker* also started their adventures. The first air test was carried out on 17th April. Taking off for the Atlantic flight on 18th May 1919 the undercarriage hit a soft spot and the Raymor was badly damaged. Freddy was uninjured but Charles was hospitalised. As repairs were initiated Lt Conrad Biddlecombe was recruited to replace Morgan. Jack Alcock and Arthur Whitten Brown departed in the Vickers Vimy on 14th June 1919 and succeeded in the first ever crossing of the Atlantic by an aeroplane. Undaunted, Freddy was determined to have another go and on 17th July the pair set off, only for the Raymor to nose-dive into the ground on take-off – Freddy and Conrad were miraculously unhurt.

Freddy Raynham demonstrating the advanced Avro 511 at Hendon, 1914. *British Aerospace*

These two misfortunes did not put Freddy off the Martinsyde 'brand'. A scaled-down Buzzard was developed as a high-performance racer and called the Semiquaver. On a sortie out of Martlesham Heath on 21st March 1920 Freddy piloted this machine, G-EAPX, to a new British record over a measured kilometre of 161.43mph. Freddy first flew the last-ever Martinsyde, F.6 two-seat tourer G-EBDK, at Brooklands on 29th September 1921. This was a very special maiden flight – Freddy was both test pilot *and* customer! He had ordered the 200hp Wolseley Viper-powered machine for his own use and, in single-seat guise, he competed in the September 1922 King's Cup air race staged from Croydon, coming second to the Airco DH.4A of Frank Barnard*.

The month after the King's Cup found Freddy soaring over Itford Hill, north of Newhaven, at the *Daily Mail*-sponsored gliding competition. Piloting a glider designed by George Handasyde – one half of the defunct Martinsyde company – and built by the Air Navigation and Engineering Company (ANEC) Freddy established a British endurance record of 113 minutes. There was spin-off work beyond the contest; Terrence Boughton in *The Story of the British Light Aeroplane* describes Freddy being catapulted off a cliff near Torquay for a film called *The Hawk*. The plot involved the heroine having been kidnapped by the villain who made his exit in his private submarine. The Handasyde glider was the means of propelling the hero to the thrilling climax – perhaps best called a cliff-hanger! (The author's many filmographies reveal nothing on this would-be blockbuster.) For the 1923 Light Aeroplane Trials at Lympne, Freddy and George Handasyde again teamed up, this time with a 15hp Douglas-powered aircraft clearly derived from the 1922 glider.

In 1921 Handley Page responded to a US Navy tender for a single-seat, deck-landing fighter and in 1923 construction of three HP.21s (or Type S) began. The prototype was first flown

Captain Bond inspecting a Bristol M.1C (probably C4909) at Biggin Hill, 1918. *Peter Green Collection*

by Arthur Wilcockson* on 7th September 1923 but, as he was employed by Handley Page Transport, there were other demands on his time. Pressure was applied by the US Navy's British agent, Major Robert Mayo (he of the Short-Mayo Composite – see John Lankester Parker) to put a full-time professional on the job. That was Freddy and he first tried out the S-1 on 10th September 1923. Freddy agreed with Arthur that there were serious directional control issues with the little monoplane. Many 'fixes' were tried, with Freddy once flying five sorties in a day. With things more or less smoothed out and the promised hand-over date slipping all the time, Freddy was at Martlesham Heath, getting ready for acceptance trials.

During a flight in S-2, the second HP.21, in February 1924 Freddy suddenly found himself at 2,000ft with no elevator control. Maintaining level flight, he groped around the base of the control column to find that the push-rod linkage for the elevator had detached. Further fumbling located the errant end of the push-rod and by holding it with one hand, his other hand on the control column and by occasionally applying the 230hp Bentley BR.2's magneto switch to drop the power – while his

The second Braemar, with Liberty engines at Filton in 1919 with the second Bristol MR.1, A5178, to the left. *Rolls-Royce*

knees steadied the stick – Freddy found he could control the S-2. He brought it in for a smooth approach, but was hampered by having the lean down to keep a hold of the push-rod; seeing forward was impossible. The S-2 bounced and turned over, Freddy crawled clear. Handley Page was weeks adrift from the small print in the contract and the US Navy pulled the plug; the third HP.21 was left unfinished. It's ironic that a much larger cancellation by the US military contributed to the demise of Handley Page in 1969 – see John Allam.

With the death of Harry Hawker in July 1921 Freddy was brought in to fly for the company that carried the gallant Australian's name. His first 'first' for Hawker was the Woodcock single-seat day fighter powered by an Armstrong Siddeley Jaguar, although production examples – Mk.IIs – had Bristol Jupiters. The Woodcock kicked off a long line of Hawker fighters; 63 were accepted by the RAF. The Hedgehog three-seat naval reconnaissance biplane of the 1924 was not taken up and remained a one-off.

Woodcock II J7960, served with 17 Squadron from late 19126 to 1928. *KEC*

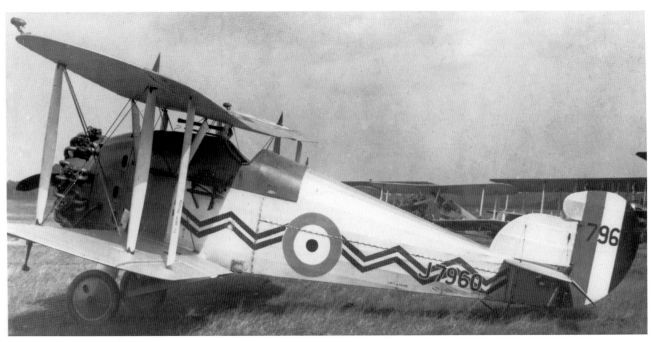

In September 1924 Freddy 'first flighted' a pair of dainty biplanes, the inaugural design of Sydney Camm – the Cygnet two-seater for the Lympne Light Aeroplane Trials. It was Freddy who had introduced Camm to Hawker designer George Carter; the two men got to know one another at Martinsyde, where Camm had been a draughtsman. At Lympne, Freddy won a £100 prize for the best take-off and landing performance flying Cygnet No.15 (later registered G-EBMB) and Sqn Ldr W H Longton competed in No.14 (G-EBJH). Both Cygnets were back for the 1926 trial with G-EBMB entered by Hawker director Fred Sigrist and flown by 'George' Bulman* and G-EBJH by the RAE Aero Club. (Cygnet G-EBMB is today on show at the RAF Museum, Cosford.) Freddy moved on from Hawker in 1925 when George Bulman was appointed as CTP.

In 1928, Freddy acquired Avro Avian III G-EBWW brand new off the production, but disposed of it in the spring of 1929 as he was bound for pastures new. Freddy joined his long-time friend 'Ronnie' Kemp in the latter's Aerial Survey Company. Ronnie and Freddy had learned to fly at the same time on a Type IV triplane of the Avro school at Brooklands, both gaining their Aviators' Certificates – respectively No.80 and 85 – on 9th May 1911. The company initially operated Airco DH.9 floatplanes on a contract to chart the Irrawaddy River in Burma, followed by another in Sarawak, Borneo. A major commission gave rise to a new organisation, the Indian Air Survey and Transport Ltd, headquartered in Calcutta. Freddy returned to Britain in 1938. During World War Two he served with the Air Ministry's Air Accident Board. Frederick Phillip Raynham OBE died on 30th April 1954, aged 60, in Colorado Springs, Colorado, USA.

Cecil Rea

Mar 1926	BP Sidestrand J7938 2 x 425hp Bristol Jupiter VI
Feb 1927	BP Bittern J7936 2 x 180hp AS Lynx IV
7 Jul 1929	BP Phoenix G-AAIT 1 x 30hp ABC Scorpion I
Jun 1930	Blackburn Sydney N241 3 x 525hp RR FXIIMS
23 Oct 1931	BP P.32 J9950 3 x 575hp Bristol Jupiter XFBM
23 Mar 1933	BP Mailplane G-ABYK 2 x 565hp Bristol Pegasus IM2
Feb 1934	BP Overstrand J9186 2 x 580hp Bristol Pegasus IIM3

Note: All took place at Mousehold other than the P.32, which was from Martlesham Heath.

Cecil Arthur Rea, born 1885. Worked for Canadian Pacific Railways before enlisting with the RNAS in 1914. By 1917 he was a trials pilot, probably at the Isle of Grain, and by 1920 he was certainly with M&AEE Isle of Grain and at MAEE Felixstowe upon its formation in March 1924. On 2nd May 1924 Cecil deliberately ditched Airco DH.18 G-EAWW offshore from Felixstowe for escape assessment: Cecil was out of the open cockpit and in the water within a minute, the DH.18 sank in just 120 seconds. Cecil was part of the British Schneider Trophy team destined to travel to Baltimore, Maryland, USA, in October 1924 but the contest was cancelled after Hubert Broad wrote off the Gloster II.*

The prototype Sidestrand, J7938, 1927. *Flight*

Phoenix G-AAIT in Mk.II guise with Salmson nine-cylinder radial at Mousehold in 1930. *Peter Green Collection*

SQN LDR CECIL ARTHUR REA AFC joined Boulton and Paul at Mousehold in July 1926, becoming the company's first full-time test pilot. Cecil's first debut was the all-metal Sidestrand biplane medium day bomber, J7938, which was issued to A&AEE at Martlesham Heath in March 1926. With a top speed of 140mph it had a lively performance and was regularly 'aerobatted' by pilots; 18 production examples served with 101 Squadron. The company had schemed a much revised version which was designated Sidestrand V until March 1934 when it was renamed Overstrand. (Both being villages on the north Norfolk coast.) The Overstrand, which Cecil flew in February 1934, was the first RAF aircraft to be equipped with a fully-enclosed, power-operated gun turret. It heralded the future for the company as it began to specialise in turrets and later power flying controls. Production of Overstrands amounted to 24 units.

Two examples of the single-seat, twin-engined Bittern heavy fighter were produced, the first being tested by Cecil in February 1927. The three-engined, 100ft-span P.32 was built to meet a requirement for a long-range night bomber. The initial quote for build of the single prototype, J9950, delivered in 1929 was £33,000 (£1,815,000 in present-day values). Taken to Martlesham Heath and assembled, it was not until 23rd October 1931 that Cecil took the giant into the air. No more were ordered.

With Cecil's vast experience with marine aircraft, he was occasionally seconded to other companies. (He had joined an organisation that throughout its history only built landplanes.) In 1929 he was at Brough for the first flight of the prototype Iris III three-engined patrol flying-boat. Cecil lifted N238 off from the Humber on 21st November with Norman Woodhead as co-pilot and designer Major J D Rennie as honorary observer. Cecil was back at Brough in June 1930, this time for the debut of the one-off Sydney three-engined monoplane flying boat. Blackburn CTP during this period was 'Dasher' Blake* who was responsible for landplane prototypes. With Short CTP John Lankester Parker* in Japan, Cecil visited Rochester on 8th June 1931 carrying out the maiden flight of a Calcutta for the French military from the River Medway.

The huge tri-motor P.32 J9950 at Martlesham Heath, 1931. *KEC*

The prototype Overstrand at Hendon in June 1934, wearing the 'new types' number '13'. *Flight*

Diversification into the civil market was essential and on 7th July 1929 Cecil flew the Phoenix two-seat parasol monoplane from Mousehold. The ABC Scorpion exhibited its cantankerous nature and a truncated circuit was followed by tinering, after which G-AAIT flew three times that day. The following year it was re-engined and re-engineered, but failed to find any buyers. The prototype was used by Cecil as a 'taxi' into the mid-1930s. The P.64 Mailplane was aimed at an Imperial Airways requirement for a high-speed mail and newspaper carrier. Cecil flew the prototype on 27th March 1933 in the early evening with most of the workforce spectating. Three days later, with company chairman Dawson Paul as co-pilot, Cecil could not correct a swing to starboard during a cross-wind take-off; G-ABYK hit the perimeter fence and ended up on its back – neither of the crew was hurt. The Mailplane remained a one-off, but two examples of the broadly similar P.71A 'feederliner' were delivered to Imperial Airways in 1935.

Cecil 'Fluffy' Feather* carried out some testing of the P.71As in late 1934, probably freelancing to help with workload. During 1935 Boulton and Paul was negotiating to relocate to Wolverhampton, with the new factory at Pendeford becoming operational in 1936 under the name of Boulton Paul Aircraft. Cecil Rea expressed a desire not to move to the West Midlands and 'Fluffy' took on the post of CTP. At this point Cecil had flown 136 types. Cecil set up his own business, John Short Ltd, in part of the Mousehold factory, carrying out sub-contract work for his former employees and building floats. In 1938 he joined the staff of the Air Ministry to help develop and deploy barrage balloons; transferring in the following year to the Ministry of Aircraft Production to oversee the manufacturer of support equipment for barrage balloons. Sqn Ldr Cecil Arthur Rea AFC died in 1975, aged 90.

Ken Reed

| 20 Jul 1958 | SARO P.531 G-APNU |
| | 1 x 325shp Turboméca Turmo 601 |

Kenneth Martin Reed, born 1921. He joined the Fleet Air Arm in 1941 and by 1944 had attended a course at the Sikorsky plant at Bridgeport, Connecticut, USA, to convert to the Hoverfly helicopter. By mid-1946 he was with 771 Squadron's Helicopter Flight, at Gosport, with Hoverflies. On 7th May 1947 the helicopter element of 771 Squadron was redesignated as 705 Squadron with Lt K M Reed as its CO. From January 1949 the unit started trials with Sikorsky Dragonflies supplied through Westland.

Lt KENNETH MARTIN REED joined Westland at Yeovil, replacing Alan Bristow* as chief helicopter test pilot, under CTP Harald Penrose*. The company was busy developing the British version of the Sikorsky S-51 Dragonfly and proving its capabilities. Loaned to the British European Airways Helicopter Unit, Ken flew a regular passenger service in Westland-built Dragonfly G-ALIL from Barnes Park, London, to Castle Bromwich, Birmingham, between 9th and 19th May, 1950. This was certainly Britain's, if not the world's, first scheduled helicopter route.

With the death of Cierva CTP Alan Marsh* in the crash of the Air Horse prototype on 13th June 1950, the Cierva company was wound up and taken over by Saunders-Roe (SARO). Ken took up the offer of becoming senior helicopter test pilot to SARO in 1952 and continued development of the Skeeter light helicopter. Ken was conducting ground resonance tests with the third prototype Skeeter, WF112, at Eastleigh on 28th April 1953 when vibrations wrecked the helicopter and

The second prototype SARO P.531, G-APNV, in the static at Farnborough, September 1958. *Roy Bonser*

Derek Reeh

| 14 Mar 1997 | Eurofighter Typhoon DA.4 ZH590 |
| | 2 x 13,490lbst Eurojet EJ200 |

Derek Reeh, born 1951. Took an aero engineering degree course from 1972 and learned to fly on DHC Chipmunk T.10s with the University of London Air Squadron at Abingdon. He joined the RAF in 1973 and flew SEPECAT Jaguars with 6 Squadron from Coltishall 1975-1979. He graduated from ETPS No.38 Course at Boscombe Down in 1979. Posted to RAE Farnborough 1980-1981. From 1981 he began a three-year exchange with the USAF, flying McD F-4 Phantoms and GD F-16 Fighting Falcons from Elgin, Florida, USA.

Ken broke his back. In 1958 he was promoted to CTP and he began ground running the prototype P.531 private-venture military helicopter on 19th July 1958. All went well and the following day he took G-APNU into the air at Eastleigh. Ken demonstrated *November-Uniform* at the SBAC airshow at Farnborough in September 1958. In the static at that show was the second P.531, G-APNV, and Ken flew this for the first time on the 30th September. (G-APNV went to 700 Squadron at Yeovilton for trials as XN332 in October 1959 and is today part of the Fleet Air Arm Museum's collection.) Westland took over SARO in 1960 and the P.531 was developed into the successful Wasp shipboard helicopter and the Scout for the Army Air Corps. Ken Reed went on to become a helicopter test pilot for the Air Registration Board (Civil Aviation Authority from 1972) – see Chapter Four. Lt Kenneth Martin Reed died in 1998, aged 77.

SQN LDR DEREK REEH left the RAF in 1985, joining British Aerospace at Warton becoming, in turn, project pilot (PP) Jaguar, PP Tornado IDS (1987), PP Tornado all variants (1992) and then Senior Test Pilot. He took ZD708, the first Panavia Tornado GR.4 upgrade for its maiden flight at Warton on 29th May 1993. He became CTP at Warton in 1997, taking over from Don Thomas* and in 1997 succeeded Chris Yeo* as Director of Flight Operations. Derek was at the controls of Typhoon DA.4, ZH590, the first British two-seater and the first with Eurojet Turbo EJ200 powerplants for an 80-minute test flight on 14th March 1997. Derek took DA.4 to the flight regime most fighters can only dream of – supercruise, Mach 1 *without* after-burner on 20th February 1998. (DA.4 ZH590 is now on show with the Imperial War Museum at Duxford.) In 2003 Derek had achieved a total of 5,845 flight hours. He retired from Warton in December 2004 taking up a post with Mission Aviation Fellowship flying humanitarian sorties in Africa; later becoming a director of the organisation. He was succeeded as Director of Flight Operations by John Turner*.

Typhoon DA.4 ZH590, the first British Eurofighter with EJ200s, was first flown by Derek Reeh. *Copyright Eurofighter – BAE Systems*

'Dick' Reynell

Richard Carew Reynell, born 1912 in Australia. He moved to Britain in 1929 to study agriculture at Oxford and learned to fly with Oxford University Air Squadron at Upper Heyford on AW Atlases. 'Dick' joined the RAF in 1931 and was flying with 43 Squadron from Tangmere in early 1932 on Hawker Fury Is. Fg Off Reynell was posted to the RAF Meteorological Flight at Duxford, with Atlases and AW Siskin IIIAs in November 1934, under the unit's CO, Jeffrey Quill*. Dick returned to Australia in 1935 for compassionate reasons, visiting the family vineyards in South Australia.

UPON the return of Flt Lt R C Reynell to the RAF in 1938, he was seconded to Hawker at Brooklands as a production test pilot, on Hinds, Henleys and, increasingly, Hurricanes. On 26th August 1940 re-joined his old unit, 43 Squadron, back at Tangmere, for operational experience to help Hawker and its test pilots perfect their work. On 2nd September Dick was credited with shooting down a Messerschmitt Bf 109. An urgent request from Brooklands was received on the morning of 7th September 1940; Dick was called back as production test pilot E G H Russell-Stacey* had been killed and the flight test office was short staffed. Dick opted to finish the day with 43 Squadron, but over south London at 16:45 while piloting Hurricane I V7257 Dick was 'bounced' by a Bf 109. Dick baled out, but his parachute did not deploy correctly and he and the Hurricane came down at Greenwich. Flt Lt Richard Carew Reynell, one of 'The Few', was killed, aged 28.

G L G Richmond

16 Jun 1940	Heston-Napier Racer G-AFOK
	1 x 2,300hp Napier Sabre I

BY the autumn of 1938 there was another UK contender for the world airspeed record. Unlike the Supermarine 'Speed' Spitfire – see Jeffrey Quill – this was without government sanction; its construction was underwritten by Lord Nuffield, founder of the Morris Motors empire. Famed aero engine manufacturer, Napier, was looking for a way to promote Major Frank B Halford's incredible 24-cylinder, H-format Sabre. This monster had first bench-run the year before and a crack at a record or two seemed ideal.

Delayed and ill-fated, the Heston Racer in early 1940. *MAP*

Heston Aircraft was contracted to build two examples of a sleek all-wooden monoplane, designed by Napier's consultant Arthur Hagg (formerly of de Havilland) and its own George Cornwall. Top speed was ultimately estimated to be 480mph. The hugely complex Sabre suffered many delays and it was well into 1940 before the Heston-Napier Type 5 Racer, G-AFOK, was ready. With World War Two into its tenth month, any record breaking was academic and perhaps it was then being touted as a lightweight fighter prototype.

On 12th June 1940 Sqn Ldr G L G Richmond took G-AFOK up for the first time but the Sabre I 'Special' encountered problems. After just seven minutes, the racer was back on the ground, wrecked beyond repair and Richmond hospitalised. Work on the more advanced second Type 5, G-AFOL, had already been halted. Two days prior to that eventful first flight the German Blitzkrieg had reached Rheims in France and Mussolini had declared war – world records could wait.

Peter Robarts

SQN LDR PETER G ROBARTS left the RAF in 1946 and joined Vickers as a test pilot. In the June 1950 King's Cup air race, staged at Wolverhampton, he piloted Supermarine Spitfire Tr.8 G-AIDN, owned by Vickers-Armstrongs, and while competing established a new world record in the Class C1 closed-circuit category of 328mph. (G-AIDN still survives, it is being restored to flying condition at Booker, Buckinghamshire.)

On 3rd February 1951 Supermarine Attacker F.1 WA477 had its first flight at South Marston. Two days later Peter took it up for a routine production test. From take-off WA477 was seen to be emitting black puffs of smoke. Shortly afterwards it rolled inverted and impacted at high speed near Marlborough. Sqn Ldr Peter G Robarts, aged 35, was killed instantly. In post-crash investigation a spanner was found within the port spoiler. This may have caused an asymmetric setting for the spoilers, which could have generated a tendency to roll at high speed.

Alex Roberts

11 Jun 1957	EE Canberra U.10 WJ624
	2 x 6,500lbst RR Avon 101

"THE test schedule that day required the auto-control system to be engaged at 2,000ft, followed by selection of auto (fast) climb, which automatically selected full power and climb at 365 knots, to be followed by fast level selection at 10,000ft, which produced high negative 'g' forces. On this occasion, during the 'bunt' [at the top of the climb] the observer's ejection seat and my own moved very rapidly up their rails, and I heard an explosion, although at that second I wasn't sure what had happened. Wedged against the canopy, quite a long way above the control wheel, I managed to cut the autopilot out, which reduced the high negative 'g', and both ejection seats slid back down to their normal positions. Looking up, I was alarmed to see that the Perspex canopy above me was fractured, and more so, when the FTO in the rear seat told me that the hatch above him was also damaged

The gear tucking up on Canberra U.10 WH733 on a test flight from Sydenham, very likely with Alex Roberts at the helm. As a drone, WH733 had a brief life, confined to 1959; first flown on 30th June, it was issued to the Weapons Research Establishment at Woomera, Australia, on 18th September and was written off in a landing accident on 30th November. *Short Brothers & Harland*

and that the drogue gun on his seat had fired... I asked him to unstrap himself and move forward and clear of his seat, but I didn't have any other place to go."

It was 12th December 1958 and Alex Roberts, Shorts Canberra project pilot, was testing U.10 drone WH742 with FTO Wilf Monteith, out of Sydenham. The day before, WH742, which had been built by English Electric as a B.2 in August 1953, had been flown for the first time as a drone. Many years later, Alex recalled the incident to Northern Ireland aviation historian Guy Warner for his book *The Last Canberra – PR.9 XH131*. Back at 10,000ft over Northern Ireland on a December day in 1958: Alex started to let WH742 down, but during the descent there was more to worry about. The barometric capsule on Wilf's seat activated, the straps fell away, the drogue parachute started to deploy – all this was as it was designed to do, starting the sequence to separate its 'passenger' from the seat and for him to float gently down under a full canopy. The hole in the hatch above Wilf was too small for much of the drogue 'chute to escape, so the two airmen were spared the main envelope filling the space within the Canberra's cramped cockpit – or worse. Alex elected for an emergency landing at Aldergrove, where the runways were longer: he made an uneventful touchdown, but emphasized that he and Wilf were going nowhere until a 'bang seat' specialist made everything safe. Investigations revealed that the latches on both seats had been removed, probably to allow access to instrumentation.

Alex Roberts joined the RAF in 1954 and two years later was flying Gloster Meteor F.8s with 615 Squadron at Biggin Hill. He moved to Shorts in 1956, under CTP Tom Brooke-Smith* during the early days of the SC.1 VTOL jet testing.

Shorts had two major Canberra contracts and Alex was put in charge of both: the PR.9 high-altitude reconnaissance variant and conversion of B.2s to U.10 drones. Readers may be thinking why does a conversion programme merit high-lighting as an important first flight? Testing the U.10's full-authority auto-control system, its self-contained approach and landing system, 'connectivity' with the ground station and the miss-distance recording equipment was a very challenging regime. The U.10 was designed to fly *very* high, and during testing Alex reached 56,700ft. Unlike contemporary target drone systems, the U.10 required no 'shepherd' aircraft, it was autonomous... once it had been fully tested courtesy of a pilot and FTO carefully monitoring how it behaved 'on its own'. The sophisticated auto-stabilisation system in the SC.1 made Shorts the perfect contractor for the U.10 programme.

Alex flew the prototype U.10, WJ624, on 11th June 1957 and the first sortie in which the full-authority control system was engaged, on WJ987 on 31st January 1958. Eighteen U.10s were converted for use at the Woomera ranges in Australia and another six U.14s were supplied to the Fleet Air Arm. Alex was also involved in the PR.9 programme, including 'first flighting' the heavily-modified SC.9 missile development test-bed, XH132, on 2nd May 1961. By 1962 he had left Shorts, buying and running a local hotel, but returned by 1964, taking part in Skyvan and Belfast development. In January 1969 Alex was appointed as Skyvan sales manager and retired from test flying. From 1973 Alexander Frederick Cecil Roberts OBE became, in turn, General Manager, Aircraft; Executive Director, Aircraft (1976); Deputy Managing Director (1989), retiring in 1995.

Chris Roberts

Christopher F Roberts, born 1945 and brought up in Rhodesia. Joined the RAF in 1963, going on to fly Hawker Hunters from Tengah, Singapore. After the CFS QFI course and a spell instructing on Hunters, he joined the 'Red Arrows' in 1971, on Folland Gnat T.1s. In 1973 he became a weapons instructor with 233 OCU on HS Harriers. He graduated from ETPS No.36 Course at Boscombe Down and was posted to A&AEE.

In 1977, at the invite of Dunsfold CTP John Farley*, Chris Roberts joined British Aerospace, working on both Harriers and Hawks. Chris first flew the second prototype Hawk 200, ZH200, on 24th April 1986. He went on to become the BAe project pilot for the McDonnell Douglas T-45 Goshawk – the fully navalised development of the Hawk for the US Navy. In 1990, Chris succeeded Heinz Frick* as Dunsfold CTP. In October 1989 he was flying ZH200 when the fin stalled and it departed violently, resulting in serious airframe damage. He retired from Dunsfold in 1994 and became a commercial pilot with Airtours, later MyTravel, flying McDonnell Douglas MD-83s and Airbus A320s, A321s and A330s. From 2003 he became an independent international consultant in addition to working with aviation safety specialists Access Aviation.

Formal 'office' portrait of 'Robbie' Robinson. *Hawker Siddeley*

'Robby' Robinson

| 6 Aug 1986 | BAe ATP G-MATP |
| | 2 x 2,653shp P&W Canada PW126 |

John Alan Robinson, born 1932. Joined the RAF in 1950, flying operationally with 10 Squadron on EE Canberra B.2s and, from 1957, 90 Squadron on Vickers Valiant B.1s from Honington. Graduated from ETPS Course No.21 at Farnborough 1962, going on to serve with A&AEE. 'Robbie' returned to ETPS in 1968 – by then at Boscombe Down – as a tutor. By 1970 he had been promoted to Wing Commander, he returned to A&AEE for another stint before 'crossing the flight line' to become Chief Instructor at ETPS in 1976.

Invited in September 1977 by Tony Blackman* to become a test pilot with Hawker Siddeley, John Alan – 'Robbie' to friends and colleagues – Robinson took up the post at Woodford in April 1978, by which time the organisation had become British Aerospace (BAe). Work was centred on Nimrod MR.2s and the AEW.3 project (which was axed in

1986) and HS.748s. Robbie was promoted to DCTP in 1979 and took over from Charles Masefield* as CTP in February 1981. With Tony Hawkes as co-pilot and Barry Lomas as FTE, Robby captained the prototype ATP, G-MATP, at Woodford on its first flight of 2 hours 45 minutes duration on 6th August 1986. The ATP – Advanced Turboprop – was a much re-engineered pure-airliner derivative of the HS.748; 65 units were built up to 1995.

Robbie retired in 1987 and was succeeded by Peter Henley*. Robbie began flying Vickers Merchantmen with Air Bridge Carriers from East Midlands Airport until 1991. He was back at Woodford in 1991 as an instructor on ATP and HS.146 simulators. He was appointed as Director of Flight Test and CTP for the Woodford-based International Test Pilot School, 1998-1999. Robbie returned to the simulator bay at Woodford in 1999, this time only on the HS.146, until finally retiring in 2001. Wg Cdr J A 'Robby' Robinson AFC has written three books, all hugely readable: *Avro One – Autobiography of a Chief Test Pilot* (2005), *Jet Bomber Pilot – Autobiography of a V-Bomber Pilot* (2006) and *I Am Saluting You, Sire – The Formative Years of a Test Pilot* (2009).

The prototype BAe ATP G-MATP on an early test flight, 1986. Note the pitot probe on the nose. *Alan Curry*

B R Rolfe

Fg Off B R Rolfe was appointed as CTP of the Blackburn-managed Greek National Aircraft Factory, Athens, from 1921 to 1929. During that time a dozen Blackburn Velos biplanes were manufactured for the Greek Navy. By the middle of 1938 Fg Off Rolfe was working as a production test pilot for Blackburn at Brough. With J B E Johnson as FTO, Rolfe took off from Brough on 5th March 1940 to test newly-built Botha I L6129. The aircraft was seen to dive into the ground, impacting at Flixborough, Lincolnshire, killed both crew.

'Tommy' Rose

15 Sep 1940	Miles M.20/2 U-5 1 x 1,300hp RR Merlin XX
Feb 1942	Miles 'X' Minor U-0233 2 x 130hp DH Gipsy Major
24 Apr 1942	Miles Martinet LR241 1 x 870hp Bristol Mercury XX
5 Apr 1944	Miles Monitor NF900 2 x 1,700hp Wright Cyclone R-2600-31
26 Jan 1945	Miles Aerovan U-0248 2 x 150hp Blackburn Cirrus Major III

Notes: All made their debut at Woodley.

Thomas Rose, born 1895. Joined the RFC in 1917 and by the end of the year was with 65 Squadron on the Western Front, flying Royal Aircraft Factory SE.5As. 'Tommy' proved to be a gifted pilot, between March and August 1918 he accounted for four enemy aircraft destroyed (two unidentified two-seaters, a Rumpler and a Fokker D.VII) plus five more as 'out of control'. Tommy stayed on with the RAF and during 1925-1927 he was a flight commander with 43 Squadron, on Sopwith Snipes and then Gloster Gamecocks, at Henlow and then Tangmere. In April 1927 he took a job in 'civvie street', becoming the manager of the Anglo-American Oil Company's aeronautical division and opening its first 'pump', at Brooklands. He became a well-known display and competition pilot and was CFI of the Northamptonshire Flying Club at Sywell for a while. He was appointed as sales manager to Phillips & Powis Aircraft (Reading) Ltd. He flew Miles Falcon Six G-ADLC in the 1935 King's Cup air race, based at Hatfield, and came first at 176.2mph. The following year, he piloted G-ADLC to Cape Town in a record-breaking 3 days, 17 hours, 37 minutes during February.

With the untimely death of Miles CTP 'Bill' Skinner* in November 1939, Flt Lt Thomas Rose DFC was appointed as his replacement. An additional responsibility was as titular commanding officer of the Woodley Aerodrome Local Defence Volunteers, more often known as the 'Home Guard'! The M.20 was conceived as a simple-to-produce fighter with fixed undercarriage with the capacity for a *dozen* 0.303in Browning machine-guns, six in each wing. Ironically first flown on what became Battle of Britain Day, the need for such a 'stop gap' fighter had receded by the time Tommy took the M.20 for its

Mrs F G 'Blossom' Miles greeting Tommy Rose at Woodley having completed his 10,000th flying hour. *via Andy Thomas*

debut. The 'X' Minor was intended as a test-bed for the wide fuselage transports schemed by 'Fred' Miles before the war and in his determination to see if such a layout would work, the scale 'X' Minor was built. Tommy flew the machine in February 1942, but it was soon confined to use as an instructional airframe.

The Martinet was a dedicated target-tug based upon the Master II advanced trainer; Tommy flying the prototype on 24th April 1942. The Martinet, and a pilot-less target drone version the Queen Martinet, was put into large scale production at Woodley – 1,789 units were built. A twin-engined target-tug, the Monitor was an advanced design of composite wood and metal construction and this took to the air on 5th April 1944. The requirement for such a machine had been a matter of some debate and the initial order for 600 units was slashed to 200, then 50 and only 20 were completed. The company had tooled up for mass production and this was certainly a factor in the parlous financial situation Miles Aircraft found itself in post-war. The Aerovan was a return to all-wood construction and a simple workhorse for the coming peace. The pod-and-boom layout allowed the rear faring to swing to starboard to provide straight-in loading, and the Aerovan could accommodate a small car. The prototype was Tommy's last inaugural flight, taking place on 26th January 1945. Aerovan production ran to 48 units.

The M.20 fighter prototype of 1940. *Miles Aircraft*

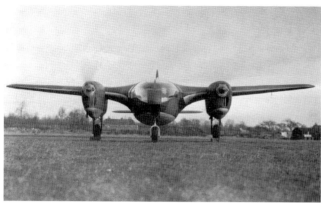

Head-on view of the 'X' Minor test-bed. *Miles Aircraft*

Martinet I HN862 on air test, August 1942. *Miles Aircraft*

Tommy retired from Miles in 1946 and was succeeded by Ken Waller*. He flew for a while for Universal Flying Services, retiring in the 1960s to Alderney in the Channel Islands where he bought the Grand Hotel. Flt Lt Thomas Rose DFC died on 20th June 1968, aged 73.

Right: Monitor TT.II NP407 was built in the spring of 1945 and retained for tests by Miles throughout its life: it was scrapped in 1947. *Miles Aircraft*

Below: George Miles flying the prototype Aerovan, U-0248 in 1945. *Miles Aircraft*

R J Ross

FLT LT R J ROSS graduated from ETPS No.11 Course at Farnborough in 1952, going on to fly for the RAE at Farnborough. By late 1954 he was a production test pilot for Gloster and on 21st October 1954 took third production Javelin FAW.1 XA546 for a routine test. During an intentional spin, Flt Ross failed to recover and the Javelin crashed off shore from Weston-super-Mare, killing its pilot.

Fg Off Rouff

THE Vickers-Armstrongs shadow factory at Byley, Cheshire, used adjacent Cranage airfield for flight testing its output of Wellingtons. On 29th July 1943 Fg Off Rouff – his initial, or initials, lost in the mists of time – and test inspector E Booth took off on the third test of Wellington X HE819. Returning from the sortie, the Wellington stalled on approach and crashed in flames on the airfield. The crash team managed to extricate both occupants, but Booth was dead on arrival at hospital and Rouff succumbed to his injuries before the day was out.

'Wally' Runciman

| 13 Aug 1953 | Short Seamew XA209 |
| | 1 x 1,435shp AS Mamba |

Walter J Runciman, born 1920, in New Zealand. Joined the Royal New Zealand Air Force and flew with Bomber Command during World War Two, on Short Stirlings and de Havilland Mosquitos. On 'demob' he departed for New Zealand, but was back in Britain in 1947, enlisting with the RAF. He graduated from ETPS Course No.9 at Farnborough in 1950. A posting with A&AEE was put on hold and he was seconded to Shorts at Sydenham.

SQN LDR WALTER J RUNCIMAN DFM AFC joined flight test team at Sydenham, under CTP Tom Brooke-Smith. Much of his work was involved in signing off Canberras, but on 12th August 1952 'Wally' and FTO Malcolm Wild were the crew for the maiden flight of the second Short Sperrin, VX161, from Aldergrove. Shorts had responded to a Fleet Air Arm requirement for a simple anti-submarine and patrol aircraft capable of a four-hour loiter with the two-crew, turboprop, fixed undercarriage Seamew. Wally took the prototype, XA209, for its first flight on 13th August 1953. On return to Sydenham, he undershot the runway and XA209 was damaged. By this time Wally had left the RAF and was full-time with Shorts with over 3,000 hours on about 50 types. Seamew XA209 was repaired and flew again on 23rd August and Wally demonstrated it at the SBAC airshow at Farnborough the following month. Production example, AS.1 XE175, was used as a demonstrator and Wally took it to Italy and Yugoslavia in February and March 1956. In the first week of June 1956 Wally was in West Germany demonstrating XE175. Wally flew XE175 at an airshow at Sydenham on 9th June 1956 and provided his usual spirited display. During a high-speed roll, while inverted the Seamew entered what is called a 'g-stall', lost height and crashed, killing 36-year-old Sqn Ldr Walter J Runciman DFM AFC. The following

One of the Seamew prototypes in a near vertical bank.
Short Brothers & Harland

year the Seamew programme was cancelled with 24 units having been completed.

E G Russell-Stacey

PRODUCTION test pilot with Hawker at Brooklands from 1939. On 28th August 1940, on the second test flight of Hurricane II Z2340 following a fuel pump problem, the fighter suffered engine failure on take-off, at about 150ft. The pilot turned Z2340 around to land downwind, but it stalled and crashed within the airfield boundary. E G Russell-Stacey died in hospital the following day.

Richard Rymer

Fg Off Richard 'Dickie' Rymer flew with Coastal Command during World War Two. In September 1942 he was with 1441 (Combined Operations) Flight at Dundonald providing target facilities for forces training for amphibious operations. Flying Hurricane I W9187 on 18th September 1942 the engine failed and Dickie had to make a forced landing near Inverkip; the Hurricane was a write off. By 1943 Dickie had been seconded to British Overseas Airways Corporation at Whitchurch, near Bristol, flying a mixture of types on diplomatic flights and services to neutral countries. By 1947 Dickie was a senior captain with British European Airways at Heathrow. On 29th July 1950 Dickie captained the world's first scheduled services with a turboprop airliner with the prototype Vickers Viscount 630, G-AHRF, which had been loaned to the airline. For a two month period Dickie flew 88 services, to Paris and to Edinburgh, carrying 1,838 fare-paying passengers.

BY 1953 Richard 'Dickie' Rymer had left British European Airways and had joined Vickers at Brooklands and Wisley under CTP 'Jock' Bryce*. Much of his work was with the Viscount and his background with the pioneer route-proving and early operation with BEA meant that he was tasked with demonstration and aircrew training as well as flight testing. He was also involved with Vanguard development. In 1960 Vickers became a part of BAC and Dickie joined the One-Eleven test team. On 22nd October 1963, Dickie was co-pilot to Mike Lithgow* on the 53rd flight of the One-Eleven prototype, G-ASHG. The rest of the crew were: Dick Wright Senior FTO, Gordon Poulter FTO, D J Clark FTO, B J Prior Assistant Chief Aerodynamicist and C J Webb Assistant Chief Designer. Among the tasks for the sortie was a series of stalls; *Hotel-Golf* crashed near Chicklade, Wiltshire, killing all on board; for more detail refer to the section on Mike Lithgow.

Howard Saint

Jan 1929	Gloster SS.18 J9125 1 x 480hp Bristol Jupiter VIIF
Jun 1929	Gloster AS.31 G-AADO 2 x 525hp Bristol Jupiter XI
23 Feb 1932	Gloster TC.33 J9832 4 x 580hp RR Kestrel IIS/IIIS
Apr 1932	Gloster TSR.38 S1705 1 x 600hp RR Kestrel IIMS
Oct 1934	Parnall G4/31 K2772 1 x 690hp Bristol Pegasus IM3

Note: All first flown from Hucclecote except the G4/31 which was from Yate. The AS.31 was also designated de Havilland DH.67B.

Howard John Thomas Saint, born 1893. By 1915 he was a chief petty officer with the Royal Navy with an armoured car unit. Transferred to the RNAS in 1916, joining 5 Wing – later 5 (Naval) Squadron – on the Western Front flying Avro 504Bs from September 1916 to July 1917. In July 1917 he was posted to 10 Squadron RNAS – 'Naval Ten' – also on the Western Front, with Sopwith Triplanes and then Camels. He was credited with seven victories, two 'destroyed' – an Albatros D.III in August 1917 and an Albatros D.V in October 1917 plus five 'out of control'. Howard left 'Naval Ten' in October 1917 and joined the Aeroplane Experimental Station at Martlesham Heath. By 1919 he was flying for Air Transport and Travel and became the holder of Britain's first commercial pilot licence. Howard re-joined the RAF in 1922 and was posted to the RAE at Farnborough.

FG OFF HOWARD JOHN THOMAS SAINT DFC became CTP for Gloster at Hucclecote in 1927, taking over from Larry Carter*. The Gamecock fighter was still providing work but the company's response to Specification F9/26 for a new day fighter was, eventually, to replace it. Designer Henry Folland created the SS.18, J9125, and Howard took this for its maiden flight in January 1929. Four years of patience and development followed, with Henry Folland astonishing pilots at Martlesham with J9125 transformed into the SS.19 with a Bristol Jupiter VII and *six* machine-guns – two Vickers in the fuselage firing through the propeller arc and two Lewis guns mounted under each lower wing, firing outside of the prop disc. The Air Ministry remained aloof, but in February 1934 relented and ordered the first of the definitive Gauntlets, but it was to be Howard's replacement, 'Gerry' Sayer* that flew the first example, K4081, in December 1934.

Line-up of Gauntlet IIs with 151 Squadron, 1936. *KEC*

The first Gloster AS.31, G-AADO, 1929. *Peter Green Collection*

In November 1928 de Havilland sub-contracted Gloster to take over its DH.67B twin-engined specialist survey biplane, two of which had been commissioned by the Aircraft Operating Company – contractors to the Ordnance Survey. Henry Folland took some time to make the machine, Gloster designation AS.31, capable of taking on a variety of roles and Howard began taxi trials at Hucclecote in June 1929. With Henry Folland 'along for the ride' Howard conducted several runs across the airfield. On the last one he gunned the throttles to overcome bumps in the aerodrome and found that the AS.31 was airborne and heading for the hangars! He kept the throttles forward and took the big biplane for a circuit. Despite hopes of attracting other customers, only two AS.31s were built.

Howard's next challenge was the 28,884lb all-up weight TC.33 bomber-transport. This was the largest, and only four-engined, aircraft that Gloster ever built. At 25ft 8in high, when it

The one-off TC.33 wearing the number 6 – its 'new types' identifier applied for the June 1932 Hendon airshow. *Rolls-Royce*

came to be brought out of the hangar at Hucclecote, two trenches had to be dug to allow the TC.33 to get into the daylight intact. The first flight was uneventful but problems with the rudders – each one 9ft high – were never fully solved. On a terminal velocity dive, Howard and FTO Basil Fielding climbed J9832 to 16,000ft and 'clocked' 200mph during the descent. Howard found that the rudder pedals were vibrating severely and to damp this out he applied so much force that he broke the back of his seat! Basil came to the rescue by sitting back-to-back with his pilot, bracing his feet on a bulkhead. The TC.33 remained a one-off, as did the TSR.38 which was a torpedo-strike, spotter, reconnaissance biplane, first flown in April 1932.

Commissioned by Italian engineer Ugo Antoni, Gloster built a wing that was capable of altering its camber in flight and this was fitted to a Breda 15 two-seat cabin monoplane. Registered as G-ABCC, the aircraft had been built in Milan in 1930 and was converted at Hucclecote to act as a test-bed for the Antoni wing. Ugo Antoni carried out the first flight in September 1933. On 1st December 1933 Howard was flying the Breda in heavy turbulence and he experienced excessive wing flutter after which the port aileron fell off. The machine crashed near Hucclecote; Howard was uninjured, but the Breda was a write off.

Howard left Gloster in 1934, with Gerry Sayer taking his place. Howard moved the short distance to Yate and took up the post of CTP to Parnall. There he 'first flighted' the Parnall G4/31 contender, K2772, for a general purpose biplane to replace the venerable Westland Wapiti, in October 1934. The requirement was scrubbed and K2722 joined Howard's list of one-offs. In 1936 he took up the post of manager of Doncaster Airport before starting a memorable administrative stint at RAE Farnborough which lasted to the mid-1960s, long beyond conventional retirement. Fg Off Howard John Thomas Saint DFC died in 1976, aged 83.

L V Sanders

Flt Lt L V Sanders dfc was a production test pilot for the Castle Bromwich Aircraft Factory who carried out a routine sortie in Spitfire Vb ER713 on 23rd October 1942. The fighter suffered structural failure and crashed near Cannock, killing its pilot. Spitfire V ER713 was rebuilt as a Mk.IX in the summer of 1943 and went on to serve with the uniquely-numbered 1435 Squadron at Luqa, Malta. There is no obvious 'clang' for the serial number – a slip of the fountain pen in the administration. Neighbouring Spitfires on the 'Castle Brom' production line (ER711, ER712, ER714) have late October 1942 issue to service dates, while ER713 was issued to 39 Maintenance Unit at Colerne on 16th June 1943 – was it replaced with another from the production flow? Anyway these things are trivia: here we record the death of a brave pilot.

H G Sawyer

| 19 Jun 1926 | Blackburn Iris I N185 |
| | 3 x 650hp RR Condor III |

A ceremony was held at Brough in the days prior to the launch of the prototype Blackburn Iris flying-boat: Robert Blackburn's wife named the three-engined biplane Iris. On 19th June 1926 a traction engine pulled N185 on its beaching dolly down to the slipway. MAEE pilot Flt Lt H G Sawyer afc climbed in and with the three Rolls-Royce Condors running it was gently lowered down the slope and into the Humber. Flt Lt Sawyer conducted an uneventful first flight and N185 was moored over-night before he ferried it to Felixstowe the following day. Between 1929 and 1933 seven more, four Mk.IIIs and three Mk.Vs, were built.

A magnificent view of the first Blackburn Iris V, S1263. It was first flown on 5th March 1932 from the Humber, embarking on a brief career: it was wrecked in Plymouth Sound in January 1933. *Flight*

'Gerry' Sayer

12 Sep 1934	Gloster SS.37 G37
	1 x 530hp Bristol Mercury IV
Dec 1937	Gloster F5/34 K5604
	1 x 840hp Bristol Mercury IX
3 Apr 1939	Gloster F9/37 L7999
	2 x 1,050hp Bristol Taurus T-Sa
15 May 1941	Gloster E28/39 W4041
	1 x 860lbst Power Jets W.1

Notes: All first flew from Hucclecote, other than the E28/39 which had its debut at Cranwell. The SS.37 was the prototype Gladiator.

After a long day of hoping the weather would co-operate, finally a westward take off was possible. At 19:48 hours the throttle was eased forward, its pilot long since used to the lag before the power kicked in. Seventeen minutes later the prototype touched down on the turf and, as the engine wound down, he was met by euphoria from the small team; the greatest smile coming from the man who had battled against the odds to create the powerplant that propelled the aircraft – Frank Whittle. Cranwell, 15th May 1941: Gloster CTP 'Gerry' Sayer had completed the first flight of a jet aircraft in Britain. In the New Year's Honours list he was awarded an Order of the British Empire. The citation mentioned services to test flying, which was accurate, but made no mention of *the* flight. It couldn't, the very existence of the Gloster E28/39 was not made public knowledge until January 1944. Gerry Sayer went to his grave without being able to bask in his achievement, but then he was not the sort to seek such adulation.

When he was 19, Philip Edward George Sayer, enlisted in the RAF and after training flew fighters, including Sopwith Snipes. Assessed as being exceptional, he was posted to

Frank Whittle congratulating 'Gerry' Sayer after the first flight of the Gloster E28/39, 15th May 1941. *KEC*

A&AEE at Martlesham Heath joining the resident 22 Squadron, tasked with service test and trials. In 1930 he was released at a request from Hawker at Brooklands, working for CTP 'George' Bullman* at Brooklands, becoming his deputy. The following year Bulman and Sayer were joined by Philip Lucas*. Always known as 'Gerry' (occasionally sources spelt it 'Jerry'), the reason for this choice of nickname remains obscure. There was no scarcity of work at Brooklands; on 14th October 1931 Gerry carried out the maiden flight of the first production Nimrod fleet fighter, S1577, and on 29th December 1931 the first Audax army co-operation biplane for the RAF, K1995. Returning from the Paris Aero Show in company-

owned Hart G-ABTN, Gerry encountered engine trouble off Ostend on 30th November 1932 and was forced to ditch in the English Channel – he was rescued by a passing vessel. His last debut for Hawker was on 7th September 1934, when he took the first production Hardy general duties biplane, K3013, for its inaugural flight.

Gerry moved to Hucclecote in late 1934, taking over as CTP for Gloster and replacing Howard Saint*. By this time designer Henry Folland was at work on a replacement for the Gauntlet. This was a private-venture multi-gun development of the Gauntlet, designated SS.37. Gerry flew this at Hucclecote for the first time on 12th September 1934 while on 17th December that year he took the first production Gauntlet I, K4081, aloft for the first time. In July 1935 the SS.37 was named Gladiator and it was ordered into volume production, the last biplane fighter for the RAF. Folland's final design for Gloster was the company's F5/34 contender, the specification that eventually gave rise to the Hurricane and the Spitfire. Gerry flew the first of two Bristol Mercury radial-engined F5/34s in December 1937, by which time both the rival Hawker and Supermarine designs were a reality. George Carter took over from Folland and he conceived the twin-engined F9/37 heavy fighter: Gerry flew the first example, L7999 on 3rd April 1939 and the Rolls-Royce Peregrine-engined second prototype, L8002, on 22 February 1940. The design went no further; George Carter turned to face a far more challenging project, while Gerry had increasing Hurricane production contracts to meet and Typhoon manufacture looming for 1942.

As related in the section on Michael Daunt*, Gerry might well have undertaken another maiden flight in 1940. Michael joined Gerry at Hucclecote in 1937 as a production test pilot, but soon became DCTP. Henry Folland had set up his own company – Folland Aircraft – at Eastleigh and it won a contract for a dedicated engine test-bed. This was the Folland Fo 108 and construction of the first two of a batch of a dozen started at Eastleigh in 1940. Lacking a test pilot, Henry turned to Gloster and the prototype Folland 43/37, P1774, powered by a Napier Sabre, first flew at Eastleigh around August 1940 with Gerry *most likely* at the controls.

As noted at the start of this section, it is with Britain's first jet, the Gloster E28/39 that Gerry Sayer is rightly most remembered. The table charts his involvement in the test

The last biplane fighter from Gloster was also the last to enter RAF service; the SS.37 at Martlesham Heath, 1935. *Peter Green Collection*

The Shuttleworth Collection Gladiator II L8032 has flown in a variety of colours schemes, including 72 Squadron in the late 1970s. *KEC*

The second prototype Gloster F5/34 was issued to the RAE at Farnborough in late 1937 for radio testing. *Peter Green Collection*

Almost certainly being flown by 'Gerry' Sayer, the first prototype Gloster F9/37, L7999. *KEC*

flying, but long before that he and George Carter worked closely on the layout of the cockpit and other elements of the prototype. Hand-in-hand with the experimental E28/39, Gloster set Carter on the path to create a viable, operational jet fighter. This emerged as the twin-engined F9/40, destined to become the spectacularly successful Meteor. Gerry was in command of the first taxi trials of the Power Jets W.2B-powered F9/40 prototype DG202 at Newmarket Heath on 22nd July 1942. But fate was to intervene and the Meteor became Michael Daunt's responsibility.

In October 1942 Gerry was at Acklington with the pilots of 1 Squadron, flying Typhoon IBs – since May 1941 Hucclecote had taken on production of the rugged Hawker fighter. Gerry was there for operational trials of a gunsight, firing against a target on the Druridge Bay ranges. On 21st October Gerry took off in R7867 with Plt Off Paul Nelson Dobie as his No.2 in R7861. They never returned and are believed to have collided out at sea. Philip Edward George

A grainy image but it captured both a momentous occasion and conveyed the 'hush-hush' nature of the event: 'Gerry' Sayer flying the Gloster E28/39 at Cranwell, 15th May 1941. *KEC*

Sayer OBE was 36. Gerry had been at pains to make sure that his deputy, Michael Daunt was up to speed on jet developments at Gloster, and he took over the demanding test schedule. *Flight's* obituary was as fulsome as it could be in the circumstances: "As a test pilot [Gerry] was outstanding and it is regretted that security reasons preclude us from giving details of what he has been doing since the outbreak of hostilities." The blanket of secrecy could only temporarily cloak Gerry Sayer's place in world aviation history.

'Gerry' Sayer and Britain's First Jet

7 Apr 1941	First taxying trials at Hucclecote, with Power Jets W.1X, not rated for flight
8 Apr 1941	Further 'straights'' at Hucclecote, including three 'hops' to about 5-6ft
14 May 1941	First taxi trials at Cranwell; flight-rated W.1 fitted
15 May 1941	First flight, taking off at 19:48 for 17 minutes
28 May 1941	Total of 17 flights made at Cranwell, flight time amounting to 10 hours, 28 minutes
Feb 1942	First taxi runs at Edgehill, W.1A engine
16 Feb 1942	First test flight from Edgehill
24 Mar 1942	Turbine blade failure on 7th Edgehill flight
2 Jun 1942	Tests resumed at Edgehill
6 Jun 1942	Premature return to Edgehill following oil system failure; turbine bearings seized
27 Sep 1942	Low oil pressure warnings brought flight to early close; fast landing port wing and rear fuselage damaged. 'Gerry' Sayer's last flight in W4041.

Harry Schofield

May 1932	General Aircraft ST-4 G-ABUZ
	2 x 85hp Pobjoy R
Jun 1934	General Aircraft ST-10 T-5
	2 x 90hp Pobjoy Niagara
May 1935	General Aircraft ST-18 Croydon T-22
	2 x 450hp P&W Wasp Junior SB9

Notes: ST-4 flown from Croydon; ST-10 and ST-18 both from Hanworth, becoming G-ACTS and G-AECB respectively.

Harry Metheun Schofield, born 1899. Joined the RNAS in 1917, serving in Italy, Albania, Greece and Malta. By 1920 he had left what had become the RAF and spent four years building church organs. He re-joined the RAF in 1925, going on to serve with the communications specialist unit, 24 Squadron, from Kenley and then Northolt. He was selected as one of the pilots for the RAF High Speed Flight to compete at Venice in the Schneider Trophy, 26th September 1927. While air testing Short-Bristow Crusader N226 after re-assembly on 11th September the floatplane rolled badly on take off and crashed at high speed upside down into the Venice Lido. Harry was found floating in the water, deeply shocked but, miraculously, hardly injured. It was discovered the aileron cables had been linked incorrectly and Harry's instinctive responses exacerbated, instead of cured, the problem. After the excitement of Venice, he instructed at the Oxford University Air Squadron.

IN 1932 Flt Lt Harry Schofield joined the newly-established General Aircraft Company at Croydon (moving to Hanworth in 1934) as CTP. The company was building a family of twin-engined types using the Monospar design techniques of Swiss-born Helmuth John Stieger. Sqn Ldr Rollo Haig*, a director of General Aircraft, had tested a 'proof of concept' light twin, Gloster-built ST-3 G-AARP in 1931. Harry piloted the first ST-4 four-seater, G-ABUZ, in 1932. On the fourth flight, the starboard Pobjoy engine failed on take-off from Croydon and Harry had few options where to put the prototype in the built-up area around the airport. He managed to keep the machine within the perimeter, colliding with a fence. Series production of the ST-4 began and included a small number of ST-6s with retractable undercarriage. Having also made the debut of the enlarged and much-refined ST-10 G-ACTS in the summer of 1934, Harry – with Stieger as navigator/observer – sizzled around the course of the King's Cup air race, based on Hatfield, to win at 134mph. In 1935 a further improved ST-10, the ST-25 with twin fins, was flown and 59 were built up to 1939. That year the company also produced a 10-passenger airliner, the Croydon, but only G-AECB was completed – see under 'Timber' Wood for more. By this time Harry had been appointed to the board as managing director and Ken Seth-Smith* replaced him as CTP.

Harry was the author of two books, both published in 1932 by John Hamilton: *High Speed and Other Flights* and *The Pictorial Flying Course*, the latter with the *Biggles* writer W E Johns. He had left General Aircraft by 1938 and settled to a life as a farmer. Flt Lt Harold Methuen Schofield died in December 1955, aged 56.

Harry Schofield taking a turning point on his way to winning the 1934 King's Cup air race in General Aircraft ST-10 G-ACTS. *Peter Green Collection*

'Tiny' Scholefield

Sep 1925	Vickers Vespa I G-EBLD
	1 x 390hp Bristol Jupiter IV
Mar 1926	Vickers Vendace I N208
	1x 275hp RR Falcon III
27 Jun 1927	Vickers Vivid G-EBPY
	1 x 500hp Napier Lion VA
Mar 1928	Vickers Vireo N211
	1 x 215hp AS Lynx IV
14 Sep 1928	Vickers Vildebeest N230
	1 x 460hp Bristol Jupiter
17 May 1928	Vickers Vellore I J8906
	1 x 515hp Bristol Jupiter IX
Apr 1929	Glenny and Henderson Gadfly G-AAEY
	1 x 34hp ABC Scorpion II

Edward Rodolph Clement Scholefield, born 1893 in Calgary, Alberta, Canada. By 1901 he was being educated in Britain. Aged 17, he learned to fly at Buc, France, as a pupil of Charles Gordon Bell*. He joined the RFC in 1914, initially as a mechanic. He was shot down and captured on the Western Front in 1915 and spent the rest of the Great War as a prisoner. Repatriated in 1918, he continued with the RAF and went on serve at RAE Farnborough, working under Roderic Hill* on inverted flat spins, among other trials.

A Vespa IV for the Irish Air Corps, delivered in April 1930. *Rolls-Royce*

Flt Lt Edward Rodolph Clement Scholefield DCM AFC was appointed as CTP for Vickers at Brooklands in the summer of 1924, succeeding 'Tommy' Broome*. At 16 stone the nickname 'Tiny' was inevitable, if inappropriate! Other than flying, he had a passion for motor racing – Tiny could find no better venue for employment than Brooklands!

As well as signing off Victoria transports for the RAF, Tiny was kept busy testing the growing family of general purpose biplanes that stemmed from the Vixen of 1923. This series had been pioneered by Tommy Broome and culminated in the all-metal Vivid of 1927. The Vendace was developed as a floatplane trainer for the Fleet Air Arm, Tiny flying the prototype in the spring of 1926 in landplane form: the Bolivian Air Force ordered three. The Vespa was a private-venture army co-operation type. While displaying the prototype at the Hendon airshow in 24th June 1926 the Bristol Jupiter played up and Tiny had to make a very public force landing, resulting in much damage to the airframe, but not the pilot. The Vespa also appealed to the Bolivians, and the Irish Air Corps also ordered eight examples. The Vireo was a single-seat monoplane fighter using the construction techniques of Michel Wibault (see below) that went no further than the prototype. Designed as a large biplane for use as a mail-carrier or freighter, the Vellore also remained a one-off, but was transformed in 1930 into a twin-engined transport – see 'Mutt' Summers.

By far the most successful of the types 'first flighted' by Tiny was the Vildebeest torpedo biplane. Initially with the Bristol Jupiter, when fully developed the Bristol Pegasus IIM3 was the standard powerplant. Production commenced in 1932: a total of 151 Vildebeests were odered by the RAF. A follow-up, the Vincent was a general purpose version and 197 were built.

Financed by A P Glenny and G L P Henderson, the Gadfly was designed by Ken Pearson as a sporting single-seater and Tiny obliged by carrying out the maiden flight, at Brooklands, in April 1929. Two Gadflies were made; both eventually using Pearson's patented rotary ailerons mounted at the wing tips.

In 1925 Vickers entered into a licence agreement with the French company Avions Michel Wibault for the 7.C1 all-metal single-seat parasol monoplane fighter. A Bristol Jupiter-powered version was manufactured in France and demonstrated to the Chilean armed forces and an order for 26 followed. Tiny flew the first Vickers-built Wibault Scout in June 1926. Around this time the Air Ministry was pressing for all test pilots to fly with parachutes and, almost without thinking, Tiny took one with him on the flight. It was a smart move, he was going to

Vildebeest III K4175 on a sortie out of Seletar, Singapore, in 1935. These biplanes were part of the opposition to the Japanese invasion of February 1942. *KEC*

The Glenny-Henderson Gadfly in its later form, from September 1929, with Pearson rotary ailerons at the wing tips. *Peter Green Collection*

Stuart Scott

28 May 1930	Saro-Segrave Meteor G-AAXP 2 x 120hp DH Gipsy III
Jul 1930	Saro Severn N240 3 x 490hp Bristol Jupiter XIFP
Jul 1930	Saro Cloud L4 2 x 300hp Wright Whirlwind J-6
16 Oct 1930	Saro Windhover ZK-ABW 3 x 120hp DH Gipsy II
Apr 1934	Saro London K3560 2 x 820hp Bristol Pegasus IIIM3

Notes: All from the River Medina at Cowes other than the Meteor which flew from Somerton.

need it. In *Flight Path*, Frank Courtney* vividly described the descent: "The plane refused to come out of the spin, no matter what he did. The earth was coming up painfully close when Tiny, who had completely forgotten his unaccustomed parachute, suddenly remembered it, and he was now forced to decide that it was the lesser of two evils. He jumped, and then realised that he had no idea what to do except that he had to pull something. His 200-plus pounds were hurtling towards the ground while he pulled wildly at anything he could reach: rings, buckles, clips, and straps. Suddenly, as he later described it to me, he was jolted as though cracked at the end of a whip, and the 'chute delivered his hefty frame into the top of a tree."

Tiny had inherited testing of the airliner development of the Victoria military transport, the Vanguard, which had been first flown by Stan Cockerell*. Neither Tiny nor his FTO Frank Sharrett took parachutes on 16th May 1929. It was not a smart move; they were going to need them. The sole Vanguard prototype, G-EBCP, had been fitted with a new tail unit configuration. The Vanguard crashed near Shepperton, killing Frank Sharrett and Flt Lt Edward Rodolph Clement Scholefield DCM AFC, aged 36. A failure of the tail unit is thought to have been the cause of the crash but a broken, wooden, propeller is also attributed by two sources. Tiny's place at Vickers was taken by 'Mutt' Summers.

The first Saro-Segrave Meteor, G-AAXP at Blackburn's airfield at Brough, 1931. *Peter Green Collection*

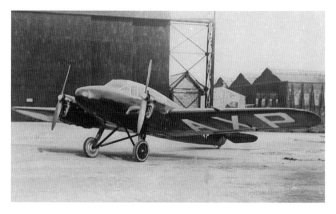

PREVIOUSLY stationed at the RAF flying-boat base at Calshot, Flt Lt Stuart D Scott signed up as CTP for Saunders-Roe (Saro), across the Solent at Cowes on the Isle of Wight in 1930. The small firm was beginning to turn the corner and achieve series production, but nevertheless, Flt Lt Scott's position was part-time. From a 'first flighting' point of view, he enjoyed a busy 1930. Scott's initial test was the Meteor twin-engined four-seater tourer prototype, G-AAXP, in May. The Meteor was designed by Sir Henry Segrave, former Great War fighter pilot and one-time holder of the world land speed record. Production of the Meteor was carried out by Blackburn at Brough, but only another two were completed. Sir Henry was killed in a motor boat accident in June 1930.

Having established the format with the Cutty Sark monoplane amphibian (see Charles Chilton) Saro developed a family of similar types. With engines mounted above the wing on pylons, a wide variety of powerplants could be offered. With two crew and up to eight passengers the Cloud was the largest. Despite its three engines the Windhover was a mid-sized option. The RAF adopted the Cloud as a trainer for the larger flying-boats and 21 were built. Only two Windhovers were manufactured, the prototype being destined for New Zealand.

Construction of the Severn long-range patrol flying-boat had started in 1928, but it was not until July 1930 that it was ready for test. It was not accepted for production. Saro's next attempt at a big 'boat was the London, first flown in April 1934. This was the turning point for Saro, the RAF ordering 31, delivered in batches from 1936 through to mid-1938. On the strength of this order, the massive Columbine assembly hall on the east shore was built – it still dominates the waterborne approach to Cowes to this day. With the London, Flt Lt Stuart D Scott's relationship with Saro was completed; the company's next CTP was Leslie Ash*.

Armstrong Siddeley Serval-powered Cloud K2898 of 'B' Flight, based at Calshot, 1934. *KEC*

Crews getting ready to beach London I K5262 of 201 Squadron at Calshot: three other examples are moored in the background. *Rolls-Royce*

Taylor Scott

TAYLOR SCOTT joined the Fleet Air Arm in 1964 and flew DH Sea Vixens and McDonnell Phantoms operationally. From 1977 to 1979 he was Royal Navy Project Liaison Officer for the Sea Harrier at Dunsfold. Taylor joined the test flight staff of British Aerospace at Dunsfold in 1979. With the Argentine invasion of the Falkland Islands Lt Cdr Scott volunteered for active duty. He helped train up personnel for the newly re-formed 809 Squadron at Yeovilton on Sea Harrier FRS.1s. The unit was officially re-activated on 27th April 1982 and the pace of work at Dunsfold was such that FRS.1 ZA194 was first flown on 23rd April and was delivered to the 809

flightline at Yeovilton five days later. With 809's departure 'down south' on the 30th, Taylor returned to Dunsfold.

On 22nd October 1987 Taylor was conducting a test flight of the sixth production Harrier GR.5, ZD325. Taking off from Dunsfold at 16:59 he climbed westwards to 30,000ft. There was no more radio contact beyond his checking in with London Military centre at 17:06. With no response to calls, London Military vectored a westbound USAF Lockheed C-5A Galaxy to the Harrier's track. The big transport drew alongside the fighter about 140 miles west of the south tip of Ireland and confirmed that ZD325 was apparently under autopilot, without its pilot-and that the ejection seat was in place. The C-5 shepherded the Harrier until 19:03 when it dropped out the sky, presumably having run out of fuel. The following day, the 40-year-old pilot's body was found 5 miles west of Boscombe Down; he was still attached to a very badly damaged parachute. The Harrier was never recovered.

The inquest recorded an open verdict, but attributed the most likely cause was a loose article lodging under the manual override (MOR) handle of the Martin-Baker Mk.12H ejector seat. Flying on autopilot into the setting sun, it was possible that Taylor adjusted the seat downwards to allow him to observe the central warning panel while he carried out the prescribed oxygen system check. Lowering the seat with a loose item in the way could have distorted the MOR, firing the drogue 'chute which dragged the pilot out through the canopy, which had been shattered by the detonation cords. The coroner described Taylor Scott as "brave, dedicated and skilled" concluding: "We in this country are very considerably in his debt."

'Slim' Sear

17 Oct 1956	Westland Whirlwind HAS.7 XG589
	1 x 750hp Alvis Leonides Major 155
17 May 1957	Westland Wessex HAS.1 XL727
	1 x 1,450shp Napier Gazelle NGa11
15 Jun 1958	Westland Westminster G-APLE
	2 x 2,920shp Napier Eland 229A
2 Sep 1959	Westland Whirlwind HAR.9 XJ398
	1 x 1,050shp BSE Gnome H.1000

Notes: All took place from Yeovil. Whirlwind Mk.9 XJ398 was flown by 'Slim' Sear from Yeovil on 28th February 1959 with an interim General Electric T58 turboshaft, before flying as the true turboshaft Whirlwind with a Gnome.

W H Sear served in the RAF 1942 to 1945. He transferred to the Fleet Air Arm in 1945, going on to serve with 891 Squadron on Grumman Hellcats, then 812 and 816 Squadrons on Fairey Fireflies. He graduated from ETPS Course No.10 at Farnborough in 1951 and was then posted to A&AEE. Flying at Boscombe Down included Westland Wyvern S.4 deck-landing trials on HMS Eagle in late 1953.

LT WILLIAM H 'SLIM' SEAR was seconded to Westland in late 1953, becoming CTP in place of Harald Penrose*, before joining the company on a full-time basis. Slim was responsible for taking Westland from 'learning the ropes' of helicopter manufacture to becoming a world-class rotorcraft design house in its own right. While the Sikorsky S-51 Dragonfly provided the basis of its new business the RAF and the Fleet Air arm required more adaptable and capable helicopters. The Sikorsky S-55 and larger S-58 were wisely chosen for the next leap. Initially Pratt & Whitney R-1820-powered S-55s were built under licence: the first example, Whirlwind G-AMJT, was flown at Yeovil on 12th November 1952 by Derrick Colvin*. But the future lay with re-engineering and 'Anglicising' the Whirlwind and Slim first flew both evolutions: the Alvis Leonides piston-engined Mk.7 and the Mk. 9 with a Bristol Siddeley Gnome turboshaft. Production of Whirlwinds ran to the early 1960s and included civilian and export sales. As the Wessex, the S-58 was transformed from the beginning as a radically different type from its American forebear. Powered by a Napier Gazelle turboshaft, a Sikorsky-built HSS-1 Seabat, XL722, served as the interim prototype and Slim carried out its maiden flight from Yeovil on 17th May 1957. The following year he piloted the first all-Westland Wessex HAS.1, XL727, on 20th June. Wessex production included civilian and export orders and ended in 1967.

The first prototype Westminster in flying space-frame guise, 1959. *Westland Aircraft*

The civilian equivalent of the military HAR.9 and HAR.10 turbine Whirlwinds was the Series 3. Westland's demonstrator G-APDY at Sywell, April 1962. *Roy Bonser*

As the next Westland project only produced two prototypes and was quietly dropped when the rotorcraft divisions of Bristol and Saro were acquired in 1960, the Westminster is often regarded as a major 'flop'. In truth it provided Westland with another large influx of 'technology transfer' – complex control systems, multi-blade main rotors and multi-engine gearboxes. Using the five-bladed, 72ft diameter main rotor, gearbox, transmission and control system of the Sikorsky S-56 (the H-37 Mojave) Yeovil schemed a large helicopter, capable of use as a 40-passenger transport or flying-crane. The first prototype Westminster, G-APLE, was intended to serve as a flying dynamics rig; behind the two-seat cockpit and FTE's position the remainder of the fuselage was a tube space-frame.

Lima-Echo was completed in February 1958 and Slim began the long and involved process of systems, controls and dynamics testing. It was not until 3rd June 1958 that engine runs began and 20 hours of tethered 'flying' began. Slim took the prototype for its first full flight on 15th June 1958 and demonstrated it at the SBAC airshow at Farnborough in September. Vibration was a continued problem and a six-bladed rotor from the Sikorsky S-64 Skycrane was fitted to the second machine, G-APTX, which Slim 'first flighted' on 4th September 1959. Integrating the Bristol and Saro product lines into Westland and the anti-submarine Wessex programme were large enough tasks and the Westminster was a casualty of this massive expansion. Lt W H 'Slim' Sear OBE was heavily involved in the anti-submarine versions of the Wessex, retiring in 1967 and handing over to Ron Gellatly*. He died in September 2015

Roger Searle

Roger W Searle, born 1946. He joined the RAF in 1964 and by 1967 was flying Hawker Hunter FGA.9s with 54 Squadron at West Raynham. In 1969 he was posted to the newly-reformed 1 Squadron at Wittering, converting to the HS Harrier GR.1. Roger moved to Boscombe Down in 1972, joining the Handling Squadron. He graduated from ETPS Course No.34 at Boscombe Down and from there was posted to RAE Farnborough; there some of his flying included sorties for the Institute of Aviation Medicine.

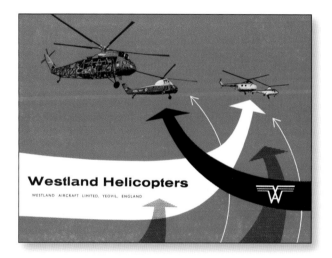

A 1959 dated Westland brochure with the product line-up on the cover, left to right: Westminster, Wessex, Whirlwind and Widgeon. Inside, the translator had been allowed to run riot with sections headed 'Helicoptères Westland', 'Westland-Hubschrauber' and 'Helicopteros Westland'.

IN January 1980 Roger Searle was appointed as a test pilot at Brough for British Aerospace and was promoted to CTP in December 1983. Roger's 'beat' was extensive, including managing Brough airfield, the flight test centre at Scampton (which closed in 1992 – Holme-on-Spalding Moor had closed in December 1983) and the offshore weapons range. As well as HS Buccaneer and McDonnell Phantom modification and refurbishment programmes, other projects included weapons store testing on the second pre-production Pilatus PC-9 HB-HPA from mid-1985. The PC-9 had been selected for the Royal Saudi Arabian Air Force, which BAe was managing as part of the massive Al Yamamah programme. In February 1993 Roger moved to Warton, heading up Hawk production test, delivery and customer training. Roger retired from testing, having amassed over 5,500 hours on 140 types. In July 1998 Roger took on a role within the Hawk Engineering Development Team at Warton, finally leaving what became BAE Systems in 1999 in December 2002. The following year he became a director of Pilotwise International, a specialist training systems and consultancy organisation.

BAe Hawker 800 and Hawker 1000 demonstrators on the ramp at Little Rock, Arkansas, USA, 1992. *Corporate Jets Inc*

Peter Sedgwick

| 16th Jun 1990 | BAe HS.125-1000B G-EXLR |
| | 2 x 5,200lbst P&W (Canada) PW305 |

SQN LDR PETER A SEDGWICK, British Aerospace Airlines Division CTP captained the maiden flight of the final iteration of the spectacularly successful HS.125 corporate jet from Hawarden, near Chester, on 16th June 1990. The 12-seater Series 1000 was a far cry form the original machine that Chris Capper* had flown from Hatfield in August 1982. Alongside Peter on Series 1000 *Lima-Romeo* was Project Test Pilot George Ellis. Nine years previously, it was Peter who was in the No.2 seat, to Mike Goodfellow* on the first flight of the HS.146-100 G-SSSH at Hatfield on 3rd September 1991. A former RAF transport pilot, Peter had graduated from ETPS Course No.30 at Boscombe Down in 1971. He was posted to RAE Farnborough before returning to Boscombe and ETPS, as an instructor. By 1978 he had left the RAF and became an airline pilot for a short period, before joining BAe as a test pilot.

John Seth-Smith

FLT LT JOHN GARDEN SETH-SMITH was a production test pilot for Fairey. On 13th October 1945, he was testing Firefly I PP417 from Heston; its third test flight. Among the tasks was to check that the canopy slid smoothly open and shut at 220 knots. Five minutes into the flight, PP417 plunged through the cloud base in a vertical spin and it impacted near Barnes. John Garden Seth-Smith – cousin of K G Seth-Smith – was killed instantly, he was 28. It was discovered that the canopy had come away from its rails, initially hitting the aerial mast and then the tail section. The tail section failed, leading to loss of control. It is likely that the canopy injured John although it appears that he had made an attempt to bale out. On 27th November 1945 a similar incident befell Colin Evans*: the canopy rails were altered and the specification increased on airframes on the production line.

Ken Seth-Smith

KENNETH G SETH-SMITH, cousin of John Seth-Smith, was an apprentice at General Aircraft, Hanworth, in 1932. By 1935 he had taken over from Harry Schofield* as CTP and was engaged in production testing of ST-25 Jubilees and Universals. He joined Hawker as a production test pilot in 1939, working from Brooklands and then Langley. He flew the first Hurricane IIC (several sources erroneously quote this as V2461) on 6th February 1941 and the twin 40mm cannon-equipped Mk.IID prototype, Z2326, on 18th September 1941 – both from Langley. Piloting Gloster-built Typhoon I R7692 from Langley on 11th August 1942 Ken put it into a spin and the tail suffered structural failure. R7692 crashed near Thorpe, Surrey, and Ken was killed. It was discovered that a bracket attaching the elevator mass balance had failed, resulting in catastrophic break up of the tail. A strengthening programme was instigated, both for the bracket and the tail section.

E J Sharp

FLT LT E J SHARP was a production test pilot for Bristol at Filton. On the first flight of Beaufort I AW215 on 14th June 1941 after 20 minutes the aircraft was observed to be on fire; it crashed at Shepperdine, killing the pilot. One of the Bristol Taurus II 14-cylinder sleeve valve radials had suffered a major seizure and fire had spread to the cockpit area through the leading edge. Production line examples had the inner centre section modified to prevent spread of fire toward the cockpit.

'Pat' Shea-Simmonds

Oct 1944	Supermarine Spitfire PR.XIX SW777
	1 x 2,025hp RR Griffon 65
6 Jul 1945	Supermarine Spitfire XVIII
	1 x 2,025hp RR Griffon 65

Notes: Both took place from High Post.

The prototype Spitfire XVIII was SM843, first flown from High Post on 6th July 1945 by 'Pat' Shea-Simmonds. *Key Publishing collection – www.keypublishing.com*

LT GEOFFREY PATRICK LA TROBE SHEA-SIMMONDS – 'Shea' to colleagues, 'Pat' to friends and family – was one of the pioneers who graduated from ETPS Course No.1 at Boscombe Down, 1943-1944. Immediately after the course, Shea was seconded to Fairey for production test pilot duties. He test flew Albacore I N4183 on 11th March 1944 at Eastleigh where it had been under repair by Cunliffe-Owen. In *Spitfire – A Test Pilot's Story*, Jeffrey Quill* described what happened next: "...somewhat to Shea's surprise, the engine fell out altogether and descended rapidly earthwards. He managed to land the aeroplane in a field [ironically, close to Chilbolton] and a working party came and fitted a new engine. Sometime later he flew it out of the field..." Although fitted with a replacement Bristol Taurus II N4183, which had been built in late 1940, was a bit long in the tooth for more service and it was placed in store, being struck off charge by mid-1945. For his efforts in saving the Albacore, Shea was awarded the MBE. In 1945 Shea undertook another forced landing of much greater significance and risk; meriting 'just' a King's Commendation.

Shea joined Supermarine, following the death of Frank Furlong* in prototype Spiteful NN660 at High Post on 13th September 1944. Working under Jeffrey Quill, Shea became his deputy, working from High Post where the small team had a large and varied output to test and despatch to operational units. In October Shea tested the prototype PR.XIX high-flying, long-range photo-reconnaissance variant and in July 1945 the first Mk.XVIII. While flying the first production Spiteful XIV, RB515, from High Post on 9th April 1945 the pilot encountered severe vibration and was unable to lower the undercarriage. He elected to use the wider expanses of Boscombe Down for a belly landing, which he accomplished safely. Piloting RB515 was Shea's 'boss', Jeffrey Quill. Repaired, it fell to Shea to test RB515 and he took it up from High Post on 27th September 1945. A mounting bracket detached from the Griffon and chronic vibration ran through the airframe. Connecting rods fractured and the propeller ground to a halt. Realising it was crucial to bring the 'evidence' back for analysis, Shea decided to stay with the Spiteful and he made a wheels-up landing at Farnborough.

In February 1946 Shea became the proud owner of Hawker Tomtit G-AFTA – it was previously in the hands of non other

than Alex Henshaw – see Chapter Two. Shea's time with this biplane was brief, he disposed of it at the end of May 1946. It later became the property of another test pilot – Neville Duke* and today the Tomtit flies with the Shuttleworth Collection. Lt Geoffrey Patrick La Trobe Shea-Simmonds MBE left Supermarine in 1946.

Ronald 'Shep' Shepherd

| 3 Aug 1954 | RR Thrust Measuring Rig XJ314 |
| | 2 x 4,900lbst RR Nene 101 IV |

Ronald Thomas Shepherd, born 1900 – perhaps as late as 1902. By at least 1915 Ronald was an apprentice with Vickers, the firearms and munitions division, in London. He enlisted with the Honourable Artillery Company in 1916 – if he was born 1900 he would be the right age, if it was 1902 he was convincingly lying about his age! 'Shep' transferred to the RFC and learned to fly. He joined 102 Squadron at Hingham, on Royal Aircraft Factory FE.2bs, in August 1917, moving to the Western Front the following month. By October 1918 he was flying Sopwith Camels with 37 Squadron at Stow Maries on home defence night duties. Leaving the RAF in 1919, he signed up again in 1921, flying Sopwith Snipes with 56 Squadron at Aboukir, Egypt. Shep was back in Britain by 1926, with 25 Squadron on Gloster Grebes from Hawkinge. In British Test Pilots, Geoffrey Dorman describes what he calls Shep's "closest squeak", which took place in 1926: "He was in a formation of Gloster Grebes, flying over Salisbury Plain when the leader saw a Bristol Fighter make a forced landing, and went down o see if the pilot was all right. Shep, following the leader, struck some rising ground with his undercart, at flying speed, and turned the Grebe over three times. He escaped with cuts, bruises, and a shaking." The Grebe is question might well have been J7409. He left the RAF in 1928 and worked briefly as CFI for Phillips & Powis at Woodley before moving to National Flying Services the following year. With NFS, Shep ran the Nottingham Flying Club at Tollerton.

ALSO at Tollerton was Rolls-Royce, using the airfield on an ad hoc basis for test purposes. With a pilot of such skills as Captain Ronald Thomas Shepherd resident, the company approached 'Shep' regarding the occasional, freelance, test flight and he readily agreed. In October 1931 he flew Fairey IIIF J9173 fitted with a Kestrel engine and other work followed. In 1934 Rolls-Royce (RR) opened its own test facility at Hucknall, north of Nottingham, and Shep was appointed as CTP. The bulk of his flying is beyond the scope of this title, including development work on the Merlin (for which he was awarded an OBE in 1946) and the early turbojets but he did carry out a very important, and challenging, maiden flight.

Co-operation between RR and the RAE starting in 1952 led to a jet-powered test-bed to produce data for a dedicated lift engine and a control and stabilisation system for hovering flight. RAE provided the control systems while RR created what was known as the Thrust Measuring Rig (TMR) but which the press readily called the 'Flying Bedstead'. Two horizontally-mounted Nene turbojets provided downward thrust. A small amount of thrust was bled away into four 'puffer' jets to provide stability, projecting starboard and port and fore and aft. The latter two could swivel to provide a limited amount of directional control; it could fly sideways, or in circles.

The TMR was rolled out at Hucknall on 3rd July 1953 and Jim Heyworth*, piloted the first successful tethered hop three days later. Following illness in 1951, Shep handed over the role of CTP to Jim, becoming flight test manager. At that point, he had over 8,000 flying hours on 77 types. It seems that the TMR was too much of a temptation: Shep made the personal transition from Sopwith Camel to Britain's first vertical take-off jet, carrying out the first free excursion on 3rd August 1954. Tests at Hucknall were completed on 15th December 1954 by which time XJ314 had clocked up 224 tethered and 16 free flights, the latter amounting to 105 minutes airborne. XJ314 was transferred to the RAE in January 1955 and is today displayed in the 'Making of the Modern World' gallery in the Science Museum, London. A second TMR, XK426, was built but crashed on 27th November 1957, killing Wg Cdr H G F Larson. Captain Ronald Thomas Shepherd OBE died in 1955, aged 55 – at the most.

'Shep' Shepherd in the cockpit of his 37 Squadron Sopwith Camel F5183 *Maisie*, 1918. *Peter Green Collection*

Below: Thirty-six years later, 'Shep' Shepherd in another, equally basic cockpit – the 'Flying Bedstead' at Hucknall, 1954. *Rolls-Royce*

Joe Shoesmith

1938	Hillson Pennine G-AFBX
	1 x 36hp Praga B

Based at Trafford Park in Manchester, the woodworking firm of F Hills and Sons set up an aircraft division in 1936, trading as Hillson, initially with a licence agreement to produce the Czechoslovakian Praga E.114 side-by-side two-seat monoplane. During 1937 the company's designer, Norman Sykes, created his own high-wing two-seater, the Pennine, with 'baffle-flaps' or spoilers in place of ailerons. Company test pilot Joe Shoesmith flew the Pennine from Barton in 1938 but nothing more is known of it – or Mr Shoesmith. Hills developed the much more conventional, but one-off, Helvellyn trainer in 1939 and during the war built Percival Proctors and carried out experimentation into auxiliary, or 'slip' wings, with the test-bed Bi-Mono leading to full-blown trials on a Hurricane.

R G Shove

Royal Marine Lt R G Shove was seconded to Hawker at Langley as a production test pilot. On 9th June 1949 he took off in Sea Fury FB.11 VX618 for an endurance test. On take-off VX618's Bristol Centaurus 18 was observed emitting black smoke and this information was transmitted to Lt Shove. He turned downwind to make a short circuit, but the Fury dived into the ground, killing the pilot.

Duncan Simpson

24 Apr 1969	HS Harrier T.2 XW174
	1 x 19,000lbst BSE Pegasus 101
21 Aug 1974	HS Hawk T.1 XX154
	1 x 5,200lbst RR/Turboméca Adour 151

Duncan Menzies Soutar Simpson, born 1928. Alan Cobham's* touring 'circus' visiting northern Scotland in 1934 and Duncan's uncle, Duncan Menzies, becoming a PTP for Fairey at Ringway by 1940 – see Chapter Seven – were both major influences on the youngster's chosen career. In 1945 he began studies at the de Havilland Technical School, Hatfield, graduating in 1949. That year he joined the RAF and by 1951 he was flying Gloster Meteor F.8s with 222 Squadron at Leuchars, followed by a posting to the Air Fighting Development Unit at West Raynham, mostly flying Hawker Hunters.

Think of Duncan Simpson and the Harrier naturally comes to mind. But Duncan was the man who first flew another money-spinner and one that is *still* in production – the Hawk. Invited by Hawker CTP Neville Duke* to join the team at Dunsfold, Duncan left the RAF in 1954. Bill Bedford* became the CTP in 1956 and in 1960 the P.1127 began its trials. Duncan was the third HSA test pilot to fly a P.1127 (Hugh Merewether* being the second), flying XP976 on 25th June 1962. His experiences at the Air Fighting Development Unit meant that he was ideal to conduct pilot training for the British-American-German Tripartite Evaluation Squadron, which used Kestrels to perfect tactics and capabilities at West Raynham from 1964 until November 1965. Harrier GR.1s became operational with 1 Squadron at Wittering in 1969 and Duncan drew up the syllabus for training pilots to master the V/STOL fighter without the aid of a two-seat trainer.

Duncan carried out the first flight of the T.2 prototype, XW174, at Dunsfold on 24th April 1969. The GR.1 had a length of 46ft 10in while the T.2 was very nearly 9ft longer; as well as the second cockpit for the instructor; the rear reaction control pipe (or 'puffer') was greatly extended to compensate for the increased length and area of the forward fuselage. The prototype two-seater had a short life – 40 days. While flying it on 4th June 1969 the Pegasus 101 failed eight minutes into the sortie at 3,000ft. Duncan aimed for Boscombe Down and had been through his second re-light sequence when he realised he wouldn't make it and he tried for the Larkhill ranges instead. At 100ft he used XW174's Martin-Baker Mk.9 ejection seat – the first time that the version had been used in anger. Duncan came down close to the burning hulk of XW174; it seems that dirt in the fuel was the culprit. Duncan broke his neck during the ejection – he had gone *through* the canopy instead of it being shattered by explosive cords attached to the inside of the glazing milliseconds before the seat launched. He needed a bone graft and the surgeons had to carry out the challenging procedure by entering via his throat. Duncan spoke with a distinctive gravel-like tone – which he describes as "permanently exhausted hoarse" – ever since. He was flying Hunters again in November and was back in a Harrier in February 1970.

Like the Harrier before it, the Hawk was a private-venture using all of the skills of the company's Hunter experience and that of the Folland team; the type initially being aimed at replacing the Gnat T.1. Duncan carried out the maiden flight

The prototype two-seat Harrier, XW174, had a brief flying life – just 40 days. *Hawker Siddeley Aviation*

Duncan Simpson first flew the Hawk in August 1974 – over 40 years later it is still in production. *Hawker Siddeley Aviation*

of the prototype Hawk, XX154, at Dunsfold on 21st August 1974, just ten days before it was due to fly into Farnborough ready for its debut at the SBAC airshow. Things went remarkably smoothly and on XX154's tenth flight, Duncan ferried it over to Farnborough. In 1998 Duncan was pleased when the author enquired if his time on the Aircraft Design Course at the de Havilland Technical School helped with the conception of the Hawk: "To be able to follow an aircraft from the drawing board to the production line was so satisfying. All that I had learned at Hatfield came flooding back."

In a report covering early experiences of XX154 *Flight* magazine for 6th March 1975 outlined typical sorties and trumpeted the prototype as it: "exceeded Mach 1 in a shallow dive on February 26 during the high-Mach-number investigations in the hands of test pilots Duncan Simpson and Andy Jones(*). Two flights were made during the afternoon, lasting one hour, 35 minutes and one hour, 30 minutes, and supersonic speed was achieved on four occasions at about 35,000ft and dive angles of 10 to 12 degrees. The following day Andy Jones made a further supersonic run at the end of a day's flying which had included a flight of two hours duration on internal fuel alone." While: "At the bottom end of the speed spectrum the Hawk has been flown down to 84 knots stalling speed, and it is expected that this may be reduced a little further. This leaves a wide training error margin for the approach since 100 to 105 knots is a normal threshold speed."

Duncan was appointed as CTP at Dunsfold in 1970, taking over from Hugh Merewether. He retired at 50, in 1978, handing over to John Farley*. Duncan Menzies Soutar Simpson OBE took charge of Harrier and Hawk service liaison until the late 1980s.

'Bill' Skinner

5 Jan 1938	Miles Mentor L4392 1 x 200hp DH Gipsy Six
21 Feb 1938	Miles Monarch U1 1 x 130hp DH Gipsy Major
Sep 1938	Miles T1/37 U1 1 x 200hp DH Gipsy Six
Oct 1939	Miles Master II N7422 1 x 870hp Bristol Mercury XXX

Notes: All had their debut from Woodley. The Monarch and the T1/37 first flew with the B Condition (or 'trade-plate') marking U1; each became G-AFCR and L7714, respectively.

MILES Aircraft's leading light, F G Miles* (FGM), was under a lot of pressure during 1938 to cease test flying and concentrate on designing and running the company. On 1st April 1938 Flt Lt Harold William Chetwynd Skinner, who had already been heavily involved in flight testing, was appointed as CTP; after the death of 'Freddie' Stent*. 'Bill' had started at Woodley as an instructor with the Phillips & Powis school. The Mentor was a three-seat monoplane to take in a wide sweep of duties from instrument flying to communications: 45 were built. The Monarch was the first design fully executed by George Miles*, intended as a replacement for the Whitney Straight. It offered excellent performance, but was stunted by the coming war, only 11 were completed. Specification T1/37 sought a higher-powered trainer to supplant the DH Tiger Moth and the Miles Magister; two prototypes were built but no orders followed.

The eighth of eleven Monarchs, G-AFLW was built in 1938 and flew until the late 1990s. It is presently in store in Berkshire. *Roy Bonser*

Bill Skinner was most strongly associated with the Master. The private-venture Kestrel had been first flown by its creator, FGM, in June 1937 and during 1938 it was considerably rebuilt to meet RAF requirements as the Master I. It was flown in the new configuration, as N3300, in January 1939 and the type went into quantity production. In October 1939 Bill was at the controls for the maiden flight of the Bristol Mercury-engined Master II. Early in November 1939 Bill took the Master I prototype, N3300, up for a maximum speed test and for some sport with the Air Ministry. Dive speed as indicated was 330mph but from 20,000ft this would give a true airspeed (TAS) of about 470mph. Climbing out of Woodley in a strong northerly gale, Bill climbed to about 25,000ft and over Oxford, turned south and dived, down wind. Streaking over Farnborough, he calculated his TAS at 504mph. FGM sent a telegram to the Air Ministry to let them know just what a 'fighter' they had in the new trainer. Days later, Flt Lt Harold William Chetwynd Skinner died of a brain haemorrhage, he was just 36. 'Tommy' Rose* became CTP for Miles. FGM Miles wrote of Bill: "He had probably tested more purely experimental wings, gadgets and aeroplanes than any other pilot over a similar period and his reports were immortal."

Production Master II AZ247, 1941. *Miles Aircraft*

Gordon Slade

19 Sep 1949	Fairey Gannet VR546
	1 x 2,950shp AS double Mamba A5MD1
12 Mar 1951	Fairey FD.1 VX350
	1 x 3,500lbst RR Derwent 5
22 May 1951	Fairey Firefly AS.7 WJ215
	1 x 1,965hp RR Griffon 59

Notes: Venues as follows: Gannet – Aldermaston; FD.1 – Boscombe Down; Firefly – White Waltham.

Richard Gordon Slade, born 1912. Joined the RAF in 1933, training at Abu Sueir, Egypt. Posted to 30 Squadron at Mosul and, from 1936, Habbaniya, both in Iraq; flying Westland Wapitis and later Hawker Hardys. Returned to Britain in 1937 and served with A&AEE at Martlesham Heath and,

from 1939, at Boscombe Down. On 11th December 1940 Gordon carried out a wheels-up landing of Blackburn Botha I L6254 at High Post on a sortie out of Boscombe when fuel starvation brought the flight to an abrupt conclusion: no injuries. After piloting the prototype DH Mosquito W4050 on 24th February 1941 taxiing back in over rough ground, the tailwheel jammed and the fuselage fractured. (W4050 was fitted with the fuselage intended for the first photo-recce Mosquito prototype, W4051, and re-flew at Boscombe. Today this aircraft is the centre-piece of the de Havilland Aircraft Museum at London Colney.) In mid-1941 Gordon was promoted to wing commander and he was attached to 604 Squadron at Middle Wallop for night-fighter experience, flying Bristol Beaufighter Is. He was tutored by John Cunningham. In December 1941 Gordon became the CO of the re-formed 157 Squadron at Castle Camps; the first RAF Mosquito night-fighter unit. On 22nd August 1942, flying a Mosquito II, Gordon shot down a Dornier Do 217. In 1942 he was posted to Hullavington and the Handling Squadron, composing Pilot' Notes from a wide range of air tests. In February 1944 he was CO of 169 Squadron at Little Snoring, flying Mosquito IIs and VIs and became a group captain. His next appointment was as OC RAF Swannignton, with 85 and 'his' 157 Squadron resident on Mosquitos. By 1945 he was OC 148 Wing at Twente, Netherlands, and then 138 Wing at Cambrai, France, also with Mosquitos.*

G P CAPT RICHARD GORDON SLADE was appointed CTP to Fairey Aviation in 1946, taking over from Foster Dixon*. At that point Fairey was using Heston for flight testing, before moving to White Waltham by 1947. In *Fairey Firefly – The Operational Record*, Bill Harrison notes that Gordon was the man who made the decision to move to White Waltham. Fairey's original airfield, the Great West Aerodrome, had been absorbed into London Airport (Heathrow) and Heston – 3 miles to the north east – was perilously close to the airliners. Gordon had a close shave while testing a Firefly, only quick reactions prevented a collision with a Lockheed Constellation.

Fireflies and Barracudas formed the bulk of the work but the company was preparing to fly the coupled-turboprop Gannet carrier-borne anti-submarine aircraft, which was to prove a very lucrative and long-term, product. The prototype Gannet, VR546, configured as a two-seater, was moved by road from the factory at Hayes to Aldermaston for the first flight. Gordon began taxying trials and 'straights' on 11th September and on the 19th he made the first flight. DCTP Peter Twiss* was piloting the 'chase' aircraft, a Firefly, with Fairey chief engineer Hollis Williams* in the rear. Slade cut the flight short as he found it nigh on impossible to trim VR546 above 170 knots. A second flight on 5th October – with Twiss shadowing in the company's Fulmar G-AIBE, see Duncan Menzies in Chapter Seven – was equally problematic, but Gordon succeeded in transferring the prototype to White Waltham. After modifications to the elevator, Gordon resumed testing on 25th November only to discover no 'feel' at all in that control and 'porpoising' began. On turning finals while fighting the Gannet, it made a series of bounces, culminating in a very heavy touch down, the nose wheel collapsed with much damage to the powerplant and forward fuselage. It was March 1950 before VR546 was back in the air and in May the problems were sufficiently ironed out for it to go to RAE Farnborough on 25th May as a preliminary for deck landing trials.

Meanwhile the Firefly had been going through a major evolution to turn it into a three-seat anti-submarine aircraft as a back up should the Gannet, or Blackburn's YB.1, be badly delayed or fail to reach production. Gordon flew the prototype AS.7, WJ215, on 22nd May 1951. Most of the production AS.7s were finished as T.7 crew trainers and other airframes became U.8 and U.9 drones.

The FD.1 delta stemmed from a Fairey design study of 1946 for a fleet defence fighter that could be deployed on destroyers or cruisers, 'sitting' on its tail for a vertical take-off. Extensive testing of radio-controlled models was carried out, the last taking place in 1949. Specification E10/47 was written around this 'tail-sitter' but as time went by the three prototypes became one (VX350) and a 'conventional' delta research vehicle. VX350 was built at Heaton Chapel, Manchester, and Gordon carried out initial taxis at Ringway, on 12th May 1950. It was not until 12th March 1951 that the the FD.1 was first flown, Gordon taking it for a 17-minute sortie from Boscombe Down. The little delta was used for research at Boscombe until it was written off in a landing accident on 6th February 1956 at the hands of Sqn Ldr Denis Tayler* of RAE.

The Gannet prototype, VR546, in September 1949. *Peter Green Collection*

Early 1950s advert for the Gannet, showing an AS.1 cruising with one of the Mamba units and propellers shut down.

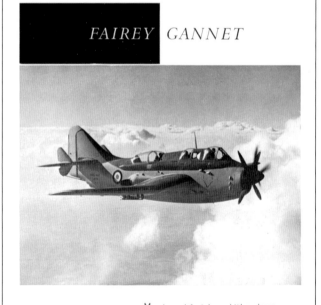

FAIREY *GANNET*

MORE than ever before Seaborne and Airborne elements are interdependent. The Royal Navy is constantly developing new weapons and new techniques to retain superiority.
To attack with these new weapons and develop new methods of keeping the sea lanes clear the Fairey Gannet anti-submarine aircraft has been ordered for the Royal Navy. It has also been ordered for the Royal Australian Navy.

FAIREY AVIATION

THE FAIREY AVIATION COMPANY LIMITED   HAYES . MIDDLESEX

The prototype Firefly AS.7, WJ215, at White Waltham. *Peter Green Collection*

Derived from a project for a 'vertical riser', the FD.1 research delta, mid-1951. *Fairey*

Beyond testing the FD.1, Gordon handed over to Peter Twiss. Gordon was appointed as a director of both Fairey Aviation and Fairey Air Surveys in 1959. The former post lasted only a year, with the acquisition of the aviation assets by Westland, but Gordon continued with the photo-mapping subsidiary to 1972. He also worked for another independent Fairey company, Fairey Hydraulics, as general manager 1961 to 1965 and as managing director to 1975. Gp Capt Richard Gordon Slade OBE became chairman of Fairey Hydraulics in 1975 and he held the post until his death in 1981, aged 69.

Brian Smith

FLT LT EDWARD BRIAN SMITH served with the RAF 1942 to 1946; later joining 501 (County of Gloucester) Squadron, flying DH Vampires from Filton. In 1950 he began flying as a production test pilot for Gloster from Hucclecote and Moreton Valence on Meteors and later Javelins. On 24th August 1956 Brian was conducting a test of Javelin FAW.4 XA644 out of Moreton Valence with Flt Lt R E Jefferies as FTO. While making a rapid descent, XA644 collided at 10,000ft with Hawker Hunter F.4 XF980 of the Central Flying School's Hunter Flight, Kemble, flown by Flt Lt P K V Hicks. The Hunter's fin ripped through the Javelin; Flt Lt Hicks was able to eject but was injured. Both Brian and Flt Lt Jefferies were involuntarily ejected from the Javelin; presumably because of the force of the impact – the Javelin's fuselage buckled at the intakes. Both aircraft crashed at Wotton-under-Edge. Flt Lt Jefferies survived, but the ejection seat of 33-year-old Flt Lt Edward Brian Smith was badly damaged and he was killed.

Roy Smith

ALL aspects of test piloting carry degrees of risk, including demonstration and ferrying. On 5th December 1957, David McIntyre, the founder and leading light of Scottish Aviation, flew to Tripoli, Libya, to catch up with Roy Smith and flight engineer R C Clapham and Twin Pioneer 3 G-AOEO. Former RAF pilot Roy Smith had worked at Prestwick post-war for the Scottish Aviation associate Scottish Airlines and made the move to test piloting on Pioneers and Twin Pioneers. By the mid-1950s, Roy had around 8,000 flying hours. *Echo-Oscar* was being used for a North African sales tour, with the Standard Oil Group of Libya as one of the 'targets'. On 7th December G-AOEO crashed in the Libyan Desert, killing Clapham, McIntyre and Smith. A failure of a wing strut was suspected.

Bob Smythe

| 10 Oct 1950 | Boulton Paul P.111 VT935 |
| | 1 x 5,100lbst RR Nene 3 |

Robert Smythe, born 1922. Joined the RAF in August 1941, training in the USA. Posted to 604 Squadron on Bristol Beaufighter VIs at Scorton by mid-1943 and, after many unit changes, he flew DH Mosquito XIIs with 256 Squadron at Foggia, Italy, by December 1944. In 1946 he swopped roles, becoming an engineering officer, whilst topping up his 'wings'. Graduated from ETPS Course No.7 at Farnborough and afterwards flew with RAE at Farnborough, becoming CO of Aero Flight.

SQN LDR ROBERT SMYTHE was called upon to make the first flight of the Boulton Paul P.111 research delta, a role that would, normally, have gone to the company's CTP, 'Ben' Gunn*. As the aircraft was destined for the RAE research fleet, Smythe was the customer's test pilot and the all-yellow delta was roaded to Boscombe Down for its debut. The citation for the Air Force Cross awarded to 'Bob' in June 1951 casts other light on why he was chosen: "This is, in fact, the first occasion on which a service pilot has been called upon to make the initial flight in a new aircraft. The Boulton Paul Delta is a highly experimental aircraft of tail-less design. There were many uncertainties regarding its longitudinal and lateral control characteristics especially in the approach and landing condition. Sqn Ldr Smythe made the first flight of this aircraft with outstanding skill and courage. Throughout the flight, he kept up a continuous running commentary on the characteristics of

the aircraft, giving a complete account of the take-off, climb and general handling qualities and of the approach and landing. In spite of carrying out the first landing of a tail-less delta aircraft with unknown characteristics at an approach speed of over 170mph he made a perfect landing." No slight was intended on Ben Gunn's abilities and the Boulton Paul CTP got to fly VT935 the same day. In 1953 VT935 was rebuilt at Pendeford, emerging as the P.111A. Today the P.111A is at the Midland Air Museum, Coventry.

After his posting to RAE, Bob returned to operational flying, joining 68 Squadron at Wahn, West Germany, on Gloster Meteor NF.11s. He left the RAF in 1961 signing up with Marshall of Cambridge, initially flying from Shawbury where the Cambridge-based company was the contractor for the Central Air Traffic Control School, using Percival Provost T.1s and DH Vampire T.11s. In 1966 Bob took up a post as test pilot for Marshall at Teversham, under CTP Leslie Worsdell*. The work was varied and challenging, including EE Canberras, the long-running contract for the RAF's Lockheed Hercules fleet and the civil certification of the Short Belfast. Bob became CTP for Marshall in 1977, retiring from the post in 1982. Sqn Ldr Robert Smythe AFC died on 12th December 1994, aged 72.

P.111A VT935 was gifted to the College of Aeronautics at Cranfield in April 1959 and it became a part of the famous 'Library of Flight'. Today it is with the Midland Air Museum at Coventry. *Roy Bonser*

Below: Bob Smythe displaying Short Belfast G-BEPS – wearing Marshall B Condition markings G-52-13 – at Duxford, September 1979. Marshall of Cambridge undertook the civilian certification of the Belfast for Trasnmeridian Air Cargo. *Roy Bonser*

George Snarey

16 Jul 1946	Auster J/2 Arrow Z-1
	1 x 75hp Continental C-75-12

By 1934, Flt Lt George Snarey was commanding officer of the RAF Meteorological Flight at Duxford, with Armstrong Whitworth Atlases and Siskin IIIAs. In November he left, leaving command to his No.2, Jeffrey Quill*. In 1938 he took up a test piloting post at Westland, under CTP Harald Penrose*, rapidly becoming his DCTP. Work centred on Lysander production testing and Whirlwind development. On 7th August 1940 George was piloting much-modified Lysander I L4673 when its Bristol Mercury failed and it was written off in a hasty forced landing; George was unscathed. The Lysander had been modified with a ventral bulge to accommodate a gunner and at Yeovil was referred to as the 'Pregnant Perch'; after the accident development was scrubbed.

During the summer of 1940 George moved to Supermarine, working for Jeffrey Quill. By October of the following year George had been put in charge of the administration of Supermarine's extensive testing commitments – including the 'out-stations' – while continuing to keep his hand in on the production flow. In 1946 George took over as CTP for Auster at Rearsby, from Geoffrey Edwards*. In July he flew the prototype Arrow, a scaled down, two-seat, version of the popular Autocar. Flt Lt George N Snarey AFC retired from Auster in 1948 and was succeeded by Ranald Porteous*.

Known as the Harrier II by McDonnell Douglas, the UK prototype, Harrier GR.5 Development Batch 1 ZD318, was first flown by Mike Snelling at Dunsfold on 30th April 1985. *British Aerospace*

Mike Snelling

30 Apr 1985	McDD/BAe Harrier GR.5 DB1 ZD318
	1 x 21, 750lbst RR Pegasus 105
19 May 1986	BAe Hawk 200 ZG200
	1 x 5,845lbst RR/Turboméca Adour 871

Michael H B Snelling, born 1941. Cadet entry into the RAF 1959, studying engineering at Cambridge and learning to fly on DHC Chipmunk T.10s with Cambridge University Air Squadron. After advanced training he was posted to Central Flying School and then 4 FTS on Folland Gnat T.1s, followed by 229 OCU at Chivenor on Hawker Hunters. From 1968 to 1970 he served with 208 Squadron on Hunter FGA.9s from Muharraq, Bahrain. Graduated from ETPS Course No.29 at Boscombe Down, 1970, and was posted 'across the ramp' to A&AEE.

Sqn Ldr Mike Snelling AFC joined Hawker Siddeley at Dunsfold, under CTP Duncan Simpson* in September 1973. Harrier production testing and, from 1978, Sea Harrier development formed the bulk of Mike's work. In 1985 he became Dunsfold CTP, taking over from Andy Jones*. Since 1976 Hawker Siddeley (part of British Aerospace from 1977) had been working with McDonnell Douglas in the USA which had taken the design lead on the AV-8B Harrier II. This was effectively a brand new aircraft, owing concept and format to the earlier Harriers, but was larger, with a supercritical wing, a substantial amount of composite construction, additional weapons stations and capable of being further developed to night/all-weather strike roles. Mike flew DB1, the first of the GR.5 development batch, ZD318 at Dunsfold on 30th April 1985. Beyond the GR.5, the Harrier was evolved through the GR.7 (from 1990) to the exceptional GR.9 (from 2003).

HAWK 200

Brochure for the Hawk 200, featuring the second prototype, ZH200.

On 19th May 1986 a new and very different version of the Hawk took to the air at Dunsfold, flown by Mike on a 78-minute sortie. This was the private-venture Hawk 200, ZG200, a single-seat, radar-capable, strike version of the very successful advanced trainer. Tragically, ZG200 crashed while displaying at Dunsfold on 2nd July 1986; 'Jim' Hawkins* was killed. Mike flew the second prototype, ZH200, on 24th April 1987. Indonesia, Oman and Malaysia became customers for the new breed. Mike Snelling retired in 1988, handing over to Heinz Frick*. By 1990 Mike was flying for Air Europe on Boeing 737s, retiring from commercial flying in 1994.

'Tommy' Sopwith

Jun 1912	COW Biplane No.10
	1 x 100 Gnome

Notes: COW – Coventry Ordnance Works – No.10 and No.11 (powered by a 110hp Chenu), were both tested by 'Tommy' Sopwith at Brooklands and attended the Military Aeroplane Competition at Larkhill in August 1912, although neither was successful.

Thomas Octave Murdoch Sopwith, born 1888. With many interests and pursuits, aviation only will be highlighted. His first flight was in a gas balloon owned by Charles Rolls on 24th June 1906 and 'Tommy' then bought an example from the Short brothers; he co-owned this with Phil Paddon, a business associate. His first fixed wing flight was with Gustav Blondeau in a Farman from Brooklands. Having acquired a Howard Wright Avis, Tommy embarked on teaching himself to fly; his first tentative expedition on 22nd October 1910 ending in a smash. He was awarded Aviators' Certificate No.31 on 22nd November 1910 on this machine. He took the Howard Wright to the USA for a successful tour. By January 1912 his school was up and running at Brooklands. With Fred Sigrist, previously the engineer on Tommy's motor yachts, the pair established the Sopwith Aviation Company in June 1912 and were soon joined by Australian Harry Hawker. Fred set about modifying an American-built Wright by fitting a 40hp ABC and the trio began creating a series of biplanes of increasing sophistication, establishing a factory in a former ice skating rink at Kingston-upon-Thames.*

HAVING gained his Aviators' Certificate, started his flying school at Brooklands and established a factory in Kingston-upon-Thames, 'Tommy' Sopwith was engaged by the Coventry Ordnance Works. Designers Howard T Wright and W O Manning came up with a pair of essentially similar biplanes as entrants to Military Aeroplane Competition at Larkhill in August 1912 and they were built at Battersea. Tommy tested both at Brooklands and was in attendance at the trials, but neither was a success. Tommy had to cut his time short as he was entered in a motor boat race in the USA and had to leave to catch his steamer. So ended Thomas Octave Murdoch Sopwith's only foray into test piloting for others. Throughout Tommy's glittering career in aviation, he led and inspired other talents that he recognised and it was Australian Harry Hawker* who took on the test flying.

Sir Thomas Sopwith retired from chairing the Hawker Siddeley Group in 1963 at the spritely age of 75. The giant grouping was formed in 1935, encompassing Armstrong Whitworth, Avro, Gloster, Hawker, although each continued to trade separately. Much of the incredible story of Sir Thomas is beyond the scope of this work; during his formative aviation years he was a designer-pilot (as defined in Chapter One) and for the bulk of his time was as a leader of industry, first with the company that carried his own name; from November 1920 a new entity in honour of Harry Hawker and on to Hawker Siddeley.

Thomas Sopwith in his modified Wright biplane, at Brooklands, 1910. *Peter Green Collection*

Alan Bramson wrote the exceptional *Pure Luck – The Authorised Biography of Sir Thomas Sopwith* (Patrick Stephens, 1990) and its second edition remains in print. Sir Thomas Octave Murdoch Sopwith CBE, aviation pioneer, balloonist, aeronautical entrepreneur and industrialist, motorcycle competition rider, national ice hockey player, accomplished yachtsman and boat owner died on 27th January 1989, aged 101. His aviation endeavours had taken him from a Farman biplane to the prototype Harrier.

Norman Spratt

Jun 1914	Royal Aircraft Factory SE.4 628
	1 x 160hp Gnome
1915	Armstrong Whitworth FK.3
	1 x 70hp Renault

Notes: SE.4 flown from Farnborough. FK.3 *probably* flown from Gosforth.

By late 1913 South African-born Lt Norman C Spratt was a test pilot for the Royal Aircraft Factory at Farnborough. On 14th May 1914 Norman took the sixth RE.5, 380, to a new record altitude of 18,900ft. He tested the prototype SE.4 single-seat scout in June 1914. Designed by Henry Folland the SE.4 featured 'I' interplane struts and a large spinner that almost blended with the cowling of the twin-row Gnome. This engine proved unreliable and the spinner did not help cooling. Despite a change to a 100hp Gnome and altering the spinner, the SE.4 did not merit further development. (The SE.5A that followed it, and was tested by Frank Gooden*, was effectively a new design.)

FK.3 B9553 proudly showing the 'AW' logo on the cowling.
Peter Green Collection

After the outbreak of the Great War, Norman enlisted with the RFC on 5th August 1914 and on 28th August 1914 he is reported to have used a series of sham attacks with an unarmed Sopwith Tabloid (reported to be with 7 Squadron although the unit did not deploy to the Western Front until 1915) to bring down an Albatros. By 1915 he was back in Britain and carried out the first flight of the Frederick Koolhoven-designed Armstrong Whitworth FK.3 prototype general duties biplane. Norman ended the war as a Captain and remained with the RAF. Grp Capt Norman C Spratt OBE died in 1944.

'Johnny' Squier

John William Copous 'Johnny' Squier, born 1920. Joined the RAF in 1939 and he was posted to 64 Squadron at Kenley in July 1940. Flying Supermarine Spitfire I P9369 on 8th August 1940 Johnny was shot down by a Messerschmitt Bf 109 of JG51 just after 11am. Johnny crash landed close to the cliffs at Capel-le-Ferne and suffered serious facial injuries; P9369 was a write-off. Johnny was taken to East Grinstead Hospital where he was treated by Dr Archibald McIndoe, the pioneer of 'plastic' surgery. Three months of surgery followed, making Johnny one of McIndoe's famous 'Guinea Pigs'. In November 1940 Johnny was back on 'ops', flying Spitfire Is with 72 Squadron from Coltishall, but by the end of the year he had been posted to 603 Squadron, with Spitfire IIs from Drem. On a patrol of the north east coast on Christmas Day in P7597, Johnny intercepted and shot down a Junkers Ju 88. From 1941 Johnny began a series of stints as maintenance unit test pilot, or attached to a ferry pilot pool.

'Johnny' Squier climbing on board a Lightning.
English Electric via Graham Pitchfork

DURING the spring of 1944 Plt Off 'Johnny' Squier was seconded to Avro at Woodford as a production test pilot under CTP 'Sam' Brown* and from early 1945 he moved across the Pennines to the 'shadow' factory at Yeadon, signing off Ansons and Lancasters. Beyond this Johnny continued ferrying work, including trips to Samlesbury to pick up English Electric-built Halifaxes and even one of the early DH Vampires made at the plant. These flights were a taste of things to come; in August 1946 he left the RAF and started work as a PTP with English Electric (EE) at Samlesbury.

On 3rd November 1947 a routine test of EE-built DH Vampire F.III 17043, destined for the Royal Canadian Air Force, went very wrong for Johnny when the engine failed on take off as Samlesbury – at just 10ft up. In *Tests of Character*, Don Middleton vividly described the outcome: "he missed the aerodrome fence and headed for a hedge with [a] farmhouse slightly to the right and a tree slightly to the left, the distance between the two being less than 30 yards. The Vampire hurtled between the two obstacles and struck the ground in a shallow, dried up, pond which hurled the aircraft back into the air. Squier went through the bottom of the seat and the canopy

shattered; he was then airborne again towards a row of trees and very conscious of the fact that half a ton of Goblin engine was behind him and a light wood shell in front. He decided that to avoid total disaster he must put one wing down by applying full aileron to starboard; the tip hit the ground and the aircraft spun round to slide backwards, stopping with its tailplane 6in from the nearest tree."

Johnny became the second pilot to fly the Canberra on 7th October 1949 in the prototype, VN799. The first person, of course, was Johnny's 'boss', EE CTP 'Bea' Beamont*. By 1951 Johnny had been appointed as Chief PTP, working on Canberras from Samlesbury, with 'Jock' Still* as his deputy. He carried out the maiden flight of the prototype Canberra B.5, VX185, on 6th July 1951. The B.5 was a radar-equipped target-marker version of the B.2 and did not enter production: VX185 was retained for a wide range of trials and was transformed into the prototype B(I).8 interdictor and given its debut in that guise by Bea in July 1954.

In 1959 Johnny made the transition to Lightnings and hit the headlines. Flying T.4 prototype XL628 on 10th October 1959 out of Warton, Johnny was detailed to carry out rapid rolls at 35,000ft. The two-seater started to yaw violently and try as he might, he could not correct this. The yawing was joined by pitching; the pitot tube bent across the air intake and the Lightning was uncontrollable. Johnny ejected, only to discover that the automatic deployment of the parachute had failed to co-operate and he used the manual over-ride. Down in the Irish Sea, Johnny sorted out his dinghy and awaited the sound of a helicopter. He was not to know it, but the battery on his personal locator beacon had long since gone flat and was way overdue replacing. There *was* a search going on, but the Irish Sea is a large place when there isn't a beacon to help you narrow down the area. Johnny made his own landfall in Wigtown Bay a staggering 28½ hours after he left XL628!

Johnny retired from test flying in December 1966 by which time he had over 6,000 hours to his credit on 75 types. He took the post of Cockpit Design Liaison and Safety Equipment Officer, the latter highly appropriate after his ditching. He worked on the escape system for the BAC TSR.2 and for the SEPECAT Jaguar and finally left what had become British Aerospace in 1997 in December 1983. John William Copous 'Johnny' Squier, one of 'The Few' and a reluctant but resilient Irish Sea sailor, died on 30th January 2006, aged 85.

Personnel examining the wreck of Vampire F.III 17043 at Samlesbury, November 1947. It was destined for the Royal Canadian Air Force. *KEC*

George Stainforth

11 Apr 1933	Airspeed Courier G-ABXN
	1 x 240hp AS Lynx IVC

THE aircraft that put the small firm of Airspeed on the road to success was the Courier five/six-seat single-engined monoplane with retractable undercarriage. Airspeed director Sir Alan Cobham* placed an order for the prototype and the company moved from a converted bus garage to a factory on Portsmouth aerodrome in 1933. When the first Courier, G-ABXN, was complete the subject turned to who should fly such a vital aircraft. Director Nevil Shute Norway suggested 34-year old Flt Lt George Stainforth with impeccable qualifications and sufficient fame to provide an endorsement of the new type. A fee was agreed and the RAF presented no objections to George's temporary 'secondment'. Having no experience of retractable undercarriage, the pilot asked for G-ABXN to be jacked up so that he could try out the process prior to flying the monoplane. The maiden flight, on 11th April 1933, was a success and George 'clocked' about five hours on G-ABXN. During that time, his meticulous preparation paid off: after take-off on an early flight the Armstrong Siddeley Lynx failed and George instinctively lowered the undercarriage as he dropped the nose and turned downwind for a faultless landing. Sixteen Couriers were built and testing a twin-engined follow up, the Envoy, was to have been offered to George, but the company appointed 'Percy' Colman* as its first CTP, again at the suggestion of Nevil Shute Norway.

Flt Lt George Hedley Stainforth AFC had joined the RAF in March 1923 and flew Gloster Grebes with 19 Squadron before being posted to MAEE at Felixstowe. He became part of the High Speed Flight and for 48 hours was the holder of the world absolute speed record just after the Schneider Trophy contest at Calshot in September 1929. Piloting Gloster VI N249 on the 10th George achieved 336.3mph only to be pipped on the 12th by Sqn Ldr Augustus Orlebar* in Supermarine S.6 N247 at 357.7mph. George was part of the outright winning 1931 team. On 13th September 1931 Flt Lt John Boothman averaged 340.08mph to take the contest and the trophy in perpetuity and on that same day George flew S1596 to 379.05mph again taking the world speed record. Promoted to squadron leader in June 1936 and to wing commander by January 1940 George took command of 600 Squadron at Manston, flying Bristol Blenheim IVs. He was at the head of the re-formed Bristol

Beaufighter-equipped 89 Squadron in October 1941, taking the unit to Egypt. While piloting Beaufighter If X7700 on 27th September 1942 Wg Cdr George Hedley Stainforth AFC was killed when it spun it near Ras Gharib.

Phil Stanbury

8th Aug 1947	Newbury Eon G-AKBC
	1 x 100hp Blackburn Cirrus Minor II

PHILIP J STANBURY was apprenticed to Bristol Aero Engines at Filton from 1938. Aged 19, he joined the RAF in 1940 and in early 1942 was seconded to the Castle Bromwich Aircraft Factory production testing Supermarine Spitfires for about six months. He returned to fighter pilot duties later in 1942, but Flt Lt P J Stanbury AFC returned to test piloting in mid-1943 when he was loaned to Gloster at Hucclecote, initially under Michael Daunt* and then Eric Greenwood*. He was involved in the production testing of Gloster-built Hawker Typhoons, moving on to development flying Meteors. By 1945 'Phil' was full-time with Gloster as Acting CTP until 'Bill' Waterton* was appointed in October 1946. In his exceptional *The Quick and the Dead*, Bill described Phil as "a handsome, boyish ex-Flight Lieutenant who had... done a fine job for them, including much of the early development work on the first Meteors". Bill also described an incident that shook Phil: "At a high altitude and speed his Perspex cockpit canopy burst, and although he suffered no wound, the terrible sub-zero cold during the greater part of his descent put Phil on his back with pneumonia. This had taken a lot out of him, and severely restricted his activities. He suffered continually from colds and sinus trouble, and was able to do little flying."

Phil left Gloster in May 1947 and joined the glider manufacturer Elliotts of Newbury, often abbreviated to EoN, inspiring the name of the company's break into the light aircraft market – the Eon. Aviation and Engineering Projects was engaged as design consultant on the all-wood four-seater. Phil carried out the first flight of the prototype, G-AKBC, from Welford in August 1947 and displayed it at that year's SBAC airshow at Farnborough; towing aloft one of EoN's glider products during the routine. The Eon got no further than prototype stage. By this stage he had over 2,000 hours on 46 types. Phil re-joined the RAF in 1948, coming back to 'civvie street' in 1953 to take up a post at Brooklands with the Vickers Servicing School and he worked there until 1955.

The prototype Courier, G-ABXN, on its belly at Hal Far, Malta, at the end of the in-flight refuelled flight from Portsmouth to the Island on 22nd September 1934 – see Chapter Three. *Peter Green Collection*

The Eon was an attempt by glider manufacturer Elliotts to break into the light aircraft market: G-AKBC remained a one-off. *Elliotts of Newbury*

Chris Staniland

3 Mar 1931	Fairey Gordon K1697 1 x 525hp AS Panther IIA
21 Mar 1933	Fairey TSR.I 1 x 625hp AS Panther VI
22 Feb 1934	Fairey S9/30 S1706 1 x 635hp RR Kestrel IIMS
29 Mar 1934	Fairey G4/31 F-1 1 x 635hp Bristol Pegasus IIM3
6 Jun 1935	Fairey Fantôme F-6 1 x 925hp Hispano-Suiza 12 Ycrs
10 Mar 1936	Fairey Battle K4303 1 x 1,030hp RR Merlin I
27 May 1936	Fairey Seafox K4304 1 x 395hp Napier Rapier VI
13 Jan 1937	Fairey P4/34 K5099 1 x 1,030 RR Merlin I
7 Dec 1940	Fairey Barracuda P1767 1 x 1,300hp RR Merlin 30
22 Dec 1941	Fairey Firefly Z1826 1 x 1,730hp RR Griffon IIB

Notes: All flown from the Great West Aerodrome, Harmondsworth, other than the Seafox which had its maiden flight as a floatplane from Hamble. S9/30 S1706 was fitted with a central float and outriggers and flown in that guise from Hamble on 15th January 1935. The improved and revised version of the TSR.I, TSR.II K4190, with a 690hp Bristol Pegasus IIIM3, had its maiden flight on 17th April 1934, also from Harmondsworth. Fantôme F-6 became G-ADIF – see Stephen Trower.

Seal I K3577 at MAEE Felixstowe, early 1934. *KEC*

Christopher Stainbank Staniland, born 1905. From an early stage he was an accomplished motorcyclist and a 'name' at Brooklands – for example winning four out of five races on his Norton in 1924 – and he had achieved a string of records. He was equally at home on four wheels, again another example being his winning of the Bugatti Handicap at 93mph in 1926. He joined the RAF in 1924 and flew Armstrong Whitworth Siskins with 41 Squadron from Northolt and proved himself to be a polished aerobatic performer. He was posted to the High Speed Flight in 1928, but did not compete in the Schneider Trophy. Chris left the RAF in 1929.

FAMED as a motorcycle and motor car racer, both in 'circuit' and long-distance racing, Chris Staniland always wore white overalls and a white leather helmet – and this garb was to become a hallmark of his test piloting years. On the track, he was known simply by his initials – 'CSS' – and the press dubbed him 'The Irrepressible Staniland'. He continued to race, on two and four wheels all the way up to the last competition at Brooklands in 1939 – during the war the famous banking was broken for a runway extension and an era came to an end. Chris was also known for his dazzling aerobatic displays over the track to 'warm up' and audience before a race meeting.

Having left the RAF in 1929 Flt Lt Christopher Stainbank Staniland moved to Southampton, joining Simmonds Aircraft as CTP. The small company was building a two-seat biplane, the Spartan, but this work held little thrall for Chris. In 1931 he joined Fairey at the Great West Aerodrome, Harmondsworth, as a production test pilot but with the death of Charles McMullin* in September 1931, Chris became CTP at a time when the company was making the transition from biplanes to monoplanes, although one of the former that he tested remained in production until 1944 and operational throughout World War Two – the Swordfish.

The Gordon and its Fleet Air Arm equivalent, the Seal, were the final extrapolation of the Fairey III dynasty. The G4/31 was a general purpose biplane chasing a catch-all Air

Royal Navy Historic Flight Swordfish II LS326 saluting the Liverpool waterfront in May 1999 on the occasion of the aircraft being officially named 'City of Liverpool'. *Courtesy and © Liverpool Daily Post and Echo, via RNHF*

Ministry specification in an era when a monoplane should have been requested and indeed Vickers took the prize with its Wellesley. The G4/31 remained a one-off as did the S9/30 spotter-reconnaissance biplane.

Fairey produced a private-venture three-seater torpedo-spotter-reconnaissance biplane – the TSR.I – and Chris took this for its maiden flight on 21st March 1933. On 11th September Chris was conducting spinning trials starting at 14,000ft with the leading edge slats unlocked but could not get the big biplane to gyrate. On his third attempt the TSR.I obeyed and started to spin but not nose-down, it adopted the dreaded 'flat' profile, increasing in speed. Corrective measures merely resulted in juddering through the entire airframe. A dozen turns were sufficient to persuade Chris that the time had come to part company with the prototype. Chris got up into the airstream only to be thrown into the rear cockpit but from there he more or less clawed his way out and parachuted down without injury. The TSR.I had shown such promise that designer Marcel Lobelle embarked upon an improved version with a longer fuselage, spin-recovery strakes on the upper rear fuselage an a slight sweep back on the upper wing. Chris flew this machine, the TSR.II, in April 1934 and the steps to the immortal Swordfish were complete.

In the mid-1930s Peter Masefield (later Sir Peter of BEA, Bristol and Beagle fame) was an assistant draughtsman at Fairey and he got to know Chris Staniland, occasionally 'cadging' a ride with him. In his autobiography *Flight Path*, written with Bill Gunston, Peter described a trip in an early Swordfish: "One day we took [it] at full throttle around the Brooklands race track very accurately, at an extremely low level, trying to break John Cobb's record of 143mph. We failed."

TSR.II K4190, the intermediate stage to the Swordfish, at the Great West Aerodrome, April 1934. *Peter Green Collection*

The Fantôme in civilian markings as G-ADIF. *KEC*

Chris was granted leave to go to the USA in September 1935 when he was part of the team supporting George Eyston who set seven world records, in 1-, 12-, 24- and 48-hour stages in the racing car *Speed of the Wind* at the Bonneville Salt Flats, Utah. Chris also took part in many air events and races and was determined to compete in the DH.88 Comet G-ACSS – which co-incidentally carried his initials. He had entered the 1938 King's Cup in G-ACSS, but it was damaged on the eve of the contest.

Above: King Edward VIII (standing in cockpit) inspecting the prototype Battle at Martlesham Heath on 8th July 1936. *Peter Green Collection*

Right: Advertisement for Fairey simply portraying the prototype Battle.

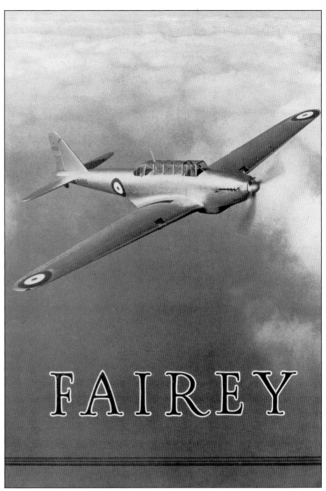

Marcel Lobelle's Fantôme and its Avions Fairey Belgian version, the Féroce, was the last throw of the dice from the company seeking orders for a single-seat fighter. Flown by Chris on 6th June 1935, the prototype lasted only until 17th July when it crashed in Belgium, killing Stephen Trower*. Components for another three had been built at the Fairey factory at Hayes and these were sent to Gosselies. Two were sold to the Soviet Union and Chris test flew both of these at Gosselies in November 1936 before they were crated and shipped. The Seafox was the last biplane to enter production at Fairey, designed for reconnaissance and to be catapulted from light cruisers. Powered by the H-format 16-cylinder

The second prototype Seafox, K4305 was first flown as a landplane from Hamble on 5th November 1936, by Chris Staniland. Converted to a floatplane, it was issued to Felixstowe in 1937. *Peter Green Collection*

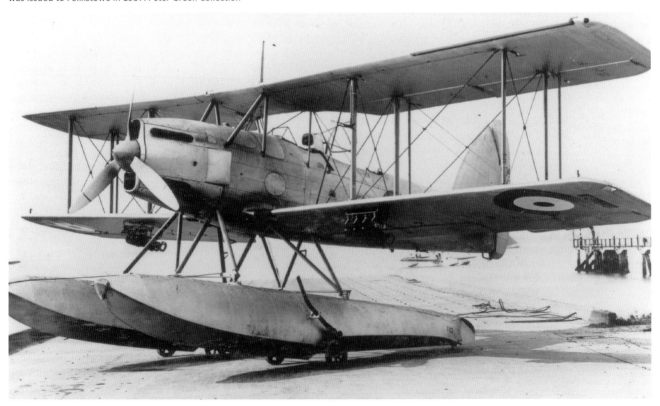

Chris Staniland in the cockpit of the P4/34 at the Great West Aerodrome, 1937. *KEC*

The prototype Barracuda, P1767, in late 1941 after having had the tailplane moved up the fin. *Peter Green Collection*

The sixth Firefly, Z1831/G, which served as the prototype for the NF.II night-fighter, at Boscombe Down during the summer of 1943. *KEC*

Napier Rapier, the prototype was flown off the Solent from Hamble in May 1936. A total of 64 followed for the Fleet Air Arm, the last retiring in 1943.

The Battle was a day bomber with fighter-like characteristics designed to replace the Hawker Hart and Hind. Such was the need to re-arm that a production order was placed before the maiden flight of the prototype, K4303, on 10th March 1936. This order also provided Rolls-Royce at Derby with its first quantity contract for the Merlin engine. Lobelle developed a smaller and lighter version of the Battle to meet Specification P4/34 which was seeking a light bomber or dive-bomber. Two prototypes were built, the first flying in January 1937, the second, K7555, on 19th April 1937. Hawker's Henley won the competition but the efforts put into the P4/34 were not wasted as it was realised that it formed the basis of a fleet fighter and this emerged as the Fulmar. The two P4/34s allowed Fairey to run straight to production, avoiding a prototype; the first Fulmar was flown from Ringway in January 1940 – see under Duncan Menzies in Chapter Seven.

Planned around the 24-cylinder X-format Rolls-Royce Exe, the Barracuda was conceived as a dive-bomber that could also serve as a torpedo-attack aircraft. The Exe was axed and the prototype, P1767, adopted the Merlin 30. When first flown by Chris on 7th December 1940 P1767 produced considerable buffeting and the problem was partially solved by raising the tailplane up the fin. The Barracuda and Fairey's next naval type, the Firefly, were to take up most of Chris's time and that of his expanding team of test pilots. The Firefly was conceived as an eight-gun fleet fighter with the added security of a navigator to lessen pilot workload. Like the Barracuda, the Firefly required a lot of development work and both types evolved considerably in shape, power and capability. Flying out of the Great West Aerodrome on 26th June 1942 in the second prototype Firefly, Z1827, Chris took it up to 10,000ft for stability trials and it entered a dive. The aircraft was seen to recover after a drop of about 4,000ft and pitch upwards whereupon parts were seen to fall away. Z1827 entered another spin, this one flat, and it crashed near Wokingham. Flt Lt Christopher Stainbank Staniland – 'The Irrepressible Staniland' – had managed to jettison the canopy, but did not bale out. The 37-year-old died as he had lived, in the fast lane. He as succeeded at Fairey by Foster 'Dickie' Dixon*.

R F Stedman

Sep 1946	Chrislea Ace G-AHLG
	1 x 125hp Lycoming O-290-3

FROM 1943 R F Stedman was a test pilot for the Blackburn-run repair organisation based at Sherburn-in-Elmet. Homespun types that were repaired or modified included Skuas and Swordfish (the latter, known as 'Blackfish' were also manufactured at Sherburn) but Grumman Wildcats were also worked on. By 1946 he had been engaged by Chrislea Aircraft Ltd of Heston to test fly its CH.3 Ace light aircraft. According to the Chrislea brochure, the Ace had a 'natural' control system. An oval-shaped control wheel, attached to a universal joint within the instrument panel accommodated *all* control inputs. Dipped to port or starboard it worked the aileron much as a conventional control. Move the wheel down and the Ace would descend; move it upwards and it would climb. Slide the wheel sideways to port and the aircraft would go left, to starboard and it would turn right – simple! Early in testing, Stedman found the single rudder inadequate and a twin rudder assembly was substituted. During 1947 Chrislea moved to new premises at Exeter and there Stedman flew the improved Super Ace prototype, G-AKFD, in February 1948. The Super Ace was of all-metal construction, whereas *Lima-Golf* had wooden wings, and was powered by a 145hp DH Gipsy Major 10. Considering that most people in a position to afford the relatively expensive Super Ace would have already learned to fly on an aircraft with a conventional control system there was a lot of sales resistance to the Super Ace – just 28 were eventually built. R F Stedman left Chrislea in 1948 and he was succeeded by D Lowry* and during 1949 Super Aces were produced with optional 'real' controls and new version, the Skyjeep, followed.

The one-off Chrislea Ace, G-AHLG, in 1946. *Chrislea Aircraft*

'Freddie' Stent

A GOOD friend of F G Miles*, Wg Cdr Frederick William Stent MC joined the company at Woodley as a member of the sales team in January 1936. Freddie was born in Cyprus in 1891 and studied engineering prior to the outbreak of the Great War, when he joined the RFC. He stayed on with the RAF, breaking to study aeronautical engineering and by January 1931 was the officer commanding 9 Squadron at Boscombe Down on Vickers Virginias.

With his piloting and academic skills test flying was a certainty and within days of his appointment at Woodley 'Freddie' had a baptism of fire. F G Miles had been spin testing Nighthawk prototype, G-ADXA, with the centre of gravity moved slightly each time. The Nighthawk was a private-venture aircrew trainer version of the Falcon Six. On 22nd January 1936 Freddie took G-ADXA to continue these tests, with full tanks. After eleven spins, the spirals flattened and the nose began to rise, recovery proved impossible and on the *twenty-third* turn, Freddie successfully took to his parachute. While ferrying Whitney Straight G-AEYI to Martlesham Heath on 28th June 1938, Freddie's luck ran out. The aircraft's engine is reported to have cut and the nose dropped. G-AEYI crashed near Hounslow, killing 47-year-old Wg Cdr Frederick William Stent MC.

'Jock' Still

James Webster Still was born in 1920. Joined the RAF in 1940 and by mid-1943 was flying Supermarine Spitfire XIIs with 41 Squadron from Westhampnett and then Tangmere. In 1944 he was briefly at Hucknall, probably testing on secondment for Rolls-Royce. His last operational unit was 1 Squadron in early 1945 flying Spitfire IXs out of Manston. 'Jock' was shipped out to India for service in Burma, but the Japanese surrender on 2nd September 1945 found him kicking his heels, carrying out some test flying of overhauled aircraft, but otherwise waiting for transport home. Once back in Britain he flew with 603 Squadron from Turnhouse, on Spitfire XVIs. In 1950 Jock took a job as test pilot for Brooklands Aviation, a repair, overhaul and modification contractor at Sywell.

'JIMMY' to some, more often 'Jock' as testament to his Edinburgh roots, Flt Lt James Webster Still joined English Electric in 1952 as assistant to the Chief PTP, 'Johnny' Squier* at Samlesbury, on Canberras. In July 1954 Jock moved to Radlett, taking up a similar post with Handley Page, under Hedley Hazelden*. ('Johnny' Allam* started with Handley Page the following month.) On 14th July 1954 the prototype Victor, WB771, had crashed fatally, and the mood in the flight shed was subdued but determined to carry out extensive testing to establish the cause.

Between October 1955 and July 1957 Jock flew WB775 on flutter trials, among other tasks. In the rear fuselage the aircraft was fitted with weights that were spun around by electric motors; these were called 'exciters' and they could be set to resonate at different frequencies. Once the exciters had set up an out-of-balance reverberation they were stopped and automatic recorders noted how the oscillations damped out. There would be a point where this flutter would not decay and potentially destroy the tail; the skill lay in getting *close* to this point, but not exceeding it! On an early sortie, with 'Jock' Ogilvy as FTO, over Lincolnshire at 20,000ft and around 400 knots, WB775 started to porpoise and yaw so Jock closed the throttles and struggled to convert speed into height while warning the *other* Jock, on his left, that they may be leaving! As the climb lowered the airspeed, WB775 became more controllable and he turned the bomber on to a southerly heading while issuing a 'Mayday' call. Listening

During 1958 a back injury, believed not aviation related, brought Jock's test piloting career to a close. By this time he had over 3,000 hours on 50-plus types. He took a post in the steel industry, rising to director level. In June 1973 Flt Lt James Webster Still returned to aviation as Base Manager at Dhahran, Saudi Arabia, under contract to BAC.

Paul Stone

P AUL STONE joined the Royal Navy in January 1988 and in 1991 was flying HS Sea Harrier FRS.1s with 800 Squadron from HMS *Invincible*. From 1993 he was shore-based at Yeovilton with 899 Squadron, working the Sea Harrier FA.2 up to operational status and engaging in 'ops' over Bosnia. Graduated from ETPS in 1995 at Boscombe Down, Paul was posted 'across the ramp' in 1996 to the Assessment and Evaluation Centre, as Sea Harrier Project Pilot and working on the Vectored-Thrust Aircraft Advanced Control (VAAC) Harrier T.2 test-bed. He moved to the USA in 1999, joining the Joint Strike Fighter (JSF) UK Project Team with the Boeing X-32, unfairly referred to as the 'Wide-Mouth Frog', and he was the first British pilot to fly it. Back in the UK in 2001, he in turn became the commanding officer of 801, 800 and back to 801 Squadrons up to 2004. In 2004 he worked for the Ministry of Defence as Joint Combat Aircraft (as the Ministry refers to JSF) desk officer.

Cdr Paul Stone left the Fleet Air Arm in May 2006 and moved to Warton, becoming a test pilot for BAE Systems on Harriers, Hawks and Tornados and, later, Typhoons. He was appointed as CTP – Combat and Training Aircraft, succeeding Mark Bowman* who became Director of Flight Operations. Throughout this time Paul was involved in all aspects of Typhoon development and delivery flights to Saudi Arabia. Paul took up the mantle of Director of Flight Operations, from John Turner*, in April 2010.

in was Peter Buggé (see Chapter Seven) of de Havilland who was up out of Hatfield, on a production test of a Comet. Peter offered to come alongside and do a 'visual' and he pronounced that a large chunk of the trailing edge of the starboard wing, inboard of the aileron, had gone and fuel was venting. Aiming for a straight in approach at Radlett, Jock found WB775 increasingly difficult to control, even more so when he dropped the flaps. He brought the Victor in for a fast, but otherwise uneventful, landing. Large amounts of debris from WB775 were strewn out along its flightpath, thankfully without hitting anyone. It was discovered that the trailing edge box structure had taken a pounding from the exciters and the entire area was strengthened before flutter tests continued.

Andy Strachan

JOHN LEE HOOKER'S *Boom, Boom* – the 1965 cover version by Eric Burden and the Animals – blasting out of the 'psywar' speakers clamped to the fuselage, heralds the arrival at an isolated stately home in the Scottish highlands of ice-cold-evil Raoul Silva – played by the outstanding Javier Bardem. This was the climax sequence of the 23rd Bond, James Bond epic *Skyfall*, superbly directed by Sam Mendes and released in 2012. A camouflaged AgustaWestland Merlin approaches the Bond ancestral home, drops the baddies and mayhem is unleashed. Needless to say, 007 has more than a few tricks up his sleeve and the Merlin crashes in flames. This being cinema, the crash is part mock-up, part CGI and the impressive Scottish baronial hall is a full-size stage set on Hankley Common, near Elstead in Surrey! And this is all in a day's work for a test pilot!

Film flying is demanding, complicated, requires split-second timing and a full and honest appreciation of what can, and cannot, be done. Several times in these two books – Volume One started with *Sound Barrier* – test pilots taking part in the aerial sequences of movies have been mentioned. Supermarine was very pleased to 'showcase' its prototype Swift in *Sound Barrier* and AgustaWestland was equally keen to be involved in *Skyfall*. AgustaWestland CTP Andy Strachan and his team flew for a total of about 16 hours during the filming. He explained: "We flew both in day and night conditions and also worked [with] a camera helicopter flying very close alongside the AW101 [Merlin] to capture the in-flight sequences. Although the flying was relatively benign, we did perform some manoeuvres and our experimental background helped because we often had the camera helicopter within half a rotor disc of our own..." There was another very high profile assignment for Andy Strachan in 2012. Using a Merlin HC.3A on loan from the RAF and painted in official colours, AgustaWestland took part in the opening event of the London Olympics, flying low level over the stadium dropping rice paper confetti as Team GB entered the area.

Andy Strachan gained his Private Pilot's Licence in 1976 through an Air Training Corps award. He joined the RAF in 1979 and spent the bulk of his career flying helicopters, both operationally and as an instructor. During the Falklands conflict of 1982, Fg Off Strachan flew with 18 Squadron on Boeing Chinook HC.1s and was Mentioned in Despatches. He graduated from ETPS Course No.49 at Boscombe Down in 1990. He joined Westland at Yeovil as a test pilot in 1997, taking the lead in the Merlin HC.3 development and was also engaged in the Wildcat 'second generation' Lynx. Andy was appointed as DCTP in 2003 and in 2012 took up the post of CTP at AgustaWestland, succeeding Donald Maclaine*. At the time of the Olympic ceremony, Andy had accumulated over 8,000 flying hours. Along with former Yeovil CTP Colin Hague*, Andy is a part owner in Vans RV-9A G-CCGU, based at Henstridge.

The Merlin flown by Andy Strachan in front of the *Skyfall* set for the climax sequence of the film. *Courtesy and © 2015 AgustaWestland*

The corporate-liveried Merlin HC.3A used during the London Olympics opening ceremony. *Courtesy and © 2015 AgustaWestland*

Louis Strange

May 1932	Spartan Cruiser I G-ABTY
	3 x 120hp DH Gipsy Major 3
14 Dec 1932	Spartan Clipper G-ACEG
	1 x 75hp Pobjoy R

Louis Arbon Strange, born 1891. By 1913 he was with the Dorset Yeomanry, but had long had a desire to learn to fly and in August 1913 he took his 'ticket' at Hendon. Louis enlisted in the RFC and while awaiting the 'call' instructed, displayed and raced, at and from Hendon. In August 1914 he was posted to 5 Squadron, which was in the process of deploying to the Western Front. Louis set about arming the unit's Avro 504s and Farmans with Lewis guns and incendiary bombs. On 22nd November 1914 he and gunner Lt F Small forced down an Aviatik behind British lines. By early 1915 Louis transferred to 6 Squadron, also in France, becoming both a captain and a flight commander. In March, flying a BE.2c modified with bomb racks for 20-pounders, Louis attacked Courtrai station from low level, hitting a troop train and killing over 70 soldiers. He returned with over 40 bullet holes in his BE.2c and was awarded the Military Cross. On 10th May came his legendary escapade with a Lewis gun-equipped Martinsyde. Standing up in the cockpit to change the ammunition drum, the biplane flipped on its back leaving Louis dangling from the gun until his gymnastics succeeded in getting him back in the cockpit and righting the aircraft. Louis formed 23 Squadron at Gosport on 1st September 1915, becoming its first CO until March 1916. He went on to set up a School of Aerial Gunnery at Hythe in September 1916 and then another at Loch Doon in May 1917. He returned to operational flying in the summer of 1918, commanding 80 Wing. He retired from the RAF in 1921 and took up farming on the Isle of Purbeck, Dorset.

In October 1928 the prototype Simmonds Spartan two-seat biplane, G-EBYU, was placed on loan to the Isle of Purbeck Flying Club, adjacent to where Lt Col Louis Strange had his farm. Louis and Fg Off H W R Banting flew it extensively, including a jaunt to Berlin. Both were convinced that it should be put into production and were instrumental in the setting up of Simmonds Aircraft at Weston, near Southampton and 49 Spartans were produced. In 1930 the company was recapitalised as Spartan Aircraft at East Cowes, Isle of Wight, and a family of biplanes based on the Spartan, as the Arrow and the Three-Seater, amounted to 34 units. After having developed the Mailplane with Edgar Percival*, Isle of Wight based Saunders-Roe passed on the design rights to the Spartan and a much refined version with more capacious all-metal fuselage was produced. This was the Cruiser I and Louis carried out the maiden flight of the prototype in May 1932. The Cruiser could take up to six passengers and it was progressively refined: 16 were produced. Alongside the Cruiser a two-seater monoplane tourer, the Clipper, was developed. Louis again carried its first flight but G-ACEG was to remain a one-off.

The 1914-1918 exploits of Louis Strange were extensive and only an abridged version appears here; likewise his service career from 1940 can only fleetingly be dealt with. At 49 he was too old for operational service but as a Volunteer Reserve Officer he flew with 24 Squadron from Hendon on communications duties. By June 1940 Louis was a squadron leader and became the CO of the Central Landing School (later Establishment) at Ringway in August 1940. The odd name was possibly a ruse; this was the origin of the British airborne forces, both parachute- and glider-borne. His next task was the establishment of the Merchant Ship Fighter Unit at Speke to train pilots who would fly 'Hurricats' – Hawker Hurricanes catapulted from converted merchantmen as stop-gap air cover to convoys. Louis was OC at Valley from September 1941, but illness was taking its toll. By late 1943 he was with 46 Group and deeply involved in planning the Allied invasion of France. He landed on the Normandy beaches on 15th June (D-Day +9) setting up a series of staging posts and landing strips. Louis returned to farming in late 1945 and acquired a Taylorcraft Plus D light aircraft which he flew, and raced, extensively. Lt Col Louis Arbon Strange DSO OBE MC DFC* died on 15th November 1966, aged 75.

Ed Strongman

| 11 Dec 2009 | Airbus A400M F-WWMT |
| | 4 x 11,000hp Europrop TP400-D6 |

Edward Strongman, born 1949. Studied for an engineering degree at Bristol, before joining the RAF and flying extensively with the Lockheed Hercules fleet. Attended the USAF Test Pilot School at Edwards Air Force Base, California, from 1979. Upon return to the UK, served for six years with the RAE at Thurleigh, ending in 1986 as Commanding Officer of the Test Squadron. He then became a certification test pilot for the Civil Aviation Authority.

In one form or another, the UK has been a part of the Airbus consortium since its formation in December 1970. Unlike the bulk of the events listed in this book, first flights take place in Toulouse, France, or Hamburg, Germany, or Seville, Spain. Throughout the incredible success story that is Airbus, the UK has been a centre of excellence for wings, with the major construction sites at Hawarden, near Chester, and Filton,

Bristol. Depending on the programme, Rolls-Royce and other UK aerostructures companies have also been involved. As a major partner in the huge operation, it would be wrong to leave Airbus out of the coverage.

Edward 'Ed' Strongman joined Airbus in 1995, initially as Project Pilot for the A330 and A340 family. He took the prototype of the stretched A340-600 variant, F-WWCA, for its first flight on 23rd April 2001. Ed was also heavily involved in the A380 development programme. With the advent of the A400M strategic military airlifter, he moved from Toulouse, France, to Seville, Madrid, and joined Airbus Military, becoming its CTP. He was in command of the first flight of the A400M prototype, F-WWMT nicknamed 'Grizzly 1', on 11th December 2009. (The A400M was named Atlas in July 2012.) Flight crew with Ed on that day were: Ignacio 'Nacho' Lombo, Experimental Test Pilot; Eric Isorce, Senior Flight Test Engineer; Didier Ronceray, FFTE; Jean-Philippe Cottet, FTE and Gerard Leskerpit, FTE. At the time of the maiden flight, Ed had 11,000 hours in his logbook, over 7,000 of which were in flight test. Ed and his team have been heavily engaged in the flight trials of the 'Grizzly' pre-production fleet, the first operational Atlas, for the French Air Force, took to the air in March 2013.

On 9th May 2015 an A400M for the Turkish Air Force crashed on its first flight from Seville, killing four and severely injuring two of the crew of six. While this tragedy is not central to the subject of this book, it serves a reminder that flight testing is still not without hazard.

Ed Strongman (left) shaking the hand of General Tan Stri Rodzali Daud, Chief of the Royal Malaysian Air Force. With an order for 4, the country is first export customer for the A400M. *Courtesy and © 2015 – Airbus*

'Hot and high' testing for the A400M was carried out at La Paz, Bolivia, in March 2012. *Courtesy and © 2015 – Airbus – S Ramadier*

L P Stuart-Smith

9 Jul 1957	Aviation Traders Accountant G-ATEL
	2 x 1,740shp RR Dart 512

L P Stuart-Smith joined the RAF in 1940 and served in Britain and the Middle East, his last posting being on DH Mosquitos. He re-joined the RAF in 1951, flying Gloster Meteors. Graduated from ETPS No.13 Course at Farnborough in 1954 and was posted to A&AEE Boscombe Down.

In 1956 Flt Lt L P Stuart-Smith joined Aviation Traders (Engineering) Ltd (ATEL) as CTP at Southend in 1956. ATEL was established by 'Freddie' Laker in 1947, specialising in freighter conversions (including Avro Tudors) and sub-contracting for other manufacturers, including Bristol. ATEL came up with the 28-seat Accountant, with Gloster Aircraft contracted to assist with design and production. The prototype, G-ATEL (an early example of a 'fixed' registration) was first flown on 9th July 1957 by Stuart-Smith and demonstrated at the

The sole Accountant performing at Farnborough, September 1957.
Peter Green Collection

SBAC airshow at Farnborough that September. This was more than a year ahead of the rival Handley Page Dart Herald – see 'Hazel' Hazelden. With no sales interest, the one-off G-ATEL was retired on 10th January 1958 and scrapped in 1960. ATEL went on to produce the radical car ferry conversion of the Douglas DC-4, the Carvair – see Don Cartledge.

Stuart-Smith went on to fly for another Laker associate company, Air Charter. Avro Super Trader 4B (an ATEL conversion of the Tudor 1) G-AGRH *Zephyr* on a Ministry of Defence charter to the ranges at Woomera, Western Australia, on 27th January 1959 impacted close to the 14,500ft summit of Mount Süphan, Turkey, killing all 12 on board, including Flt Lt L P Stuart-Smith.

Neville Stack

May 1929	Blackburn Nautilus N234
	1 x 525hp RR F.XIIMS

T Neville Stack AFC flew with the RFC and on into the RAF. By 1921 he was a musician in a prominent London dance band but was tempted back into aviation to become the first full-time flying instructor at the Lancashire Aero Club (LAC) in 1926. This did not last long, he gave up the post for what was to become a large number of point-to-point flights; his place at LAC was taken by 'Sam' Brown*. In November 1926, Neville and B M T S Leete flew a pair of DH Moths (respectively G-EBMO and G-EBKU) to Karachi, India, in 54 days, arriving on 8th January 1927. By 1928 Neville was retained by the Air Disposal Company at Croydon as a test pilot for the aero engines it manufactured, mainly the Cirrus.

WITH Blackburn CTP 'Dasher' Blake* apparently unavailable Neville Stack, who had demonstrated and raced Bluebird biplanes for Blackburn at times, was engaged to carry out the first flight of the Nautilus, a two-seat carrier-borne fighter. The lower wing was placed well below the fuselage (in the same manner as the Bristol F.2B Fighter) and the gap was used to house the radiator of the Rolls-Royce F.XIIMS (later Kestrel II). Neville took the biplane up from Brough in May 1929 only to report cooling and directional issues. N234 was modified and by August 1929 Dasher resumed testing but the Nautilus did not progress beyond the prototype stage.

In September 1929 Neville was appointed as the chief pilot for the newly-established National Flying Services chain of flying clubs, headquartered at Hanworth. From April to June 1931, Neville and J R Chaplin flew Vickers Vivid G-EBPY on a series of record-breaking 'out-and-backs': Berlin, Istanbul, Copenhagen and Warsaw. By early 1939 Neville was flying as Chief PTP at Longbridge, testing Austin-built Fairey Battles. Returning to Longbridge on 25th July 1939 in L5254, 'Stacko' encountered difficulties and was caught by a downdraught at the railway cutting on approach; the Battle crashed into the embankment and he was badly injured. He was succeeded by Geoffrey Alington – see Chapter Two – in late 1941. Before he left Longbridge, Neville did return to limited flying and later did ferrying work for the Fleet Air Arm.

The Waterhen on Lake Windermere, 1913. *Peter Green Collection*

H Stanley-Adams

30 Apr 1912	Lakes Waterhen
	1 x 50hp Gnome
1912	Lakes Seabird
	1 x 50hp Gnome

H STANLEY-ADAMS gained Aviators' Certificate No.97 at the Avro school at Brooklands on 27th June 1911. By November he was the chief pilot for E W Wakefield's Lakes Flying Company at Lake Windermere. That month he started flying the company's Avro-built Waterbird biplane floatplane. Oscar Gnosspelius designed the Waterhen, a two-seat pusher biplane floatplane, for use by the company and Stanley-Adams carried out the first flight in April 1912. This machine lasted through to 1914 and was used to train RNAS seaplane pilots. Later in 1912 a two-seat tractor biplane floatplane, the Seabird, was created using the fuselage of the Avro Duigan biplane. Stanley-Adams also tested this and instructed on all three types. As an aside, the Lakes Flying Company became the Northern Aircraft Company in 1915, with both Rowland Ding* and John Lankester Parker* flying for it. The latter first flew the Gull, designed by Oscar Gnosspelius, in 1923.

Reg Stock

28 Feb 1967	BAC Jet Provost T.5 XS230
	1 x 2,500lbst AS Viper 202
26 Oct 1967	BAC Strikemaster Mk.80 G-27-8
	1 x 3,410lbst AS Viper 535

Reginald Trevor Stock, born 1933. Joined the RAF in 1951; his first operational posting was with 94 Squadron at Celle, West Germany, on DH Vampire FB.5s and Venom FB.1s. In 1957 he flew HP Hastings C.1As at Colerne with the co-located 24 and 511 Squadrons. After that he became an instructor on Hunting Jet Provosts. Reg left the RAF in 1961, becoming the Jet Training Officer with the Marshall-operated Central Air Traffic Control School at Shawbury.

The first Strikemaster Mk.87 for the Kenyan Air Force, 601, on a test flight out of Warton. This machine was displayed at the 1970 Farnborough airshow before being delivered in January 1971. *British Aircraft Corporation*

Reg Stock became a test pilot for Hunting at Luton in March 1962 by which time the company was busy building Jet Provost T.4s for the RAF. The British Aircraft Corporation (BAC) took over Hunting in June 1964 and Reg transferred to Warton in May 1966, becoming the Strikemaster Project Pilot. Under BAC the Jet Provost was significantly re-engineered to produce the pressurised Mk.5 for the RAF, replacing the earlier T.3s and T.4s, and the Strikemaster with much more powerful Bristol Siddeley Viper turbojet and the ability to carry up to 3,000lb of stores under wing. With BAC CTP 'Jimmy' Dell* in the right-hand seat, Reg carried out the first flight of the prototype Jet Provost T.5 XS230 (a converted T.4) in February 1967 at Warton. That October, Reg followed up the programme with the maiden flight of the first Strikemaster, a Mk.80 destined for the Royal Saudi Air Force as 901. Reg was heavily involved in Jet Provost production testing and much development work with the Strikemaster, perfecting armament and 'kit' options for the type's many export customers. He carried out many demonstration flights, among them consecutive displays at the biennial SBAC airshow at Farnborough from 1962 to 1970, and delivery sorties. In August 1980 he checked out the first Strikemaster off the re-located production line at Hurn; a Mk.90 destined for Sudan. Reg retired from British Aerospace (as BAC had been since 1977) to fly for Dan-Air: now retired from flying, he lives in Lancashire.

'Mutt' Summers and Maurice Summers

11 Jun 1929	Vickers 143 1 x 450hp Bristol Jupiter VIA
30 Nov 1929	Vickers B19/27 J9131 2 x 480hp RR FXVIVS
Mar 1930	Supermarine Southampton X N252 3 x 570hp Bristol Jupiter XFBM
Apr 1930	Vickers Jockey J9122 1 x 480hp Bristol Mercury IIA
24 Jun 1930	Vickers Vellore III G-AASW 2 x 525hp Bristol Jupiter XIF
21 Jan 1931	Vickers 163 O-2 4 x 480hp RR FXIVS
1 Oct 1930	Vickers Viastra I G-AAUB 3 x 270hp AS Lynx Major
21 Jan 1931	Vickers COW Gun Fighter J9566 1 x 480hp Bristol Jupiter VIIF
8 Jul 1932	Supermarine Scapa S1648 2 x 525hp RR Kestrel IIIMS
11 Jan 1933	Vickers M1/30 1 x 825hp RR Buzzard IIIMS
21 Jun 1933	Supermarine Seagull V N-1 1 x 625hp Bristol Pegasus IIM2
23 Jan 1934	Vickers Vellox G-ABKY 2 x 600hp Bristol Pegasus IM3
19 Feb 1934	Supermarine F7/30 K2890 1 x 600hp RR Goshawk II
27 Jul 1934	Supermarine Stranraer K3973 2 x 820hp Bristol Pegasus IIIM
16 Aug 1934	Vickers G4/31 Biplane K2771 1 x 635hp Bristol Pegasus IIM3
19 Jun 1935	Vickers G4/31 Monoplane PVO-9 1 x 925hp Bristol Pegasus XX
5 Mar 1936	Supermarine Spitfire K5054 1 x 890hp RR Merlin C

15 Jun 1936	Vickers Wellington K4049
	2 x 915hp Bristol Pegasus X
17 Jun 1936	Vickers Venom PVO-10
	1 x 625hp Bristol Aquila AE3S
3 Mar 1939	Vickers Wellington II L4250
	2 x 1,145hp RR Merlin X
13 Aug 1939	Vickers Warwick K8178
	2 x 1,800hp RR Vulture II
5 Apr 1940	Vickers Warwick L9704
	2 x 2,300hp Bristol Centaurus CE4SM
23 Oct 1943	Vickers Windsor DW506
	4 x 1,635hp RR Merlin 65
22 Jun 1945	Vickers Viking G-AGOK
	2 x 1,675hp Bristol Hercules 130
6 Apr 1948	Vickers Nene Viking VX856
	2 x 5,000lbst RR Nene 1
16 Jul 1948	Vickers Viscount 630 G-AHRF
	4 x 1,380shp RR Dart 502
17 Jul 1949	Vickers Varsity T.1 VX828
	2 x 1,950hp Bristol Hercules 264
15 Mar 1950	Vickers Tay Viscount VX217
	2 x 6,250lbst RR Tay Ta1
18 May 1951	Vickers Valiant WB210
	4 x 6,500lbst RR Avon RA3

Notes: First flight venues as follows: Brooklands, all except the following: Eastleigh: F7/30, Spitfire; Farnborough: Windsor; Hamble: Viastra; Martlesham Heath: Jockey; Woolston/Solent: Southampton X, Scapa, Stranraer, Seagull V; Wisley: Viking, Nene Viking, Varsity, Viscount, Tay Viscount, Valiant. The Scapa was originally known as the Southampton IV; Seagull V was the name adopted by the original customer, the RAAF; in RAF and FAA service this was the Walrus; the Stranraer was originally known as the Southampton V.

Joseph Summers, born 1904. Joined the RAF in 1924 and went on to fly with 29 Squadron from Duxford on Sopwith Snipes, quickly converting to Gloster Grebe IIs. His flying skills were so good that he was soon posted to A&AEE at Martlesham Heath. With the death of Vickers CTP 'Tiny' Scholefield* in May 1929, Joseph asked for release to take over at Brooklands, and this was granted.

MILES FALCON G-ADTD touched down at Eastleigh on 5th March 1936 on a flight from Martlesham Heath. It was piloted by Jeffrey Quill* and with him as a passenger was his boss, Joseph 'Mutt' Summers, who had an appointment with a sleek, powerful aircraft that was waiting outside the Supermarine factory – the Type 300, K5054. Vickers had acquired Supermarine in November 1928, but the Southampton-based company continued to keep its name. As CTP for Vickers, Mutt held responsibility for the products of the parent organisation at Brooklands and at Eastleigh, although both sites had 'resident' test pilots:

George Pickering* looked after production testing the flying-boats and amphibians. Jeffrey had not long been appointed by Mutt as his No.2, across both airfields, although the new fighter was destined to dominate his flying career. Mutt's team faced an increasingly busy time in 1936. Already on the CTP's mind was an important project at Brooklands; in 103 day's time he would test fly B92/32 K4049, the nascent Wellington bomber.

Hand-built, the Type 300 was unpainted and without covers to its main undercarriage legs – the gear would stay locked down for the maiden flight. A small crowd of onlookers had gathered, including the pale-looking Reginald Joseph Mitchell, the man in charge of the design of this thoroughbred. Mutt took K5054 into the air and, typical of his inaugural flights, was back in 15 minutes. Clearly well pleased, he is reported as telling the ground crew: "Don't touch anything" – he was *that* happy with its behaviour. The legend of the Spitfire was born and Mutt had assured his place among the 'greats' of the nation's test pilots.

Before outlining a career that ran from 1929 to 1951, taking him from biplane fighters to the Walrus, Spitfire and Wellington, to the first four-turbine airliner and the inauguration of the V-bomber era, the nickname 'Mutt' needs examining. It's very likely that its true origin will remain lost in the mists of time but it *can* be said that it was at Martlesham that this piece of test piloting folklore was born. The 'majority vote' goes with his habit of urinating on the tail skid or wheel before a flight, like a dog marking its territory and slang for a dog is 'Mutt'. Sources as unimpeachable as George Edwards – who started in the design office in 1935, designed the Viscount and Valiant, was knighted in 1957 and took Vickers and then BAC through to Concorde wrote of Mutt's firm belief that some pilots who had been flying with full bladders died in accidents whereas they may have survived having relieved themselves pre-flight. There is also the pioneering American 'Mutt and Jeff' strip cartoon, but Joseph Summers bears no resemblance to the nice-but-dim Mutt character. A couple of sources allude to the cockney rhyming slang that 'Mutt and Jeff' is 'deaf'. Most pilots suffered from the roaring noise around them, but there is no evidence that Joseph Summers suffered hearing problems.

Fg Off Joseph 'Mutt' Summers became CTP at Vickers following the death of 'Tiny' Scholefield* in May 1929 and inherited an expanding and challenging 'in' tray. He kicked off in June with the so-called 'Bolivian Scout', the Type 143 fighter, the latest of a series of single-seat fighters for export customers. The 143 was used as the basis for the broadly similar Type 177, which Mutt first flew at Brooklands on 26th November 1929: it was aimed at a British requirement for a ship-board fighter, but got no further than the prototype. (Four days later, Mutt was 'first flighting' the B19/27 – see below.) In complete contrast was the monoplane single-seat Jockey intended for Specification F20/27 which was looking for a new-fangled need, an 'interceptor'. This was taken by road to Martlesham Heath for its first excursion. On 15th July 1932 with an A&AEE flyer at the helm, the Jockey failed to recover from a spin. Its pilot successfully took to the silk; the Jockey project was shelved but was rethought in 1936 as the Venom.

Informal gathering at Eastleigh after the first flight of the Spitfire prototype, 5th March 1936. Left to right: 'Mutt' Summers, H J 'Agony' Payn*, R J Mitchell, Stuart Scott-Hall, Mr Hall, Jeffrey Quill*. *KEC*

The first in-house monoplane fighter from Vickers was the Vireo of March 1928 – see Tiny Scholefield – and the Jockey underlined the future. Yet in early 1931 Mutt was at the controls of an aircraft that, other than its form of construction and some aerodynamic advances, would not have looked out of place in 1915 – here was the ultimate 'Gunbus'. This throwback was the COW Gun Fighter – designed around an upward-firing Coventry Ordnance Works (hence COW) 37mm gun that fired 1½lb shells. Specification F29/27 was chasing a 'bomber destroyer', capable of flying under a bomber stream and decimating the enemy with well-aimed heavy firepower. A couple of 'straights' to try out the integrity of the tail skid on 21st January 1931 turned into a classic Summers quick 'circuit'. Mutt believed that inaugural flights should be just so, proving that the type could aviate; the detailed, exacting test schedule was for the following days and months. He was a great believer in lifting the morale of one and all with the success of a 'first', leaving any damning analysis to another day. Despite its looks, the COW Gun Fighter was full of engineering and aerodynamic innovations, but the entire concept of F29/27 was quietly dropped. The Jockey design was dusted off for Specification F5/34 and it emerged as the retractable undercarriage Venom. The machine stuck to the

'spec' and while it was a very workmanlike fighter, Mutt must have known he was flying a redundant airframe when he took it up for the first time at Brooklands on 17th June 1936. Sixty-three days earlier he had flown the Spitfire, which reflected what the design team thought was needed: Woolston was the future of fighters, not Weybridge.

It was on bombers and transport biplanes that Vickers had built its reputation and the company's prototype to replace the long-lived, lumbering Virginia was predictably a cleaned-up version. First flown in November 1929 and the subject of considerable revision and modification, J9131 remained a one-off. A troop-carrier based upon the B19/27 followed, with its four engines arranged in tandem, two pulling, two pushing. The Type 163 was equally unsuccessful.

Tiny Scholefield had flown the Vellore in May 1928, a large single-engined biplane intended for air mail and freight. This machine had potential as a twin and Mutt flew Vellore III G-AASW from Brooklands in June 1930. In March 1932, fitted with twin floats, Supermarine CTP Henri Biard* flew G-AASW from Southampton Water, and Mutt also took a hand in testing it as a seaplane. A second twin Vellore followed in February 1932. A final extrapolation was the Vellox, a ten-passenger airliner for Imperial Airways: only the prototype flew.

The prototype Viastra in Mk.III guise with a pair of Armstrong Siddeley Jaguars. *Peter Green Collection*

The construction techniques of Frenchman Michel Wibault (see Tiny Scholefield) influenced Vickers thinking in fighters (Vireo and the Jockey/Venom) and also gave rise to the Viastra transport which was intended for developing countries and from the start was offered with powerplant options. Assembly of the prototype, G-AAUB, powered by three Armstrong Siddeley Lynx Majors, was carried out at the Supermarine Woolston plant and it was towed on a lighter down the Solent to Hamble, where Mutt took it into the air in October 1930. This was followed by the Viastra II with twin 525hp Bristol Jupiters in late 1930 and the single-Jupiter powered Viastra VI freighter in April 1931. Despite a plethora of engine combinations, only four Viastras were built; Vickers receiving Royal approval with the order of Mk.X G-ACCC for the Prince of Wales.

As CTP across both the Supermarine and Vickers product line, Mutt conducted first flights and initial trials on the final flying-boats from the Woolston stable. The final trio of big 'boats were all designed to replace the successful Southampton series. The first of these was the Southampton X, which was a radical departure for R J Mitchell, a three-engined sesquiplane – with the lower wing of greatly decreased span. Its maiden flight, in the hands of Mutt, was from the Solent in March 1930 and he was not happy with its performance; only the prototype was built. The Southampton IV, a much more conservative design, was first flown by Mutt for ten minutes in July 1932. It was so different from its Southampton forebears that it was renamed Scapa in October 1933 and the RAF ordered a dozen. The last of the line was the Southampton V, a bigger Scapa, which had its debut in July 1934 and was renamed Stranraer in

August 1935. The RAF ordered 23 and Stranraers were also built by Canadian Vickers at St Hubert, Montreal. The three 'Southamptons' paled against the small pusher amphibian which Mutt took on its maiden flight from Southampton Water in June 1933. Ordered by the Royal Australian Air Force as the Seagull V, it was an entirely new type with only the name in common with the previous series of amphibians. Mutt made enquiries with Mitchell about the strength of the airframe and then surprised everyone – including its designer – by *looping* the prototype at the Hendon airshow, *four* days after the maiden flight! The RAF and Fleet Air Arm adopted the type from April 1935 and named it Walrus. The story of this amazingly adaptive and long-lived design need not be repeated here.

Vickers had taken on former airship designer Barnes Wallis as head of structures to work alongside the company's chief designer Rex Pierson. Using airship principles the Vickers M1/30 prototype biplane torpedo bomber was first flown by Mutt, along with FTO John Radcliffe, on 11th January 1933. With an inert torpedo under the M1/30's centre section, Mutt and John were engaged in a high speed dive on 23rd November 1933 when the wings began to break up and the aircraft started a roll to starboard. As it inverted, the wings parted company with the fuselage and the tail section was soon to do likewise. Mutt was thrown out and he pulled the handle on his parachute instantly. John found himself dangling out of the rear compartment, snagged by his parachute back strap; adrenaline solved this and, like his CTP, he drifted down for a safe landing. Wallis abandoned airship techniques and his geodetic system came to the fore: through this Vickers were set on the dynasty that arose from the Wellington. The first application of geodetics was in response to Specification G4/31 for a general purpose bomber, which was hotly contested. Vickers took an exceptional brave move and opted to meet G4/31 with *two* aircraft, a predictable biplane and a big-winged monoplane, both using geodetics. Mutt flew both, in turn August 1934 and March 1935 and the contrast of both performing together at the Hendon airshow that year was extreme. The powers that be wisely opted for the monoplane and the first pre-production Wellesley appeared in March 1936 – 175 more followed.

The bizarre COW Gun fighter, J9566, at Martlesham Heath in 1931. *KEC*

The prototype Seagull V wearing the B Condition markings N-2, at MAEE Felixstowe, 1934. *Vickers-Armstrongs*

The F7/30 prototype K2890 of 1934, saddled with a Goshawk engine. Two years later, freed from Air Ministry specifications, R J Mitchell created the Spitfire. *Vickers-Armstrongs*

Both Vickers G4/31 contenders, biplane and monoplane, displaying at Hendon in 1935. *Vickers-Armstrongs*

The Spitfire was dealt with in the introduction to Mutt and its story really belongs with that of his deputy, Jeffrey Quill. But there was a 'stepping stone' to the Spitfire that taught R J Mitchell and all at Vickers-Supermarine that radical new thinking was needed in fighters – Sydney Camm and his team at Kingston-upon-Thames had come to the same conclusion. Specification F7/30 sought a single-seat day fighter, ideally powered by a Rolls-Royce Goshawk with evaporative cooling. The gull-winged, faired undercarriage, open cockpit, Type 224 first flew on 19th February 1934 and proved disappointing from the very start. None of the bidders for F7/30 were successful and in the end the requirement was re-written as F14/35 and won by the Gloster Gladiator, destined to be the RAF's last biplane fighter.

Robert Gardner's marvellous biography of Sir George Edwards, *From Bouncing Bombs to Concorde*, provides a telling aside on the rise of Germany and Mutt's morale. Mutt was a frequent visitor to friends in Germany and he returned from such a trip in October 1937 having sampled among others, the Junkers Ju 87 'Stuka' dive-bomber. Sir George describes Mutt as being in a state of "complete depression" – despite having flown the Spitfire 20 months previously. Perhaps this was because, until May 1938 there was only *one* Spitfire, whereas the Stuka was in mass production.

For the first flight of the Wellington, on 15th June 1936, Mutt had company. In another case of too many 'eggs' in the one basket Barnes Wallis and production supremo Trevor Westbrook were along for the ride; which thankfully was uneventful. With the experience of the Wellesley, the geodetic structure allowed the Vickers interpretation of Specification B9/32 to be a very advanced medium bomber. It went on to be produced in huge numbers with a series of powerplant alternatives, including the Rolls-Royce Merlin, and was the backbone of Bomber Command during the first years of the war. Mutt and his expanding team faced a hugely increasing workload as production increased and the support structure expanded. For example, Mutt was at Sywell in April 1940 to test Mk.I L4349, the first to go through a repair programme by Brooklands Aviation. Prior to that, he flew the most unusual variant, the so-called DWI equipped with an on-board petrol engine to generate sufficient charge to power a huge magnetic coil suspended under the wings and the forward and rear fuselage. DWI stood for the wholly misleading Directional Wireless Installation, but the Wellington was an airborne mine-sweeper. Barnes Wallis increasingly turned his mind to special weapons, including the famous 'Bouncing Bombs' for the Dams raid of May 1943. In the run up to this, Mutt was heavily involved in development of the UPKEEP 'mine' and the later HIGHBALL anti-shipping weapon, at first in Wellingtons and later in Avro Lancasters.

Hopefully, readers will have become accustomed to the occasional tangent taken by the narrative. Given the name of this book's illustrious publisher, Crécy, an aside on the Duke of Wellington might be in order. The monoplane G4/31 was named in honour of the brilliant soldier Arthur Wellesley, who became the 1st Duke of Wellington after his dazzling defeat of Napoleon at the Battle of Waterloo on 18th June 1815. So, the Wellington bomber *also* carried Arthur's name – how did the Duke manage to get his name on two aircraft? When the Vickers B9/32 first flew at Brooklands in June 1936 it was going to be called the Crécy after Edward III's victory over Philip VI's forces on 26th August 1346. That battle changed the face of warfare with longbows decimating the French. By the summer of 1936 it was clear that the new bomber was very likely going to fight *alongside* France. So it was best not to have Britain's 20th century longbow equivalent commemorating a conflict France would sooner forget. Why not one of Britain's greatest Field Marshals? To add insult to injury, the man who provided decisive help to Wellington in crushing the French at Waterloo was Gebhard von Blücher who was Prussian – that would be German, then!

Strongly showing its familial legacy the Warwick was an entirely new type and considered to be a heavy bomber, while the Wellington was in the medium class. Alterations in the requirement and a complete change of role to maritime patrol delayed and dogged the Warwick. Mutt flew the Rolls-Royce Vulture-engined prototype in August 1939. It was not until April 1940 the second example appeared, also acting as a test-bed for the Bristol Centaurus engine. Directional stability was a major problem with 'round engined' Warwicks and within the space of 24 hours there were two accidents in January 1945. On the 5th Mutt, along with FTO 'Jimmy' Green, were testing GR.II HG364 at 3,000ft over Weybridge when the rudder overbalanced, giving only full starboard deflection. Mutt realised he could keep a form of control by banking and putting full power into the opposite engine and forced landed near Chobham; HG364 was written off, Mutt and Jimmy escaped relatively unscathed. The following day Vickers PTP 'Shorty' Longbottom* died when a similar mishap befell GR.V PN778 and it spun in. More trouble was to follow.

The four-engined Windsor was much like the Warwick in so far as it was a bomber without a purpose when it appeared. Using geodetic construction it was an exceptionally advanced, long-range, design and Vickers built an assembly building at Farnborough to house the project. Only three were completed, Mutt flying the first example, DW506, on 23rd October 1943.

This brings us to Mutt's younger brother, Maurice. He was the pilot for the maiden flight of the second Windsor, DW512, from Farnborough on 15th February 1944. Maurice had joined the flight test team at Vickers by 1943. Wellingtons were the main pre-occupation, but as well as the Windsor programme, Maurice tested Warwicks and in February 1945 was involved in a third directional control incident. After Mutt's accident on 5th January and the tragic death of 'Shorty' Longbottom the following day, Maurice and FTO George Hemsley took GR.V PN777 up from Brooklands on 1st February to investigate what had happened to the previous two. The rudder control could be limited in flight so that rudder deflection could be slowly increased as sideslip trials continued. At 13,000ft the rudder over-balanced to starboard and Maurice could do nothing to alter the situation. He instructed George to jump and then followed him – George broke a leg, but Maurice was badly injured and did not return to test flying. Warwick PN777 came down at Ewell, near Surbiton, ploughing into houses in Ruxley Lane and killing Mrs Annie Swan (43) and Mrs Edith Connor (42). 'Tommy' Lucke* had to bale out of Warwick

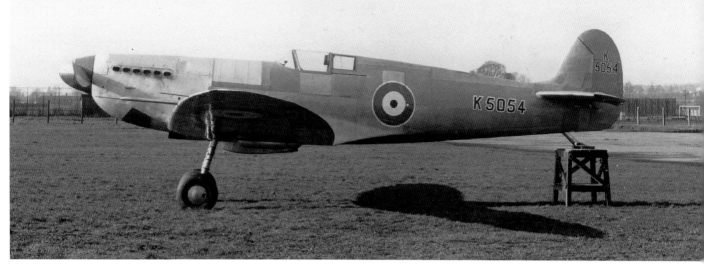

The Supermarine Type 300 – the Spitfire prototype – with the tail on a trestle at Eastleigh, 1936. *Vickers-Armstrongs*

The prototype Wellington, K4049, at Brooklands, with fairings in place of the nose and tail turrets, 1936. *Vickers-Armstrongs*

PN780 on 27th March 1945, but this was a fluke accident not attributed to the rudder issue. Dorsal fins and restricting rudder travel eventually cured the Warwick fleet.

Maurice Summers was born in 1911. He joined the RAF in 1929 and served until 1935 when he became a PTP for Gloster at Hucclecote. Returning to the RAF in 1940, he served the Air Ministry on bomber development, including procurement of US-built aircraft. He transferred to Vickers at Brooklands by 1943 and, following the accident to Warwick PN777 in February 1945 he took a post in the technical publication department. In 1950, Maurice became a member of the New York Stock Exchange, later becoming a director of international brokers E F Hutton. In 1973 he retired and returned to flying, aged 62, taking up aerobatic competition flying. Later in the 1970s he became a property developer in Florida. Wg Cdr Maurice Summers died in Bermuda on 29th March 2001, aged 89.

The Vulture-powered Warwick prototype, K8178, early 1940. *Peter Green Collection*

The third and last Windsor, NK136, in 1944. *Vickers-Armstrongs*

From as early as May 1939 an airliner version of the Wellington had been postulated, but events overtook this. Mutt was at the controls of the prototype Viking, G-AGOK, from Wisley on 22nd June 1945. The Viking was essentially a new stressed-skin fuselage attached to Wellington outer wings, undercarriage and many other components and sub-assemblies. Production was completed in 1947 by which time 163 had been built – by far and away the largest production run for any British airliner up to that date. A version powered by a pair of Rolls-Royce Nene turbojets flew in April 1948; it was the first British pure jet transport. Mutt flew the Nene Viking from Heathrow to Villacoublay, Paris, on 25th July 1948 in 43 minutes 7 seconds, averaging 384mph. A military transport version, the Valetta, was first flown by Mutt on 30th June 1947 from Brooklands:

prototype VL249 was followed by 251 others. The final Wellington descendent was the tricycle undercarriage Varsity crew trainer, first flown by Mutt in July 1949: this long-serving workhorse was built up to 1954, with 163 produced.

Schemed by Rex Pierson but designed and brought into reality by George Edwards, the Viscount four turboprop airliner eclipsed all that the Viking achieved with 459 built, becoming the most produced British airliner ever. With his deputy 'Jock' Bryce* as co-pilot, Mutt took the prototype for its 'traditional' ten-minute first flight on 16th July 1948. Mutt had developed a radio code to convey his thought to George and to throw anyone 'eves dropping' off the scent. He often reported "swithering" which sounded dire, but actually meant that all was well! Mutt was very impressed with the Viscount,

Viking 1A G-AHOS *Valiant*, delivered to BEA in September 1946. *British European Airways*

The Nene Viking flat out and low down, probably at Hucknall. *Rolls-Royce*

adding another quote to his repertoire by describing the Viscount as: "The smoothest and best I have ever known." In a similar manner to the Viking, the Viscount was turned into a twin-jet as a test-bed for the Rolls-Royce Tay turbojet and this was first flown in May 1950.

Mutt's final 'first' was the prototype Valiant V-bomber, WB210. There was friction between Mutt and George Edwards when the latter announced plans that the Valiant would make its debut from the then all-grass airfield of Wisley. Mutt wanted it moving by road to Boscombe Down, but George would not be swayed. Mutt and Jock took WB210 on its maiden flight on 18th May 1951, for 18 minutes. Three more flights were made from Wisley and then it was ferried to Hurn where testing continued while a concrete runway was laid down at Wisley.

Mutt, aged 47, handed over to Jock Bryce later in 1951. At that point he had over 5,000 hours in an astonishing 366 types. Fg Off Joseph 'Mutt' Summers CBE died following a stomach operation on 16th March 1954 – six days after his 50th birthday. In the obituary in *Flight* magazine for 26th March 1954 George Edwards wrote: "He was essentially an individualist. His early days of test flying were those of personal assessment, the qualitative rather than the quantitative analysis. Mutt's approach to test flying was much more in sympathy with the knee-pad than with the complicated automatic observers which nowadays are an indispensable part of test flying. He vigorously defended the feel of an aeroplane as measured by his hand or by the seat of his pants... He had extraordinarily quick reactions. His ability to extract himself from a tight corner was the result of a powerful blend of experience, judgement and reaction. To those who designed the aeroplanes he tested he was a tower of strength."

The prototype Viscount, G-AHRF, in BEA colours for the route-proving trials with fare-paying passengers July to September 1950 – see 'Dickie' Rymer. *Vickers*

The Tay Viscount displaying at the 1950 Farnborough airshow. *Rolls-Royce*

First of the V-bombers, Valiant WB210, 1951. *Vickers-Armstrongs*

W H Sutcliffe

| 11 Aug 1929 | Civilian Coupé I G-AAIL |
| | 1 x 75hp ABC Hornet |

THE Civilian Aircraft Company of Burton-on-Trent developed a high-wing two seat light aircraft, the Coupé and built the prototype, G-AAIL, at Hedon, Hull. The chief flying instructor of the Midland Flying Club was contracted to carry out the first flights, from 11th August 1929. The prototype was followed by five Mk.IIs before the company closed down in 1933.

The first indigenous Nieuport, the one-off BN.1 C3484. *Peter Green Collection*

The second of two Nieuport London night bombers, H1741.
Peter Green Collection

Chequerboard-painted Nieuport Nighthawk K-151 flown by Leslie-Tait-Cox at the 1919 Hendon Aerial Derby. *Peter Green Collection*

Leslie Tait-Cox

Feb 1918	Nieuport BN.1 C3484 1 x 230hp Bentley BR.2
Apr 1919	Nieuport Nighthawk F2909 1 x 320hp ABC Dragonfly
13 Apr 1920	Nieuport London H1740 2 x 320hp ABC Dragonfly

In 1916 Nieuport (England) Ltd was set up at Cricklewood to licence build the French Nieuport 11 single-seat scout, but instead manufactured Sopwith Camels. By 1918 the company had been re-established as Nieuport and General Aircraft (N&G) to develop its own designs and engaged Henry Folland as designer and Lt Leslie R Tait-Cox as test pilot. The first design, intended to replace the Camel, was the BN.1 (British Nieuport 1), which first flew in February 1918, only to suffer an engine problem and crash in flames on 10th March 1918. In April or May 1919 Leslie took the Nighthawk prototype for its maiden flight and this machine showed great promise, other than the choice of the notoriously unreliable ABC Dragonfly engine. The first of two London night bombers, H1740, was flown in April 1920.

In August 1920 N&G announced that it was closing down and negotiations began with Gloucestershire Aircraft (Gloster from 1926) to acquire the design rights to the Nighthawk and a substantial stock of airframes and components. Henry Folland later joined, going on to design a string of Gloster biplane fighters. Leslie Tait-Cox flew the one-off Gloster Mars III G-EAYN in the 1922 Hendon Aerial Derby, probably having been retained by the company. By 1925 Leslie was flying Royal Aircraft SE.5As for Jack Savage's skywriting organisation.

The Manx tail-less research test-bed at Radlett with twin-wheel main undercarriage, late 1943. *Handley Page*

'Jamie' Talbot

25 Jun 1943	Handley Page Manx H-0222 2 x 130hp DH Gipsy Major
2 Dec 1945	Handley Page Hermes I G-AGSS 4 x 1,650hp Bristol Hercules 101

FLT LT JAMES R TALBOT had joined Handley Page at Radlett by 1941 as production of the Halifax got into swing. On 17th July 1941, 'Jamie' was airborne in former 35 Squadron Halifax I L9490 along with two FTOs. There was a fuel transfer problem and Jamie carried out a forced landing near North Mimms; with slight injury to those on board. Fourteen days later Jamie was appointed CTP as 'Jim' Cordes* moved on to run 7 Aircraft Assembly Unit at Hooton Park. Halifaxes were the major commitment throughout Jamie's time at Radlett. He took the 'working' prototype of the Bristol Hercules VI-engined Mk.III, converted from Mk.II R9534, for its maiden flight on 12th October 1942 and the first production Mk.III and 700th Halifax, HX226, airborne in August 1943.

Jim Cordes had taken the Manx tail-less research aircraft for its first fast taxis at Radlett in February 1940. As the project was being conducted on a 'when time permits' basis it was not until 12th September 1942 that J F Marsh (see Chapter Seven) *nearly* succeeded in flying it. After a series of modifications, on 14th May 1943, the Manx was ready for test by Jamie but severe undercarriage shimmy precluded more than fast runs. More modifications followed; the Manx gaining twin-wheel main undercarriage and a damping unit on the nose wheel. On 25th June 1943 a fast taxi turned into the maiden flight as the Manx reached a slight rise in the Radlett runway and stayed aloft. At 100ft the canopy blew off and the flight lasted only ten minutes. Jamie flew the Manx several more times and from October 1944 Robert Kronfeld* also tried it out; he carried out its last sortie on 2nd April 1946.

The Hermes four-engined airliner prototype, G-AGSS, was assembled at Radlett by November 1945 and with rival firms achieving maiden flights of new peacetime designs, Don Middleton in *Test Pilots* asserts that there was pressure for Handley Page to get the Hermes airborne before year's end. Jamie undertook taxi tests on 1st December and the following day put the throttle forward. Don described the next few minutes: "It was clear immediately that they were in serious trouble; the Hermes climbed in a violent switchback path,

diving steeply and then climbing again as the pilots fought to retain control. Finally it stalled, turned upon its back and crashed on farmland three miles from the aerodrome, miraculously missing Radlett itself." Flt Lt James R Talbot and FTO E A 'Ginger' Wright were killed instantly. It was considered that the elevators were seriously over-balanced; an increased span tailplane and a large fin were introduced as a consequence. Hedley Hazelden* took over as CTP.

Denis Tayler

17 Jan 1963	Short Skyvan 1 G-ASCN 2 x 390hp Continental GTSIO-520
5 Jan 1964	Short Belfast C.1 XR362 4 x 5,730shp RR Tyne 101

Denis Graham William Tayler, born 1915. Joined the RAF in 1939 and was operational with 50 Squadron on Avro Lancasters from Skellinghorpe by 1942, going on to the Pathfinder Force with DH Mosquito XVIs at Upwood with 139 Squadron. He was posted to RAE Farnborough in July 1945. Ferrying former Luftwaffe Siebel Fh 104A twin-engined light transport 'Air Min 119' from Schleswig, Germany, to Farnborough on 28th November 1945 Denis experienced engine problems and force landed on the Goodwin Sands, where he and his passengers were rescued and the Siebel was abandoned. Graduating from ETPS No.7 Course at Farnborough 1948, Denis continued to fly with RAE Farnborough, and later with Aero Flight at RAE Thurleigh. After a general handling sortie of Fairey FD.1 VX350 on 6th February 1956 one of the main undercarriage legs would not lower and Denis carried out a wheels-up landing at Farnborough. Denis was unhurt, the one-off FD.1 was scrapped – see under Gordon Slade for its details.

SQN LDR DENIS TAYLER DFC joined Shorts at Sydenham in 1960 as CTP, succeeding Tom Brooke-Smith*. In January 1963 he carried out the maiden flight of an aircraft that transformed the fortunes of the Northern Ireland manufacturer – the Skyvan light freighter and mini-airliner. *Charlie-November* was fitted with an interim pair of Continental piston engines and it returned to the factory shortly afterwards to

Dennis Tayler taking the piston-egined Skyvan prototype, G-ASCN, for its first flight, Sydenham, 17th January 1963. *Short Brothers and Harland*

receive its intended powerplants, 520shp Turboméca Astazou XII turboprops. As the Skyvan 1A G-ASCN was flown again by Denis on 2nd October 1963 and the type entered production, as the Mk.2. Denis was at the helm on 15th December 1967 for the first flight of the Skyvan 3, G-ASZI, with 715shp Garrett AiResearch TPE331-201 turboprops with much wider export appeal. The last Skyvan appeared in 1986 and the type formed the basis for the Short 330 and 360 commuterliners.

At the other end of the spectrum was the 136ft 5in span, 125,000lb empty weight Belfast strategic airlifter the for the RAF. Dennis was captain for the inaugural flight of XR362 on 5th January 1964, taking the prototype to Aldergrove where the longer runway would greatly aid testing. With Denis on that flight were: Peter Lowe (co-pilot, see chapter Seven); Malcolm Wild (chief engineer); Ricky Steel (FTE), Bill

Skyvan 3M G-BBRU on its way to the South Yemen Air Force, April 1974. Royal Saudi Air Force BAC Strikemaster Mk.80 to the right. *Airwork*

Mortimer (radio); Alex Mackenzie and Gil Thomas (FTOs). Despite an extensive marketing exercise, other than the ten RAF Belfasts, no others were built. Denis handed over to Don Wright* on 1st January 1969. Sqn Ldr Denis Graham William Tayler OBE DFC died in 2006, aged 91.

The mighty Belfast prototype soaring skyward on its maiden flight, Sydenham 5th January 1964, bound for the longer runway at Aldergrove. The famous cranes of the Harland and Wolff shipyard in the background. *Short Brothers and Harland*

'Teddy' Tennant provides the scale for the 23ft 4in wingspan of the Midge, G-39-1, 1954. *Folland Aircraft*

'Teddy' Tennant

11 Aug 1954	Folland Midge G-39-1 1 x 1,640lbst AS Viper 5
18 Jun 1955	Folland Gnat G-39-2 1 x 4,520lbst BS Orpheus 701
31 Aug 1959	Folland Gnat T.1 XM691 1 x 4,230lbst BS Orpheus 100

Notes: Midge and Gnat prototypes both flew from Boscombe Down; the Gnat T.1 from Chilbolton.

Edward A Tennant, born 1924. Joined the RAF in 1940 and flew with 256 and 153 Squadrons, both on Boulton Paul Defiant night-fighters, followed by extensive operations on Hawker Typhoons. Graduated from ETPS No.8 Course at Farnborough 1948 and was posted to A&AEE Boscombe Down.

S QN LDR EDWARD 'TEDDY' A TENNANT DFC was appointed as CTP to Folland Aircraft at Hamble in June 1953. Under W E W 'Teddy' Petter, acting as managing director and chief engineer, Folland was developing as a private-venture a small jet fighter primarily for export, but with hopes of attracting the RAF. The one-off Midge used an Armstrong Siddeley Viper turbojet to enable testing to get started while the much more powerful BSE Orpheus became available for the definitive Gnat. The Midge was roaded to Boscombe Down and Teddy Tennant carried out a 'straight' during the afternoon of 11th August 1954. Back-tracking, he got ready for another and put the throttle forward, realised he'd let the 'straight' go a greater distance than before and, to save severe braking, Teddy converted the 'hop' into a maiden flight. After a couple more sorties he flew the short distance to Chilbolton, where Folland had established its test centre.

The Gnat's fuselage was considerably changed to accept the Orpheus and a pair of ADEN cannon had been shoe-horned in. Teddy took the first Gnat, G-39-2, for its maiden flight from Boscombe Down on 18th June 1955. Just over a year later, on

31st July 1956, Teddy was engaged in a high speed, low level, sortie when the control column began to shake, followed by a loud noise and total loss of pitch control. Unbeknown to Teddy, the tailplanes had failed and fallen off. He was down to about 600ft and jettisoned the canopy, prior to ejecting. With the canopy gone, Teddy founds that his arms were sucked out of cockpit and that the seat blind (which would ordinarily have been pulled over his face to initiate ejection) was flapping in the airflow. He struggled and brought his arms back within the cockpit and, fumbling at the base of the blind, yanked at it and was suddenly in the air, his parachute deploying. Gnat G-39-2 crashed just to the north of Boscombe Down. Teddy alighted not that far away and later even raised a smile by noting that where he landed was just a short walk to his house! The tailplanes were strengthened on production versions. A batch of six Gnat fighters were ordered by the Ministry of Supply, a dozen by Finland and two went to Yugoslavia. The real bonanza was a licence production deal with India, with 30 built and flown from Chilbolton followed by 'kits' being sent to Hindustan Aircraft at Bangalore, until Gnats and the improved Ajeet were manufactured entirely in India.

RAF interest in the fighter never gelled, but the Gnat was considerably redesigned to become a two-seat advanced trainer to replace the venerable DH Vampire T.11s. Teddy flew the prototype Gnat T.1 from Chilbolton in August 1959 and the type entered service with the Central Flying School the following year. During 1961 Michael Oliver* succeeded Teddy as CTP. Sqn Ldr Edward A Tennant DFC died in 1981, aged 57.

Gnat T.1s of the 'Red Arrows' lined up during the team's second year, 1966. *KEC*

D A Terrill

BLACKBURN-BUILT Fairey Barracuda II BV825 was first flown from Brough on 13th October 1943. Two days later Blackburn PTP D A Terrill took it up for a routine test. After about 30 minutes an aircraft engine was heard running intermittently in cloud near Scunthorpe. Moments later BV825 dived into ground to the south of Scunthorpe, killing its pilot instantly. Another Barracuda, with the same serial number, was supplied off contract in January 1944.

Don Thomas

Donald L J Thomas joined the RAF in 1963 and, after initial training, flew English Electric Canberra B.15s and B.16s with 32 Squadron from Akrotiri, Cyprus, 1966 to 1969. He converted to HS Buccaneer S.2s, flying with 12 Squadron at Honington until 1973. A 'slot' at the US Navy Test Pilot School at Patuxent River, Maryland, was delayed, so he 'sat in' on the ETPS course at Boscombe Down; before heading over to 'Pax River'. He returned in 1974 for a posting at A&AEE.

FLT LT DON THOMAS joined British Aerospace at Warton in October 1979 working mostly on the Tornado programme, including the first 'buddy-buddy' in-flight refuelling trials in May 1981. He also flew the EAP and Typhoon prototypes. Don succeeded Chris Yeo* as CTP in 1987, serving as such until 1995 when he handed over to Derek Reeh*. He flew with the BAE communications fleet until 1996 when he became a commercial pilot, flying HS.146s and later Airbus A320s. He retired from flying in 2005 with over 10,000 hours on 58 types.

Arthur Thompson

27 Feb 1942	Blackburn Firebrand I DD804
	1 x 2,305hp Napier Sabre III
21 Dec 1943	Blackburn Firebrand III DK372
	1 x 2,400hp Bristol Centaurus VII

Notes: DD804 first flew from Leconfield; DK372 from Brough.

FLT LT ARTHUR C R THOMPSON joined Blackburn at Brough by 1941, having taken over from 'Bill' Bailey*. Fairey Swordfish at the Sherburn-in-Elmet factory and Short Sunderlands from the Dumbarton plant and Fairey Barracudas at Brough were keeping the workforce going. Great hope was vested in the Firebrand, single-seat carrier-borne torpedo strike fighter and Arthur flew the Sabre-powered prototype in February 1942 and the second example, DD810, on 15th July 1942. On a routine test flight on 20th February 1943 Arthur encountered engine failure while making a westerly approach to Brough. About a mile short, DD810 impacted with a cable from the bucket conveyor system on the C and T Earle cement works. The cable tore through the rear fuselage and the Firebrand crashed on the airfield: Arthur was slightly injured, DD810 was rebuilt as NV636. Firebrand development suffered from changing requirements and engines and Specification S8/43 was written around a Centaurus-powered version. Arthur took the Mk.III prototype, DK372, for its maiden flight in December 1943. The Mk.III led in turn to the Mk.IV and it was the Mk.V that was the definitive version, although it did not enter Fleet Air Arm service until April 1947. Charles Flood* took over from Arthur in 1947.

The second prototype Firebrand, DD810, in which Arthur Thompson had a lucky escape following an engine failure at Brough on 20th February 1943. *KEC*

Blackburn FIREBRAND V
THE NAVY'S STRIKE AIRCRAFT
BLACKBURN AIRCRAFT LTD., BROUGH E.YORKS

A 1948 advert showing the definitive TF.5 version, which entered service during the previous year.

'Bill' Thorn

24 Mar 1935	Avro Anson K4771
	2 x 290hp AS Cheetah VI
14 Jun 1945	Avro Tudor 1 G-AGPF
	4 x 1,750hp RR Merlin 102
10 Mar 1946	Avro Tudor 2 G-AGSU
	4 x 1,750hp RR Merlin 102
17 Apr 1946	Avro Tudor 7 G-AGRX
	4 x 1,750hp Bristol Hercules 120

Notes: Anson and Tudor 7 flew from Woodford; Tudor 1 and 2 from Ringway.

Sidney Albert Thorn, born 1901. 'Cadged' a ride in an RFC Avro 504 at Shoreham and was not enamoured with the experience. By 1918 he was working in a factory manufacturing gauges and piping for warships. In August 1919 he joined the Coldstream Guards. Known as 'Bill' to everyone, he left the Guards after an inheritance in 1922 allowed him to become a partner with his brothers in a farm; but this venture foundered in 1925. So Bill enlisted in the RAF; one of his instructors at 5 FTS Sealand was 'Jim' Cordes*. Posted to 17 Squadron at Hawkinge, he flew Hawker Woodcock IIs. In June 1927 the RAF lent Charles Lindbergh a

17 Squadron Woodcock, J8295, to enable him to return to Paris prior to taking a ship back to the USA. (He had flown the Atlantic solo in the Ryan NYP Spirit of St Louis *in the previous month and his aircraft had been packed and freighted back to the States.) Bill was detailed to make his way by surface transport to Le Bourget and bring the Woodcock back. Fg Off Thorn spent time at RAE Farnborough and A&AEE Martlesham Heath in 1927 and among the types he tested at the latter was the prototype Arrow Active G-ABIX early in 1931 – later owned by Alex Henshaw, see Chapter Two. Bill succeeded Neville Stack* as test pilot for the Air Disposal Company's engine division; he was retained to test Cirrus, and possibly Nimbus, variants. From March 1931 came a string of short-lived positions: instructor at the Southern Aero Club at Shoreham, a sales post with Brooklands Aviation at Sywell (while part-time instructing at the Northampton Aero Club), charter pilot for Brian Allen Aviation at Croydon, likewise for Birkett Air Service at Heston.*

FLT LT SIDNEY ALBERT THORN – always known as 'Bill' – joined Avro as a test pilot under 'Sam' Brown* in 1934. With 'Tommy' Tomkins* as co-pilot, Bill had the honour of taking a prototype of huge importance to Avro, and a legend in aviation, the Anson, for its 25-minute first flight on 24th March 1935. (Tommy had flown the first of two Type 652s for Imperial Airways in January 1935 – this design formed the basis for the 'Annie'.) See under the section on Tommy for a reason why Bill was given the first flight of the Anson. After the Anson debut Bill settled down to the unrelenting task of signing off Avro output as the war approached and materialised. In July 1939, Bill was the co-pilot when Sam took the prototype Manchester for its maiden flight from Ringway and he was P2 to his boss again in November 1941 for the first outing of the Bristol Hercules-engined Lancaster prototype. One of Bill's duties during the early years of the war was to organise Local Defence Volunteers for the airfield, more often known as the Home Guard. For this Bill was bestowed with the rank of major and increasingly 'Major' became a new nickname for him!

Sam Brown retired in the spring of 1945 and Bill took his place as CTP and he prepared for the Tudor 1 four-engined airliner ordered by BOAC. 'Jimmy' Orrell was co-pilot to Bill for the first flight of G-AGPF from Woodford on 14th June 1945. The type needed considerable modifications to cure longitudinal instability, behaviour up to and beyond the stall and a myriad other necessary alterations and a string of 'tweaks' requested by the customer. In April 1947 BOAC abandoned the Tudor and long before the term was coined, Avro was left with a lot of 'white tails'. In parallel with the Tudor 1, BOAC had requested a high-capacity version, the Tudor 2, with the fuselage diameter increased by 12in and stretched by 26ft 1in. This made for a radically different aircraft and it was the longest British type at the time. Sam and Jimmy piloted the prototype, G-AGSU, in May 1946. With a stretch of 6ft, the Tudor 4 was produced for British South American Airways and Bill flew the first of these, G-AHNJ, on 9th April 1947.

On August 23, 1947 Bill prepared to take Tudor 2 *Sierra-Uniform* for a test with a crew of three and a trio of keen

A charming portrait of 'Bill' Thorn is his favourite 'office' – an Anson. The grin is for the photographer, friend and colleague Alex 'Sandy' Jack. *Avro*

passengers: Roy Chadwick CBE, Avro's visionary designer; Stuart Davies, his nominated successor; and Sir Roy Dobson, the company's indomitable boss. An important telephone call pulled Dobson back to the flight office and the sortie continued without him. Bill put the throttles forward and the airliner climbed into the air and banked to starboard, violently. It cartwheeled, the fuselage broke in two places and the wreck plummeted into a large pond. Miraculously, FTE Eddie Talbot and Stuart Davies survived; Thorn and Sqn Ldr David Wilson drowned in the cockpit, Roy Chadwick and radio operator John Webster both died of fractured skulls.

During maintenance, G-AGSU's ailerons had been rigged wrongly – starboard down on the control wheel produced 'up' and the opposite to port. Before he could establish this cross-over, Bill's control inputs put the Tudor into an ever-deepening roll. The stretched fuselage meant that a visual check from the cockpit to see that the ailerons were working as they should be was not possible; this could only be done with help from ground crew, physically signing 'starboard aileron down' etc.

Everyone at Woodford was stunned; the loss of the flight crew was grievous enough, but Roy Chadwick was synonymous with Avro – a giant of his time. Among Chadwick's last work had been sketches confirming the delta configuration of what would become the Vulcan. The Tudor 2 never recovered from this tragedy and was a rare dismal failure for Avro. A Bristol Hercules-engined version of the Tudor 2, the Tudor 7 – Bill's last 'first' in April 1946 – did not alter the type's image; only one was built.

Flt Lt Sidney Albert Thorn was 46 when he died. He had at least 5,500 hours to his name. He was succeeded by 'Jimmy' Orrell. In *Flight* magazine for 28th August 1947, Sir Roy

Dobson wrote that Bill: "...our chief test pilot, was one of the first in the country, with long and varied experience – steady and enthusiastic. As a friend I feel his loss extremely deeply."

The prototype Anson, K4771, first flown on 24th March 1935.
Peter Green Collection

The one-off Tudor 7, G-AGRX, first flown by 'Bill' Thorn on 17th April 1946.
Bristol Siddeley

Peter Tisshaw

10 Jul 1948	BP Balliol T.2 VW897
	1 x 1,245hp RR Merlin 35

Kingsley Peter Henry Tisshaw, born 1923. Joined the RAF in 1941 and trained in the USA. He returned and instructed at several venues. In 1945 he took part in a training delegation to Turkey, returning to Britain in January 1947.

PETER TISSHAW joined Boulton Paul at Pendeford in August 1947 as assistant to CTP Lindsay Neale*. Peter took the first Merlin-powered Balliol, T.2 VW897, on its maiden flight in July 1948. The variant was found to suffer so-called 'reversal' of the elevator at high speed. On 3rd February 1949 Lindsay *and* Peter took VW897 up for stability trials. During a high speed dive the port windscreen collapsed and the entire canopy was wrenched from the airframe. It would seem that both pilots were incapacitated and the Balliol crashed at Coven, near Wolverhampton. Robert Lindsay Neale (37) and Kingsley Peter Henry Tisshaw (25) were killed instantly.

'Tommy' Tomkins

7 Jan 1935	Avro Type 652 G-ACRM
	2 x 270hp AS Cheetah V

FLT LT FRANK B 'TOMMY' TOMKINS, described in Harald Penrose's *Architect of Wings* as "ex-Armstrong", joined Avro as a test pilot during 1930, as assistant to 'Sam' Brown*. On 30th October 1930 Tommy, one of three passengers, boarded Imperial Airways Handley Page W.8 G-EBIX at Le Bourget, Paris, bound for Croydon. The aircraft encountered fog and crashed near Boulogne. Two members of the crew and a passenger perished in the impact, another passenger died in hospital. Despite being badly injured, Tommy crawled a mile to raise the alarm. The only survivors, Tommy and the Imperial Airways Captain, J J Flynn, each had to have a leg amputated.

With his boss in Chile delivering an Avro 626 trainer, ironically Tommy was detailed to make the first flight of a twin-engined four-passenger charter aircraft for Imperial Airways, the Type 652. Designer Roy Chadwick had come up with a clean-looking cabin twin with retractable undercarriage and at the same time realised it had great military potential. After

The second Avro Type 652, G-ACRN Avatar *on early air test; March 1935.*
Peter Green Collection

engine runs on 6th January 1935, Tommy carried out a series of 'straights' in G-ACRM the following day, then took it for a brief test flight. Afterwards he noted: "She is so directionally stable, even with feet off the rudder pedals..." adding "She flies much like the old 504". Tests of the Type 652 went well, but the Imperial Airways order remained at just the pair. But this had spurred the creation of the Anson and when 'Jimmy' Orrell* flew the last example in May 1952 production had reached a staggering 11,020 examples.

On 11th March 1935 Sam Brown, back from his adventures over the Andes, and Tommy delivered both of the Type 652s, G-ACRM *Avalon* and G-ACRN *Avatar* to Imperial Airways at Croydon. Sam, with minimal experience of retractable undercarriage, disgraced himself when his machine *slid* to a halt, having omitted to wind the gear down. Thankfully, the undercarriage retracted in such a way that about a third of the mainwheels projected below the line of the engine nacelles to provide a 'buffer' on just such an occasion. This must have helped in many an absent-minded landing in Ansons over the next three decades! This faux pas *may* explain why, 13 days later, Bill Thorn captained the first flight of the prototype Anson, with Tommy as his co-pilot, whereas Sam would ordinarily have presided over the occasion. After this maiden flight, references to Tommy dry up.

Graham Tomlinson

Graham J Tomlinson, born 1950. Learned to fly with Bristol University Air Squadron at Filton on DHC Chipmunk T.10s from 1968. Joined the RAF in 1971 and from 1974 was flying HS Harrier GR.1s with 3 Squadron at Wildenrath, West Germany. Flt Lt Tomlinson graduated from ETPS Course No.37 at Boscombe Down 1978 and the following year was posted 'across the ramp' to A&AEE. In 1982 he was detached to the Naval Air Test Center at Patuxent River, Maryland, USA on the AV-8B Harrier II programme. He was flight commander of 1417 Flight in Belize during 1985 flying Harrier GR.3s.

SQN LDR GRAHAM J TOMLINSON, nicknamed 'GT' by test pilots on both sides of the Atlantic, took up the post of test pilot at British Aerospace Dunsfold in January 1986, becoming CTP in 1994, taking over from Chris Roberts*. With project pilot Rod Frederikson in the rear seat, Graham flew the first Harrier T.8, ZB605. from Dunsfold on 27th July 1994. The T.8 was the Fleet Air Arm version of the RAF two-seat conversion trainer T.4. With the closure of Dunsfold in September 2000, Graham transferred to Warton, taking up the role of CTP Strike and STOVL. He headed westwards in April 2002, as Lead STOVL test pilot on the Joint Strike Fighter programme at Lockheed Martin, Fort Worth, Texas, USA. There Graham became the fourth pilot, and the first British pilot, to fly the F-35A on 28th May 2008. The following month, he took the first F-35B STOVL, BF-1, variant on its maiden flight on 11th June 2008. Graham retired in late 2010.

Stephen Trower

FORMER RNAS and Fleet Air Arm Lt Stephen H G Trower had joined Fairey at the Great West Aerodrome, Harmondsworth under CTP Chris Staniland* by 1934. On 6th June 1935 Chris first flew the Fantôme single-seat fighter aimed at a Belgian Air Force requirement. Stephen flew the prototype, by then civil registered G-ADIF, to Evère to take part in demonstrations and a ministry competition. On approach to a landing on 17th July 1935 the Fantôme crashed, killing Lt Stephen H G Trower.

Brian Trubshaw

30 Jun 1967	BAC One-Eleven 500 G-ASYD
	2 x 12,500lbst RR Spey 25 Mk.512
9 Apr 1969	BAC/Sud Concorde 002 G-BSST
	4 x 35,080lbst RR/SNECMA Olympus 593

André Turcat (left) with Brian Trubshaw in the cockpit of Concorde 001, F-WTSS, at Toulouse, 1969. *British Aerospace*

Notes: One-Eleven first flew from Hurn; Concorde from Filton.

Ernest Brian Trubshaw, born 1924. Aged ten, Brian witnessed an aircraft land close to his home on the beach at Pembrey, south Wales. He later learned that this was Flt Lt E H 'Mouse' Fielding on a 'recce' for a visit by the Prince of Wales. Brian's first flight was in a Blackburn Shark at Worthy Down in 1938 when he was a member of the Winchester School Officers Training Corps. He joined the RAF in August 1942, training in the USA. He returned to Britain in December 1943, and flew Vickers Wellingtons at an operational training unit before a posting to 46 Squadron, equipped with Short Stirling V transports, at Stoney Cross in early 1945, converting to Douglas Dakotas from February 1946. He joined the King's Flight in September 1946 flying Vickers Vikings and, briefly, Sikorsky Hoverflies. The King's Flight was commanded by Air Cdre 'Mouse' Fielden and also on the unit was 'Jock' Bryce. Brian's final RAF posting was to the Empire Flying School at Hullavington.*

BRIAN TRUBSHAW joined Vickers at Brooklands and Wisley on 1st May 1950. In his autobiography, *Brian Trubshaw – Test Pilot*, he notes that the salary was £1,200 which was up on what the RAF had been paying – £900 – although that was 'all-in'. (The Vickers salary would be about £36,000 in present-day values.) CTP was 'Mutt' Summers* at the time of Brian's appointment but in 1951 he retired and 'Jock' Bryce became Brian's boss – the two having served together on the King's Flight. Straight off, in May 1950, Brian flew a Vickers Valetta as support ship to a tour of the Middle East by Mike Lithgow* in a Supermarine Attacker. (Vickers had acquired the Supermarine as far back as 1928.) Later in the year Brian flew an Avro Lincoln out of Wisley on trials of the Vickers air-to-ground TV-guided weapon, the Blue Boar. Other weapons work included the huge Vickers Red Dean air-to-air missile, which was launched from English Electric (EE) Canberra B.2 WD935; trials began in January 1954.

The production standard Viscount prototype was Series 700 G-AMAV which was first flown by Mutt, with Jock as co-pilot, from Brooklands on 28th August 1950. Squeezed in behind them, as a supernumerary, was Brian and he found the experience exceptionally informative about maiden flight procedure, particularly the relative roles of a two-pilot test crew. Jock and Brian shared most of the development flying of the Series 700. Just prior to his retirement, Mutt captained the first flight of the Valiant prototype, WB210, from Wisley on 18th May 1951 with Jock alongside him. Jock and Brian crewed up in WB210 for the first time on 20th June and Brian went solo on it on the 24th. As with the Viscount, the pair handled the bulk of the Valiant trials work.

During 1952 Brian was involved in Valiant 'special' weapon release trails from RAE Farnborough, dropping inert 10,000lb Blue Danube nuclear bombs. During the tests, the Valiant was taxied to a special area at Farnborough, where the weapon could be loaded behind screens. On these sorties Brian flew up to the Suffolk coast for a drop off the coast at Orfordness. On 30th July 1952 as Brian was en route to Orfordness he felt a lurch within the fuselage. Inspection by an FTO revealed that the Blue Danube had detached from the shackles and was resting on the closed bomb doors! Brian steered the Valiant to the Thames estuary, dropped the weapon and made an emergency landing at Manston. The bomb doors were badly buckled. Brian helped to develop a special tight turn 'escape' manoeuvre for the Valiants engaged in testing Britain's first hydrogen bombs near Christmas Island in the Pacific in May 1957: he also put in a lot of air time on in-flight refuelling development on Valiants.

With the setting up of the British Aircraft Corporation in 1960, Jock was appointed as CTP for the entire combine and Brian became CTP of the Weybridge division. By this point the Vanguard was in production and in June 1962 Jock took the VC-10 into the skies – with Brian as co-pilot- with the Super VC-10 following it in May 1964. Jock flew the first One-Eleven twin-jet in August 1963; this was destined to be the mainstay for 'Vickers' to the end of the 1980s. Brian was deeply involved in all three development programmes. Returning to Brian's autobiography, he recorded that by the late 1960s: "strength at Wisley and Hurn peaked at 35 pilots,

The first production One-Eleven 500, G-AVMH for British European Airways, was first flown from Hurn on 7th February 1968. *BAC*

most of whom were training captains in order to cope with the size of the [One-Eleven] programme." On 30th June 1967 Brian captained the prototype 'Super' One-Eleven, G-ASYD, with Roy Radford* as co-pilot.

By this stage the Concorde programme was gaining in momentum and the input of its pilot-to-be became increasingly important. On 5th August 1965 Brian was appointed as General Manager of Flight Operations for Filton and Weybridge (which included the One-Eleven facility at Hurn). Filton would be the venue for the first flight of British-assembled Concordes, but was wholly unsuitable for testing. Brian studied other possible sites and settled on Fairford and began turning it into the test centre: at its peak there were 500 personnel working there. Brian's title changed with promotion, he became Director of Flight Test and CTP. To prepare him for this task, Brian flew a variety of aircraft: EE Lightning T.4 XL629 of ETPS at Farnborough; a Vulcan B.2 from A&AEE, Boscombe Down; a Hawker Hunter from RAE Farnborough;

the BAC 221 and Handley Page HP.115 with Aero Flight at RAE Thurleigh; a French Air Force Dassault Mirage IV seconded to Sud Aviation at Toulouse, France; and a Convair B-58 Hustler at Edwards Air Force Base, California, USA.

Although both test teams – British and French – had long agreed to remain separate for at least the early, high-risk, flights, Sud Aviation (Aérospatiale from January 1970) CTP André Turcat invited Brian in to the cockpit of 001 F-WTSS for the initial taxi trials at Toulouse in August 1968. The Concorde programme broke with most British developmental procedure as the prototypes were what today would be called proof-of-concept items with pre-production airframes providing the bridge to production standard. (The English Electric Lightning had pioneered this approach – see Roland Beamont.) André Turcat and his team took 001 for its 42-minute maiden flight from Toulouse on 2nd March 1969. On 001's fifth sortie – 21st March – Brian took the co-pilot's seat, providing him with enormous experience ready for the big moment at Filton.

Concorde 002 G-BSST at its flight test centre, Fairford, 1970. *BAC*

On 6th April 1969 taxying commenced on 002 G-BSST. (The specially-granted out-of-sequence civil registration – a rare thing in 1960s – stood for: 'Great Britain's Super Sonic Transport.) For a long time before this, the aircrew had gone through the pre-flight, systems, emergency procedures and countless other checks and had put in a vast number hours in simulators and procedure rigs. Including going through the status of all of the monitoring stations, the pre-flight check list took an hour to read through. Brian had decided that there would come a moment during fast taxying when the team would decide that all was ready and that the next time 002 ventured on to Filton's runway would be for a one-way trip to Fairford. It was on 9th April 1969 that all the heads nodded and the nearby A38 road was closed to traffic ready for take-off. Brian captained G-BSST with John Cochrane* as co-pilot; Brian Watts, flight engineer; Roy Lockhart, navigator; John Allan senior FTO and Mike Addley and Peter Holding as FTOs. The 22-minute sortie was not without its difficulties, *both* radio altimeters failed as 002 engaged the instrument landing system at Fairford; Brian and John having to 'eyeball' the touchdown. Thanks to his previous experience on 001 this was a *British* maiden flight, but not a 'first-first'. Brian was already aware of the somewhat alarming view forward when the 'droop snoot' was lowered. On the prototypes it dropped to 17½-degrees which Brian wrote "was rather like looking over a precipice as there was no reference in front of one's eyes", the droop was standardised at 12.5-degrees. *Sierra-Tango's* second flight took place on 16th April. In June, 001 and 002 both displayed at the Paris airshow at Le Bourget.

It was not until 17th December 1971 that another Concorde had its maiden flight – 01 G-AXDN stopped the traffic again on the A38 on its trip to Fairford. *Delta-November* was the third of six aircraft used in the extensive 6½ year testing programme that preceded Concorde's entry into airline service. In April 1974, in a sortie out of Tangier, 01 reached Mach 2.23 (1,450 mph), and in November of the same year it flew from Fairford to Bangor, Maine, in 2 hours 56 minutes, a record for a commercial aircraft crossing the Atlantic in a westerly direction. (G-AXDN is today preserved at Duxford.)

A marketing tour in the summer of 1972 took it on a 12-country excursion, including Singapore, Japan and Australia. South Africa was its next overseas venue in early 1973 for 'hot and high' trials at Johannesburg. Back in the UK, G-BSST switched from the tropical to testing the de-icing system. These were conducted by flying behind tanker-configured Canberra B2/8 hybrid WV787 of A&AEE Boscombe Down. The test schedule for 002 was completed on 10th April 1975 when it was put into temporary storage at Fairford while the debate about its final resting place was finalised. Presented to the Science Museum, 001 was to become the centre piece of a major new display hall at the Fleet Air Arm Museum, Yeovilton. With Brian at the controls, G-BSST touched down at Yeovilton for the 438th and final time on 4th March 1976, completing 723½ flying hours, 173½ of which had been at beyond the speed of sound.

Fifty-three days before *Sierra-Tango's* last flight, the type's commercial life had begun with a simultaneous inauguration by Air France and British Airways from Charles de Gaulle and

Brian Trubshaw leading the way down the steps of Concorde 002 at Fairford on 7th August 1969. Behind him is Sir George Edwards, the British Aircraft Corporation supremo, who had just become the first non-flight test member to fly (as P2) 002. *BAC*

Heathrow airports, respectively. The tenth and final British-assembled Concorde and the last of the combined production run of 20, G-BFKX, had its maiden flight at Filton on 20th April 1979 and it was delivered to British Airways in June 1980. (See Chapter Four, *Airbuses to Puddle-jumpers*, for insights into the Concorde certifications process.)

From 1977 Brian was project director on the first phase of the Vickers VC-10 tanker conversion programme for the RAF. Brian, Peter Baker* and John Cochrane ferried nine examples to Filton and Roy Radford carried out the maiden flight of the first K.2 in June 1982. In 1980 Brian was appointed as Director and General Manager of Filton, with Roy Radford taking on the role of CTP in 1981. Brian and Roy flew the final flight of the pre-series Concorde 202, G-BBDG, on 24th December 1981, bringing it to Filton for storage: it was the last sortie by a development airframe. (*Delta-Golf* was moved by road to Brooklands in 2004.)

Brian retired from British Aerospace in 1986 and he helped Wensley Haydon-Baillie to establish his exceptional private collection of 'Concordalia'. He also had a long association with aerospace design specialists SAC Ltd and became a director of A J Walter (Aviation) Ltd, among other posts. As well as his autobiography *Brian Trubshaw Test Pilot*, written with Sally Edmondson in 1998, Brian also penned *Concorde – The Inside Story* in 2000. Ernest Brian Trubshaw CBE MVO died on 25th March 2001, he was 77.

John Turner

26 Aug 2004	BAE Systems Nimrod MRA.4 ZJ516
	4 x 15,500lbst RR BR710 Mk.101

John Turner, born 1952. Gained his private pilot's licence aged 17 through an Air Training Corps scholarship. Joined the RAF in 1972 and from 1980 flew McDonnell Phantom FGR.2s with 92 Squadron at Wildenrath, West Germany. Graduated from ETPS Course No.45 at Boscombe Down, 1986. John was posted to RAE Farnborough, commanding the Experimental Flying Squadron.

RETIRING from the RAF, Sqn Ldr John Turner joined the team at British Aerospace Warton in September 1990. He worked initially as a lead pilot on the Panavia Tornado ADV, moving to the Eurofighter Typhoon programme in 1992. John was appointed as Project Pilot on the Nimrod MRA.4 in April 2000 and in 2003 succeeded Al McDicken* as BAE Systems CTP Nimrod MRA.4 and Strategic Aircraft. The MRA.4 was the replacement for the Nimrod MR.2 maritime reconnaissance aircraft, with entirely new systems, engines, wing and a host of other changes. MR.2 airframes were used as the basis for each MRA.4, but effectively the programme was producing a new aircraft. With John as captain and Bill Ovel as co-pilot, Paul Bayley as FTE and Harry Nockolds as mission crew manager, the prototype MRA.4 PA01 ZJ516 was first flown from Woodford on 26th August 2004. (This machine started life as MR.1 XV234 at Woodford in 1969, later being upgraded to MR.2 status.) The two-hour flight was a resounding success and ended at Warton, the flight test centre for the project. John's 'beat' extended to the BAe ATP and HS.146 and RJ airliners at Woodford and by 2009 unmanned aerial vehicles (UAVs) were also part of his remit. John piloted the BAE Systems Mantis twin-turboprop 'pusher' configured technology UAV demonstrator ZK210 on its debut at Woomera, Australia, on 21st October 2009. (See Chapter Six in Volume One for more on BAE Systems UAV programmes.) John Turner retired in March 2010 and was succeeded by Paul Stone*.

On 10th March 2010 the Ministry of Defence accepted the fourth Nimrod MRA.4 at Woodford and the type was cleared to commence training crews, which initially took place at Warton. On 19th October 2010 the whole MRA.4 projected was terminated in the government's Strategic Defence Review. By the spring of 2011 all traces of the project had gone from Woodford. It was horrifically over budget and long delayed, an example of how a requirement can be strangled from birth by naive procurement expectations, political 'salami-slicing' and air force officers of stratospheric rank pleasantly 'lost' in the 'system'. Along with the MRA.4, the RAF's Nimrod MR.2 fleet was also axed and an island nation found itself without a dedicated maritime patrol capability.

Charles Turner-Hughes

25 Jun 1934	AW Scimitar G-ACCD
	1 x 640hp AS Panther VII
6 Dec 1936	AW AW.29 K4299
	1 x 920hp AS Tiger VIII
24 Jan 1938	AW Ensign G-ADSR
	4 x 850hp AS Tiger VIII
20 Mar 1940	AW Albemarle P1360
	2 x 1,590hp Bristol Hercules XI
2 Mar 1945	AW AW.52G RG324
	glider

Notes: Scimitar flown from Whitley Abbey; AW.29 and AW.52G from Baginton; Ensign and Albemarle from Hamble.

Charles Keir Turner-Hughes, born 1908. Joined the RAF in 1926 and flew Gloster Grebe IIs and later Armstrong Whitworth Siskin IIIAs with 56 Squadron at Biggin Hill. Charles became commander of 'A' Flight. His next posting was to 24 Squadron at Northolt, flying a variety of types on communications duties, including Westland Wapitis. In 1931 he was offered the post of CFI of the Aero Club of New York, but this was short-lived as the depression in the USA brought the job to an end. From New York, Charles moved to Kingston, Jamaica, to become the Chief Pilot of Caribbean Airways. Flying a Liberty-engined Vickers biplane flying-boat at night, the nose section partially collapsed and the aircraft was wrecked as Charles force-landed into the sea – he was picked up. Returning to Britain, Charles took the job of chief aerobatic pilot with the Sir Alan Cobham National Aviation Day 'flying circus', performing in DH Tiger Moth G-ABUL for £25 a week. At the end of the 1932 season, the 'circus' moved to South Africa for a two-month tour. Armstrong Whitworth lent AW XVI fighter demonstrator G-ABKF for the tour and so that it could be demonstrated to the SAAF. Throughout the tour, it was flown by Charles. On return, Armstrong Whitworth requested Charles to display another Type XVI, G-ACCD, at the SBAC airshow at Hendon in June 1933.*

As Charles Turner-Hughes (CTH) demonstrated Type XVI G-ACCD at the SBAC display at Hendon in June 1933, the company's general manager, S W Hiscocks, was watching and was very impressed. Hiscocks offered CTH a job and in October Charles joined Armstrong Whitworth (AW) at Whitley Abbey and, from 1936, Baginton. Charles was known as 'T-H' from his initials and also as 'Toc H', probably after the British-based charitable fellowship. When CTP Alan Campbell-Orde* retired in 1936, CTH took over.

His first 'first' was the much redesigned Type XVI, renamed as the Scimitar. The machine retained the registration of its predecessor, G-ACCD, so CTH had the odd experience of carrying out the maiden flight of an aircraft he *already* had in his logbook! Considerably rebuilt with a more powerful Armstrong Siddeley Panther, Scimitar G-ACCD was taken aloft by CTH on 25th June 1934. The Scimitar was a contender for Specification F7/30 which was ultimately won by the

Gloster Gladiator. An order for four was received from the Royal Norwegian Air Force and a licence production agreement was signed. The AW.29 was a two-seat day bomber aimed at Specification P27/32 but when the prototype was first flown by CTH on 6th December 1936 it was already six months behind the Fairey Battle, which convincingly won the contest. Having established the new factory and airfield at Baginton, embarked on testing the Whitley bomber and gearing up to build the Ensign airliner; the AW.29 was always going to be at the back of the queue. Early in K4299's testing a different pilot landed the prototype with the wheels retracted; it was not repaired and the project was quietly forgotten.

Designed to replace the venerable Handley Page HP.42s, the Ensign was the largest ever British airliner when it was rolled out at Hamble in the first days of 1938. (Whitley Abbey and Baginton were by then mass manufacturing Whitleys and spare capacity at associate company Air Service Training, was utilised.) Imperial Airways went on to order 14 of the 123ft span, 114ft length, 48,500lb all-up weight monsters. With Eric Greenwood* as co-pilot, CTH took prototype G-ADSR for several 'straights' on 24th January 1938 before lifting it off. From the moment the Ensign was in the air, the presence of Eric was revealed to be providential. The rudder was hugely heavy and it took both pilots straining on both sets of rudder pedals to counter the loading. After 15 minutes the exhausted pair brought the Ensign back to Hamble. With the rudder adjusted, CTH took G-ADSR into the air again two days later and he was able to observe for the first time the agonising 90 seconds required to raise the massive main undercarriage as he set course for Baginton. On G-ADSR's fourth flight, 8th March 1938, also with Eric alongside, at about 8,000ft all went very quiet – Britain's largest airliner had morphed into

Britain's largest glider. CTH at first steered towards Upper Heyford, but that would involve an into sun approach, so he casually turned and made an impressive 'dead-stick' landing on the all-grass flying field at Bicester. It was discovered that ambiguous fuel cock settings had deprived the Armstrong Siddeley Tigers of more than half the available fuel.

The Albemarle was obsolete before it was ready to enter production. It was conceived as a medium bomber using as many non-strategic materials as possible, including wooden structures, and to be modular in its design, allowing for major assemblies to be created by sub-contractors. Demands on the midlands plants of Armstrong Whitworth meant that the first two prototypes were built at Hamble. With its tricycle undercarriage, CTH wanted to get to know how P1360 behaved on the ground and in 'hops' as much as possible before he committed to a take-off. On one of the runs across Hamble on 20th March 1940 CTH realised that he'd left things far too late to apply the brakes and taxi back for another go. Pulling back manically on the control column he was amazed to find that he could only just claw P1360 into the air for a much-truncated circuit. Take-off performance was improved by extending the wing span by 10ft and testing was transferred to Baginton. A total of 602 Albemarles was built, the majority at Hucclecote.

As Whitley production tapered off, the Baginton plant built initially Bristol Hercules-engined Avro Lancasters from 1941 and later Packard-built Merlin-engined Mk.IIIs, amounting to 1,328 units up to 1945. Between them CTH and Eric Greenwood were responsible for the testing of the bulk of Whitley and Lancaster output. Before Lancaster production really ramped up, the pair also commuted down to Hucclecote to help out signing off Gloster-built Hurricanes. A subsidiary factory assembling Lancaster IIs was set up at Sywell and on

Scimitar G-ACCD in the line up at the 1934 SBAC display at Hendon. *Ray Davies Collection*

The one-off AW.29 K4299, 1937. *KEC*

12th August 1942 CTH tested the first example, DS601, from the new production line. It was while testing an AW-built Lancaster that CTH had a close shave. A flock of plovers collided with the Lancaster, at least one of the birds crashing through the windscreen and hitting CTH full in the face. Charles remembered coming around to find the FTE mopping his face, trying to revive him and get rid of copious amounts of blood. CTH had broken his nose in several places; he managed to put the Lancaster down on the ground safely, only to pass out again. Charles spent some time in hospital and suffered with sinus problems for the rest of his life: indeed: he cited problems with breathing and face masks as a reason for his early retirement.

CTH was seconded to both Boscombe Down and Farnborough during his tenure with AW. While flying de Havilland Mosquito IV DK327 at A&AEE on 24th September 1942 CTH believed he was selecting undercarriage 'down', instead he opened the bomb doors and was deeply embarrassed by the subsequent belly-landing. The Mosquito was repaired and returned to service. AW chief designer John Lloyd had for some time been studying laminar flow airfoils, particularly regarding his rapidly maturing concept for a flying-wing bomber. Between John's team and the National Physical Laboratory an 8ft section was devised and wind tunnel tested. A full-scale test-bed was then demanded and a new wing was devised and fitted to Hawker Hurricane II Z3687. This was extensively evaluated at RAE by many pilots, including CTH, from 1944 through to at least 1946.

As a stepping stone to the AW.52 flying-wing jet – see Eric Franklin and 'Jo' Lancaster – John Lloyd devised an all-wooden two-seat tail-less glider to gain experience of the concept. While construction of the AW.52G was going ahead, CTH went down to Portsmouth where he received tuition on an Airspeed Horsa assault glider from George Errington*. The AW.52G was towed aloft from Baginton for the first time on 2nd March 1945 behind the last Whitley built, Mk.V LA951 which had been retained by AW for trials work, and released at 12,000ft. Later RG324 was released at around 20,000ft; this gave CTH about 30 minutes of useful trials time.

The first Ensign, G-ADSR, dominating another Armstrong Siddeley group product. *British Airways*

Albemarle I V1599, served as the prototype for the ST.I transport version. *KEC*

Right: A poor, but fascinating photo of the laminar flow experimental Hurricane II, Z3687 which was flown by Charles Turner-Hughes at Farnborough, circa 1945. Note the roundels positioned well inboard of the wing; it is believed that this was to allow the remainder of the wing to remain finely polished to monitor airflow. *Peter Green Collection*

The AW.52G under tow, 1945. *Armstrong Whitworth*

Sinus problems got the better of CTH and he retired in April 1946, with over 7,000 hours and 158 types to his credit. He was succeeded by 'Midge' Midgley*. Charles Keir Turner-Hughes died in 1973, aged 65.

Peter Twiss

6 Oct 1954	Fairey FD.2 WG774
	1 x 9,500lbst RR Avon RA14R
20 Aug 1958	Fairey Gannet AEW.3 XJ440
	1 x 3,875shp AS Double Mamba 102

Notes: FD.2 flown from Boscombe Down, AEW.3 from Northolt.

Lionel Peter Twiss, born 1921. His initial attempt to join the Fleet Air Arm was turned down, but he succeeded in 1939. By 1941 he was with the Hawker Sea Hurricane-equipped 804 Squadron, attached to Catapult Armed Merchantmen – CAM Ships. He then spent time shore-based with 804's 'A' Flight at Gibraltar. Peter transferred to 807 Squadron, with Fairey Fulmars operating from HMS Ark Royal. He had not been with the ship long when it was torpedoed by a U-boat, sinking on 14th November 1941. Peter was airborne at the

time and landed at Gibraltar. Peter took part in Operation PEDESTAL, *the re-supply of Malta in August 1942, flying from HMS Argus and shot down an Italian Fiat CR.42. No.807 Squadron converted to Supermarine Seafire Is and in September 1942 was detached to HMS Furious during Operation TORCH, the invasion of Morocco and Algeria. Peter was detached to A&AEE Boscombe Down and involved in development flying with Fairey Fireflies and was posted to the British Air Mission in the USA. By 1944 he was with the Naval Fighter Interception Unit (746 Squadron) working alongside the RAF Fighter Interception Unit (FIU) at Ford. No.746 had Fairey Fireflies and operationally developing tactics. Peter managed to convert to FIU DH Mosquitos and took part in several intruder 'ops' prior to D-Day; he is credited with shooting down two Junkers Ju 88s. He graduated from ETPS Course No.3 at Boscombe Down in 1945 and was posted to the Naval Test Squadron at A&AEE.*

LT CDR PETER TWISS OBE DSC* joined Fairey in 1946, becoming DCTP to Gordon Slade*. Fireflies formed the bulk of the development and production test work, but on 19th

Peter Twiss, in 1956. *via Don Middleton*

September 1949 Gordon flew the prototype of the next money-spinner for Fairey, the Gannet shipborne anti-submarine patroller. Peter conducted the first deck landing trials in the prototype, VR546, on HMS *Illustrious* in July 1950. A major problem on the prototype was elevator authority and Peter fell foul of this while landing VR546 at White Waltham on 23rd August 1950. Getting the nose up was a problem, a heavy landing resulted and the nose leg collapsed. He was in good company, this had happened to his boss the previous November! Major 'surgery' was carried out to turn the Gannet into a replacement for the Douglas Skyraider AEW.1 airborne early warning radar picket. Peter flew the first Gannet AEW.3, XJ440, from Northolt on 20th August 1958. This was a 'bare shell' machine, acting as aerodynamic prototype as the installation of all the radar equipment and systems was a long and complex process. The first 'full' AEW.3, XL450 was flown on 31st January 1959. The last AEW.3 flew in April 1963, by which time Fairey had been a part of Westland for three years.

Peter was back on the *Ark Royal* in October 1957. The first example had been torpedoed almost from under him while Peter was flying a Fairey Fulmar of 807 Squadron in November 1941. He arranged to visit its replacement, which entered service in 1955, in a *very* different Fairey aircraft. Associated company Avions Fairey had built a series of light aircraft at Gosselies under the brand name Tipsy, after their designer Ernest Oscar Tips. Fairey had helped to market them in Britain and retained single-seat Tipsy Junior G-AMVP as a runabout. Talking to him in 2000, Peter explained that flying something that light and slow on to an aircraft carrier was "far trickier" but did not have the need for an arrester wire!

Sharing White Waltham with Fairey was ML Aviation which developed an inflatable wing aircraft, the Utility, for the British military between 1954 and 1958. Fairey PTP David Masters (see Chapter Seven) carried out much of the testing on behalf of ML before evaluation by A&AEE at Boscombe Down. In February 1958 Peter piloted the prototype, XK784, during two sessions and wrote a report on the curious aircraft. He managed reach the giddy heights of 150ft and noted that even when the machine was in its equivalent of a power-on dive, the airspeed indicator never exceeded 37mph! Talking to Peter in 2000 he was pleased that the author was not discussing the Fairey Delta Two and the world record – "I never escape that topic!" – and was very happy to tell of his experiences of the ML Utility. As a portable aeroplane, capable of being deployed in knocked-down state, aircrew rescue and 'special duties' were possible applications for the aircraft. Peter explained: "it was fun and challenging but the control responses were best measured with a calendar, not a stop-watch!" He added: "It was supposed to have a role as a modern-day Lysander, covertly dropping off personnel or picking them up. We had great difficulties to get it to carry anything more than the pilot and it was so loud, you could hear it coming a long, long time before it would appear."

Peter's world airspeed record in the Delta Two is the stuff of legend, but perhaps much more so is his airmanship on its 14th flight when its Avon turbojet famously ceased to function at 30,000ft and Peter brought it in for a 'dead-stick' landing at Boscombe Down. In his outstanding book *Faster than the Sun* Peter is self-effacing about the exploit: "I was awarded the Queen's Commendation for bringing us both back on that occasion, dented but otherwise unbowed. But the honest truth is that I brought the Delta back as much as a matter of self-preservation as anything else." He explained some of the personal attributes he summoned up that day: "An innate inquisitiveness, together with a lot of cussedness and plain everyday luck on the occasion of the dead-stick landing, saved us months of time in the development in the Delta. Had we lost the aircraft, we would have lost our clues at the same time."

Peter took over as CTP not long after Gordon Slade flew the Fairey Delta 1 in 1951. Other than their delta planform, the FD.1 and the FD.2 were unrelated, both intended to do *very* different things. Ignoring the major reconfiguration of the Gannet to become a radar picket, the FD.2 was the last fixed-wing Fairey design to see the light of day. Specification ER.103 was issued by the Ministry of Supply (*Faster than the Sun* explains that many pilots referred to this institution as the *Misery* of Supply!) for two supersonic research aircraft. Design and manufacture had to take second place to the Gannet programme which had been determined a 'super-priority' to combat the Soviet submarine menace. Much work was put into making the Delta Two a practical aircraft so that it could evolve into a fighter – English Electric achieved this spectacularly with the P.1 transforming into the Lightning. Peter took FD.2, WG774, for its maiden flight of 25 minutes from Boscombe Down on 6th October 1954 and was so pleased with it he flew it again the following day.

He was a 30,000ft on the 14th flight on 17th November 1954 when the fuel tank collapsed under pressure and the Rolls-Royce Avon went silent, never to re-light. With bearings supplied from

Fairey Delta 2 WG774 in celebratory world airspeed record breaker colours. *Fairey*

Boscombe, Peter elected to bring WG774 home. He broke through the cloud layer at 2,500ft six miles out from the airfield and perfectly lined up. There was not enough hydraulic pressure to completely deploy the undercarriage; only the nose wheel indicated a 'green' for locked and the 'droop snoot' was equally uncooperative. Peter went 'over the numbers' at the threshold at an estimated 265mph. The Delta slithered to a halt and Peter was unharmed. The wings from the 'iron bird' static test airframe were grafted on and WG774 was rebuilt in the jigs with several improvements, including strengthening the fuel tank system. It was back in the air in August 1955 and on 28th October went supersonic for the first time. In November WG774 sizzled along at Mach 1.56 which at 36,000ft was 1,028mph. The world airspeed record was held by the USA in a North American F-100C Super Sabre at a 'mere' 822mph. A fully promulgated record by WG774 would not just smash that wide open; it would add another 'magic' digit. While Peter was busy practicing and calibrating for the record attempt, he carried out the maiden flight of the second FD.2, WG777, from Boscombe Down on 15th February 1956. The record-breaking runs were made on 10th March at an average speed of 1,132mph or Mach 1.7. (As will be seen in the section on Godfrey Auty, WG774 was converted into the ogival delta wing test-bed BAC.221 in 1964. Both it and WG777 survive; at the Fleet Air Arm Museum, Yeovilton, and the RAF Museum, Cosford, respectively.)

With the acquisition of Fairey's aviation assets by Westland in 1960, Peter did not see a future for himself with the company. He turned instead to another love and still part of the Fairey Group – Fairey Marine. He took up a post in sales and development of a family of motor cruisers and power boats. In 1962 Peter had an on-screen part in the 1963 Bond, James Bond film *From Russia with Love*. All of the vessels in the famed boat chase were Fairey Marine craft and the closest boat in hot pursuit of Sean Connery and Daniela Bianchi was captained by Peter Twiss.

In the year that *From Russia with Love* was released (1963) Peter's book *Faster than the Sun* was published; a new edition appeared in 2000 and it remains 'must read' material. Peter left Fairey Marine in 1988, continuing to sail and to fly gliders. Lt Cdr Peter Twiss OBE DSC* died on 31st August 2011, aged 90.

Third production Gannet AEW.3 XL451 during deck landing trials on HMS Victorious in May 1959. *Bristol Siddeley*

Jack Tyler

DE HAVILLAND'S chief engineer at Stag Lane, Jack Tyler, learned to fly at the in-house flying school in 1927. Early in 1932 he was appointed by CTP Hubert Broad as an assistant test pilot as his experience with the 'spanner' would provide invaluable insight. Tragically, Jack was killed testing a DH Moth on 28th April 1932. It seems that a locking pin in the wings was not correctly seated and the wings folded in flight.

Geoffrey Tyson

7 Jun 1946	Short Sturgeon RK787 2 x 2,080hp RR Merlin 140
16 Jul 1947	Saro SR.A/1 TG263 2 x 3,230lbst Metropolitan-Vickers Beryl F2/4
22 Aug 1952	Saro Princess G-ALUN 10 x 2,500shp Bristol Proteus 2

Notes: The Sturgeon first flew from Rochester, the SR.A/1 and the Princess from the waters off Cowes, Isle of Wight.

Geoffrey Arthur Virley Tyson, born 1907. Initially training to be an estate agent, he joined the RAF in 1925. He was CFI with the Maidstone Aero Club at West Malling from 1930, moving on to the Scarborough Aero Club in 1932. Geoffrey took the role of chief aerobatic pilot for Sir Alan Cobham's* National Aviation Day touring 'flying circus' in 1933, taking over from Charles Turner-Hughes*. On 7th July 1933 Geoffrey and four passengers in DH Fox Moth G-ABWF had a lucky escape while pleasure flying at Limerick, Ireland, when a curious Irish pilot flew too close and collided with G-ABWF's underside. The Fox Moth's undercarriage was whipped off; Geoffrey executed a successful belly landing. The two occupants of the other aircraft, DH Moth EI-AAI were killed.

GEOFFREY TYSON left the National Aviation Day organisation in 1934 to fly as a test pilot with Avro at Woodford, under CTP 'Sam' Brown*. Geoffrey flew the first production Anson I, K6152, on the last day of 1935. That machine was destined for a life of trials, but the next one, K6153, was taken on charge by 48 Squadron at Manston on 6th March 1936, beginning the transformation of maritime reconnaissance for the newly-formed Coastal Command. The link that had been established with Sir Alan Cobham* during Geoffrey's stint with the National Aviation Day travelling 'circus' was renewed is 1937 when Geoffrey took up a pioneering role with Flight Refuelling Ltd (FRL). This work required exacting flying skills that could certainly be described as 'test piloting' and the development of in-flight refuelling in Britain, and Geoffrey's part in it, is dealt with in Chapter Three.

Personal connections continued to play a major role in the direction of Geoffrey's career. During the trials with FRL, Geoffrey met with Shorts CTP John Lankester Parker* (JLP) and in September 1939 he moved to Rochester to help the great man with the expanding work on Sunderlands and Stirlings. Geoffrey spent the bulk of his time testing the output from the Short & Harland factory at Sydenham, Belfast, along with 'Pip' Piper* and George Wynne-Eyton*. Geoffrey flew on a raid to Cassel, Germany, in a Stirling captained by Wg Cdr 'Bobby' Gilmour to gain an appreciation of how the manufacturer could help the men of Bomber Command. On 14th December 1944 Geoffrey was co-pilot to JLP when the prototype Shetland, DX166, had its maiden flight from the River Medway. The veteran JLP retired in 1945 and Geoffrey succeeded him as Shorts CTP. From 1943 Shorts had had been designing a twin-engined torpedo bomber for the Fleet Air Arm, but as the war evolved it was revised as a strike fighter and by the time it came to production was a catch-all type with two versions, strike and target-tug. Geoffrey took the prototype Sturgeon into the air on 7th Jun 1946 – it was the last wholly new type to fly from Rochester – either the airfield or the Medway – as the company decamped to Belfast.

Geoffrey Tyson piloting the prototype Short Sturgeon, RK787, 1946.
Short Brothers and Harland

The prototype Saro SR.A/1, TG263, in its final form, 1948. *Saunders-Roe*

Launching Princess G-ALUN into the waters of the Medina, August 1952. *Saunders-Roe*

The liner of the skies, the Saro Princess, saluting more conventional vessels moored at Southampton. *Saunders-Roe*

As might be expected from having developed a close working relationship with JLP, Geoffrey was very much a 'flying-boat man' and he became a disciple of Short designer Arthur Gouge. In 1943 Arthur had taken up the post of Vice-Chairman of Saunders-Roe and set about the design of a massive passenger-carrying 'boat intended to re-ignite the hey-days of Imperial Airways and the Empire routes. This proved very tempting to Geoffrey and in 1946 he moved to East Cowes to take up the post of CTP for Saro as the company re-commenced original design.

Geoffrey's first prototype for Saro could not have been further away from the Empire flying-boat revival. The war in the Far East and the Pacific had thrown up a need for fighters that could operate without the need for scarce runways; Saro came up with a single-seat twin-jet flying-boat fighter. Specification E6/44 was written around this idea and three SR.A/1 prototypes were ordered. Geoffrey took the first one, TG263, off from the mouth of the Medina River off Cowes on 16th July 1947. He developed a quick reaction take-off technique, by retracting the wing floats as soon as the hull was up on the step, the drag was lowered considerably and the SR.A/1 could conduct the flying-boat equivalent of a scramble. TG263 caused a stir at the SBAC airshow at Farnborough that September but nowhere near as much as at the 1948 event when Geoffrey flew the third example, TG271, in a prolonged, low-level, inverted flypast. (Emulating the hallmark aerobatic manoeuvre performed by Geoffrey, and Charles Turner-Hughes before him, at the pre-war National Aviation Day displays, albeit in a Tiger Moth.)

By the late 1940s any practical use for the SR.A/1 had vaporised but trials and marketing continued. On 12th August 1949 an RAE Farnborough pilot was trying out TG271 off Cowes when it hit an object in the water which holed the hull and the jet turned over and sank. Geoffrey Tyson was in the safety boat and he dived in to rescue the pilot – a very grateful Lt Cdr Eric 'Winkle' Brown! The following month, the second SR.A/1, TG267, crashed killing its MAEE pilot, through no fault of the aircraft. The first example, TG271 flew intermittently until the middle of 1951 – today it is on show at Solent Sky, Southampton.

By 1950 the 209ft 6in span, 190,000lb empty weight, *ten* turboprop (four coupled with contra-rotating propellers, two singles). pressurised, double-decker SR.45 flying-boat design was well advanced and construction of three prototypes began. British Overseas Airways Corporation showed 'interest' and much of the project seems to have been predicated on the airline buying the behemoths, no matter what. The first Princess, as the 'boat was called, was launched into the Medina on 21st August 1952 and flown for 30 uneventful minutes the following day. With Geoffrey on the flight deck was DCTP John Booth* and nine other personnel; they had completed the debut of the largest aircraft ever built in Britain. Geoffrey displayed G-ALUN at the SBAC airshow at Farnborough in 1952 and again in 1953. No orders materialised and the other two examples were never completed. *Uniform-November* flew 47 times and was mothballed in June 1954.

Geoffrey Arthur Virley Tyson OBE left Saro in 1955, taking up a post with Dunlop's Aviation Division before retiring in 1958: he died in 1987, aged 80.

Cyril Uwins

4 Sep 1918	Bristol Scout F1 B3989 1 x 200hp Sunbeam Arab
4 Feb 1919	Bristol Badger F3495 1 x 320hp ABC Dragonfly Ia
13 May 1919	Bristol Badger X K-110 1 x 230hp Siddeley Puma
28 Nov 1919	Bristol Babe 1 x 45hp Viale
Jun 1920	Bristol Bullet G-EATS 1 x 450hp Bristol Jupiter II
Jul 1920	Bristol Seely G-EAUE 1 x 240hp Siddeley Puma
21 Jun 1921	Bristol Ten-Seater G-EAWY 1 x 450hp Napier Lion
Jul 1922	Bristol Racer G-EBDR 1 x 510hp Bristol Jupiter
Nov 1922	Bristol Bullfinch J6901 1 x 425hp Bristol Jupiter III
13 Feb 1923	Bristol Taxiplane G-EBEW 1 x 120hp Bristol Lucifer
6 Aug 1924	Bristol Brownie G-EBJK 1 x 32hp Bristol Cherub I
5 Mar 1925	Bristol Berkeley J7403 1 x 650hp RR Condor III
5 May 1925	Bristol Badminton G-EBMK 1 x 510hp Bristol Jupiter VI
8 Jun 1925	Bristol Boarhound G-EBLG 1 x 425hp Bristol Jupiter IV
Nov 1925	Bristol 92 1 x 450hp Bristol Jupiter VI
17 May 1927	Bristol Bulldog 1 x 480hp Bristol Mercury IIA
15 Jul 1927	Bristol Bagshot J7767 2 x 450hp Bristol Jupiter VI
8 Aug 1927	Bristol 101 G-EBOW 1 x 450hp Bristol Jupiter VI
7 Sep 1928	Bristol 109 G-EBZK 1 x 480hp Bristol Jupiter VIII
25 Oct 1929	Bristol 110A G-AAFG 1 x 220hp Bristol Titan
22 Jan 1931	Bristol 118 G-ABEZ 1 x 590hp Bristol Jupiter XFA
8 Jun 1934	Bristol 133 R-10 1 x 640hp Bristol Mercury VIS.2
12 Jun 1934	Bristol 123 1 x 695hp RR Goshawk III
12 Apr 1935	Bristol 142 R-12 2 x 650hp Bristol Mercury VIS.2
11 May 1935	Bristol 138A K4897 1 x 500hp Bristol Pegasus PE6S
23 Jun 1935	Bristol Bombay K3583 2 x 750hp Bristol Pegasus IIIM3
20 Jan 1936	Bristol 143 R-14 2 x 500hp Bristol Aquila I
25 Jun 1936	Bristol Blenheim K7033 2 x 840 Bristol Mercury VIII
15 Oct 1937	Bristol 148 K6551 1 x 840hp Bristol Mercury IX
11 Feb 1938	Bristol 146 K5119 1 x 840hp Bristol Mercury IX
15 Oct 1938	Bristol Beaufort L4441 2 x 1,130hp Bristol Taurus VI
17 Jul 1939	Bristol Beaufighter R2052 2 x 1,400hp Bristol Hercules III
4 Feb 1943	Bristol Buckingham DX249 2 x 2,400hp Bristol Centaurus IV
4 Dec 1944	Bristol Brigand MX988 2 x 2,400hp Bristol Centaurus VII
2 Dec 1945	Bristol 170 G-AGPV 2 x 1,675hp Bristol Hercules 632

Cyril Frank Uwins, born 1896. He enlisted in the army in 1914, serving with the London Irish Rifles. Cyril transferred to the RFC in 1916 flying operationally over the Western Front with 13 Squadron (Royal Aircraft Factory BE.2s) and 64 Squadron (Royal Aircraft Factory FE.2s). His next posting was to the Royal Aircraft Factory at Farnborough and Cyril was involved in an accident, perhaps with a Nieuport, and he was badly injured, breaking his neck. After a spell in hospital during 1917 he began flying at the recently-formed 5 Aircraft Acceptance Park, Filton – establishing a link with the airfield that lasted for six decades.

WITH the greatest of respect to the remainder of the alphabet, we turn to the last of the 'big beasts'. The place that Cyril, occasionally 'Cy', Uwins held among his colleagues was emphasized by his nickname: 'Papa Uwins'. Already working at Filton – the venue for all of his maiden flights – Cyril was seconded to the British and Colonial Aeroplane Company (renamed the Bristol Aeroplane Company in 1920 but referred to here only as Bristol) on 24th October 1918, taking over following the death in the USA of 'Joe' Hammond*.

Cyril's first prototype was the Scout F1, the first of four, which had only the name in common with the single-seater flown by 'Harry' Busteed* back in February 1914. In the space of a fortnight in February 1919 Cyril faced two extremes of prototypes. The Badger, on the 4th, was a hopeful replacement for the F.2B Fighter and indeed was originally designated F.2C. On take off the engine failed and Cyril force landed the

Cyril Uwins, complete with his Irvin parachute, poses for the press before piloting a Blenheim I, circa 1938. *Bristol Aeroplane Co*

The Babe of 1919, the first of three. *British Aircraft Corporation*

Flt Lt Cyril Uwins joined Bristol as a civilian in May 1919 and he flew the Badger Experimental, soon referred to as the Badger X. Designer Frank Barnwell* created a very simple box-fuselage biplane with Badger wings which he wished to compare with models of the 'X' in the company's newly-installed wind tunnel to calibrate results. Nine days after Cyril put the Badger X through its maiden flight, Frank Barnwell, also a pilot, nosed it over and it was wrecked, never to be repaired. Cyril had no plans to fly the Babe single-seat sporting biplane on 28th November 1919, but while he was undertaking some 'straights' a flock of sheep wandered in the way and a maiden flight seemed a much more reasonable outcome. Cyril enjoyed the Babe, but it was a handful for a novice pilot – the intended market – and only three were completed.

With so many prototypes to his name, some of the aircraft 'first flighted' by Cyril need to be treated in the briefest manner. The Bullet was a one-off test-bed single seat biplane for the Jupiter engine which had been acquired by the company from the defunct Cosmos Engineering in 1920 – so founding the Bristol aero engine empire. The Seeley was a much redeveloped Tourer, itself a civilian version of the ubiquitous F.2B Fighter, with a single passenger carried behind the pilot in an enclosed cabin – it remained a one-off. The Ten-Seater did just that, a large biplane that could take nine passengers in

prototype, breaking its undercarriage and engine mount. For once it was not the fault of the notoriously unreliable ABC Dragonfly, there was an airlock in the fuel system. Four Badgers were built, but no production order was placed. On the 18th he was piloting the second Braemar triplane, Mk.II C4297, powered by four 400hp Liberty 12s – the first example had been flown by 'Freddy' Raynham* in August 1918.

The prototype Ten-Seater of August 1922. *Peter Green Collection*

The corpulent Racer boasted retractable main gear. *Rolls-Royce*

the cabin; two were built for civil purposes and a military troop-carrier or ambulance was evaluated as the Brandon.

The Bullfinch was a single-seat Jupiter-powered parasol monoplane single-seat fighter; the third example was completed as a two-seater with a gunner behind the pilot and an auxiliary wing attached to the lower fuselage. The Taxiplane was a small biplane with accommodation for two passengers side-by-side in front of the pilot; this found little appeal but a primary trainer version did, half-a-dozen being used by the Bristol school at Filton – 28 units in all were built. Three two-seat Brownies were built for the 1924 Light Aeroplane Trials at Lympne. The Berkeley was a two-seat day or night biplane bomber aimed at Specification 26/23 – three were produced. The Boarhound was another attempt to replace the F.2B in RAF service; it was further developed as the Beaver, but only four appeared. The Type 92 was a one-off biplane designed to investigate the cooling of radial engines and was given the unofficial name 'Laboratory'. Replacing the F.2B remained a holy grail and the Type 101 biplane was followed by the Type 118 capable of carrying out a wide range of roles and, as the Type 120, featured an enclosed gun turret. The Type 110A was a four-passenger biplane air taxi and the Type 109 a private-venture biplane intended for long-distance record-breaking: one of each was built. Types 146 and 148 were single-seat six-gun fighter and two-seat army co-operation prototypes, with one and two produced, respectively. Ignoring the BAC.221 ogival delta wing test-bed (see Godfrey Auty) and the Sycamore helicopter, these were the last single-engined Bristol types to see the light of day.

The second Bullfinch, J6902, during its service with RAE Farnborough. The '3' on the fuselage is its 'New Types' number for the Hendon display, June 1924. The aircraft behind also has a test pilot connection; it is the Handley Page W.8 G-EBIX in which 'Tommy' Tomkins had a miraculous escape – as a passenger – when it crashed in fog in October 1930. *Peter Green Collection*

The third Berkeley, J7405, at Filton in March 1926. *Bristol Aeroplane Co*

The one-off Badminton racer, 1925. *Peter Green Collection*

The prototype Bulldog, Filton, May 1927. *British Aircraft Corporation*

To showcase the Jupiter nine-cylinder engine a radical single-seat racer was conceived in 1922. It was initially to be called the Blizzard but the more pedestrian Racer was settled upon. The big radial was submerged within the fuselage, with a very large spinner allowing airflow into the engine for cooling and a bullet-like nose. The short span wing was fitted with full-span ailerons and the main undercarriage was

retractable. On the first flight, in July 1922, Cyril was in trouble as soon as he lifted off, the full-span ailerons were far too powerful and caused the thin wing to bend. A quick, very low-level circuit was accomplished. The wing was wire-braced for the second excursion but suddenly the fabric on the port wing was badly ripped and the pitot head on the leading edge of that wing had vanished. Another short circuit! While the Racer was being fitted with bracing wires, the huge spinner had received several coats of paint: this was sufficient to unbalance the plywood moulded structure and it had broken, damaging the wing surface and stripping off the pitot head as the debris departed. The ailerons were reduced in size, but by the seventh flight it was clear that the Racer was a step too far and it was quietly forgotten.

With over 400 built including export orders, the Bulldog single-seat fighter was a major success for Bristol. The prototype was flown on May 1927 and production continued through to 1935. A revised version, the Bullpup, failed to extend the programme. While calibrating speed-to-height in the one-off Bulldog IV with a Bristol Mercury IVS2, Cyril was the victim of what all pilots call 'finger trouble' – self-induced

Roy Fedden, the Bristol aero engine supremo, Cyril Uwins complete with electrically-heated flying suit and Rex Pierson, chief designer for Vickers. They are standing in front of Vickers Vespa G-ABIL, in which all three combined their talents in the altitude record of 16th September 1932. *via Tony Buttler*

wrongful selection, or lack of selection, of a switch, a setting, a lever... Having reached 27,000ft, Cyril put his mask on and selected oxygen. Before long, he blacked out; recovering to find the Bulldog had dropped 9,000ft. Up he went again, only to lose consciousness a second time. So Cyril did a physical check of all of the likely suspects: the first being that the oxygen was *on* all the time and that he'd turned it *off*. Not so, he'd hung his mask around his neck, but failed to connect the bayonet fitting to the supply pipe!

The Bagshot was a disaster for Bristol and underlined just how badly Air Ministry requirements could be devised. Responding to a need for a twin-engined monoplane fighter, the armament was not specified. Seven months after issuing the contract for a prototype and with construction well advanced, the weaponry was revealed as a pair of 37mm Coventry Ordnance Works cannon. These were so-called COW-guns, which fired a 1½lb shell, each gun weighed a cool 120lb, without its shell feed mechanism, magazine and mountings. Cyril took J7767 for its first flight in July 1927 and soon found that the wing flexed so much as to induce aileron reversal. Eventually the Ministry took on the one-off for structural testing: it never carried armament.

Under the title *Experimental Test Flying*, in 1929 Cyril gave a well-greeted lecture to the Royal Aeronautical Society and among the audience was Harald Penrose*, newly-appointed assistant test pilot at Westland. Cyril was manager and CFI of the Bristol Flying School at Filton, where Harald had learned to fly, and his mentor provided clarity about the assessment of fins and rudders, elevators and tailplanes; their relationship with one another and with dives and spins. The words were absorbed and appreciated by all attending, and those reading the post-talk write-up, because this was 'Papa Uwins' and he had been testing for over a decade at one of the largest and most respected manufacturers.

Carrying the B Condition (or 'trade-plate') identity R-10, the Type 133 at Filton, 1934. *Bristol Aeroplane Co*

Rare use of a non-Bristol engine – a Rolls-Royce Goshawk – on the unmarked Type 123 at Filton in June 1934. *Peter Green Collection*

Britain First, the Type 142 executive transport that gave rise to the Blenheim. *Bristol Aeroplane Co*

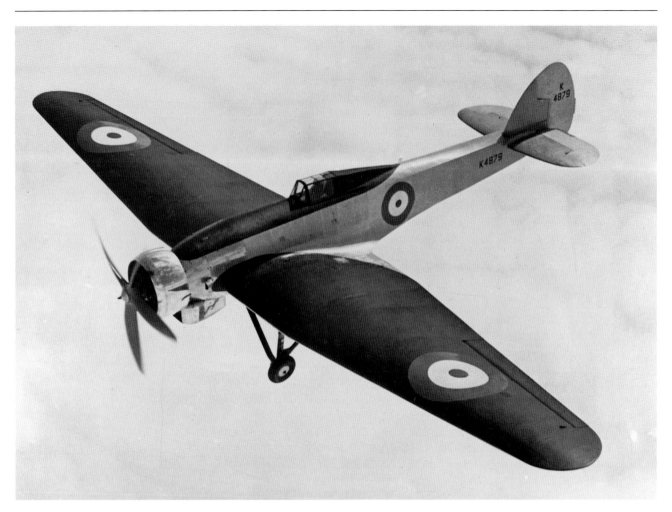

Above: The one-off high-flying Type 138A, K4897. *Bristol Aeroplane Co*

Left: Wearing the Hendon 'New Types Park' number '9', Type 130 – named Bombay in 1937 – K3583 in July 1935. *Peter Green Collection*

Below: With very significant differences from the Type 142, the Bristol 142M, the prototype Blenheim, K7033. *Bristol Aeroplane Co*

The first of two Type 148s, K6551, in October 1937. *Peter Green Collection*

At Brooklands, Vickers realised that its 50ft-span Vespa biplane had the ability – with the right engine – to have a crack at the world altitude record. In a superb example of co-operation among competitors, a supercharged Bristol Pegasus 'S' was fitted to G-ABIL. Roy Fedden of the Bristol engine division assisted the Vickers chief designer, Rex Pierson, with the installation and Bristol designer, Frank Barnwell, tackled much of the 'what if' mathematics of the project. There could only be one pilot for the job... Wearing an electrically-heated flying suit and with decidedly 'low-tech' Vaseline smeared over his face to fend off frost-bite, Cyril took G-ABIL to 43,976ft on 16th September 1932 to establish a new word record. This experience was put to good use in May 1935 when Cyril flew the Type 138A, a monoplane dedicated to high-altitude research. With Flt Lt M J Adam of RAE Farnborough at the helm, K4897 reached 53,937ft in a 95-minute climb on 30th June 1937.

Specification F7/30 called for an interceptor of considerably improved performance with the ultimately doomed Rolls-Royce Goshawk as the preferred powerplant. Bristol produced two very different private-ventures for this requirement, with Cyril taking both for their debut within four days of one another. Remarkably compact, the biplane Type 123 was derided by Cyril almost from the first flight and it was shelved. The Type 133 was more conventional-looking although the main undercarriage retracted into underwing spats. This flew well and was ready for despatch to Martlesham Heath for evaluation. 'Jock' Campbell* took the prototype up for spinning and dive trials on 8th March 1935 and he was lucky to parachute away from a spin. With one prototype rejected and the other wrecked in a field east of Filton, Specification F7/30 passed Bristol by.

By the middle of the following year the loss of this potentially lucrative fighter contract was forgotten. In yet another private-venture initiative the nation was about to gain an aircraft that contributed to giving Britain the edge in the coming war with Germany. Lord Rothermere of the *Daily Mail* heard that Barnwell was scheming a six-passenger high-speed twin-engined type for business use. The newspaper magnate

The Beaufort prototype, L4441, late 1938. *Bristol Aeroplane Co*

The first Beaufighter, R2052, at Filton in July 1939. *Bristol Aeroplane Co*

DX255, the second prototype Buckingham, 1943. *Bristol Aeroplane Co*

The second prototype Brigand, MX991, with torpedo under the centre section. *Bristol Aeroplane Co*

placed an order for the Type 142, which he named *Britain First* and Filton set to producing it and a larger version, the Type 143, that might attract Imperial Airways. It was the stuff of legend, the Air Ministry was far from put out; it could see the military application of such a machine and followed the project closely. 'Gerry' Sayer* flew the prototype of what became the Gloster Gladiator on 12th September 1934; this was the winner of the rethought Specification F7/30 – for which Bristol had proffered the ill-fated Type 123 and 133. When Cyril flew *Britain First* on 12th April 1935 it was soon clocking 50mph *faster* than the Gladiator – Britain's next generation fighter! In August 1935 an off-the-drawing-board order for 150 Type 142Ms was placed. The prototype Blenheim – one of the most versatile and prolific warplanes ever built – had its maiden flight in the hands of Cyril on 25th June 1936 and it transformed Bristol into a giant of the British aviation industry.

The Blenheim set Bristol on to a dynasty of twin-engined military types, some exceptional, others less so. The Beaufort was a torpedo bomber based on the Blenheim and from it came the incredible Beaufighter, essentially a thin fuselage fighter and strike version of its predecessor. Using the Beaufighter as the next design basis, the Buckingham was a bomber, but the requirement was overtaken by events and it was developed

instead into the Buckmaster transport. The Brigand followed the thinking of the Beaufort-Beaufighter and was a Buckingham with a fighter fuselage. It was 1950 when the last Brigands, T.4 crew-trainers, came off the line at Filton.

After its experience with the Bombay bomber-transport of 1935, Bristol devised the twin-engined Type 170 commercial freighter/airliner with clam-shell doors in the nose. Simply called Freighter, or Wayfarer in its all-passenger version, it was affectionately known as 'Biffo', although the reason is obscure. The company built 214 examples up to 1958 – this figure eclipsing the *total* of large civil landplane airliners built in the UK from 1919 to 1939. The prototype, G-AGPV, first flew on 2nd December 1945 and was the last of a long line of maiden flights carried out by Cyril.

By 1946 Cyril had around 4,400 hours and during the following year he handed over to his deputy, 'Bill' Pegg*. Cyril's time with Bristol was far from over, he was appointed as Assistant Managing Director of the Aircraft Division. In 1954 Bristol took a small share in Shorts and Cyril took a post on the board of the Northern Irish concern. He became Deputy Chairman of the Bristol Aircraft Division in 1957 until retiring in 1964. Cyril Frank Uwins OBE AFC died on 11th September 1972, aged 76.

The prototype Bristol 170, G-AGPV, first flown on December 2 1945, had a long and productive life. It was taken on by Trans European Airways in 1960 – illustrated at Coventry in February 1961. The opportunity to preserve this important prototype was missed; it was scrapped at Gatwick in 1965. *Roy Bonser*

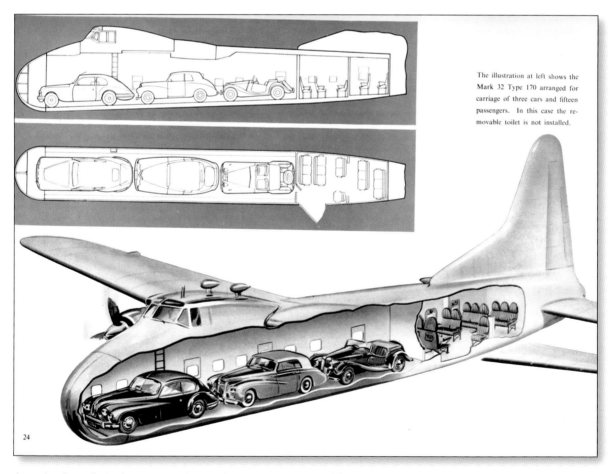

The illustration at left shows the Mark 32 Type 170 arranged for carriage of three cars and fifteen passengers. In this case the removable toilet is not installed.

A page from a brochure of Bristol 170 variants, showing the car-carrying capacity of the Mk.32 – the Superfreighter.

'Wimpy' Wade

19 Nov 1948	Hawker P.1052 VX272
	1 x 5,000lbst RR Nene 2
19 Jun 1950	Hawker P.1081 VX279
	1 x 5,000lbst RR Nene 4

Trevor Sidney Wade, born 1920. Joined the RAFVR in 1938 and was posted to 92 Squadron at Northolt in May 1940 flying Supermarine Spitfire Is and later Vs. He had his share of incidents and scrapes: baling out of N3287 on 28th July 1940 on a night patrol out of Pembrey near Exeter in bad weather. On 19th August 1940, flying R6703 again from Pembrey, he was hit by return fire from a Junkers Ju 88 over the Solent and wrote the Spitfire off in a forced landing near Selsey. 'Wimpy' was injured when W3264 was hit by a Messerschmitt Bf 109 on 25th June 1941 on a patrol out

of Biggin Hill; both he and the Spitfire returned to service. On 27th September 1940, in P9544 from Biggin Hill he was caught in the cross fire created by Dornier Do 17s and force landed on Lewes Race Course, coming to rest upside down. Finally on 2nd December 1940, again on a sortie from Biggin Hill Wimpy shot down a Bf 109E but he also took damage and force landed at Gravesend. For all this, he achieved six victories: an He 111, a Do 17 and four Bf 109s. He was posted to 123 Squadron at Turnhouse in late June 1941, also flying Spitfire Is; transferring briefly to 602 Squadron at Kenley on Spitfire Vs. There followed a posting as Gunnery Officer for 9 Group. In late 1943 he moved to Wittering, as OC Flying of the Air Fighting Development Unit, which evaluated captured enemy aircraft. In early 1945 he was despatched to the USA to test captured Japanese types at Wright Field, Ohio. Wimpy left the RAF in 1946 and joined the editorial staff of the Temple Press magazine The Aeroplane, *writing light aircraft air tests and piloting the company Auster J/1 Autocrat G-AERO.*

The first P.1052, VX272, in 1949. Note the jet outlets behind the wing root and the 'straight' tailplane. *British Aerospace*

'Wimpy' Wade flying the P.1081, VX279, July 1950. The tailplane is sweptback and the jet exhausts under the tail. *Hawker*

S QN LDR 'WIMPY' WADE DFC AFC was rescued from the rigours of magazine work by 'Bill' Humble*, CTP for Hawker at Langley with the offer of a test piloting post in 1947. Bill retired in 1948 and handed over to Wimpy. As can be seen from his background, there were no Vickers Wellingtons in Wimpy's career to explain the origin of his nickname. In *British Test Pilots*, Geoffrey Dorman most likely hits it on the head, describing the former Battle of Britain 'ace' as a hearty eater, just like the character in the *Popeye* cartoon!

Wimpy began signing off Sea Furies at Langley but quickly gravitated to trials of the prototype Sea Hawk, the P.1040, which Bill Humble had flown for the first time in September 1947. The bulk of Wimpy's testing was to lie with Sea Hawks and developments of the design. Reading up on the story of the P.1052 and P.1081 sweptwing prototypes is to enter a quagmire of 'definitive' references and even the date of Wimpy's tragic demise can shift by plus-or-minus 24 hours. Fitting a sweptwing was a logical progression for the P.1040 and Wimpy flew the first of two P.1052s, VX272, on 19th November 1948 with the second, VX279, following on 13th April 1949; both from Boscombe Down. (Today, VX272 is held by the Fleet Air Arm Museum, Yeovilton.)

A month after its maiden flight, Wimpy took VX279 to Villacoublay, Paris, and created a city-to-city record in the process; taking 21 minutes, 27 Seconds to travel 221 miles – averaging 618mph. Beyond this, VX279 was rebuilt, doing away with the trailing edge twin jet nozzles and replacing them with a single exhaust at the end of the fuselage; the tailplane was also swept. In this guise, VX279 was re-designated as the P.1081 and the format, if not the proportions, of the next thoroughbred – the Hunter – took form. Wimpy flew the all-swept machine on 19th June 1950 and four days later took it to the Belgian Aero Show demonstrating its agility at Antwerp. In September at the Farnborough SBAC airshow, he had extended the routine to show off the type's exceptional rate of roll. On a test sortie out of Farnborough on 3rd April 1951 Wimpy experienced some form of difficulty, analysis failed to define its nature as recording devices were not activated for the flight. He ejected at about 2,000ft and the body of 31-year-old Sqn Ldr 'Wimpy' Wade DFC AFC was found still strapped to the ML Aviation ejection seat, near Lewes. The seat was not automatic, the pilot had to initiate unstrapping and dropping of the seat post-ejection; it was surmised that the seat rotated at such a rate that Wimpy could not physically extract himself and thus deploy his parachute. At Langley, he was succeeded by Neville Duke*. In 1950 this most charismatic personality, incredibly determined fighter pilot, gifted test and demonstration pilot had accrued about 2,200 hours on 72 types.

Bob Waight

20 May 1937	DH Albatross E-2
	4x 525hp DH Gipsy Twelve Srs 1

Robert John Waight, born 1909. Apprenticed to de Havilland at Stag Lane, Edgware, as an engineer in May 1928. Learned to fly with the company in 1932 at Hatfield and was soon involved in production testing.

By 1934 'Bob' Waight was an assistant to de Havilland CTP Hubert Broad*; the following year Hubert left and Bob was promoted. From mid-April 1937 de Havilland's new airliner, the Albatross, was ready for testing and Bob undertook a careful series of ground runs, taxi runs and 'straights'. Designed as a mailplane with the potential to fly the Atlantic and as a medium range 22-passenger airliner, the Albatross used moulded plywood techniques in its construction. Unusually, the press were invited to the first flight and many of those present within the factory were also allowed to watch on 20th May 1937. Placarded for 07:00, Bob and co-pilot G D Tucker got the airliner off at 06:55 and they were confident enough to retract the undercarriage during the 30-minute sortie. Between 1937 and 1939 a total seven Albatrosses was built, five entering service with Imperial Airways.

In September 1937 Bob flew the single-seat TK.4 G-AETK, designed and built by students of the de Havilland Technical School, in the Hatfield-based King's Cup air race; he came ninth at 230mph. The performance of the diminutive retractable undercarriage racer was such that it was believed it could be used to break the 100km closed-circuit record for its class. In preparation for this on 1st October 1937 Bob was flying the TK.4 when it was observed that the undercarriage had not retracted completely. While *probably* using one hand to re-cycle the undercarriage, the TK.4 was seen to porpoise at low level, then bank steeply and crash in flames. Robert John Waight was killed instantly, three days short of his 28th birthday. He had 2,150 hours in his logbook and was succeeded by Geoffrey de Havilland JR.

Johnnie Wakefield

Fleet Air Arm pilot Lt 'Johnnie' Wakefield had been a successful alpine skier and motor racing driver pre-war; in the latter case mostly with Maseratis. By 1942 he was a production test pilot for Supermarine and on 24th April 1942 he was embarking on a routine test flight of Spitfire IV BR413 from the dispersed assembly factory at Aldermaston. On take-off he lost control while avoiding a landing Miles Magister: the Spitfire crashed in a ball of flame, killing the 27-year-old outright.

Jack Wales

Jack Bertram Wales, born 1917. Apprenticed as an engineer while serving in the Territorial Army, with the 9th Battalion, Manchester Regiment. He joined Avro at the Chadderton factory as an engineer in 1938. Transferring to the RAF in September 1940, Lt Wales became Plt Off Wales and began flying training. By August 1941 Jack was with 4 Squadron at Clifton, Yorkshire, flying Westland Lysander IIIs. On the 14th while on approach at night, he was attacked by a Junkers Ju 88: Jack and his gunner were unhurt as he force landed his damaged aircraft. Jack was posted to the joint RAF and Fleet Air Arm-crewed 273 Squadron at China Bay on Ceylon, flying Fairey Fulmars. Promoted to squadron leader, Jack was sent to the Hawker Hurricane-equipped 28 Squadron operating in the Imphal, Burma, area. Two non-operational postings followed, before he returned to the fray with 60 Squadron in May 1945 in Burma, on Hurricane IIs and later Republic Thunderbolt IIs. By October 1945 the unit had moved to Kuala Lumpur, Malaya, for 'ops' against insurgents in Surabaya province. Jack returned to Britain in April 1946 and the following year he joined 613 (City of Manchester) Squadron RAuxAF at Ringway, flying Supermarine Spitfire XIVs and F.22s and later DH Vampires: in 1949 he became the unit's CO.

The first three Albatrosses at Hatfield in 1938. Left to right: the second prototype E-3 (later G-AEVW); first production example E-2 (later G-AFDI) and the prototype G-AEVV (flown initially as E-2). *via Don Middleton*

Sqn Ldr Jack Wales became a production test pilot for Avro at Woodford in April 1949 under CTP 'Jimmy' Orrell and he was soon appointed Senior PTP. During his time he test flew Lancasters, Shackletons, Vulcans and Avro-built EE Canberra B.2s. On 1st July 1953 he was at Waddington to carry out the first flight of the last of five Avro 707 delta test-beds: two-seater 707C WZ744 which had been assembled just up the A15 at the Avro facility at Bracebridge Heath. (WZ744 is now displayed at the RAF Museum, Cosford.)

On 7th December 1956 Jack was captaining the prototype Shackleton MR.3, WR970, on a sortie out of Woodford to assess the stall characteristics with the bomb doors open and the radar 'dust bin' fully extended behind the bomb bay. Also on board were: FTE G A Blake and FTOs R A Greenhalgh and C O'Neill. Jack set WR970 up for the stall and it entered a spin, which became inverted. South-west of Sheffield WR970 broke through cloud and was seen to have been righted, but with a considerable sink rate. Near Foolow, west of Eyam in the Peak District, the Shackleton banked to port, side-slipped and cartwheeled in open ground, bursting into flames and killing all on board. Sqn Ldr Jack Bertram Wales DFC OBE TD, 39, had about 3,150 flying hours to his credit, 1,300 of which were testing with Avro. He had been awarded the OBE in January 1952 for services to the Royal Auxiliary Air Force and the Territorial Decoration for his time with the Manchester Regiment.

Ken Waller

19 May 1946	Miles Marathon U-10
	4 x 330hp DH Gipsy Queen 71
7 Aug 1947	Miles Merchantman U-21
	4 x 250hp DH Gipsy Queen 30

Notes: Both flown from Woodley and both wore B Condition ('trade-plate') markings: U-10 became G-AGPD; U-21 became G-AILJ.

Kenneth Fraser Herbert Waller, born 1908. Learned to fly with the Cinque Ports Flying Club at Lympne 1930. Along with Owen Cathcart-Jones, he flew de Havilland DH.88 Comet G-ACSR in the MacRobertson race from Mildenhall to Melbourne, Australia. Setting off on 20th October 1934 they came fourth but then achieved a record out-and-back, arriving in Britain after 13½ days elapsed time. On 20th December 1934 with Frenchman Maurice Franchomme and again in G-ACSR Ken flew from Evere, Belgium, to Leopoldville, Congo, returning on the 28th. Ken was second pilot to Max Findlay in the Schlesinger Race from Portsmouth to Johannesburg, South Africa, flying Airspeed Envoy III G-AENA. They got as far as Abercorn in Northern Rhodesia: on take off on 1st October 1936 the Envoy crashed, killing Max and radio operator A H Morgan, Ken was thrown clear but was badly injured. By 1938 he was instructing at the Brooklands School of Flying but with the onset of war he trained to instruct for the RAF and plied his trade at 6 EFTS, Sywell.

The RAF quickly realised that while Ken Waller had much to offer as an instructor, he had particular skills and that a secondment to Phillips & Powis – the Miles types manufacturer – as a test pilot was a better placing. He started work at Woodley in January 1940, under CTP 'Tommy' Rose*. Ken took the prototype Pratt & Whitney Wasp Junior-powered Master III N7994 for its first flight on 17th December 1940 and daily routine involved in a relentless procession of trainers requiring signing off. His instructing skills came back to the fore in late 1941 when he was despatched to South Africa to assist the SAAF in the use of Master IIs within the Joint Air Training Scheme.

Tommy Rose retired early in 1946 and Ken was appointed as CTP of Miles Aircraft, the name the company traded under

Gleaming prototype Marathon U-10, 1946. *Miles Aircraft*

The Merchantman at Woodley during the last phase of its flight test: with enlarged outer fins and rudders, deleted ventral fin and rudder and a dorsal fin fillet. Note the pitot tube above the nose undercarriage leg. *Miles Aircraft*

from 1943. Ken's first maiden flight following his promotion was – like the Master III – a sub-variant: Martinet Trainer JN275 on 11th April 1946. This was envisaged as a stop-gap until the new generation turboprops, Avro's Athena or Boulton Paul's Balliol, came about. The Martinet Trainer did not go into production and only two were built. In Don Brown's book *Miles Aircraft since 1925* is a wonderful description of pilot and aircraft: "The Martinet Trainer was on the controls and the author vividly remembers accompanying Ken Waller on the spinning trials of the prototype JN275. These trials included spins in both directions and in every possible configuration. The flight concluded with a high speed dive, a half roll into the inverted position at a height of 100ft, followed by an inverted climb in the course of which the undercarriage and flaps were lowered, upwards! This manoeuvre was as much testimony to the handling qualities of the Martinet Trainer as to the pilot's skill."

The month after the debut of the Martinet Trainer, Ken was at the helm of the largest and heaviest type built by Miles, the four-engined Marathon airliner on 19th May 1946. Production and development continued under the aegis of Handley Page – see Hugh Kendall. The final Woodley Miles prototype was typical of the company philosophy, the Merchantman was essentially a Marathon wing mated to a pod-and-boom freighter fuselage and a 'Boxcar' palletised freighter version (see George Miles and the M.68) was also envisaged. Testing of the Merchantman included an intriguing time trying to work out the origin of a loud double bang heard by Ken during diving tests. Ken asked his deputy, Hugh Kendall, to accompany him to try and chase down the errant noise. Don Brown described the detective work: on entering a dive – perhaps descent is a better phrase – both pilots heard the bang and another occurred as Ken started to level out. Hugh declared it was coming from the front and the penny dropped. The metal skinned nose was caving inwards under the extreme pressure of the airflow – Bang No.1. As the stick was pulled back, the metal flexed back into its normal position – Bang No.2. Miles Aircraft foundered in late 1947 and as part of

attempts to rescue the situation in early 1948, Ken flew the Merchantman to Kirkwall in Orkney delivering a Hillman Minx car – registered conveniently MNX 1948 – to customer John Nicholson for a cost stated as £35 (£1,050 in present-day values). Such publicity was beyond helping the company. By late 1948 Ken had renewed his association with South Africa and taken up the post of manager and chief pilot of Strathair, operating a Beech 18 out of Germiston, near Johannesburg.

Ken Wallis

2 Aug 1961	Wallis WA-116 Agile G-ARRT
	1 x 72hp McCulloch 4318A
28 Dec 1972	Wallis WA-121 G-BAHH
	1 x 100hp Wallis-McCulloch
1987	Wallis WA-201 G-BNDG
	2 x 64hp Rotax 532

Notes: With so many variants and powerplant options, it is difficult to define a 'first-of-type': the three given are representative of the 'baseline' models.

Kenneth Horatio Wallis, born 1916. Started working for his father's and uncle's business – Wallbro Cycle and Motor Works in Ely. In 1910 the brothers, Horace (Ken's father) and Percival (uncle) had designed and built the Wallbro Monoplane of steel tube construction and powered by a 25hp JAP, this was flown with some success at Cambridge. Ken had a series of cars and also designed, built and raced powerboats and hyroplanes. He learned to fly at the Cambridge University Aero Club in 1938. A problem with his right eye meant that he was turned down by the RAF twice, but in late 1938 he succeeded and he got his 'wings' in 1939. By February 1941 he was flying Westland Lysander IIIs with 268 Squadron at Bury St Edmunds. In June 1941 he was posted to 103 Squadron at Elsham Wolds, on Vickers Wellington Is. On 21st September 1941, returning from a raid on Frankfurt in L7886 fog precluded a return to base and eventually the Wellington ran out of fuel; all crew abandoned the aircraft, taking to their parachutes safely. After an 'op' to Mannheim in R1459 the Wellington hit a balloon cable and Ken force-landed it with only minor injuries to the crew. From April 1942 Ken was 'rested' at 21 OTU, Moreton-in-Marsh before returning to 'ops' with 37 Squadron at Tortorella in Italy, on Wellington Xs, where he completed 36 'ops'. Post-war he became an armament specialist and in 1950 was Station Armament Officer at Scampton, among many other postings.

It is perhaps sad that it is for *Little Nellie*, the inanimate star of the 1967 Bond, James Bond movie *You Only Live Twice* that Ken Wallis will be remembered. Then again, the film did much of what Ken was determined to do, to demonstrate that the autogyro was capable of many roles and was a safe and reliable form of aviation. Ken belongs to that hallowed band of designer-pilots and in *some* ways that precludes him having an entry in this work. However, his output was prolific and there can be few readers who would not consider him a 'manufacturer' and there have been several attempts to 'industrialise' his designs.

As well as his passion for motorcycles, fast cars, powerboats and many other aspects of engineering, Ken began to get interested in the mechanics of flight from the 1930s. He started the construction of a Mignet 'Flying Flea' during the so-called 'craze' of the mid-1930s, but did not complete this project. In 1947 he converted a Slingsby Petrel glider to a self-launching sailplane by adapting a former Luftwaffe 270cc Riedel starter motor to drive a pusher propeller. By the late 1950s his interest had focussed on autogyros and he was convinced that the type represented a multi-purpose platform for pleasure, commercial and military purposes. Ken acquired a kit of a US-designed Bensen B-7, registered as G-APUD, this he flew for the first time from Shoreham on 23rd May 1959. (*Uniform-Delta* is on display at the Museum of Science and Industry, Manchester, on loan from The Aeroplane Collection.) From this Ken began to develop a series of patents, including the off-set gimbal rotor head

providing exceptionally stable flight and a spin-up drive for the rotor. On 2nd August 1961 Ken flew the prototype WA-116 Agile, G-ARRT, from Boscombe Down; this was a completely original design and formed the basis for the family of more than 20 autogyros that followed up to the late 1980s.

In 1961 Ken came to an agreement with Beagle Aircraft to develop and certificate the WA-116; five were completed at Shoreham and three were evaluated by the Ministry of Defence. Among the many intentions of Beagle, the WA-116 was ultimately shunted to one side. In 1970 Airmark Ltd also inaugurated a venture to market the type. (For more on the Beagle era and Airmark, see under 'Pee Wee' Judge.) A final co-operative agreement was reached with East Anglian-based Vinten, specialists in cameras, mounts, reconnaissance systems and more. Vinten-Wallis Ltd offered the WA-117 series for a variety of roles, but again this came to nought.

With his cousin Geoffrey, Ken established Wallis Autogyros Ltd and continued to experiment and develop the small 'working' autogyro. As an aside, Geoffrey and Ken built a replica of the Wallbro Monoplane designed and built by their fathers in 1910. Registered as G-BFIP, Ken piloted this on its maiden flight on 10th August 1978. As well as film contracts such as *You Only Live Twice*, Ken and the company embarked on many record-breaking flights and by 1998 Ken had no fewer than *sixteen* world records to his name; nine of which he still held in 2001. For example: 28th September 1975 non-stop in a straight line 543 miles and duration 6 hours 25 minutes both in a flight from Lydd to Wick in WA-116 G-ATHM; 17th April 1985 100km closed circuit, 118.3mph in a WA-116; 19th March 1998 time to climb to 3,000m, 7 minutes, 20 seconds in WA-121 G-BAHH. (The Wallbro Monoplane, WA-116 G-ARRT, *Little Nellie* G-ARZB and many of the other Wallis autogyros are presently held in store.)

Wg Cdr Kenneth Horatio Wallis MBE died on 1st September 2013, aged 97. The *Lives of Ken Wallis – Engineer and Aviator Extraordinaire* by Ian Hancock is an excellent testament to a remarkable man.

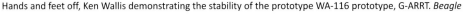

Hands and feet off, Ken Wallis demonstrating the stability of the prototype WA-116 prototype, G-ARRT. *Beagle*

Ken Wallis inside the hangar at his home at Reymerston Hall in Norfolk, with a selection of what he called "his girls" – G-ARZB *Little Nellie* alongside him. *via Ian Hancock*

Alan Washer

C Alan Washer, born 1910. Joined the RAF in 1929 and in September 1930 was flying Armstrong Whitworth Atlas Is with 13 Squadron from Netheravon. Other postings included the Hal Far Station Flight on Malta from March 1932.

FLT LT ALAN WASHER joined Bristol at Filton in 1935 as a PTP. That year he demonstrated the prototype Bullpup, J9051, at the SBAC airshow at Hendon on 1st July. In November 1937 Alan and CTP Cyril Uwins* ferried Blenheims G-AFCE and G-AFCF out to Yugoslavia to act as patterns for Icarus at Zemun, Belgrade, where a licence production line was planned. As with most Bristol test pilots, Alan was also engaged to carry out engine trials work for the company's aero engine division. Vickers Wellesley I K7717 had been fitted with a Bristol Pegasus XXII and was undergoing trials for the Upper Heyford-based Long Range Development Unit. On 13th May 1938 Alan took K7717 for routine trials but at about 3,000ft the engine caught fire. Alan successfully baled out but the FTO, P H Warren, was killed when the Wellesley crashed near Alveston, Bristol.

History repeated itself, at least in part, on 12th June 1940 when Alan and two FTOs took off from Filton in the third prototype Beaufort, L4443, for engine cooling trials. First flown in 1939, L4443 and the second prototype, L4442, had been retained by Bristol. The Beaufort suffered engine failure and fire broke out: the two un-named FTOs on board successfully took to their parachutes, but 30-year-old Flt Lt Alan Washer was killed when L4443 crashed at South Hinksey. Ten days previously, sister-ship L4442 had taken off from Filton and crashed in unspecified circumstances: its pilot survived.

Graham Wardell

Graham Wardell, born 1954. Joined the RAF in 1972 and became the first student to train on the HS Hawk, at 4 FTS Valley, in 1977. He was posted to 14 Squadron at Brüggen, West Germany, in 1978, flying SEPECAT Jaguar GR.1s. On 18th July 1979 Graham was flying GR.1 XX960 as No.4 in a four-ship tactical formation; his Jaguar collided with a 90ft TV mast on a promontory and he ejected successfully. Posted to 41 Squadron at Jaguars at Coltishall in 1982, he later instructed on Jaguars and Panavia Tornados. In 1987 he was sent to the USA on an exchange, becoming the first non-American pilot to fly the Lockheed F-117A Nighthawk 'stealth' fighter. He returned to the UK and graduated from ETPS at Boscombe Down.

SQN LDR GRAHAM WARDELL joined the British Aerospace test team at Warton in March 1996. Much of his work was involved with Tornado, including the GR.4 upgrade programme. On 6th June 1999 Graham was demonstrating BAe Hawk 200 ZJ701 at M R Stefanik Airport, Bratislava, Slovakia, at an airshow. News reports noted that the Hawk failed to pull out of a turn at low level, a wing tip hit the ground and the aircraft exploded. Sqn Ldr Graham Wardell, 45, was killed instantly; a woman in the crowd was killed by the blast from the crash.

Brian Wass

Brian Oscar Wass, born 1926. Worked in a bank from 16; enlisted in the Army in 1944 and trained with the Glider Pilot Regiment. No operational details, left the service in 1946. Brian joined the RAF in 1948 and was trained in Rhodesia. He was posted to 92 Squadron at Linton-on-Ouse, flying Gloster Meteor F.8s. He left the RAF in 1953 and flew in Sudan and Kenya with the British crop-spraying company Pest Control Ltd.

BRIAN WASS joined Marshall of Cambridge at Teversham in 1954. As a major contractor to the armed forces and the aircraft industry, the work was varied, at the time it included a lot of modification work on Canberras under sub-contract to English Electric. Marshall had developed a boundary layer control test-bed for Cambridge University, MA.4 VF665 and operated the radically converted Auster T.7 on the engineering faculty's behalf – see under Leslie Worsdell for more details. On 8th March 1966 Brian and FTO Ramaswamiah Krishnamirthy, an engineering student, took off for the MA.4's 140th flight. The aircraft was last seen in an inverted spin and it crashed, killing both occupants, near West Wratting in Suffolk.

'Bill' Waterton

9 Mar 1948	Gloster E1/44 TX145 1 x 5,200lbst RR Nene 2
19 Mar 1948	Gloster Meteor T.7 G-AKPK 2 x 3,600lbst RR Derwent 5
19 Jan 1950	Avro Canada CF-100 18101 2 x 6,500lbst RR Avon RA.2
26 Nov 1951	Gloster Javelin WD804 2 x 8,000lbst AS Sapphire Sa.6 10201/10301

Notes: E1/44 flown from Boscombe Down; T.7 and Javelin from Moreton Valence; CF-100 flew at Malton, Ontario, Canada.

William Waterton, born 1916 in Edmonton, Canada. From 1935 'Bill' studied at the Royal Military College at Kingston, Ontario, and served for a short period with the 19th Alberta Dragoons. He applied for a commission with the Canadian Army and the RCAF, but this came to nought. Bill was accepted by the RAF and he sailed to Britain in March 1939. By the early spring of 1940 he was posted to the Hawker Hurricane equipped, Canadian-staffed, 242 Squadron at Church Fenton. From 16th May the unit supported British forces in France and, from the 26th took part in Operation DYNAMO, the retreat through Dunkirk. Bill suffered oxygen starvation and miraculously came to with sufficient altitude to recover; he nursed his aircraft towards England, its Merlin was vibrating badly and he force landed near Dover; suffering back and head injuries. It was August 1940 before he was back in action and he caught up with 242 at Coltishall, only to be posted to 61 OTU at Heston as an instructor. He became a very gifted at this and spent all of 1942 back in Canada teaching. Bill returned to Britain in 1943 and flew high-altitude Supermarine Spitfire VIs and VIIs, perhaps with 124 Squadron, before joining a Meteorological Flight. From May 1944 Bill was posted to the Air Fighting Development Unit – part of the Central Fighter Establishment (CFE) from October 1944 – at Wittering where he flew captured enemy aircraft and helped to develop tactics. CFE also had Gloster Meteors on strength and Bill got his first experience of jets. His skill with jets was recognised when he joined the RAF High Speed Flight at Tangmere, under Gp Capt E M 'Teddy' Donaldson – also on the Flight was Neville Duke*. On 7th September 1946 Donaldson flew Meteor F.4 EE549 around a calibrated course to achieve a world speed record of 616mph.

IF you read no other test pilot autobiography than 'Bill' Waterton's *The Quick and the Dead*, it will serve you well. It has all the derring-do that you would expect, but this is of far less importance than the matter-of-fact analysis of the job, the state of the industry and the stresses and angst of a tradesman not being allowed to fulfil his task. Bill writes exceptionally well; you will return to read it again. When you've put down the *Quick and the Dead*, it's time to pick up James Hamilton-Paterson's *Empire of the Clouds – When Britain's Aircraft Ruled the World* in which Bill Waterton's

experiences are inter-woven through a punchy, absorbing, narrative of the post-war British aircraft industry. That's enough product-placement, on with a tribute to a great individual and very skilled pilot.

Sqn Ldr William 'Bill' Arthur Waterton AFC* would have loved an RAF commission, but while one was occasionally promised, such status was never forthcoming. He took up a test piloting post with Gloster at Hucclecote and Moreton Valence on 21st October 1946 for a salary of £1,000 (£30,000 in present-day values). The following March, Bill was appointed as CTP, for an additional £500 a year, and he became responsible for the day-to-day schedules, the remainder of the test team and the flight office. Bill officially took over from Eric Greenwood* but it was Phil Stanbury* who was acting CTP – Phil left Gloster in May 1947. In *The Quick and the Dead*, Bill describes the odd situation: "The appointment of chief test pilot was still held by a man who was doing no flying when I joined the firm, and had done little in the previous twelve months. He was occupied with something on the executive side."

The success of the Meteor, with large orders for the RAF and increasing interest from overseas made Moreton Valence a very busy airfield. The factory at Hucclecote (also called Brockworth) was not far away to the north-east was the venue for first flights that merely positioned the aircraft to Moreton Valence. Having been part of the RAF High Speed Flight for the world airspeed record in September 1946, Bill was the ideal candidate for Gloster to have a crack in its own right at the 100km closed-circuit. Flying out of Moreton Valence, Bill piloted F.4 VT103 to a new record on 6th February 1948 at 542.9mph. This was temporary glory: 20 days later, flying the prototype Supermarine Attacker, TS409, Mike Lithgow* took the record to 560.6mph and – to show it was no fluke – raised it again the following day, to 564.8mph.

Gloster had responded to Specification E1/44 for an experimental single-seat jet with the potential to become a fighter. Bill first flew TX145 in March 1948 from Boscombe Down and did the same with the second example, TX148 in 1949. Both performed well enough, but the E1/44 was not followed up; Gloster was close to saturation with Meteors. Ten days after the debut of TX145, Bill was at the controls of a very significant Meteor prototype. There was a pressing need, especially with export customers, for a conversion trainer and this was created by stretching the forward fuselage to create space for a second cockpit under a 'glasshouse'-like canopy. The private-venture demonstrator F.4 was rebuilt and emerged as Meteor T.7 G-AKPK, which was used for a series of far-ranging sales tours.

In a 'combined operation' by Bristol, Gloster and Westland, on 30th September 1948 Sir Frederick Wells delivered a message from the Lord Mayor of London to the Deputy President of the Municipality of Paris in 46 minutes 29 seconds. Eric Swiss* flew Bristol 171 helicopter VL963 from a car park behind St Paul's cathedral to Biggin Hill in 9½ minutes. There, Sir Frederick boarded G-AKPK and was flown by Bill to Orly Airport, Paris, in 27½ minutes. Then Alan Bristow* whisked the passenger to the Place des Invalides in 8½ minutes in a Westland WS-51 helicopter.

The first of two Gloster E1/44s, TX145, at Moreton Valence. To the left is a Royal Netherlands Air Force North American Harvard. *KEC*

Several times in these two volumes, maiden flights outside of Great Britain have been included when the test pilot involved was seconded by his employers and as such the debut was an extension of his 'day job'. In late 1949 Bill was informed that he was going to Malton, Ontario, to fly the prototype CF-100 Canuck, a twin-engined all-weather fighter being developed by Avro Canada. Gloster and Avro had been part of the Hawker Siddeley Group since 1935 and 'exchanges' such as this were common within Britain, far less so for the overseas 'branches'. So Bill was to return, temporarily, but he could not have realised that he would be away for 15 months. The Malton CTP, Don Rogers, and his successor, Bruce Warren, had no twin-engined jet fighter time and it was appropriate that someone of Bill's experience initially take charge. Bill took the prototype up for the first time on 19th January 1950 and it was quickly discovered that the centre section needed strengthening as the wing was twisting in flight. The team at Malton set to this task with a speed that eclipsed Gloster, but the delay to the programme was appreciable. The second CF-100, 18102, was flown by Bill in July 1950. With his return to Britain, Gloster sent out 'Zura' Zurakowski* as Bill's replacement.

On his return Bill was horrified to find his office at Moreton Valence a morass of paperwork that had been allowed to pile up in his absence. Out on the airfield, Meteors were parked at every available space; it appeared that all had been put on 'hold' to await his return. Bill worked hard to clear both the desk and the ramp – looming was the next Gloster project and this would dominate his time. Early in its gestation the all-weather Javelin was declared a 'super-priority' programme and this gave the complex delta project an urgent pace when what was really needed was a steady learning curve. Both the management and the designers – or as Bill regarded them "accountants and long-haired boffins" respectively – at Gloster tended to see the Javelin as a big Meteor, not the huge leap that it was. The Meteor was a first generation jet: the Javelin represented what later would be called a 'weapon system', a complicated mixture of aerodynamics, powered flying controls, sophisticated weaponry and radar. The Javelin had all the potential to be an even bigger money-spinner for Gloster, by overall value if not by unit.

Javelin prototype WD804 was assembled at Moreton Valence and was ready for ground runs in October 1951. Bill began taxying trials and was alarmed to discover that the delta reared up during low speed runs with the flaps down. Reporting back he was astounded that it took considerable badgering to get the trim changed to correct this, when it would have been reasonable to expect that such a request would be addressed overnight. More ground runs were carried out and on 26th November Bill took WD804 on its maiden flight. He was back after 34 minutes for a perfectly smooth landing, giving the impression that all went well. This was far from the case. There was chronic buffeting coming from the rear and at more than 200mph the whole airframe shook. The 'snag list' got longer with each flight: there was control reversal near the stall and with the flaps down the jet pitched up frighteningly. Within the flight sheds, the 'feel' of the hydraulically-assisted controls was altered as was the centre of gravity -without a word to Bill, or even by entering it on the flight dockets. The list of items requiring attention grew and very few of them were addressed, it seemed to be a case of 'grin and bear it'.

There is a *brilliant* assessment of what a test pilot strives for in *The Quick and the Dead*: "I have always tried to get an aeroplane to a state in which an ordinary, inexperienced junior squadron pilot would feel at home. I remembered my earliest flying days and recalled how little I really knew about flying and aeroplanes. Joe Prune, and not Bill Waterton with 5,000 flying hours behind him, was the chap for whom the 'plane was built. But what was the good of such idealism when people ignored warnings and let faults go uncorrected?"

Frustrated, Bill tendered his resignation in April 1952, only to be talked around. On 29th June 1952, on WD804's 99th sortie Bill put the nose down for a full-chat dive and the aircraft "turned itself into a sort of crazy pneumatic drill". He brought it back to Moreton Valence in a momentous piece of

CF-100 Canuck Mk.3s with indigenous Avro Canada Orenda 1 turbojets. *Avro Canada*

flying. Bill was awarded a George Medal and the *London Gazette* for 25th July 1952 carried the citation: "...whilst travelling at high speed at the height of about 3,000ft, elevator flutter developed and both elevators became detached from the aircraft. This left the pilot with practically no controls of his aircraft in pitch. Waterton climbed the aircraft to 10,000ft and experimented with what was left of the control, the paramount factor in effecting a safe landing. He found that it was possible to retain some control down to a speed roughly half as fast again as the normal landing speed. Knowing that a crash would put back seriously the development and production he decided to land the aircraft despite having at his command an ejector seat and parachute. He landed the machine heavily owing to the lack of control and the undercarriage gave way.

The prototype Javelin, WD804, with a host of Meteors in the background, Moreton Valence, 1952. *Russell Adams – Gloster*

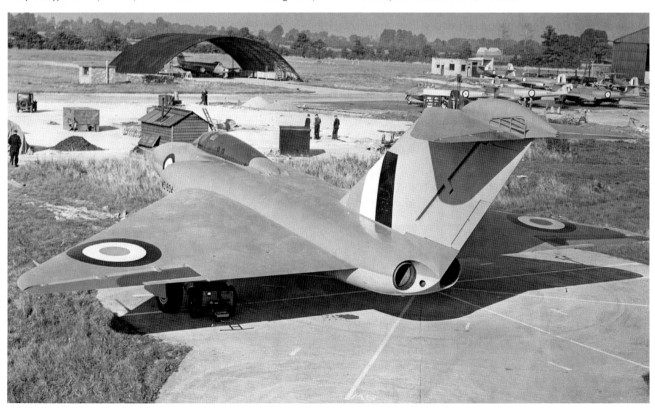

"After the crashed aircraft came to rest, fire broke out and Waterton found great difficulty in freeing himself owing to a jammed hood. Eventually he did get out of the wreck. By then the flames had reached the area of the cockpit but despite this, he climbed back into the fuselage and salvaged the automatic records relating to the original aerodynamic and structural failures.

"The behaviour of Chief Test Pilot Waterton was exemplary and beyond the call of duty and his courage was outstanding." That merely paraphrases the event; Bill's words in his autobiography covering the incident are some of the best aviation writing you'll ever read.

There had been two fatal accidents at Moreton Valence on Bill's 'watch': one pilot error, the other open to debate. Both occurred within a matter of weeks of his becoming CTP and 'winnowing' out of pilots who didn't cut the mustard was work for the coming months. With these tragedies at the back of his mind and the memory of his own traumatic last ride in WD804 still fresh in his mind Bill took the second Javelin, WD808 which he'd flown on 21st August, to the 1952 SBAC airshow at Farnborough, staged 1st-7th September. In the pilot's tent on the 6th Bill stood behind Eve Derry as everyone watched her husband, John Derry*, display DH.110 WG236, only for it to end in tragedy.

In the autumn of 1952 Bill appointed Peter 'PG' Lawrence* as his deputy, to share the considerable load of Javelin development flying. Bill regarded Peter as heir apparent to the post of CTP: some in the crew room saw him as 'leap-frogging' into a post that should have been offered within. The second Javelin prototype, WD808, was grounded early in 1953 for modifications to the wings to improve manoeuvrability at height and at high Mach numbers – as revealed in Bill's ill-fated sortie of 29th June 1951. In the meantime, Bill 'first flighted' the third example, WT827. With its new wing, WD808 was ready and Bill re-flew it on 28th May 1953. Fourteen days later, on his second flight in WD808 that day Peter Lawrence called: "I'm in trouble". The wreckage of WD808 came down on a playing field near Flax Bourton in Somerset. PG's body, still strapped in his ejector seat, was found nearby- see his section for more details.

In late 1953 Bill secured the services of 'Dickie' Martin* as his deputy. Early in March the following year Bill presented a dossier of grievances about pay, conditions and the string of modifications that needed implementing on the Javelin to the management. The inevitable greeted him: it was best he go, and he could do that the following day. Amazed that the powers-that-be did not seem to place any value on a fully-

The Javelin had a protracted development programme and it was not until 1956 that the first operational unit, 46 Squadron at Odiham accepted its first FAW.1s. Illustrated is an FAW.2 of 46 Squadron in 1958. *RAF Odiham*

briefed handover with his successor, Bill stuck to his guns and declared he would see the month out.

Bill's pent-up frustration and bitterness turned to acquiescence in the final days, so vividly conveyed towards the end of *The Quick and the Dead*: "I continued with my job as though nothing were amiss, quietly gathering together my correspondence and belongings and went on flying as usual. I brought the Javelin [fourth prototype WT830] back from Boscombe Down and briefed my No.1 ['Dickie' Martin, soon to be appointed CTP] on it. The Ministry of Supply showed no apparent concern that almost all of the handling and flying background to their important aeroplane was to be lost immediately... [On 31st March 1954] I went round making my farewells. It came as a bombshell to most people, and many others weren't actors enough to conceal their pleasure at my departure. One said: 'Shall I say I'm sorry?' I replied: 'Hell, no, why perjure your soul at this stage of the game?' I flew my last aeroplane that afternoon, tested one of the last production Meteor VIIIs, had a photograph taken to commemorate the event and drove out of the gate of Moreton Valence for the last time. I had done exactly seven years as Gloster's chief test pilot. Tomorrow was another April Fool's Day."

Bill turned his forthright nature and writing skills to good use and was appointed as the aviation correspondent for the *Daily Express*. True to form, he was deeply critical in much of what he penned. In 1955 *The Comet Riddle* (Frederick Muller,

Major Accidents at Moreton Valence 1949-1954

22 Apr 1947	Meteor F.4 RA394	Final production test flight; starboard engine failed in dive – apparently unnoticed by the pilot, Lt J Bridge. Landing in a crosswind, RA394 yawed, stalled and crashed killing Bridge.
15 Jun 1949	Meteor FR.5 VT347	First flight of prototype, a conversion of an F.4 airframe. On returning to the airfield, the Meteor went into a high-g pull-over and it broke up and crashed, killing Acting CTP Flt Lt Rodney Dryland. For more see Volume One.
29 Jun 1952	Javelin WD804	Flight 99 of prototype, CTP Bill Waterton – see text.
11 Jun 1953	Javelin WD808	Test flight of modified second prototype by DCTP, aircraft entered stable stall and did not recover. Lt Peter Lawrence killed – see his section.

London) was published, jointly written by Bill and Tim Hewat, it was a controversial examination of the DH Comet jetliner accidents. The same publisher produced Bill's *The Quick and the Dead* the following year with its incisive criticism of the ramshackle state of the British aircraft industry. The reaction to the books and his newspaper column was such that the *Daily Express* felt that it had no option but to let Bill go; the axe fell in July 1956. Bill returned to Canada, settling at his birthplace, Owen Sound, Ontario, where he took up instructing, among other pursuits. Sqn Ldr William 'Bill' Arthur Waterton AFC* GM died on 17th April 2006 in Canada, aged 90.

I leave it to John Farley*, the writer of the foreword to this volume, as quoted in James Hamilton-Paterson's *Empire of the Clouds* to sum up a determined and skilled pilot: "In response to a posting on an internet forum in early 2003, Farley wrote that Bill Waterton had recently been made a member of the ETPS Association. He added: 'He was considered a bad trouble-maker back in the 1950s because of his insistence on telling the truth about the aeroplanes he tested. Jeffrey Quill* was his biggest fan – which says it all, really.' *The Quick and the Dead* was my bible when I was in the business and I still read the preface a couple of times a year – lest I forget what being a test pilot is actually about.'"

Douglas Weightman

Graduate of No.1 ETPS Course at Boscombe Down in 1943, former RAE Farnborough pilot Sqn Ldr D D Weightman DFC was appointed as a test pilot for the Air Registration Board (see Chapter Four) in 1948. (He is incorrectly given as D W Weightman in Chapter One, Volume One.) Douglas also served as a PTP for Bristol at Filton and on 14th October 1948 he was testing Brigand B.1 RH824. The port engine failed and the propeller blades sheared off, impacting in the nose section and starboard engine. Over a populated area, he struggled with the controls and force-landed at Northwick and was killed when RH824 impacted with trees.

Alfred Weyl

| Aug 1936 | Dart Pup G-AELR |
| | 1 x 27hp Ava 4a |

Alfred Richard Oscar Weyl, born in Berlin, Germany, 1898. Served with the Imperial German Air Force during the Great War. Post-war he became a senior member of the Deutsche Versuchsanstalt für Luftfahrt – the national aviation research institute. He also held a research post at Berlin University, designed for Udet Flugzeugbau and acted as a test pilot.

Alfred Weyl came to Britain in 1935 as a refugee and established Zander and Weyl Ltd, re-named Dart Aircraft in 1936, with E P Zander at Dunstable. After a series of gliders, Alfred designed the parasol-wing single-seat pusher Pup which, in true designer-pilot style, he first flew in July 1936. It is *very likely* that Alfred also did the honours with his next two creations, the single-seat pusher Flittermouse G-AELZ and the firm's most well-known product, Kitten G-AERP, both

having their debut in 1936. The first two types remained one-offs; eventually four Kittens were built. Alfred was interned during World War Two, later becoming a consultant on a wide range of subjects including ballistics, guided missiles, composites and tail-less aircraft formats. (Lindsay Neale* was a director of Dart Aircraft in 1937.) Alfred Richard Oscar Weyl, died on 23rd February 1959, aged 61. In 1965 his book *Fokker – The Creative Years* was completed by 'Jack' Bruce and published by Putnam.

'Dickie' Wheldon

23 Feb 1950	Percival Provost WE522
	1 x 385hp AS Cheetah 17
26 Jan 1954	Percival Jet Provost T.1 XD674
	1 x 1,750lbst AS Viper 5

Richard J Wheldon, joined the RAF in 1936 and in his early operational career flew Bristol Blenheims. Later in the war he was a test pilot for Maintenance Command.

'Dickie' Wheldon joined Percival Aircraft at Luton in 1947 under CTP 'Sandy' Powell*. He succeeded Sandy in early 1950 and flew the prototype Provost in February. The Provost was a replacement for the Prentice and also became a major export success; production running to 1960. Originally fitted with an Armstrong Siddeley Cheetah, the third example, WG503 first flown in March 1951, adopted an Alvis Leonides and it was that engine that powered production examples. The design underwent a radical evolution, becoming the Jet Provost in 1954 and again Dickie carried out the maiden flight of the long-legged T.1s. A batch of Jet Provost T.1s was ordered for the RAF for a comparative training course at 2 Flying Training School, Hullavington. A set of pupils were trained on the Leonides-powered Provost T.1 to later convert to jets; others were trained on the Jet Provost T.1s from the start in what the RAF called 'all-through' jet training. The 'JP' remained in production until 1982 as the much-developed Strikemaster – see Reg Stock.

The third Provost prototype, WG503, the first to be powered by an Alvis Leonides. *Percival Aircraft*

By 1957 the prototype Jet Provost, XD674, had been retired and it became an instructional airframe – 7570M – at Gaydon, where it is illustrated in 1964. Today, it is on display with the RAF Museum at Cosford. *Roy Bonser*

Derek Whitehead

30 Apr 1958	Blackburn NA.39 XK486
	2 x 7,100lbst DH Gyron Junior 101
17 May 1963	Blackburn Buccaneer S.2 XK526
	2 x 11,100lbst RR Spey 101

Notes: NA.39 prototype first flown at Thurleigh; S.2 XK526 flew from Holme-on-Spalding Moor.

Derek J Whitehead, born 1925. Joined the RAF in 1945, after learning to fly he transferred to the Fleet Air Arm. By the summer of 1951 Derek was with 801 Squadron on Hawker Sea Fury FB.11s from the shore-base at Lee-on-Solent and embarked on HMS Indomitable. *The following year he was instructing at the Naval Air Fighter School – 759 Squadron – at Culdrose, flying Supermarine Seafire F.17s and F.47s. On 16th May 1952 Derek had to crash land F.17 SX297 at the satellite airfield of Predannack; it was written off, he was uninjured. He graduated from ETPS Course No.13 at Farnborough 1954 and was then posted to A&AEE Boscombe Down and among his responsibilities was the introduction to service of the Supermarine Scimitar F.1.*

WITH his intimate knowledge of the Supermarine Scimitar naval strike fighter, Lt Cdr Derek Whitehead AFC was the perfect candidate to take its replacement – what became the Buccaneer – through conception and into flight test. Derek joined Blackburn in 1957, working for CTP 'Tim' Wood* but his 'boss' was to have no part in the new programme and retired in April 1959, handing on to Derek. Initially known as the NA.39, the Buccaneer was an exceptionally advanced design, featuring area rule aerodynamics and boundary layer control (BLC) over the wings and tail. The first prototype was taken by road from Brough to RAE Thurleigh and Derek began ground runs and taxying in mid-April 1958. On one run the brakes overheated and a fire broke out, XK486 ran off the runway and burst a main tyre. Repairs complete, Derek and Bernard J Watson, head of flight test, took XK486 for its debut on the last day of April, the 42-minute sortie going up to 17,000ft. XK486 operated out of Thurleigh and Boscombe Down until 9th July 1958 when Derek brought it to Holme-on-Spalding Moor, which had been acquired by Blackburn as a test centre for the programme. On 27th August 1958 Derek flew the second prototype, XK487, from Holme and all other Buccaneers started life in similar manner, being roaded from Brough for flight test.

The third (XK488 background) and fourth (XK489 foreground) NA.39s in April 1959 – both appeared at the Paris Airshow at Le Bourget that June. (See under David Lockspeiser for more on XK488.) *Blackburn Aircraft*

An RAF Buccaneer S.2B during the type's just prior phase out celebrations, September 1993. *British Aerospace – Brough*

With J Pearson as FTO, Derek took the prototype Buccaneer S.2 (XK526, a converted S.1) for its maiden flight in May 1963. The S.2 represented a mighty leap in performance thanks to its Spey turbofans and greater use of BLC. Production continued to 1977 and the RAF became a major customer of the type. Lt Cdr Derek Whitehead AFC had retired from Hawker Siddeley (as Blackburn became in 1963) by 1980: he died in 1989, aged 64.

Geoffrey Wikner

| 21 Sep 1936 | Foster Wikner Wicko G-AENU |
| | 1 x 85hp 'Wicko F' (Ford V8) |

Geoffrey Neville Wikner, born Australia, 1904. Cousin of Edgar Percival*. Designed and built several aircraft – and at least one sports car – in his homeland, including the Sports Monoplane, the Lion and the Wizard. He sailed to Britain in 1934 to continue as an aircraft designer.

GEOFFREY WIKNER teamed up with V 'Jack' Foster in Britain and established Foster Wikner Aircraft to produce a two-seat tourer powered by a converted Ford V8 engine. The prototype was flown by the designer from Stapleford Tawney in September 1936. Changing to a 90hp Cirrus Minor and other in-lines, another nine Wickos were built at Eastleigh. During the war, Geoffrey flew for the Air Transport Auxiliary carrying out over 1,000 ferry flights. In 1946 Geoffrey purchased an ex-RAF Handley Page Halifax III which was civilian registered as G-AGXA and inevitably named *Waltzing Matilda*. With 14 fare-paying 'crew' (one source quotes 21 in total on board) Geoffrey piloted G-AGXA from Hurn on 25th May 1946 and arrived at Mascot, New South Wales, Australia, on 20th June. Designer-pilot Geoffrey Neville Wikner died in 1990, aged 86.

The fifth Wicko, DH Gipsy Major-powered G-AFJB at Coventry in September 1962. *Juliet-Bravo* was briefly owned by its designer, Geoffrey Wikner, from October 1945 to April 1946 and survives in airworthy trim, with an Irish-based owner. *Roy Bonser*

The HP.20 slotted wing test-bed, built around an Airco DH.9A fuselage, 1921. *Peter Green Collection*

Arthur Wilcockson

24 Feb 1921	HP HP.20 J6914
	1 x 400hp Liberty 12-N
3 Jan 1922	HP Hanley N143
	1 x 450hp Napier Lion IIB
7 Sep 1923	HP Type S
	1 x 230hp Bentley BR.2
7 Jul 1924	HP Hendon N9724
	1 x 450hp Napier Lion IIB
19 Oct 1926	HP Hamlet G-EBNS
	3 x 120hp Bristol Lucifer IV

Arthur Sydney Wilcockson served with the RFC during the Great War and during 1918-1919 flew the Army personnel and document 'shuttle' service from Folkestone to Cologne. By 1920 he was a pilot with Handley Page Transport, based at Cricklewood.

FREDERICK HANDLEY PAGE tended to 'second' pilots from his airline, Handley Page Transport (HPT), to act as test pilots for his aircraft manufacturing business – it was much more 'cost effective' than hiring in a specialist. (See Robert Bager, Gordon Olley and particularly Sholto Douglas for examples of that 'arrangement'.) By 1921 Arthur Wilcockson could be considered as the 'resident' Handley Page test pilot above and beyond his requirements with HPT. Arthur's first 'first' – all of which were flown from Cricklewood – was a challenging and important test-bed, the HP.20 (also known as the X.4B) a thick-winged monoplane to try out the patented full-span slots. The HP.20 was based upon the fuselage of Westland-built Airco DH.9A F1632. At first Arthur flew the

parasol with the slats sealed, then he and Geoffrey Hill* shared trials with the devices fully operable. Frank Courtney* was contracted to deliver the HP.20 to RAE Farnborough – see under his section for more.

The Hanley was a single-seat shipborne torpedo bomber of which five were built and the Hendon, an enlarged two-seat derivative, with six completed. (This was the first use of the name 'Hendon', Fairey later built a monoplane bomber of the same name – see Norman Macmillan.) The Hamlet was a seven-seater air taxi tri-motor that remained a one-off. The HP.21, or Type S, single-seat shipborne fighter was aimed at a potentially lucrative US Navy requirement and was to prove the point to Frederick Handley Page that a 'full-timer' was needed. An order for three prototypes was placed, with conditional deadlines littering the contract. Major Robert Mayo was the UK agent and the debut was arranged for the morning of 7th September 1923 in the presence of the US Navy's Cdr Robert Towers. Captain Wilcockson was delayed in France with a recalcitrant HPT O/400 and it was not until 17:40 that he could take the little machine into the air. The following day, Arthur ground-looped the Type S, having already declared that the rudder was ineffectual. Mayo was unhappy with this situation and insisted that 'Freddie' Raynham be brought in to keep the project on time: despite this the US Navy cancelled the contract the following year.

In 1924 Arthur became a founder-pilot of the newly-formed Imperial Airways and the Hendon and the Hamlet had to be tested with special dispensation from the airline. The situation was resolved with the appointment of Tom Harry England* as CTP in 1927. Arthur remained as a senior pilot with Imperial Airways through its transformation into British Overseas Airways Corporation (BOAC) in 1939 and his skills pop up twice more within this volume. In January 1938 he was the pilot of Short C-Class flying-boat G-ADUV *Cambria* during the first hook-up with the Flight Refuelling's Armstrong Whitworth AW.23 K3585 – flown by Geoffrey Tyson* – and detailed in Chapter Three. The remainder of 1938 was dominated by the Short-Mayo composite experiments, with Arthur flying the 'mother ship' *Maia* on the inaugural transatlantic service on 21st July 1938 – see the section of John Lankester Parker. In August 1940 Arthur was in charge of establishing the Atlantic Ferry Organisation, along with former Imperial Airways pilots Don Bennett and Griffith Powell, at Montreal, Canada. The following year this was to become Ferry Command. Arthur stayed with BOAC until his retirement in 1964.

The third Handley Page Hanley, N145, 1922. *Peter Green Collection*

Hollis Williams

1939	General Aircraft Cygnet II G-AFVR
	1 x 150hp Blackburn Cirrus Major II

DAVID L HOLLIS WILLIAMS served as a pilot in the RAF before joining the Hawker design office in 1923. Two years later he moved to Fairey, again as a designer but with the portfolio of acting as a 'second pilot' as and when needed under CTP Norman Macmillan*. During his time, Hollis led the design team that created the Long Range Monoplane (see A Jones-Williams) and the Hendon bomber (first flown by Macmillan). To digress a little, while at Hawker Hollis discovered the remains of a Sopwith Dove (the civil version of the Pup) at Kingston-upon-Thames and bought it. He and his friend, Charles Lowe-Wylde* restored it to flying condition, as G-EBKY, in 1927. Lowe-Wilde was killed in 1933 and Hollis left Fairey in the same year and the Dove was sold off – today it flies with the Shuttleworth Trust at Old Warden.

In 1934 Hollis was appointed as chief engineer to General Aircraft at Hanworth. In 1938 the company acquired the design rights to the CW Cygnet two-seat light aircraft. The prototype, G-AEMA, had been test flown by Hubert Broad* in May 1937 and also moved to Hanworth. Hollis undertook a major redesign, intending to produce a viceless aircraft with many more modern features than the somewhat pedestrian types of the day. G-AEMA was used to try out several concepts before the Cygnet II was ready and Hollis flew the prototype, G-AFVR, in 1939. With its easy access, side-by-side, cockpit, generous flaps and above all, tricycle undercarriage with rudder-bar actuated ground steering, the Cygnet II was well greeted. Only a small production run was achieved before General Aircraft became a major contractor in the war effort. Included in this was the tank-carrying Hamilcar assault glider, designed by Hollis and test flown by Charles Hughesdon*. Post-1945 Hollis returned to the design office at Fairey, playing a major part in Firefly and Gannet development.

A Wilson

FG OFF A WILSON, a production test pilot at Hucclecote, engaged on testing Armstrong Whitworth Albemarles being built at the Gloster plant under the aegis of A W Hawksley. (Gloster and Armstrong Whitworth were part of the Hawker Siddeley Group and 'A W Hawksley' was an administrative creation to manage the manufacture of Albemarles at Hucclecote.) On 6th September 1943, Fg Off Wilson and F Cole, B Latham and R Sands took off in Mk.II V1708 for a routine test flight. After about 40 minutes the Albemarle was seen approaching Hucclecote at low level and with the port engine feathered; at about 100ft the aircraft yawed, crashed and burst into flames: all on board died.

Hugh 'Willie' Wilson

17th Sep 1936	Broughton-Blayney Brawny G-AENM
	1 x 32hp Carden-Ford
23rd Dec 1938	Blackburn Roc I L3057
	1 x 890hp Bristol Perseus XII

Notes: Brawney first flown at Hanworth, Roc at Brough.

Hugh John Wilson, born 1908. Joined the RAF in September 1929, going on to Armstrong Whitworth Siskin IIIAs with 111 Squadron at Duxford. In 1935 he became an instructor at the Blackburn-managed 5 Elementary & Reserve Flying Training School (E&RFTS) at Hanworth where, among many others, he taught 'Sandy' Powell to fly.

WHILE instructing at Hanworth, Flt Lt Hugh Wilson, inevitably called 'Willie', first flew the prototype Broughton-Blayney Brawny single-seat parasol sporting monoplane being developed at the aerodrome. This debut took place during the annual Garden Party, in full view of the gathered worthies. Only two Brawnys were completed. Blackburn moved

Designed and first flown by Hollis Williams, the prototype Cygnet II G-AFVR was impressed into the RAF during the war. It was regularly flown from 1949 until destroyed in a fatal crash in August 1969. *KEC*

The third prototype Roc, L3059, was completed as a floatplane and tested at MAEE in 1939. *Peter Green Collection*

Hugh to its other school, 5 Elementary and Reserve Flying Training School, at Brough, where he was appointed CFI by 1937. During 1938 he was transferred from tutoring at Brough to test piloting at the airfield, under 'Bill' Bailey*. In December 1938 Bill was away on HMS *Courageous*, helping 800 Squadron to work up on the Blackburn Skua fleet fighter and Willie was deputed to test fly the turreted version, the Roc. Production of the Roc was sub-contracted to Boulton Paul.

By 1940 Hugh was at RAE Farnborough, rising to wing commander and chief pilot. He was succeeded by 'Roly' Falk* in 1943. By 1946 he was officer commanding ETPS. On 7th November 1946 he flew Gloster Meteor IV EE454 to a new world record of 606.25mph. (For more details, see Eric Greenwood.) Having left the RAF, in 1948 Hugh was retained by Planet Aircraft as test pilot for the company's radical four-seater, the Satellite, powered by a DH Gipsy Queen mounted within the mid-fuselage, driving a pusher propeller. The prototype, G-ALOI, was shown off in the static at the 1948 Farnborough SBAC airshow and then taken to Blackbushe for flight test. Try as he might, Hugh could not get *Oscar-India* to fly and the project was abandoned. Hugh was back in the employ of Blackburn by the mid-1950s, as sales manager for the engine division. Gp Capt Hugh John Wilson CBE AFC* died on 5th September 1990, aged 82.

The flightless Planet Satellite on show at the 1948 SBAC airshow at Farnborough. *via Don Middleton*

John Wilson

22 Aug 1950	DH Venom NF.2 G-5-3 1 x 4,850lbst DH Ghost 103
15 Nov 1950	DH Vampire T.11 G-5-7 1 x 3,500lbst DH Goblin 35

Notes: Venom first flew from Hatfield, Vampire from Christchurch.

John William Wilson, born 1924. Joined the RAF in 1942 and trained in Canada. Flew DH Mosquito VIs operationally in Malaya, 1945, then Gloster Meteor IIIs in Britain. John was posted in 1947 to the Air Fighting Development Squadron element of the Central Fighter Establishment at West Raynham and was involved in Vampire tropical trials in Malaya during 1948.

Jᴏʜɴ Wɪʟsᴏɴ joined de Havilland at Hatfield in 1948 and on 27th July 1949 was on John Cunningham's* right hand side for the first flight of the Comet prototype. During 1950 he carried out the maiden flights of the Venom night-fighter and the trainer version of the Vampire. The latter was an important boost to the sales potential of both the Vampire and the Venom, particularly with overseas customers. John was also involved in Sea Vixen development flying before he became Chief Operations Engineer. He went on to oversee the development of the Trident, HS.125 and HS.146.

The prototype Venom NF.2, G-5-3, in 1950. *Peter Green Collection*

Vernon Wilson

Vernon Gorry Wilson, born 1902. Apprenticed as an engineer to Avro in 1918. Served with the RAF 1919 to 1930, flying Supermarine Southamptons and later instructing in Iraq. Joined Imperial Airways in 1930, piloting AW Atalantas, Handley Page HP.42s, Short Calcuttas and Kents. Vernon was the sole survivor of the crash of Calcutta G-AASJ City of Khartoum off Alexandria, Egypt, on 31st December 1935. He flew for Croydon-based International Air Freight flying Curtiss Condors from 1937 until 1938 when he signed up with Jersey Airways.

Vᴇʀɴᴏɴ Wɪʟsᴏɴ became a test pilot for Fairey in 1939 and by 1941 was working at Ringway signing off aircraft from the Heaton Chapel factory. On 6th November 1942 he was piloting Barracuda I P9661 on a routine test flight, it failed to come out of a dive and crashed just outside of the airfield perimeter. Vernon Gorry Wilson, aged 40, was killed.

'Timber' Wood at the helm of the Beverley prototype, XB289, Farnborough, September 1956. *Peter Green Collection*

Harold 'Timber' Wood

20 Jun 1950	Blackburn Universal Freighter Mk.1 WF320 4 x 2,020hp Bristol Hercules 730
14 Jun 1953	Blackburn Universal Freighter Mk.2 WZ889 4 x 2,840hp Bristol Centaurus 171

Notes: Both flown at Brough. WZ889 was the interim prototype for the Beverley.

Harold Wood, born 1903. Learned to fly at Filton in 1925, taught by Cyril Uwins. In 1931 he was appointed as the chief pilot for the newly-formed Hillman's Airways based at Maylands, Essex. Harold took up a post as personal pilot to Major Claude Ronald Anson to fly General Aircraft Monospar Croydon G-AECB to and from Australia. (Harry Schofield* first flew this machine in May 1935.) Leaving Croydon on 30th July 1936, G-AECB arrived in Melbourne in just short of 73 hours flying time. On the return journey Harold had to force land the Croydon on a coral reef in the Timor Sea off the north Australian coast. Harold and his crew were rescued, but G-AECB was abandoned to the waves. After this he took up a post as instructor for Flying Training Ltd before becoming the chief pilot for Heston-based British American Air Services. Harold served in the RAF 1939-1941.*

Fʟᴛ Lᴛ Hᴀʀᴏʟᴅ Wᴏᴏᴅ was a tall man and the combination of this and his surname resulted in the nickname 'Timber', most often shortened to 'Tim'. In 1941 he joined General Aircraft at Hanworth as CTP. Flying was varied, including development work on the Hamilcar assault glider and sub-contract work, including de Havilland Mosquitos and Fairey Fireflies. Designer F F Crocombe used the experience of the massive Hamilcar to develop a series of designs for a tactical airlifter and these gelled into the Universal Freighter, which was pitched to Specification

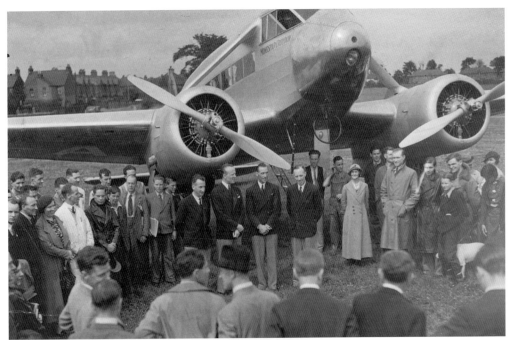

A ceremony prior to the departure of the General Aircraft Monospar Croydon for Australia, July 1936. In blazers below the starboard Pratt & Whitney Wasp Junior for left to right are: Mr Davies, engineer; Lord Sempill; 'Timber' Wood'; Charlie Gilroy, radio operator. *General Aircraft Ltd*

Left: A 1952 brochure for the Blackburn Universal.

Below: Troops embarking into a Beverley C.1 – the boom at the rear carried seating for personnel, which could use the hatch for parachuting. *KEC*

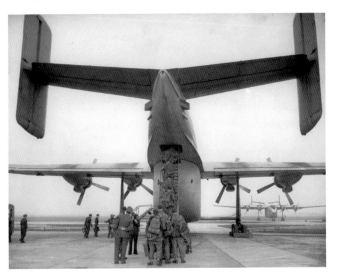

C3/46. Construction of the 162ft-span double-deck monster with an empty weight of 62,860lb began at the Feltham factory. On 1st January 1949 General Aircraft and Blackburn merged and Timber was appointed as CTP. Brough's CTP, Peter Lawrence* concentrated on naval prototypes, leaving the freighter project to his new boss. The prototype Universal Freighter was erected at Brough and Timber flew WF320, with D G Brade as co-pilot, in June 1950. Meanwhile the design was considerably revised to meet RAF needs for air-dropping heavy loads, with greatly increased power and very nearly double the load-carrying capability. Known as the Universal Freighter Mk.2, this was essentially the Beverley and a contract for 47 was placed. Interim prototype WZ889 was flown by the same crew in June 1953 and production was completed in 1958. In June 1954 Timber competed in the King's Cup air race at Baginton and entered the history books by winning in Miles Messenger G-AKBO at 133mph – this machine was airworthy in 2015. With the end of Beverley production, Timber retired in April 1959, handing on to Derek Whitehead*. Flt Lt Harold Wood died in 1980, aged 77.

Herbert Wood

1912	Vickers No.3 Monoplane
	1 x 60hp REP

Herbert Frederick Wood, a captain in the cavalry, learned to fly with the Bristol school at Brooklands, gaining Aviators' Certificate No.37 on 29th November 1910 on a 'Bristol' – ie Boxkite. He flew Boxkites for Bristol at Larkhill, but probably not in a test pilot capacity.

Captain Herbert Wood – 'Bertie' to his friends – retired from the Army in 1911 and via his friendship with Vickers director Sir Trevor Dawson was appointed manager of the company's newly-founded aviation department. An agreement was reached with French designer Robert Esnault-Pelterie (REP) and three of his monoplanes, and at least one engine, were acquired. On 28th March 1911 Bertie flew the first of these from the newly founded Joyce Green flying field at Dartford.

Meanwhile Major Archibald Low had been recruited as designer and he set about altering the REPs significantly. In *British Aviation – The Pioneer Years 1903-1914*, Harald Penrose quotes Archibald's scarifying assessment of Bertie: "A first class horseman who had the correct shibboleths for a society gentleman, but outside that range had the mentality of a boy ten years old or even younger". (If, like the author, you need a refresher on 'shibboleths', allow me: language or phraseology signifying belonging to a particular social class.) Needless to say, the Captain and the Major were at loggerheads most of the time: Bertie got the upper hand: Archibald was dismissed in 1913.

The No.3 was a two-seat side-by-side monoplane and can be regarded as the first 'indigenous' Vickers machine. Bertie is known to have been flying a Vickers-Farman biplane from Brooklands in May 1913 but beyond this date he appears to increasingly take a managerial role, for example gaining a contract to build Royal aircraft Factory BE.2s in 1913 and laying down a production run of FB.5 'Gunbuses' as a private-venture in 1914 – in both cases significantly advancing Vickers as an aircraft manufacturer – not bad for a 'ten-year-old'! With the onset of the Great War, Bertie re-joined the Army, with the 12th Lancers building a reputation for leading from the front and with great courage. Major Herbert Frederick Wood died on 12th December 1918.

Geoff Worrall

Geoffrey Worrall, born 1922. Joined the RAF in 1940, training as an electrical technician but in 1943 started flying training, which was completed in South Africa. He flew operationally with 81 Squadron in India and later Java, flying Republic Thunderbolt IIs up to June 1946. Geoff was posted to 60 Squadron, also on Thunderbolts, converting to Supermarine Spitfire FR.18s in 1947, and was based at Kuala Lumpur, Malaya, and Tengah, Singapore. 'Demobbed' in 1948, Geoff flew for a while with 616 (South Yorkshire) Squadron RAuxAF, from Finningley, on Gloster Meteor F.3s and F.4s.

In September 1950 Flt Lt Geoffrey Worrall joined Gloster at Moreton Valence testing Meteors and also taking part in conversion training in the Middle East for customer air forces. In 1954 he was appointed Chief PTP by 'Dickie' Martin*, Gloster CTP, and Geoff became increasingly a part of Javelin development flying as well as production testing of the delta. On 8th April 1960 Dickie was in command of Javelin FAW.8 XJ128, taking off from Hucclecote and finishing at the flight test airfield at Moreton Valence. This was the final maiden flight of the long line of Gloster fighters. Geoff took over as CTP in 1960, but work was limited to upgrades and in 1962 the Hucclecote factory closed. By 1967 Geoff had moved to BAC at Filton and was at work on various aspects of the Concorde programme in non-pilot roles. Geoff retired from what had become British Aerospace in 1984.

Henry Worrall

5 Apr 1932	Airspeed Ferry G-ABSI
	2 x 120hp upright DH Gipsy II and
	1 x 120hp inverted DH Gipsy II

Henry Vernon Worrall, born in 1888 in Fiji. (Sir Alan Cobham in* A Time to Fly, *referred to him as a New Zealander.) By 1914 he was in Britain and he trained as a pilot in the RNAS. In January 1918 he was flying with 2 Wing RNAS and was involved in the action against the former Imperial German warship* Goeben, *then sailing with the Ottoman Navy. Sub*

The prototype Airspeed Ferry, G-ABSI, at Shoreham in 1939. *KEC*

Lt Worrall piloted one of two aircraft that attacked at night the beached vessel in the Dardanelles, hitting it with bombs. By 1920 Henry was flying Fairey III floatplanes with 230 Squadron RAF from Felixstowe. In 1927 he travelled to South America where he carried out demonstrations of a Blackburn Velos floatplane on behalf of the manufacturer: Brazil was the main 'target' but other countries were also visited. From November 1927 to June 1928 Henry was co-pilot to Sir Alan Cobham in the around-Africa route survey flight in Short Singapore I G-EBUP. In January 1929 Henry became CFI of the Yorkshire Aeroplane Club at Sherburn-in-Elmet.

PRESUMABLY in crisp notes, the sum of £30 was passed to Henry Worrall, chief flying instructor of the Yorkshire Aeroplane Club (YAC), at Sherburn-in-Elmet on 5th April 1932. In present-day values that fee equates to £1,650 and it had been negotiated by the management of Airspeed Aircraft to test fly the nascent company's first powered aircraft, the tri-motor biplane Ferry. The Ferry had been built in York and in the previous days had been wheeled on its own undercarriage to Sherburn. Henry carried out a 19 minute test flight; he asked for rudder to be re-balanced and felt that it flew slightly nose down, but otherwise was happy. Four Ferries were built.

YAC re-located to Yeadon in late 1931 and by 1933 Henry was its general manager. In 1942 the massive Avro 'shadow factory' was built at Yeadon and Henry was appointed as its Chief PTP, testing Ansons, Lancasters and Yorks through to 1948. 'Jimmy' Orrell*, Avro CTP from August 1947, referred to Henry as 'Digger' – presumably because of his antipodean roots. Flt Lt Henry Vernon Worrall DSC* CDG left Britain in 1956 to settle in Australia.

Leslie Victor Worsdell

28 Feb 1959	Marshall MA.4 VF665
	1 x 145hp DH Gipsy Major 7

Leslie Victor Worsdell, born 1917. He learned to fly at Hatfield in 1935 under the RAF reserve scheme and completed his course at Marshall of Cambridge at Teversham. After this he became an instructor at the Marshall-operated Cambridge Aero Club. Leslie was called up in September 1939 and instructed at 12 SFTS Grantham. In January 1942 Leslie was posted to 3 OTU at Chivenor and converted to the Bristol Beaufort torpedo bomber. In July 1942 he joined 39 Squadron, variously based in Egypt but mostly flying from Luqa, Malta. Leslie was involved in extensive 'ops' against shipping in the Mediterranean. In September 1943 he was instructing on Bristol Beaufighters at 132 (Coastal) OTU, East Fortune.

SQN LDR LESLIE VICTOR WORSDELL DFC was 'demobbed' in November 1945 and immediately took up the post of CTP for Marshall of Cambridge. A major sub-contractor, modifier and operator, the bulk of the work of 'Marshalls' is beyond the scope of this work but the creation of the unique MA.4 boundary layer control (BLC) test-bed certainly merits detailing. Using the prototype Auster T.7 VF665 as the basis, the airframe was radically restructured to provide Cambridge University's Engineering Laboratory with a practical BLC test-bed. A new wing with small retractable spoilers and the 'blown' surface was created; the ailerons were made to droop; a variable incident tailplane was fitted, a 60hp Budworth gas turbine, venting under the rear fuselage, was installed to provide suction for the BLC; a rearward facing FTO position was shoehorned into the crowded fuselage. Leslie took VF665 for a brief circuit at Teversham in February 1959 and beyond that began to expand the performance envelope, processing the BLC and readying the MA.4 for hand-over to the University. The aircraft was operated for the University throughout its life by Marshall, with a pilot provided by the company. On 8th March 1966 Brian Wass* and FTO Ramaswamiah Krishnamirthy, an engineering student, took off for the MA.4's 140th flight. The aircraft was last seen in an inverted spin and it crashed, killing both occupants, near West Wratting in Suffolk. Leslie retired from test piloting at Teversham in 1977, but continued to fly in other capacities with Marshall for several more years. Sqn Leslie Victor Worsdell OBE DFC died on 24th January 2008, aged 91.

The Marshall MA.4 – the cylinder under the rudder is the housing for an anti-spin parachute.
MAP

Supermarine S.5 N219 at Calshot in 1929. *via John Lowry*

Oscar Worsley

| 7 Jun 1927 | Supermarine S.5 N219 |
| | 1 x 875hp Napier Lion VIIA |

OCCASIONALLY aircraft ordered directly for research or other special purposes have been first flown by the 'client' and not by a manufacturer's test pilot. Sometimes the reason was that time was pressing... For former MAEE Felixstowe pilot Flt Lt Oscar E Worsley of the RAF High Speed Flight both reasons came into play. Oscar was to compete in the tenth Schneider Trophy contest to be held in Venice on 26th September 1927. The first of three Supermarine S.5 floatplanes, N219, was roaded to Felixstowe and was ready for flight test in the first week of June, Oscar carrying out the flight on the 7th. The machine was then dismantled and placed on the MV *Eworth*, which arrived at Venice on 31st August. Oscar took second place in the competition, N219 averaging 273mph: the race was won by Flt Lt S N Webster in S.5 N220 at 281mph. N219 was also in contention in the 1929 Schneider Trophy at Calshot, when it was flown by Flt Lt D D'Arcy Greig into third place at 282mph.

Don Wright

| 22 Aug 1974 | Short 330 G-BSBH |
| | 2 x 1,120shp P&W Canada PT6A-45A |

Donald Burn Wright, born 1930. Joined the merchant navy in 1946 working for the Blue Star Line and then Athel Line. In 1953 he enlisted with the RAF and learned to fly in Canada. In 1954 he was posted to 115 Squadron at Marham, on English Electric Canberra B.2s. He graduated from ETPS Course No.19 at Farnborough in 1960 and was posted to RAE.

DON WRIGHT joined Shorts at Sydenham, becoming Project Pilot for the Skyvan. He succeeded Denis Tayler* as CTP in 1969. In August 1974 he flew the prototype of the Short 330 twin-turboprop airliner, based on the main wing, tails and fuselage sections of the Skyvan. (*Bravo-Hotel* is just about extant, lying in a scrapyard in Portadown, Northern Ireland.) Don retired from the post in 1976, handing on to Lindsay Cumming*. Don became personal pilot to HRH Prince Mohammed Bin Faisal Al Saud, flying an HS.125 and later a BAC One-Eleven out of Jeddah, Saudi Arabia. From 1979 he was a captain for Air Europe, later becoming training captain on Boeing 737s for the airline. In 1990 he took up part-time piloting for Channel Express, flying Handley Page Heralds. Donald Burn Wright OBE died in 2005, aged 75.

The prototype Short 330, G-BSBH, on an early test flight, 1974. *Shorts*

Howard Wright

13 May 1913	Wight Seaplane No.1
	1 x 160hp Gnome

Howard Theophilus Wright, born 1867. Apprenticed to his father's engineering works at Tipton, near Dudley. The company acted as a sub-contractor to Hiram Maxim, building the boiler for his unsuccessful 1894 biplane. Howard later went to work for Hiram at his workshops in Kent. In 1905 Howard and his brothers formed Howard T Wright Brothers Co Ltd a general engineering concern based in Putney and later Battersea. In 1907 Howard decided that the business should concentrate on building and designing for aviators and about 30 different projects were embarked upon. With William Manning, Howard designed a biplane in 1908 and in 1910 a very successful biplane on classic Farman lines. Howard sold the company to the Coventry Ordnance Works in 1911 and he and William initially worked with the new set up.

B Y early 1913 Howard Wright accepted the post of manager and chief designer for the East Cowes, Isle of Wight-based J Samuel White and Company's newly-established aviation department. The designs of the new concern were marketed under the trade name Wight, a convenient combination of Wright, White and the island. In May 1913 the Wight Seaplane No.1, a two-seater pusher twin-float biplane, was ready for test and Howard determined to be a designer-pilot. Launched on the Medina, it was towed out into the open waters of the Solent for its maiden flight. On take-off the No.1 reared upwards at an alarming angle, stalled and crashed into the water. Howard and the No.1 were rescued; Howard suffering back injuries. The 'bones' of the No.1 were used in the second Wight Seaplane, but the company opted to bring in renowned test pilot 'Freddie' Raynham* to do the honours. Later Wight machines were piloted by Gordon England*. Howard left J Samuel White in September 1917, establishing himself as a technical adviser and later as a management consultant.

Maurice Wright

8 Apr 1923	English Electric Wren J6973
	1 x 3hp ABC

Maurice Edward Arthur Wright, born 1893. Flew a Wright-type glider at Eastchurch in 1913 and befriended Richard Fairey, this became a long-lasting comradeship. Joined the RNAS in 1914 and flew operationally in the North Sea, the Dardanelles and the Middle East, mostly in Short 184 floatplanes. Later tested aircraft for the RNAS at the Isle of Grain, Kent. This role was continued when Maurice transferred to the RAF in 1918 and he was later seconded to the Air Ministry for similar duties. His elder brother was Kenneth Wright – see Charles McMullin.*

W ITH no resident test pilot, the English Electric Company had Maurice Wright highly recommended to them to carry out the maiden flight of the first machine to carry the 'EE' name. This was the Wren single-seat ultralight. On 5th April 1923 it was taken to Ashton Part in Preston and Maurice conducted three 'hops'. It was moved to the more expansive vistas of Lytham St Anne's and on the 8th Maurice managed a seven-minute excursion and was soon taking the delicate craft for longer and longer sorties. Maurice and Flt Lt W Longton flew the second and third Wrens at Lympne during the 1923 Light Aeroplane Trials. In 1925 Maurice was invited to become a director of Fairey and later he took up a similar position with the Belgian sister company, Avions Fairey. Sqn Ldr Maurice Edward Arthur Wright AFC died in 1957, aged 64.

The third Wren survives at the Shuttleworth Collection, Old Warden (here in September 1977) and flies when conditions are co-operative. *KEC*

George Wynne-Eaton

7 May 1938	Arpin A.1 G-AFGB
	1 x 70hp Salmson AD.9R
24 Apr 1939	Taylorcraft Auster Plus C G-AFNW
	1 x 55hp Lycoming O-145-A2

THE first record of George Wynne-Eaton is his appointment as test pilot for CW Aircraft of Slough in 1937 when he was demonstrating the prototype Cygnet G-AEMA, which had been first flown by Hubert Broad*. The company folded in March 1938 and George moved on to test Morris Arpin's two-seat, tricycle undercarriage, pusher monoplane, the A.1. This he first flew at Hanworth on 7th May 1938 – the A.1 remained a one-off. The opposite could be said for his next prototype, the first British-built Taylorcraft Plus C, the first of the very successful Auster dynasty. George flew G-AFNW from Ratcliffe and its descendants remained in production, finally under the 'Beagle' label until the late 1960s. George moved to Northern Ireland during the war, becoming a PTP with Short Brothers and Harland, testing Stirlings alongside Harold Piper* and Geoffrey Tyson*. George flew Mk.IV PW405, the last of 134 Stirlings tested from Aldergrove on 3rd February 1945.

The Arpin A.1, probably at RAeS Garden Party at the Great West Aerodrome, Harmondsworth, May 1938. *Peter Green Collection*

The founder-member of the Auster dynasty, Plus C G-AFNW, at Rearsby 1939. *KEC*

Chris Yeo

20 Oct 1981	SEPECAT Jaguar GR.1 ACT XX765
	2 x 7,305lbst Rolls-Royce/Turboméca RT 172 Adour 104
6 Apr 1994	Eurofighter 2000 DA.2 ZH588
	2 x 9,100lbst Turbo Union RB.199-34R-104E

Christopher John Yeo, born 1946. Joined the RAF in 1965 and from March 1968 to March 1970 flew EE Canberra B.15s with 45 Squadron from Tengah, Singapore. The McDonnell Douglas Phantom FGR.2 was pioneered into RAF frontline service by 6 and 54 Squadrons at Coningsby from June 1969 and Chris joined the latter; helping perfect tactics and becoming an instrument rating examiner. Graduated from ETPS Course No.34 at Boscombe Down, 1975 and he was then posted to A&AEE 'A' Squadron.

ALONGSIDE the banks of the River Ribble on 6th April 1994 a prototype fighter screamed into the air from the British Aerospace (BAe) airfield at Warton. That machine was DA.2, the first British Eurofighter 2000, later named Typhoon. Today, Typhoons continue to blast off from the same runway and look set to do so for many years to come. Piloting DA.2 that day in 1994 was Chris Yeo, he and everyone else around him could not be aware that it was to be the *last* 'first' of any significant *manned* British aircraft programme to the present day.

Sqn Ldr Chris Yeo joined BAe at Warton in 1978 from Boscombe Down. Chris provided the foreword for Volume One of *Testing to the Limits* and the author asked him what he thought of ETPS. Chris explained that he found: "the technical bit was hard work, but I could see the point of it all". The task of the tutors was to transform the intake from experienced pilots to "something *very* different, a test pilot. [The course was] the toughest thing I've ever done in my life, but also the most rewarding – you're never the same again."

Chris Yeo with the EAP test-bed. Chris flew the second sortie of this machine, on 10th August 1986. *BAE Systems via Chris Yeo*

Life at Warton was very varied, Chris was involved with Hawk, Jaguar and Tornado trials; he flew the HS Buccaneer S.2 Tornado radar test-beds and delivered refurbished Canberras. Jaguar work included asymmetric stores carriage, operating from grass strips and Low Light Television experiments, among many others. The very different nature of test piloting was reinforced at Warton: "the work was always new and original and test pilots are a fundamental part of the design team." This is not confined to the ergonomics of the cockpit and how the software displays should look; Chris had a remit that ran across all elements of the complex airframe and its systems. His input was valued at every stage, although he: "didn't win all the battles, but you wouldn't expect to."

I wanted to talk about the lead up to the first flight of DA.2 and the mind-set needed. Chris explained that the build up took in all forms of presentation: written reports and estimations, procedure diagrams, static displays, functionality rigs through to simulators. "As the project crystalizes, the rigs and simulators become more and more representative and this means that you

begin to fly the first flight endlessly; long before the real thing comes along." As the flight control laws are developed, fault presentation is built up in complexity on the simulator. For the actual test schedule, a 'to do' list is created with a vast number of checks – in many configurations and combinations – to go through. This does not preclude 'free-flying' as it is important for fault-finding to think out how the 'customer' will fly the aircraft in routine and 'un-planned' manners.

Liaison with the DASA test pilot, Peter Weger, at Manching, Germany, was important as both men were going through the process more or less in parallel. Peter was the first man to fly a Eurofighter 2000, DA.1 on 27th March 1994, and this gave Chris a few days to quiz him. All of the prototypes carried telemetry and other devices recording vast amounts of data, but: "you can't beat talking things through with a colleague". Nothing that Peter passed on was out-of-the-blue; as Chris said, "we had tried and tested every possible element, including all sorts of failures – both physical and system". So, the canopy goes down, all the systems and comms have been checked, what

On 15th March 1984, Chris flew the Jaguar ACT with large leading edge strakes. *British Aerospace*

goes through the mind of a man about to fly something as ground-breaking as Typhoon? "The checks, the procedures and talk with the tower dominate, you consciously put the occasion away – there will be time enough for that after shut-down."

Two aircraft provided the stepping stones to Typhoon and Chris was involved in both. After a brief operational life, Jaguar GR.1 XX765 was ferried back to Warton on 4th August 1978 where BAe undertook a complex rebuild to turn it into the ACT – Active Control Technology – demonstrator. ACT is perhaps best known as fly-by-wire, no physical linkage from the pilot's controls to the spoilers, 'elevators' and rudder, all being moved by digitally-controlled actuators. This Jaguar was destined to be the world's first aircraft to fly with a digital quadruplex control system with no physical back-up. Such systems would allow future fighter designs to be inherently unstable, allowing regimes that could not be obtained with 'conventional' controls. Chris was at the helm when XX765 first flew in this new form on 20th October 1981. BAe, A&AEE and the RAE were all involved in testing this pioneer. The FBW Jaguar programme successfully completed all of its objectives including demonstrating exemplary flying characteristics and retired in November 1984: it is now on show at the RAF Museum Cosford.

By July 2000 Typhoon DA.2 ZH588 had gained its all-over black colour scheme adopted when the airframe was covered with 490 pressure sensors. *Courtesy and © British Aerospace*

From the ACT Jaguar, BAe could take the leap to the EAP test-bed, ZF534, first flown by David Eagles* on 8th August 1986. Two days later Chris experienced the EAP for the first time, a 90-minute familiarisation sortie. It was Chris that piloted the EAP on its public debut, at the SBAC airshow at Farnborough in September 1986. EAP was retired on 1st May 1991, but by then it had paved the way for the incredible Typhoon.

Chris was in command of ZH588, the first UK-assembled Typhoon to fly, at Warton on 6th April 1994. Both the German-assembled DA.1 and DA.2 were fitted with RB.199 Mk.104E turbofans in place of the intended Eurojet EJ200s. (Derek Reeh* flew two-seater DA.4, the first EJ200-fitted example on 14th March 1997.) DA.2 was in the static at the Paris Salon, Le Bourget, in June 1995 and was displayed at Farnborough in September 1996. Sqn Ldr Simon Dyde became the first RAF pilot to sample the new type, flying ZH588 from Warton on 9th November 1995. ZH588 was grounded at Warton during 1998 for installation of EJ200-01A turbofans to continue its part in the development programme. On 29th July 2007 it was retired to Coningsby for spares recovery and now graces the 'Milestones of Flight' hall at the RAF Museum, Hendon.

Chris was appointed as CTP in 1985 and two years later became Director of Flight Operations, with Don Thomas* taking on the role of CTP. For the latter post Chris was not only responsible for the day-to-day running of the flight test team at Warton, he was also in charge of activities at Brough and Dunsfold. Chris left BAe in 1997 and was succeeded by Derek Reeh.

Chris joined FRA – Flight Refuelling Aviation – operating civil registered Dassault Falcon 20s on special mission tasks, including target simulation and target-towing, on contract to the Ministry of Defence and other agencies. With his test piloting experience, Chris was also involved in testing modifications to the fleet; the Falcons having wing pylons for a variety of payloads. From January 2000 Chris instructed at ETPS, setting up and tutoring the first two Civil Flight Test courses. He took a one-year contract with Airbus at Toulouse, France, from August 2001 testing twin-jet A320s and A330s and the four-jet A340-500s and -600s. Re-joined FRA – soon to be renamed Cobham – in June 2003, becoming Deputy Chief Training Captain, retiring from the operation in 2011. Sqn Ldr Christopher John Yeo OBE AFC now has over 9,300 hours on over 60 types; these days he enjoys high performance on two wheels, as a globe-trotting mountain biker.

'Jan' Zurakowski

| 12 Oct 1948 | Gloster Meteor F.8 VT150 |
| | 2 x 3,600lbst RR Derwent 8 |

Janusz Zurakowski, born 1914 in the Ukraine, then part of Imperial Russia. He learned to fly in 1935, joining the Polish Air Force the following year. With the German invasion of Poland, 'Jan' claimed a Luftwaffe Dornier shot down before he managed to escape to France and then to Britain. He was posted to 234 Squadron, flying Supermarine Spitfire Is from Middle Wallop. He opened his RAF 'score' with a Messerschmitt Bf 110 on 15th August 1940. On the 24th he

was shot down over the Isle of Wight by a Bf 109 of JG 53: he crash landed, but was unhurt. Damaged in combat on 5th September, Jan force landed N3279 on 5th September: both man and machine returned to the fray. Posted to 609 Squadron, also at Middle Wallop and on Spitfire Is, on 5th October 1940. Jan was 'rested' in March 1941, instructing at several OTUs before flying with a series of Polish-manned units: 315 (December 1941, Northolt), 306 (April 1942, Kirton-in-Lindsey) and 315 (June 1942, Woodvale) Squadrons, the latter as CO. Jan's victory tally was as follows: two 'kills', two shared, one shared 'probable', one damaged. He was awarded the Cross of Valour, with two Bars, and the Virtuti Militari. Graduated from ETPS No.2 Course at Boscombe Down 1944-1945, going on to fly with A&AEE. On 3rd December 1945 Jan was demonstrating the first English Electric-built DH Vampire F.I TG274 at Boscombe Down to a delegation from the USSR. During a slow pass, he let the speed decay and TG274 – first flown at Samlesbury by Geoffrey de Havilland JNR on 20th April 1945 – ended up on its belly in a cloud of dust. TG274 was a write off; Jan was OK, but red-faced!*

SQN LDR JANUSZ ZURAKOWSKI – variously referred to as 'Jan' and 'Zura' – joined Gloster at Moreton Valence under CTP 'Bill' Waterton* in 1947, becoming senior development test pilot. In October 1948 Jan first flew the prototype of the definitive Meteor day fighter, the exceptional F.8. He also carried out the maiden flights of two sub-variant prototypes, the tactical reconnaissance FR.9 VW360 on 23rd March 1950 and the dedicated photo-recce PR.10 VS968 six days later. On 4th April 1950 Jan flew Meteor F.8 VZ468 from Northolt to Kastrup in Denmark to create a new city-to-city record of 1 hours 5 minutes 55 seconds, averaging 541.4mph: his out and back time was 2 hours 29 minutes 8 seconds, at 478.6mph.

Jan's test piloting career is best known for two very different exploits – his astonishing 'cartwheel' aerobatic sequence and the maiden flight of Canada's incredible CF-105 Arrow. In Mike Lithgow's *Vapour Trails*, Neville Duke paid fine tribute to Zura's manoeuvre while demonstrating the Gloster Meteor F.8 demonstrator G-AMCJ fully loaded with rockets at the 1950 Farnborough SBAC airshow. "It consisted of a vertical climb at full throttle, to some 4,000ft where, at an appropriately low speed, one engine was fully throttled back; with the other engine at full throttle the Meteor performed a perfect cartwheel, nose over tail and tail over nose."

Jan described his signature airshow set piece in *Janusz Zurakowski – Legend in the Skies* by Bill Zuk and Jan. "I tried it on the Meteor by zooming at full power until I reached a vertical climb and when my speed dropped to about 80 knots I cut the power of one engine. When the aircraft started cartwheeling (rotation in the yawing plane), I would cut power of the other engine after one turn. Rotation would slow down, and in half a turn, vertical down speed was increased enough to stop the aircraft rotation. In the vertical position speed was building rapidly and at about 250 knots I was pulling out of the dive. ...At the end of the cartwheel the Meteor flicked into a spin; I put it intentionally into two turns of a spin to lose excess altitude. If the cartwheel was badly executed it could spin, but properly executed it stopped even without any oscillation at the end. The manoeuvre was a bit of fun but not of combat value..." Several names were devised by the media and commentators for this spectacular gyration: 'Catherine Wheel', the 'Zurabatic Cartwheel', 'Zurabatics', 'Zuras' but the inventor preferred to refer to it as the 'Fin Sling'.

When Bill Waterton returned from Avro Canada at Malton, Ontario, in 1950 having flown the first two CF-100 Canucks, Gloster sent Jan out as a follow-up; this 'secondment' was to help him determine Jan's future. Relations within Gloster were strained, Jan and Bill certainly had their 'moments', and in April 1952 Jan accepted the post of Chief Development Pilot for Avro Canada. At this point, Jan leaves the coverage of this book, but as he went on to fly an aircraft immersed, like the BAC TSR.2 programme, in angst and conspiracy theories, we'll continue... Jan worked on production testing and demonstrating the CF-100 and in this capacity he was back in Britain during September 1955 displaying a RCAF Mk.4B at the SBAC airshow at Farnborough. Jan's main purpose was getting ready for the incredibly advanced CF-105 Arrow, a twin-engined, delta wing interceptor way beyond the capabilities of the Gloster Javelin. Jan 'first flighted' the prototype CF-105, 25201, at Malton on 25th March 1958 and was greeted with adulation by the crowds upon his return. He went on to fly the next two of the five CF-105s completed. The entire project was axed by the Canadian government on 20th February 1959, by which time Jan had left Avro Canada. Sqn Ldr Janusz Zurakowski died on 9th February 2004, aged 89.

Crowds mobbing around the prototype Avro Canada CF-105 Arrow 25201 at Malton after the first flight, 25th March 1958: 'Zura' is standing in the cockpit. *Hawker Siddeley Canada*

CHAPTER SEVEN

They Also Serve

Each and every name that follows has stories to tell, just as significant as those given in Chapter Six and in Volume One but either they do not fit the criteria for entry as outlined at the beginning of Chapter Six or the information gleaned is so fleeting. To not include them at all would be a crime. Space restrictions mean that coverage is limited to the idividual's time as a test pilot.

This section is far from exhaustive and is a poor tribute to a largely unsung band: for example, inevitably, a lot of 1914-1918,

1939-1945 and late 1940s-1950s 'Cold War' surge production tests pilots – many of short-term postings – have slipped the net. A whole host of Supermarine production test pilots appears below, courtesy of Jeffrey Quill's *Spitfire – A Test Pilot's Story*, the great man being determined to 'credit' his small army if only in the briefest of manners. As with the rest of the work, with the help of readers, this study can only grow...

Gloster production test pilot Jack Hathorne hurtling low over Hucclecote in a locally-built Hurricane, past a yet to be deployed barrage balloon. Approaching from the east, he had flown down the Witcombe ridge and crossed the Cheltenham to Stroud road. Jack was killed testing a Hurricane in December 1940 at Hucclecote; ironically he is thought to have been avoiding the balloon barrage in mist when he came to grief. *KEC*

Alexander 'Sandy' Ian Aitken: Joined BAC at Warton by January 1977, mostly on Jaguars. In 1983 he took responsibility for chase aircraft and air-to-air photography sorties. Later flew for the communications fleet; he retired in 1995.

Cyril Geoffrey Marmaduke Alington: Flew for Austin Motors at Longbridge from 1940 and became Chief PTP from 1941, testing Battles, Hurricanes, Stirlings and Lancasters. Flew his last Lancaster on 27th July 1946. In 1949 became Chief PTP for Fairey, operating from White Waltham, Hamble and Ringway on Fireflies and Gannets. Became CTP of Fairey Australia in 1956. Geoffrey is profiled in Chapter Two and see the reference for Desmond Norman.

Flt Lt J P B Almack: Supermarine on Spitfires.

Clive Anderton: Seconded from 33 Maintenance Unit, Lyneham, to Supermarine at High Post, August to September 1944 – see Chapter Two.

Flt Lt A J Andrews DFC: Supermarine on Spitfires. Killed circa 1943 in a Spitfire XII while serving with 91 Squadron.

Lt Cdr Edward 'Ted' R Anson: Blackburn development flying Buccaneer S.1, seconded from Fleet Air Arm, 1959-1961.

Flt Lt Pierre Arend: Belgian – Supermarine on Spitfires.

Ken Ashley: Shorts, Sydenham 1955 on Britannias. By 1958 was with Hunting on Jet Provosts at Luton. Finally with Bristol at Filton, early 1960s.

John Ayres: Pilatus Britten-Norman at Bembridge on Islanders from circa 1986.

C A Ball: Blackburn, Brough, circa 1935.

Flt Lt F S Banner DFC*: Supermarine. Killed while practising ADDLs (aerodrome dummy deck landings) at High Post 31st August 1945 in Seafire XVII SW987. (Aircraft signed off from test and ready for collection by Fleet Air Arm early May 1945.)

Fg Off H W R 'Sonny' Banting: Assistant to 'Mutt' Summers at Vickers, Brooklands, late 1928. Testing the Supermarine F7/30 at Eastleigh 1934.

Jim 'Binnie' Barnes: Westland, Yeovil, Scouts, Wasps, Sea Kings. Suffered double engine failure ferrying Sea King HAS.1 XV372 from Filton to Yeovil, 12th July 1962. Executed forced landing at Harptree, Somerset; helicopter rolled over on landing, Barnes and crew OK.

Mr Barraclough: Bristol, Filton. Along with A Bolton radio operator; E C Brunt flight engineer; F C T Pullen electrical engineer, killed in flight test of Bristol Freighter Mk.21 G-AHJJ at Cowbridge, Wales, 21st March 1950. See J A C Northway in Chapter Six. (Second hand aircraft, refurbished for new customer, Silver City.)

Flt Lt Anthony 'Tony' C Bartley DFC: Seconded to Supermarine July 1941 to February 1942.

David M Bay: Percival, Luton, circa 1938-1940. Joined Fleet Air Arm and later served with Air Fighting Development Unit. Hawker at Langley on Hurricanes, seconded from MAP, 1941.

Christopher D Beaumont: Seconded to Vickers, Brooklands; Hawker, Langley; and Westland, Yeovil during World War Two, then DH Engines, Hatfield as CTP.

Flt Lt W R L Beaumont: Supermarine on Spitfires.

Sqn Ldr J L N Bennett-Baggs: Director of Blackburn Aircraft 1931-1950 and he combined these duties with production testing and sales work.

Arthur Berkeley: Gloster, Hucclecote, 1938-1941 on Henleys and Hurricanes.

W Birchenough: Airco, Hendon, circa 1916.

James 'Jim' Birnie: Pilot with Crop Culture (Aerial) Ltd, a Britten-Norman company, from late 1950s. Joined Britten-Norman in 1966; testing and delivering Islanders and Trislanders up to 1971.

C J Blackburn: Testing flying-boat production from English Electric, Lytham St Anne's, 1924-1926.

Richard 'Dickie' L C Blyth DSO DFC: English Electric, Samlesbury, Vampires 1945-1947.

Andy Blythe: BAE Systems, Warton, on Hawks from 2008, then Typhoons.

Lt Cdr D A Bowler: Westland, Yeovil, mid-1980s on Lynx.

Wg Cdr Archibald 'Archie' Douglas McNeill Boyd DSO DFC: Vickers, Brooklands and Wisley 1946 on Warwicks, Vikings, Valettas, Viscounts. Became an Assistant Sales Manager and later transferred to the nuclear submarine division.

D G Brade: Blackburn, Brough, co-pilot to 'Timber' Wood, see Chapter Six, on first flight of both Universal Freighters, 1950 and 1953.

Lt Cdr Roy S Bradley: Westland, Yeovil, helicopters from 1950.

Flt Lt J H Brew: (Omission from Chapter Seven, Volume One.) Castle Bromwich Aircraft Factory, killed 11th October 1944 in first test of Spitfire IX RR237 when it dived into ground near Nuneaton airfield.

Lt James 'Jimmy' Bridge: (Omission from Chapter Seven, Volume One – see also 'Bill' Waterton.) Gloster, Hucclecote and Moreton Valence, from 1946, killed in Meteor IV RA394 during asymmetric approach to Moreton Valence, 22nd April 1947.

Forrester Robin John Britten: See Desmond Norman in Chapter Six.

Flt Lt F J 'The Count' Brunton: Westland 1928-1931, Wapitis plus some Pterodactyl development flying.

Eric 'Buckers' Bucklow: BAC Wisley, 1953-1966 on VC-10s and One-Eleven. During 1964-1965 he was seconded to Hunting at Luton, on Jet Provosts. BAC Warton from February 1967 to 1987 on Canberras, Jet Provosts, Strikemasters, Jaguars and Tornados. Eric is profiled in Chapter Three, Volume One.

Peter Buggé: Test pilot and then Chief Development TP for de Havilland and HSA, Hatfield, 1949-1962. P2 to John Cunningham on first flight of the Comet 3 and Trident. Joined Airbus at Toulouse in 1980 on customer liaison.

G Frank Bullen: With Blackburn 1947-1949, development flying on the B-48 and work on Firebrand and Prentice. Joined Hawker 1949, becoming Senior PTP 1955 to 1960.

K A Butler: Westland, previously with RAE Farnborough. Killed in 1946-built, refurbished Spitfire F.22 PK545 near Yeovil, 16th February 1950.

Flt Lt T Burke: Supermarine on Spitfires and Seafires.

John Goodwin 'Bobby' Burns: Hunting Aircraft, Luton, from 1958 on Jet Provosts. Ferrying Jet Provost T.3 XM348 from Farnborough 4th September 1958 when engine fire warnings came on. Force landed near Twyford; XM348 written off, Bobby OK. Joined Blackburn at Brough 1959 on Buccaneers.

Peter Cadbury: Hawker, Langley, up to 1943 on Hurricanes. Gloster at Hucclecote 1943-1946 on Typhoons and then Meteors (at Moreton Valence).

William 'Bill' B Cairns AFC: Vickers/BAC from 1953, Valiants, Vanguards, at Brooklands and Wisley. Was flight engineer on first flight of the VC-10 – see 'Jock' Bryce in Volume One – and project pilot on VC-10 tropical trials.

Alan Calder: Testing flying-boat production from English Electric, Lytham St Anne's, 1924-1926.

Alf Camp: Former RAE autoland test pilot at Thurleigh. Joined Handley Page on Victor development flying from 1964.

Walter G Capley: (Formerly Kaepelli.) Swiss-born stressman and pilot working for Miles Aircraft; designed the M.18 trainer (see F G Miles in Chapter Six) and provided substantial input to the M.20 'stop-gap' fighter (see Tommy Rose). Put in charge of the M.52 supersonic research aircraft programme, also ran the Woodley Repair and Service Department *and* set up Miles Aircraft (Northern Ireland) Ltd in late 1944. Acted as a PTP for the company when he could; killed while flight testing Spitfire IX MH349 after servicing 8th February 1945 (some sources quote the 10th).

Major R H Carr with an Avro 504K; the date 16th May 1920 and the altitude – 2,000ft – deserve further investigation. *Peter Green Collection*

Swiss-born Walter Capley flying his creation, the M.18 prototype U2. Conceived as a Magister replacement, the previous design held sway! *Miles Aircraft*

Sqn Ldr John Michael Vowles 'Chips' Carpenter DFC*: Hawker, Langley, 1944-1945 on secondment.

Major Reginald H Carr: Mechanic for Claude Grahame-White from at least 1910, but 1913 was flying for him in displays, but also almost certainly in the manner of a PTP.

Lt John A Carrodus: PTP and development test for BAC 1962-1965 on Lightnings and occasionally Canberras. Later test pilot to the Air Registration Board and then the Civil Aviation Authority – see Chapter Four.

Keith H Chadbourn: PTP and instructor Fairey on Gannets, late 1950s-1962. Joined Westland 1976 on Wasps, Gazelles, Sea Kings and Lynx.

P R T Chamberlayne: Pilot for the Grahame-White Aviation Company, circa 1919.

R J Chandler: Blackburn, Holme-on-Spalding Moor, Buccaneer S.1s, circa 1964.

Flt Lt Clennell: Austin at Longbridge on Battles, 1940.

Flt Lt P J Clive: Supermarine on Spitfires and Seafires.

S M Collins: Westland on Lynx, c1980s.

Albert Coltman: Auster at Ratcliffe during 1939 and from Rearsby until at least 1940.

Flt Lt H A G Comerford: Supermarine on Spitfires.

Sqn Ldr A Ken 'Cookie' Cook DFC: Avro on Lancasters, late production Ansons and Avro XIXs, Lincolns, Athenas, Shackletons. Became senior air traffic controller at Woodford until retirement in 1971.

Sqn Ldr Peter Roland Cope: Armstrong Whitworth, Bitteswell, 1951-192 on Meteors. Joined Avro Canada in 1951, testing CF-100 Canuck and then CF-105 Arrow.

Plt Off Digby 'Digger' Cotes-Preedy GM: Gloster at Hucclecote and Moreton Valence 1946-1949 on Meteors.

Douglas 'Doug Cotton': Austin at Longbridge, deputy to Geoffrey Alington from early 1942. Wrote off Stirling III BK660 when he took off from Elmdon 23rd February 1943 with the elevators locked. Cotton, the flight engineer and a passenger escaped unhurt.

Ronald Arthur Cowpe: Rolls-Royce flight test at Filton from 1980. BAe at Brough from 1988 on the Pilatus PC-9 programme. BAE Warton from 1992-1996 on Hawks.

Lt Cdr Ron R Crayton: Westland initially on Wyverns, finishing on Whirlwind, Wessex, Sea King as Senior TP.

Flt Lt T Craxton DFC: Supermarine on Spitfires.

C B Critchley: (Omission from Chapter Seven, Volume One.) PTP for de Havilland. During the first air test of Mosquito VI HJ664 out of Hatfield on 14th February 1943 was observed executing slow rolls at around 3,000ft. The aircraft impacted two miles south of the airfield at Colney Heath, killing Critchley.

Lt Cdr Robert Michael Crosley DSC*: ATP Shorts, Sydenham, from 1948 to early 1950s.

Ken Cook and a Vickers Vildebeest I at Turnhouse during his time with 22 Squadron in 1934. *Peter Green Collection*

'Digger' Cotes-Preedy flew Bristol Blenheims with 236 Squadron during the Battle of Britain. By 1947 he was training Argentinean pilots to convert to the Meteor. *via Andy Thomas*

Sqn Ldr John Goodwin Cruse AFC: Joined Bristol Siddeley Engines at Filton on Olympus development for Concorde, flying the Vulcan B.1 test-bed XA903. To HSA Woodford on HS.748, P2 to Charles Masefield* on the first flight of Nimrod AEW.3 XZ286 at Woodford 16th July 1980, becoming AEW project pilot. Appointed DCTP under 'Robbie' Robinson* 1981, retired 1982.

Keith Davies: By 1914 was an experimental pilot with the Royal Aircraft Factory at Farnborough. Joined Parnall & Sons at Bristol in 1916 as test pilot, probably working on Hamble Babies. Helped in the conception/design of the company's Scout, which was to have been powered by a 250hp Sunbeam Maori II but the project was not completed. Left circa 1917 to run an aircraft factory in London.

Wg Cdr Neil Dawson: Joined BAE Systems at Warton in June 2003 on the Nimrod MRA.4 project – which was axed in 2010. Became CTP Large Aircraft Projects and Unmanned Air Systems – see also Chapter Six Volume One.

Sqn Ldr Leo Charles Evan de Vigne DSO DFC AFC: CTP for Armstrong Siddeley Motors at Bitteswell 1952-1953. Leo joined Westland in 1954 flying Wyverns but specifically testing the Westland-modified Gloster Meteor F.4 RA490 with up to 60% jet deflection between May and August 1954 before it moved on to RAE. Leo stayed with Westland and was testing and demonstrating Whirlwind HAR.10s in 1962.

Desmond 'Dizzy' de Villiers: South African. In 1944 he was seconded to de Havilland at Hatfield as ACTP. Left the RAF in 1946 and became CTP for DH Engines at Hatfield. Joined English Electric at Warton in 1955, becoming Chief PTP on Canberras and Lightnings. Retired 1966.

Flt Lt A Deytrikh: Supermarine on Spitfire and Seafires.

Jon S Dickens: Westland, Yeovil, on Lynx and Merlins, becoming Senior TP on Merlins. Testing second UK prototype EH101 PP4, ZF644, at 12,000ft on 7th April 1995 when uncommanded tail rotor pitch rendered the helicopter uncontrollable; Dickens, Don Maclaine* and FTOs G Douthwaite and A Wood all successfully baled out.

Angus Alan Douglas-Hamilton: 15th Duke of Hamilton. Joined Scottish Aviation 1967, later testing ferrying and displaying Bulldogs up to circa 1988.

George 'Loopy' Dunworth: Joined Boulton Paul on 15th June 1953, mostly on Canberras from Defford, but also flew the Tay-engined Viscount. Retired in 1966.

Philip Desmond Dye: South African. Joined BAe at Warton in December 1987, on Jaguars and Strikemasters. Hawk Project Pilot in 1993 and later Deputy CTP. Retired February 2001.

J Easdown: English Electric at Samlesbury on Hampdens and Halifaxes, 1940-1945.

Angus Douglas-Hamilton owned the second prototype Bulldog 104 G-AXIG from 1997 up to his death in 2010 – it is now displayed in the National Museum of Scotland, Edinburgh. *Scottish Aviation*

'**Jock' Eassie**: Shorts, DTP to Tom Brooke-Smith, flying such types as Sealand, Seamew, Sperrin, SB.4 and SC.1. First flew the first Sperrin, VX158, with a DH Gyron in the lower port nacelle on 7th July 1955 and then with a Gyron in the lower starboard position, 26th June 1956.

George Ellis: BAe at Hatfield from 1980; became project pilot HS.125-800 and -1000 at Hawarden, plus additional HS.146 work based at Woodford. (P2 to Peter Sedgwick* on first flight of HS.125-1000B.) Moved to USA in 1990s, testing HS.125s for Raytheon.

Ronald C W Ellison: CTP of MAP at Oldmixon, Weston-super-Mare, 1st January 1941 to 1945, on Beaufighters, Beaufort IIs and Tempest IIs. From 1945 at Filton and in 1949 became ACTP, types including Buckingham, Buckmaster, Brigand and Type 170 until 1952. He is featured in Chapter Three of Volume One.

Major Evans: RNAS pilot seconded to J Samuel White and Co upon the death of Ralph Lashmar*. Tested second prototype Wight Quadruplane (which became N546) October 1916.

Peter Gordon-Johnson at Binbrook, having delivered Lightning F.6 XR724 to the Lightning Association, 23rd July 1992. *Peter Green*

Don F Farquharson: Westland from 1960, Sycamores through to Sea King and Lynx.

Flt Lt G Farquharson: Supermarine on Spitfires.

John Samuel Fay, Westland PTP and instructor, circa 1949 to 1960s.

B Field: PTP with Airspeed at Christchurch, testing and ferrying Oxfords (including some to Turkey in the spring of 1940) and later Horsas. Joined Miles at Woodley for similar duties. He was killed during an air test of former 17 (P)AFU Master II DM239 on 26th August 1943; his FTO managed to bale out.

T B Fitzgerald: Seconded from MAP to Hawker, Langley, on Hurricanes 1942-1943.

Steve Formoso: Joined BAE Systems at Warton on Hawks and Typhoons, 2012.

Frankie H S Fox: Seconded from MAP to Hawker on Hurricanes and Typhoons 1942-1943.

Bob Fraser: BAE Systems Taranis Project Pilot – see Chapter Six Volume One.

Mike H Fuller, Westland, Yeovil from 1967, Wessex, Gazelle, Lynx, EH.101.

Peter Julian Ginger: Joined BAe at Warton, flying Canberras, Lightnings and Jaguars. Became Chief PTP and on 20th June 1972 he flew the last Lightning built, F.53 53-700, from Samlesbury. Appointed Manager Operations India in March 1979 and from 1984 was with the Hawk and Harrier marketing team. Retired 2004.

Michael Charles Gann AFC: Westland Senior Engineering Test Pilot and Project Pilot on Sea Kings and testing on Lynx, late 1960s to mid-1970s.

Dave Glaser: Senior BAC One-Eleven test pilot at Hurn mid-1970s.

John Goddard: BAe Warton from January 1987, becoming Deputy Project Pilot Tornado ADV: left 1990.

Lt Cdr Nick Goodhart: Loaned by Fleet Air Arm to Westland, Yeovil, for Wyvern testing, 1951.

Lt F B Goodwin-Castleman: Chief pilot of the Central Aircraft Co, Kilburn, by 1920, testing production Centaur IVs from Northolt. Killed in the second Centaur IIA G-EAPC, when it span in from 500ft on 25th September 1920 following the failure of the port engine at Hayes. Goodwin-Castleman and five passengers were killed. (Frank Courtney* had carried out the testing on both Centaur IIs.)

Peter Gordon-Johnson: Known as 'PGJ'. Joined BAe at Warton November 1979, flying Lightnings before becoming Tornado ADV Project Pilot and then DCTP, piloting the EAP. Left Warton in late 1992.

Flt Lt R C Gosling Supermarine on Spitfires.

Flt Lt Michael Graham Supermarine on Spitfires.

Wg Cdr Donald Salisbury Green OBE: Test pilot for Armstrong Whitworth. Co-pilot to Alan Campbell-Orde* testing Atalanta prototype G-ABPI from Whitley 20th October 1932. Aircraft force-landed and Green was injured, curtailing his test piloting career.

Clement Gresswell: Airco at Hendon circa 1916; later the aerodrome manager at Hendon.

Lyndon 'Pee-Wee' Griffith RNZAF: Armstrong Siddeley, Bitteswell, by 1954 (see Volume One Chapter Four under 'Witt' Wittridge). By 1961 was joint chief pilot for Aviation Traders (see Donald Cartlidge in Volume One) on Carvair certification.

John C Hall: Joined English Electric at Warton in December 1955, on Canberras and Lightnings. Transferred to BAC at Filton in September 1961 before leaving for commercial flying in 1964.

R C Handasyde: FTO when the Vickers G4/31 monoplane, piloted by 'Mutt' Summers* force landed at Brooklands 23rd July 1935. With Summers he flew much of the Wellington and Warwick development flying; eg P2 to Summers on the first flight of the Wellington III prototype L4251 at Brooklands, 19th May 1939 and he carried out the first flight of the initial Warwick C.I for BOAC, G-AGEX, at Brooklands on 22nd February 1943. Along with FTO J M Warner, he baled out of Warwick VI PN826 on 7th June 1945 when an engine caught fire.

John Aubrey Hanslip: de Havilland at Hatfield on Mosquitos 1943, then served with Fleet Air Arm. Back with de Havilland Hatfield by 1946 before transferring to Hawarden 1948 and Christchurch in 1953. By 1958 he was involved in pilot training. Saudi Royal Flight Comet 4 SA-R-7 was handed over on 15th June 1962 and entered an extensive crew training regime, with John supervising. On a flight from Geneva to Nice on 20th March 1964, the Comet hit a mountain close to Nice, killing John and eight others on board.

Maurice Hare: Production test at Vickers Brooklands from 1937. By 1940 he was CPTP at Hawarden on Wellingtons, including first flight of Mk.IV prototype R1220 that December.

Cdr Simon N Hargreaves OBE: Joined BAe at Dunsfold as Harrier/Sea Harrier PTP in 1996. Transferred to Lockheed Martin in 1997 to take part in the X-35 Joint Strike Fighter contest, BAe being a partner in the Lockheed Martin/Northrop-Grumman team. He flew the X-35A in November 2000 and on 25th June 2001 piloted the X-35B STOVL version on its maiden hover and on 10th July 2001 its first transition. Later in the year he was at Warton as DCTP; retiring in 2005.

Flt Lt S Harris RNVR: Supermarine on Spitfires and Seafires.

T S 'Staff' Harris: BAC One-Eleven development pilot, Wisley, 1960s – see Peter P Baker.

Keith Hartley: Joined BAe at Warton in 1979 on Lightnings, Jaguars, Hawk (deliveries), Tornado and also flew the EAP. Joined the International Test Pilots School at Cranfield in 1989. Returned to BAe at Warton in 1992, under contract from IPTS, then full-time from 1994. Tornados and then Typhoons, becoming Typhoon Project Pilot from 2001. Moved to Australia in August 2002.

Jack W Hathorne: PTP for Gloster at Hucclecote, 1939-1940, flying Henleys and Hurricanes. He was killed testing repaired Hurricane I N2497 at Hucclecote on 4th December 1940.

Sqn Ldr Ralph E 'Titch' Havercroft: Supermarine on Spitfires mid-1944 to December 1944. See also 'Bill' Else.

A J 'Tony' Hawkes: Harriers at HSA Dunsfold, 1970s. In late 1970s moved to BAe at Woodford. Co-pilot to 'Robbie' Robinson* on first flight of BAe ATP 6th August 1986.

Flt Lt Osborne 'Ossie' James Hawkins: New Zealander. Gloster at Hucclecote and Moreton Valence of Javelins 1957-1960. By 1961 was with Avro at Woodford on Shackletons, Vulcans and HS.748s. Ossie was captaining A&AEE Vulcan B.2 XH535 on flight from Woodford to Boscombe Down 11th May 1964. Close to Boscombe control was lost: Ossie and A&AEE Flt Lt R L Beeson ejected and were badly injured; *four* occupants of the rear flight deck were killed.

Alex Henshaw: Appointed by Jeffrey Quill* as production test for Supermarine on Spitfires at Eastleigh; became CPTP at Castle Bromwich – profiled in Chapter Two.

Lt P Hill: Supermarine on Spitfires.

Tom Hope: Scottish Aviation at Prestwick on Twin Pioneers, from 1956.

'Chunky' Horne: Supermarine at Chilbolton, post-1945, moving to Vickers at Wisley in 1956.

Trevor Howard: Joined Auster ex-RAF in 1951 as an aerodynamicist, becoming chief aerodynamicist in 1959. Also appointed as senior pilot in 1961 when Auster was acquired by Beagle. Seriously injured in crash of demonstrator D.5/180 G-ASBV in Switzerland 20th October 1963. Still flying from Rearsby and Shoreham on collapse of Beagle, 1970.

John F Howman: Bristol at Filton, including time as instructor on Type 170s, late 1940s.

Merrick S C Hymans: Hawker at Langley 1942-1945, Hurricanes, Typhoons, Tempests.

Richard Ingham: BAC at Warton on Lightnings, including Saudi ferrying and instruction, to 1983.

Wg Cdr Michael Roscoe Ingle-Finch DFC: Shorts at Sydenham 1952 to at least 1967 on Belfasts and Skyvans.

J Keith Isherwood: English Electric at Warton on Canberras and Lightings 1956-1967.

Jasper Jarvis: Vickers and BAC at Wisley on VC-10, also undertook Supermarine Swift wet runway trials 1958-1962 – see Dizzy Addicott.

John J M Jeffrey: Saunders-Roe, Eastleigh, then Westland 1950-1964: Skeeter, P.531, Scout, Wasp.

Flt Lt Jennings: Supermarine on Spitfires.

Flt Lt Venda Jicha DSO CDG DFC AFC: Castle Bromwich Aircraft Factory, circa 1944.

Flt Lt Will Jonas MBE: BAE Systems at Warton as Typhoon Project Pilot, 2005-2007.

Henri Jullerot: One of a group of French 'mercenaries' hired by Sir George White, founder the British and Colonial Aeroplane Company, hired to test, demonstrate and instruct on Boxkites, along with Maurice Tétard*. By the summer of 1913, Henri was instructing at the Halberstadt school in Germany.

Steve Long in his 'office', a Typhoon at Warton. Prior to his time with BAE Systems, Steve had flown the Lockheed Martin F-35B at Patuxent River, Maryland, in 2008. *Courtesy and © BAE Systems*

Flt Lt Hugh V Kennedy: By 1938 was Assistant CTP for Miles Aircraft at Woodley on a wide range of types, including the M.20 fighter and in July 1943 he carried out the second flight of the M.39B Libellula.

Sqn Ldr Michael Plaistow 'Slim' Kilburn DFC CDG: Gloster at Hucclecote and Moreton Valence 1949-1953 on Meteors and Javelins. Joined de Havilland at Hatfield 1953, becoming CTP for the Propeller Division in 1955-1965.

Flt Lt 'Reg' J Knight: Lancasters, late 1940s, Avro Woodford.

Sqn Ldr Peter 'Kos' Kosogorin: BAE Systems at Warton from July 2006. Attached to the Lockheed Martin F-35 JSF Programme team in the USA from 2010.

Robert Langley: Chief pilot for Channel Air Bridge, he also acted as PTP for Aviation Traders Carvair conversions, Southend and Stansted, circa 1962-1964.

Richard John Lawson: BAE Systems, Warton from 2002 as Harrier Project Pilot, later on Typhoons.

Steve Long: Joined BAE Systems in March 2011 on Typhoons and Hawks. Left in 2013.

Fg Off R 'Ronnie' Louis: Vickers at Brooklands, early 1930s; by 1936 was also testing Supermarine flying-boats.

Peter D Lowe: Shorts at Sydenham from 1963. Was P2 to Denis Tayler* on the first flight of Belfast XR362 5th January 1964.

Thomas Donald Lucey: Chief PTP at Hawker, Dunsfold, in 1951. Moved to same role at the Squires Gate 1956-1958. Seconded to Gloster as PTP on Javelins up to 1961.

Flt Lt L Lundsten: Norwegian, Supermarine on Spitfires, 1944.

Lt Cdr Nigel John Maggs: Westland/AgustaWestland at Yeovil on Merlins from circa 1997. Captain of first flight of Merlin HM.2 prototype conversion, ZH826 at Yeovil 30th September 2010.

Sqn Ldr Nat Makepeace: BAE Systems at Warton from October 2005, initially Hawk Project Pilot, then Typhoon Project Pilot. In August 2014 he clocked up 5,000 hours on fast jets.

Sqn Ldr R Manlove: Supermarine on Spitfires and Seafires.

Flt Lt F W Markham: Seconded from 9 Squadron to fly the Vickers Virginia VII prototype J6993 in place of CTP 'Tiny' Scholefield*. By 1938 he was CTP of the Rootes Securities 'shadow' factory at Speke, on Blenheims.

D J Marpole: Westland at Yeovil on Lynx, circa 1980s.

J F Marsh: Assistant to 'Jamie' Talbot* at Handley Page. Managed a 'near' flight in the HP Manx at Radlett 12th September 1942.

David Masters displaying 'Flying Mattress' ML Utility XK776 to the incredulous press at White Waltham on 21st May 1957. *KEC*

Sqn Ldr David J Masters: Joined Fairey at Ringway in 1946, becoming CPTP there. Graduated ETPS No.5 Course 1946-1947, Cranfield. Later PTP at White Waltham on Gannets. He was heavily involved in test flying the ML Utility inflatable wing aircraft at White Waltham, 1954-1958 – see Peter Twiss. He retired from Fairey in 1961.

Sqn Ldr John Oliver Mathews DSO DFC: Joined Fairey in 1946 and in 1950 was appointed as operations manger for the company's guided weapons division, including stints at Woomera, Australia. With the take over by Westland in 1960 he tested Scouts and Wasps before retiring in 1963.

Wg Cdr Terry McComb OBE: Miles at Long Kesh and Newtownards, on Messengers, 1947-1948.

James 'Jim' Gibson 'Mac' McCowan: Armstrong Whitworth at Bitteswell from circa 1946, by the early 1950s on Meteors.

Gordon J McClymont: Joined BAe at Warton in 1996 on Hawks, Jaguars and Tornados. On 12th May 2000 Gordon carried out the maiden flight of the first Australian-assembled Hawk 127 for the RAAF at Williamtown, New South Wales and on 17th January 2005 did likewise for the first Denel-assembled Hawk 120 for the SAAF from Johannesburg, South Africa. Gordon left BAE Systems in 2008.

Eddie McNamara: BAC at Wisley on VC-10s and One-Elevens and by mid-1970s Concordes at Fairford.

Flt Lt Ian McNicol: Austin at Longbridge on Battles, 1940, then Supermarine on Spitfires.

Flt Lt Duncan Menzies: (Uncle of Duncan Simpson*.) By 1936 worked for Fairey, test flying production Hendons from the Heaton Chapel plant at Barton. He became senior production test pilot for Fairey, conducting Battle, Fulmar and Firefly testing from Ringway.

Robert E M B 'Bob' Milne AFC: Joined Phillips & Powis at Woodley as an instructor with some test flying on Miles Hawks. In 1939 joined Airspeed at Portsmouth as PTP carrying out extensive testing of Oxfords and was involved in testing the Cambridge trainer. By the late 1940s he was testing de Havilland Doves and later Comets at Hatfield.

Vyrell Baillie Mitchell: Beagle at Shoreham from circa 1960 to 1967. Later Hunting at Luton on Jet Provosts.

Flt Lt J F Moir: CFI of 8 EFTS, Woodley, occasionally testing Miles types, example: the Nighthawk 1935.

Peter Moore: Bristol at Oldmixon and Filton, Sycamores, 1950s.

Kevin Moorhouse: Originally an FTO at Avro, Woodford, in the mid-1960s. Later took his PPL and then CPL and by 1979 was flying HS.748s on pre-delivery and demonstrations, later also flying Nimrods. On 1st July 1996 he was killed, along with Steve Watson, in the BAE-operated DH Mosquito T.3 RR299 (G-ASKH) while displaying at Barton.

Graham Morgan: Joined BAe at Woodford in 1999 initially on the 'comms' fleet. Pilot on the Nimrod MRA.4 project from 1996. Retired by 2010.

Duncan Menzies carried out the maiden flight of the first production Fairey Fulmar, N1854, at Ringway on 4th January 1940. It was flown post-war by Fairey as a chase plane and for special occasions, illustrated at Farnborough in September 1962. Today, it is preserved at the Fleet Air Arm Museum, Yeovilton. *Roy Bonser*

Sqn Ldr Guy Morgan DFC: Deputy to Jeffrey Quill at the Supermarine test office, running the 'desk' as well as signing off Spitfires and Seafires. By 1952 was at Vickers, Wisley, on Viscounts.

E S 'Doc' Morrell: Hawker at Langley on Sea Furies, 1948-1949.

Michael Morss: Gloster at Hucclecote and Moreton Valence on Meteors and Javelins, 1955-1957.

Sam Moseley: Fairey at Ringway on Fireflies from 1945.

Lt Roger M Mowbray: AugustaWestland on Merlins circa 2002 at Yeovil and Vergiate, Italy.

Leonard Roy Moxam OBE: Joined Westland in the early 1960s, becoming DCTP under Ron Gellatly*. He was co-pilot on the first flight of the Lynx prototype XW835. On 1st July 1972 Ron flew development batch Lynx AH.1 XX153 around a 100km closed-circuit to clinch the record at 197.91mph.

Malcolm Christison Muir: With de Havilland at Hawarden, on Vampires and Venoms, early 1950s. Joined Rolls-Royce in 1958 as TP – see Chapter Four in Volume One.

Flt Lt Ralph S Munday: Hawker at Langley on Hurricanes and Typhoons, 1942. With Fairey by 1944 on Fireflies. Later test piloting with Heston Aircraft.

Flt Lt Richard Vivian Muspratt DFC: Hawker, Hurricanes and Typhoons, 1942 to circa 1945.

J E M Mustard: Senior TP Westland/AgustaWestland on Sea Kings and Merlins 1988-2003 at Yeovil; at Vergiate, Italy from 2004.

Colin Newnes: Britten-Norman on Islanders and Trislanders at Bembridge from 1967.

Thomas Henry Newton: RNAS officer, tested at least the first Dick, Kerr and Co, Preston-built Felixstowe F.3, N4230 *Pauline* (named after his wife), at South Shields, 20th February 1918.

Wg Cdr Rupert Oakley: Testing Valiants for Vickers from Wisley before fronting 138 Squadron at Gaydon, 1955.

Sqn Ldr Kenneth Peter Orme AFC: Joined BAe at Warton on 1981 and Jaguars, becoming EAP project Pilot in 1983 and DCTP in 1992. Flying with the comms fleet from 1993, he retired in 2002.

Sqn Ldr Bill Ovel: BAe at Woodford from 1998 as part of the Nimrod MRA.4 development team; also taking part in ATP and 146 testing. Was P2 to John Turner* for the first flight of MRA.4 prototype ZJ516 on 26th August 2004 from Woodford. In 2004 he was appointed CTP Nimrod and UAVs.

Flt Lt G Page DSO DFC: Supermarine on Spitfires and Seafires.

Flt Lt H Parry: Supermarine on Spitfires and Seafires.

Major Timothy Nigel Peake: AgustaWestland production test pilot from 2009. Selected same year for training in the European Space Agency programme. Blasted off to the International Space Station on 15th December 2015.

Flt Lt John Desmond Penrose: Joined de Havilland (HSA from 1963) at Hatfield 1961 on Sea Vixens and Tridents.

Harry Phillips: Saunders-Roe, then Westland, 1958-1971.

'Doug' Potter, English Electric, Samlesbury, 1940s.

Brian A Powell: Vickers at Brooklands on Vikings, Valettas and early Viscounts. Joined Airspeed, testing Ambassadors, transferring to de Havilland at Hatfield on Comets, circa 1950, then to Hawarden on Vampires, Venoms, Doves and Herons. Left test flying to join Hunting Clan – later British United – as a Viscount captain. Seconded to BAC in 1963 to circa 1966 as BAC One-Eleven test pilot and training captain.

John Powers: Joined Boulton Paul at Pendeford in the mid-1950s, retiring in early 1960s.

Former AgustaWestland production test pilot Major Tim Peake aboard the International Space Station, December 2015. *Courtesy and © ESA/NASA*

Barry Radley: Circa 1951 senior test pilot with Percival (Hunting-Percival from 1954) and part-time instructor with Luton Flying Club. By 1957 he was DCTP.

James Ramsden: Appointed as assistant TP at Westland, Yeovil, 1940, on Lysanders, Spitfires and Seafires. Ferrying the third production Welkin I DX280 back from A&AEE Boscombe Down on 9th September 1943 (another source gives 24th August 1943) he landed long, skidded and ground-looped; coming to a halt beyond the airfield perimeter. DX280 was repaired. Ramsden left Westland in 1945.

Sub Lt Peter Rawson: Seconded to Fairey at Ringway as a PTP on Barracudas.

Harry W Rayner: Assistant CTP, Handley Page. Victor B.2 spinning trials 1960-1961 and co-pilot on first flight of Jetstream prototype G-ATXH 18th August 1967 – both with John Allam*.

Flt Lt George Reston: ACTP at MAP Oldmixon, Weston-super-Mare, from 9th September 1941 on Beaufighters.

Don Riches: Seconded to HS Dunsfold early 1970s, then testing Harriers from 1973-1979,

Lew Roberts: Bristol at Filton, early 1960s.

Peter Roberts: Supermarine at Chilbolton on Swift development, early 1950s.

Lt Don R Robertson DFC: Supermarine at Worthy Down, particularly on Seafires, July 1942 to April 1943.

Mark Robinson: Joined Avro International Aerospace (aka BAe) at Woodford June 1997 on 146 and RJX testing and Nimrod MRA.4. Left 2005.

W L Rogers: Handley Page Transport Ltd from 1922 and was testing HP Hendon Is at Cricklewood, 1924.

John Duello Rose MBE: CPTP for English Electric at Samlesbury from 1939 to September 1946, testing HP Hampdens and Halifaxes and then DH Vampires.

Flt Lt J Rosser AFC: Castle Bromwich Aircraft Factory, circa 1944.

Flt Lt C Rudland: Supermarine on Spitfires.

R N Rumbelow: Hunting at Luton on Jet Provosts circa 1958.

Bernie Scott: BAe Dunsfold December 1989 to 1999 on Harriers, Sea Harriers and Hawks, becoming DCTP. Transferred to Warton 1999, but left in November 2000. Flew commercially with My Travel on Airbus A320s. Returned to Warton (then BAE Systems) October 2003 on Nimrod MRA.4; retiring April 2011.

Jack Scott: Standard Motors, Coventry, on Mosquitos, later Rolls-Royce at Hucknall, then CTP of Power Jets and the National Gas Turbine Establishment. CTP Martin-Baker Aircraft 1946 to 1960 – see Chapter Four in Volume One.

Sempill, The Master of: (later Lord Sempill – see also 'Timber' Wood in Chapter Six), Testing for Robey & Co, Lincoln, and also Sopwith 'Gun Buses' 1915.

Flt Lt Jack Sherburn DFC: DCTP Shorts at Sydenham on Skyvans, 1962-1970.

Flt Lt Francis 'Frankie' H Silk DFC: Seconded to Hawker at Langley on Hurricanes, Typhoons, Tempests, 1943-1945.

C W 'George' Simpson: Armstrong Whitworth at Bitteswell, on Argosies.

George Skelton: DCTP to Cecil Feather* at Boulton Paul Pendeford from 1936 and heavily involved in Defiant production testing. Returned to the RAF by 1940, flying Defiants with 264 Squadron. On 13th May 1940 Flt Lt Skelton was flying L6969 and was shot down by Messerschmitt Bf 109s over Dunkirk. He became a prisoner of war and was repatriated in 1943.

Stuart N 'Scotty' Sloan MVO CGM DFC: Vickers at Wisley on Viscounts and then Vanguards from 1952.

'Bob' Smith: Bristol at Oldmixon on Sycamores, 1950s.

Winfield Smith: Assisting Geoffrey de Havilland* at the Royal Aircraft Factory, Farnborough, circa 1912-1913.

Ernest Hugh Statham: PTP for MAP at the Oldmixon plant on Beaufighters from June 1943. Later worked for Bristol at Filton; he was killed in the crash of Britannia G-ANCA in the USA on 6th November 1957. More details in the profile of 'Ronnie' Ellison in Chapter Three of Volume One.

Rex Stocken: Gloster at Hucclecote 1927 to 1930, on Grebes and Gamecocks. Also flew the Breda 15 wing test-bed (see Howard Saint*).

H N Sweetman: Seconded from MAP, Hawker at Langley in 1943 on Tempests.

Eric A Swiss: Bristol rotorcraft, on Sycamores. Flew Bristol 171 VL963 in the London to Paris 'dash which also involved a Westland S-51 flown by Alan Bristow* and Meteor T.7 G-AKPK flown by 'Bill' Waterton*. Eric is illustrated in the ETPS No.1 Course line-up in Chapter One Volume One.

Flt Lt H A Taylor: Supermarine on Spitfires – see also Chapter Five Volume One.

Lt J C Teasdale: Westland at Yeovil on Sea Kings, Lynx and Merlins, 1980s.

Maurice Tétard: One of a group of French 'mercenaries' Sir George White, founder the British and Colonial Aeroplane Company, hired to test, demonstrate and instruct on Boxkites, along with Henri Jullerot. He returned to France in 1911.

Flt Lt Thomas: Supermarine on Spitfires.

Flt Lt John B 'Tommy' Thompson, Westland, 1945-1946 on Seafires and Welkins.

Flt Lt George Irving Thomson DFC: CFI of the Hampshire Aeroplane Club at Hamble, took on the post of part-time test pilot for Cierva Autogiro after the resignation of Bert Hinkler* in February 1928. He was succeeded by 'Dizzy' Rawson five months later.

Barry J Tonkinson: HSA Dunsfold on Harriers from 1970. On 11th July 1970 he suffered engine failure in Harrier T.2 XW264 and carried out a force landing at Boscombe Down; undercarriage collapsed and fire broke out. XW264 written off, Barry injured.

John 'Johnnie' G Towle: Gloster at Hucclecote and Moreton Valence on Javelins, 1957-1960.

Jeremy 'Jerry' Pettican Tracy MBE: By 1977 was with Westland, first flying the initial Oldmixon-built Gazelle AH.1 XZ338 on 28th October 1977; going on to test flying Lynx. By April 1998 he was DCTP to Colin Hague* on Merlins. By 2010 he took up the post with AgustaWestland as Canada Head of Region.

Keith Trow: Scottish Aviation at Prestwick on Twin Pioneers, late 1950s.

Richard 'Dick' Trueman: AgustaWestland on Lynx, Merlins and Wildcats, 2004-2010.

G D Tucker: Co-pilot to 'Bob' Waight* on first flight of the DH Albatross, Hatfield, 20th May 1937.

'Dickie' Turley-George DFC: Shorts at Sydenham, late 1950s, Canberra PR.9s.

Cyril Turner: Reported as testing for the British Aerial Transport Co; raced Bantam F1657 (K-155) at Hendon in May 1919 on the company's behalf.

Captain Olav Ullstad DSC DFC: Norwegian. Supermarine on Spitfires; Castle Bromwich Aircraft Factory circa 1944.

Lt J Underwood MBE: Supermarine on Spitfires.

James Valentine: Bristol 1911-1912 on Boxkites. In late 1911 he flew Bristol-Prier Monoplane No.58 and in December piloted it around the Eiffel Tower, Paris, before the aero show in the city. In 1912 he flew a Bristol-Coanda Monoplane '15' in readiness for the Larkhill trials but had to force land and his 'trail' runs dry after that.

Flt Lt Peter W Varley: Joined Gloster in 1955 as DCTP to 'Dicky' Martin*, testing Meteors and Javelins. First flew the prototype Javelin FAW.4, XA629, 19th September 1955. By 1959 he was at Bitteswell, testing and demonstrating Argosies for Armstrong Whitworth.

'Johnnie' Walker: BAC on Concorde 1970s, Filton and Fairford.

Flt Lt J B 'Johnnie' Walker: Avro on Lancasters at Woodford; first flew Tudor 3 G-AIYA 27th September 1946 at Woodford.

Lt A S Walls: Westland at Yeovil on Sea Kings, Lynx and Merlins circa 1979-1999.

Ronald Whitehouse with the Handley Page Type E Monoplane with passenger at Lincoln, June 1913. *Peter Green Collection*

Peter Martin R Walton: Armstrong Whitworth at Bitteswell on Sea Hawks, Hunters and Argosies. On 14th August 1954 testing Hunter F.2 WN905 during a low-level high speed pass at Bitteswell, part of the starboard undercarriage dislodged, damaging the flaps and the hydraulics stopped functioning. Peter took WN905 to height, put it into a spin and ejected. The Hunter crashed near Market Harborough, Peter alighting safely close by.

J C V K 'Watty' Watson: Hawker at Langley on Hurricanes 1941-1942.

Flt Lt J H Wedgwood DFC: Supermarine on Spitfires November 1940 to December 1941.

E Ronald Whitehouse: By Easter 1913 Ronald had been taken on by Frederick Handley Page as a pilot and flew the Type E Yellow Peril in May, taking it on an extensive tour. He was testing the Type G biplane, ready for handing on to Rowland Ding* in early 1914.

Charlie Whittaker: Joined BAE Systems at Woodford in 2000 on the comms fleet and in preparation for the Nimrod MRA.4. After cancellation of the project in 2010, he took up a commercial piloting post.

Sqn Ldr Leslie Morris 'Dick' Whittington DFC: Canberra PTP at English Electric Warton from 1953. Moved to Folland at Chilbolton in February 1955 becoming assistant CTP to 'Teddy' Tennant* on Gnat development. Worked as PTP at HSA Dunsfold 1961-1970.

Flt Lt P Wigley DFC: Supermarine Spitfires at High Post. See Frank Furlong in Chapter Six.

Ian 'Willie' Wilkinson: Bristol at Oldmixon on Sycamores, 1950s.

Maxwell 'Max' Williams: Austin at Longbridge on Battles 1940. Gloster at Hucclecote on Hurricanes and Typhoons, 1941-1944.

Neil R Williams: Canadian. Flew for Handley Page at Radlett up to 1970 on development and certification of the Jetstream; thereafter a stellar career as a champion aerobatic pilot.

J Ian 'Willy' Williamson: Deputy to Godfrey Auty at Bristol, Filton, early 1960s; carried out last flight of Bristol 188 XF926 on 11th January 1964, bringing its total flying time to a dismal 26 hours 11 minutes.

Peter 'Wizzer' Wilson: Joined BAE Systems at Warton as Hawk Deputy Project Pilot before moving to the USA in 2006 to become the Joint Strike Fighter Project Pilot. On 3rd October 2011 he was one of a team of pilots carrying out the first ship trials of the Lockheed Martin F-35B on the USS *Wasp*.

Peter A Wilson: de Havilland at Hatfield on Comet 4s.

Peter R D Wilson: Bristol at Oldmixon on Sycamores, Belvederes from 1951, then Westland at Yeovil on Pumas, Gazelles and Sea Kings to 1974.

Flt Lt Norman Hargreave Woodhead: Carried out the first flight of the AS Genet-powered Blackburn Bluebird at Brough on 4th June 1926 – this was the re-engined prototype originally flown by Arthur Loton*. Norman was P2 to Cecil Rea* for the first flight of Iris III N238 from the Humber, November 1929.

CHAPTER EIGHT

Prototype Legacy

<big>B</big>y their very nature, prototypes lead a perilous existence. Those that survive the rigours of test and development flying might be dusted down and sold on to a customer, but most likely they will be scrapped as there is no profit in sentiment. Only with the dramatic expansion of the 'heritage movement' from the 1960s onwards have prototypes been sought out for saving and manufacturers been so moved as to hand on these treasures for posterity.

When finalising *Testing to the Limits*, it was felt that readers might appreciate an indication of just *what* has survived into to the 21st century; hence this chapter. Some reference has been made in the biographies in both volumes, but the table herewith provides a 'catch all'. As might be imagined, the bulk of the survivors are from the post-war era, with examples from earlier times very thin on the ground. Half-a-dozen date from before 1939 with four gracing the Shuttleworth Collection and a pair of rotorcraft pioneers in Scotland. 'King' of these is the Blackburn Monoplane: now in its 104th year, it is the oldest *airworthy* British aeroplane in the world.

Of those prototypes on public view, there are two venues that dominate. The Science Museum at South Kensington in London holds a galaxy of 'stars' from all eras of British aviation achievement; many of which get a mention within the two volumes. There can be found the largest concentration of 'pioneer' aircraft in the country, including the Cody biplane and the Roe triplane. In terms of 'true' prototypes the Gloster E28/39 and the Hawker P.1127 automatically draw the author in during his regular pilgrimages to the museum. The former remained a prototype but opened up jet propulsion to the industry; the latter presaged one of the most successful of British military programmes, the peerless Harrier.

Hangar 2, entitled 'Test Flight', at the Royal Air Force Museum at Cosford, Shropshire, holds a treasure trove of prototypes and development test-beds and the museum is to be congratulated for going 'off piste' from its central collecting policy to secure these jewels for the nation. Installed in March 2012, the British Aerospace EAP contrasts wonderfully with the Bristol 188; it is hard to credit that only 24 years separate their maiden flights.

The plan for this chapter was to include a 'case study', to zoom in on the career of just one prototype and how it came to be preserved. Selection was a simple matter, an aircraft I have admired since the days when I first became fascinated by aircraft and one I have followed closely since I discovered, in the late 1960s, that it still existed. Personal reasons aside, the choice was easy, de Havilland Mosquito W4050, the only surviving British World War Two combat aircraft prototype.

With a few details still to be finalised, the prototype Mosquito W4050 was rolled out of its hangar at the de Havilland Aircraft Museum, London Colney, on 11th October 2015. This was a rehearsal for a ceremony held on 25th November to celebrate the 75th anniversary of the first flight; then W4050 was rolled out at the very moment that Geoffrey de Havilland jr put the throttles forward. *Ken Ellis*

Out-of-the way but nearby

If you find yourself on the M25 motorway on the northern edge of London, close to Junction 22, take a look south. Across a few fields, you will catch a glimpse of an impressive hall and the tails of a couple of aircraft. If you have not been to the de Havilland Heritage Aircraft Museum at London Colney in Hertfordshire, you *have* to make amends and go. Impressive building developments were in hand as these words were typed, but that should not stop you. The most important airframe within the impressive collection never ceases to give me the goose bumps. This is the rarest of rare things, the prototype of a World War Two icon. The very first Hurricane, Spitfire, Wellington, Halifax and Lancaster - to name a few British giants - are long since gone. Likewise the initial Thunderbolt, Warhawk, Mitchell, Flying Fortress and Liberator as examples of US legends. The EAA Air Venture Museum at Oshkosh, Wisconsin, has a XP-51 Mustang, but *not* the seminal NA.73X. Then of course there are the inaugural German, Italian and Japanese combat types to consider. All of these are extinct.

This is not the case for the Mosquito, but this is just part of the story. It is on show to the public in the *very* place that it was designed and conceived. The survival of W4050 is an incredible story that involves a string of visionary and determined de Havilland employees, a man who bought a ramshackle hall in Hertfordshire and discovered its 'unseen' heritage and a team of people who founded, expanded and run Britain's oldest established pure aviation collection.

In 1958 Major Walter Goldsmith moved into the 17th century moated manor house of Salisbury Hall, London Colney. A substantial dwelling on this site can be traced back to the 9th century, if not before. The present house was built in the 1670s and can boast illustrious residents. These include King Charles II and Eleanor 'Nell' Gwynne, who occupied a cottage in the grounds. In more recent times, during 1905 Lady Randolph Churchill, along with her son, Winston, and in the 1930s Sir Nigel Gresley, designer of locomotives such as *The Flying Scotsman* and *Mallard* stayed a while.

Walter was bemused by scribblings of wing sections on the wall of a toilet and he asked around to get answers. He also pondered the large patch of concrete adjacent to the hall. He soon discovered that less than two decades earlier, the concrete had been the base of a Robin hangar and the house had been a design office for de Havilland (DH). In October 1939, the month after World War two broke out, chief designer R E Bishop and his team re-located from Hatfield, less than 4 miles to the north. The aircraft factory was too tempting a target for the Luftwaffe and Salisbury Hall represented a quiet, out-of-the-way, yet neighbouring retreat.

Wooden Wonder No.1

Inside the hangar a mock-up of a private venture twin-engined fighter-cum-bomber was hastily erected and the initial design was given the go-ahead. From 1939 the little building resounded to the clamour of construction while rooms in the hall witnessed the creation of thousands of drawings. The prototype Mosquito was taking shape. The revolutionary machine was dismantled and taken by road to Hatfield for flight testing. Three developmental airframes were also built at Salisbury Hall, but they made their maiden flights from the extensive grounds, landing only moments later at Hatfield. The same process was followed with the next project: the prototype Airspeed Horsa assault glider was sketched, planned and built at the hall. (See under George Errington in Volume One for more.) Salisbury Hall was used by DH until 1947, when it fell into disuse and its future looked bleak.

Wearing the B Condition (or 'trade plate') identity E-0234 and overall yellow colours, Geoffrey de Havilland jr took the prototype 'Wooden Wonder' on its first flight on 25th November 1940. It flew to Boscombe Down in Wiltshire for evaluation by the Aeroplane & Armament Experimental Establishment on 19th February 1941, by which time it was wearing the RAF serial W4050. After its 12th flight at Boscombe on the 24th, Gordon Slade - see Chapter Six - was taxying the prototype over rough ground when the tail wheel jammed and the fuselage fractured. W4050 was hastily fitted with the fuselage- also built at Salisbury Hall - intended for the first photo-recce prototype, W4051, and it re-flew on 14th March. A very busy schedule of trials at Boscombe, Hatfield, with Rolls-Royce at its test airfield at Hucknall, Nottinghamshire, among others, followed. The airframe was modified many times, adapted for trial installations and tests. There is so much that could be written of this stage of W4050's life, but this will have to suffice: in late October 1942 John de Havilland flew W4050 to 29,000ft at an incredible 437mph - 20mph *faster* that a production Spitfire HF.VIII at the same altitude. In December 1943 W4050 was flown for the last time but it was needed as an instructional airframe and it was put to good use. In 1946 it was transferred to the DH Technical School which was then at W4050's birthplace, Salisbury Hall. It appeared in the static at the 1946 and 19746 Society of British Aircraft Constructors displays at Radlett, a mere 2 miles to the east of the hall.

Common sense and subterfuge

When DH moved out of Salisbury Hall, the prototype 'Mossie' started a somewhat migratory life, with periods in store at the DH-run aerodrome at Panshanger, near Hertford, the company factory at Hawarden, near Chester, before settling again on Hatfield. Several times the significant, but industrially redundant, airframe faced destruction but common sense, and the occasional subterfuge, prevailed.

When Walter Goldsmith acquired Salisbury Hall, the pressure of space at Hatfield and the Major's wish to foster his home's aviation legacy coincided. In September 1958 W4050 was again oved to Salisbury Hall and it was put into a hangar similar to the one it had been built in 18 years previously. While the Imperial War Museum and the Science Museum have had airframes on charge since 1920 and 1913 respectively, both have a much wider remit than aviation. The Shuttleworth Collection - aircraft *and* vehicles - traces its origins to 1932; but it was the 1960s before it opened, at first only occasionally, to the public. W4050 was publically unveiled on 15th May 1959 and from this humble beginning came the pioneering Mosquito Aircraft Museum and the present-day De Havilland Aircraft Museum.

To help celebrate W4050's 75th birthday, the Heritage Lottery Fund (HLF) said 'yes' to a grant of £41,000 towards the epic four-year restoration of this incredibly significant survivor. At 14:45 hours on 25th November 2015 it was rolled out at exactly the time that it started its maiden flight at nearby Hatfield 75 years before. This precious prototype has been conserved to the configuration in which it last flew, from the first half of 1943, with two-speed, two-stage supercharged Merlin 70s. Since its grounding W4050 had survived several corporate attempts to have it scrapped or burnt and each time it was quietly moved to another venue to keep the 'suits' off the scent! Eventually, 'top brass' at Hatfield agreed to recognise the status quo by presenting W4050 on permanent loan to the Mosquito Aircraft Museum.

With the advent of the restoration grant, HLF could not pour money into an artefact that was on loan and BAE Systems agreed to make the prototype's existence official. At the 75th anniversary ceremony a representative of the multi-national giant presented a scroll that transformed an airframe that had relied on skulduggery for its initial survival and then a 'nod and a wink' into a national treasure on *permanent* loan - W4050 had secured perpetuity, at its birthplace.

Surviving British Prototypes as featured in Volumes One and Two

Prototype	Pilot	Location
Airbus A350 F-WXWB	Peter Chandler	Airbus, Toulouse, France, airworthy
Airbus A400M F-WWMT	Ed Strongman	Airbus, Toulouse, France, preserved
ANEC II G-EBJO	'Jimmy' James	Shuttleworth Collection, Old Warden, airworthy
Avro 707A WD280	'Roly' Falk	Privately owned, Australia
Avro Canada Jetliner CF-EJD-X	'Jimmy' Orrell	Canada Aviation Museum, Rockcliffe, Canada, cockpit
BAC 221 WG774	Godfrey Auty	Fleet Air Arm Museum, Yeovilton (See also Fairey FD.2)
BAC Jet Provost T.5 XS230	Reg Stock	Privately owned, Kent owner, airworthy as G-VIVM
BAC One Eleven 500 G-ASYD	Brian Trubshaw	Brooklands Museum, Weybridge
BAC/Sud Concorde 002 G-BSST	Brian Trubshaw	Fleet Air Arm Museum, Yeovilton
BAe EAP ZF534	David Eagles	Royal Air Force Museum, Cosford
BAe 146-100 G-SSSH	Mike Goodfellow	National Environmental Research Council, Cranfield, airworthy
BAe Jetstream 31 G-JSSD	Len Houston	National Museum of Flight Scotland, East Fortune
Beagle E.3 G-25-12	Ranald Porteous	Privately owned, Northamptonshire
Beagle Pup 100 G-AVDF	'Pee Wee' Judge	Privately owned, Buckinghamshire
Beagle 206X G-ARRM	John Nicholson	Farnborough Air Sciences Trust, Farnborough
Beagle Bulldog G-AXEH	'Pee Wee' Judge	National Museum of Flight Scotland, East Fortune

Another porotype can be found at Salisbury Hall, de Havilland-built Cierva C.24 G-ABLM which was first flown by its designer, Juan de la Cierva, in September 1931. *Ken Ellis*

Among the treasures at the Science Museum is the first Gloster E28/39 W4050. *Ken Ellis*

Blackburn Single-Seat Monoplane	'Harry' Blackburn	Shuttleworth Collection, Old Warden, airworthy
Boulton Paul P.111 VT935	Bob Smythe	Midland Air Museum, Coventry
Bristol Type 188 XF923	Godfrey Auty	Royal Air Force Museum, Cosford
Britten-Norman BN-1 G-ALZE	Desmond Norman	Solent Sky, Southampton
Britten-Norman Nymph G-AXFB	Desmond Norman	Private owner, Isle of Wight, airworthy as G-NACI
Chilton DW.1 G-AESZ	Ranald Porteous	Shuttleworth Collection, Old Warden, airworthy
Cierva C.24 G-ABLM	Juan de la Cierva	De Havilland Aircraft Museum, London Colney
CMC Leopard G-BKRL	Angus McVitie	Bournemouth Aviation Museum, Bournemouth
Cranfield A1 G-BCIT	Angus McVitie	Cranfield Institute of Technology, Cranfield, stored
De Havilland Humming Bird G-EBHX	Hubert Broad	Shuttleworth Collection, Old Warden, stored
De Havilland Mosquito E-0234	Geoffrey de Havilland jr	De Havilland Aircraft Museum, London Colney
EHI EH.101 ZF641	Trevor Egginton	RNAS Culdrose, training aid
English Electric Canberra B(I).8 VX185	Roland Beamont	National Museum of Flight Scotland, East Fortune, cockpit
English Electric P.1A WG760	Roland Beamont	Royal Air Force Museum, Cosford
Eurofighter 2000 DA.2 ZH588	Chris Yeo	Royal Air Force Museum, Hendon
Eurofighter Typhoon DA.4 ZH590	Derek Reeh	Imperial War Museum, Duxford
Fairey FD.2 WG774	Peter Twiss	Fleet Air Arm Museum, Yeovilton, as BAC 221 - see above
Fairey Jet Gyrodyne XJ389	John Dennis	Museum of Berkshire Aviation, Woodley
Fairey Rotodyne XE521	Ron Gellatly	The Helicopter Museum, Weston-super-Mare, substantial components
Garland-Bianchi Linnet G-APNS	Neville Duke	Privately owned, East Sussex, stored
Gloster E28/39 W4041	'Gerry' Sayer	Science Museum, London
Gloster Meteor F.8 prone-pilot WK935	Eric Franklin	Royal Air Force Museum, Cosford
Handley Page Gugnunc G-AACN	Tom Harry England	Science Museum, Wroughton
Handley Page HP.115 XP841	Jack Henderson	Fleet Air Arm Museum, Yeovilton
Handley Page Jetstream 1 G-ATXH	John Allam	South Yorkshire Aircraft Museum, Doncaster, cockpit
Hawker P.1052 VX272	'Wimpy' Wade	Fleet Air Arm Museum, Yeovilton, stored
Hawker P.1067 WB188	Neville Duke	Tangmere Military Aviation Museum, Tangmere

'Hovering' above a Bristol Siddeley Pegasus vectored thrust engine at the Science Museum, the P.1127 'father of the Harrier'. *Ken Ellis*

A portion of Cosford's 'Test Flight' hangar. Left to right: Avro 707C WZ744, BAC TSR.2 XR220, Hunting 126 XN714, Saro SR.53 XD145, SEPECAT Jaguar GR.1 ACT XX765. *Ken Ellis*

Prototype	Pilot	Location
Hawker P.1127 XP831	'Bill' Bedford	Science Museum, London
Hawker Siddeley HS.125-700B G-BFAN	Mike Goodfellow	Privately owned, Congo Democratic Republic as 9Q-CBC, *probably* airworthy
Hawker Siddeley Nimrod XV148	John Cunningham	Privately owned, Malmesbury, cockpit
Hunting 126 XN714	'Olly' Oliver	Royal Air Force Museum, Cosford
Kay 33/1 Gyroplane G-ACVA	'Dizzy' Rawson	National Museum of Scotland, Edinburgh
Miles Mohawk G-AEKW	F G Miles	Royal Air Force Museum, stored
Miles Sparrowjet G-35-2	George Miles	Privately owned, Gloucestershire, restoration project
Miles Student G-35-4	George Miles	Museum of Berkshire Aviation, Woodley
NDN Fieldmaster G-NRDC	Desmond Norman	Aerial Application Collection, Lincolnshire, stored
Panavia Tornado P.01 D-9591	Paul Millett	Erding, Germany, preserved
Panavia Tornado P.02 XX946	Paul Millett	Royal Air Force Museum, Cosford
Percival Jet Provost T.1 XD674	'Dickie' Wheldon	Royal Air Force Museum, Cosford
Reid and Sigrist Desford G-AGOS	C F French	Leicestershire Museums, stored
Reid and Sigrist Bobsleigh VZ728	A G Bullmore	Much-modified from G-AGOS, see above
Rolls-Royce TMR XJ314	'Jim' Heyworth	First tethered flight
	'Shep' Shepherd	First free flight: Science Museum, London
Saro SR.A/1 TG263	Geoffrey Tyson	Solent Sky, Southampton
Saro SR.53 XD145	John Booth	Royal Air Force Museum, Cosford
Scottish Aviation Bullfinch G-BDOG	John Blair	Privately owned, Netherthorpe, airworthy
SEPECAT Jaguar S.06 XW560	'Jimmy' Dell	Boscombe Down Aviation Collection, Old Sarum, cockpit
SEPECAT Jaguar GR.1 ACT XX765	Chris Yeo	Royal Air Force Museum, Cosford
Short SB.4 G-14-1	Tom Brooke-Smith	Ulster Aviation Collection, Long Kesh
Short SB.5 WG768	Tom Brooke-Smith	Royal Air Force Museum, Cosford
Short SC.1 XG900	Tom Brooke-Smith	Science Museum, London
Short SC.1 XG905	Tom Brooke-Smith	Ulster Folk and Transport Museum, Holywood
Short 330 G-BSBH	Don Wright	Scrapyard at Portadown, Northern Ireland
Short Tucano T.1 ZF135	Allan Deacon	RAF Linton-on-Ouse, training aid
Slingsby T.67 Firefly G-BKAM	'Norrie' Grove	Privately owned, Kent, airworthy

The incredible, but problematical, Bristol 188 XF926 with its ingenious air brakes (see inset) deployed. *Ken Ellis*

Prototype	Pilot	Location
Somers-Kendall SK.1 G-AOBG	Hugh Kendall	Believed extant, UK
Supermarine 510 VV106	'Mike' Lithgow	Fleet Air Arm Museum, Yeovilton, stored
Trago Mills SAH-1 G-SAHI	Geoffrey Cairns	Privately owned, Bedfordshire, airworthy
Wallis Autogyros types	Ken Wallis	Wallis family estate, held in store
Weir W.2 W-2	Alan Marsh	National Museum of Flight Scotland, East Fortune, stored
Westland Whirlwind HAR.9 XJ389	'Slim' Sear	Yorkshire Helicopter Preservation Group, Doncaster
Westland Wildcat ZZ400	Donald Maclaine	Finmeccanica-Helicopters, Yeovil, stored

Notes: Test pilots 'A' to 'H' appeared in Volume One. Airframes may not necessarily be owned by the organisation given in the third column.

Cosford's latest 'Test Flight' exhibit, BAe EAP ZF534. *Ken Ellis*

Appendix A

UK Aviation Manufacturers – A Brief Genealogy

To help keep track of changing names, below is a *brief* look at who-became-who in the main players of the UK aircraft industry.

Airspeed: Acquired by de Havilland in 1940, still trading under its own name; absorbed into **de Havilland** in 1951.

Armstrong Whitworth: Part of the Hawker Siddeley Group from 1935 – along with Avro, Gloster and Hawker – but trading under its own name. With the setting up of **Hawker Siddeley Aviation** in 1963, the use of its original name stopped by 1965.

Auster: Taken over by **Beagle** in 1960.

Avro: Part of the Hawker Siddeley Group from 1935 – along with Armstrong Whitworth, Gloster and Hawker – but trading under its own name. With the setting up of **Hawker Siddeley Aviation** in 1963, the use of its original name stopped by 1965.

Blackburn: Renamed **Blackburn and General Aircraft** in 1949. Became part of **Hawker Siddeley Aviation** in 1963 and use of its original name stopped by 1965.

Bristol Aeroplane Co: Became part of **British Aircraft Corporation** in 1960. The helicopter division was acquired by **Westland** at the same time.

British Aerospace: Merged with Marconi in 1999, becoming **BAE Systems**.

British Aircraft Corporation: Merged into **British Aerospace** in 1977.

British and Colonial Aeroplane Co: Renamed as Bristol Aeroplane Co in 1920.

Britten-Norman: Has had several owners in its time with changes of name/title, but essentially keeping the original 'BN' identity.

Cierva Autogiro: Merged its organisation with **G & J Weir** in 1943, but used Cierva as trade name. Absorbed into **Saunders-Roe** in 1951. Cierva Autogiro remained a separate legal entity post-1951 and it acquired Rotorcraft Ltd in 1966, becoming **Cierva Rotorcraft Ltd**.

Comper Aircraft: Re-organised as **Heston Aircraft** in 1934.

Coventry Ordnance Works: Became part of the combine that formed **English Electric** in 1918.

de Havilland Aircraft: Became part of **Hawker Siddeley Aviation** in 1963 and use of its original name stopped by 1965.

Dick, Kerr and Co: Became part of the combine that formed **English Electric** in 1918.

Edgar Percival Aviation: Independently established by the founder of Percival Aircraft in 1954; acquired by **Lancashire Aircraft** (Samlesbury Engineering) in 1960.

English Electric: Closed its aviation element in 1926. Re-entered aircraft manufacture in 1938 and became part of **British Aircraft Corporation** in 1960.

Fairey: Acquired by **Westland** in 1960.

Folland: Became part of **Hawker Siddeley Aviation** in 1963 and use of its original name stopped by 1965.

General Aircraft: Merged with Blackburn as **Blackburn and General Aircraft**, in 1949.

Gloucestershire Aircraft: Known as **Gloster** from 1926. For convenience, throughout this book, the company is referred to as 'Gloster'. Part of the Hawker Siddeley Group from 1935 – along with Armstrong Whitworth, Avro and Hawker – but trading under its own name. With the setting up of **Hawker Siddeley Aviation** in 1963, the use of its original name stopped by 1965.

Hawker Aircraft: Officially H G Hawker Engineering until 1933, part of the Hawker Siddeley Group from 1935 – along with Armstrong Whitworth, Avro and Hawker – but trading under its own name. With the setting up of **Hawker Siddeley Aviation** in 1963, the use of its original name stopped by 1965.

Hawker Siddeley Aviation: Merged into **British Aerospace** in 1977.

Hendy Aircraft: Amalgamated into **Parnall Aircraft** in 1935.

Hunting Aircraft: Acquired by **British Aircraft Corporation** in 1960.

Martin & Handasyde: Became **Martinsyde** in 1913.

Miles: Trading from 1933 through **Phillips & Powis Aircraft**, then **Miles Aircraft** formed in 1943, but collapsed 1947. Marathon and other design rights, plus Woodley airfield acquired by **Handley Page (Reading) Ltd** in June 1948. **F G Miles Ltd** formed in 1951; aviation activities to **Beagle** in 1960.

NDN Aircraft: Established independently by Desmond Norman (see Britten-Norman) in 1976; re-named **Norman Aeroplane** in 1985.

Pemberton-Billing: Renamed **Supermarine Aviation Works** in 1916.

Percival Aircraft: Acquired by Hunting Group 1944, but traded under its own name. Renamed **Hunting Percival Aircraft** in 1954 and **Hunting Aircraft** in 1957. Edgar Percival formed **Edgar Percival Aircraft** in 1954 to manufacture the EP.9; the design rights were sold to **Lancashire Aircraft** in 1959.

Petters Ltd: building aircraft at the Westland Aircraft Works, Yeovil, from 1915. Universally referred to as 'Westland'; taking the name **Westland Aircraft** in 1935.

Phoenix Dynamo: Became part of the combine that formed **English Electric** in 1918.

Saunders-Roe: Also known as Saro. Acquired by **Westland** in 1959.

Scottish Aviation: Became part of **British Aerospace** in 1977.

S E Saunders Ltd: Became **Saunders-Roe** in 1928.

Short Brothers: To avoid confusion with the word 'short', throughout this book the company is referred to as 'Shorts' where it is used singly. (From late 1947, the company announced it was to be known as Shorts. This was explained as not being plural, or possessive, but as a contraction of Short Brothers.) Formed 1908 and in 1938 **Short & Harland** was established in Belfast. Both companies were nationalised in 1943 and merged, becoming **Short Brothers and Harland** in 1947. Renamed **Short Brothers** in 1977. Acquired by the Canadian Bombardier Group in 1989, becoming known as **Bombardier Aerospace Belfast**.

Sopwith Aviation: went into liquidation in 1920, re-emerging as **H G Hawker Engineering**, renamed as **Hawker Aircraft** 1933.

Southern Aircraft: Name under which F G Miles developed the Martlet biplanes. From 1933 Miles traded through **Phillips & Powis Aircraft**.

Supermarine Aviation Works: Acquired by Vickers in 1928, but continued to trade under its own name. Restructured as **Vickers-Armstrongs (Supermarine Division)** in 1938 but universally referred to as Supermarine all the way up to the Scimitar. Vickers aviation assets became part of **British Aircraft Corporation** in 1960.

Taylorcraft Aeroplanes (England): Renamed as **Auster** in 1946.

Vickers: Via Vickers Ltd (Aviation Dept) and Vickers (Aviation) Ltd re-organised as **Vickers-Armstrongs (Aircraft) Ltd** in 1955, but continued to be universally referred to as Vickers. Aviation assets became part of **British Aircraft Corporation** in 1960.

Westland Aircraft: Re-organised as **Westland Helicopters** in 1966 and renamed **GKN Westland** in 1994. Merged into Italian-British **AgustaWestland** in 2000. Renamed **Finmeccanica-Helicopters** on 1st January 2016

Appendix B

Abbreviations and Acronyms

These have been kept to a minimum, but those mostly used are as follows:

AAP	Aircraft Acceptance Park
ABC	ABC Motors – or All British Engine Co
ADC	Aircraft Disposal Company – or Airdisco
AEE	Aeroplane Experimental Establishment, Martlesham Heath, became A&AEE 1924
A&AEE	Aircraft and Armament Experimental Establishment, Martlesham Heath then, from 1939, Boscombe Down
AES	Aeroplane Experimental Station, Martlesham Heath, 1917 to 1920: became AEE
AFC	Air Force Cross
AFS	Advanced Flying School
AFDU	Air Fighting Development Unit
AFEE	Airborne Forces Experimental Establishment
Air Cdre	Air Commodore
ANEC	Air Navigation and Engineering Company
ARB	Air Registration Board (became CAA 1972)
AS	Armstrong Siddeley
ATP	Assistant Test Pilot
AVM	Air Vice-Marshal
AW	Armstrong Whitworth
AuxAF	Auxiliary Air Force (RAuxAF from 1947)
BAC	British Aircraft Corporation
BAe	British Aerospace
BAT	British Aerial Transport
BEA	British European Airways
B&GS	Bombing and Gunnery School
BHP	Beardmore-Halford-Pullinger aero engines
BOAC	British Overseas Airways Corporation
B&P	Boulton & Paul (Boulton Paul from 1934)
BP	Boulton Paul
BS	Bristol Siddeley
BSE	Bristol Siddeley Engines
CAA	Civil Aviation Authority
CAACU	Civilian Anti-Aircraft Co-operation Unit
CB	Companion of the Order of the Bath
CBE	Commander of the Order of the British Empire
CDG	Croix de Guerre
CFI	Chief Flying Instructor
CFS	Central Flying School
CO	Commanding Officer
CTP	Chief Test Pilot

DFC	Distinguished Flying Cross – DFC* with Bar
DCTP	Deputy Chief Test Pilot
DH	de Havilland
DHC	de Havilland Canada
DSC	Distinguished Service Cross – DSC* with Bar
DSO	Distinguished Service Order – DSO* with Bar
EE	English Electric
EFTS	Elementary Flying Training School – Elementary & Reserve Flying Training School (E&RFTS) prior to 1919
ENV	English designed, French-built engine; acronym derived from the French for V-configuration – 'En V'
EoN	Elliotts of Newbury
ETPS	Empire Test Pilots' School
FAA	Fleet Air Arm
FAI	Fédération Aéronautique Internationale
Fg Off	Flying Officer
Flt Lt	Flight Lieutenant
FTE	Flight Test Engineer
FTO	Flight Test Observer
FTS	Flying Training School
GCB	Knight Grand Cross of the Order of the Bath
Gp Capt	Group Captain
hp	horse power, relating to the power rating of a piston engine
HP	Handley Page
HS(A)	Hawker Siddeley (Aviation)
ITS	Initial Training School
JAP	J A Prestwich – engine manufacturer
lbst	pounds of static thrust, relating to the power rating – without reheat/afterburner – of a jet engine
Lt	Lieutenant
Lt Cdr	Lieutenant Commander
KBE	Knight Commander of the Order of the British Empire
MAEE	Marine Aircraft Experimental Establishment, Grain until 1924, then Felixstowe, Helensburgh 1939-1945, Felixstowe 1945-1956. Formed out of the MAES at Grain, 1920
M&AEE	Marine & Armament Experimental Establishment (MAEE from 1924)
MAES	Marine Aircraft Experimental Station – see MAEE
MAP	Ministry of Aircraft Production

MBE	Member of the Order of the British Empire		RR	Rolls-Royce
McDD	McDonnell Douglas		RTM	Rolls-Royce/Turboméca
MOS	Ministry of Supply		RAuxAF	Royal Auxiliary Air Force
MP	Member of Parliament		RFC	Royal Flying Corps
MRAF	Marshal of the Royal Air Force		RNAS	Royal Naval Air Service
NACA	National Advisory Committee for Aeronautics, renamed NASA in 1958		RNZAF	Royal New Zealand Air Force
			SAL	Scottish Aviation Ltd
NAG	Nationale Automobil Gessellschaft		Saro	Saunders-Roe
NASA	National Aeronautics and Space Administration		SBAC	Society of British Aircraft (Aerospace from 1964) Companies
NATO	North Atlantic Treaty Organisation			
OBE	Civil: Order of the British Empire; military Officer of the Order of the British Empire		shp	shaft horse power, relating to the power rating of a turboprop or turboshaft
OCU	Operational Conversion Unit		Sqn	Squadron
OM	Order of Merit		Sqn Ldr	Squadron Leader
OTU	Operational Training Unit		st	Static thrust, power measurement for jets
(P)AFU	(Pilots) Advanced Flying Unit		STOL	Short take-off and landing
P&W	Pratt & Whitney		STOVL	Short take-off, vertical landing
PPL	Private Pilot's Licence		Sub Lt	Sub Lieutenant
PRU	Photographic Reconnaissance Unit		UAS	University Air Squadron
PTP	Production Test Pilot		UN	United Nations
P1	Pilot-in-command, or captain		USAF	United States Air Force – from 1947
P2	2nd pilot		USAAC	United States Army Air Corps, 1926-1941
QFI	Qualified Flying Instructor		USAAF	United States Army Air Force, 1941-1947
RAE	Royal Aircraft Establishment		USAAS	United States Army Air Service – to 1926
RAF	Royal Air Force		V/STOL	Vertical/Short take-off and landing
RAFVR	Royal Air Force Volunteer Reserve		Wg Cdr	Wing Commander

Appendix C

Bibliography

Amos, Peter, *Miles Aircraft – The Early Years*, Air-Britain, Tonbridge, 2009

Miles Aircraft – The Wartime Years, Air Britain, Tonbridge, 2012

Andrews, C F and Morgan, E B, *Supermarine Aircraft since 1914*, Putnam, London, 1981

Vickers Aircraft since 1908, Putnam, London, 1988

Armstrong Whitworth Aircraft, *Pioneers of Progress – A Brief Illustrated History of Sir W G Armstrong Whitworth Aircraft Ltd, Coventry*, company brochure, 1982

Ashworth, Chris, *Avro's Maritime Heavyweight: The Shackleton*, Aston, Bourne End, 1990

Balfour, Christopher, *Spithead Express – The Pre-War Island Air Ferry and Post-War Plans*, Magna Press, Leatherhead, 1999

Barnes, C H, *Bristol Aircraft since 1910*, Putnam, London, 3rd Ed, 1988

Handley Page Aircraft since 1907, Putnam, London, 1976

Shorts Aircraft since 1900, Putnam, London, 1967

Barnett-Jones, Frank, *Tarnish 6 – Biography of Test Pilot James L Dell* OBE, Old Forge, Cowbit, 2008

Beamont, Roland, *Fighter Test Pilot – From Hurricane to Tornado*, Patrick Stephens, Wellingborough, 1986

Bingham, Victor F, *Folland Gnat – Sabre-Slayer and Red Arrow*, J&KH Publishing, Hailsham, 2000

Blackburn Aircraft Co, *Blackburn Story 1909-1959*, Brough, 1960

Blackman, Tony, *Nimrod – Rise and Fall*, Grub Street, London, 2011

Test Pilot – My Extraordinary Life in Flight, Grub Street, London, 2009

Vulcan Boys – From the Cold War to the Falklands, Grub Street, 2014

Vulcan y' S Test Pilot, Grub Street, London, 2007

Blackmore, L K, *Hawker – One of Aviation's Greatest Names*, David Bateman Ltd, Auckland, New Zealand, 1990

Blake, John and Hooks, Mike, *40 Years at Farnborough – SBAC's International Showcase*, Haynes, Sparkford, 1990

Bonser, Roy, *Aviation in Leicestershire and Rutland*, Midland, Hinckley, 2001

Boughton, Terence, *The Story of the British Light Aeroplane*, John Murray, London, 1963

Bowyer, Chaz, *The Short Sunderland*, Aston, Bourne End, 1989

Bramson, Alan, *Pure Luck – The Authorised Biography of Sir Thomas Sopwith*, 2nd ed, Crécy Publishing, Manchester, 2005 edition

Brett, Dallas, R, *History of British Aviation 1908-1914*, Air Research, Surbiton, 1987

Brew, Alec, *Boulton Paul Aircraft since 1915*, Putnam, London, 1993

Brooks, Peter W, *Cierva Autogiros – The Development of Rotary-Wing Flight*, Smithsonian, USA, 1988

Brooks, Roger R, *Handley Page Victor – History and Development of a Classic Jet*, Pen & Sword, Barnsley, Vols 1 and 2, 2007

Brown, Don L, *Miles Aircraft since 1925*, Putnam, London, 1970

Bruce, J M, *Aeroplanes of the Royal Flying Corps (Military Wing)*, Putnam, London, 1982

Butler, Phil and Buttler, Tony, *Avro Vulcan – Britain's Famous Delta-Wing B-Bomber*, Midland, Hinckley, 2007

Butler, P H and Buttler, Tony, *Handley Page Victor – Crescent-Winged V-Bomber*, Midland, Hinckley, 2009

Buttler, Tony, *British Experimental Combat Aircraft of World War Two – Prototypes, Research Aircraft and Failed Production Designs*, Hikoki, Manchester, 2012

Carter, Graham, *ML Aviation Ltd – A Secret World*, Keyham Books, Chippenham, 2006

Chacksfield, J E, *Sir Sydney Camm – From Biplanes and Hurricanes to Harriers*, Oakwood, Usk, 2010

Chartres, John, *BAe Nimrod*, Ian Allan, Shepperton, 1986

Church, Richard J, *The One-Eleven Story*, Air-Britain, Tonbridge, 1994

Clarke, Bob, *Jet Provost – The Little Plane with the Big History*, Amerberley, Stroud, 2008

Clegg, Peter V, *Test Pilots of A V Roe – R J 'Roly' Falk*, GMS Enterprises, Peterborough, 2010

The Quiet Test Pilot – The Story of Jimmy Orrell, Greater Manchester Museum of Science and Industry, Manchester, 1989

Cobham, Sir Alan, *A Time to Fly*, Shepheard-Walwyn, London, 1978

Cooper, Peter J, *Farnborough – 100 Years of British Aviation*, Midland, Hinckley, 2006

Courtney, Frank T, *Flight Path – My Fifty Years of Aviation*, Kimber, London, 1972

Cowell, G, *Handley Page Herald*, Jane's, London, 1980

Cruddas, Colin, *In Cobham's Company*, Cobham plc, Wimborne, 1994

Cummings, Colin, *Category Five – A Catalogue of RAF Aircraft Losses 1954 to 2009*, Nimbus, Yelvertoft, 2009

Final Landings – A Summary of RAF Aircraft and Combat Losses 1946-1949, Nimbus, Yelvertoft, 2001

Last Take-off – A record of RAF Aircraft Losses 1950 to 1953, Nimbus, Yelvertoft, 2000

Curtis, Howard, *Sabre – The Canadair Sabre in RAF Service*, Sutton, Stroud, 2005

de Havilland, Sir Geoffrey, *Sky Fever*, Hamish Hamilton, London, 1961

Delve, Ken, Green, Peter and Clemons, John, *English Electric Canberra*, Midland Counties, Earl Shilton, 1992

Donne, Michael, *Pioneers of the Sky – A History of Short Brothers*, Nicholson and Bass, Belfast, 1987

Dorman, Geoffrey, *British Test Pilots*, Forbes Robertson, London, 1950

Dudley, Roger and Johnson, Ted, *Weston-super-Mare and the Aeroplane 1910-2010*, Amberley, Stroud, 2010

Duke, Neville, *Test Pilot*, Grub Street, London, 2nd ed 1992

Ellison, Norman, *British Gliders and Sailplanes 1922-1970*, Adam and Charles Black, London,1971

Farley, John, *A View from the Hover – My Life in Aviation*, Seager Publishing, 2nd ed, 2010

Floyd, Jim, *Avro Canada C102 Jetliner*, Boston Mills Press, Erin, Ontario, Canada, 1986

Gardner, Charles, *British Aircraft Corporation – A History*, Book Club Associates, London, 1981

Gardner, Robert, *From Bouncing Bombs to Concorde – The Biography of Sir George Edwards*, Sutton, Stroud, 2006

Gearing, David W, *On the Wings of a Gull – Percival and Hunting Aircraft*, Air-Britain, Staplefield, 2012

Gibbings, David, *Fairey Rotodyne*, History Press, Stroud, 2009

Gibson, Michael L, *Aviation in Northamptonshire – An Illustrated History*, Northamptonshire Libraries, Northampton, 1982

Goodall, Michael H, *Wight Aircraft: The History of the Aviation Department of J Samuel White and Co Ltd 1913-1919*, Gentry Books, London, 1973

Gunston, Bill, *British Aerospace EAP*, Linewrights, Chipping Ongar, 1986

Nimrod – The Centenarian Aircraft, Spellmount, Stroud, 2009

World Encyclopaedia of Aircraft Manufacturers – From Pioneers to the Present Day, Patrick Stephens, Sparkford, 1993

Hamilton-Paterson, James, *Empire of the Clouds – When Britain's Aircraft Ruled the World*, Faber and Faber, London, 2010

Hancock, Ian, *The Lives of Ken Wallis – Engineer and Aviator Extraordinaire*, self-published, Flixton, 2001

Hare, Paul R, *Royal Aircraft Factory*, Putnam, 1990

Harkins, Hugh, *Eurofighter 2000 – Europe's Fighter for the New Millennium*, Midland, Earl Shilton, 1997

Harrison, William, *Fairey Firefly – The Operational Record*, Airlife, Shrewsbury, 1992

Hayward, Keith, *British Aircraft Industry*, Manchester University Press, Manchester, 1989

Hayes, Paul and King, Bernard, *de Havilland Biplane Transports*, Gatwick Aviation Society, Coulsdon, 2003

Henshaw, Alex, *Sigh for a Merlin – Testing the Spitfire*, Crécy Publishing, Manchester, 1996 edition

Hitchman, Ambrose and Preston, Mike, *History of the Auster Aeroplane*, International Auster Club Heritage Group, Ratcliffe on the Wreake, 3rd Ed, 1989

Holmes, Harry, *Avro Lancaster – The Definitive Record*, Airlife, Shrewsbury, 2nd Ed, 2001

Avro – The History of an Aircraft Company, Airlife, Shrewsbury, 1994

Hudson, R K, *A Sound in the Sky – Reminiscences of Geoffrey Alington*, self-published, London, 1994

Hygate, Barrie, *British Experimental Jet Aircraft*, Argus, Hemel Hempstead, 1990

Jackson, A J, *Avro Aircraft since 1908*, Putnam, London, 2nd Ed, 1990

Blackburn Aircraft since 1909, Putnam, London, 2nd Ed, 1989

British Civil Aircraft since 1919, Putnam, London, Vol 1 and Vol 2nd Eds 1973, Vol 3 2nd Ed 1974

de Havilland Aircraft since 1909, Putnam, London, revised ed, 1978

Jackson, Robert, *Avro Vulcan*, Patrick Stephens, Cambridge, 1984

Hawker Tempest and Sea Fury, Blandford, London, 1989

James, Derek N, *Gloster Aircraft since 1917*, Putnam, London, 2nd Ed 1987

Schneider Trophy Aircraft 1913-1931, Putnam, London, 1981

Spirit of Hamble – Folland Aircraft, Tempus, Stroud, 2000

Westland Aircraft since 1915, Putnam, London, 1991

Kay, Derek R, *The Last Grand Adventure in British Aviation?* (A personal history of Britten-Norman), Anthony Rowe Publishing, Croydon, 2008

King, Derek A, *The Bristol 170 Freighter, Wayfarer and Superfreighter*, Air-Britain, Staplefield, 2011

King, H F, *Sopwith Aircraft 1912-1920*, Putnam, London, 1980

Kingsley-Jones, Max, *Hawker Siddeley Trident*, Ian Allan, Shepperton, 1993

Kinsey, Gordon, *Boulton & Paul Aircraft – History of the Companies at Norwich and Wolverhampton*, Terrence Dalton, Lavenham, 1992

Kirby, Robert, *Avro Manchester – The Legend Behind the Lancaster*, Midland, Earl Shilton, 1995

Lake, Jon, and Crutch, Mike, *Tornado – Multi-Role Combat Aircraft*, Midland, Earl Shilton, 2000

Lewis, Peter, *British Aircraft 1809-1914*, Putnam, London, 1962

British Racing and Record-Breaking Aircraft, Putnam, London, 1970

Lithgow, Mike, *Mach One*, Allan Wingate, London, 1954

(ed), *Vapour Trails – Thrilling Exploits of Men Who Fly at Supersonic Speeds*, Allan Wingate, London, 1956

London, Peter, *Saunders and Saro Aircraft since 1917*, Putnam, London, 1988

Longworth, James, H, *Test Flying in Lancashire from Samlesbury and Warton Aerodromes – Military Aviation at the Leading Edge*, Vol 1 *World War One to the 1960s*, Vol 2 *From the 1960s to 1980s*, Vol 3 *From the 1980s into the New Millennium*, BAE Systems, Warton, 2012, 2013 and 2014

Triplane to Typhoon – Aircraft Produced by Factories in Lancashire and the North West from 1910, Lancashire County Developments, Preston, 2005

Lumsden, Alec S C, *British Piston Aero-Engines and Their Aircraft*, Airlife, Shrewsbury, 1994

Macmillan, Norman, *Freelance Pilot*, William Heinemann, London, 1937

Masefield, Sir Peter, with Gunston, Bill, *Flight Path*, Airlife, Shrewsbury, 2002

Mason, Francis K, *Harrier*, Patrick Stephens, Cambridge, 2nd Ed, 1983

Hawker Aircraft since 1920, Putnam, London, 1961

Hawker Hunter, Biography of a Thoroughbred, Patrick Stephens, Cambridge, 1981

Hawker Hurricane, Aston, Bourne End, 1987

Tornado, Patrick Stephens, Wellingborough, 1986

Mason, Tim, *British Flight Testing Martlesham Heath 1920-1939*, Putnam, London, 1993

Cold War Years – Flight Testing at Boscombe Down, 1945-1975, Hikoki Publications, Ottringham, 2001

Seaplane Years – M&AEE and MAEE 1920-1956, Hikoki, Manchester, 2010

Secret Years – Flight Testing at Boscombe Down, 1939-1945, Hikoki, Manchester, 2010

Matthews, Henry, *Husky One – A E 'Ben' Gunn Boulton Paul Chief Test Pilot*, HPM Publications, Beirut, Lebanon, 1999, 2nd ed

Prelude to Eurofighter – EAP, HPM Publications, Beirut, Lebanon, 2001

Prelude to the Sea Vixen: DH.110, HPM Publications, Beirut, Lebanon, 2001

and Peter Davison, *Prelude to Concorde – HP.115 Slender Wing Research Aircraft*, HPM Publications, Beirut, Lebanon, 2004

and Allan Wood, *The Saga of SR.53 – A Pictorial Tribute*, HPM Publications, Beirut, Lebanon, 2004

McIntyre, Dougal, *Prestwick's Pioneer – A Portrait of David F McIntyre*, Woodfield, Bognor Regis, 2004

McKay, Stuart, *de Havilland Tiger Moth – Legendary Biplane Trainer*, Midland, Earl Shilton, 1999

Merewether, H C H, *Prelude to the Harrier: P.1127 Prototype Flight Testing at Kestrel Evaluation*, X-Planes Vol.3, HPM Publications, Beirut, Lebanon, 2003

Merrick, K A, *Handley Page Halifax – From Hell to Victory and Beyond*, Classic, 2009

Middleton, Donald H, *Airspeed – The Company and its Aeroplanes*, Terence Dalton, Lavenham, 1982

Tests of Character – Epic Flights by Legendary Test Pilots, Donald Middleton, Airlife, Shrewsbury, 1995

Test Pilots – The Story of British Test Flying 1903-1984, Willow Books, London, 1985

Midland Counties Aviation Research Group, *Beagle Aircraft – A Production History*, Hinckley, 1974

Molson, K M and Taylor, H A, *Canadian Aircraft since 1909*, Putnam, London, 1982

Morgan, Eric B, and Shacklady, Edward, *Spitfire the History*, Key Publishing, Stamford, 1987

Neil, William T, *Just One of the Pioneers – My Days With Scottish Aviation and de Havillands*, Cirrus, Gillingham, 2002

Nicholl, Lt Cdr G W R, *Supermarine Walrus – The Story of a Unique Aircraft*, G T Foulis, London, 1966

Odr-Hume, Arthur W J G, *British Light Aeroplanes – Their Evolution, Development and Perfection, 1920-1940*, GMS, Peterborough, 2000

Oliver, David, *Hendon Aerodrome – A History*, Airlife, Shrewsbury, 1994

Painter, Martin, *DH.106 Comet – An Illustrated History*, Air-Britain, Tunbridge Wells, 2002

Pardoe, Alan J, *Jetstream – A Production History*, Central Scotland Aviation Group, Bearsden, 1979

Pasco, Dennis, *Tested – Marshall Test Pilots and Their Aircraft in War and Peace 1919-1999*, Grub Street, London, 1999

Penrose, Harald, *Adventure with Fate*, Airlife, Shrewsbury, 1984

Architect of Wings – A Biography of Roy Chadwick, Airlife, Shrewsbury, 1985

British Aviation – The Pioneer Years 1903-1914, Putnam, London, 1967

British Aviation – The Great War and Armistice 1915-1919, Putnam, London, 1969

British Aviation – The Adventuring Years 1920-1929, Putnam, London, 1973

British Aviation – Widening Horizons 1930-1934, HMSO, London, 1979

British Aviation – Ominous Skies 1935-1939, HMSO, London, 1980

Philpott, Bryan, *Lightning*, Patrick Stephens, Wellingborough, 1984

Meteor, Patrick Stephens, Wellingborough, 1986

Pixton, Stella, *Howard Pixton – Test Pilot and Pioneer Aviator*, Pen & Sword, Barnsley, 2014

Powell, H P 'Sandy', *Men With Wings*, Allan Wingate, London, 1957

Test Flight, Allan Wingate, London, 1956

Quill, Jeffrey, *Spitfire – A Test Pilot's Story*, Crécy Publishing, Manchester, 1996 edition, reprinted 2008

Ransom, Stephen and Fairclough, Robert, *English Electric Aircraft and their Predecessors*, Putnam, London, 1987

Rawlings, John and Sedgwick, Hilary, *Learn to Test, Test to Learn – The History of the Empire Test Pilots' School*, Airlife, Shrewsbury, 1991

Reed, Arthur, *BAe Hawk*, Ian Allan, Shepperton, 1985

SEPECAT Jaguar, Ian Allan, Shepperton, 1982

Riding, Richard, *Ultralights – The Early British Classics*, Patrick Stephens, Wellingborough, 1987

Robertson, Alan, *Lion Rampant and Winged, A Commemorative History of Scottish Aviation Ltd*, self-published, Brarassie, 1986

Robinson, Wg Cdr J A 'Robby', *Avro One – Autobiography of a Chief Test Pilot*, Old Forge, Cowbit, 2005

Tester Zero One – The Making of a Test Pilot, Old Forge, Cowbit, 2007

Scott, J D, *Vickers – A History*, Weidenfeld and Nicolson, London, 1962

Scott, Stewart A, *English Electric Lightning – Volume One, Birth of a Legend*, GMS Enterprises, Peterborough, 2000

Sharp, C Martin, *DH – A History of de Havilland*, Airlife, Shrewsbury, 1982

Shores, Christopher and Williams, Clive, *Aces High*, and *Aces High Volume 2*, Christopher Shores, Grub Street, London, 1994 and 1999

Shores, Christopher and Franks, Norman, and Guest, Russell, *Above the Trenches*, Grub Street, London 1990

Silvester, R John, *Percival and Hunting Aircraft*, self-published, Luton, 1987

Skinner, Stephen, *Marshall of Cambridge*, Tempus, Stroud, 2003

Smith, Constance Babington, *Testing Time – A Study of Man and Machine in the Test Flying Era*, Cassell, London, 1961

Sturtivant, Ray, *British Research and Development Aircraft – 70 Years at the Leading Edge*, Foulis, Sparkford, 1990

Sturtivant, Ray, with Hamlin, John, *Flying Training and Support Units since 1912*, Air-Britain, Staplefield, 2007

Tapper, Oliver, *Armstrong Whitworth Aircraft since 1913*, Putnam, London, 1988

Taylor, H A, *Airspeed Aircraft since 1931*, Putnam, London, 1970

Fairey Aircraft since 1915, Putnam, London, 1988

Test Pilot at War, Ian Allan, Shepperton, 1970

Temple, Julian C, *Wings over Woodley – The Story of Miles Aircraft and the Adwest Group*, Aston, Bourne End, Bucks, 1987

Thetford, Owen, *Aircraft of the Royal Air Force since 1918*, Putnam, London, 9th Ed, 1995

British Naval Aircraft since 1912, Putnam, London, 1971

Trevor, Hugh, *Lightnings Live On!*, Lightning Preservation Group, Bruntingthorpe, 1996

Trubshaw, Brian and Edmondson, Sally, *Brian Trubshaw – Test Pilot*, Sutton, Stroud, 1998

Turnill, Reginald, and Reed, Arthur, *Farnborough – The Story of the Royal Aircraft Establishment*, Robert Hale, London, 1980

Twiss, Peter, *Faster than the Sun – The Compelling Story of a Record-Breaking Test Pilot*, Peter Grub Street, London, 2nd ed 2000

Unwin, N H F, *Geoffrey de Havilland – Log Book of Test Flying and Some Design Notes*, Royal Aircraft Establishment Museum, Farnborough, 1971

Wallace, Graham, *Claude-Grahame-White – A Biography*, Putnam, London, 1960

Walpole, Nigel, *Swift Justice – The Full Story of the Supermarine Swift*, Astonbridge, Ruardean, 2000

Warner, Guy, *The Last Canberra – PR.9 XH131*, Ulster Aviation Society, Belfast, 2011

Warner, Guy, and Cromie, Ernie, *Aircraft and Aerospace Manufacturing in Northern Ireland*, Colourpoint Books, Newtownards, 2014

Waterton, William Arthur, *The Quick and the Dead – The Perils of Post-War Test Flying*, Grub Street, 2012 edition

Watkins, David, *de Havilland Vampire – The Complete History*, Sutton, Stroud, 1996

Venom – de Havilland Venom and Sea Venom, The Complete History, Sutton, Thrupp, 2003

Webb, Derek Collier, *UK Flight Testing Accidents 1940-1971*, Air-Britain, Tunbridge Wells, 2002

Williams, Paul, *The James Brothers – Pembrokeshire's Aviation Pioneers*, Pembrokeshire Aviation Group, Kilgetty, Wales, 1992

Winkler, Eduard F, *Civilian Affair – A Brief History of the Civilian Aircraft Company of Hedon*, Flight Recorder Publications, Ottringham, 2003

Wittridge, Flt Lt A H 'Witt', *An Evil Boy*, Wunjo Press, Loftus, 2004

Wixey, Kenneth E, *Parnall Aircraft since 1914*, Putnam, London, 1990

Zuk, Bill, with Zurakowski, Janusz, *Janusz Zurakowski – Legend in the Skies*, Crécy Publishing, Manchester, 2007

In his poem *The Rock* of 1934 Thomas Stearns Eliot predicted the minefield that is the 'web', long before pixels became all-dominant:

Where is the wisdom we have lost in knowledge?

Where is the knowledge we have lost in information?

So, bearing in mind that only a *fraction* of things beginning-with-www are helpful – let alone reliable, and that the rest ranges from the well-meaning but ill-informed, to fantasists shrouded in anonymity, to the outright malicious; the following occupy the 'real' world:

afleetingpeace.org – 'Golden Age Aviation' in the British Empire, Terry Mace's study of the inter-war years

agustawestland.com – Europe's innovative rotorcraft combine

airbus.com – Comprehensive site on a global triumph

airsciences.org – Superbly informative site from FAST, the Farnborough Air Sciences Trust

auster.org – Incredibly detailed site of the International Auster Club

baesystems.com – BAE Systems vast and informative site

eurofighter.com – 'Home' of Europe's world-beater

flightglobal.com – *Every* page of every *Flight* and *Flight International*

hatfieldaviationheritage.co.uk – Dedicated to the aviation heritage of the town and airfield

martin-baker.co.uk – Excellent material on the history of the company

museumofberkshireaviation.co.uk – Detailed tribute to all things Miles

theaerodrome.com – 'Aces' and aircraft of World War One

thetartanterror.blogspot.co.uk – Neil Corbett's affectionate tribute to worldwide test pilots

thunder-and-lightnings.co.uk/memorial – Damien Burke's testament to UK test flight fatalities

And which of the books does the author consider should be on the 'bucket list' of anyone wanting to read about British test pilots? Courtney, Farley, Hamilton-Paterson, Henshaw, Lithgow, Quill, Constance Babington Smith, Twiss, Waterton and *everything* by Harald Penrose!

Index I

Test Pilots by Manufacturer

Listed alphabetically – initials only, no honours, decorations or rank – by manufacturer. This index includes *all* of the pilots mentioned in Chapter Seven Volume One *and* integrates those listed in Chapter Seven, *They Also Serve...* in this volume (marked ”).

Airborne Forces Experimental Establishment: I M D Little

Airbus: P Chandler, E Strongman

Aircraft Manufacturing Co (Airco): W Birchenough”, F T Courtney, G de Havilland, C Gresswell”, B C Hucks

Airmark: J W C Judge

Air Navigation and Engineering Company (ANEC): J H James, P J R King

Airspeed: R E Clear, C H A Colman, G B S Errington, B Field”, R E M B Milne”, B A Powell”, G H Stainforth

Armstrong Whitworth (including Siddeley-Deasy): F L Barnard, A C Campbell-Orde, P R Cope”, F T Courtney, W H Else, E G Franklin, D S Green”, E S Greenwood, D Hughes, J H James, F Koolhoven, J O Lancaster, P Legh, R M Mace, J G McCowan”, F R Midgley, C B Prodger, C W Simpson”, N C Spratt, C K Turner-Hughes, P W Varley”, P M R Walton”

Arpin Aircraft: G Wynne-Eyton

Auster (British Taylorcraft): A Coltman”, G Edwards, T Howard”, R L Porteous, G N Snarey, G Wynne-Eyton

Austin Motors: C G M Alington”, D Cotton”

Aviation Traders: D B Cartlidge, L Griffith”, R Langley”

Avro: C Allen, J D Baker, A L Blackman, H A Brown, K Cook”, S E Esler, R J Falk, H A Hamersley, J G Harrison, O J Hawkins”, H J L Hinkler, R C Kemp, J Knight”, F L Luxmoore, R F Martin, J C Nelson, J H Orrell, W Parke, C H Pixton, F P Raynham, J W C Squier, S A Thorn, F B Tomkins, G A V Tyson, J B Wales, J B Walker

Baynes: R Kronfeld

Beagle: T Howard”, J W C Judge, G H Miles, V B Mitchell”, J M Nicholson, R L Porteous

Beardmore: R A W H Haig, A N Kingwill, J Noakes, M W Piercey

Blackburn: E R Anson”, H Bailey, C A Ball”, H Blackburn, A M Blake, J L N Bennett-Baggs”, D G Brade”, G F Bullen”, J G Burns”, R J Chandler”, W R Ding, C G P Flood, B C Hucks, R W Kenworthy, P G Lawrence, A G Loton, J Neilan, H Oxley, G R I Parker, C B Prodger, C A Rea, B R Rolfe, T N Stack, D A Terrill, A C R Thompson, D J Whitehead, H J Wilson, H Wood, N H Woodhead”

Boulton (and) Paul: F T Courtney, G Dunworth”, C Feather, A E Gunn, J O Lancaster, R B Mancus, R L Neale, C H Pixton, J Powers”, W B Price-Owen, C A Rea, G Skelton”, R Smythe, K P H Tisshaw

Brennan/RAE: R G Graham

Bristol (also British and Colonial): G L Auty, Barraclough”, H R Busteed, A C Capper, R A Cowpe”, R C W Ellison”, E C G England, G W England, W F Gibb, J J Hammond, Capt Hooper, C T D Hosegood, J F Howman”, H Jullerot”, L F Macdonald, N Macmillan, H A Marsh, P Moore”, J A C Northway, A J Pegg, C H Pixton, F P Raynham, G Reston”, L Roberts”, E J Sharp, R Smith”, E

H Statham”, E A Swiss”, M Tétard”, C F Uwins, J Valentine”, C A Washer, D D Weightman, I Wilkinson”, J I Williamson”, P R D Wilson”

British Aerial Transport: C Draper, P Legh, C Turner”

British Aerospace / BAE Systems: T N Allen, P Baker, R P Beamont, A L Blackman, J Blair, A Blythe”, J W A Bolton, M N Bowman, J Cochrane, J J Cockburn, N Dawson”, P D Dye”, J D Eagles, G Ellis”, J F Farley, S Formoso”, R Fraser”, H E Frick, P J Ginger”, J Goddard”, M S Goodfellow, P Gordon-Johnson”, S N Hargreaves”, K Hartley”, A J Hawkes”, J S Hawkins, P Henley, L Houston, W Jonas”, A P S Jones, P Kosogorin”, R J Lawson”, J J Lee, S Long”, G J McClymont; A A McDicken, P Millett, G Morgan”, P Murphy, K P Orme”, W Ovell, R Pengelly, C Penrice, H R Radford, D Reeh, C F Roberts, J A Robinson, M Robinson”, B Scott”, T Scott, R W Searle, D M S Simpson, M H B Snelling, R T Stock, D L J Thomas, G J Tomlinson, E B Trubshaw, J Turner, C Whittaker”, P Wilson”, C J Yeo

British Aircraft Company: C H Lowe-Wylde

British Aircraft Corporation: D G Addicott, A I Aitken”, G L Auty, P Baker, G R Bryce, E Bucklow”, W B Cairns”, J A Carrodus”, J Cochrane, J J Cockburn, J L Dell, J D Eagles, T M S Ferguson, D Glaser”, J C Hall”, T S Harris”, P D Hillwood, R Ingham”, J Jarvis”, D M Knight, J J Lee, M J Lithgow, D Lockseiser, A M Love, E McNamara”, P Millett, R Pengelly, B A Powell”, H R Radford, R Rymer, J W C Squier, R T Stock, E B Trubshaw, ‘J’ Walker”

British Deperdussin: J C Porte

British Klemm / British Aircraft: E G Hordern

Britten-Norman: J Ayres”, J Birnie”, F R J Britten”, P D Hillwood, H M Kendall, J Neilan, C Newnes”

Carden-Baynes: H S Broad

Central Aircraft: F T Courtney, F B Goodwin-Castleman”

Chichester-Miles: A M McVitie

Chilton Aircraft: R L Porteous

Chrislea Aircraft: D Lowry, R F Stedman

Cierva Autogiro (and **G & J Weir**): R A C Brie, F J Cable, J de Cierva, H A Hamersley, H A Marsh, R A Pullin, A H C Rawson, G I Thomson”

Civilian Aircraft Co: W H Sutcliffe

CLW Aviation: A N Kingwill

Comper: N Comper

Coventry Ordnance Works: T O M Sopwith

Cranfield Institute of Technology: A M McVitie

Cranwell Light Aeroplane Club: N Comper

Cunliffe-Owen: A G Corbin, P D Hillwood

CW Aircraft: G Wynne-Eyton

de Havilland: G Aird, P Barlow, R P Beamont, H S Broad, P Buggé”, A C Capper, A J Cobham, C B Critchley”, J

Index II

Aircraft Types and 'First Flighting' Pilots

All listed by manufacturer/design house and are British-built unless noted in *round* brackets (). To further aid reference, pilots listed in Chapter Seven who made the first flight are given in *square* brackets [].

"What is it like to fly?"

"We just fly the cockpit and the rest of its trails along behind!"

Bristol chief test pilot A J 'Bill' Pegg talking to the press after the first flight of the Brabazon, 4th September 1949